Lecture Notes in Computer Science 1762
Edited by G. Goos, J. Hartmanis and J. van Leeuwen

**Springer**
*Berlin*
*Heidelberg*
*New York*
*Barcelona*
*Hong Kong*
*London*
*Milan*
*Paris*
*Singapore*
*Tokyo*

us-Dieter Schewe
nhard Thalheim (Eds.)

# oundations
# f Information and
# nowledge Systems

t International Symposium, FoIKS 2000
g, Germany, February 14-17, 2000
ceedings

 Springer

ies Editors

chard Goos, Karlsruhe University, Germany
is Hartmanis, Cornell University, NY, USA
van Leeuwen, Utrecht University, The Netherlands

ume Editors

us-Dieter Schewe
chnische Universität Clausthal, Institut für Informatik
us-Albert-Str. 4, 38678 Clausthal-Zellerfeld, Germany
nail: schewe@informatik.tu-clausthal.de

rnhard Thalheim
chnische Universität Cottbus, Institut für Informatik
stfach 101344, 03013 Cottbus, Germany
nail: thalheim@informatik.tu-cottbus.de

taloging-in-Publication Data applied for

Deutsche Bibliothek - CIP-Einheitsaufnahme

ndations of information and knowledge systems : first international
nposium ; proceedings / FoIKS 2000, Burg, Germany, February 14-17,
)0. Klaus-Dieter Schewe ; Bernhard Thalheim (ed.). - Berlin ;
idelberg ; New York ; Barcelona ; Hong Kong ; London ; Milan ; Paris ;
igapore ; Tokyo : Springer, 2000
(Lecture notes in computer science ; Vol. 1762)
ISBN 3-540-67100-5

Subject Classification (1998): H.2, H.3, H.5, I.2.4, F.3.2, G.2

N 0302-9743
3N 3-540-67100-5 Springer-Verlag Berlin Heidelberg New York

pringer-Verlag Berlin Heidelberg 2000
ted in Germany

setting: Camera-ready by author
V: 10719669      06/3142 – 5 4 3 2 1 0      Printed on acid-free paper

# Preface

This volume contains the papers presented at the "First International Symposium on Foundations of Information and Knowledge Systems" (FoIKS 2000), which was held in Burg, Germany from February 14th to 17th, 2000.

FoIKS is intended to be a biannual event focussing on theoretical foundations of information and knowledge systems. It aims to take up the old tradition of the conference series "Mathematical Fundamentals of Database Systems" (MFDBS) which encouraged East-West collaboration in the field of database theory. Former MFDBS conferences were held in Dresden in 1987 (Springer LNCS 305, edited by Joachim Biskup, János Demetrovics, Jan Paredaens, and Bernhard Thalheim), in Visegrád in 1989 (Springer LNCS 364, edited by János Demetrovics and Bernhard Thalheim), and in Rostock in 1991 (Springer LNCS 495, edited by Bernhard Thalheim, János Demetrovics, and Hans-Detlef Gerhard).

Another goal of the MFDBS conference series has always been to attract researchers working in mathematical fields such as discrete mathematics, combinatorics, logics, and finite model theory who are interested in applying their theories to research on database and knowledge base theory. To that end, FoIKS takes up the tradition of providing a forum for mathematical foundations in a specific branch of computer science. A first attempt to reestablish the MFDBS tradition was made in 1995 with a follow-up workshop "Semantics in Databases" to ICDT (Springer LNCS 1358, edited by Bernhard Thalheim and Leonid Libkin).

In addition, the FoIKS symposium is intended to be a forum for intensive discussions. For this reason, the time slot of long and short contributions is 60 and 30 minutes, respectively, followed by 30 and 15 minutes for discussions, respectively. Furthermore, participants are asked in advance to prepare to act as correspondents to a contribution of another author. There are also special sessions for the presentation and discussion of open research problems.

The FoIKS 2000 call for papers solicited contributions dealing with any foundational aspect of information and knowledge systems, e. g.

    logical foundations and semantics of datamodels,
    dependency theory,
    integrity and security,
    temporal aspects,
    foundations of information systems design including Web-based information services,
    query languages and optimization,

database dynamics,
intelligent agents,
non-monotonic reasoning,
application of non-classical logics,
finite model theory,
deduction, abduction, and induction in data and knowledge bases.


The programme committee received 45 submissions by authors from 22 different countries. Each paper was carefully reviewed by at least three experienced referees. Fourteen papers were chosen for long presentations, four papers for short presentations. This volume contains polished versions of these papers modified according to comments made in the reviews. A few papers will be selected for further extension and publishing in a special issue of the journal "Annals of Mathematics and Artificial Intelligence".

We would like to thank all authors who submitted papers and all workshop participants for the fruitful discussions. We are grateful to the members of the programme committee and the external referees for their timely expertise in carefully reviewing the papers, and we would like to express our thanks to our hosts for the enjoyable week in the pleasant surroundings of the Spreewald.



**February 2000**                                            **Klaus-Dieter Schewe**
                                                             **Bernhard Thalheim**

## Programme Committee Co-chairs

Klaus-Dieter Schewe      Technical University of Clausthal (Germany)
Bernhard Thalheim        Technical University of Cottbus (Germany)

## Programme Committee

Joachim Biskup           University of Dortmund (Germany)
Leopoldo Bertossi        Catholic University of Chile (Chile)
François Bry             Ludwig Maximilian University at Munich (Germany)
Thomas Eiter             Technical University of Vienna (Austria)
Marc Gyssens             University of Limburg (Belgium)
Hele-Mai Haav            International University of Estonia (Estonia)
Stephen J. Hegner        Umeå University (Sweden)
Hans-Joachim Klein       Christian Albrechts University at Kiel (Germany)
Mark Levene              University College London (United Kingdom)
Leonid Libkin            Bell Labs (USA)
Takao Miura              Hosei University at Tokyo (Japan)
Janaki Ram               Indian Institute of Technology, Madras (India)
Domenico Sacca           University of Calabria (Italy)
Vladimir Sazonov         Russian Academy of Sciences (Russia)
Dietmar Seipel           University of Würzburg (Germany)
Nicolas Spyratos         University of Paris South (France)
Millist W. Vincent       University of South Australia, Adelaide (Australia)
Roel Wieringa            University of Twente (The Netherlands)

## External Referees

| | | |
|---|---|---|
| Marcelo Arenas | Herman Balsters | Hans H. Brüggemann |
| Uwe Egly | Wolfgang Faber | Thomas Feyer |
| Sergio Flesca | Floris Geerts | Sergio Greco |
| Claire Kenyon | Bart Kuijpers | Gabriel Kuper |
| Nicola Leone | Jana Lewerenz | Alexei Lisitsa |
| Irina Lomazova | Thomas Lukasiewicz | Fatma Ozcan |
| Luigi Palopoli | Michel de Rougemont | Marie-Christine Rousset |
| Isamu Shioya | Jerome Simeon | Srinath Srinivasa |
| Daniel Stamate | V. S. Subrahmanian | Hans Tompits |
| Mars Valiev | Paul Van der Vet | Luc Vandeurzen |
| Gottfried Vossen | Jan Wendler | |

## Organisation

FoIKS 2000 was organised by the Database and Information Systems team from the Technical University of Cottbus:

| | | |
|---|---|---|
| Thomas Feyer | Karla Kersten | Thomas Kobienia |
| Jana Lewerenz | Günter Millahn | Srinath Srinivasa |
| Bernhard Thalheim | Vojtech Vestenicky | |

# Table of Contents

# Low Discrepancy Allocation
# of Two-Dimensional Data*

Richard Anstee[1], János Demetrovics[2], Gyula O.H. Katona[3], Attila Sali[3] **

[1] Mathematics Department, University of British Columbia
Vancouver, Canada V6T 1Y4
[2] Computer and Automatization Institute of HAS
Budapest, Lágymányosi u. 11 H-1111 Hungary
[3] Alfréd Rényi Institute of Mathematics, Hungarian Academy of Sciences
Budapest P.O.B. 127 H-1364 HUNGARY

**Abstract.** Fast browsing and retrieval of geographically referenced information requires the allocation of data on different storage devices for concurrent retrieval. By dividing the two-dimensional space into tiles, a system can allow users to specify regions of interest using a query rectangle and then retrieving information related to tiles covered by the query. Suppose that there are $m$ I/O devices. A tile is labeled by $i$ if the data corresponding to this area is stored in the $i$th I/O device. A labeling is efficient if the difference of the numbers of occurrences of distinct labels in any given rectangle is small. Except for some simple cases this discrepancy exceeds 1. In the present paper constructions are given to make this discrepancy small relative to $m$. The constructions use latin squares and a lower bound is given, which shows that the constructions are best possible under certain conditions.

## 1 Introduction

Todays information systems often use the two dimensional screen as a tool for retrieval of detailed data that is associated with a specific part of the screen. A standard example is a geographic database, where first a low resolution map is displayed on the screen and then the user specifies a part of the map that is to be displayed in higher resolution. Another application is when pictures of famous historical monuments or sightseeing spots of an area are to be displayed. Efficient support of such queries is quite important for image databases in particular, and for browsing geographically referenced information in general. In the Alexandria Digital Library project [7] a large satellite image is divided into tiles and each tile is decomposed using wavelet decomposition [8]. A wavelet decomposition of

---

* The work of the second and third authors was partially supported by the Hungarian National Foundation for Scientific Research grant number T016389, and European Communities (Cooperation in Science and Technology with Central and Eastern European Countries) contract number CIPACT930113
** This research was done while the third author visited The University of British Columbia on a grant of the first author.

K.-D. Schewe, B. Thalheim (Eds.): FoIKS 2000, LNCS 1762, pp. 1–12, 2000.

an image results in a lower resolution image of the original one together with higher order coefficients that can be used to retrieve higher resolution versions of the same image. Similar approaches are common to other systems for browsing large image databases [4,5]. A user would usually browse the lower resolution images fast and then specify areas to be displayed in higher resolution. This requires the retrieval of the higher resolution components for the various tiles that overlap with the specific region. For a more detailed review of the current state of art the reader is referred to [1].

In the present paper the model introduced in [1] is analised further. It is assumed that data is associated with the tiles of a two-dimensional grid. The data corresponding to individual tiles is usually large, so it is preferable to store them on parallel I/O devices in such a way, that for a given query, retrieval from these parallel devices can occur concurrently. The ideal situation, when information related to each individual tile could be stored on a distinct I/O device and hence data for any query could be retreived concurrently is not realizable in general, because the number of tiles is usually much larger than the number of I/O devices available. Thus, the only hope is to "spread out" data as evenly as possible. In the following, a measure of optimality of data allocation is defined as smallest possible discrepancy in the number of access requests for different I/O devices for any rectangular set of tiles. Upper bounds for this discrepancy are derived that give simple, but efficient allocation methods. These upper bounds are shown to be best assymptotycally for certain types of data allocation. This could be viewed as a generalization of *strict optimality* of [1].

## 2   The General Model

Let $\mathcal{R}$ be an $n_1 \times n_2$ array, whose elements $(i, j)$ where $0 \leq i \leq n_1 - 1$ and $0 \leq j \leq n_2 - 1$ are called *tiles*. Each tile is supposed to contain detailed information on the area it covers. For example, if the array is a low resolution image of a geographic region, the higher resolution wavelet coefficients may be associated with the individual tiles. Given two tiles $(i_1, j_1)$ and $(i_2, j_2)$, where $i_1 \leq i_2$ and $j_1 \leq j_2$, two dimensional query is defined by

$$\mathcal{R}[(i_1, j_1), (i_2, j_2)] = \{(i, j) : i_1 \leq i \leq i_2 \text{ and } j_1 \leq j \leq j_2\}.$$

This represents a rectangle, whose opposite corners are $(i_1, j_1)$ and $(i_2, j_2)$ and area is $(i_2 - i_1 + 1)(j_2 - j_1 + 1)$, the number of tiles contained in the rectangle. To each tile $(i, j)$ in $\mathcal{R}$ is assigned a number $f(i, j)$ from the set $\{1, 2, \ldots, m\}$. The number $f(i, j)$ refers to one of $m$ available I/O devices on which the information related to the given tile is stored. $f$ is called an $m$-*assignment* for $\mathcal{R}$. The *degree* of $k$ ($1 \leq k \leq m$) with respect to rectangle $\mathcal{R}[(i_1, j_1), (i_2, j_2)]$ is

$$d_{i_1, j_1, i_2, j_2}(k) = |\{(i, j) \in \mathcal{R}[(i_1, j_1), (i_2, j_2)] : f(i, j) = k\}|,$$

that is the number of ocurrences of $k$ as assignments to tiles in the rectangle. An $m$-assignment is called $d$-*discrepancy assignment* iff for any given rectangle

$\mathcal{R}[(i_1, j_1), (i_2, j_2)]$

$$\delta(i_1, j_1, i_2, j_2) = \max_k d_{i_1, j_1, i_2, j_2}(k) - \min_k d_{i_1, j_1, i_2, j_2}(k) \le d$$

holds. $\delta(i_1, j_1, i_2, j_2)$ is called the *discrepancy* of the rectangle $\mathcal{R}[(i_1, j_1), (i_2, j_2)]$. Clearly, $d$-discrepancy $m$-assignments with small $d$ are sought for efficient retrieval of data using as many I/O devices concurrently, as possible. The *optimality* $d(m)$ of $m$ is the minimum $d$, such that a $d$-discrepancy $m$-assignment exists for arbitrary $n_1$ and $n_2$. 1-discrepancy $m$-assignments were called *strictly optimal* in [1] and the following theorem was proved.

**Theorem 2.1 (Abdel-Ghaffar,El Abbadi'97).** *A 1-discrepancy $m$-assignment exists for an $n_1 \times n_2$ array $\mathcal{R}$ iff one of the following conditions holds:*
- $\min\{n_1, n_2\} \le 2$,
- $m \in \{1, 2, 3, 5\}$,
- $m \ge n_1 n_2 - 2$,
- $m = n_1 n_2 - 4$ *and* $\min\{n_1, n_2\} = 3$,
- $m = 8$ *and* $n_1 = n_2 = 4$.

**Corollary 2.1.** $d(m) \ge 2$ *if* $m \notin \{1, 2, 3, 5\}$.

Theorem 2.1 shows that strict optimality can be achieved only in very restricted cases, hence it is natural to ask, how good an assignment can be in general, i.e., good upper bounds for $d(m)$ are of interest. In the rest of the paper $d$-discrepancy assignments are given, where $d$ is of order of magnitude $\log m$ It is shown to be best possible apart from a multiplicative constant, if the assignment is of *latin square* type.

Because $d(m)$ is defined as the lowest discrepancy that can be achieved for arbitrary $n_1$ and $n_2$, we will consider $m$ assignments for an $\infty \times \infty$ array, like an infinite checkerboard covering the plane. In other words, an $m$-assignment is a map $f: \mathbb{Z} \times \mathbb{Z} \longrightarrow \{1, 2, \ldots, m\}$.

The proof of Theorem 2.1 and most of the previous results use *modular assignments*, i.e. maps of type $f(i, j) = \alpha i + \beta j \mod m$. Our methods are different: good assignments are constructed for $p\,m$ provided good ones exist for some $m$ via *blow up* technique. This results in $d(m) = O(\log m)$ for $m = p^t$. Then using special transversals in latin squares the construction is extended for all values of $m$.

## 3   The Blow Up

The following construction is crucial in the proofs. Let $M$ be an $m$-assignment, i.e., an $\infty \times \infty$ array, whose rows and columns are indexed by $\mathbb{Z}$. Furthermore, let $A(p)$ be an $\infty \times p$ array, whose rows are indexed by $\mathbb{Z}$ and each row is a permutation of $\{1, 2, \ldots, p\}$. The *blow up* $A(pM)$ of $M$ by $A(p)$ is defined as follows. In each column of $M$ the $i$ entries are replaced by $i \times$ rows of $A(p)$, i.e., each $1 \times 1$ entry $i$ becomes a $1 \times p$ block, a permutation of $\{(i, 1), (i, 2), \ldots, (i, p)\}$. Each $i$

entry of the given column is mapped this way to a row of $A(p)$, different entries to different rows, and consecutive entries to consecutive rows. For example, if

$$A(p) = \begin{array}{l} 1\,2\,3\ 4\ 5\,6\ldots p \\ 4\,5\,6\ldots p\,1\ 2\ 3 \end{array}$$

then the substitution of the $1 \times 1$ blocks of $i$-entries are as follows (* denotes entries different from $i$)

$$
\begin{array}{c}
\vdots \\
* \\
i \mapsto (i,1)\,(i,2)\,\ldots\,(i,p) \\
* \\
i \mapsto (i,4)\,(i,5)\,\ldots\,(i,3) \\
* \\
\vdots
\end{array}
$$

This substitution is performed for each different entries $i$ ($1 \le i \le m$), independently of each other, thus replacing each column of $M$ with $p$ columns, whose entries are from $\{1, 2, \ldots, m\} \times \{1, 2, \ldots p\}$.

Let us recall that the discrepancy of the (possibly infinite) array $M$, $\delta(M)$ is defined as the supremum of $\delta(M')$ for finite subrectangles $M'$ of $M$.

**Theorem 3.1.** *Let $M$ be an $\infty \times \infty$ $m$-assignment array of discrepancy $\delta(M)$. Suppose that $A(p)$ is a $\infty \times p$ array whose rows are permutations of $\{1, 2, \ldots, p\}$ of discrepancy $\delta(A(p))$. Then*

$$\delta(A(pM)) \le \delta(M) + 6\,\delta(A(p)).$$

*Proof (of Theorem 3.1).* Consider a rectangle $R$ in $A(pM)$. It can be decomposed into three parts $A, B$ and $C$, where $B$ consists of complete blown up columns, $A$ is the "left chunk", and $C$ is the "right chunk", i.e, they consist of only a part of a blow up of one column, respectively, see Figure 1. Let $A', B'$ and $C'$ denote corresponding entries of $M$. Notice, that $A'$ and $C'$ are single columns. Let $\#_X\alpha$ denote the number of $\alpha$-entries in the block $X$ of an array. Then the following are immediate facts.

(i) $|\#_{A'}i - \#_{A'}j|,\ |\#_{B'}i - \#_{B'}j|,\ |\#_{C'}i - \#_{C'}j| \le \delta(M)$
(ii) $|\#_{A'}i + \#_{B'}i - \#_{A'}j - \#_{B'}j|,\ |\#_{B'}i + \#_{C'}i - \#_{B'}j - \#_{C'}j| \le \delta(M)$
(iii) $|\#_{A'}i + \#_{B'}i + \#_{C'}i - \#_{A'}j - \#_{B'}j - \#_{C'}j| \le \delta(M)$
(iv) $\#_{B'}i = \#_B(i,k)$ for $k = 1, 2, \ldots, p$
(v) $|\#_{ABC}(i,k) - \#_{ABC}(j,l)| \le |\#_{ABC}(i,k) - \#_{ABC}(i,l)| + |\#_{ABC}(i,l) - \#_{ABC}(j,l)|$

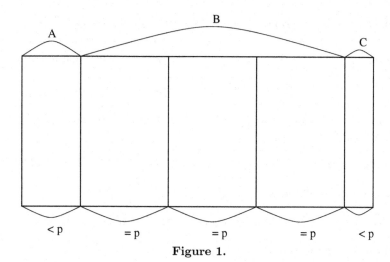

**Figure 1.**

Now

(vi) $|\#_{ABC}(i,k) - \#_{ABC}(i,l)| \leq |\#_A(i,k) - \#_A(i,l)| + |\#_B(i,k) - \#_B(i,l)| + |\#_C(i,k) - \#_C(i,l)| \leq \delta(A(p)) + 0 + \delta(A(p))$

by definition of $\delta(A(p))$ and by (iv). Also, $|\#_{ABC}(i,l) - \#_{ABC}(j,l)| \leq |\#_{AC}(i,l) - \#_{AC}(j,l)| + |\#_{B'}i - \#_{B'}j|$ by (iv). Assume $A$ has $a$ columns $(0 \leq a < p)$ and $C$ has $c$ columns $(0 \leq c < p)$. Then

$$\frac{a}{p}\#_{A'}i - \delta(A(p)) \leq \#_A(i,l) \leq \frac{a}{p}\#_{A'}i - \delta(A(p))$$

is obtained using the fact that the expected number of $(i,l)$'s in $A$ is $\frac{1}{p} \times$ size of the array $= \frac{a\#_{A'}i}{p}$. Thus,

$$\frac{a}{p}(\#_{A'}i - \#_{A'}j) + \frac{c}{p}(\#_{C'}i - \#_{C'}j) - 4\,\delta(A(p)) \leq$$
$$\leq \#_{AC}(i,l) - \#_{AC}(j,l) \leq$$
$$\leq \frac{a}{p}(\#_{A'}i - \#_{A'}j) + \frac{c}{p}(\#_{C'}i - \#_{C'}j) + 4\,\delta(A(p))$$

Again, using (iv) the following is obtained.

(vii) $\frac{a}{p}(\#_{A'}i - \#_{A'}j) + \frac{c}{p}(\#_{C'}i - \#_{C'}j) + (\#_{B'}i - \#_{B'}j) - 4\,\delta(A(p))$
$\leq \#_{ABC}(i,l) - \#_{ABC}(j,l)$.

If $\#_{A'}i - \#_{A'}j \geq 0$ and $\#_{C'}i - \#_{C'}j \geq 0$ then from (vii) $(\#_{B'}i - \#_{B'}j) - 4\,\delta(A(p)) \leq \#_{ABC}(i,l) - \#_{ABC}(j,l)$ follows, which in turn, using (i) implies that

$$-\delta(M) - 4\,\delta(A(p)) \leq \#_{ABC}(i,l) - \#_{ABC}(j,l).$$

For $\#_{A'}i - \#_{A'}j < 0$ and $\#_{C'}i - \#_{C'}j < 0$ we get $\#_{A'}i - \#_{A'}j \leq \frac{a}{p}(\#_{A'}i - \#_{A'}j)$ and $\#_{C'}i - \#_{C'}j \leq \frac{c}{p}(\#_{C'}i - \#_{C'}j)$ so inequality (vi) becomes $\#_{A'B'C'}i - \#_{A'B'C'}j - 4\,\delta(A(p)) \leq \#_{ABC}(i,l) - \#_{ABC}(j,l)$, which again results in

$$-\delta(M) - 4\,\delta(A(p)) \leq \#_{ABC}(i,l) - \#_{ABC}(j,l)$$

using (i). By similar arguments for the remaining two cases using $A'B'$ or $B'C'$, respectively,

(viii) $\quad -\delta(M) - 4\,\delta(A(p)) \leq \#_{ABC}(i,l) - \#_{ABC}(j,l) \leq \delta(M) + 4\,\delta(A(p))$

is obtained. Combining (v), (vi), and (viii) we deduce

$$|\#_{ABC}(i,k) - \#_{ABC}(j,l)| \leq \delta(M) + 6\,\delta(A(p))$$

which proves the result.         $\square$

**Corollary 3.1.** *If the prime factorization of $m$ is $m = p_1^{e_1}\, p_2^{e_2} \ldots p_k^{e_k}$ then*

$$d(m) \leq \sum_{i=1}^{k} 6\, e_i\, d(A(p_i)).$$

*In particular, for $m = 2^k$ $d(m) = O(\log m)$.*

Theorem 3.1 suggests finding $A(p)$ arrays for all prime $p$ of low discrepancy. Clearly, for small $p$ one can do that. For arbitrary $p$ the modular assignment $f(i,j) = s\,i + j \bmod p$ where $s = \lfloor \sqrt{p} \rfloor$ gives $\delta(A(p)) = O(\sqrt{p})$ (To be strict, we should replace symbol 0 with $p$ in this case). We only sketch the simple proof of this observation, because in the next section a better upper bound is proved by a different method.

Let $A(p)$ given by the above $f$. Because $s$ and $p$ are relative primes, each consecutive $p$ entries in a column are permutations of $\{0, 1, \ldots, p-1\}$. Thus, calculating the discrepancy it is enough to consider only rectangles with at most $p$ rows. $A(p)$ is tiled with "L" shaped tiles (see Figure 2)

| $s^2$ | $\ldots$ | | $p-1$ | | |
|---|---|---|---|---|---|
| $s^2 - s$ | $s^2 - s + 1$ | $s^2 - s + 2$ | $\ldots$ | $s^2 - 1$ | |
| $\vdots$ | | | | $\vdots$ | |
| $s$ | $s+1$ | $s+2$ | $\ldots$ | $2s-1$ | |
| $0$ | $1$ | $2$ | $\ldots$ | $s-1$ | |

Each such tile contains every different entry exactly once. A rectangle of at most $p$ rows cuts $O(\sqrt{p})$ such tiles, each cut tile adds at most one to the discrepancy of the rectangle.

This construction and Corollary 3.1 gives $d(m) = O(\sqrt{m})$ for all $m$.

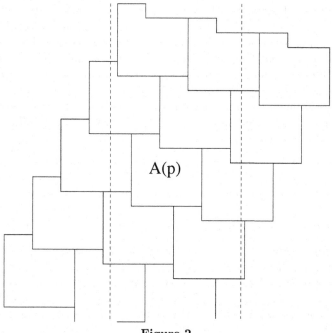

**Figure 2.**

## 4   Latin Square Type Assignments

In the previous section a construction was given that allows "multiplication", i.e. if good assignments for $m$ and $p$ are given, then a good one can be generated for $pm$. In this section we show how to "add". To this end, we consider assignments of *latin square type*. Let us recall that a latin square is an $m \times m$ array consisting of $m$ different symbols, such that each symbol occurs in each row and column exactly once. An $m$-assignment is called latin square type, if

$$f(i,j) = f(i+m,j) = f(i,j+m) \qquad (*)$$

and the array $M = [f(i,j)]_{\substack{i=1,2,\ldots,m \\ j=1,2,\ldots,m}}$ forms a latin square. In this case $M$ is called the *generator* of the assignment. The discrepancy of such an assignment, denoted by $\delta(M)$, is clearly attained by a rectangle whose number of rows and columns, respectively, is not larger than $m$.

A *transversal* of an $m \times m$ latin square $M = [f(i,j)]_{\substack{i=1,2,\ldots,m \\ j=1,2,\ldots,m}}$ is a set of pairwise distinct entries $\{f(i_1,j_1), f(i_2,j_2), \ldots, f(i_m,j_m)\}$ such that in each row and column there is exactly one of them. In other words, $\{i_1, i_2, \ldots, i_m\}$ and $\{j_1, j_2, \ldots, j_m\}$ are both permutations of $\{1, 2, \ldots, m\}$.

The *discrepancy of an entry* in a rectangle $\mathcal{R}$ of an $m$-assignment is the maximum deviation of the number of occurrences of that entry in any sub-rectangle of $\mathcal{R}$ from the expected value, that is from $\frac{1}{m}$th of the area of the subrectangle. That is, the discrepancy of entry $k$ in subrectangle $\mathcal{R}[(a, b), (c, d)]$ is $|\frac{1}{m}(c - a)(d - b) - d_{a,b,c,d}(k)|$. Clearly, an $m$-assignment is of low discrepancy iff each entry is of low discrepancy in every rectangle. The *discrepancy of a transversal* in a latin square defined similarly, namely the maximum deviation of the number of entries (positions) of the transversal in a subregtangle of the latin square from the $\frac{1}{m}$th of the area of the subrectangle. This is extended for the $m$-assignment generated by the latin square by extending the transversal via (*). The next definition allows formulating a strong enough induction hypotheses that can be carried over.

**Definition 4.1.** *Number $m$ is said to have* property O *if there exists a $m \times m$ latin square $M$ that generates an $c \log m$ discrepancy $m$-assignment, such that $M$ has a transversal of discrepancy $c_1 \log m$, where $c$ and $c_1$ are absolute constants.*

**Theorem 4.1.** *If $m$ has property O, then so do $3m$, $3m + 1$, $3m + 2$, as well.*

*Proof (of Theorem 4.1).* The idea of the proof is as follows. Let $M$ be the $m \times m$ latin square showing that $m$ has property O. First, $M$ is blown up to a $3m \times 3m$ latin square $B$ by Theorem 3.1. Then using a transversal of $M$, three new ones of $B$ are constructed. $B$ is extended to a $(3m + 1) \times (3m + 1)$ latin square $C$ by putting symbol $3m + 1$ to the positions of one of the transversals and to entry $(3m + 1, 3m + 1)$, while the original entries of the transversal are placed in column and row $3m + 1$, respectively. Using that $C$ has two transversals left, one can extend it with one more column and row, and preserve one transversal to carry over the induction.

Let $A(3)$ be the $\infty \times 3$ matrix generated by the latin square

$$L = \begin{bmatrix} 1 & 2 & 3 \\ 3 & 1 & 2 \\ 2 & 3 & 1 \end{bmatrix}.$$

Then $\delta(A(3M)) \leq \delta(M) + 6$, by Theorem 3.1. Also, it is generated by the $3m \times 3m$ latin square

$$B = \begin{bmatrix} [1\,2\,3] \times M \\ [3\,1\,2] \times M \\ [2\,3\,1] \times M \end{bmatrix}.$$

$L$ has three transversals:

$$\begin{bmatrix} \bigcirc & \triangle & \square \\ \triangle & \square & \bigcirc \\ \square & \bigcirc & \triangle \end{bmatrix},$$

the *circle*, the *triangle* and the *square* transversals. The product of any of these and a transversal of $M$ yields a transversal for $B$ that are also called circle, triangle and square transversals, respectively.

In order to prove the statement for $3m$ we need to show that any of these product transversals has low discrepancy. Consider a subrectangle $R$ of the $3m$-assignment generated by $B$. We may assume without loss of generality, that $R$

has at most $3m$ columns. $R$ can be decomposed in the same way as in the proof of Theorem 3.1 into 3 parts: $R = S \cup T \cup V$, where $T$ consists of the fully blown up parts, while $S$ and $V$ consist of 1 or 2 extra columns on the left-hand side and right-hand side, respectively. Because $T$ is a fully blown up part, the product transversal has the same number of entries in $T$, as the transversal of $M$ has in the subrectangle, which is blown up to $T$. That is, the density of the product transversal in $T$ is just 1/3rd of that of the original, which is needed exactly. The parts $S$ and $V$ add at most 4 to the discrepancy of the product tranversal, so it has $O(\log 3m)$ discrepancy.

Now, from $B$ a $(3m + 1) \times (3m + 1)$ latin square $C$ is constructed as follows. Take the square transversal of $B$. For each entry $t$ of it at position $(i, j)$ we replace it by $3m + 1$ and place $t$'s in positions $(3m + 1, j)$ and $(i, 3m + 1)$. Furthermore, let the $(3m + 1, 3m + 1)$ entry of $C$ be $3m + 1$.

The $3m+1$-assignment generated by $C$ has discrepancy $O(\log(3m+1))$, since each entry has low discrepancy. In order to obtain a transversal of $C$ use the triangle (or circle) transversal of $B$ and add the $3m + 1$ entry in lower right (i.e. in position $(3m + 1, 3m + 1)$).

We would like to repeat this construction to go from $3m + 1$ to $3m + 2$ by using a transversal of $C$. However, to find a transversal of the resulting latin square $D$, such a transversal of $C$ is needed that does not include the lower right entry. To this end, let us consider an entry $i$ of the low discrepancy transversal of $M$. After the blow up, this becomes

$$
\begin{array}{ccc}
(i,1) & (i,2) & (i,3) \\
\vdots & \vdots & \vdots \\
(i,3) & (i,1) & (i,2) \\
\vdots & \vdots & \vdots \\
(i,2) & (i,3) & (i,1)
\end{array}
$$

in $B$. It is transformed further in $C$ to

$$
\begin{array}{cccccc}
(i,1) & \underline{(i,2)} & \underline{3m+1} & \cdots & (i,3) \\
\vdots & \vdots & \vdots & & \vdots \\
(i,3) & 3m+1 & (i,2) & \cdots & \underline{\underline{(i,2)}} \\
\vdots & \vdots & \vdots & & \vdots \\
3m+1 & \underline{\underline{(i,3)}} & (i,1) & \cdots & (i,2) \\
\vdots & \vdots & \vdots & & \vdots \\
\underline{\underline{(i,2)}} & (i,1) & (i,3) & \cdots & \underline{3m+1}
\end{array}
$$

Here the single underlined entries are from the triangle transversal. Instead of them, take the doubly underlined entries from this part of $C$ together with the rest of the triangle transversal to obtain $(3m + 2) \times (3m + 2)$ latin square $D$ in the same way as $C$ was generated from $B$. This new transversal is also of low discrepancy, because it is a slight perturbation of the triangle transversal, which is of low discrepancy. Hence, $D$ generates a $O(\log(3m+2))$ discrepancy $3m+2$-assignment. The only thing left to finish the proof is to find a good transversal of $D$. Now, in $D$ we have

| $(i,1)$ | $(i,2)$ | $3m+2$ | $\ldots$ | $(i,3)$ | $3m+1$ |
|---|---|---|---|---|---|
| $\vdots$ | $\vdots$ | $\vdots$ | | $\vdots$ | $\vdots$ |
| $\underline{(i,3)}$ | $3m+1$ | $(i,2)$ | $\ldots$ | $3m+2$ | $(i,1)$ |
| $\vdots$ | $\vdots$ | $\vdots$ | | $\vdots$ | $\vdots$ |
| $3m+1$ | $3m+2$ | $\underline{(i,1)}$ | $\ldots$ | $(i,2)$ | $(i,3)$ |
| $\vdots$ | $\vdots$ | $\vdots$ | | $\vdots$ | $\vdots$ |
| $3m+2$ | $(i,1)$ | $(i,3)$ | $\ldots$ | $\underline{3m+1}$ | $(i,2)$ |
| $(i,2)$ | $(i,3)$ | $3m+1$ | $\ldots$ | $(i,1)$ | $3m+2$ |

The underlined entries and the rest of the triangle transversal from the rest of $B$ forms a low discrepancy transversal of $D$.                                    □

**Corollary 4.1.**
$$d(m) = O(\log m)$$
*for all $m > 0$.*                                    □

# 5    A Lower Bound

In this section we use the following deep result of Schmidt [6] to prove that Theorem 4.1 is best possible for latin square type assignments.

**Theorem 5.1.** *Let $P$ be an arbitrary set of $N$ points in the unit square $[0,1)^2$. Then there exisits a rectangle $B \subset [0,1)^2$ with sides parallel to the coordinate axes such that*
$$\left| |P \cap B| - N\,area(B) \right| > c \log N \qquad (**)$$
*where $c$ is an absolute constant.*

To prove a lower bound for the discrepancy of an assignment it is enough to consider a finite part of it, in our case, the generating lating square.

**Theorem 5.2.** *Let $M$ be an $m \times m$ latin square. Then any entry has discrepancy at least $c \log m$, where $c$ is an absolute constant.*

*Proof (of Theorem 5.2).* Let us partition the unit square into $m^2$ little squares of side $1/m$. Consider entry $t$ of $M$ and put a point in the center of the little square in the $i$th row and $j$th column if the $(i,j)$ entry of $M$ is equal to $t$. Apply Theorem 5.1 with $N = m$ to find subrectangle $B$. We may assume without loss of generality, that $B$'s sides coincide with the sides of some little squares, so $B$ corresponds to some $\mathcal{R}[a,b,c,d]$ subrectangle of $M$. The number of points in $B$ is equal to $d_{a,b,c,d}(t)$, while $N\,area(B) = m\,\frac{c-a}{m}\,\frac{d-b}{m}$, so inequality $(**)$ states that the deviation of entry $t$ from the expected value in the subrectangle of $M$ corresponding to $B$ is at least $c \log m$.                                    □

## 6   Conclusions, Open Problems

We have shown that the optimality of every $m$ is $O(\log m)$. However, the lower bound works only for latin square type assignments. Thus, it is natural to ask, whether it holds in general?

In the proof of Theorem 4.1 triple-fold blow-up is used. One might ask why was it neccessary, could not the proof be done using only double blow-up? The reason for the seemingly more complicated induction is that transversals of the $3 \times 3$ latin square are essentially used, however, a $2 \times 2$ latin square does not have any.

Applying the blow up for $p = 2$ the the obtained assignments are generated by the following latin squares for $m = 2^t$ $t = 1, 2, 3, 4$:

$$\begin{bmatrix} 1 & 2 \\ 2 & 1 \end{bmatrix} \qquad \begin{bmatrix} 1 & 2 & 3 & 4 \\ 3 & 4 & 1 & 2 \\ 2 & 1 & 4 & 3 \\ 4 & 3 & 2 & 1 \end{bmatrix} \qquad \begin{bmatrix} 1 & 2 & 3 & 4 & 5 & 6 & 7 & 8 \\ 5 & 6 & 7 & 8 & 1 & 2 & 3 & 4 \\ 3 & 4 & 1 & 2 & 7 & 8 & 5 & 6 \\ 7 & 8 & 5 & 6 & 3 & 4 & 1 & 2 \\ 2 & 1 & 4 & 3 & 6 & 5 & 8 & 7 \\ 6 & 5 & 8 & 7 & 2 & 1 & 4 & 3 \\ 4 & 3 & 2 & 1 & 8 & 7 & 6 & 5 \\ 8 & 7 & 6 & 5 & 4 & 3 & 2 & 1 \end{bmatrix}$$

$$\begin{bmatrix}
1 & 2 & 3 & 4 & 5 & 6 & 7 & 8 & 9 & 10 & 11 & 12 & 13 & 14 & 15 & 16 \\
9 & 10 & 11 & 12 & 13 & 14 & 15 & 16 & 1 & 2 & 3 & 4 & 5 & 6 & 7 & 8 \\
5 & 6 & 7 & 8 & 1 & 2 & 3 & 4 & 13 & 14 & 15 & 16 & 9 & 10 & 11 & 12 \\
13 & 14 & 15 & 16 & 9 & 10 & 11 & 12 & 5 & 6 & 7 & 8 & 1 & 2 & 3 & 4 \\
3 & 4 & 1 & 2 & 7 & 8 & 5 & 6 & 11 & 12 & 9 & 10 & 15 & 16 & 13 & 14 \\
11 & 12 & 9 & 10 & 15 & 16 & 13 & 14 & 3 & 4 & 1 & 2 & 7 & 8 & 5 & 6 \\
7 & 8 & 5 & 6 & 3 & 4 & 1 & 2 & 15 & 16 & 13 & 14 & 11 & 12 & 9 & 10 \\
15 & 16 & 13 & 14 & 11 & 12 & 9 & 10 & 7 & 8 & 5 & 6 & 3 & 4 & 1 & 2 \\
2 & 1 & 4 & 3 & 6 & 5 & 8 & 7 & 10 & 9 & 12 & 11 & 14 & 13 & 16 & 15 \\
10 & 9 & 12 & 11 & 14 & 13 & 16 & 15 & 2 & 1 & 4 & 3 & 6 & 5 & 8 & 7 \\
6 & 5 & 8 & 7 & 2 & 1 & 4 & 3 & 14 & 13 & 16 & 15 & 10 & 9 & 12 & 11 \\
14 & 13 & 16 & 15 & 10 & 9 & 12 & 11 & 6 & 5 & 8 & 7 & 2 & 1 & 4 & 3 \\
4 & 3 & 2 & 1 & 8 & 7 & 6 & 5 & 12 & 11 & 10 & 9 & 16 & 15 & 14 & 13 \\
12 & 11 & 10 & 9 & 16 & 15 & 14 & 13 & 4 & 3 & 2 & 1 & 8 & 7 & 6 & 5 \\
8 & 7 & 6 & 5 & 4 & 3 & 2 & 1 & 16 & 15 & 14 & 13 & 12 & 11 & 10 & 9 \\
16 & 15 & 14 & 13 & 12 & 11 & 10 & 9 & 8 & 7 & 6 & 5 & 4 & 3 & 2 & 1
\end{bmatrix}$$

The discrepancies are 1, 2, 2, 3, respectively. Studying the pattern of these latin squares one can find an explicit, non-recursive method for constructing them, starting from the first row $[1, 2, \ldots, 2^t]$. We strongly believe that for $m = 2^t$ our construction is best possible.

Theorem 5.2 works also for modular assignments, as well. However, there are not known bounds for their performance, in general. The construction for $A(p)$, $p$ prime, gives an $O(\sqrt{m})$ upper bound, for certain $m$'s. The question is, whether the lower, or the upper bound is sharp in that case?

In the present paper we studied low discrepancy allocation of two-dimensional data. It is natural to extend the scope of investigations to higher dimensions. For example, one can have a database of temperature distribution in a three-dimensional body. How well can three- (or higher-) dimensional data distributed?

## References

1. K. A. S. Abdel-Ghaffar and A. El Abbadi, *Optimal Allocation of Two Dimensinal Data*, in: Database Theory – ICDT'97, F. Afrati and Ph. Kolaitis (Eds.), *Lecture Notes in Computer Science 1186*, 1997, 409-418.
2. C. Y. Chen and C. C. Chang, On GDM allocation method for partial range queries, *Information Systems*, **17** 1992, 381-394.
3. H. C. Du and J. S. Sobolewski, Disk allocation for cartesian product files on multiple disk systems, *ACM Trans. Database Syst.*, **7** 1982, 82-101.
4. C. Faloutsos, R. Barber, M. Flickner, J. Hafner, W. Niblack, D. Petkovic and W. Equitz, Efficient and effective querying by image content, *Journal of Intelligent Information Systems*, **3** 1994, 231-262.
5. V. E. Ogle and M. Stonebraker, Chabot: Retrieval from relational database of images, *Computer* **28**(9) 1995, 40-48.
6. W. M. Schmidt, Irregularities of distribution VII, *Acta Arithm.* **21**, (1972) 45-50.
7. T. R. Smith, A digital library for geographically referenced materials, *Computer*, **29**(5) 1996, 54-60.
8. M. Vitterli and C. Herley, Wavelets and filter banks: Theory and design, *IEEE Transactions on Signal Processing*, **40**(9) 1992, 2207-2232.

# A Family of Nested Query Languages for Semi-structured Data

Nicole Bidoit, Sofian Maabout, and Mourad Ykhlef

LaBRI. Université de Bordeaux I
351 cours de la libération 33405 Talence
{bidoit,maabout,my}@labri.u-bordeaux.fr

**Abstract.** Semi-structured data are commonly represented by labelled graphs. The labels may be strings, integers, ... Thus their type is atomic. They are carried by edges and/or nodes. In this paper, we investigate a nested graph representation of semi-structured data. Some nodes of our graphs may be labelled by graphs. Our motivation is to bring the data model in use closer to the natural presentation of data, in particular closer to the Web presentation. The main purpose of the paper is to provide query languages of reasonable expressive power for querying nested db-graphs.

## 1 Introduction

Recently, semi-structured data attracted a lot of attention from the research database community (see for example [8, 4, 3, 10, 9, 5, 6]). This interest is motivated by a wide range of applications such as the genome databases, scientific databases, libraries of programs, digital libraries, on-line documentation, electronic commerce. Semi-structured data arises under a variety of forms: data in BibTex or Latex files, HTML or XML files, data integrated from independent sources. Clearly enough, the main challenge is to provide suitable data models and languages to represent and manipulate semi-structured data. Several proposals have been made [13, 7, 6]. The representation of semi-structured data by graphs with labels on edges and/or vertices is shared by almost all proposals.

In a previous paper [6], we have proposed a model for semi-structured data, called the db-graph model together with a logic query language in the style of relational calculus. The contribution of [6] resides in a sound theoretically founded language. Furthermore the language, called Graph(Fixpoint), has been shown more expressive than other proposals such as Lore [3], UnQL [8], WebSQL [10].

In this paper, we study an extension of our db-graph model for representing semi-structured data. This extension allows one to have db-graphs whose vertex labels are db-graphs themselves. It is widely recognized that the difficulties arising when defining a model and a language to describe and manipulate semi-structured data are *(i)* a partial knowledge of the structure and *(ii)* a potentially "deeply nested" structure.

K.-D. Schewe, B. Thalheim (Eds.): FoIKS 2000, LNCS 1762, pp. 13–30, 2000.
© Springer-Verlag Berlin Heidelberg 2000

Bringing the data model closer to the natural presentation of data stored via Web documents is the main motivation behind nesting db-graphs. To illustrate the use of nested graphs, let us consider the case of XML documents. Assume we have a XML file `book.xml`. Its contents and its graph representation are described below.

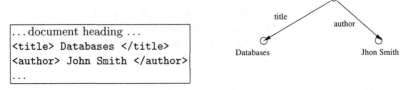

```
... document heading ...
<title> Databases </title>
<author> John Smith </author>
...
```

Clearly, `title` and `author` are considered as attribute names whereas `Databases` and `John Smith` are data. Now suppose that we add to this document the lines which describe an anchor pointing to the file `contents.xml`.

```
<contents>
<A HREF ="file://contents.xml">Table of contents
</A></contents>
```

The view of `books.xml` becomes:

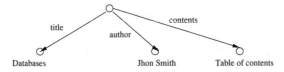

Furthermore, assume that `contents.xml` is as described below

```
... document heading ...
<Section1> Relational Databases </Section1>
<Section2> Object Databases </Section2>
...
```

Thus, we may enrich our initial graph to represent the contents of the second document. To this purpose, we may consider two alternatives. The first one uses a "flat graph" while the second uses a "nested graph". Both representations are respectively described below. We believe that the second graph is a more faithful representation of the real world. Indeed, it helps to distinguish between the structure of `book.xml` and that of the file

```
... document heading ...
<title> Databases </title>
<author> John Smith </author>
<contents> Table of Contents
        <Section1> Relational databases</Section1>
        <Section2> Object databases</Section2>
</contents>
...
```

whose graph representation is actually a flat graph identical to the one in Figure 1(a).

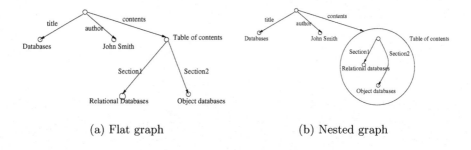

(a) Flat graph                           (b) Nested graph

**Fig. 1.** Two possible representations

Let us now consider another situation. The Web can be viewed as a graph. Its nodes are files in particular formats. A node of the Web db-graph may well be a structured document (e.g., the annual report of the LaBRI database group in PDF format). As such, this node can itself naturally be represented by a graph. Another node of the Web may be a simple text file (e.g., describing the topics of interest of the LaBRI database group). This node will carry a simple label. Finally, there may exist a node providing an interface to an integrated movie database build from several sources containing information about movies, movie theaters in Bordeaux, ... , comments about movies provided by the LaBRI database group members. In this case again, the Web node is in fact valued by a db-graph: the db-graph (let us call it the movie db-graph) represents the integrated sources of information. It is easy to go one step further in the modeling process. Let us consider those nodes of the movie db-graph corresponding to the LaBRI database group member comments about movies. Some of these nodes may well be simple and carry simple text. Others may be complex and contain structured documents. This situation leads to having a second level of nesting in the Web db-graph.

Applications bring many examples of this kind. It is of course possible to represent these semi-structured data by "flat" db-graphs. The work presented in this paper investigates the gain in using a nested representation. The approach is similar to that of the nested relational model [1] compared to the relational model. We mainly focus on providing languages to query nested db-graphs. Two languages are proposed. They both are formally defined in a calculus style as extensions of the language introduced in [6]. The two languages differ in the knowledge of the "structure" required to express queries. The first language, called Graph(Nest-Path), is based on a nested path language Nest-Path. In order to specify a query with this language, it is required that the user knows the levels of nesting of the searched information. In contrast, the second language, called Graph(Emb-Path), has a higher degree of declarativeness: the user does not need to have any knowledge about the level of nesting of the "wanted" information.

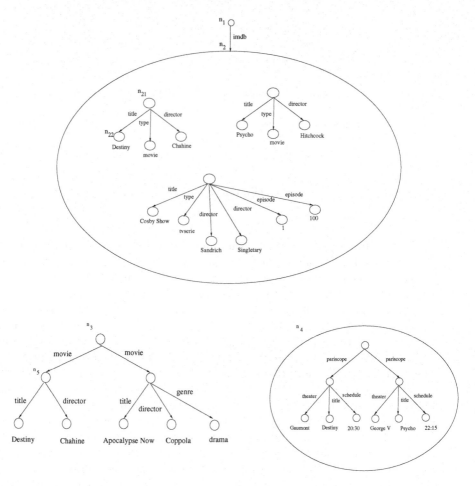

**Fig. 2.** A nested db-graph.

The paper is organized as follows. Section 2 is devoted to the presentation of our nested semi-structured data model. Section 3 prepares to the definitions of the graph query languages by introducing common notions. In fact, Section 3 introduces a parameterized graph query language Graph($\mathcal{L}$) where $\mathcal{L}$, the parameter, is a path query language. In section 4, we instantiate $\mathcal{L}$ by a path query language based on nested path formulas called Nest-Path which extends the language Path introduced in [6]. The advantages and drawbacks of Graph(Nest-Path) are discussed. The main problem arising while using Graph(Nest-Path) to query a nested db-graph is that it requires to have knowledge of the levels of nesting. Section 5 tries to solve this problem and provides a new instantiation of $\mathcal{L}$ called Emb-Path. Further research topics conclude the paper.

## 2    Data Model

Nested db-graphs (db-graphs for short) are a generalization of flat db-graphs in the sense that some nodes are allowed "to be" themselves db-graphs. Hence, in the next definition, we shall distinguish two sets of nodes: a set $N_s$ of simple nodes and a set $N_c$ of complex nodes.

**Definition 2.1 (Nested db-graph).** *Let $\mathcal{V}$ be an infinite set of atomic values. Let $N_s$ be a set of simple nodes and $N_c$ a set of complex nodes. Let $E$ be a set of edges (identifiers). Let $org$ and $dest$ be functions assigning to an edge respectively its origin and its destination. Let $\lambda$ be a polymorphic labelling function for nodes and edges such that labels of simple nodes and edges are atomic values in $\mathcal{V}$ whereas labels of complex nodes are db-graphs.*

*A nested db-graph $G = (N_s, N_c, E, \lambda, org, dest)$ is defined recursively by:*

1. *If $N_c$ is empty then $G = (N_s, N_c, E, \lambda, org, dest)$ is a nested db-graph. In this case, $G$ is called a flat db-graph.*
2. *$G = (N_s, N_c, E, \lambda, org, dest)$ is a nested db-graph over the db-graphs $G_1, .., G_k$ if for each $n \in N_c$, $\lambda(n)$ is one of the db-graphs $G_1, .., G_k$*

*Example 2.1.* Figure 2 is an example of a nested db-graph. It contains two complex nodes $n_2$ and $n_4$. The destination $n_2$ of the edge labelled by imdb, contains a db-graph providing information about movies and tv-series. The complex node $n_4$ is labelled by a db-graph representing a relational database having a single relation *pariscope(theater, title, schedule)*. The simple node $n_3$ is the *root* of a flat db-tree giving information about movies too.

Let us consider a nested db-graph $G = (N_s, N_c, E, \lambda, org, dest)$ over the db-graphs $G_1, \ldots, G_k$. We provide the reader with few remarks and notations:

- In order to avoid ambiguity, we use the term *node* of $G$ to refer to an element of $N_s$ or $N_c$ and we use the term *embedded node* of $G$ to refer to either a node of $G$ or a node of $G_i$ or an embedded node of $G_i$.
  For instance, if one considers the db-graph drawn in Figure 2, the nodes $n_1$, $n_2$, $n_3$ are nodes of $G$; the nodes $n_{21}$ and $n_{22}$ are not "direct" nodes of $G$, they are embedded in the node $n_2$.
  When necessary, we use the notations $N_s(G)$, $N_c(G)$ and $N_{emb}(G)$ to refer respectively to the set of simple nodes of $G$, the set of complex nodes of $G$ and the set of embedded nodes of $G$.
- We make the assumption that $N_s$ and $N_c$ are disjoint sets (a node cannot be simple and complex at the same time). We also make the assumption that $N_s$ and $N_c$ both have an empty intersection with $N_{emb}(G_i)$, for any $i$. Intuitively, a node cannot belong to several levels of nesting in $G$ (see below).
- Two nodes can be linked by several edges although each pair of such edges should carry different labels. Thus an edge is totally defined by its origin $o$, its destination $d$ and its label $l$. We sometimes use the notation $(o, d, l)$ to refer to that edge.

- A *path* is a sequence of edges $\langle e_1, e_2, \ldots, e_k \rangle$ s.t $dest(e_i) = org(e_{i+1})$ for $i=1..k\text{-}1$.

  In the following, as it is usually done, we restrict our attention to *simple paths* that is paths with no multiple occurrences of a same edge.

  Note here again that when considering a path of $G$, embedded db-graphs are not expanded.

  The empty path is denoted $\epsilon$.

  The mappings $org$ and $dest$ are extended to paths in a natural way.

- The embedded db-graphs $G_1, \ldots, G_k$ of $G$ are at level 1 of nesting in $G$. The set of all embedded db-graphs of $G$ is composed of $G_1, \ldots, G_k$ and of theirs embedded db-graphs. The notion of *level of nesting* in $G$ of an embedded db-graph is the natural one.

  By a path $p$ of level $l$ in $G$, we mean a path $p$ of an embedded db-graph of level $l$. Recall that we make the assumption that an embedded node cannot belong to more than one level of nesting. Thus the same holds for a path.

- Atomic labels are carried by simple nodes and edges of $G$ and also by simple nodes and edges of embedded db-graphs of $G$. This entails that a label may occur at different levels of nesting in $G$. For instance, in figure 2, the atomic value `title` labels two embedded edges, one at level 0 and the other at level 1.

  In the following, atomic values labelling nodes are called *data* and atomic values labelling edges are called *labels*.

- A node $r$ of a graph $G$ is a source for $G$ if there exists a path from $r$ to any other node of $G$. A graph is rooted if it has at least one source.

## 3   Querying Semi-structured Data: Preliminaries

In this section, we introduce the general setting which serves the definition of our languages. In the literature, most of the languages proposed for querying semi-structured data represented by a graph are based on a similar approach, although the paradigms used are different. A query is meant to extract sub-graphs from the initial graph or equivalently the roots of these sub-graphs. What are the criteria participating in the specification of the sub-graph retrieval? Essentially, the languages allow one to express two kinds of properties: *(i)* reachability of the root of the output sub-graphs via a specific path; *(ii)* existence, in the output sub-graph, of some specific paths. It is easy to see that both kinds of property rely on some paths. This explains why most languages like ours [6] are based on an intermediate language which retrieves paths in a graph. These path languages often use path expressions as their basic constructs. Their expressive power determines the expressive power of the semi-structured query language based on it. In the following, for the purpose of the presentation, we will view a semi-structured query language as a language parameterized by a path formulas $\mathcal{L}_{path}$.

The languages considered in this paper are calculus. Thus we suppose that four sorts of variables are on hand: path and graph variables denoted by

$X, Y, Z, \ldots$, label variables denoted by $x, y, z, \ldots$ and data variables denoted by $\alpha, \beta, \gamma, \ldots$ We sometimes use bold capital characters $\mathbb{X}, \mathbb{Y}, \ldots$ when the sort of the variable is irrelevant. A *term* is defined as usual.

A path formula $\varphi$ of $\mathcal{L}_{path}$ may have free variables. All free variables of $\varphi$ are forced to be of the sort path. Defining the semantics of $\mathcal{L}_{path}$ is done by defining the relation $G, \nu \models \varphi$ for any db-graph $G$ and any valuation $\nu$ of the free variables in $\varphi$.

We now have all the ingredients to define a db-graph query language parameterized by the path formulas in $\mathcal{L}_{path}$.

**Definition 3.1.** *A query in the language Graph($\mathcal{L}_{path}$) is an expression of the form $\{X_1, \ldots, X_n \mid \phi\}$ where $X_i$'s are graph variables and moreover $X_i$'s are the only free variables of the graph formula $\phi$.*

*An atomic graph formula is an expression of one of the following forms:*

1. *A path formula in $\mathcal{L}_{path}$,*
2. *$t : X$ where $t$ is a graph term and $X$ is a path variable,*
3. *$X[t]$ where $X$ is a path variable and $t$ is a graph term,*
4. *$t_1 \sim t_2$ where both $t_1$ and $t_2$ are graph terms and where $\sim$ is the symbol of bisimulation [12].*

*A general graph formula is defined in the usual way by introducing connectives and quantifiers.*

Roughly speaking, $t : X$ means that $X$ is a path whose origin is a root of the graph $t$. Hence the formula of the kind $t : X$ expresses what has been formerly introduced as a retrieval condition of the kind *(i) existence, in the output subgraph, of some specific path.*

Intuitively, the atom $X[t]$ checks whether the graph $t$ is rooted at the destination of the path $X$. This formula illustrates what we have previously introduced as a retrieval condition of the kind *(ii) reachability of the root of the output sub-graphs via a specific path.*

The formal definitions of graph formula satisfaction and of graph query answering are not developed here. The interested reader can find these definitions in [6].

As a matter of fact, in [6] we defined three path languages, namely Path, Path-Fixpoint and Path-While. The expressive power of the graph languages G-Fixpoint defined as Graph(Path-Fixpoint) and G-While defined as Graph(Path-While) were investigated.

In the next sections, using the same technics as [6], we define two nested db-graph query languages. The first one is based on a path language called Nest-Path and the second one is based on Emb-Path.

## 4   Nest-Path: A Nested Path Calculus

In this section, we introduce Nest-Path, a path expression language which extends Path by nesting (simple) path expressions. A path expression in Path is an abstraction for describing paths which have a level of nesting equal to 0. Here we need a mechanism to abstract paths belonging to any level of nesting. Let us first illustrate the language Nest-Path.

A (simple) path expression (in Path) can be of the form $x \triangleright \alpha$ and then the intention is to describe all paths reduced to a single edge labelled by $x$ whose destination is a *simple* node labelled by $\alpha$.

We extend these simple expressions by considering the more general form $l \triangleright q$ where $q$ is a path query. Such a nested path expression is meant to specify paths reduced to a simple edge labelled by $l$ and whose destination is a *complex* node on which the query $q$ should evaluate to a non-empty set of paths.

*Example 4.1.* Let q : {Y | Y ∈ title} be a path query. Then imdb $\triangleright$ q is a nested path expression. It specifies paths of level 0 reduced to a single edge labelled by imdb and whose destination is a complex node labelled by a nested graph $G_i$ on which the query q evaluates to a non-empty set of paths of level 1, reduced to one edge labelled by title. The single path of the db-graph of figure 2 spelled by imdb $\triangleright$ q} is the edge $(n_1, n_2, imdb)$. Note that the query $q$ evaluated on the contents of the complex node $n_2$ returns the 3 edges whose destinations are respectively labelled by "Destiny", "Psycho" and "Cosby Show".

## 4.1   Nest-Path's Syntax

We now formally define nested path expressions.

**Definition 4.1 (Nest-Path).** *A nested path expression is recursively defined by:*

1. *A path variable or a label term is a nested path expression. In this case, it is both pre-free (the origin of the path is not constrained) and post-free (the destination of the path is not constrained).*

2. *(a) $s \triangleright t$        (b) $t \triangleleft s$*
   *(c) $s \triangleright q(X_1, \ldots, X_n)$ (d) $q(X_1, \ldots, X_n) \triangleleft s$  are nested path expressions if*
   - *$s$ is a nested path expression. In cases (b) and (d), s is required to be pree-free and in cases (a) and (c), s is required to be post-free.*
   - *$t$ is a data term.*
   - *$q$ is a nested path query of arity $n$ [1]*
   - *$X_i$ are path variables.*
   *The nested path expressions of types (a) and (c) are post-bound. Those of types (b) and (d) are pre-bound.*

3. *$s_1.s_2$ is a nested path expression when $s_1$ and $s_2$ are nested path expressions, resp. post-free and pree-free. $s_1.s_2$ is pre-free (resp. post-free) as soon as $s_1$ (resp. $s_2$) is.*

---

[1] See definition 4.2.

*Example 4.2.* The expression `movie.title` captures every path $p$ having two edges labelled successively by `movie` and `title`. It is pre-free and post-free since neither the destination nor the origin of $p$ is bound by a data term or a query. The path expression `movie.title ▷ "Destiny"` captures paths of the same form whose destination brings the data "Destiny". This expression is pre-free and post-bound. The expression `imdb ▷ q(X)` is a pre-free, post-bound nested path expression.

We are now going to complete the former definition to make precise what is a path query. A path formula is build from path expressions as follows:

1. It is a nested path expression.
2. It is $t_1 = t_2$ where $t_1$ and $t_2$ are terms of the same sort.
3. It is $t \in s$ where $t$ is a path term and $s$ is a nested path expression.
4. $\phi \wedge \psi$ (resp. $\phi \vee \psi$, $\neg \phi$, $(\exists X) \phi$ and $(\forall X) \phi$ where $\phi$ and $\psi$ are path formulas.

Intuitively, $t \in s$ intends to check that the path $t$ is among the paths spelled by the path expression $s$.

**Definition 4.2 (Nested path query).** *A nested path query of arity $n$ is of the form $\{X_1, \ldots, X_n \mid \varphi\}$ where $\varphi$ is a nested path formula, for $i = 1..n$, $X_i$ is a path variable, and the set $Free(\varphi)$ of free variables of $\varphi$ is exactly $\{X_1, \ldots, X_n\}$.*

*Example 4.3.* Let us consider the nested path query $r : \{X \mid \text{imdb} \triangleright q(X)\}$ where $q$ is the unary query $\{Y \mid Y \in \text{title}\}$.

This query is meant to return paths of level 1 embedded in a node which is the destination of an edge of level 0 labelled by `imdb`. These output paths are reduced to single edges labelled by *title*.

The preceding example suggests that a level of nesting is associated to variables in path expressions and queries. The notion of level of a variable in a path expression or query is necessary in order to define the semantics. We will restrict our presentation to meaningful examples.

*Example 4.4.* In the previous example, the level of the variable X occurring in r is 1. This is implied by the fact that the level of the variable Y in q is 0 and X is linked to Y by q in the nested path expression `imdb ▷ q(X)`.

*Example 4.5.* Consider the path query r defined by $\{X \mid X \in \text{title} \vee \text{imdb} \triangleright q(X)\}$ where q is $\{Y \mid Y \in \text{title}\}$.
The query r returns the edges of level 0 labelled by `title` (this comes from $X \in \text{title}$) as well as the edges of level 1 labelled by `title` (this comes from `imdb ▷ q(X)`). Note that, in this case, two levels (0 and 1) are associated to the variable X. This situation is considered valid in the framework of nested db-graphs. The motivation is to allow one to retrieve paths at different levels of nesting. In fact, the only case where it is sound to assign multiple levels to a variable arises in disjunctive queries. Note here that the query r could have been split into two conjunctive queries.

*Example 4.6.* The expression $\{X \mid X.\mathtt{imdb} \triangleright \mathtt{q}(X)\}$ where $\mathtt{q} : \{Y \mid Y \in \mathtt{title}\}$ is not a query because the variable $X$ is assigned two levels (0 and 1) and a concrete path cannot be assigned two different levels.

In [15], a procedure has been defined that assigns levels of nesting to the variables of a path query or path expression. In the following we assume that expressions are "well nested" and moreover that variables have a unique level (disjunction is ruled out without loss of generality).

## 4.2   Nest-Path's Semantics

The semantics of Nest-Path is provided by giving a precise definition of the function *Spell*. Given a db-graph $G$ and a path expression $s$, the function *Spell* gives the paths of $G$ or embedded in $G$ which conform to the expression $s$. In order to define *Spell*, we first need to tell how variables are valuated. As usually in the framework of calculus for querying databases [2], valuations rely on the active domain of the underlying db-graph $G$ and expression $s$. The formal definition of the active domain is cumbersome and we will avoid its presentation here. The general idea is that a variable $X$, for instance a path variable, cannot be valuated by any path. It should be valuated by a path $p$ in $G$ or in an embedded graph of $G$, depending on the level of nesting associated to the variable $X$. So in fact, we always valuate a pair $(X, l)$ composed of a variable and its level in the path expression $s$ or in a query $r$ by a "value" in the graph of corresponding level $l$ of nesting.

For sake of simplicity, in the rest of the paper, we use the term *valuation* to abbreviate *active domain valuation sound w.r.t. level assignment*.

**Definition 4.3 (Spelling).** *Let* $G = (N_s, N_c, E, \lambda, org, dest)$ *be a db-graph.* $Var(s)$ *is the set of variables appearing in the expression* $s$. *Let* $\nu$ *be a valuation of* $Var(s)$. *The set of simple paths spelled by* $s$ *in* $G$, *with respect to* $\nu$ *denoted by* $Spell_G(\nu(s))$ *is defined as follows:*

1. *if* $s$ *is* $X$ *then* $Spell_G(\nu(s)) = \{\nu(X)\}$,

2. *if* $s$ *is a label term* $t$ *then* $Spell_G(\nu(s)) = \{\langle e \rangle \mid e \in E$ *and* $\lambda(e) = \nu(t)\}$,

3. *if* $s$ *is* $s_1 \triangleright t$ *then* $Spell_G(\nu(s)) = \{p \mid p \in Spell_G(\nu(s_1))$ *and*
$$\lambda(dest(p)) = \nu(t) \qquad \}$$
$Spell_G(\nu(t \triangleleft s_1)$ *is defined in a similar fashion.*

4. *if* $s$ *is* $s_1 \triangleright q(X_1, \ldots, X_n)$ *then*
$Spell_G(\nu(s)) = \{p \mid p \in Spell_G(\nu(s_1)) \qquad\qquad$ *and*
$\qquad\qquad\qquad q(\lambda(dest(p))) \neq \emptyset \qquad\qquad$ *and*
$\qquad\qquad\qquad (\nu(X_1), \ldots, \nu(X_n)) \in q(\lambda(dest(p))) \qquad \}$
*where* $q(\lambda(dest(p)))$ *denotes the answer (see definition 4.5 below) of the path query* $q$ *evaluated on the db-graph labelling the destination of the path* $p$. $Spell_G(\nu(q(X_1, \ldots, X_n) \triangleleft s_1))$ *is defined in a similar way.*

5. *if $s$ is $s_1.s_2$ then $Spell_G(\nu(s)) = \{p_1.p_2 \mid$* $p_1 \in Spell_G(\nu(s_1))$ *and*
$$p_2 \in Spell_G(\nu(s_2)) \quad and$$
$$dest(p_1) = org(p_2) \quad and$$
$$p_1.p_2 \ is \ simple \qquad \}$$

*Example 4.7.* Let $G$ be the db-graph of figure 2. Let $s$ be the path expression
imdb $\triangleright$ q(X) where q : $\{$Y $\mid$ Y $\in$ title$\}$
Consider the valuation $\nu$ of X (whose level in $s$ is 1) by the path $\langle(n_{21}, n_{22}, title)\rangle$
of level 1, then it is easy to see that $\nu(X)$ belongs to the answer of the query q
evaluated on the db-graph labelling the complex node $n_2$. In fact, $Spell_G(\nu(s)) = \{\langle(n_1, n_2, imdb)\rangle\}$.

**Definition 4.4 (Satisfaction of a path formula).** *Let $\varphi$ be a path formula
and $\nu$ a valuation of $Free(\varphi)$. A db-graph $G$ satisfies $\varphi$ w.r.t $\nu$, denoted $G \models \varphi[\nu]$, if*

1. *$\varphi$ is a path expression and $Spell_G(\varphi[\nu]) \neq \emptyset$.*
2. *$\varphi$ is $t_1 = t_2$ where $t_1$ and $t_2$ are both terms and $\nu(t_1) = \nu(t_2)$.*
3. *$\varphi$ is $t \in s$ where $t$ is a path term and there exists an embedded db-graph $G'$
   of level equal to that of $t$ such that $\nu(t) \in Spell_{G'}(\nu(s))$.*
4. *Satisfaction for $(\phi \wedge \psi)$, $\neg \phi$, $(\exists X) \phi$ or $(\forall X)$ is defined as usual.*

**Definition 4.5 (Path query answer).** *Let $q = \{X_1, \ldots, X_n \mid \varphi\}$ be a path
query and $\nu$ be a valuation of $Free(\varphi)$. The answer of $q$ evaluated over the
db-graph $G$ is*

$$q(G) = \{(\nu(X_1), \ldots, \nu(X_n)) \mid G \models \varphi[\nu]\}.$$

Hence, a path query takes a db-graph as an input and outputs tuples of paths.
The following example illustrates how the language Nest-Path can be used to
combine data which may reside in different embedded graphs.

*Example 4.8.* Let us consider once more the db-graph of Figure 2. Assume that
the user knows about the "structure" of the information in node $n_2$ as well as
the "structure" of the information in node $n_4$ (These structures may have been
extracted by an intelligent engine). Thus he/she knows that $n_2$ provides titles
together with directors of movies and $n_4$ provides titles together with theaters.
Now assume that the user just wants to combine these information to have
together titles, directors and theaters. He/she may express this by the following
query r : $\{$F, D, T $\mid$ s$\}$ where $s$ is the following path expression
   imdb $\triangleright$ q$_1$(F, D) $\wedge$ $(\exists$U$)(\exists$Fm) (U $\triangleright$ q$_2$(Fm, T) $\wedge$
$$(\exists\alpha) \ (\text{F} \in \text{title} \triangleright \alpha \ \wedge \ \text{Fm} \in \text{title} \triangleright \alpha))$$
   and
   q$_1$ : $\{$X$_1$, Y$_1$ $\mid$ $(\exists$Z$_1)$ (Z$_1$.X$_1$ $\wedge$ X$_1$ $\in$ title $\wedge$ Z$_1$.Y$_1$ $\wedge$ Y$_1$ $\in$ director)$\}$
   q$_2$ : $\{$X$_2$, Y$_2$ $\mid$ $(\exists$Z$_2)$ (Z$_2$ $\in$ pariscope $\wedge$ Z$_2$.X$_2$ $\wedge$ X$_2$ $\in$ title
$$\wedge \ \text{Z}_2.\text{Y}_2 \ \wedge \ \text{Y}_2 \in \text{theater})\}$$

The query $q_1$ collects information (title and director) from the complex node $n_2$ and the query $q_2$ returns information (title and theater) from $n_4$. The combination is performed by the condition $(\exists \alpha)$ $(F \in \texttt{title} \triangleright \alpha \wedge Fm \in \texttt{title} \triangleright \alpha)$ that appears in $r$. This combination acts like a join.

Now that we have a way to select paths (and embedded paths) in a db-graph, we naturally can select sub-graphs (and embedded sub-graphs) via the language Graph(Nest-Path). Let us reuse the preceding example to illustrate this language.

*Example 4.9.* The reader may have noticed that the path query $r$ returns triples of paths although it seems more natural for a user to get triples of nodes (the destinations of the paths) as an answer. Intuitively, this is what is performed by the following graph query:

$\{X, Y, Z \mid (\exists F \exists D \exists T)\ s \wedge F[X] \wedge D[Y] \wedge T[Z]\}$ where $s$ is the path expression defined in the previous example.

## 4.3    Expressiveness

In this section we investigate the expressive power of Nest-Path. Essentially, we compare the new path language Nest-Path with the simple path language Path. The next result relies on a translation of nested db-graphs into "flat" db-graphs and it shows that a Nest-Path query $q_{nest}$ can be translated into a Path query $q$ in such a way that evaluating $q_{nest}$ over a db-graph $G$ is equivalent to evaluating $q$ over the corresponding "flat" db-graph. Intuitively, this result tells that Nest-Path is not more expressive than Path. It can be compared in its spirit to the result [14, 1] which bridges a gap between the nested and the "flat" relational models.

The simple language Path is not redefined here. The reader can assume that Path is just like Nest-Path without nesting that is without the constructs of 2.(c) and 2.(d) of definition 4.1.

**Theorem 4.1.** *There exist a mapping $S$ from db-graphs to flat db-graphs, and a mapping $T$ from Nest-Path to Path such that*
*if $q \in$ Nest-Path and $G$ is a nested db-graph then $q(G) = T(q)(S(G))$.*

Before we proceed to a short proof, let us recall [6] the notion of maximal sub-graph of a graph $G$. A graph $G'$ rooted at $r$ is maximal w.r.t. $G$ if each path in $G$ starting at the source $r$ is also a path in $G'$. Moreover $G'$ is assumed to be a sub-graph of $G$. Finally, $G'$ is a cover of $G$ if it is maximal and if it is not a sub-graph of any other maximal sub-graph.

**Sketch of proof** The mapping $S$ unnests a nested db-graph $G$ by repeating the process described below until $G$ becomes totally flat.

1. Every complex node $n$ of $G$ is replaced by a simple node $n_{flat}$. Consider the label of $n$ that is a graph $G_n$.

2. Nodes, edges etc of $G_n$ are added to nodes, edges ... of $G$.
3. For each cover $G'$ of $G_n$, a root $r$ is selected and an edge $(n_{flat}, r, \%)$ is added to the edges of $G$. Note here that $\%$ is a new special label for the purpose of unnesting.

Notice that $\mathcal{S}$ is not deterministic because of the choice of a root (see point 3. above) for a cover of $G_n$.

The figure 3 shows a flat db-graph which is the result of unnesting the db-graph of figure 2 by applying $\mathcal{S}$.

The translation of a path expression $s_{nest}$ of Nest-Path is not very complicated (although it is overly technical) once the transformation of nested db-graph into flat db-graph is defined. In fact, the only difficulty is to capture in the flat path expression translating $s_{nest}$ the nested path queries $q$ that appear in sub-expressions of the kind $X \triangleright q(Y)$. The level of $Y$ is the information allowing one to make the translation. Let us consider the expression $s_{nest} = X \triangleright q(Y)$ where $q$ is the path query $\{Z \mid Z \in title\}$. The translation of $s_{nest}$ is $X.\%.Y \wedge Y \in title$. The fact that the level of $Y$ in $s_{nest}$ is 1 is reflected by the requirement of one edge labelled by $\%$ before $Y$.

It is quite trivial to see that Graph(Nest-Path) can be simulated by Graph(Path) by using the transformations $\mathcal{S}$ and $\mathcal{T}$ of theorem 4.1.

## 5   Emb-Path: A Fixpoint Nested Path Calculus

When using Graph(Nest-Path) for extracting data from a semi-structured database represented by a nested db-graph, the following problem arises. How could the user write a query if he does not know about the level of nesting of the data that he wants to retrieve? For instance, consider that the user is seeking all possible movie or tv-serie titles. The database of interest is the one depicted in figure 2. Hence, the user may ignore that some of the data he is looking for are at level 1 of nesting and try to get what he wants by writing the query $\{X \mid \texttt{title}[X]\}$. The answer returned by this query is not complete w.r.t. the user expectation. Now, the user may have already navigate in the database and happen to know that data are nested at least one level. Thus he probably will write the following expression to retrieve movie and tv-serie titles:
$$\{X \mid \texttt{title}[X] \vee (\exists U) \, U \triangleright r(X)\} \text{ where } r : \{Y \mid \texttt{title}[Y]\}.$$
However, it may well be the case that the data are nested one level more etc.

First, it is unrealistic to require that the user (and even the data management system) knows about the depth of nesting. Secondly, even in the case where the depth $d$ of the nested db-graph is known, writing a query such as the one above may become highly complicated if $d$ is large.

In this section, we introduce a new path language called *Emb-Path* to overcome the above mentioned problem and gain a degree of declarativeness by allowing the user to write queries such as the one of the motivating example without knowing the depth of the db-graph.

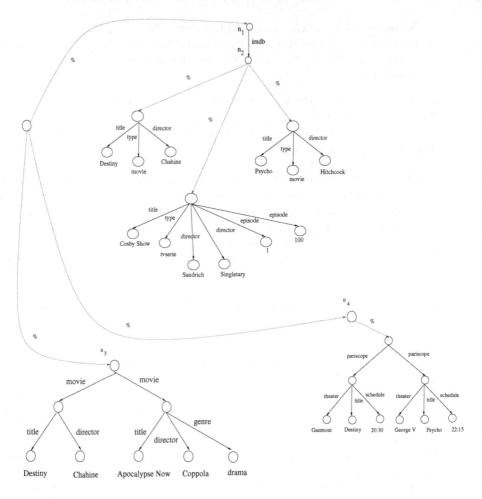

**Fig. 3.** Flattening a nested db-graph

## 5.1   Emb-Path's Syntax and Semantics

Roughly speaking, an embedded path formula is specified by two Path formulas. The evaluation of the embedded path formula specified by $\varphi$ and $\psi$ is an iterative process. At each step, the role of the first formula $\varphi$ is simply to extract paths of interest. At each step, the second formula $\psi$ serves to access some specific complex nodes in the db-graph, the ones which are going to be unnested in the sense that the labels of these complex nodes which are db-graphs are going to be processed (queried) at the next iteration. Thus in fact the second formula allows one to navigate in depth into the db-graph (not necessarily in the whole db-graph). Formally,

**Definition 5.1 (Emb(Path,Path)).** *Let $\varphi$ be a Path formula with $n$ free path variables $X_1, \ldots, X_n$ and let $\psi$ be a Path formula with one free path variable $Y$. Then $Emb(\varphi, \psi)$ (read $\varphi$ is embedded in $\psi$) is an embedded path expression of arity $n$. Given a db-graph $G$, $Emb(\varphi, \psi)$ denotes the $n$-ary relation which is the limit of the sequence $\{x_k\}_{k \geq 0}$ defined by:*

1. *$x_0$ is the answer to the query $\{(X_1, \ldots, X_n) \mid \varphi\}$ evaluated on $G$.*
   *$y_0$ is the answer to the query $\{(Y) \mid \psi\}$ evaluated on $G$.*
2. *$x_{k+1} = x_k \cup \varphi(y_k)$ and $y_{k+1} = y_k \cup \psi(y_k)$ where*
   *$\varphi(y_k)$ (resp. $\psi(y_k)$) is the union of the answers to the query $\{(X_1, \ldots, X_n) \mid \varphi\}$ (resp. $\{(Y) \mid \psi\}$) evaluated on the db-graphs labelling the destination of the paths $p \in y_k$ (when this destination is a complex node).*

An atomic embedded formula is an expression of the form $Emb(\varphi, \psi)(t_1, \ldots, t_n)$ where $t_1, \ldots, t_n$ are path terms and an embedded path expression $Emb(\varphi, \psi)$ of arity $n$. Note that a Path formula $\varphi$ having $n$ free variables can be "translated" by embedding $\varphi$ in false. The language of embedded formulas is denoted Emb-Path as an abbreviation of Emb(Path,Path). It leads to a graph query language in a straightforward manner by considering Graph(Emb-Path).

Note that the above definition can be generalized in a standard way by allowing $\varphi$ and $\psi$ to be embedded formulas themselves. In this case, the language of embedded formulas is called Emb(Emb-Path,Emb-Path).

*Example 5.1.* Let us consider the introductory query example: the user is trying to gather all movie or tv-serie titles in the database no matter at which level of nesting they are. In order to write this query, we will use the Emb-Path expression $\mathbf{Emb}(\varphi, \psi)$ of arity one where: $\varphi$ is U $\in$ `title` and $\psi$ is V
The graph query which returns all the titles is written in Graph(Emb-Path) as:
   { X | ∃ Y $\mathbf{Emb}(\varphi, \psi)$(Y) ∧ Y[X] }
This graph query just extracts the subgraphs rooted at the destination of the paths Y satisfying the embedded formula $Emb(\varphi, \psi)$(Y). What kind of paths does the embedded formula select? Because the path formula $\varphi$ is U $\in$ `title`, $Emb(\varphi, \psi)$ returns embedded paths reduced to edges labelled by `title`. Because the path formula $\psi$ is V, all complex nodes are explored and unnested and thus $Emb(\varphi, \psi)$ returns all paths reduced to edges labelled by `title` and belonging to any level of nesting.

*Example 5.2.* Let us consider a second example having the same structure as the previous one except for the formula $\psi$ which is now replaced by V $\in$ `imdb`. As in the previous example, because the path formula $\varphi$ is U $\in$ `title`, $Emb(\varphi, \psi)$ returns embedded paths reduced to edges labelled by `title`. However, now, because the path formula $\psi$ is V $\in$ `imdb`, the only complex nodes explored and unnested are the one at the destination of an edge labelled by `imdb`. Thus $Emb(\varphi, \psi)$ here returns all paths reduced to edges labelled by `title` and belonging to any embedded db-graph reachable by an edge labelled by `imdb`.

Note here that there is another slightly different way to define a graph query language (in the same style). It consists in embedding a graph formula in a path formula instead of embedding a path formula in a path formula and linking it to a graph formula.

**Definition 5.2 (Emb(Graph,Path)).** *Let $\varphi$ be a Graph(Path) formula with $n$ free graph variables $X_1, \ldots, X_n$ and let $\psi$ be a Path formula with one free path variable $Y$. Then $Emb(\varphi, \psi)$ (read $\varphi$ is embedded in $\psi$) is an embedded graph expression of arity $n$. An atomic formula of Emb(Graph, Path) is an expression of the form $Emb(\varphi, \psi)(t_1, \ldots, t_n)$ where $t_1, \ldots, t_n$ are graph terms.*

We do not develop the semantics of the language Emb(Graph, Path). The definition is similar as the one for Emb-Path. We simply illustrate it by the following example.

*Example 5.3.* Let us consider the introductory example. It can be expressed in Emb(Graph, Path) by the query { X | $\texttt{Emb}(\varphi, \psi)(\texttt{X})$ } where $\varphi$ is $\texttt{title}[\texttt{Y}]$ and $\psi$ is V

## 5.2   Expressiveness

Let us now address the following question with respect to expressive power: how are related the path languages Nest-Path and Emb-Path when the depth of the db-graph is known. We first show that Emb-Path is subsumed by Nest-Path although in a rather weak sense.

**Theorem 5.1.** *For a given db-graph $G$ whose depth is known we have: for each query $q_{emb}$ in Emb-Path, there exists a query $q_{nest}$ in Nest-Path such that $q_{emb}(G)$ and $q_{nest}(G)$ are equal.*

The result above does not imply the inclusion of Emb-Path into Nest-Path because the translation of the query $q_{emb}$ depends strongly on the queried db-graph $G$. In fact this result could be compared to the one showing that the transitive closure of a binary relation can be computed within the relational calculus as soon as one can use the number of tuples of the relation.

*Proof.* Let $k$ be the depth of $G$.
The atomic embedded formula $Emb(\varphi, \psi)(X_1, \ldots, X_n)$ can be simulated by the formula

$$\varphi(\mathsf{X}_1, \ldots, \mathsf{X}_n)$$
$$\vee \ (\exists \mathsf{V}_1) \ ( \ \psi(\mathsf{V}_1) \ \wedge \ \mathsf{V}_1 \in \mathsf{V}_1 \triangleright \mathsf{q}(\mathsf{X}_1, \ldots, \mathsf{X}_n) \ )$$
$$\vee \ (\exists \mathsf{V}_1)(\exists \mathsf{V}_2) \ ( \ \psi(\mathsf{V}_1) \ \wedge \ \mathsf{V}_1 \in \mathsf{V}_1 \triangleright \mathsf{r}(\mathsf{V}_2) \ \wedge \ \mathsf{V}_2 \in \mathsf{V}_2 \triangleright \mathsf{q}(\mathsf{X}_1, \ldots, \mathsf{X}_n) \ )$$
$$\vdots$$
$$\vee (\exists \mathsf{V}_1) \ldots (\exists \mathsf{V}_{k-1}) \ ( \ \psi(\mathsf{V}_1) \wedge \ \mathsf{V}_1 \in \mathsf{V}_1 \triangleright \mathsf{r}(\mathsf{V}_2) \wedge \ldots \mathsf{V}_{k-1} \in \mathsf{V}_{k-1} \triangleright \mathsf{q}(\mathsf{X}_1, \ldots, \mathsf{X}_n) \ )$$

$$q : \{(U_1, \ldots, U_n) \mid \varphi\}$$
$$r : \{(V) \mid \psi\}$$

Concerning the inverse inclusion, proving that Nest-Path $\subseteq$ Emb-Path remains an open question. In contrast to the preceding inclusion, this one would be strong. It would imply that the language Emb-Path enables at the same time (1) to write queries without having to know about the depth of the data to be retrieved, (2) to write queries exploring the db-graph at a given level of nesting. For the time being, even for a simple Nest-Path query like $\{X \mid (\exists U)\ X \in \text{imdb} \rhd q(U)\}$ where q is $\{Y \mid Y \in \text{title}\}$, we have no translation in Emb-Path neither a proof showing that it cannot be translated. The difficulty that arises here is finding a mechanism that stops embedding at a specific level of nesting.

## 6    Concluding Remarks

To conclude we would like to stress that although the current paper does not address it, the problem of restricting the languages to tractable queries i.e. queries computable in polynomial time has been investigated in [15]. To illustrate the problem let us consider the path query $\{X \mid X\}$ which returns all simple paths in a db-graph. For instance suppose that the db-graph nodes are $1, 2, \ldots, 2n$, and its edges are from $i$ to $i+1$ and $i+2$, for $i = 1, \ldots, 2n-2$. Thus the db-graph has $O(2^n)$ simple paths from node 1 to node $2n$. This entails that the evaluation of the query $\{X \mid X\}$ is not polynomial. In order to avoid such situation, syntactic restrictions can be used (see [15, 11]).

We are currently studying the open problem mentioned in the previous section. As a matter of fact, we separate the problem into couple of questions: *(i)* is Nest-Path included in Emb-Path=Emb(Path,Path)? *(ii)* is Nest-Path included in Emb(Emb(Path),Emb(Path))? *(iii)* how Emb(Graph,Path) is related to Graph(Emb-Path)?

## References

1. S. Abiteboul and N. Bidoit. Non first normal form relations: An algebra allowing data restructuring. *Journal of Computer and System Sciences, Academic*, 33, 1986.
2. S. Abiteboul, R. Hull, and V. Vianu. *Foundations of Databases*. Addison-Wesley, 1995.
3. S. Abiteboul, D. Quass, J. McHugh, J. Widom, and J. L. Wiener. The lorel query language for semistructured data. *International Journal on Digital Libraries*, 1(1):68–88, April 1997.
4. Serge Abiteboul. Querying semistructured Data. In *ICDT*, pages 1–18, 1997.
5. Nicole Bidoit and Mourad Ykhlef. Fixpoint Path Queries. In *International Workshop on the Web and Databases WebDB'98 In Conjunction with EDBT'98*, pages 56–62, Valencia, Spain, 27–28 March 1998. `http://www.dia.uniroma3.it/webdb98/papers.html/`.

6. Nicole Bidoit and Mourad Ykhlef. Fixpoint Calculus for Querying Semistructured Data. *Lecture Notes in Computer Science*, 1590:78–98, 1999.
7. P. Buneman, S. B. Davidson, M. Fernandez, and D. Suciu. Adding Structure to Unstructured Data. In *Proceedings of International Conference on Database Theory (ICDT)*, Delphi, Greece, January 1997.
8. P. Buneman, S. B. Davidson, G. Hillebrand, and D. Suciu. A query language and optimization techniques for unstructured data. In *Proceedings of ACM SIGMOD Conference on Management of Data*, pages 505–516, Montreal, Canada, June 1996.
9. M. Fernandez, D. Florescu, J. Kang, A. Y. Levy, and D. Suciu. System demonstration - strudel: A web-site management system. In *Proceedings of ACM SIGMOD Conference on Management of Data*, Tucson, Arizona, May 1997. Exhibition Program.
10. A. Mendelzon, G. Mihaila, and T. Milo. Querying the World Wide Web. *International Journal on Digital Libraries*, 1(1):54–67, 1997.
11. A. Mendelzon, and P. Wood. Finding Regular Simple Paths in Graph Databases. *SIAM Journal on Computing*, 24, 1995.
12. R. Milner. *Communication and concurrency*. Prentice Hall, 1989.
13. Y. Papakonstantinou, H. Garcia-Molina, and J. Widom. Object exchange across heterogeneous information sources. In *Proceedings of IEEE International Conference on Data Engineering (ICDE)*, pages 251–260, Taipei, Taiwan, March 1995.
14. J. Paredaens and D. Van Gucht. Possibilities and limitations of using flat operators in nested algebra expressions. In *Proceedings of PODS conference*, 1988.
15. M. Ykhlef. *Interrogation des données semistructurées*. PhD thesis, Univ. of Bordeaux, 1999.

# Decomposition of Database Classes under Path Functional Dependencies and Onto Constraints

Joachim Biskup and Torsten Polle

Universität Dortmund, FB Informatik, D-44221 Dortmund
biskup@ls6.informatik.uni-dortmund.de
Torsten.Polle@t-online.de

**Abstract.** Based on F-logic, we specify an advanced data model with object-oriented and logic-oriented features that substantially extend the relational approach. For this model we exhibit and study the counterpart to the well-known decomposition of a relation scheme according to a nontrivial nonkey functional dependency. For decomposing a class of a database schema the transformation pivoting is used. Pivoting separates apart some attributes of the class into a newly generated class. This new class is declared to be a subclass of the result class of the so-called pivot attribute. Moreover the pivot attribute provides the link between the original class and the new subclass. We identify the conditions for the result of pivoting being equivalent with its input: the expressive power of path functional dependencies, the validity of the path functional dependency between the pivot attribute and the transplanted attributes, and the validity of the onto-constraint guaranteeing that values for the transplanted attributes can be referenced from the remaining part of the original class.

## 1 The Problem: An Introduction into Decomposition

The theory of database schema design (see any suitable database textbook or [10, 2, 1, 3]) aims at formally characterizing "good" schemas and at inventing algorithms to test and to improve the quality of a given schema. Semantic constraints play a key role for both tasks. On the one side, semantic constraints are purely syntactic items, and as such they can be algorithmically examined and manipulated by the schema administrator at design time. On the other side, they represent the collection of all instances of the schema, and as such they essentially determine the performance of the database application during its future lifetime. As a general heuristic, a schema is considered "good" if it consists of atomic and independent components where atomicity and independence are expressed relative to the features of the data model, in particular, of the available semantic constraints. Accordingly, the semantic constraints of a schema can indicate whether there are still compound components and how to decompose them into simpler ones.

K.-D. Schewe, B. Thalheim (Eds.): FoIKS 2000, LNCS 1762, pp. 31–49, 2000.

In the past, this approach has been successfully elaborated for the relational data model where, roughly simplified, the features are restricted to flat relation schemes, functional dependencies and some kinds of inclusion dependencies. Here a relation scheme is considered to be compound (not in "normal form") if it contains a nontrivial nonkey functional dependency, and a compound scheme can be decomposed by separating apart the left-hand side of such a dependency with some or all attributes of its implicational closure. With the advent of more powerful data models, we are challenged to extend the insight gained for the relational model for the new models.

This paper contributes a fundamental response to this challenge for an advanced data model with object-oriented and logic-oriented features. For the sake of presentation, the model is based on F-logic [8] but the response is applicable to any similarly powerful model. Basically, the model combines object-orientation (allowing in particular class declarations with signatures, class hierarchies with inheritance, scalar attributes and object identifiers) with deductive capabilities for query processing and enforcement of semantic constraints, both of which allow to navigate along arbitrary paths (sequences of attributes) in the schema. Thus, besides some built-in semantic constraints and further application-dependent constraints, the model supports arbitrary path functional dependencies [14, 15] which significantly generalize the functional dependencies as known from the relational model. A path functional dependency of syntactic form $c(p_1 \cdots p_k \rightarrow p_{k+1} \cdots p_n)$ declares that whenever the path-functions $p_1 \cdots p_k$ in the left-hand side applied to two different objects of class $c$ return the same objects, respectively, so do the path-functions $p_{k+1} \cdots p_n$ in right-hand side. Path functional dependencies are a powerful means to describe sophisticated application semantics yet in general demand for extensive computations to enforce them.

The expressive power of path functional dependencies is also strong enough to avoid the well-know problem of relation schemes with functional dependencies all nontrivial lossless decompositions of which are not dependency preserving. As an example consider the relation scheme $R = \{A, B, C, D, E\}$ with functional dependencies $\{A \rightarrow CD, B \rightarrow CE\}$. If, for instance, we separate apart the attributes of $A \rightarrow CD$, the original scheme is decomposed into relation schemes $S = \{A, C, D\}$ and $T = \{A, B, E\}$ none of which can embody the functional dependency $B \rightarrow C$.

To state this semantic constraint in the decomposed schema, we basically would have to say that whenever two tuples for $T$ agree on the $B$-value, two tuples for $S$ that agree on their $A$-values with the $A$-values of the tuples for $T$ have to agree on their $C$-value. In our advanced data model such a statement can be captured by a path functional dependency $c_T(.B \rightarrow .A.C)$ where the class $c_T$ corresponds to the scheme $T$, and $A.C$ is a path which starts at class $c_T$ and passes the class $c_S$ corresponding to scheme $S$ via attribute $A$. Additionally, in the relational model, we would need inclusion dependencies to ensure the existence of matching tuples. In our advanced data model such conditions are expressed by an interplay between built-in object-oriented features and so-called onto constraints [13]. An onto constraint of syntactic form $c\{m \mid c_m\}$ is used to guarantee that every object $v$ of class $c_m$ is referenced by some object $o$ of class $c$ via attribute $m$, i.e., if the attribute $m$ is considered as a path-function of length 1 with domain $c$ and range $c_m$, then this function is required to be surjective (onto).

So, given our advanced data model as an extension of the simple relational model, we can ask for also extending the above mentioned known results on decomposing compound relation schemes. Our earlier work [4–6] has already given some preliminary and partial answers which can be summarized as follows.

First, we have to identify an appropriate notion of decomposition. In the relational model decomposition is formally done by the operation of taking multiple projections: in the simplest case, a first projection separates apart the attributes of the nonkey functional dependency under consideration by introducing a new relation scheme, and a second projection retains the left-hand side of the functional dependency and all remaining attributes in the original scheme. Thus, in some sense, the second projection preserves the essential part of the original scheme, some (only "transitively dependent") attributes of which have been shifted into the first projection. This view motivated the introduction of the operation pivoting for decomposition in the advanced data model. Roughly speaking, pivoting transplants some attributes of a class to a newly generated subclass of another class. The new subclass plays the role of the first projection.

Second, as in the relational case, also for pivoting all original semantic constraints have to be adjusted. However, if we are restricted to use only functional dependencies, then the analysis of [6] confirmed that the problem of decompositions that are not dependency preserving arises again. But fortunately, at least we could precisely characterize the well behaving cases.

Now, for our advanced data model this paper studies the decomposition of classes by pivoting allowing arbitrary path functional dependencies and onto constraints. Thereby the paper contributes a fully exhaustive and fundamental response to the challenge of extending the classical results on relational decompositions. This response is semi-formally outlined in more detail in the following Sect. 2. Then, assuming an intuitive understanding of the sophisticated formalism of the full data model, in Sect. 3 we sketch the proofs of our formal theorems.

## 2    The Solution: A Semi-formal Outline

### 2.1    F-Logic

We base our advanced data model with object-oriented and logic-oriented features on F-logic [8] because of its precise syntax and semantics combined with high flexibility. Its flexibility facilitates to define appropriate formal notions for the concepts needed, in particular for schema, instances, semantic constraints, schema equivalence and schema transformations. Its precision allows to state and to prove formal theorems. F-logic can be considered as a tailored version of predicate logic, and, accordingly, it plays the same role for our advanced data model as generic predicate logic for the relational model. Assuming the reader's familiarity with predicate logic and with object-oriented and logic-oriented database features, we refrain from presenting all formal details of our data model (which can be found in [11]) but rather expose only a rough outline.

## 2.2 Schema and Instances

For using F-logic we assume a fixed set of object constructors $\mathcal{F}$. $\mathcal{F}_0 \subset \mathcal{F}$ denotes the set of constant symbols, and $\mathcal{HB}(\mathcal{F})$ denotes the Herbrand base, i.e. the set of the ground molecules constructed from $\mathcal{F}$ and the built-in predicate symbols.

A data model describes two things, the schema and its possible instances.

**Definition 2.1 (Schema).** *A schema $D$ is of the form*

$$D = \langle \underbrace{\mathrm{CL}_D \cup \mathrm{AT}_D \cup \mathrm{HR}_D \cup \mathrm{SG}_D}_{\mathrm{ST}_D :=} \mid \mathrm{SC}_D \rangle$$

*with the following finite sets*

- *a set of constants, $\mathrm{CL}_D \subset \mathcal{F}_0$, for class names,*
- *a set of constants, $\mathrm{AT}_D \subset \mathcal{F}_0$, for attribute names,*
- *a set of ground class is-a assertions, $\mathrm{HR}_D \subset \{c :: d \mid c, d \in \mathrm{CL}_D\}$, to form the class hierarchy,*
- *a set of ground object molecules consisting only of scalar signature expressions,*

$$\mathrm{SG}_D \subset \{c[a \Rightarrow r] \mid c, r \in \mathrm{CL}_D, a \in \mathrm{AT}_D\} \ ,$$

   *to declare signatures for classes and attributes, and*
- *a set of sentences, $\mathrm{SC}_D$, as semantic constraints to restrict the set of allowed instances.*

The classes in a schema form a hierarchy given by the set $\mathrm{HR}_D$ of class is-a assertions. We demand that the class hierarchy is acyclic throughout this work. On classes we declare attributes and their signatures by means of the set $\mathrm{SG}_D$ of object molecules with signature expressions. Due to the semantics of inheritance these signature declarations are inherited to subclasses. The set $\mathrm{SC}_D$ of sentences contains the application-dependent semantic constraints, which restrict the data stored under a schema to meaningful data.

*Example 2.1.* Suppose we have to formalise a relationship set for administrating telecommunication costs in an environment with entity sets for faculty members, phone equipments and schools which are grouped into departments. A (not necessarily good) formalization is obtained by giving the entity sets as well as the relationship set the status of a class. Then an object of the relationship class represents a specific relationship among some objects of the entity classes. This representation is achieved by referencing the entity objects involved by the attributes of the relationship object. More formally, we consider a schema $ADM$ with the following structural components:

$$\mathrm{CL}_{ADM} := \{\text{Phone-admin, Faculty, School, Phone, Department}\}$$
$$\mathrm{AT}_{ADM} := \{\text{fac, sch, ph, dep}\}$$
$$\mathrm{HR}_{ADM} := \emptyset$$
$$\mathrm{SG}_{ADM} := \{\text{Phone-admin[fac} \Rightarrow \text{Faculty; sch} \Rightarrow \text{School;}$$
$$\text{ph} \Rightarrow \text{Phone; dep} \Rightarrow \text{Department]}\}$$

The semantic constraints $\mathrm{SC}_{ADM}$ are specified later on in Sect. 2.3.

Sometimes we add to a given schema $D$ new semantic constraints $\Phi$. We denote this addition by $D \cup \Phi$,

$$D \cup \Phi := \langle \mathrm{ST}_D \mid \mathrm{SC}_D \cup \Phi \rangle .$$

Besides the application-dependent constraints we also use a set AX of *built-in axioms*: As we usually want syntactically different things to be semantically different as well, we use *unique-name* axioms UN [12] for this purpose. In addition, attributes should always return a value if the attributes are declared for an object. A fact that is ensured by the *not-null* axiom NN. The connection between signature expressions and data expressions is ensured by the presence of *well-typedness* axioms WT.

Later on we are often interested in the set of attributes declared for a class and in attributes that are declared for exactly one class.

**Definition 2.2 ((Proper) Attribute).** *Let $D$ be a schema.*

- *The set $\{a \mid \mathrm{HR}_D \cup \mathrm{SG}_D \models c[a \Rightarrow ()]\}$ of attributes for a class $c$ is denoted $\mathrm{At}_D(c)$.*
- *An attribute $a \in \mathrm{AT}_D$ is called a* proper attribute *for a class $c \in \mathrm{CL}_D$ :iff $\mathrm{SG}_D \models c[a \Rightarrow ()]$ and $\mathrm{SG}_D \not\models d[a \Rightarrow ()]$ holds for all classes $d \in \mathrm{CL}_D$ with $d \not\equiv c$.*

Having described a schema, we come to the data, which is the objects populating classes and their attribute values. Both aspects are formalised as formulae, which we separate according to their nature, object is-a assertions for class populations and scalar data atoms for attribute value definitions.

**Definition 2.3 (Extension).** *An extension $f \in \mathrm{ext}(D)$ of a schema $D$ is of the form $f = \langle \mathrm{pp}_f \mid \mathrm{ob}_f \rangle$ with the following sets*

- *a set of ground object is-a assertions,*

$$\mathrm{pp}_f \subset \{o : c \mid o \in \mathcal{F}_0 \setminus (\mathrm{CL}_D \cup \mathrm{AT}_D), c \in \mathrm{CL}_D\} ,$$

*populating classes, and*
- *a set of ground object molecules with only scalar data expressions,*

$$\mathrm{ob}_f \subset \{o[a \rightarrow v] \mid o, v \in \mathcal{F}_0 \setminus (\mathrm{CL}_D \cup \mathrm{AT}_D), a \in \mathrm{AT}_D\} ,$$

*for the definition of attribute values for objects.*

A *completion* of an extension under a schema comprises all that can be deduced from the extension and the schema, in this case ground molecules.

**Definition 2.4 (Completion).** *Let $f$ be an extension of a schema $D$. The completion of the extension $f$ under the schema $D$ is $\mathrm{compl}_D(f) := \{\tau \in \mathcal{HB}(\mathcal{F}) \mid \mathrm{ST}_D \cup \mathrm{pp}_f \cup \mathrm{ob}_f \models \tau\}$.*

Completions are the smallest H-models of the union $\mathrm{ST}_D \cup \mathrm{pp}_f \cup \mathrm{ob}_f$.

An instance is an extension of a schema that obeys the semantic constraints given in the schema. In addition, instances or better their completions must satisfy unique-name, not-null and well-typedness axioms.

**Definition 2.5 (Instance).** *Let $f$ be an extension of a schema $D$. Then the extension $f$ is called a(n) (allowed) instance of the schema $D$, $f \in \mathrm{sat}(D)$, if $\mathrm{compl}_D(f)$ is an H-model of the axioms AX and the semantic constraints $\mathrm{SC}_D$.*

## 2.3   Path Functional Dependencies and Onto Constraints

For our study on decompositions we consider two kinds of application-dependent semantic constraints, path functional dependencies and onto constraints.

Path functional dependencies [14, 15] generalize functional dependencies. While, in the relational context, a functional dependency relates some of the attribute values contained in a tuple, in the object-oriented context, a path functional dependency relates some of the objects reachable by path-functions from an object. Here a path-function $p \equiv .m_1^p \cdots .m_l^p$ for a class $c$ is given by a sequence of attributes which is well-defined relative to the declarations of the schema $D$. The set of all path-functions starting at class $c$, including the "this-path" .Id, is denoted by $\mathrm{PathFuncs}_D(c)$.

**Definition 2.6 (Path Functional Dependency).** *Let $D$ be a database schema, and $c \in \mathrm{CL}_D$ be a class.*

**Syntax:** *A path functional dependency for the class $c$ over the schema $D$ is of the form*

$$c(p_1 \cdots p_k \to p_{k+1} \cdots p_n) \ ,$$

*where $0 < k < n$, and where $p_i \in \mathrm{PathFuncs}_D(c)$ for $i \in \{1, \ldots, n\}$.*

**Semantics:** *To define that an extension satisfies a path functional dependency, we can construct F-sentences which roughly express the following statement: If for two argument objects $x$ and $y$ the path-functions $p_1, \ldots, p_k$ all yield the same result objects, respectively, and any of the path-functions $p \in \{p_{k+1}, \ldots, p_n\}$ is defined for one of the argument objects, then it is also defined for the other argument object, and the returned result objects are the same.*

The set of (F-sentences for) path functional dependencies in $\mathrm{SC}_D$ is denoted by $\mathrm{PFD}_D$.

Onto constraints can be considered as a special kind of inclusion constraints, as known in the relational model. Generally, inclusion constraints are employed to express certain interrelational conditions, like for foreign keys. In object-oriented models, some of these conditions are built-in or captured by axioms like the not-null axiom. Others have to be made explicit, in particular the condition of an onto constraint that every object $v$ of class $c_m$ is referenced by some object $o$ of class $c$ via attribute $m$. Such a condition, first mentioned in [13], can be used to form the class $c_m$ as a subclass of some further class $c_p$ by comprehending the pertinent subpopulation of $c_p$, namely just those objects of $c_p$ which are attainable from class $c$ via the attribute $m$. Indeed, such conditions are crucial for separating apart some aspects of the class $c$ into a newly generated subclass, here $c_m$.

**Definition 2.7 (Onto Constraint).** *Let $D$ be a database schema, and $c \in$ $\mathrm{CL}_D$ be a class.*

**Syntax:** *An onto constraint for the class $c$ over the schema $D$ is of the form $c\{m \mid c_m\}$, where $m \in \mathrm{At}_D(c)$ is an attribute for $c$ and $c_m \in \mathrm{CL}_D$ is a class.*
**Semantics:** *To define that an extension satisfies an onto constraint, we can construct an F-sentence which expresses the condition given above.*

*The set of (F-sentences for) onto constraints in $\mathrm{SC}_D$ is denoted by $\mathrm{OC}_D$.*

*Example 2.2.* For our example database schema $ADM$ we declare some simple path functional dependencies all path-functions of which have length one or length zero:

$$\mathrm{SC}_{ADM} := \mathrm{AX} \cup$$
$$\{\mathsf{Phone\text{-}admin}(.\mathsf{fac} \to .\mathsf{sch}),$$
$$\mathsf{Phone\text{-}admin}(.\mathsf{fac} \to .\mathsf{ph}),$$
$$\mathsf{Phone\text{-}admin}(.\mathsf{sch} \to .\mathsf{dep}),$$
$$\mathsf{Phone\text{-}admin}(.\mathsf{ph} \to .\mathsf{dep}),$$
$$\mathsf{Phone\text{-}admin}(.\mathsf{fac} \;\; .\mathsf{sch} \;\; .\mathsf{ph} \;\; .\mathsf{dep} \to .\mathsf{Id})\}$$

Up to now there are no onto constraints. Such a constraint will be introduced in Sect. 2.5.

As usual, having explicitly declared a set of path functional dependencies and onto constraints for a schema, we are interested in all further implied constraints of the same kinds.

**Definition 2.8 (Implicational Closure).** *Let $D$ be a database schema with application-dependent constraints $\mathrm{SC}_D$. The closure of the set $\mathrm{SC}_D$ (with respect to $D$), written $\mathrm{SC}_D^{+_D}$, is the set of all constraints $\xi$ over the schema $D$, where $\mathrm{sat}(D) \subset \mathrm{sat}(D \cup \{\xi\})$.*

In order to handle constraints and their closures algorithmically, we need a correct and complete set of inference rules to infer further constraints from given ones. For path functional dependencies alone, such rules are already exhibited in [14, 15], and [13] suggests a further rule to deal with situations as described by onto constraints. Finally, in [7, 11] we embed all these rules into our advanced data model, add some further rules for dealing with inclusion of class populations and then prove their correctness as well as their completeness, provided the class hierarchy of the schema obeys some minor restriction.

## 2.4   Equivalence of Schemas

In this paper we are mainly concerned with the decomposition of classes, more generally with transforming a given schema $S$ into a (hopefully) improved schema $T$. Surely, in order to be useful the new schema $T$ should at least "capture the intended application semantics" of the original schema $S$. This intuitive requirement has been formalized in seemingly different though essentially equivalent ways, as discussed for instance in [1, 11, 9]. For the purpose of our investigations, we found the following formalization most appropriate. Basically, this formalization requires that the original schema is "supported" as a view of the transformed schema. Here a view is provided by a query which returns extensions of the original schema $S$ when applied to instances of the transformed schema $T$. We distinguish three degrees of "support" depending on the set theoretical relationship between the set of instances of the original schema and the set of query results.

The following formal definition is based on the skipped formal syntax and semantics of a class of simple queries. Roughly sketched, a query $Q$ is a set of F-Horn-rules, $Q \subset \{H \longleftarrow B \mid H \longleftarrow B$ is an F-Horn-rule$\}$, that when applied to an extension $f$ of a schema $D$ returns all nonrecursive implications according to $Q$,

$$\mathrm{eval}_D(Q, f) := \bigcup_{H \longleftarrow B \in Q} \{\nu(H) \mid \mathrm{compl}_D(f) \models_\nu B\} \ .$$

**Definition 2.9 (View Instance Support).**

- *A schema $T$ provides* view instance support *for a schema $S$ if there exists a query $Q$ such that*

$$\{\mathrm{compl}_S(f_S) \mid f_S \in \mathrm{sat}(S)\} \subset \{\mathrm{compl}_S(\mathrm{eval}_T(Q, f_T)) \mid f_T \in \mathrm{sat}(T)\} \ .$$

- *If we have equality, the view instance support is called* faithful.
- *If additionally the supporting query $Q$ is injective on the saturated elements of $\mathrm{sat}(T)$, i. e., if $\mathrm{eval}_T(Q, f) = \mathrm{eval}_T(Q, f')$, then $\mathrm{compl}_T(f) = \mathrm{compl}_T(f')$, the view instance support is called* unique.

## 2.5    Decomposition of Classes by Pivoting

Having presented our advanced data model so far, we are finally ready to formally present the central topic of this paper, namely the schema transformation pivoting which can be used to decompose a class under path functional dependencies and onto constraints.

Pivoting comprises three actions. First, it decomposes a class $c$ of a schema $S$ by transplanting some of its attributes, those of $\mathbb{M}$, to a newly generated subclass $p$ of another class $c_p$ which is the unique result class of a further attribute of class $c$, the so-called pivot attribute $m_p$. Figure 1 visualizes the structure of an object of class $c$ before the decomposition, and Fig. 2 shows the effect of transplanting the pivoted attributes. Second, it adjusts the original semantic constraints of $S$ according to the transplantation of the pivoted attributes. Third, it provides appropriate queries for treating the original schema as a view of the pivoted schema, and vice versa. These actions are formalized by the following definition. Subsequently, in the next subsection, we characterize those parameters of pivoting which guarantee that the resulting pivoted schema $T$ "uniquely supports" the input schema $S$.

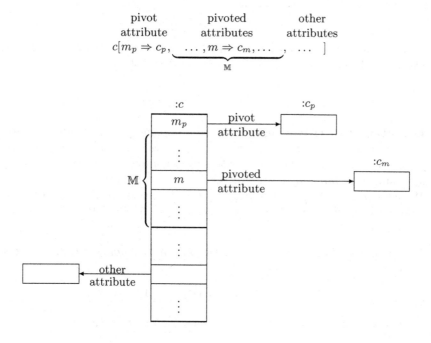

**Fig. 1.** Visualization of an object of class $c$ with pivot attribute $m_p$ and pivoted attributes $\mathbb{M}$ together with the directly accessible objects.

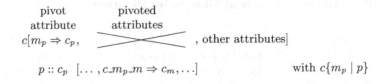

$$p :: c_p \quad [\ldots, c\_m_p\_m \Rightarrow c_m, \ldots] \qquad\qquad \text{with } c\{m_p \mid p\}$$

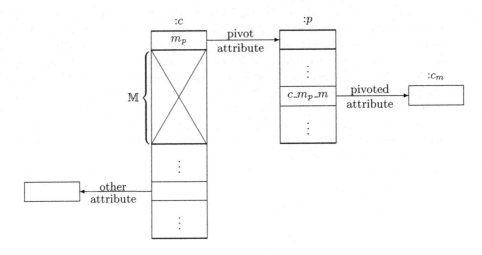

**Fig. 2.** Visualization of the transformed objects where the attributes $m \in \mathrm{M}$ are transplanted to the referenced object of the new subclass $p$ of $c_p$.

**Definition 2.10 (Pivoting).** *Let $S$ be a schema, $p$ be a constant symbol not used elsewhere, $c \in \mathrm{CL}_S$ be a class, $\mathrm{M} \subset \mathrm{At}_S(c)$ be a set of proper attributes for class $c$, and $m_p \in (\mathrm{At}_S(c) \setminus \mathrm{M})$ be a proper attribute for class $c$, called* pivot attribute, *with the unique result class $c_p$, called* pivot class. *We assume that $c\{m_p \mid c_p\} \notin \mathrm{SC}_D^{+_D}$, otherwise we do not have to introduce the class $p$. Then the pivoted schema $T := \langle \mathrm{CL}_T \cup \mathrm{AT}_T \cup \mathrm{HR}_T \cup \mathrm{SG}_T \mid \mathrm{SC}_T \rangle$ is obtained as follows:*

- *For introducing a new subclass, we add the constant symbol $p$ to the set of classes,*

$$\mathrm{CL}_T := \mathrm{CL}_S \cup \{p\} \;,$$

  *and we make the new class $p$ a subclass of the pivot class $c_p$,*

$$\mathrm{HR}_T := \mathrm{HR}_S \cup \{p :: c_p\} \;.$$

- *For transplanting attributes, we introduce new attributes and remove the obsolescent ones. The constant symbols for denoting these new attributes are chosen in a way that it is possible to keep track of the transformation process and avoid name clashes with already existing symbols,*

$$\mathrm{AT}_T := (\mathrm{AT}_S \setminus \mathrm{M}) \cup \{c\_m_p\_m \mid m \in \mathrm{M}\} \ ,$$

*and we add appropriate signatures $p[c\_m_p\_m \Rightarrow c_m]$ for all attributes $m \in \mathrm{M}$ and for their result classes $c_m$,*

$$\{p[c\_m_p\_m \Rightarrow c_m] \mid m \in \mathrm{M} \text{ and } \mathrm{SG}_S \models c[m \Rightarrow c_m]\} \ ,$$

*and, accordingly, we remove the obsolescent signatures for class $c$ of the form $c[m \Rightarrow c_m]$ for all attributes $m \in \mathrm{M} \cup \{m_p\}$ and their result classes $c_m$,*

$$\mathrm{SG}_S \setminus \{c[m \Rightarrow c_m] \mid m \in \mathrm{M} \cup \{m_p\} \text{ and } c_m \in \mathrm{CL}_S\} \ .$$

*Finally we add the signature $c[m_p \Rightarrow p]$ in order to enable navigation to the new subclass $p$, and further onto the pivoted attributes, from the class $c$,*

$$\{c[m_p \Rightarrow p]\} \ .$$

*Thus the new signatures are summarised as*

$$\begin{aligned} \mathrm{SG}_T := {} & \{p[c\_m_p\_m \Rightarrow c_m] \mid m \in \mathrm{M} \text{ and } \mathrm{SG}_S \models c[m \Rightarrow c_m]\} \cup \\ & \mathrm{SG}_S \setminus \{c[m \Rightarrow c_m] \mid m \in \mathrm{M} \cup \{m_p\} \text{ and } c_m \in \mathrm{CL}_S\} \cup \\ & \{c[m_p \Rightarrow p]\} \ . \end{aligned}$$

– *For adjusting the semantic constraints, we replace the obsolescent attributes $m \in \mathrm{M}$ with the new navigational paths $m_p.c\_m_p\_m$ wherever they occur in the set of path functional dependencies,*

$$\mathrm{PFD}_T := \mathrm{PFD}_S[m_p.c\_m_p\_m/m \mid m \in \mathrm{M}] \ .$$

*Correspondingly, for an onto constraint of the form $c\{m \mid c_m\}$ with an obsolescent attribute $m$, we replace the class $c$ with the new subclass $p$ and the attribute $m$ with the new attribute $c\_m_p\_m$. We add the onto constraint $c\{m_p \mid p\}$ as a means to ensure the equivalence of both schemas.*

$$\begin{aligned} \mathrm{OC}_T := {} & \{p\{c\_m_p\_m \mid c_m\} \mid m \in \mathrm{M} \text{ and } c\{m \mid c_m\} \in \mathrm{OC}_S\} \cup \\ & \{d\{m \mid c_m\} \in \mathrm{OC}_S \mid m \notin \mathrm{M}\} \cup \\ & \{c\{m_p \mid p\}\} \ . \end{aligned}$$

*For treating the original schema $S$ as a view on the pivoted schema $T$, we define a query $Q_{T \to S}$ that collapses the new navigational path $m_p.c\_m_p\_m$ to the obsolescent attribute $m$, for $m \in \mathrm{M}$, and suppresses objects of the new subclass $p$, while leaving the rest of an instance unchanged,*

$$Q_{T \to S} := \{O : d \longleftarrow O : d \mid d \in \mathrm{CL}_S\} \cup \tag{1}$$
$$\{O[m \to R] \longleftarrow O[m \to R] \mid m \in (\mathrm{AT}_S \setminus \mathrm{M})\} \cup \tag{2}$$
$$\{O[m \to R] \longleftarrow O : c[m_p \to P] \wedge P : p[c\_m_p\_m \to R] \mid m \in \mathrm{M}\} \tag{3}$$

*For treating the pivoted schema $T$ as a view on the original schema $S$, we define a query $Q_{S \to T}$ that retains the class population and the values for most attributes. The obsolescent attributes and their values are transplanted to the pivot class p and its objects, respectively. This class is populated with objects of class $c_p$ that are referenced by an object of class c via the pivot attribute $m_p$.*

$$Q_{S \to T} := \{O : d \longleftarrow O : d \mid d \in \mathrm{CL}_S\} \cup \tag{4}$$
$$\{O[m \to R] \longleftarrow O[m \to R] \mid m \in (\mathrm{AT}_S \setminus \mathbb{M})\} \cup \tag{5}$$
$$\{P : p[c\_m_p\_m \to R] \longleftarrow O : c[m_p \to P; m \to R] \mid m \in \mathbb{M}\} \tag{6}$$

*Finally, we define the tuple* $\mathrm{piv}(S, p, c, \mathbb{M}, m_p) := (T, Q_{T \to S}, Q_{S \to T})$.

*Example 2.3.* To demonstrate pivoting, we perform it on class Phone-admin of the schema $ADM$ with pivot attribute fac. In order to simplify, we first reduce the left-hand side of the key path functional dependency

$$\text{Phone-admin}(.\text{fac} \quad .\text{sch} \quad .\text{ph} \quad .\text{dep} \to .\text{Id})$$

to .fac and get the key path functional dependency

$$\text{Phone-admin}(.\text{fac} \to .\text{Id}) \ .$$

The reduction is possible, because the attribute fac determines all other attributes functionally.

The pivot class is the class Faculty. As pivoted attributes we choose the attributes sch and dep. To render the example more readable, we do not introduce the cryptic names of attributes. Instead we use the original names. As subclass for the pivot class Faculty we introduce the class Phoning-faculty. It is populated with the objects that are referenced by Phone-admin-objects via attribute fac.

The outcome is then the schema $ADM_P$ with

$\mathrm{CL}_{ADM_P} := \{\text{Phone-admin, Faculty, Phoning-faculty, School, Phone, Department}\}$

$\mathrm{AT}_{ADM_P} := \{\text{fac, sch, ph, dep}\}$

$\mathrm{HR}_{ADM_P} := \{\text{Phoning-faculty::Faculty}\}$

$\mathrm{SG}_{ADM_P} := \{\text{Phone-admin}[\text{fac} \Rightarrow \text{Phoning-faculty}; \text{ph} \Rightarrow \text{Phone}],$
$\qquad\qquad \text{Phoning-faculty}[\text{sch} \Rightarrow \text{School}; \text{dep} \Rightarrow \text{Department}] \}$

$\mathrm{SC}_{ADM_P} := \mathrm{AX} \cup$
$\qquad\qquad \{\text{Phone-admin}(.\text{fac} \to .\text{fac.sch}),$
$\qquad\qquad \text{Phone-admin}(.\text{fac} \to .\text{ph}),$
$\qquad\qquad \text{Phone-admin}(.\text{fac.sch} \to .\text{fac.dep}),$
$\qquad\qquad \text{Phone-admin}(.\text{ph} \to .\text{fac.dep}),$
$\qquad\qquad \text{Phone-admin}(.\text{fac} \to .\text{Id}),$
$\qquad\qquad \text{Phone-admin}\{\text{fac} \mid \text{Phoning-faculty}\}\} \ .$

The transformation pivoting removes in the class Phone-admin the declarations for the attributes sch and dep. These declarations occur again as declarations for the class Phoning-faculty. This change in the signature declarations has to be reflected by the path functional dependencies. For example, whenever the path function .sch appears in a path functional dependency, we replace it by the path function .fac.sch. This replacement is done for the path functional dependency

$$\text{Phone-admin}(.\text{fac} \rightarrow .\text{sch})$$

and leads to the path functional dependency

$$\text{Phone-admin}(.\text{fac} \rightarrow .\text{fac.sch}) \ .$$

We do not have to change any onto constraints in this example, because there is no onto constraint in the original schema. But we have to introduce the onto constraint

$$\text{Phone-admin}\{\text{fac} \mid \text{Phoning-faculty}\} \ .$$

## 2.6   Equivalence of Pivoted Schema

At design time a schema administrator has to decide on whether pivoting a given schema is useful or not. As argued before, a necessary condition is that the pivoted schema "supports" the original one. This condition has been formalized in terms of the instances of the schemas under consideration. These instances, however, are not explicitly available at design time. Rather the administrator can only deal with the purely syntactic items given in the schemas. In particular he can investigate the consequences of the semantic constraints. The following theorem precisely tells the schema administrator which property the semantic constraints must satisfy. This property is stated in terms of the implicational closure of the semantic constraints involved, and thus it is algorithmically tractable.

The theorem provides a fundamental response to the decomposition problem for advanced data models. Moreover, it nicely generalizes and extends the corresponding result for the simple relational model. For the relational model, it is well-known that the attributes transplanted apart into a new relation scheme should be functionally dependent on the attributes retained in the original scheme. More precisely, if the nonkey functional dependency $X \rightarrow Y$ is used for the decomposition, then the attributes of the right-hand side $Y$ are transplanted apart, together with the attributes of the left-hand side $X$. The latter are also retained in the original scheme in order to allow a reconstruction using $X$ as join attributes. A "lossless" reconstruction is just guaranteed by the validity of the functional dependency, or, speaking otherwise, by the attributes transplanted apart being in the implicational closure of the connecting join attributes. The announced theorem exhibits a corresponding property for the object-oriented context, where the pivot attribute $m_p$ plays the role of the join attributes $X$ in the relational context. Moreover, now the decomposition is not only "lossless" but also "dependency preserving", due to the expressive power of path functional dependencies.

**Theorem 2.1 (Equivalence).** *Let $S$ be a schema, and the vector $(T, Q_{T \to S}, Q_{S \to T}) := \mathrm{piv}(S, p, c, \mathbb{M}, m_p)$ be the outcome of pivoting the schema $S$. Then the following statements are equivalent.*

1. *$c(.m_p \to \mathbb{M}) \in \mathrm{SC}_S^{+s}$, i.e., all pivoted attributes are functionally dependent on the pivot attribute.*
2. *The schema $T$ provides unique view instance support for the schema $S$ with supporting query $Q_{T \to S}$.*
3. *The schema $S$ provides unique view instance support for the schema $T$ with supporting query $Q_{S \to T}$.*

## 2.7   Simplifying a Pivoted Schema

Knowing when a pivoted schema $T$ is equivalent to the original schema $S$, we can start to compare the quality of both schemas.

First, pivoting removes (potential) redundancy, and thus ameliorates the efficiency of constraint enforcement, since the attribute values of the pivoted attributes $c\_m_p\_m$, $m \in \mathbb{M}$, for an object $o_p$ of the new subclass $p$ can be shared. Here sharing occurs among all objects $o$ of the class $c$ which reference $o_p$ via the pivot attribute $m_p$. Clearly, sharing actually pays off only if $o_p$ is referenced by more than just one object of $c$. Surely, this cannot happen if the pivot attribute $m_p$ is a key for the class $c$. Thus, pivoting should be applied only if $c(.m_p \to \mathbb{M}) \in \mathrm{SC}_S^{+s}$ is a nonkey path functional dependency. This advice for our data model exactly corresponds to the normalization procedures in the relational framework where a relation scheme is decomposed if it is not in "normal form" (saying that a nontrivial nonkey functional dependency is implied).

Second, pivoting adjusts path functional dependencies by formally replacing a simple obsolescent attribute $m$ with the new navigational path $m_p.c\_m_p\_m$, and thus, at first glance, pivoting appears to deteriorate the efficiency of constraint enforcement. A second thought, however, reveals that deterioration will rarely happen, hopefully, since the formally adjusted path functional dependencies can be simplified as follows:

- We completely remove path functional dependencies that stem from path functional dependencies of the form $c(L \to R)$ where $\{.m_p\} \subset L \subset \{.m_p\} \cup \mathbb{M}$ and $R \subset \mathbb{M}$ (because these are naturally supported, see [5]).
- We simplify path functional dependencies that stem from path functional dependencies of the form $c(L \to R)$ where $L \cup R \subset \mathbb{M}$, by making them a constraint of the new subclass $p$ and, accordingly, deleting all occurrences of the prefix $.m_p$.

Let denote the resulting schema by $\mathrm{sim}(S, p, c, \mathbb{M}, m_p)$. The following theorem states that we can always use the simplified schema instead of the pivoted schema. Thus we can hope that amelioration prevails.

**Theorem 2.2 (Equivalence of Simplified Schemas).** *Let $S$ be a schema, and the vector $(T, Q_{T \to S}, Q_{S \to T}) := \mathrm{piv}(S, p, c, \mathbb{M}, m_p)$ be the outcome of pivoting the schema $S$. Then the schema $T$ provides unique view instance support for the schema $\mathrm{sim}(S, p, c, \mathbb{M}, m_p)$ with supporting query $\mathrm{id}_Q$ and vice versa.*

*Example 2.4.* Looking at the semantic constraints of the schema $ADM_P$ reveals that the path functional dependency

$$\text{Phone-admin(.fac} \rightarrow \text{.fac.sch)} \qquad (7)$$

is redundant because it can be derived from the trivial path functional dependency

$$\text{Phoning-faculty(.Id} \rightarrow \text{.sch)} \ ,$$

which in turn can be derived from (7) and the onto constraint

$$\text{Phone-admin\{fac} \mid \text{Phoning-faculty\}}$$

by "simple prefix reduction". In fact, each path functional dependency in the original schema of the form

$$\text{Phone-admin(.fac} \rightarrow \text{.}m)$$

with $m$ a pivoted attribute is transformed into a path functional dependency

$$\text{Phone-admin(.fac} \rightarrow \text{.fac.}m) \ ,$$

which is redundant in the pivoted schema. Furthermore, the path functional dependency

$$\text{Phone-admin(.fac.sch} \rightarrow \text{.fac.dep)}$$

can be simplified to

$$\text{Phoning-faculty(.sch} \rightarrow \text{.dep)}$$

## 2.8   Pivoting with Functional Dependencies Only

Although in general pivoting might increase the path length of path functional dependencies, by adding the pivot attribute $m_p$ as a prefix, in most practical cases simplification is hoped to actually avoid such an increase. In particular, when the original schema $S$ comprises only normal functional dependencies (i.e. all path functional dependencies have only path-functions of length 1), then simplification will come up with functional dependencies again in many cases. But not in all cases, as demonstrated by the example in the introductory section. A precise characterization of the good cases has already been provided by Theorem 6 of [6]. This characterization is fully expressed by properties of the implicational closure of the semantic constraints.

## 2.9   Recursive Pivoting

In [6] we have also studied the options to apply pivoting recursively in order to achieve natural enforcement of all functional constraints, i.e. to get rid of all functional dependencies by the simplification of pivoted schemas. The outline of results, as presented in [6], has been further refined in [11]. A full treatment of this topic is beyond the scope of this paper.

# 3   The Justification: Proofs for Formal Theorems

For the sake of distinctness, the following proof sketches sometimes blur the subtle distinction between an extension $f$ and its completion.

In order to justify Theorem 2.1, i.e. the conditions for a pivoted schema $T$ supporting the original schema $S$, we have to relate the following sets:

$$\{\mathrm{compl}_S(f_S) \mid f_S \in \mathrm{sat}(S)\} \text{ , for the original schema } S, \text{ and} \tag{8}$$

$$\{\mathrm{compl}_S(\mathrm{eval}_T(Q_{T \to S}, f_T)) \mid f_T \in \mathrm{sat}(T)\}, \text{ for the pivoted schema } T. \tag{9}$$

We first note that the query $Q_{T \to S}$ always yields an instance of the original schema, i.e. we have the following inclusion:

**Lemma 3.1.**

$$\{\mathrm{compl}_S(f_S) \mid f_S \in \mathrm{sat}(S)\} \supset \{\mathrm{compl}_S(\mathrm{eval}_T(Q_{T \to S}, f_T)) \mid f_T \in \mathrm{sat}(T)\} \tag{10}$$

*Proof.* Let $f_T \in \mathrm{sat}(T)$ be an instance of the schema $T$, and recall the form of the query $Q_{T \to S}$. While the rules in (1) and (2) merely copy data (either objects or their attributes values), the rules in (3) perform somewhat more. Nevertheless it is easy to see that the image $\mathrm{eval}_T(Q_{T \to S}, f_T)$ is an extension of the schema $S$, and its completion $\mathrm{compl}_S(\mathrm{eval}_T(Q_{T \to S}, f_T))$ satisfies the built-in axioms AX. Moreover, it also satisfies all application-dependent constraints, i.e. all onto constraints and path functional dependencies of the original schema $S$, because a corresponding onto constraint or path functional dependency has been generated for the pivoted schema $T$ and is satisfied by the completion $\mathrm{compl}_T(f_T)$.

Note that we need the expressive power of path functional dependencies in order to generate all constraints required for $T$.                                       □

So the crucial property of support, and then even for faithful support, is the inverse of the inclusion stated in the preceding lemma. Basically, the crucial inclusion means that the query $Q_{T \to S}$ restricted to $\mathrm{sat}(T)$ is surjective with respect to $\mathrm{sat}(S)$. This surjectivity in turn is well-known to be equivalent with the existence of a function $Q$ on $\mathrm{sat}(S)$ such that $Q$ followed by the restricted $Q_{T \to S}$ is the identity. Clearly, the query $Q_{S \to T}$ is the canonical candidate for the role of $Q$. Indeed we have the following equivalence.

**Lemma 3.2.**

$$\{\mathrm{compl}_S(f_S) \mid f_S \in \mathrm{sat}(S)\} \subset \{\mathrm{compl}_S(\mathrm{eval}_T(Q_{T \to S}, f_T)) \mid f_T \in \mathrm{sat}(T)\} \tag{11}$$

*if and only if*

$$c(.m_p \to \mathbb{M}) \in \mathrm{SC}_S^{+s}. \tag{12}$$

*Proof.* Consider the query $Q_{S \to T}$. Then we have for all instances $f_S \in \text{sat}(S)$:

$Q_{S \to T}$ applied to $f_S$ yields an instance of T

iff for all data generated by (6) the unique-name axioms hold

iff $f_S$ satisfies $c(.m_p \to \mathbb{M})$.

From this equivalence we easily derive the equivalence stated in the lemma.

□

Now, if both properties of the preceding lemma are valid, then the queries $Q_{T \to S}$ and $Q_{S \to T}$ are actually full inverses of each other, since we have added the onto constraint $c\{m_p \mid p\}$ to $T$. More precisely:

**Lemma 3.3.** $Q_{T \to S}$ *restricted to* $\text{sat}(T)$ *is injective (on the saturated elements).*

*Proof.* Since rules in (1) and (2) merely copy data, they cannot violate injectivity. Thus, only rules in (3) could cause a violation if there existed an object $o_p$ in the new subclass $p$, $o_p : p$, which is not referenced by any object $o_c$ in the class $c$, $o_c : c$, via the pivot attribute $m_p$. However, this unhappy situation has been excluded by adding the onto constraint $c\{m_p \mid p\}$.                                             □

The lemmas and the reasoning so far indicate that the first and the second statement of Theorem 2.1 are equivalent. Furthermore, if they both hold then $Q_{T \to S}$ and $Q_{S \to T}$ can be proven to be fully inverses indeed. This shows that the second statement implies the third statement. The inverse implication can be verified by carefully elaborating the observation that $Q_{T \to S}$ and $Q_{S \to T}$ are the canonical candidates for being inverses to each other, i.e., basically, the former is a bijection iff the latter is the inverse bijection.

Concerning Theorem 2.2 we only note that we can infer the simplified path functional dependencies of the schema $\text{sim}(S, p, c, \mathbb{M}, m_p)$ from those of the pivoted schema, and vice versa, using the inferential system studied in [7, 11]. For the former direction, we employ the inference rule of "simple prefix reduction" which requires the onto constraint $c\{m_p \mid p\}$ added to the pivoted schema. For the latter direction, basically we have to combine the inference rules of "simple prefix augmentation" with further auxiliarily used rules.

# 4   Summary and Conclusions

We specified an advanced data model with object-oriented and logic-oriented features that substantially extend the relational approach. For this model we exhibited and studied the counterpart to the well-known decomposition of a relation scheme according to a nontrivial nonkey functional dependency.

For decomposing a class of a database schema the transformation pivoting can be used. Pivoting separates apart some attributes of a class to a newly generated class. This new class is declared to be a subclass of the result class of the so-called pivot attribute. Moreover the pivot attribute provides the link between the original class and the new subclass.

We identified the conditions for the result of pivoting being equivalent to its input. Basically, we need three features:

- The expressive power of path functional dependencies allowing to capture connections between classes, in order to be able to transform all original constraints (see Lemma 3.1).
- The validity of the path functional dependency between the pivot attribute and the transplanted attributes, in order to achieve support of the original schema (see Lemma 3.2).
- The validity of the onto constraint guaranteeing that values for the transplanted attributes can be referenced from the remaining part of the original class, in order to make the support of the original schema unique and to simplify the pivoted schema (see Lemma 3.3 and Theorem 2.2).

The decompositions studied in this paper have a special form: First, the link between the original class $c$ and the new subclass $p$ is provided by just one attribute, the pivot attribute $m_p$. Second, the decomposition produces two components (with the option of further decompositions by recursion).

From the relational context we know that in some cases more decompositions are possible which are not covered by the special ones.

First, the relational link consists of the join attributes, which are specified by the left-hand side of the nonkey functional dependency under consideration. Clearly this link can comprise several attributes. If we want to simulate such cases with pivoting, we first have to lift a value tuple for the join attributes into the status of an object, i.e. on the schema level to introduce an appropriate class. Then the new compound objects could be referenced by a single suitably adapted pivot attribute, which would serve as the link needed to simulate the join.

Second, in general relational decompositions are characterized by join dependencies, and there exist binary join dependencies (multivalued dependencies) which are not implied by a functional dependency, and there exist join dependencies with more than two components which are not implied by a set of binary join dependencies. If we want to simulate such cases within our data model, we could suitably adopt and combine the following approaches: lift attribute values into the status of an object, use the option of object-oriented systems to declare set-valued attributes (rather than only scalar attributes), employ the more general form of pivoting as originally introduced in [4], and simulate relational decompositions directly as discussed in [4]. A complete analysis of these approaches, however, is beyond the scope of the present paper, and is suggested for interesting further research.

# References

1. Joachim Biskup. Database schema design theory: Achievements and challenges. In Subhash Bhalla, editor, *Proceedings of the 6th International Conference Information Systems and Management of Data*, number 1006 in Lecture Notes in Computer Science, pages 14–44, Bombay, 1995. Springer-Verlag.
2. Joachim Biskup. *Grundlagen von Informationssystemen*. Vieweg, Braunschweig-Wiesbaden, 1995.

3. Joachim Biskup. Achievements of relational database schema design theory revisited. In Bernhard Thalheim and Leonid Libkin, editors, *Semantics in Databases*, number 1358 in Lecture Notes in Computer Science, pages 29–54. Springer-Verlag, Berlin, 1998.

4. Joachim Biskup, Ralf Menzel, and Torsten Polle.    Transforming an entity-relationship schema into object-oriented database schemas. In J. Eder and L. A. Kalinichenko, editors, *Advances in Databases and Information Systems, Moscow 95*, Workshops in Computing, pages 109–136. Springer-Verlag, 1996.

5. Joachim Biskup, Ralf Menzel, Torsten Polle, and Yehoshua Sagiv. A case study on object-oriented database schema design. In Hele-Mai Haav and Bernhard Thalheim, editors, *International Baltic Workshop on Databases and Information Systems*, Tallinn, Estonia, 1996.

6. Joachim Biskup, Ralf Menzel, Torsten Polle, and Yehoshua Sagiv. Decomposition of relationships through pivoting. In Bernhard Thalheim, editor, *Proceedings of the 15th International Conference on Conceptual Modeling*, number 1157 in Lecture Notes in Computer Science, pages 28–41, Cottbus, Germany, 1996.

7. Joachim Biskup and Torsten Polle.    Constraints in object-oriented databases. Manuscript in preparation, 1999.

8. Michael Kifer, Georg Lausen, and James Wu.    Logical foundations of object-oriented and frame-based languages. *Journal of the ACM*, 42(4):741–843, 1995.

9. J. A. Makowsky and E. V. Ravve. Dependency preserving refinements and the fundamental problem of database design. *Data & Knowledge Engineering*, 24(3):277–312, 1998.

10. Heikki Mannila and Kari-Jouko Räihä.    *The Design of Relational Databases*. Addison-Wesley, Wokingham, England, 1992.

11. Torsten Polle. *On Representing Relationships in Object-Oriented Databases*. PhD thesis, Universität Dortmund, FB Informatik/LS6, D-44221 Dortmund, 1999.

12. R. Reiter. Equality and domain closure in first-order databases. *Journal of the ACM*, 27(2):235–249, 1980.

13. Bernhard Thalheim. Foundations of entity-relationship modeling. *Annals of Mathematics and Artificial Intelligence*, 1993(7):197–256, 1993.

14. Grant E. Weddell. A theory of functional dependencies for object-oriented data models. In Won Kim, Jean-Marie Nicolas, and Shojiro Nishio, editors, *Proceedings of the 1st Deductive and Object-Oriented Databases (DOOD '89)*, pages 165–184, Kyoto, Japan, 1989. Elsevier Science Publishers (North-Holland).

15. Grant E. Weddell. Reasoning about functional dependencies generalized for semantic data models. *ACM Transactions on Database Systems*, 17(1):32–64, March 1992.

# Imprecision and User Preferences
# in Multimedia Queries:
# A Generic Algebraic Approach*

Paolo Ciaccia[1], Danilo Montesi[2], Wilma Penzo[1], and Alberto Trombetta[3]

[1] DEIS - CSITE-CNR, Bologna, Italy, {pciaccia,wpenzo}@deis.unibo.it
[2] DSI, Dept. of Computer Science, Milano, Italy, montesi@dsi.unimi.it
[3] DI, Dept. of Computer Science, Torino, Italy, tromb@di.unito.it

**Abstract.** Specification and efficient processing of similarity queries on multimedia databases have recently attracted several research efforts, even if most of them have considered specific aspects, such as indexing, of this new exciting scenario. In this paper we try to remedy this by presenting an integrated algebraic framework which allows many relevant aspects of similarity query processing to be dealt with. As a starting point, we assume the more general case where "imprecision" is already present at the data level, typically because of the ambiguous nature of multimedia objects' content. We then define a *generic* similarity algebra, $SAME^W$, where semantics of operators is deliberately left unspecified in order to better adapt to specific scenarios. A basic feature of $SAME^W$ is that it allows user preferences, expressed in the form of *weights*, to be specified so as to alter the default behavior of most operators. Finally, we discuss some issues related to "approximation" and to "user evaluation" of query results.

## 1 Introduction

The fact that "traditional" (Boolean) queries are not really appropriate for dealing with multimedia (MM) data has been early recognized, and many systems now exist that allow users to issue queries where some form of "imprecision" is allowed. For instance, in the QBIC system [10] one can look for images which are "similar" to a target one, according to color, texture, and shape of embedded objects. Since MM queries can lead to (very) high response times, many efforts have been spent in order to devise access methods able to efficiently deal with complex features [6]. This line of research has been somewhat complemented by activity aiming to provide users with a full-fledged query language able to express complex similarity queries [17]. Although the processing of such complex queries has been the subject of some recent works [1,7,8,15], a full understanding of the implications (both at a formal and at a system level) of similarity query processing is still lacking. In particular, several important issues have only partially been addressed, such as models able to capture the "essential" aspects of

---

* This work has been partially supported by the InterData MURST Italian project.

K.-D. Schewe, B. Thalheim (Eds.): FoIKS 2000, LNCS 1762, pp. 50–71, 2000.
© Springer-Verlag Berlin Heidelberg 2000

MM objects needed by similarity queries, the impact of "user preferences" on query processing, the management of "approximate" queries (and the relationship of this concept to those of query equivalence and query containment), the complexity and expressiveness of similarity-based query languages, and so on. Furthermore, contributions to above issues typically consider ad-hoc scenarios and/or completely ignore the other coordinates of the problem, thus resulting in a set of difficult-to-integrate recipes.

In this work we address several of the above points in a unified algebraic framework. We have deliberately chosen to "start simple" from the modeling point of view, in order to better focus on those aspects which are peculiar to similarity query processing. Thus, we consider a (extended) relational framework which takes into account the two major sources of "imprecision" arising when querying MM databases [21]: 1) imprecision of *classification* of MM data, and 2) imprecision in the *matching of features* that characterize the content of MM objects. As to the first point we rely on basic concepts from *fuzzy set theory*, and allow representation of "vague classification" both at tuple and at attribute level (Sect. 2). This reflects the fact that in some cases imprecision characterizes an object as a whole, whereas in others it only affects some of its attributes. We then introduce a "similarity algebra", called $SAME^W$,[1] which extends relational algebra in a conservative way and incorporates the use of "weights" in most of its operators, in order to adapt to user preferences (Sect. 4). We show how complex similarity queries can be easily expressed in $SAME^W$ (Sect. 5) and how equivalence rules can be exploited for the purpose of query rewriting and optimization (Sect. 6). In Sect. 7 we present some extensions to our framework that consider such relevant issues as "approximation of results" and user feedback. Finally, we briefly discuss related work and conclude.

## 2   The Data Model

For the sake of clarity, we first remind some standard notation and definitions. Given a set of attribute names, $\mathcal{A}$, and a function $dom()$ which associates to each $A \in \mathcal{A}$ a value domain, $dom(A)$, a (named) relation schema is formed by a relation name, $R$, and a subset of attributes $X = \{A_1, \ldots, A_n\} \subseteq \mathcal{A}$.[2] A tuple $t$ over $R(X)$ is any element of $dom(X) = dom(A_1) \times \ldots \times dom(A_n)$, and $t.A_i \equiv t[A_i]$ denotes the value of $A_i$ in $t$. For any $Y \subseteq X$, $t[Y]$ denotes the restriction of $t$ on $Y$, that is, the (sub-)tuple obtained from $t$ by considering only the values of the attributes in $Y$.

Our data model extends the relational one by allowing both *fuzzy attributes* and *fuzzy relations*. Remind that a fuzzy set $F$ over a "universe" $U$ is a set characterized by a *membership function* $\mu_F : U \rightarrow \mathcal{S}$, where $\mu_F(x)$ is the *degree of membership* of $x$ in $F$, also called "score" or "grade". In the following we will always consider a normalized *score domain* $\mathcal{S} = [0, 1]$.

---

[1] $SAME^W$ stands for "Similarity Algebra for Multimedia Extended with Weights".

[2] We will adopt the conventional list notation for sets, thus writing $A$ for $\{A\}$ and $XY$ for $X \cup Y$.

Imprecision at the attribute level is captured by the notion of "fuzzy domain". We say that $A_i$ is a fuzzy attribute if its values are pairs of the form $F_j : s_j$, where $F_j$ is a fuzzy set and $s_j \in \mathcal{S}$. The two components of $A_i$ can be referred to as $A_i^v$ (the "value") and $A_i^\mu$ (the "score"), respectively. Intuitively, given a tuple $t$, $t.A_i$ is interpreted as "$t.A_i^v$ is an appropriate value, with score $t.A_i^\mu$, of attribute $A_i$ for $t$ ", or, equivalently, that "$t$ fits $A_i^v$ with score $A_i^\mu$". In practice, $t.A_i^v$ will be a real-world, application-specific concept, used to classify $t$ according to $A_i$. For instance, an image can be classified, considering its Brightness, as dark with score 0.8.[3] For lack of space, in this paper we do not explicitly consider the case where $t.A_i$ is set-valued, which is appropriate when multiple non-exclusive classifications are possible (for instance, an image could be classified, according to its Color, as red with score 0.8 and as orange with score 0.7). However, as shown in [4], this is not restrictive, since set-valued attributes can be easily "normalized" into single-valued attributes.

Non-fuzzy (*crisp*) domains include "ordinary" sets of values, like integer and string, as well as more complex domains, like, say, color_histogram, which are required to represent feature values extracted from MM objects. We conveniently call *feature attribute* an attribute defined over such domains, in order to emphasize that for such attributes *similarity predicates* (rather than exact-matching) are the usual way to compare feature values (see Sect. 3.1).

Imprecision can also occur at the whole tuple level, and motivates the introduction of fuzzy relations. A fuzzy relation $r$ over $R(X)$ is a fuzzy subset of $dom(X)$, $r \subseteq dom(X)$, characterized by a membership function $\mu_R$ (or simply $\mu$ if $R$ is clear from the context)[4] which assigns to each tuple $t$ a grade $\mu_R(t) \in \mathcal{S}$. The notation $t.\mu_R$ will be used with the same meaning of $\mu_R(t)$. We say that $t$ belongs to $r$ ($t \in r$) iff $t.\mu_R > 0$, and $r$ is called a *crisp* instance iff $t.\mu_R = 1$ for each $t \in r$. The intuition about fuzzy relations is that, if a schema $R(X)$ represents some real-world "fuzzy" concept, the introduction of *tuple imprecision* permits to model how much a given object (tuple) "fits" the concept expressed by $R(X)$.

## 3    The SAME$^W$ Algebra: Preliminaries

SAME$^W$ extends relational algebra (RA) with a set of peculiarities that make it amenable to easily formulate complex similarity queries. SAME$^W$ expressions operate on fuzzy relations and always return a fuzzy relation, and can use ordinary (Boolean), *similarity*, and *fuzzy* predicates. Semantics of expressions is *parametric* in the semantics of logical operators, which can therefore be varied in order to better adapt to user and application requirements. "Weights" can also be used to bias the behavior of most operators.

---

[3] Clearly, the fuzzy sets which can occur as values of $A_i^v$ must be defined over the same universe.

[4] There is a slight notational inconsistency here, since the membership function should be denoted by $\mu_r$. In practice, however, the best thing is to use, when needed, the relation name, since instances are usually unnamed.

## 3.1 Predicates and Formulas

A logical formula $f$ is obtained by combining predicates with logical connectives, respecting the syntax $f ::= p|f \wedge f|f \vee f|\neg f|(f)$, where $p$ is a predicate. The *evaluation* of $f$ on a tuple $t$ is a score $s(f, t) \in \mathcal{S}$ which says how much $t$ satisfies $f$. We simply say that $t$ *satisfies* $f$ iff $s(f, t) > 0$. How $s(f, t)$ depends on (the evaluation on $t$ of) the predicates in $f$ is intentionally left unspecified, in order to achieve parametricity with respect to the semantics of logical operators. The basic constraint we impose is that $s(f, t)$ has to be computed by means of a so-called "scoring function" [8], $s_f$, whose arguments are the scores, $s(p_i, t)$, of $t$ with respect to the predicates in $f$, that is:

$$s(f(p_1, \ldots, p_n), t) = s_f(s(p_1, t), \ldots, s(p_n, t)) \ . \tag{1}$$

Besides Boolean predicates, which evaluate to either 1 (true) or 0 (false), we also consider similarity and fuzzy predicates. A similarity predicate has either the form $A \sim v$, where $A$ is a feature attribute, $v \in dom(A)$ is a constant (*query value*), and $\sim$ is a *similarity operator*, or $A_1 \sim A_2$, where both $A_1$ and $A_2$ are over the same domain.[5] Then, the evaluation of $p : A \sim v$ on $t$ returns a score, $s(p, t) \in \mathcal{S}$, which says how much $t.A$ is similar to the query value $v$. For instance, evaluating the predicate Color $\sim$ red over an image $t$ returns a score assessing the "redness" of $t$.[6]

Fuzzy predicates, on the other hand, operate on fuzzy attributes. Remind that if $A$ is a fuzzy attribute, then $t.A$ is a pair $t.A^v : t.A^\mu$, where $t.A^v$ is (the name of) a fuzzy set and $t.A^\mu$ is the membership degree of $t$ in $t.A^v$. The evaluation on $t$ of a fuzzy predicate $q : A = w$, where $w$ is a fuzzy set, is the score $s(q, t) = t.A^\mu$, if $t.A^v = w$, otherwise $s(q, t) = 0$. This is to say that we assume that different fuzzy sets are incomparable. The same applies to the predicate $q : A_1 = A_2$. In this case $s(q, t) = 0$ if $t.A_1^v \neq t.A_2^v$, otherwise the score is computed as a "parametric conjunction" of the two membership degrees, that is, $s(q, t) = s_\wedge(t.A_1^\mu, t.A_2^\mu)$, where $s_\wedge$ denotes the AND scoring function.

For the sake of definiteness, in the following we restrict our focus on the class $\mathcal{F}$ of scoring functions corresponding to fuzzy *t-norms* and *t-conorms* [13,8], for which the AND ($\wedge$) and OR ($\vee$) operators satisfy the following properties:

1. They are both associative and commutative;
2. $s_\wedge(x, 1) = x$ and $s_\vee(x, 0) = x$ (*boundary* condition);
3. $x_1 \leq x_2 \Rightarrow s_\wedge(x, x_1) \leq s_\wedge(x, x_2)$ and $s_\vee(x, x_1) \leq s_\vee(x, x_2)$ (*monotonicity*).

As to the NOT ($\neg$) operator, it is assumed to satisfy the two properties:

1. $s_\neg(1) = 0$ and $s_\neg(0) = 1$ (*boundary* condition);
2. $x_1 \leq x_2 \Rightarrow s_\neg(x_1) \geq s_\neg(x_2)$ (*monotonicity*).

---

[5] This is a simplification. It suffices that the domains are compatible for '$\sim$' to be well-defined.

[6] Note that red is just a name for a value of $dom$(Color), and not a string constant.

For instance, $\mathcal{FS}$ (fuzzy standard) and $\mathcal{FA}$ (fuzzy algebraic) [13] semantics are given by the following set of rules:

| | $\mathcal{FS}$ | $\mathcal{FA}$ |
|---|---|---|
| $s(f_1 \wedge f_2, t)$ | $\min(s(f_1,t), s(f_2,t))$ | $s(f_1,t) \cdot s(f_2,t)$ |
| $s(f_1 \vee f_2, t)$ | $\max(s(f_1,t), s(f_2,t))$ | $s(f_1,t) + s(f_2,t) - s(f_1,t) \cdot s(f_2,t)$ |
| $s(\neg f, t)$ | $1 - s(f,t)$ | $1 - s(f,t)$ |

Considering the general case of $n$-ary t-norms and t-conorms, the following inequalities hold $\forall x_1, \ldots, x_n \in \mathcal{S}$ [13]:

$$s_\wedge(x_1, \ldots, x_n) \leq \min(x_1, \ldots, x_n) \leq x_i \qquad \forall i \in [1..n] \qquad (2)$$
$$s_\vee(x_1, \ldots, x_n) \geq \max(x_1, \ldots, x_n) \geq x_i \qquad \forall i \in [1..n] \ . \qquad (3)$$

## 3.2 Dealing with User Preferences: Weights

With a non-Boolean semantics, it is quite natural and useful to give the user the possibility to assign a different relevance to the conditions he states to retrieve tuples. Such "user preferences" can be expressed by means of *weights*, thus saying, for instance, that the score of a predicate on Color is twice as important as the score of a predicate on the Texture of an image. The seminal work by Fagin and Wimmers [9] shows how *any* scoring function $s_f$ for a formula $f(p_1, \ldots, p_n)$ can be properly extended into a weighted version, $s_{f_\Theta}$, where $\Theta = [\theta_1, \ldots, \theta_n]$ is a vector of weights (also called a "weighting"), in such a way that:

1. $s_{f_\Theta}$ reduces to $s_f$ when all the weights are equal;
2. $s_{f_\Theta}$ does not depend on $s(p_i, t)$ when $\theta_i = 0$;
3. $s_{f_\Theta}$ is a continuous function of the weights, for each fixed set of argument scores.

Let $x_i = s(p_i, t)$ denote the score of $t$ with respect to $p_i$, and assume without loss of generality $\theta_1 \geq \theta_2 \geq \ldots \geq \theta_n$, with $\theta_i \in [0,1]$ and $\sum_i \theta_i = 1$. Then, Fagin and Wimmers' formula is:

$$s_{f_\Theta}(x_1, \ldots, x_n) = (\theta_1 - \theta_2) \cdot x_1 + 2 \cdot (\theta_2 - \theta_3) \cdot s_f(x_1, x_2) + \cdots + n \cdot \theta_n \cdot s_f(x_1, \ldots, x_n) \ .$$
$$(4)$$

Although above formula is usually used to weigh the predicates appearing in a (selection) formula, our position is that *whenever scores have to be "combined", then a weighting should be allowed*. For instance, if we take the union of two relations, it might be reasonable to require that tuples in the first relation are "more important" than tuples in the second one. A meaningful example is when we want to integrate results from different search engines, but we trust more one than the other. Accordingly, most of the SAME$^W$ operators[7] that compute new tuples' scores can use weights.

---

[7] We only leave out Difference, because we were not able to conceive any meaningful "weighted Difference" query. As to Projection, since the duplicate tuples to be combined together are not a priori known, it is not possible to assign weights to them.

## 4 The SAME$^W$ Algebra

Basic operators of SAME$^W$ conservatively extend those of RA in such a way that, if no "imprecision" is involved in the evaluation of an expression, the semantics of RA applies (see Theorem 4.1). Genericity with respect to different semantics is achieved by defining SAME$^W$ operators in terms of the (generic) scoring functions of the logical operators. Thus, if a given semantics is adopted for formulas, the same is used by SAME$^W$ operators, which avoids counter-intuitive phenomena and preserves many RA equivalence rules. As an example, the semantics of Union ($\cup$) is based on that of the OR ($\vee$) operator.

In the following, $E(X)$ denotes an expression with schema $X$, and $e = E[db]$ is the fuzzy set of tuples with schema $X$ obtained by evaluating $E(X)$ over the current database $db$. We say that a tuple $t$ belongs to $e$ ($t \in e$) iff $t.\mu_E > 0$ holds. Two tuples $t_1$ and $t_2$ with attributes $X$ are *equal* iff $t_1[A_i] = t_2[A_i]$ holds for each $A_i \in X$. In case of fuzzy attributes, tuple equality thus requires that also the attributes' grades are the same. Two relations $e_1$ and $e_2$ are equal iff: 1) they consist of the same set of tuples, and 2) $\forall t_1 \in e_1, \forall t_2 \in e_2 : t_1 = t_2 \Rightarrow t_1.\mu = t_2.\mu$.

We start by extending "traditional" operators of RA, and then introduce new operators which have no direct counterpart in RA.

**Selection ($\sigma$)** The Selection operator applies a formula $f$ to the tuples in $e$ and filters out those which do not satisfy $f$. The novel point here is that, as an effect of $f$ and of weights, *the grade of a tuple $t$ can change*. Weights can be used for two complementary needs: In the first case, they weigh the importance of predicates in $f$, as in [9], thus leading to use the scoring function $s_{f_{\Theta_f}}$ in place of $s_f$.[8] In the second case they are used to perform a *weighted conjunction*, $s_\wedge^\Theta$, between the score computed by $f$ and the "input" tuple score, $t.\mu_E$. This determines the new tuple score, $t.\mu$:

$$\sigma_{f_{\Theta_f}}^\Theta(e) = \{t \mid t \in e \wedge t.\mu = s_\wedge^\Theta(s(f_{\Theta_f}, t), t.\mu_E) > 0\} \ . \tag{5}$$

**Projection ($\pi$)** As in RA, the Projection operator removes a set of attributes and then eliminates duplicate tuples. Projection can also be used to *discard* scores, both of fuzzy attributes and of the whole tuple. In this case, however, in order to guarantee consistency of subsequent operations, such scores are simply set to 1, so that they can still be referenced in the resulting schema. This captures the intuition that if we discard, say, the tuples' scores, then the result is a crisp relation, that is, a fuzzy relation whose tuples all have score 1.

Formally, let $e$ be a relation with schema $E(X)$, $Y \subseteq X$, and $V$ a set of *v-annotated* fuzzy attributes, $V = \{A_i^v\}$, where $V$ contains exactly those fuzzy attributes for which scores are to be discarded. Note that $V$ can include $A_i^v$ only if $A_i \in X - Y$. Finally, let $F$ stand for either $\mu$ or the empty set. Then, the projection of $e$ over $YVF$ is a relation with schema $YW$, where if $A_i^v \in V$ then

---

[8] When using weights, $f$ is restricted to be either a conjunction or a disjunction of predicates.

$A_i \in W$, defined as follows:

$$\pi_{YVF}(e) = \{t[YW] | \exists t' \in e : t[YV] = t'[YV] \wedge \forall A_i^v \in V : t.A_i^\mu = 1 \qquad (6)$$
$$\wedge\, t.\mu = s_\vee\{t''.\mu_E | t''[YV] = t[YV]\} \text{ if } F = \mu, \text{ otherwise } t.\mu = 1\} \ .$$

Thus, tuples' scores are discarded (i.e. set to 1) when $F = \emptyset$, whereas they are preserved when $F = \mu$. In the latter case, new scores are computed by considering the "parametric disjunction", $s_\vee$, of the scores of all duplicate tuples with the same values for $YV$.

**Union** ($\cup$) In SAME$^W$ the Union is an $n$-ary operator,[9] which, given $n$ relations $e_i$ with schemas $E_i(X)$, computes the score of a tuple $t$ as a *weighted disjunction*, $s_\vee^\Theta(t.\mu_{E_1}, \ldots, t.\mu_{E_n})$, with $\Theta = [\theta_1, \ldots, \theta_n]$, of the input tuples' scores, that is:

$$\cup^\Theta (e_1, \ldots, e_n) = \{t \,|\, (t \in e_1 \vee \ldots \vee t \in e_n) \wedge t.\mu = s_\vee^\Theta(t.\mu_{E_1}, \ldots, t.\mu_{E_n}) > 0\} \ .$$
$$(7)$$

Note that, because of the presence of weights, Union is not associative anymore. This implies that the $n$-ary Union cannot be defined in terms of $n - 1$ binary unions, as it happens in RA.

**Join** ($\bowtie$) Also the weighted (natural) Join is an $n$-ary operator, where the score of a result tuple $t$ is a *weighted conjunction*, $s_\wedge^\Theta(t_1.\mu_{E_1}, \ldots, t_n.\mu_{E_n})$, of the scores of matching tuples:

$$\bowtie^\Theta (e_1, \ldots, e_n) = \{t[X_1 \ldots X_n] \,|\, \exists t_1 \in e_1, \ldots, \exists t_n \in e_n : \qquad (8)$$
$$t[X_1] = t_1[X_1] \wedge \ldots \wedge t[X_n] = t_n[X_n] \wedge t.\mu = s_\wedge^\Theta(t_1.\mu_{E_1}, \ldots, t_n.\mu_{E_n}) > 0\} \ .$$

**Difference** ($-$) Given relations $e_1$ and $e_2$ with schemas $E_1(X)$ and $E_2(X)$, respectively, their Difference is defined as:

$$e_1 - e_2 = \{t \,|\, t \in e_1 \wedge t.\mu = s_\wedge(t.\mu_{E_1}, s_\neg(t.\mu_{E_2})) > 0\} \ .$$
$$(9)$$

**Renaming** ($\rho$) The Renaming operator is as in RA, thus we do not repeat its definition here.

The following result proves that the "RA-fragment" of SAME$^W$, that is, SAME$^W$ restricted to the above operators, is indeed a conservative extension of relational algebra.

**Theorem 4.1.** *Let $E$ be a SAME$^W$ expression that does not use weights and that includes only operators in $\{\sigma, \pi, \cup, \bowtie, -, \rho\}$. If $E$ does not use similarity operators, the database instance db is crisp and the semantics of the scoring functions is in $\mathcal{F}$, then $E[db] = E_{RA}[db]$, the latter being evaluated with the Boolean semantics of RA.*

*Proof.* (sketch) It is sufficient to show that every operator in $\{\sigma, \pi, \cup, \bowtie, -, \rho\}$, when applied to crisp relations, yields a crisp relation. Here we only consider

---
[9] We also use the infix notation, $E_1 \cup^{[\theta_1, \theta_2]} E_2$, when only two operands are present.

the case of Selection, arguments for the other operators being similar. A Selection $\sigma_f(E)$, where $f$ does not contain similarity predicates and $E[db]$ is a crisp relation, computes the score of a tuple $t \in E[db]$ as $s_\wedge(s(f, t), t.\mu_E)$. Since $s_\wedge$ is a t-norm, $t.\mu_E$ is equal to 1, and $s(f, t)$ is either 0 or 1, the Selection outputs a tuple score that equals either 0 or 1, thus yielding a crisp relation.        □

Two other operators of SAME$^W$, that can be derived from those already introduced, are:

**Boolean difference** ($\overset{B}{-}$) The Boolean difference behaves "as expected", in that if a tuple $t$ belongs to both $e_1$ and $e_2$, with schemas $E_1(X)$ and $E_2(X)$, respectively, then it is not part of the result, regardless of its scores (in general, this is not the case for the Difference), that is:

$$e_1 \overset{B}{-} e_2 = \{t \mid t \in e_1 \wedge t \notin e_2 \wedge t.\mu = t.\mu_{E_1} > 0\} \ . \tag{10}$$

Boolean difference can be defined in terms of other operators as $e_1 \overset{B}{-} e_2 = e_1 - \pi_X(e_2)$, where $\pi_X(e_2)$, according to the semantics of Projection, simply discards the scores of the tuples in $e_2$.

**Intersection** ($\cap$) As in RA, the Intersection can be defined as a particular case of Join, where all the $n$ operands have the same schema $X$:

$$\cap^\Theta (e_1, \ldots, e_n) = \{t \mid (t \in e_1 \wedge \ldots \wedge t \in e_n) \wedge t.\mu = s_\wedge^\Theta(t.\mu_{E_1}, \ldots, t.\mu_{E_n}) > 0\}$$
$$= \bowtie^\Theta (e_1, \ldots, e_n) \ . \tag{11}$$

The two new operators introduced in SAME$^W$ are the *Top* and the *Cut*.

**Top** ($\tau$) The Top operator retrieves the first $k$ ($k$ is an input parameter) tuples of a relation $e$, according to a *ranking criterion*, as expressed by a ranking function $g$. If weights are used to rank tuples according to $g_{\Theta_g}$, then $g$ has to be a formula of predicates over the schema of $e$.[10] If $e$ has no more than $k$ tuples, then $\tau_{g_{\Theta_g}}^k (e) = e$, otherwise:

$$\tau_{g_{\Theta_g}}^k (e) = \{t \mid t \in e \wedge |\tau_{g_{\Theta_g}}^k (e)| = k \wedge \forall t \in \tau_{g_{\Theta_g}}^k (e) :$$
$$\nexists t' : t' \in e \wedge t' \notin \tau_{g_{\Theta_g}}^k (e) \wedge g_{\Theta_g}(t') > g_{\Theta_g}(t)\} \tag{12}$$

with ties arbitrarily broken. When $g$ is omitted, the *default* ranking criterion, based on the score of tuples, applies, thus the $k$ tuples with the highest scores are returned.

**Cut** ($\gamma$) The Cut operator "cuts off" those tuples which do not satisfy a formula $g$, that is:

$$\gamma_g(e) = \{t \mid t \in e \wedge s(g, t) > 0 \wedge t.\mu = t.\mu_E > 0\} \ . \tag{13}$$

Unlike Selection, Cut *does not change tuples' scores*. Thus, if $g$ includes non-Boolean predicates, the two operators would behave differently. However, the

---

[10] If "bottom" tuples are needed, the *ranking directive* $<$ can be used, written $g_{\Theta_g, <}$.

major reason to introduce Cut is the need of expressing *(threshold) conditions on tuples' scores*, e.g. $\mu > 0.6$. Such a predicate cannot be part of a Selection, since it does not commute with others. This is also to say that the expressions $\gamma_{\mu>0.6}(\sigma_f(E))$ and $\sigma_f(\gamma_{\mu>0.6}(E))$ are *not* equivalent. Indeed, the first expression is *contained* in the second one, that is:

$$\gamma_{\mu>\alpha}(\sigma_f(E)) \sqsubseteq \sigma_f(\gamma_{\mu>\alpha}(E)) \ . \tag{14}$$

*Proof.* ($\sqsubseteq$) Let $E_L$ and $E_R$ stand for the left and right hand side expression, respectively. Since the Cut does not modify tuples' scores, if a tuple $t$ satisfies both $E_L$ and $E_R$, then its score will be the same, i.e. $t.\mu_{E_L} = t.\mu_{E_R}$. If $t \in E_L[db]$, then $t.\mu_{E_L} = s_\wedge(s(f,t), t.\mu_E) > \alpha$ holds. From the monotonicity and boundary condition of t-norms it follows that $t.\mu_E > \alpha$ holds too, thus $t \in \gamma_{\mu>\alpha}(E)[db]$. This is enough to prove that $t \in E_R[db]$.

($\not\sqsupseteq$) Consider a tuple $t$ for which both $t.\mu_E > \alpha$ and $0 < s_\wedge(s(f,t), t.\mu_E) \leq \alpha$ hold. This implies that $t \in E_R[db]$ but $t \notin E_L[db]$. $\qquad\square$

## 5   Examples

Examples in this section, aiming to show the potentialities and flexibility of $\text{SAME}^W$, refer to a *biometric DB* using faces and fingerprints to recognize the identity of a person. Stored data include extracted features relevant for identification,[11] and modeled by the **FaceFV** and **FP_FV** attributes, respectively. Because of the huge size of biometric databases, a viable way to improve performance is, at face and fingerprint acquisition time, to *classify* them with respect to some predefined classes. As to fingerprints, as demonstrated in [14], a "continuous" classification approach, where a fingerprint is assigned with some degree to many (even all) classes, can perform better than an approach based on "exclusive" classification. As to faces, we consider that the **Chin** and the **Hair** are also preventively classified.

Our simplified biometric DB consists of the following relations, where the '*' denotes fuzzy attributes and relations that can have fuzzy instances, and primary keys are underlined. The **Freq** attribute is the relative frequency of a fingerprint class.[12] This can be computed by considering the *scalar cardinality* (also called the *sigma count* [13]) of the fuzzy set corresponding to the fingerprint class. A partial instance is shown in Fig. 1.

Persons(<u>PId</u>,Name)
Faces(<u>PId</u>,FaceFV,Chin*,Hair*)
FingerPrints(<u>FPId</u>,PId,FingerNo,FP_FV)
FPClasses(<u>Class</u>,Freq)
FPType*(<u>FPId,Class</u>)

---

[11] For fingerprints these can be "directional vectors", positions of "minutiae", etc. For faces, position of eyes, nose, etc., can be considered.

[12] Class names are among those adopted by NIST (U.S. National Institute of Standards and Technology).

**Persons**

| PId | Name |
|-----|------|
| P00001 | John |
| P00002 | Mary |
| P00003 | Bill |

**FPClasses**

| Class | Freq |
|-------|------|
| Arch | 3.7% |
| LeftLoop | 33.8% |
| RightLoop | 31.7% |

**Faces**

| PId | FaceFV | Chin | Hair |
|-----|--------|------|------|
| P00001 | FFV0001 | pointed:0.74 | black:0.87 |
| P00002 | FFV0002 | rounded:0.65 | brown:0.75 |
| P00003 | FFV0003 | pointed:0.93 | brown:0.84 |

**FingerPrints**

| FPId | PId | FingerNo | FP_FV |
|------|-----|----------|-------|
| FP0001 | P00001 | 1 | FPFV0001 |
| FP0002 | P00001 | 2 | FPFV0002 |
| FP0011 | P00002 | 1 | FPFV0011 |
| FP0015 | P00002 | 5 | FPFV0015 |
| FP0017 | P00002 | 7 | FPFV0017 |

**FPType**

| FPId | Class | $\mu$ |
|------|-------|-------|
| FP0001 | Arch | 0.65 |
| FP0001 | RightLoop | 0.25 |
| FP0003 | LeftLoop | 0.95 |
| FP0005 | Arch | 0.60 |
| FP0005 | LeftLoop | 0.20 |

**Fig. 1.** An instance of the biometric database

The first query aims to retrieve those persons who have black hair, and whose facial features match the ones (`inFace`) given in input:

$$\sigma_{(Hair=`black')\wedge(FaceFV\sim\text{inFace})}(Faces) \ .$$

The final score of a tuple $t$ is obtained by combining the scores of both Selection predicates and the initial score of the tuple (this is 1, since `Faces` is a crisp relation). For instance, if the $\mathcal{FA}$ semantics is used, it is $t.\mu = (s(p_1,t){\cdot}s(p_2,t)){\cdot}1$. Assuming the following similarity table:

$\sim$ inFace

| FaceFV | score |
|--------|-------|
| FFV0001 | 0.60 |
| FFV0002 | 0.84 |
| FFV0003 | 0.33 |

the result of the query is therefore $(0.87 \cdot 0.60 = 0.522)$:

| PId | FaceFV | Chin | Hair | $\mu$ |
|-----|--------|------|------|-------|
| P00001 | FFV0001 | pointed:0.74 | black:0.87 | 0.522 |

Trusting more hair classification than feature matching is achieved by giving the first predicate a weight $> 0.5$, say 0.7:

$$\sigma_{(Hair=`black')^{0.7}\wedge(FaceFV\sim\text{inFace})^{0.3}}(Faces) \ .$$

The score of the resulting tuple is now computed as (the score of the crisp relation is omitted since it equals 1 and does not influence the computation):

$$(0.7-0.3){\cdot}s(p_1,t)+2{\cdot}0.3{\cdot}s_\wedge(s(p_1,t),s(p_2,t))=0.4{\cdot}0.87+0.6{\cdot}(0.87{\cdot}0.60)=0.6612 \ .$$

On the other hand, if the $\mathcal{FS}$ semantics is used, the final score would be:

$$0.4 \cdot 0.87 + 0.6 \cdot \min(0.87, 0.60) = 0.708 \ .$$

If we want only the persons' id's and the scores of the 10 best matching tuples, we can use the Top and Projection operators:

$$\pi_{PId,\mu}(\tau^{10}(\sigma_{(Hair='black')^{0.7}\wedge(FaceFV\sim\texttt{inFace})^{0.3}}(Faces)))\ .$$

In order to see, for the only persons returned by above expression, call it $E$, how well the fingerprint of the left thumb (`FingerNo = 1`) matches a given fingerprint (`inFP`), we can write:

$$\sigma_{(FingerNo=1)\wedge(FP\_FV\sim\texttt{inFP})}(FingerPrints)\bowtie\pi_{PId}(E)$$

or, equivalently:

$$\sigma_{(FingerNo=1)\wedge(FP\_FV\sim\texttt{inFP})}(FingerPrints)\bowtie^{[1,0]}E$$

since both expressions discard the scores computed by $E$. Indeed, the Projection of $E$ on $PId$ returns a crisp relation, thus the final scores of the resulting tuples are, because of the boundary condition of t-norms, those of the component tuples returned by the Selection expression, call it $E'$. On the other hand, the weighted Join in the second expression returns a set of tuples whose scores are given by the following rule, where $E'$ still denotes the left operand of the Join:

$$(\theta_1-\theta_2)\cdot t.\mu_{E'}+2\cdot\theta_2\cdot s_\wedge(t.\mu_{E'},t.\mu_E) = (1-0)\cdot t.\mu_{E'}+2\cdot0\cdot s_\wedge(t.\mu_{E'},t.\mu_E) = t.\mu_{E'}\ .$$

For a more complex query, assume we want to perform a combined match on fingerprints and faces, giving as input an `inFP` and an `inFace`. We then join the result, weighting more (0.6) the match on faces, combine the tuples of a same person (since each person has more than one fingerprint in the DB), and discard all the tuples whose overall score is less than 0.5:

$$\gamma_{\mu\geq0.5}(\pi_{PId,\mu}(\sigma_{FaceFV\sim\texttt{inFace}}(Faces)\bowtie^{[0.6,0.4]}\sigma_{FP\_FV\sim\texttt{inFP}}(FingerPrints))).$$

Given the following similarity table:

$\sim$ `inFP`

| FP_FV | score |
|---|---|
| FPFV0001 | 0.72 |
| FPFV0002 | 0.48 |
| FPFV0011 | 0.84 |
| FPFV0015 | 0.38 |
| FPFV0017 | 0.55 |

consider the case of person P00001 ('John'), thus the join of the first tuple of `Faces` with the first two tuples of `FingerPrints`. The scores computed by the weighted Join (when the $\mathcal{FS}$ semantics is used) are, respectively:

$$(0.6-0.4)\cdot0.60+2\cdot0.4\cdot\min(0.60,0.72) = 0.2\cdot0.60+0.8\cdot0.60 = 0.60$$
$$(0.6-0.4)\cdot0.60+2\cdot0.4\cdot\min(0.60,0.48) = 0.2\cdot0.60+0.8\cdot0.48 = 0.504\ .$$

Then, the Projection combines the two tuples and returns (P00001,0.60), since $\max(0.60, 0.504) = 0.60$. Since $0.60 \geq 0.5$, the tuple is preserved by the Cut operator.

As a final example query, we want to know who are those persons with an 'Arch' fingerprint and with a pointed chin, giving these conditions weights 0.6 and 0.4, respectively. This can be expressed by means of a weighted Join, where a 0 weight is used for the Fingerprints relation on which no predicates are specified:

$$\bowtie^{[0.6, 0.4, 0]} (\sigma_{Class='Arch'}(FPType), \sigma_{Chin='pointed'}(Faces), FingerPrints) .$$

## 6    Reasoning in SAME$^W$

Equivalence and containment rules in SAME$^W$ can only partially rely on results from RA since, unless we consider the $\mathcal{FS}$ semantics, rules based on *idempotence* and/or *distributivity* of logical operators are no longer valid (e.g., $E \cup E \not\equiv E$ in $\mathcal{FA}$). Nonetheless, many opportunities for query rewriting are still left. For lack of space, here we present only a selected sample of such rules, focusing on Cut and Top operators and on the effect of weights. Complete proofs are given only for some of the results. In order to simplify the notation, when no direct manipulation of weights is involved, we understand the presence of weights, thus writing, say, $f$ in place of $f_{\Theta_f}$. In general, $E_L$ and $E_R$ will be used to denote the left hand side and the right hand side expression, respectively. As to proofs' style, in order to demonstrate that $E_L \equiv E_R$ ($E_L \sqsubseteq E_R$) holds, we usually split the proof in two parts:

1. We first show that, if $t \in E_L[db]$ and $t \in E_R[db]$ both hold for a generic tuple $t$, then $t.\mu_{E_L} = t.\mu_{E_R}$.
2. Then we prove that $E_L$ is "Boolean equivalent" to ("Boolean contained" in, respectively) $E_R$, written $E_L \equiv_b E_R$ ($E_L \sqsubseteq_b E_R$, resp.), that is that the sets of tuples computed by the two expressions are the same (the first is a subset of the second, resp.), *regardless of tuples' scores.*

We start with some basic rules that are also useful for proving more complex results. The following containment relationships hold for any expression $E$:

$$\gamma_f(E) \sqsubseteq E \tag{15}$$
$$\tau_g^k(E) \sqsubseteq E \tag{16}$$

whereas $\sigma_f(E) \not\sqsubseteq E$, since $\sigma$ modifies the tuples' grades.

As to monotonicity of unary operators, assume that $E' \sqsubseteq E$ holds. Then:

$$\gamma_f(E') \sqsubseteq \gamma_f(E) \tag{17}$$
$$\sigma_f(E') \sqsubseteq \sigma_f(E) . \tag{18}$$

On the other hand, the Top operator is not monotone, that is, $E' \sqsubseteq E$ does not imply $\tau_g^k(E') \sqsubseteq \tau_g^k(E)$, as it can be easily proved.

The weighted Join is monotone. For this, assume that $E_i' \sqsubseteq E_i$ holds $\forall i \in [1..n]$. Then:

$$\bowtie^{\Theta}(E_1', \ldots, E_n') \sqsubseteq \bowtie^{\Theta}(E_1, \ldots, E_n) . \tag{19}$$

Indeed, if a tuple $t$ belongs to $E_L[db]$, then it also belongs to $E_R[db]$. Since the joining sub-tuples leading to $t$ are necessarily the same in both cases, then also the score of $t$ will be the same.

**Moving Cut's Around.** Consider the "canonical" Cut condition, $\gamma_{\mu > \alpha}$, abbreviated $\gamma_\alpha$, applied to a weighted Join. Our first equivalence rule shows that a Cut $\gamma_{\alpha_i}$ can be applied to the $i$-th Join operand, where $\alpha_i$ depends on the values of weights. Assuming $\theta_1 \geq \theta_2 \geq \ldots \geq \theta_n$, we have:

$$\gamma_\alpha(\bowtie^{[\theta_1, \ldots, \theta_n]}(E_1, \ldots, E_n)) \equiv \gamma_\alpha(\bowtie^{[\theta_1, \ldots, \theta_n]}(\gamma_{\alpha_1}(E_1), \ldots, \gamma_{\alpha_n}(E_n))) \tag{20}$$

where:

$$\alpha_i = \frac{\alpha - \sum_{j=1}^{i-1} j \cdot (\theta_j - \theta_{j+1})}{1 - \sum_{j=1}^{i-1} j \cdot (\theta_j - \theta_{j+1})} \qquad i \in [1..n] . \tag{21}$$

For instance, when $n = 3$, $[\theta_1, \theta_2, \theta_3] = [0.5, 0.3, 0.2]$, and $\alpha = 0.6$, it is $\alpha_1 = 0.6$, $\alpha_2 = 0.5$, and $\alpha_3 = 1/3$. Note that $\alpha_1 = \alpha$ and that $\alpha_i = \alpha$ when all the weights are equal, i.e. $\gamma_\alpha(\bowtie(E_1, E_2, \ldots, E_n)) \equiv \gamma_\alpha(\bowtie(\gamma_\alpha(E_1), \gamma_\alpha(E_2), \ldots, \gamma_\alpha(E_n)))$.

*Proof.* First observe that, since $\gamma$ does not change the tuples' grades, $t.\mu_{E_L} = t.\mu_{E_R}$ holds for all tuples $t$ which belong to both $E_L[db]$ and $E_R[db]$.

($\sqsubseteq$) Let $t_i \in E_i[db]$, and let $x_i = t_i.\mu_{E_i}$. A tuple $t = \bowtie^{[\theta_1, \theta_2, \ldots, \theta_n]}(t_1, t_2, \ldots, t_n)$ belongs to $E_L[db]$ iff $t.\mu_{E_L} > \alpha$, where $t.\mu_{E_L}$ is computed according to (4), with the t-norm $s_\wedge$ which takes the place of $s_f$. In order to show that the $\alpha_i$ cut-off value computed by (21) is safe, first observe that, due to (2), $x_i \geq s_\wedge(x_1, \ldots, x_j)$ holds $\forall j \in [i..n]$, whereas, when $j < i$, we can exploit the inequality $1 \geq s_\wedge(x_1, \ldots, x_j)$. Then, we can majorize $t.\mu_{E_L}$ as follows:

$$(\theta_1 - \theta_2) \cdot 1 + \cdots + (i-1) \cdot (\theta_{i-1} - \theta_i) \cdot 1 + i \cdot (\theta_i - \theta_{i+1}) \cdot x_i + \cdots + n \cdot \theta_n \cdot x_i \geq t.\mu_{E_L} > \alpha .$$

Considering that $\sum_{i=1}^n \theta_i = 1$, above inequality can be rewritten as:

$$x_i > \frac{\alpha - \sum_{j=1}^{i-1} j \cdot (\theta_j - \theta_{j+1})}{\sum_{j=i}^{n-1} j \cdot (\theta_j - \theta_{j+1}) + n \cdot \theta_n} = \frac{\alpha - \sum_{j=1}^{i-1} j \cdot (\theta_j - \theta_{j+1})}{1 - \sum_{j=1}^{i-1} j \cdot (\theta_j - \theta_{j+1})} \stackrel{def}{=} \alpha_i .$$

It follows that if $t \in E_L[db]$, then the corresponding $t_i$ has a score $t_i.\mu_{E_i} > \alpha_i$, thus passing the $\gamma_{\alpha_i}$ filter.

($\sqsupseteq$) Trivial, since $\gamma_{\alpha_i}(E_i) \sqsubseteq E_i$, $\forall i \in [1..n]$. $\qquad \square$

A similar rule applies when the Cut has the form $\gamma_{\mu < \alpha}$ and follows a weigthed Union:

$$\gamma_{\mu < \alpha}(\cup^{[\theta_1, \ldots, \theta_n]}(E_1, \ldots, E_n)) \equiv \gamma_{\mu < \alpha}(\cup^{[\theta_1, \ldots, \theta_n]}(\gamma_{\mu < \alpha_1}(E_1), \ldots, \gamma_{\mu < \alpha_n}(E_n))) \tag{22}$$

where $\alpha_i = \alpha / (1 - \sum_{j=1}^{i-1} j \cdot (\theta_j - \theta_{j+1}))$, and $\alpha_i = \alpha$ if weights are not used.

*Proof.* (sketch) The proof almost follows the same steps used to demonstrate (20). The only difference is that, if a tuple $t$ belongs to both $E_L[db]$ and $E_R[db]$, then, in order to have that $t.\mu_{E_L} = t.\mu_{E_R}$, we have to prove that no occurrence of $t$ in the $E_i[db]$'s is filtered out by the inner Cut's appering in $E_R$.        □

A simple yet useful rule to manipulate Cut expressions is:

$$\gamma_{\alpha_1}(\sigma_f(\gamma_{\alpha_2}(\sigma_g(E)))) \sqsubseteq \gamma_{\alpha_1}(\sigma_{f \wedge g}(E)) \tag{23}$$

$$\gamma_{\alpha_1}(\sigma_f(\gamma_{\alpha_2}(\sigma_g(E)))) \equiv \gamma_{\alpha_1}(\sigma_{f \wedge g}(E)) \qquad \text{if } \alpha_1 \geq \alpha_2 \ . \tag{24}$$

*Proof.* (sketch) The validity of (23) directly follows from monotonicity of Cut and Selection ((17) and (18), respectively), after observing that $E_R$ can be rewritten as $\gamma_{\alpha_1}(\sigma_f(\sigma_g(E)))$ and that $\gamma_{\alpha_2}(\sigma_g(E)) \sqsubseteq \sigma_g(E)$ holds due to (15). To prove (24) we exploit the associativity of $s_\wedge$ and Cut's definition to show that if $t \in E_R[db]$ then $t$ also necessarily belongs to $\gamma_{\alpha_2}(\sigma_g(E))[db]$, from which the result easily follows.        □

Let us now consider the case where we apply to a *crisp* relation $E[db]$ a "cheap" predicate, $p_1$, and a "costly" one, $p_2$, after which we Cut the result. If predicates are weighted, and $\theta_1 \geq \theta_2$, we can apply a Cut just after evaluating $p_1$, which can lead to considerable cost saving. This also shows how weights on predicates can be transformed into weights on tuples' scores:

$$\gamma_\alpha(\sigma_{p_1^{\theta_1} \wedge p_2^{\theta_2}}(E)) \equiv \gamma_\alpha(\sigma_{p_2}^{[\theta_2, \theta_1]}(\gamma_\alpha(\sigma_{p_1}(E)))) \ . \tag{25}$$

*Proof.* (sketch) Since the Cut does not modify tuples' scores, if $t$ is in the result of both expressions then $t.\mu_{E_L} = t.\mu_{E_R} = s_\wedge^{[\theta_1, \theta_2]}(s(p_1, t), s(p_2, t)) > \alpha$.

($\sqsubseteq$) It is sufficient to show that if $t \in E_L[db]$, then its score is high enough to pass the inner Cut in $E_R$. This is proved by showing that above inequality implies $s(p_1, t) > \alpha$.

($\sqsupseteq$) It can be shown that $E_L$ can be rewritten as $\gamma_\alpha(\sigma_{p_2}^{[\theta_2, \theta_1]}(\sigma_{p_1}(E)))$, after which containment follows from (17), (18), and (15).        □

Note that above equivalence *does not* hold if $p_1$ is commuted with $p_2$, when $\theta_1 > \theta_2$ holds. In this case, indeed, a tuple $t$ can satisfy $\sigma_{p_1^{\theta_1} \wedge p_2^{\theta_2}}(E)$ but not $\sigma_{p_1}^{[\theta_1, \theta_2]}(\sigma_{p_2}(E))$. In particular, this is the case when $s(p_2, t) = 0$. The reason of this asymmetry directly stems from the asymmetry of Expression (4).

**Moving Top's around.** Turning to the Top operator, consider the case where the ranking criterion, $g_{\Theta_g}$ (or simply $g$) *does not* refer to tuples' scores. If no ties, according to $g$, occur in $E_i[db]$ ($i \in [1..n]$), then it is safe to apply a Top to each operand of a weighted Union, that is:

$$\tau_g^k(\cup^{[\theta_1,\dots,\theta_n]}(E_1,\dots,E_n)) \equiv \tau_g^k(\cup^{[\theta_1,\dots,\theta_n]}(\tau_g^k(E_1),\dots,\tau_g^k(E_n))) . \qquad (26)$$

*Proof.* First observe that if $E'$ and $E$ are two expressions such that $E' \sqsubseteq_b E$ (note that we do not require equality of scores), and $t$ belongs to $E'[db]$ (thus to $E[db]$) and to $\tau_g^k(E)[db]$, where $g$ is a ranking criterion which does not consider tuples' scores, then $t$ also belongs to $\tau_g^k(E')[db]$. Since Top does not change tuples' scores, the score of $t$ will be the same in the two top-relations iff so it is in $E'[db]$ and $E[db]$. Now, let $E = \cup^{[\theta_1,\dots,\theta_n]}(E_1,\dots,E_n)$ and let $E' = \cup^{[\theta_1,\dots,\theta_n]}(\tau_g^k(E_1),\dots,\tau_g^k(E_n))$.

($\sqsubseteq$) Consider a tuple $t \in E_L[db] = \tau_g^k(E)[db]$. Thus, $t$ is among the $k$ best tuples in $E[db]$ according to the ranking established by $g$. We have to prove that if $t \in E_i[db]$ then $t$ also belongs to $\tau_g^k(E_i)[db]$. Furthermore, we can limit to consider those sub-expressions for which $\theta_i > 0$ holds, the others being uninfluential at all. Since $E_i \sqsubseteq_b E$ (provided $\theta_i > 0$, as we are considering), from the above observation we have that $t \in \tau_g^k(E_i)[db]$. Therefore, whenever $t \in E_i[db]$ holds, then $t \in \tau_g^k(E_i)[db]$ holds too. This proves that $t.\mu_E = t.\mu_{E'}$. Since Top does not change grades, and $E' \sqsubseteq_b E$, we have that $t \in E_R[db] = \tau_g^k(E')[db]$ and that $t.\mu_{E_L} = t.\mu_{E_R}$.

($\sqsupseteq$) Straightforward. □

On the other hand, if the ranking criterion is based on tuples' scores, the above rule can be applied only if Union is unweighted and the $\mathcal{FS}$ (max) semantics is used:

$$\tau^k(\cup(E_1,\dots,E_n)) \equiv \tau^k(\cup(\tau^k(E_1),\dots,\tau^k(E_n))) . \qquad (27)$$

*Proof.* ($\sqsubseteq$) Assume that $t \in \tau^k(\cup(E_1,\dots,E_n))[db]$. Since $\mathcal{FS}$ semantics applies, this means that $t.\mu_{E_L} = \max(t.\mu_{E_1},\dots,t.\mu_{E_n})$ is among the $k$ highest scores considering all the tuples in $\cup(E_1,\dots,E_n)[db]$. Without loss of generality, assume that $t.\mu_{E_L} = t.\mu_{E_1}$, i.e. tuple $t$ achieves its best score in $E_1[db]$. We can prove that $t \in \tau^k(E_1)[db]$ as follows. Reasoning by absurd, assume that $t \notin \tau^k(E_1)[db]$, thus in $E_1[db]$ there are at least other $k$ tuples $t^h$ ($h \in [1..k]$) such that $t^h.\mu_{E_1} > t.\mu_{E_1}$ holds. From this we can conclude that $t^h.\mu_{E_L} \geq t^h.\mu_{E_1} > t.\mu_{E_1} = t.\mu_{E_L}$, thus $t$ would not belong to $E_L[db]$, which is a contradiction.

($\sqsupseteq$) Straightforward. □

As a negative result, we state that in no case operands of a (weighted) Join followed by a Top can be reduced by pushing down the Top (as done for Union). Let $g = p_1 \wedge p_2 \wedge \dots \wedge p_n$, with $p_i$ over the schema of $E_i$. If the $\mathcal{FS}$ semantics is used and no score ties occur with respect to the $p_i$'s and to $g$, it is:

$$\tau_g^k(\bowtie^{[\theta_1,\dots,\theta_n]}(\tau_{p_1}^k(E_1),\dots,\tau_{p_n}^k(E_n))) \sqsubseteq \tau_g^k(\bowtie^{[\theta_1,\dots,\theta_n]}(E_1,\dots,E_n)) . \qquad (28)$$

*Proof.* Omitted.  □

Considering the relationship between Top and Cut operators, in general we have the following containment result:

$$\gamma_f(\tau_g^k(E)) \sqsubseteq \tau_g^k(\gamma_f(E)) \ . \tag{29}$$

*Proof.* Assume that $t \in E_L[db]$. Then $t$ also belongs to $\tau_g^k(E)$ (due to (15)) and to $\gamma_f(E)$ (due to (16) and (17)). Since $\gamma_f(E) \sqsubseteq E$ also holds due to (15), we can conclude that $t \in \tau_g^k(\gamma_f(E))[db]$.  □

On the other hand, equivalence is obtained when $f = g$ or when both operators have their "canonical" form, that is $\tau^k(\gamma_\alpha(E)) \equiv \gamma_\alpha(\tau^k(E))$.

**Moving Selection.** Since the Selection operator changes tuples' scores, particular care has to be paid when reasoning about it. For instance, the following equivalence holds only for the $\mathcal{FS}$ semantics (and unweighted Union):

$$\sigma_f(\cup(E_1,\ldots,E_n)) \equiv \cup(\sigma_f(E_1),\ldots,\sigma_f(E_n)) \ . \tag{30}$$

*Proof.* We first show that if $t$ satisfies both $E_L$ and $E_R$, then $t.\mu_{E_L} = t.\mu_{E_R}$. As to $E_L$, it is:

$$t.\mu_{E_L} = s_\wedge(s(f,t), s_\vee(t.\mu_{E_1},\ldots,t.\mu_{E_n})) \tag{31}$$

whereas

$$t.\mu_{E_R} = s_\vee(s_\wedge(s(f,t), t.\mu_{E_1}),\ldots,s_\wedge(s(f,t), t.\mu_{E_n})) \ . \tag{32}$$

Equality of scores then follows from the distributivity of $s_\wedge$ over $s_\vee$, which indeed holds only under $\mathcal{FS}$ semantics. It remains to show that $E_L \equiv_b E_R$. This part is straightforward and we omit the detailed steps here.  □

Consider the case where $f = p_1 \wedge p_2 \wedge \ldots \wedge p_n$, with $p_i$ over the schema of $E_i$, and $\Theta_f = [\theta_1, \theta_2, \ldots, \theta_n]$. The following rule shows what happens if predicates are pushed down a Join, provided Join operands are crisp relations:

$$\bowtie^{\Theta_f}(\sigma_{p_1}(E_1),\ldots,\sigma_{p_n}(E_n)) \sqsubseteq \sigma_{f\Theta_f}(\bowtie(E_1,\ldots,E_n)) \ . \tag{33}$$

*Proof.* Let $t = \bowtie(t_1,\ldots,t_n)$ be a tuple which belongs to both $E_L[db]$ and $E_R[db]$, with $t_i \in E_i[db]$. Since all the $E_i$'s are crisp, it is

$$t.\mu_{E_L} = s_\wedge^{\Theta_f}(s(p_1,t_1),\ldots,s(p_n,t_n))$$

and

$$t.\mu_{E_R} = s(f_{\Theta_f}, t) = s_\wedge^{\Theta_f}(s(p_1,t),\ldots,s(p_n,t)) \ .$$

Since $s(p_i,t) = s(p_i,t_i)$ holds $\forall i \in [1..n]$, equality of scores is guaranteed. Finally, showing that $E_L \sqsubseteq_b E_R$ is trivial.  □

On the other hand, when no weights are used it is immediate to conclude, by exploiting the definition of Join and Selection and the associativity of t-norms, that:

$$\bowtie(\sigma_{p_1}(E_1),\ldots,\sigma_{p_n}(E_n)) \equiv \sigma_f(\bowtie(E_1,\ldots,E_n)) \ . \tag{34}$$

# 7  Other Issues

## 7.1  Approximation vs Equality

Although SAME$^W$ is a "similarity" algebra, it still preserves some aspects where similarity is not considered at all. This has the advantage of allowing for a clean definition of operators' semantics, yet in some cases a more flexible view would be desirable. In particular, we observe that equality of expressions' results requires equality of scores for corresponding tuples, a fact that in some scenarios can be exceedingly restrictive. In particular, consider the case when alternative similarity operators can be used for a same feature (e.g. $\sim_1$, $\sim_2$, etc.). As an example, the similarity of two color histograms can be assessed by using a complex quadratic-form distance which takes into account colors' cross-correlations [19], but even using the simpler Euclidean distance. In general, if $\sim_1$ is a "cheap" operator, what are the implications of using it in place of a (much) costly $\sim_2$ operator? In the following we provide some preliminary results on the problem of "approximate answers" in SAME$^W$ by relying only on rather generic assumptions, which therefore can be strenghtened on need. The starting point is the definition of $\epsilon$-*compatibility* of scores.

**Definition 7.1.** *A binary relation of $\epsilon$-compatibility over the elements of $\mathcal{S}$, $\simeq_\epsilon$, where $\epsilon \geq 0$, is a symmetric relation closed under interval containment, i.e. a relation which for all $x_1, x_2, x_3 \in \mathcal{S}$ satisfies $x_1 \simeq_\epsilon x_2 \iff x_2 \simeq_\epsilon x_1$ and $x_1 \leq x_2 \leq x_3, x_1 \simeq_\epsilon x_3 \Rightarrow x_1 \simeq_\epsilon x_2, x_2 \simeq_\epsilon x_3$.*

Intuitively, $\epsilon$ represents the "tolerance" we have on discrepancies of scores. For instance, specific cases of $\epsilon$-compatibility relations are:

$$|x_1 - x_2| \leq \epsilon \iff x_1 \simeq_\epsilon x_2 \quad \text{and} \quad x_2/(1+\epsilon) \leq x_1 \leq x_2(1+\epsilon) \iff x_1 \simeq_\epsilon x_2 \ .$$

The relationship between the different $\simeq_\epsilon$ relations arising from different values of $\epsilon$ is established by two basic axioms:

1. $x_1 \simeq_0 x_2 \iff x_1 = x_2$
2. $\epsilon_1 \leq \epsilon_2, x_1 \simeq_{\epsilon_1} x_2 \Rightarrow x_1 \simeq_{\epsilon_2} x_2$ .

Above extends to relations and expressions as follows (both $e_1$ and $e_2$ are over set of attributes $X$):

$$e_1 \simeq_\epsilon e_2 \iff \pi_X(e_1) = \pi_X(e_2) \wedge \forall t_1 \in e_1, \exists t_2 \in e_2 : t_1 = t_2 \wedge t_1.\mu \simeq_\epsilon t_2.\mu$$
$$E_1 \cong_\epsilon E_2 \iff \forall db : E_1[db] \simeq_\epsilon E_2[db] \ .$$

Turning to consider algebraic operators, a basic problem is to understand how they influence errors on scores. The following holds for the $\mathcal{FS}$ semantics:

**Lemma 7.1.** *Let $x_i \simeq_{\epsilon_i} x_i'$, $i \in [1..n]$. Then, $\min(x_1, \ldots, x_n) \simeq_\epsilon \min(x_1', \ldots, x_n')$ and $\max(x_1, \ldots, x_n) \simeq_\epsilon \max(x_1', \ldots, x_n')$ both hold, where $\epsilon = \max(\epsilon_1, \ldots, \epsilon_n)$.*

*Proof.* We prove the statement for the min scoring function, being the case for max analogous. Since $\epsilon_i \leq \epsilon$, it follows that $x_i \simeq_{\epsilon_i} x_i'$ implies $x_i \simeq_\epsilon x_i'$. Assume that $\min(x_1, \ldots, x_n) = x_i < x_j$ and that $\min(x_1', \ldots, x_n') = x_j' < x_i'$, otherwise the result would trivially hold by hypothesis. Without loss of generality, let $x_j' < x_i$. Since $x_j' \simeq_\epsilon x_j$, from $x_j' < x_i$ and $x_i < x_j$ we derive that both $x_j' \simeq_\epsilon x_i$ and $x_i \simeq_\epsilon x_j$ hold, thus proving the result. $\square$

We have the following result which shows that errors will stay limited to $\epsilon$ even for arbitrarily complex SPJU (Select, Project, Join, Union) queries.

**Theorem 7.1.** *Let $E$ be a $SAME^W$ expression with no weights, no negated predicates, and using operators in $\{\sigma, \pi, \bowtie, \cup\}$, and let $E'$ be an expression obtained from $E$ by changing a similarity operator from $\sim$ to $\sim'$ so that $(v_1 \sim v_2) \simeq_\epsilon (v_1 \sim' v_2)$ holds for any pair of values $v_1, v_2$ in the domain of $\sim$. Then $E \cong_\epsilon E'$ holds under $\mathcal{FS}$ semantics.*

*Proof.* (sketch) The complete proof considers each operator in $\{\sigma, \pi, \bowtie, \cup\}$. Here we limit the analysis to the Selection operator. Consider the two expressions $E = \sigma_p(E_1)$, where $p : A \sim v$, and $E'$ obtained from $E$ by replacing $\sim$ with $\sim'$. By definition of Selection under $\mathcal{FS}$ semantics, the scores of tuples satisfying $E$ and $E'$ are respectively given by $\min(s(A \sim v, t), t.\mu_{E_1})$ and $\min(s(A \sim' v, t), t.\mu_{E_1})$. By hypothesis, it is $s(A \sim v, t) \simeq_\epsilon s(A \sim' v, t)$. From Lemma 7.1 it follows that $\min(s(A \sim v, t), t.\mu_{E_1}) \simeq_\epsilon \min(s(A \sim' v, t), t.\mu_{E_1})$. This is to say that $\sigma_{A \sim v}(E_1) \cong_\epsilon \sigma_{A \sim' v}(E_1)$. $\square$

Extending the Theorem to the general case of *weighted* SPJU expressions is indeed possible (we omit the proof here). For this, however, we need the following additional assumption of *linearity* on the behavior of $\epsilon$-compatibility relations:

$$x_1 \simeq_\epsilon x_1', x_2 \simeq_\epsilon x_2' \;\Rightarrow\; \beta \cdot x_1 + (1 - \beta) \cdot x_2 \simeq_\epsilon \beta \cdot x_1' + (1 - \beta) \cdot x_2' \quad (\beta \in [0, 1]) \;.$$

Intuitively, linearity means that if discrepancies of scores stay limited at the extremes of an interval, then they are also limited in the whole interval, which seems quite reasonable to demand. Note that both sample $\epsilon$-compatibility relations we have considered are linear, as it can be easily proved.

The Theorem does not apply to expressions with negated predicates and/or Difference. For instance, consider the second sample $\epsilon$-compatibility relation $(x_1 \in [x_2/(1 + \epsilon), x_2(1 + \epsilon)])$, and take $x_1 = 0.8$, $x_2 = 0.9$, and $\epsilon = 0.2$. Clearly $0.8 \simeq_{0.2} 0.9$, but $(1 - 0.8) \not\simeq_{0.2} (1 - 0.9)$.

Finally, the reason why the Theorem does not extend to expressions using Cut and Top is that such operators explicitly consider tuples' scores for determining which tuples are to be part of the result. For the Cut, however, the relationship between different similarity operators can be exploited as follows.[13] Assume that $\sim'$ is *weaker* than $\sim$. This means that, for any pair of values $v_1, v_2$ in the domain

---

[13] This is tightly related to "filter-and-refine" strategies used to speed-up the processing of range queries over complex (multi-dimensional) domains, where one adopts a "simplified" distance function which lower bounds the original one [2].

of $\sim$, $(v_1 \sim' v_2) \geq (v_1 \sim v_2)$ holds. Then the following applies, where $\pi_X$ is just used to get rid of scores, $p : A \sim v$, and $p' : A \sim' v$:

$$\gamma_\alpha(\sigma_p(\pi_X(E))) \equiv \gamma_\alpha(\sigma_p(\pi_X(\gamma_\alpha(\sigma_{p'}(\pi_X(E)))))) \ . \tag{35}$$

If $\sim'$ is cheaper to evaluate than $\sim$, one can use the expression on the right to first filter out all those tuples that do not satisfy the condition $p'$ at least with score $> \alpha$. Since $\sim'$ is weaker than $\sim$, the result of this first filter is guaranteed to contain all the tuples returned by the expression on the left.

## 7.2   Adapting Weights to User Evaluation

As a final issue, we consider the case where the result of an expression $E$ is "evaluated" by the user, who assigns to each tuple $t_i \in e = E[db]$ a "goodness" value $g_i$. Basically, $g_i$ represents how much the user considers $t_i$ "relevant" for his information needs. The fact that the result of a query does not exactly match user expectation is common in MM systems, and leads to a "closed-loop" interactive process, where user evaluation is fed back to the query engine and then taken into account to compute a (possibly) "better" result, and so on.

For our purpose, *relevance feedback* algorithms that have been proposed in the Information Retrieval (IR) field are not appropriate for two reasons. First, they do not apply to complex algebraic expressions [11]. More precisely, such algorithms work only for keyword-based similarity search, when queries and documents are interpreted as vectors and weights as coordinate values. Second, they do not explicitly consider weights at predicate and expression levels. Recently, Ishikawa et al. [12] have proposed a method ("MindReader") to compute an optimal set of weights (according to a specific objective function), given user goodness values and assuming a "range query" whose shape indeed depends on weights. In our context, this amounts to "guess" the best similarity operator to be used for a certain feature, a problem somewhat orthogonal to the one we consider here.

The generic framework we propose to deal with user judgments is as follows. Let $E_{\{\Theta_j\}}$ be an expression using a set $\{\Theta_j\}$ of weightings, and let $e = E_{\{\Theta_j\}}[db]$. For each tuple $t_i \in e$, let $\mu_i = \mu_{E_{\{\Theta_j\}}}(t_i) = t_i.\mu_{E_{\{\Theta_j\}}}$, and let $g_i = G(t_i)$ be the "goodness" that the user assigns to $t_i$ ($G$ is called a *goodness function*). Then, consider an *objective function* $\mathcal{O}$, $\mathcal{O}(G, \mu_{E_{\{\Theta_j\}}}; e) \in \Re$, that measures the overall goodness of $e$. A set of weightings $\{\Theta_j^{opt}\}$ is called *optimal* with respect to $\mathcal{O}$ if:

$$\mathcal{O}(G, \mu_{E_{\{\Theta_j^{opt}\}}}; e) \geq \mathcal{O}(G, \mu_{E_{\{\Theta_j\}}}; e) \qquad \forall \{\Theta_j\} \ .$$

As an example, assume that $\mathcal{O}$ is a function which is maximum when $\mu_i = g_i$ $\forall i$ (thus the $g_i$'s are values in $\mathcal{S}$), say, $\mathcal{O}(G, \mu_{E_{\{\Theta_j\}}}; e) = -\sum_i (\mu_i - g_i)^2$, and consider the expression $\sigma_{f_1}(R_1) \cup^{[\theta_1, \theta_2]} \sigma_{f_2}(R_2)$, where we take the weighted Union of two (crisp) relations, to which the (unweighted) formulas $f_1$ and $f_2$ are applied. One can think of this as a weighted integration of results from different search engines, where $f_1$ and $f_2$ are tailored to the engine at hand, and $[\theta_1, \theta_2]$ are the initial weights we assign to the two engines, reflecting how much we "trust" them. The objective is therefore to minimize:

$$\sum_i \left( s_\lor^{[\theta_1, \theta_2]}(s_{i,1}, s_{i,2}) - g_i \right)^2$$

where $s_{i,1} = s(f_1, t_i)$ and $s_{i,2} = s(f_2, t_i)$. Since numerical methods exist to minimize above expression, we can consequently determine optimal values for $\theta_1$ and $\theta_2$, that is, the relative importance to be assigned to the two engines in order to make the overall scores as close as possible to their goodness values.

Although we have not explored yet all the (numerical) intricacies of adjusting weights to maximize $\mathcal{O}$, we claim that *it is indeed possible to compute* $\{\Theta_j^{opt}\}$ *for any* SAME$^W$ *expression.* Clearly, the real challenge here appears to be the determination of a good tradeoff between the "soundness" of the objective function and the corresponding cost of computing (at query time) an optimal set of weightings.

## 8   Related Work

In the last two decades, many works have focused on problems related to extending data models so as to allow representation of "imprecision" in databases. These works are only marginally relevant here, since they mostly concentrate on modeling aspects (see e.g. [18]) and typically ignore issues related to advanced processing of similarity queries, which are a major concern in multimedia environments. Indeed, it is a fact that similarity queries arise even if the database does not store imprecise information at all, provided "similarity operators" are defined. This is also the scenario considered by the VAGUE system [16], where, however, important features are missing, such as weights, the Top operator, and fuzzy attributes. Further, problems related to query optimization are not considered in [16]. Recent work by Adali et al. [1] addresses issues similar to ours, but important differences exist. First, they do not consider weights, that we have shown to introduce new interesting problems in the query optimization scenario. Second, they are mainly concentrated on problems related to the *integration* of heterogeneous "similarity measures", coming from different sources, into a common framework. This results in a quite complex "multi-level" algebraic scenario, on which reasoning becomes difficult and tricky. In this light, we believe that SAME$^W$ is much "cleaner", and that it highly simplifies the (inherently difficult) task of reasoning about similarity queries.

Finally, several works are related to ours from the point of view of query processing and execution. Besides Fagin's works, here we mention our previous work in the area and recent activity related to "Top queries". In [7] we have considered problems related to the efficient index-based execution of similarity queries, where all the predicates refer to a single feature (e.g. find objects which are similar to *this* shape, but not to *that* one). Results in [7] show how important performance improvements are obtainable by using access methods able to process the "query as a whole", rather than one predicate at a time.

Recent research on so-called Top queries [3] addresses issues arising in a DBMS when the cardinality of the result is limited by the user. In this case, it is assumed that the result set is sorted (using the ORDER BY SQL clause), and that the result stream is stopped after $k$ tuples have been produced. There is a tight connection here with our Top $(\tau)$ operator, with our "ranking criterion" playing the role of the ORDER BY clause. Optimization techniques considered in [3] to "push-down" the Top basically exploit primary key-foreign key joins (as well as analysis of residual predicates) – a thing which we could embed into $SAME^W$ by means of functional dependencies.

## 9    Conclusion

In this paper we have introduced a "similarity algebra with weights", called $SAME^W$, that generalizes relational algebra to allow the formulation of complex similarity queries over multimedia databases. $SAME^W$ combines within a single framework several aspects relevant to multimedia queries, such as new operators (Cut and Top) useful for "range" and "best-matches" queries, weights to express user preferences, and "scores" to rank tuples. These aspects, together with other issues which we have only partially addressed here, such as "approximate results" (see Sect. 7.1) and user evaluation (Sect. 7.2), pose new challenges to a query engine, which have not been considered yet in their full generality. For instance, if the user evaluates the result of a query, thus the system should adapt to this by adjusting weights, how does this affect execution costs? Indeed, as shown in Sect. 6, changing the weights will modify the numerical values, thus the processing costs, used by some operators (like the Cut) to limit the cardinality of the arguments of $n$-ary operators, such as Join and Union.

A point which would also deserve a much more careful investigation concerns the definition of "notions of approximation" which are both practical and useful. This is an issue whose importance is likely to considerably grow in the near future, and that have only partially been addressed in recent years [20,5].

## References

1. S. Adali, P. Bonatti, M.L. Sapino, and V.S. Subrahmanian. A Multi-Similarity Algebra. In *Proc. of the 1998 ACM-SIGMOD Int. Conf. on Management of Data*, pages 402–413, Seattle, WA, June 1998.
2. R. Agrawal, C. Faloutsos, and A. Swami. Efficient Similarity Search in Sequence Databases. In *Proc. of the 4th Int. Conf. on Foundations of Data Organizations and Algorithms (FODO'93)*, pages 69–84, Chicago, IL, October 1993.
3. M.J. Carey and D. Kossmann. On Saying "Enough Already!" in SQL. In *Proc. of the 1997 ACM SIGMOD Int. Conf. on Management of Data*, pages 219–230, Tucson, AZ, May 1997.

4. P. Ciaccia, D. Montesi, W. Penzo, and A. Trombetta. SAME$^W$: A Fuzzy Similarity Algebra for Web and Multimedia Databases. Technical Report T2-R26, InterData project, 1999. Available at URL ftp://ftp-db.deis.unibo.it/pub/interdata/tema2/T2-R26.ps.

5. P. Ciaccia and M. Patella. PAC Nearest Neighbor Queries: Approximate and Controlled Search in High-Dimensional and Metric Spaces. In *Proc. of the 16th Int. Conf. on Data Engineering (ICDE 2000)*, San Diego, CA, March 2000.

6. P. Ciaccia, M. Patella, and P. Zezula. M-tree: An Efficient Access Method for Similarity Search in Metric Spaces. In *Proc. of the 23rd VLDB Int. Conf.*, pages 426–435, Athens, Greece, August 1997.

7. P. Ciaccia, M. Patella, and P. Zezula. Processing Complex Similarity Queries with Distance-based Access Methods. In *Proc. of the 6th Int. Conf. on Extending Database Technology (EDBT'98)*, pages 9–23, Valencia, Spain, March 1998.

8. R. Fagin. Combining Fuzzy Information from Multiple Systems. In *Proc. of the 15th ACM Symposium on Principles of Database Systems (PODS'96)*, pages 216–226, Montreal, Canada, June 1996.

9. R. Fagin and E.L. Wimmers. Incorporating User Preferences in Multimedia Queries. In *Proc. of the 6th ICDT Int. Conf.*, pages 247–261, Delphi, Greece, January 1997.

10. M. Flickner, H. Sawhney, W. Niblack, J. Ashley, Q. Huang, B. Dom, M. Gorkani, J. Hafner, D. Lee, D. Petkovic, D. Steele, and P. Yanker. Query by Image and Video Content: The QBIC System. *IEEE Computer*, 28(9):23–32, September 1995.

11. D. Harman. Relevance Feedback and Other Query Modification Techniques. In W.B. Frakes and R. Baeza-Yates, editors, *Information Retrieval: Data Structures and Algorithms*, chapter 11, pages 241–263. Prentice Hall PTR, 1992.

12. Y. Ishikawa, R. Subramanya, and C. Faloutsos. MindReader: Querying Databases through Multiple Examples. In *Proc. of the 24th VLDB Int. Conf.*, pages 218–227, New York, NY, August 1998.

13. G.J. Klir and B. Yuan. *Fuzzy Sets and Fuzzy Logic*. Prentice Hall PTR, 1995.

14. A. Lumini, D. Maio, and D. Maltoni. Continuous versus Exclusive Classification for Fingerprint Retrieval. *Pattern Recognition Letters*, 18:1027–1034, 1997.

15. D. Montesi and A. Trombetta. Similarity Search through Fuzzy Relational Algebra. In *Proc. of the 1st Int. Workshop on Similarity Search (IWOSS'99)*, Florence, Italy, September 1999.

16. A. Motro. VAGUE: A User Interface to Relational Databases that Permits Vague Queries. *ACM Trans. on Office Information Systems*, 6(3):187–214, July 1988.

17. S. Nepal, M.V. Ramakrishna, and J.A. Thom. A Fuzzy Object Language (FOQL) for Image Databases. In *Proc. of the 6th Int. Conf. on Database Systems for Advanced Applications (DASFAA'99)*, pages 117–124, Hsinchu, Taiwan, April 1999.

18. K. Raju and A. Majumdar. Fuzzy Functional Dependencies and Lossless Join Decomposition of Fuzzy Relational Database Systems. *ACM Trans. on Database Systems*, 13(32):129–166, June 1988.

19. T. Seidl and H.-P. Kriegel. Efficient User-Adaptable Similarity Search in Large Multimedia Databases. In *Proc. of the 23rd VLDB Int. Conf.*, pages 506–515, Athens, Greece, August 1997.

20. N. Shivakumar, H. Garcia-Molina, and C.S. Chekuri. Filtering with Approximate Predicates. In *Proc. of the 24th VLDB Int. Conf.*, pages 263–274, New York, NY, August 1998.

21. A. Soffer and H. Samet. Integrating Symbolic Images into a Multimedia Database System using Classification and Abstraction Approaches. *The VLDB Journal*, 7(4):253–274, 1998.

# Maximal Expansions of Database Updates*

Michael Dekhtyar[1], Alexander Dikovsky[2,3], and Sergey Dudakov[4],
and Nicolas Spyratos[4]

[1] Department of Computer Science, Tver State University
3 Zheljabova str. Tver, Russia, 170013
[2] Université de Nantes, IRIN, UPREF, EA No 2157
2, rue de la Houssinière BP 92208
F 44322 Nantes Cedex 3 France
[3] Keldysh Institute for Applied Mathematics
4 Miusskaya sq. Moscow, Russia, 125047
[4] Université de Paris-Sud, LRI, U.R.A. 410 du CNRS, Bât. 490
F-91405 Orsay Cedex, France

Michael.Dekhtyar@tversu.ru, Alexandre.Dikovsky@irin.univ-nantes.fr,
Nicolas.Spyratos@lri.fr

**Abstract.** Databases with integrity constraints (IC) are considered. For each DB update, i.e. a set of facts to add and of facts to delete, the IC implies its *correct expansion*: new facts to add and new facts to delete. Simultaneously, each expanded update induces a *correct simplification* of the IC. In the limit this sequence of expansions and simplifications converges to the maximal correct update expansion independent from the initial DB state.
We show that such maximal expansion is computed in square time for partial databases, and that its computation is a co-$NP$-complete problem in classical databases. However, it is also square time computable in classical DBs under ICs with some restrictions on the use of negation.
Computing the real change of the initial DB state after accomplishing an update is a hard problem. The use of maximal update expansion in the place of initial update can substantially simplify computation of a new correct DB state.

## 1 Introduction

Conventional databases roll back after updates violating integrity constraints (IC). Meanwhile, some developed contemporary databases (for instance, Oracle), enable its administrators or application developers to present IC in the form of systems of rules (e.g., business rules), and use automatic means, such as triggers, which enforce these rules after updates. The intensive recent work on active databases (cf. [14]) shows that in the future this ability of intelligent update enforcement will be developed.

* This work was sponsored by the Russian Fundamental Studies Foundation (Grants 97-01-00973, 98-01-00204, 99-01-00374).

K.-D. Schewe, B. Thalheim (Eds.): FoIKS 2000, LNCS 1762, pp. 72–87, 2000.

The effect of extensional updates on data can be specified declaratively by expressions of algorithmic algebras generalizing SQL (cf. [1]), or by formulas of a logical language (see e.g. [4]). However, when IC are presented in the form of rule systems, the effect of an update manifests itself indirectly: either following to some intentional semantics of rules, or operationally, in the form of a derivation. Let us consider the following simplified example.

**Example 1** *The IC $\Phi$ below expresses a typical case of an exception from a general rule. It consists of two clauses. The first one expresses the general rule: "children (proposition* children*) can bathe (*bathe*) when with parents (*parents*)". The other one expresses an exception from this rule: "children cannot bathe while the ebb tide (proposition* ebb*)":*

$$\text{bathe} \leftarrow \text{children}, \text{parents}$$
$$\neg\text{bathe} \leftarrow \text{children}, \text{ebb}.$$

*Let us consider a DB state where children cannot bathe because of the ebb. This state is materialized differently in classical and partial databases. In classical databases the absence of a fact means that its negation holds. In a partial database $S$ a holds if $a \in S$, $\neg a$ holds if $\neg a \in S$ explicitly, otherwise a is unknown.*

*Let us consider first the classical databases. This means that we have the DB state $I = \{\text{children}, \text{ebb}\}$. Suppose that the parents arrive, which is expressed as the addition of the fact* parents *to $I$. This addition causes the conflict with the first rule. The possible solutions are simple but nontrivial. The first solution is to replace* ebb *by* bathe. *The result is the DB state where children's bathing is allowed: $I_1 = \{\text{children}, \text{parents}, \text{bathe}\}$. The other is just to eliminate* children. *The resulting DB state is that where no children's bathing is needed: $I_2 = \{\text{parents}, \text{ebb}\}$.*

*Now, let us consider the case of partial databases. The initial DB is in this case $I = \{\text{children}, \text{ebb}, \neg\text{bathe}\}$. The first solution is then to replace* ebb *and* $\neg$bathe *by* bathe, *the resulting DB state being: $I_1 = \{\text{children}, \text{parents}, \text{bathe}\}$. The other solution is again to eliminate* children, *the resulting DB state being this time: $I_2 = \{\text{parents}, \text{ebb}, \neg\text{bathe}\}$.*

In logical terms, the result of such an intensional update is defined as a model of a logical theory (*knowledge base (KB) update*), or as a set of consequences of an extensional DB state (*DB view update*), or else, its effect is defined through logical inference, e.g. abduction ( see e.g. [20,12,15,10]), sometimes enforced by bottom-up hypothesis generation for integrity checking (e.g. [5]). Sometimes updates are specified indirectly as a minimal (in a sense) change of the given state sufficient to attain an intended KB state (see e.g. [18,19]), sometimes they are specified by an update program, so the change is defined by both programs: KB and update ([2]). In the case where negative knowledge is treated, these approaches work exclusively with some sort of intended models: for instance, stable [11] or well founded [21].

In this paper we develop the conflict resolution approach to updates, proposed in [6,7,13]. It departs from the premise that IC have nothing to do with data or knowledge definition. They only specify the conflicts to avoid after the update. So the use of exclusively "intended" models of IC may lead to the loss of information or to unjustified conflict resolution failures. The above example shows such a loss [1]. So in our approach one should consider all classical models of IC, but among these models one should find a model minimally deviating from the model before update. A bit more formally, the problem we tackle is formulated as follows. Given a logic program $\Phi$ which formalizes the IC, a correct initial DB state $I \models \Phi$, and an external update $\Delta$ which specifies the facts $D^+$ to be added to $I$ and the facts $D^-$ to be deleted from it, one should find the minimal real change $\Psi(I)$ of $I$, sufficient to accomplish $\Delta$ and to restore $\Phi$ if and when it is violated (i.e. to guarantee that $D^+ \subseteq \Psi(I), \Psi(I) \cap D^- = \emptyset$, and $\Psi(I) \models \Phi$).

Unfortunately, the problem of minimal real change with respect to IC is still harder from the complexity point of view than the problem of intended knowledge update. The latter is of the type "guess and check" (which corresponds to $NP$), whereas, the former is proven in [8] to be $\Sigma_2^p$-complete for classical databases. In this paper we prove that its solution is co-$NP$-complete for partial databases.

In our earlier papers [6,7] we introduce a broad class of update operators $\Psi(\Phi, \Delta, I)$ (we call them *conservative*), which apply to generalized logic programs $\Phi$ with explicit negation (possible in the bodies as well as in the heads of clauses) and are based on a mixed minimal change criterion which is a combination of the maximal intersection, and of the minimal symmetric difference of states. We describe various nondeterministic and deterministic conservative update algorithms based on a conflict resolution techniques. In the recent paper [8] we propose a practical method of speeding up the conservative update algorithms. The method is based on the idea that the initial update $\Delta = (D^+, D^-)$ can be incrementally and correctly expanded to a broader update after being iteratively propagated into the IC $\Phi$. *Correctness* of an expansion means that it preserves the set $Acc(\Phi, \Delta)$ of DB states in which $\Delta$ is accomplished and which satisfy $\Phi$. $\Phi$ being fixed, each compatible update $\Delta$ implies correct expansions: $\Delta_1 = (M^+, M^-) \sqsupseteq \Delta$ and simultaneously correct IC simplifications $\Phi_1 \preceq \Phi$. Using $\Phi_1, \Delta_1$ in the place of $\Phi, \Delta$ can substantially simplify the choice of a new correct DB state after accomplishing update. Indeed, this new state separates $M^+$ from $M^-$, so the expansion narrows the choice space.

In this paper we obtain a result which gives a definitive theoretical foundation to our uproach, and has a clear practical sense. We describe the optimal update expansion and IC simplification as those which imply all others and preserve the models in $Acc(\Phi, \Delta)$. The optimal expansion is the maximal real

---

[1] It seems that the "intended model" methods fail to find the solutions it demonstrates. Indeed, since there are no rules with •• ••• •• in the head, there is no direct refutation or abduction proof of the added fact. $I, I_1, I_2$ are not stable models of $\Phi$. One could propose to add the clauses •• ••• •••  ←   and  •••  ←   to $\Phi$ and then to update the resulting program $\Phi'$ by the update program $\{\bullet \bullet \bullet \bullet \bullet \bullet \bullet \ \leftarrow\ \}$. In this case the states would become stable models of $\Phi'$, but again the inertia rules of [2,19] would prevent to infer $\neg ebb$. The answer set semantics of [3,16] does not help because there is no negation as failure in $\Phi$.

change independent from the initial DB state. We show that both, the optimal update expansion and the optimal IC simplification are incrementally computed from $\Phi$ and $\Delta$ in square time for partial databases. Unfortunately, their computation is a co-$NP$-complete problem in classical databases. Nevertheless, we find an important class of ICs where their computation is easily reduced to that in partial databases, so they are again computable in square time.

The paper is organized as follows. All preliminary notions and notation are given in the next section. The conservative update problem is formulated in Section 3, and its complexity is established in Section 4. Update expansion operators are defined in Section 5. The maximal update expansion is explored in Section 6 for partial DBs, and in Section 7 for classical DBs.

## 2    Preliminaries

We assume that the reader is familiar with the basic concepts and terminology of logic programming (see [17]).

**Language.** We fix a 1st order signature $\mathbf{S}$ with an infinite set of constants $\mathbf{C}$ and no other function symbols. A *domain* is a finite subset $\mathbf{D}$ of $\mathbf{C}$. For each domain $\mathbf{D}$ by $\mathbf{A(D)}$, $\mathbf{L(D)}$, $\mathbf{B(D)}$ and $\mathbf{LB(D)}$ we denote respectively the sets of all atoms, all literals, all ground atoms, and all ground literals in the signature $\mathbf{S}$ with constants in $\mathbf{D}$. A literal contrary to a literal $l$ is denoted by $\neg.l$. We set $\neg.M = \{\neg.l \mid l \in M\}$.

**Logic programs.** We consider generalized logic programs in $\mathbf{S}$ with explicit negation, i.e. finite sets of clauses of the form $r = (l \leftarrow l_1, ..., l_n)$ where $n \geq 0$ and $l, l_i \in \mathbf{L(D)}$, (note that negative literals are possible in the bodies and in the heads of the clauses). For a clause $r$    $head(r)$ denotes its *head*, and $body(r)$ its *body*. We will treat $body(r)$ as a set of literals. Integrity constraints (IC) are expressed by a logic program $\Phi$ of this kind. $\mathbf{IC(D)}$ denotes the set of all *ground* integrity constraints in the signature $\mathbf{S}$ with constants in $\mathbf{D}$. We consider the following *simplification order* on $\mathbf{IC(D)}$: $\Phi_1 \preceq \Phi_2$ if $\forall r \in \Phi_1 \; \exists r' \in \Phi_2 \; (head(r) = head(r') \; \& \; body(r) \subseteq body(r'))$. This relationship between $\Phi_1$ and $\Phi_2$ means that $\Phi_1$ consists of stronger versions of some clauses of $\Phi_2$.

**Correct DB states.** In this paper we consider both kinds of interpretations of ICs, total and partial, over *closed domains*. This means that a certain domain $\mathbf{D}$ is fixed for each problem. A *partial* interpretation (*DB state*) over $\mathbf{D}$ is a finite subset of $\mathbf{LB(D)}$. For such an interpretation $I \subseteq \mathbf{LB(D)}$ we set $I^+ = I \cap \mathbf{B(D)}$ and $I^- = I \cap \neg.\mathbf{B(D)}$. $I$ is *consistent* if it contains no contrary pair of literals $l, \neg.l$. Intuitively, in a consistent partial DB state $I$ the atoms in $I^+$ are regarded as true, the atoms in $\neg.I^-$ are regarded as false, and all others are regarded as unknown. A partial interpretation $I$ is *total* if $I^+ \cup \neg.I^- = \emptyset$ and

$I^+ \cup \neg.I^- = \mathbf{B(D)}$. So the total interpretations are consistent by definition. They are completely defined by their positive parts, therefore, we will identify total interpretations with subsets of $\mathbf{B(D)}$. $\mathbf{D}$ being fixed we consider ICs with constants in $\mathbf{D}$ and groundisations over $\mathbf{D}$. Given an IC $\Phi \in \mathbf{IC(D)}$ and a DB state $I$ over $\mathbf{D}$, a (ground) clause $r = (l \leftarrow l_1, ..., l_n)$ of $\Phi$ is *valid* in $I$ (denoted $I \models r$) if $I \models l$ whenever $I \models l_i$ for each $1 \leq i \leq n$. For a partial DB state $I$ and a ground literal $l$ $I \models l$ means $l \in I$. For a total DB state $I$ and a ground atom $a$ $I \models a$ means $a \in I$, and $I \models \neg.a$ means $a \notin I$. $I$ is *a correct DB state* or a *model* of $\Phi$ (denoted $I \models \Phi$) if it is consistent (which is always true for total DB states) and every clause in $\Phi$ is valid in $I$.

**Consequence closure.** Let $\Phi \in \mathbf{IC(D)}$. For a partial interpretation $I$ we set $cl_\Phi(I) = \{l | \exists r = (l \leftarrow l_1, ..., l_n) \in \Phi \ ( \bigwedge_{i=1}^{n} I \models l_i )\}$. A strong immediate consequence operator is the total operator

$$T_\Phi^\in(I) = \begin{cases} cl_\Phi(I) & : & cl_\Phi(I) \text{ is consistent} \\ \mathbf{LB(D)} & : & cl_\Phi(I) \text{ is inconsistent.} \end{cases}$$

Being continuous, $T_\Phi^\in$ has the least fixed point $lfp(T_\Phi^\in) = \bigcup_{i=0}^{\infty} (T_\Phi^\in(\emptyset))^i$. We denote this set by $M_\Phi^{min}$. It is clear that if $M_\Phi^{min}$ is consistent, then it is the least (partial) model of $\Phi$. For any partial DB state $I$ we set $M_\Phi^{min}(I) = M_{\Phi \cup I}^{min}$.

**Updates.** When partial interpretations over $\mathbf{D}$ are considered, an *update* is a pair $\Delta = (D^+, D^-)$ where $D^+, D^-$ are subsets of $\mathbf{LB(D)}$. In the case of total interpretations $D^+, D^-$ are subsets of $\mathbf{B(D)}$. In both cases $D^+ \cap D^- = \emptyset$. Intuitively, the literals of $D^+$ are to be added to DB state $I$, and those of $D^-$ are to be removed from $I$. For both kinds of interpretations $\mathbf{UP(D)}$ will denote the set of all updates in the signature $\mathbf{S}$ and with constants in $\mathbf{D}$. We say that $\Delta = (D^+, D^-)$ is *accomplished* in $I$ if $D^+ \subseteq I$ and $D^- \cap I = \emptyset$. A partial DB state $I$ *agrees* with (partial or total) $\Delta$ if $I \cap (D^- \cup \neg.D^+) = \emptyset$. The updates in $\mathbf{UP(D)}$ will be partially ordered by the componentwise inclusion relation: $\Delta_1 \sqsubseteq \Delta_2$ iff $D_1^+ \subseteq D_2^+$ and $D_1^- \subseteq D_2^-$.

**Update operators.** Let $\Gamma$ be an operator of the type $\Gamma : \mathbf{IC(D)} \times \mathbf{UP(D)} \to \mathbf{IC(D)} \times \mathbf{UP(D)}$, $\Gamma(\Phi, \Delta) = (\Phi', \Delta')$, and $\Delta' = (D'^+, D'^-)$. In the definitions to follow $\Phi'$, $\Delta'$, $D'^+$, and $D'^-$ are denoted respectively by $\Gamma(\Phi, \Delta)^{ic}$, $\Gamma(\Phi, \Delta)^{up}$, $\Gamma(\Phi, \Delta)^+$, and $\Gamma(\Phi, \Delta)^-$. We denote by $\Gamma^n$ the $n$-fold composition of $\Gamma$ and by $\Gamma^\omega$ the operator $\Gamma^\omega(\Phi, \Delta) = \lim_{n \to \infty} \Gamma^n(\Phi, \Delta)$.

In the sequel we will omit $\mathbf{D}$ when it causes no ambiguity. So when $\mathbf{D}$ is subsumed, in the place of $\mathbf{A(D)}, \mathbf{L(D)}, \mathbf{B(D)}, \mathbf{LB(D)}$ we will use the notation $\mathbf{A, L, B, LB}$.

## 3    Conservative Update Operators

In general an update may contradict a constraint. So a reasonable definition of an update operator should either contain a requirement of "compatibility" of an update and a constraint, or specify a part of the update "compatible" with the constraint. The requirement of compatibility is easy to formalize.

**Definition 1** *For $\Phi \in \mathbf{IC}$ and $\Delta \in \mathbf{UP}$ let us denote by $Acc(\Phi, \Delta)$ the set of all models $I \models \Phi$ where $\Delta$ is accomplished. An update $\Delta$ is* compatible *with an IC $\Phi$ if $Acc(\Phi, \Delta) \neq \emptyset$.*

Compatibility of $\Phi$ with $\Delta = (D^+, D^-)$ means that there is a model $I \in Acc(\Phi, \Delta)$. For partial interpretations this guarantees the existence of the *least model* $M_\Phi^{min}(D^+)$ which is in fact the set of all ground consequences of the facts in $D^+$ with respect to $\Phi$. We denote this model by $M_\Delta^\Phi$. $M_\Delta^\Phi$ is constructed in time linear with respect to the summary size of $\Phi$ and $\Delta$. This means that for partial interpretations compatibility of $\Phi$ and $\Delta$ is recognized in linear time. For total interpretations the consistency of $M_\Delta^\Phi$ does not guarantee compatibility of $\Phi$ and $\Delta$, as the following example shows.

**Example 2** *Let us consider IC $\Phi = \{r_1 : \neg c \leftarrow a, b;\ r_2 : \neg b \leftarrow \neg a, c\}$ and update $\Delta = (\{b, c\}, \emptyset)$. Then it is easy to see that $M_\Delta^\Phi = \{b, c\}$. But of course, there is no total DB state satisfying $\Phi$, where $\Delta$ is accomplished.*

As we show in [8], the compatibility problem for total interpretations is $NP$-complete.

Conservative update operators provide in a sense a minimal real change of the initial DB state after its update. In [6] we propose the following minimal change criterion intended to keep as much initial facts as possible, and then to add possibly fewer new facts.

**Definition 2** *Let $I, I_1$ be two DB states, and $\mathbf{K}$ be a class of DB states. We say that $I_1$ is* minimally deviating *from $I$ with respect to $\mathbf{K}$ if $\forall I_2 \in \mathbf{K}\ (\neg(I \cap I_1 \subsetneq I \cap I_2)\ \&\ ((I \cap I_1 = I \cap I_2) \rightarrow \neg(I_2 \setminus I \subsetneq I_1 \setminus I)))$.*

Conservative update operators [7] have the following definition (for interpretations of both kinds).

**Definition 3** *Let $\Delta$ be an update compatible with IC $\Phi$. An operator $\Psi$ on the set of DB states $\mathbf{UP}$ is a* conservative update operator *if for each DB state $I$ :*
- *$\Psi(I)$ is a model of $\Phi$,*
- *$\Delta$ is accomplished in $\Psi(I)$,*
- *$\Psi(I)$ is minimally deviating from $I$ with respect to $Acc(\Phi, \Delta)$.*

Clearly, the conservative update operators are nondeterministic. The "children-ebb-tide" example in the Introduction describes two different DB states minimally deviating from the initial one for the interpretations of both kinds. The problem of finding one of the conservative update operator values for given IC, update and initial DB state is called in [6] the *enforced update problem (EUP)*.

As it is shown in [7], these operators have the following model completeness property: for any two DB states $I_1, I_2$ satisfying IC $\Phi$ there exists an update $\Delta$ such that $I_2 = \Psi(I_1)$.

# 4   Complexity of Conservative Updates

In order to measure the complexity of conservative updates we consider two standard algorithmic problems: *Optimistic and Pessimistic Fall-Into-Problem* (**OFIP, PFIP**) (cf. [9]).

**OFIP:** Given some $\Delta \in$ **UP** compatible with $\Phi \in$ **IC**, an initial DB state $I$, and a literal $l \in$ **LB**, one should check whether there exists a DB state [2] $I_1$ such that:
(a)  $I_1 \in Acc(\Phi, \Delta)$,
(b)  $I_1$ is minimally deviating from $I$ with respect to $Acc(\Phi, \Delta)$, and
(c)  $I_1 \models l$.

**PFIP:** requires (c) be true *for all* DB states $I_1$ satisfying (a) and (b).

We consider the combined complexity of these problems with respect to the problem size evaluated as $N = |\mathbf{D}| + |I| + |\Delta| + |\Phi| + |l|$   (| | is the size of constant or literal sets and of programs in some standard encoding). We denote respectively by **OFIP** and **PFIP** the sets of all solutions $(I, \Delta, \Phi, l)$ of these problems. These problems are "co-problems" in total interpretations in the sense that $(I, \Delta, \Phi, l) \in$ **PFIP** iff $(I, \Delta, \Phi, \neg.l) \notin$ **OFIP**. In [8] we show that for total DBs **OFIP** is $\Sigma_2^p$-complete, so **PFIP** is $\Pi_2^p$-complete. For partial DBs these problems are simpler.

**Theorem 1** *(Case of partial DBs)*
*(1)* **OFIP** *and* **PFIP** *belong to P in the case where:*
   *a) $\Phi$ is normal (i.e. there are no negations in the heads of clauses),*
   *b) there are no deletions and negations in $\Delta$, i.e. $D^+ \subseteq \mathbf{B}$ and $D^- = \emptyset$, and*
   *c) there are no negations in $I$, i.e. $I \subseteq \mathbf{B}$.*
*(2) If any of conditions a), b), c) is violated, then* **OFIP** *is NP-complete and* **PFIP** *is co-NP-complete.*

The following standard algorithm $Dp\_search$ resolves $EUP$ in partial interpretations [3].

---

[2]  We remind that some finite domain $\mathbf{D}$ is fixed.
[3]  Since DB states and updates are finite, and the domain is closed, the space of DB states resulting from updates is finite as well. For each subset $X$ of this space we fix the topological order with respect to set inclusion on subsets of $X$, with the successor function $next_X$. We set $next_X(X) = \bot$ for some constant $\bot$.

**Algorithm** $Dp\_search(I, \Phi, \Delta)$

*Input:* a DB state $I$, and some compatible update $\Delta = (D^+, D^-)$ and $\Phi \in \mathbf{IC}$.
*Local variables:* $\tilde{I}, H^-, H_{del}$ : sets of literals; $b$ : boolean.
*Output:* $I_1$.

(1)  $\tilde{I} := (I \cup D^+) \setminus D^-$;
(2)  $H^- := \tilde{I} \setminus D^+$;
(3)  $H_{del} := \emptyset$;  $b := false$;
(4)  **WHILE** $\neg b$ **AND** $H_{del} \neq \perp$ **DO**
(5)      $I_1 := M_\Phi^{min}(\tilde{I} \setminus H_{del})$;
(6)      **IF** $I_1$ is inconsistent **OR** $I_1$ does not agree with $\Delta$
(7)      **THEN** $H_{del} := next_{H^-}(H_{del})$
(8)      **ELSE** $b := true$
(9)      **END_IF**
(10) **END_DO**;
(11) **Output** $I_1$.

**Theorem 2** *Algorithm Dp_search implements conservative update operators for partial interpretations in linear space and in time $O(2^d N)$, where $N = |\Phi| + |\Delta|$ and $d$ is the size (the number of literals) of $H^-$.*

In [8] we describe a similar algorithm $D\_search$ which implements a conservative update operators for total interpretations in linear space and in time $O(2^{d+a} N)$, where $a$ is the size of the choice space for facts to add.

This complexity analysis leaves no hope to optimize substantially the standard algorithms by some general theoretical method. However, there may exist some practical speed-up methods. Below we propose one such efficient method.

## 5   Update Expansion Operators

If we look at the *EUP* solutions, we see that $\Phi$, $\Delta$, and $I$ being fixed, each solution $I_1$ is represented as $I_1 = (I \cup M^+) \setminus M^-$, where $M^+ \supseteq D^+$, $M^- \supseteq D^-$, and $M^+ \cap M^- = \emptyset$. In [8] we have proposed an operator $\Gamma_{lim}$ which gives an approximation $(D_0^+, D_0^-)$ to $(M^+, M^-)$ in the case of total interpretations: $M^+ \supseteq D_0^+ \supseteq D^+$, $M^- \supseteq D_0^- \supseteq D^-$. The expansion $(D_0^+, D_0^-)$ of $(D^+, D^-)$ does not depend on $I$. It is computed from $\Phi$ and $\Delta$ incrementally in deterministic square time. Moreover, $\Gamma_{lim}$ equivalently simplifies the IC $\Phi$ itself with respect to the expanded update. So to find $(M^+, M^-)$ we use this simplified IC in the place of $\Phi$. Our new idea is to provide a more powerful operator $\Gamma_{max}$ which gives the maximal update expansion and IC simplification implied by $\Phi$ and $\Delta$. To arrive at its definition we modify the concepts of [8].

We start by the following factorization of the space $\mathbf{IC} \times \mathbf{UP}$.

**Definition 4** *The pairs* $(\Phi, \Delta), (\Phi', \Delta') \in \mathbf{IC} \times \mathbf{UP}$ *are* update-equivalent *(notation:* $(\Phi, \Delta) \equiv_u (\Phi', \Delta')$*) if* $Acc(\Phi, \Delta) = Acc(\Phi', \Delta')$*. We set* $Equ(\Phi, \Delta) = \{(\Phi', \Delta') \mid (\Phi', \Delta') \equiv_u (\Phi, \Delta)\}$*.*

The orders $\sqsubseteq$ on $\mathbf{UP}$ and $\preceq$ on $\mathbf{IC}$ induce the following natural partial order on $\mathbf{IC} \times \mathbf{UP}$ :

$$(\Phi_1, \Delta_1) \preceq (\Phi_2, \Delta_2) \text{ iff } \Delta_1 \sqsubseteq \Delta_2 \text{ and } \Phi_2 \preceq \Phi_1.$$

This order has evident computational sense: expansions of updates narrow the search space of standard algorithms *D_search* and *Dp_search*, and simplifications of IC at least simplify model checking.

The general definition of expansion operators is as follows.

**Definition 5** *An operator* $\Gamma : \mathbf{IC} \times \mathbf{UP} \to \mathbf{IC} \times \mathbf{UP}$ *is an* update expansion operator *if*
- $(\Phi, \Delta) \equiv_u \Gamma(\Phi, \Delta)$ *and*
- $(\Phi, \Delta) \preceq \Gamma(\Phi, \Delta)$

*for all compatible* $\Phi \in \mathbf{IC}$ *and* $\Delta \in \mathbf{UP}$*.*

Quite evidently, the set of update expansion operators is closed under composition.

We are interested in expansion operators which provide the best expansion independent of the initial DB state. As it concerns updates, such a best expansion always exists. Indeed, let us remark that $(\Phi, (D_1^+ \cup D_2^+, D_1^- \cup D_2^-)) \in Equ(\Phi, \Delta)$ for any $(\Phi_1, (D_1^+, D_1^-)), (\Phi_2, (D_2^+, D_2^-)) \in Equ(\Phi, \Delta)$. So the following proposition is true.

**Lemma 1** *(For interpretations of both kinds)*
*1)* $Equ(\Phi, \Delta)$ *contains pairs with the greatest update* $\Delta_{max}^\Phi = (D_{max}^+, D_{max}^-)$*, where* $D_{max}^+ = \bigcup\{D^+ \mid (\Phi', (D^+, D'^-)) \in Equ(\Phi, \Delta)\}$ *and* $D_{max}^- = \bigcup\{D^- \mid (\Phi', (D'^+, D^-)) \in Equ(\Phi, \Delta)\}$*.*
*2)* $D_{max}^+ \subseteq \bigcap \{I \mid I \in Acc(\Phi, \Delta)\}$*.*
*3)* $D_{max}^- \cap \bigcup \{I \mid I \in Acc(\Phi, \Delta)\} = \emptyset$*.*

As it concerns IC simplification, it is possible that two or more minimal equivalent programs are $\preceq$-incomparable.

**Example 3** *Let* $\Phi_1 = \{r_1 : a \leftarrow b; \ r_2 : b \leftarrow a; r_3 : c \leftarrow a\}$ $\Phi_2 = \{r_1, r_2\} \cup \{r_3' : c \leftarrow b\}$ *and* $\Delta = (\{d\}, \emptyset)$*. Then* $Equ(\Phi_1, \Delta)\}$ *includes two incomparable maximal pairs:* $((\{d\}, \emptyset), \Phi_1)$ *and* $((\{d\}, \emptyset), \Phi_2)$*.*

So we propose the following definition.

**Definition 6** *An expansion operator* $\Gamma$ *is* optimal *if for all compatible* $\Phi$ *and* $\Delta$
- $\Gamma(\Phi, \Delta)^{up} = \Delta_{max}^\Phi$ *and*
- $\Phi' \prec \Gamma(\Phi, \Delta)^{ic}$ *for no* $\Phi'$ *such that* $(\Phi', \Delta') \in Equ(\Phi, \Delta)$ *for some* $\Delta'$*.*

The update expansion operators in [8] propagate into $\Phi$ the initial update $\Delta = (D^+, D^-)$ and so define the set of literals $l$ which it requires ($\Delta \models l$), and those to which it contradicts ($\Delta \not\models l$). Table 1 below describes the primary relations

$\models$ and $\not\models$ between $\Delta$ and ground literals $a, \neg a \in D^+$ and $a, \neg a \in D^-$ in the case of partial interpretations. Table 2 describes these relations for total DB states and for ground atoms $a \in D^+$ and $a \in D^-$. These relations can be extended to conjunctions of ground literals $l_1, ..., l_k \in \mathbf{BL} : \Delta \models l_1, ..., l_k$ if $\forall j\ (\Delta \models l_j)$, and $\Delta \not\models l_1, ..., l_k$ if $\exists j\ (\Delta \not\models l_j)$. In particular, $\Delta \models \emptyset$, and $\Delta \not\models \emptyset$ is not true.

Table 1. Relations $\Delta \models l$ and $\Delta \not\models l$ for partial DB states.

| $\in$ | $D^+$ | $D^-$ |
|---|---|---|
| $a$ | $\Delta \models a,\ \Delta \not\models \neg a$ | $\Delta \not\models a$ |
| $\neg a$ | $\Delta \models \neg a,\ \Delta \not\models a$ | $\Delta \not\models \neg a$ |

Table 2. Relations $\Delta \models l$ and $\Delta \not\models l$ for total DB states.

| $\in$ | $D^+$ | $D^-$ |
|---|---|---|
| $a$ | $\Delta \models a,\ \Delta \not\models \neg a$ | $\Delta \models \neg a,\ \Delta \not\models a$ |

These definitions allow to carry over the validity of literals from updates to the DB states in which the updates are accomplished. Namely, an update $\Delta$ being accomplished in an DB state $I$,

(1) if $\Delta \models l_1, ..., l_k$ then $I \models l_1, ...l_k$ and if $\Delta \not\models l_1, ..., l_k$ then $\neg(I \models l_1, ...l_k)$,

(2) if $I \models l_1, ...l_k$ then it is not the case that $\Delta \not\models l_1, ..., l_k$.

Both relations $\models$ and $\not\models$ are monotone with respect to updates.

The simplification order on programs we use conforms with the following residue operator simplifying logic programs via updates.

**Definition 7** *The residue of $\Phi \in \mathbf{IC}$ with respect to $\Delta$ is defined as:*
$res(\Phi, \Delta) = \{l \leftarrow \alpha \mid \exists r \in \Phi\ (head(r) = l\ \&\ \neg(\Delta \models l)\ \&\ \neg(\Delta \not\models body(r))\ \&\ \alpha \subseteq body(r)\ \&\ body(r) \setminus \alpha = max\{\beta \subseteq body(r) \mid \Delta \models \beta\})\}$.

The effect of the residue operator is different in total and partial interpretations. However, in both cases it is correct with respect to $Acc(\Phi, \Delta)$, confluent with respect to updates, and computable in linear time.

The particular update expansion operators we propose in this paper generalize those in [8]. They also propagate the relations $\Delta \models l$ and $\Delta \not\models l$ into the clauses of $\Phi$ in opposite directions: from bodies to heads and back.

## The case of partial DBs

*Forward operator $F$ on $\Phi \in \mathbf{IC}$ and $\Delta = (D^+, D^-) \in \mathbf{UP}$ :*
$$F(\Phi, \Delta)^+ = D^+ \cup \{l \mid \exists r \in \Phi\ (l = head(r)\ \&\ \Delta \models body(r))\}$$
$$F(\Phi, \Delta)^- = D^- \cup \{\neg.l \mid l \in F(\Phi, \Delta)^+\}.$$

*Backward operator $B$ on $\Phi \in \mathbf{IC}$ and $\Delta = (D^+, D^-) \in \mathbf{UP}$ :*
$$B(\Phi, \Delta)^+ = D^+$$
$$B(\Phi, \Delta)^- = D^- \cup \{l \mid M_\Phi^{min}(D^+ \cup \{l\})\ does\ not\ agree\ with\ \Delta\}.$$

The case of total DBs

*Forward operator $F$ on $\Phi \in \mathbf{IC}$ and $\Delta = (D^+, D^-) \in \mathbf{UP}$ :*
$$F(\Phi, \Delta)^+ = D^+ \cup \{a \in \mathbf{B} \mid \exists r \in \Phi \; (a = head(r) \; \& \; \Delta \models body(r))\}$$
$$F(\Phi, \Delta)^- = D^- \cup \{a \in \mathbf{B} \mid \exists r \in \Phi \; (\neg a = head(r) \; \& \; \Delta \models body(r))\}.$$

*Backward operator $B$ on $\Phi \in \mathbf{IC}$ and $\Delta = (D^+, D^-) \in \mathbf{UP}$ :*
$$B(\Phi, \Delta)^+ = D^+ \cup \{a \in \mathbf{B} \mid M_\Phi^{min}(D^+ \cup \neg.D^- \cup \{\neg a\}) \text{ does not agree with } \Delta\}\,^4.$$
$$B(\Phi, \Delta)^- = D^- \cup \{a \in \mathbf{B} \mid M_\Phi^{min}(D^+ \cup \neg.D^- \cup \{a\}) \text{ does not agree with } \Delta\}.$$

It is clear that both operators $F$ and $B$ are monotone with respect to the order on $\mathbf{UP}$. They are also invariant with respect to the residue operator $res$ and do not change models in $Acc(\Phi, \Delta)$.

We now use these operators to define the forward and backward update expansions.

*Forward update expansion $\Gamma_f$ :*         *Backward update expansion $\Gamma_b$ :*

$$\gamma_f^0(\Phi, \Delta) = (\Phi, \Delta)$$
$$\gamma_f(\Phi, \Delta) = (res(\Phi, \Delta), F(res(\Phi, \Delta), \Delta))$$
$$\gamma_f^{n+1}(\Phi, \Delta) = \gamma_f(\gamma_f^n(\Phi, \Delta))$$
$$\Gamma_f(\Phi, \Delta) = \lim_{n \to \infty} \gamma_f^n(\Phi, \Delta).$$

$$\gamma_b^0(\Phi, \Delta) = (\Phi, \Delta)$$
$$\gamma_b(\Phi, \Delta) = (res(\Phi, \Delta), B(res(\Phi, \Delta), \Delta))$$
$$\gamma_b^{n+1}(\Phi, \Delta) = \gamma_b(\gamma_b^n(\Phi, \Delta))$$
$$\Gamma_b(\Phi, \Delta) = \lim_{n \to \infty} \gamma_b^n(\Phi, \Delta).$$

The operators $F, B$, and $res$ we have introduced, have good properties which guarantee the existence of limits for the directed sets of their iterations, and that the operators $\Gamma_f$ and $\Gamma_b$ are update expansion operators (see [8]). Meanwhile, their properties in partial and in total interpretations are very different.

# 6   Optimal Update Expansion in Partial Databases

The composition of operators $(\Gamma_f \circ \Gamma_b)$ is again an expansion operator. One can consider the powers of this composition of the form $(\Gamma_f \circ \Gamma_b)^n$, $n > 1$. It is surprising that in partial and in total DBs these operators have different properties. In [8] we show that for total DBs these powers can form a proper hierarchy. The expansion operator $\Gamma_{lim}$ mentioned in Section 5 is the limit of this power hierarchy: $\Gamma_{lim} = (\Gamma_f \circ \Gamma_b)^\omega$. In partial DBs the powers hierarchy degenerates.

**Theorem 3** *In the case of partial DBs $(\Gamma_f \circ \Gamma_b)^n = \Gamma_f \circ \Gamma_b$ for all $n \geq 1$.*

In order to reach the optimal expansion we introduce the following nondeterministic refinement operator on ICs.

---

[4] We remind that $M_\Phi^{min}$ is syntactic, i.e. is understood as in partial interpretations.

**Definition 8** *Let $\Phi \in \mathbf{IC}$ and $\Delta = (D^+, D^-) \in \mathbf{UP}$. The* refinement *of $\Phi$ by $\Delta$ is a maximal program $\Phi' = ref(\Phi, \Delta) \preceq \Phi$ in which every clause $r$ meets the conditions:*

*(a) if $head(r)$ agrees with $\Delta$, then $M_{\Phi'}^{min}(body(r))$ agrees with $\Delta$;*
*(b) $r \in \Phi'$ is independent of $\Phi' \setminus \{r\}$ (i.e. $head(r) \notin M_{\Phi' \setminus \{r\}}^{min}(body(r))$);*
*(c) $body(r) \setminus M_{\Phi'}^{min}(\alpha) \neq \emptyset$ for any $\alpha \subsetneq body(r)$.*

The refinement operator is correct, i.e. $Acc(ref(\Phi, \Delta), \Delta) = Acc(\Phi, \Delta)$, and is computable in square time. Together with the limit expansion operator it gives the needed optimal expansion.

**Theorem 4** *Let $\Gamma_{max}$ be the operator on $\mathbf{IC} \times \mathbf{UP}$ defined by the equalities:*

*(i) $\Gamma_{max}(\Phi, \Delta)^{up} = \Gamma_f \circ \Gamma_b(\Phi, \Delta)^{up}$,*
*(ii) $\Gamma_{max}(\Phi, \Delta)^{ic} = ref(\Gamma_f \circ \Gamma_b(\Phi, \Delta)^{ic}, \Gamma_f \circ \Gamma_b(\Phi, \Delta)^{up})$.*

*Then:*

*1) $\Gamma_{max}$ is an optimal update expansion operator.*
*2) $\Gamma_{max}$ is computable in square time.*

## 7    Optimal Update Expansion in Total Databases

Unfortunately, in the case of total DBs the update $\Delta_{max}^{\Phi}$ is rather complex.

**Theorem 5** *For total DBs the set $\{(\Phi, \Delta, a) \mid a \in (\Delta_{max}^{\Phi})^+\}$ is co-NP-complete.*

The composition of the limit operator $(\Gamma_f \circ \Gamma_b)^{\omega}$ and of the refinement operator $ref$ is computed in square time, but it does not give the optimal expansion in general. It can serve as a more or less good approximation to the optimal expansion operator. Nevertheless, there is an interesting subclass of total DBs for which the optimal expansion operator is computable in polynomial time. It is the class of DBs with ICs whose clauses have positive bodies: $\mathbf{IC^{pb}} = \{\Phi \in \mathbf{IC} \mid (\forall r \in \Phi)( body(r) \subseteq \mathbf{B})\}$. For this class there exists a close relationship between maximal elements of $Equ(\Phi, \Delta)$ in total interpretations and those in partial ones [5].

**Theorem 6** *Let a total update $\Delta = (D^+, D^-)$ be compatible with an IC $\Phi \in \mathbf{IC^{pb}}$. Then*

*(1) if $\Delta_{max}^p$ is the maximal update in $Equ^p(\Phi, \Delta)$, then $\Delta_{max}^t = (\neg.D_p^- \cap \mathbf{B}, D_p^- \cap \mathbf{B})$ is the maximal update in $Equ^t(\Phi, \Delta)$;*

*(2) if $\Delta_{max}^t$ is the maximal update in $Equ^t(\Phi, \Delta)$, then $\Delta_p = (D_t^+ \cup \{\neg a \mid \exists r \in \Phi \ (head(r) = \neg a \ \& \ body(r) \subseteq D_t^+)\}, \neg.D_t^+ \cup D_t^-)$ is the maximal update in $Equ^p(\Phi, \Delta)$.*

We should amend the definition of partial refinement because it does not give the t-simplest IC, as the following example shows.

---

[5]    In order to distinguish notation in partial and total interpretations we will use in this section upper indices $p$ and $t$ respectively. Considering updates $\Delta = (D^+, D^-)$ with $D^+ \cup D^- \subseteq \mathbf{B}$ in the context of partial DBs we will call them *total*.

**Example 4** *Let* $\Phi_1 = \{\neg a \leftarrow b, c; \; c \leftarrow a\}$ *and* $\Phi_2 = \{\neg a \leftarrow b; \; c \leftarrow a\}$. *Clearly,* $\Phi_2 \prec \Phi_1$. *For* $\Delta = (\emptyset, \emptyset)$ *the partial DB state* $\{b\}$ *belongs to* $Acc^p(\Phi_1, \Delta) \setminus Acc^p(\Phi_2, \Delta)$. *However,* $Acc^t(\Phi_1, \Delta) = Acc^t(\Phi_2, \Delta) = \{\emptyset, \{b\}, \{c\}, \{a, c\}, \{b, c\}\}$.

**Definition 9** *Let* $\Phi \in \mathbf{IC^{pb}}$ *and* $\Delta = (D^+, D^-) \in \mathbf{UP}$. *The t-refinement of* $\Phi$ *by* $\Delta$ *is a maximal program* $\Phi' = ref^t(\Phi, \Delta) \preceq \Phi$ *in which every clause* $r$ *meets the conditions (a)-(c) of definition 8 and also the conditions:*

*(d) if* $head(r)$ *is a negative literal, then* $M_{\Phi'}^{min}(body(r) \cup \neg.head(r))$ *agrees with* $\Delta$;

*(e) if* $head(r)$ *is a negative literal, then* $body(r) \setminus M_{\Phi'}^{min}(\alpha \cup \neg.head(r)) \neq \emptyset$ *for any* $\alpha \subsetneq body(r)$.

This nondeterministic operator is correct with respect to $Acc^t(\Phi, \Delta)$ for ICs in $\mathbf{IC^{pb}}$ and computable in square time. Being combined with partial limit expansion operator it gives the optimal expansion.

**Theorem 7** *Let* $\Gamma_{max}^t$ *be the operator on* $\mathbf{IC^{pb}} \times \mathbf{UP}$ *defined by the equalities:*

*(i)* $\Gamma_{max}^t(\Phi, \Delta)^+ = \neg.(\Gamma_f \circ \Gamma_b(\Phi, \Delta)^-) \cap \mathbf{B}$,

*(ii)* $\Gamma_{max}^t(\Phi, \Delta)^- = \Gamma_f \circ \Gamma_b(\Phi, \Delta)^- \cap \mathbf{B}$,

*(iii)* $\Gamma_{max}^t(\Phi, \Delta)^{ic} = ref^t(\Gamma_f \circ \Gamma_b(\Phi, \Delta)^{ic}, \Gamma_f \circ \Gamma_b(\Phi, \Delta)^{up})$.

*Then:*

*1)* $\Gamma_{max}^t$ *is an optimal update expansion operator for total DBs with ICs in* $\mathbf{IC^{pb}}$.

*2)* $\Gamma_{max}^t$ *is computable in square time.*

Restricting ourself to ICs in $\mathbf{IC^{pb}}$ we find a simple relation between the solutions of the *EUP* in partial and total DBs.

**Theorem 8** *Let a total update* $\Delta = (D^+, D^-)$ *be compatible with IC* $\Phi \in \mathbf{IC^{pb}}$ *and* $I \subseteq \mathbf{B}$ *be a DB state. Then:*

*(1) if a partial DB state* $I_1 \in Acc^p(\Phi, \Delta)$ *is minimally deviating from* $I$ *with respect to* $Acc^p(\Phi, \Delta)$, *then the total DB state* $I_1^+$ *belongs to* $Acc^t(\Phi, \Delta)$ *and is minimally deviating from* $I$ *with respect to* $Acc^t(\Phi, \Delta)$;

*(2) if a total DB state* $I_1 \in Acc^t(\Phi, \Delta)$ *is minimally deviating from* $I$ *with respect to* $Acc^t(\Phi, \Delta)$, *then the partial DB state* $I_1' = I_1 \cup \{\neg a \mid \exists r \in \Phi \; (head(r) = \neg a \; \& \; body(r) \subseteq I_1\}$ *belongs to* $Acc^p(\Phi, \Delta)$ *and is minimally deviating from* $I$ *with respect to* $Acc^p(\Phi, \Delta)$.

**Example 5** *Consider the following IC* $\Phi \in \mathbf{IC^{pb}}$:

$r_1 : salary(100) \leftarrow dept(cs), pos(programmer)$;

$r_2 : \neg pos(programmer) \leftarrow dept(cs), salary(30), edu(high)$;

$r_3 : \neg salary(30) \leftarrow salary(100)$;

$r_4 : \neg dept(cs) \leftarrow edu(low)$;

$r_5 : edu(high) \leftarrow pos(programmer)$.

*Clearly,* $I = \{salary(30), pos(programmer), edu(high)\}$ *is a partial as well as a total model of* $\Phi$. *Suppose we add a new fact to this DB state:* $D^+ = \{dept(cs)\}$.

*There are two ways to treat this update. We can consider it partial. Then the operator $\Gamma_{max}$ returns $\Phi_1$ :*

$r_1'$ : $salary(100) \leftarrow pos(programmer)$;
$r_2'$ : $\neg pos(programmer) \leftarrow salary(30), edu(high)$;
$r_3$ : $\neg salary(30) \leftarrow salary(100)$;
$r_5$ : $edu(high) \leftarrow pos(programmer)$.

*and $D_p^+ = \{dept(cs)\}$, $D_p^- = \{\neg dept(cs), edu(low)\}$. Applied to this expansion, Dp_search gives the DB state $I_1 = \{salary(100), pos(programmer), edu(high), dept(cs), \neg salary(30)\}$ minimally deviating from $I$ with respect to $Acc^p(\Phi, \Delta)$. By theorem 8 it is transformed into the total DB state: $I_1^+ = \{salary(100), pos(programmer), edu(high), dept(cs)\}$ minimally deviating from $I$ with respect to $Acc^t(\Phi, \Delta)$.*

*We can also consider this update total. Then the operator $\Gamma_{max}^t$ returns a slightly simpler IC $\Phi_1''$ :*

$r_1'$ : $salary(100) \leftarrow pos(programmer)$;
$r_2''$ : $\neg pos(programmer) \leftarrow salary(30)$;
$r_3$ : $\neg salary(30) \leftarrow salary(100)$;
$r_5$ : $edu(high) \leftarrow pos(programmer)$.

*and $D_t^+ = \{dept(cs)\}$, $D_t^- = \{edu(low)\}$. The resulting total DB state $I_t = \{dept(cs), edu(high), salary(100), pos(programmer)\}$ minimally deviating from $I$ is the same as above. $r_2''$ results from $r_2$ by point (e) of the definition of $ref^t$ because $edu(high) \in M^{min}(\neg.head(r_2')) = M^{min}(pos(programmer))$.*

## 8   Conclusion

The problem of computing the minimal real change restoring the correctness of an updated DB state, is proven to be hard. We subdivide this problem into two parts:

- first part is to maximally expand the update, taking into account all its consequences with respect to IC, and simultaneously to maximally simplify the IC itself with respect to this expansion;

- second part is to find the minimal real change of a given DB state.

The first part does not depend on the initial DB state, so it should be included in any DB update procedure. We show that in partial DBs this part is computable in square time. In classical DBs this problem is itself quite hard. So we propose its reasonable approximation computed in square time. Moreover, we show that for ICs with positive clause bodies the maximal expansion is computed in square time for classical DBs. As it concerns the second part, even standard complete choice procedures solving this part of the update problem can be substantially simplified, being applied to the expanded update and the simplified IC in the place of the initial ones (cf. the dynamic optimization method in [8]). Moreover, this techniques may lead to efficient interactive update algorithms, where the maximal expanded update is accomplished in current DB state, then conflicts are proposed to resolve, which leads to a new update, etc.

# 9  Acknowledgements

We are grateful to the anonymous referees for their helpful comments.

# References

1. Abiteboul, S.:Updates a new Frontier. In: *Proc. of the Second International Conference on the Theory of Databases, ICDT'88*. LNCS **326** (1988) 1-18.
2. Alferes, J.J.,Pereira, L.M.: Update-Programs Can Update Programs. In: J.Dix, L.M. Pereira, T.C. Przymusinski, editors: *Second International Workshop, N-MELP'96. Selected Papers*. LNCS **1216** (1997) 110-131.
3. Chitta Baral and Michael Gelfond: Logic programming and knowledge representation. *Journal of Logic Programming*, 12:1–80, 1994.
4. Bonner, A.J., Kifer, M.: An Overview of Transaction Logic. *Theoretical Computer Science*, **133**(2) (1994), 2-5-265.
5. Decker H.: An extension of SLD by abduction and integrity maintenance for view updating in deductive databases. In: *Proc. of the 1996 International Conference on Logic Programming*. MIT Press, (1996), 157-169.
6. Dekhtyar, M., Dikovsky, A., Spyratos, N.: On Conservative Enforced Updates. In: Dix, J., Furbach, U., Nerode, A., editors: *Proceedings of 4th International Conference, LPNMR'97*. Dagstuhl Castle, Germany, LNCS **1265** (1997) 244-257.
7. Dekhtyar, M., Dikovsky, A., Spyratos, N.: On Logically Justified Updates. In: J. Jaffar, editor: *Proc. of the 1998 Joint International Conference and Symposium on Logic Programming*. MIT Press, (1998), 250-264.
8. Dekhtyar, M., Dikovsky, A., Dudakov S., Spyratos, N.: Monotone expansion of updates in logical databases. To be published in the Proc. of LPNMR'99.
9. Eiter, T., Gottlob, G.: On the complexity of propositional knowledge base revision, updates, and counterfactuals. *Artificial Intelligence*. **57** (1992) 227-270.
10. Eshghi, K., Kowalski, R. A.: Abduction Compared with Negation by Failure. In: *Proc. of the 1989 International Conference on Logic Programming*. (1989)
11. Gelfond, M., Lfschitz, V.: The stable semantics for logic programs. In: R.Kovalsky and K.Bowen, editors, *Proc. of the 5th Intern. Symp. on Logic Programming*. Cambridge, MA, MIT Press (1988) 1070-1080.
12. Guessoum A., Lloyd J.W.: Updating knowledge bases. *New Generation Computing*. **8** (1990), 71-89.
13. Halfeld Ferrari Alves, M., Laurent, D., Spyratos, N., Stamate, D.: Update rules and revision programs. Rapport de Recherche Université de Paris-Sud, Centre d'Orsay, LRI **1010** (12 / 1995).
14. Hanson, E.N., Widom, J., An Overview of Production Rules in Database Systems. *The Knowledge Engineering Review*. **8** (1993), N. 2, 121-143.
15. Kakas A.C., Mancarella P.: Database updates through abduction. In: *Proc. 16th VLBD Conference*. (1990) 650-661.
16. Vladimir Lifschitz: Foundations of logic programming. In: Gerhard Brewka, editor, *Principles of Knowledge Representation*, pages 69–128. CSLI Publications, 1996.
17. Lloyd, J.W., Foundations of Logic Programming. Second, Extended Edition. Springer-Verlag. (1993)
18. Marek, V.W., Truszciński, M.: Revision programming, database updates and integrity constraints. In: *International Conference on Data Base theory, ICDT*. LNCS **893** (1995) 368-382.

19. Przymusinski, T.C., Turner, H.: Update by Means of Inference Rules. In: V.W.Marek, A.Nerode, M.Truszczyński, editors, *Logic Programming and Non-monotonic Reasoning.* Proc. of the Third Int. Conf. LPNMR'95, Lexington, KY, USA (1995) 166-174.

20. Tomasic A.: View update translation via deduction and annotation. In: *Proc. of the Second International Conference on the Theory of Databases, ICDT'88.* LNCS **326** (1988) 338-352.

21. Van Gelder, A., Ross, K.A., and Schlipf, J.S.: The Well-Founded Semantics for General Logic Programs. *Journal of the ACM.* **38** (1991) 620-650.

# Error-Correcting Keys in Relational Databases

János Demetrovics[1], Gyula O.H. Katona[2], and Dezső Miklós[2]⋆

[1] Comp. and Autom. Institute
Hungarian Academy of Science
Kende u. 13-17, H-1111, Hungary
dj@ilab.sztaki.hu
[2] Alfréd Rényi Institute of Mathematics
Hungarian Academy of Sciences
Budapest P.O.B. 127 H-1364 Hungary
ohkatona@math-inst.hu, dezso@math-inst.hu

**Abstract.** Suppose that the entries of a relational database are collected in an unreliable way, that is the actual database may differ from the true database in at most one data of each individual. An error-correcting key is such a set of attributes, that the knowledge of the actual data of an individual in this set of attributes uniquely determines the individual. It is showed that if the minimal keys are of size at most $k$, then the smallest sizes of the minimal error-correcting keys can be $ck^3$ and this is the best possible, all minimal error-correcting keys have size at most $3k^3$.

## 1 Introduction

A database can be considered as an $m \times n$ matrix $M$, where the rows are the data of one individual, the data of the same sort (*attributes*) are in the same column. Denote the set of attributes (equivalently, the set of columns of the matrix) by $\Omega$, its size is $|\Omega| = n$. It will be supposed that the data of two distinct individuals are different, that is, the rows of the matrix are different. We write $A \rightarrow b, A \subset \Omega, b \in \Omega$ if the matrix contains no two row identical in the columns belonging to $A$ and different in $b$, that is, if the data in $A$ uniquely determine the data in $b$. $A \rightarrow b$ is called a *functional dependency*. A subset $K$ of $\Omega$ is called a *key* if $K \rightarrow b$ holds for all $b \in \Omega$, that is, if the data in $K$ determine the individual (row) uniquely. In other words, there are no two distinct rows of the matrix which are equal in $K$. A key is a *minimal key* if its no proper subset is a key. Denote the family of all minimal keys by $\mathcal{K}$.

Suppose that the data are collected in a non-reliable way, for instance the data come through a noisy channel, or simply the input is handled with typos. One might have complicated probabilistic assumption on the occurance of the errors, but these assumptions are difficult to use. We simply suppose that the probability of an error is so small, that at most $e$ of the data of each individual can be incorrect.

---

⋆ The work of the second and third authors was supported by the Hungarian National Foundation for Scientific Research grant numbers T029255

K.-D. Schewe, B. Thalheim (Eds.): FoIKS 2000, LNCS 1762, pp. 88–93, 2000.

Consider the situation of data mining. Then a large set of data is given and rules, connections (dependencies) are sought among the data. The most important case is when we are looking for functional dependencies. They are useful only when $|A|$ is small, on the other hand, finding functional dependencies with large $|A|$ has computational obstacles, too. The errors make the recognition of functional dependencies harder. The aim of the paper is to give some insight into these difficulties.

We consider here only the special case when keys are sought in the database. If $K$ is a key, it may seem not to be a key since certain row equal in $K$ might differ at an erroneous entry. If all these attributes are added to $K$ then these two row do not serve as a counter-example, but there might exist other pairs of rows with this property. Can we find a $K \subset K'$ which behaves as a key for the database with errors? How large they can be? Suppose that the "real keys" have size at most $k$. How large these new "keys" $K'$ can be? Our main theorem will answer this question.

First we will formalize the questions asked above. Let $M$ denote the matrix of the real data and $M^*$ ($m \times n$, again) the collected ones. We know that $M$ and $M^*$ differ in at most $e$ entries in each row. Although it is here also supposed that the real data of two distinct individuals are different, that is the rows of $M$ are different, this cannot be stated about $M^*$. Moreover a key $K$ cannot determine the row if the entries of the unreliable matrix $M^*$ are given in the columns belonging to $K$. In the present paper we will investigate such sets of attributes (columns) which uniquely determine the individual from $M^*$. We say that $C$ is an *e-error-correcting key* if it has this property, that is, knowing the entries of $M^*$ in the columns belonging to $C$, the individual (and its row in $M$) can be uniquely determined.

The number of different entries in two rows is called the *Hamming distance* of these two rows. The $m \times |C|$ submatrix of $M$ determined by the set $C$ of its columns is denoted by $M(C)$. If the Hamming distance of any two rows of $M(C)$ is at least $2e + 1$ then the Hamming distance of any two rows of $M^*(C)$ is at least 1, that is, knowing the entries of the unreliable matrix in $C$ it determines the row uniquely, $C$ is an $e$-error correcting key. The converse is true, too: if the Hamming distance of two rows of $M(C)$ is at most $2e$ then it may happen that the rows are equal in $M^*(C)$, that is, $C$ is not an $e$-error-correcting key. We obtained the following proposition.

**Proposition 1.1.** $C \subset \Omega$ *is an e-error-correcting key iff the pairwise Hamming distance of the rows of $M(C)$ is at least $2e + 1$.*    $\square$

## 2    Error Correcting Keys

It is easy to see that if the pairwise Hamming distance of the rows of $M(C)$ is at least $2e$ then the knowledge of $M^*(C)$ detects the error, but does not determine the row uniqely. This case is less interesting, but it makes worth introducing the more general definition: $C \subset \Omega$ is called a *d-distance key* iff the pairwise Hamming distance of the rows of $M(C)$ is at least $d$.

The main aim of the present investigations is to find connections between the family of keys and the family of $d$-distance keys. The next proposition is the first step along this line.

**Proposition 2.1.** $C \subset \Omega$ is a $d$-distance key iff for any choice $a_1, \ldots, a_{d-1} \in C$ one can find a $K \in \mathcal{K}$ such that $K \subset C - \{a_1, \ldots, a_{d-1}\}$.

*Proof.* The necessity will be proved in an indirect way. Suppose that there exist $a_1, \ldots, a_{d-1} \in \Omega$ such that $C - \{a_1, \ldots, a_{d-1}\}$ contains no member of $\mathcal{K}$, that is, $C - \{a_1, \ldots, a_{d-1}\}$ is not a key. Therefore there are two distinct rows of $M$ which are equal in $M(C - \{a_1, \ldots, a_{d-1}\})$. The Hamming distance of these two rows in $M(C)$ is less than $d$. This contradiction completes this part of the proof.

To prove the sufficiency suppose, again in an indirect way, that $M(C)$ contains two distinct rows with Hamming distance $< d$. Delete those columns where these columns are different. We found a set $C - \{a_1, \ldots, a_{d-1}\}$ satisfying the condition that $M(C - \{a_1, \ldots, a_{d-1}\})$ contains two distinct rows which are equal everywhere, therefore $C - \{a_1, \ldots, a_{d-1}\}$ is not a key in $M$, it cannot contain a member of $\mathcal{K}$. $\qquad\square$

It is easy to see that the family $\mathcal{K}$ of minimal keys is non-empty and *inclusion-free*, that is, $K_1, K_2 \in \mathcal{K}, K_1 \neq K_2$ implies $K_1 \not\subset K_2$. On the other hand, it is known ([1], [2]) that there is a database for any non-empty inclusion-free family $\mathcal{K}$ in which this is the family of all minimal keys. This is why it is sufficient to give a non-empty inclusion-free family rather than constructing the complete database or matrix. Note that, by Proposition 1.2, $\mathcal{K}$ and $d$ determine $\mathcal{C}_d$ — where $\mathcal{C}_d$ denotes the family of all minimal $d$-distance keys —, therefore the notation $\mathcal{C}_d(\mathcal{K})$ will be used, if it is necessary to emphasize that $\mathcal{C}_d$ is generated by $\mathcal{K}$.

Our first observation is that it may happen that there is no $d$-distance key at all. Fix an element $a \in \Omega$ (that is, a column) and an integer $2 \leq k$. Define $\mathcal{K}$ as the family of all $k$-element sets $(\subset \Omega)$ containing $a$. Then $C - \{a\}$ cannot contain any key, so the condition of Proposition 2 does not hold for any $C$ if $2 \leq d$: there is no $d$-distance key in this database for $2 \leq d$.

On the other hand, if $\mathcal{K}$ consists of all $k$-element subsets of $\Omega$ then all sets $C$ with at least $k + d - 1$ elements are $d$-distance keys. In the case when there are $d$-distance keys, it is enough to consider the minimal ones. Our last example suggests that the sizes of the members of $\mathcal{C}_d$ do not exceed the sizes of the members of $\mathcal{K}$ by too much. We will show that this is not really true.

Now we introduce some notations. Let $\binom{\Omega}{\leq k}$ denote the family of all subsets of $\Omega$ with size not exceeding $k$. Furthermore

$$f_1(\mathcal{K}, d) = \min\{|C| : C \in \mathcal{C}_d(\mathcal{K})\},$$

$$f_2(\mathcal{K}, d) = \max\{|C| : C \in \mathcal{C}_d(\mathcal{K})\},$$

$$f_i(n, k, d) = \max_{\mathcal{K} \subset \binom{\Omega}{\leq k}} f_i(\mathcal{K}, d).$$

We will prove the following theorem in Section 2.

**Theorem 2.1.**

$$c_1 k^d \leq f_1(n, k, d) \leq f_2(n, k, d) \leq c_2 k^d$$

*holds for $n_0(k, d) \leq n$ where $c_1$ and $c_2$ depend only on d.*

Section 3 contains suggestions how to continue this research.

## 3   The Proof

Let $\mathcal{K}$ be a family of subsets of $\Omega$. We say that the elements $a_1, \ldots a_{d-1} \in \Omega$ *represent* $\mathcal{K}$ if each $K \in \mathcal{K}$ contains one of the $a$s. Proposition 1.2 can be said in the form that $C \subset \Omega$ is a $d$-distance key iff no $d-1$ elements can represent the family $\{K : K \in \mathcal{K}, K \subset C\}$. If $C$ is minimal with respect to this property then no proper subset of $C$ has the above property, that is, for all $a \in C$ the family $\{K : K \in \mathcal{K}, K \subset C - \{a\}\}$ can be represented by $d-1$ elements. This gives a new variant of Proposition 1.2:

**Proposition 3.1.** $C \in \mathcal{C}_d$ *iff* $\{K : K \in \mathcal{K}, K \subset C\}$ *cannot be represented by $d-1$ elements, but it can be represented by $d$ elements $a, a_1, \ldots, a_{d-1}$ where $a$ can be given arbitrarily in $C$, in advance.*

$\square$

**Lower estimate.** We give a non-empty, inclusion-free family $\mathcal{K}$ consisting of $k$-element sets which generates a $\mathcal{C}_d$ consisting of one member having size at least $ck^d$.

Fix an integer $1 \leq i$ and take a subset $A \subset \Omega$ of size $i + d - 1$. Let $A_1, A_2, \ldots$ be all the $\binom{i+d-1}{i}$ $i$-element subsets of $A$ and

$$\mathcal{K}(i) = \{A_1 \cup B_1, A_2 \cup B_2, \ldots\},$$

where $A, B_1, B_2, \ldots$ are pairwise disjoint and $|B_1| = |B_2| = \cdots = k - i$. This can be carried out if

$$i + d - 1 + \binom{i+d-1}{i}(k-i) \leq n. \tag{2.1}$$

Show that the only member of $\mathcal{C}_d(\mathcal{K}(i))$ is $C = A \cup \cup_i B_i$. It is easy to see that $\mathcal{K}(i)$ cannot be represented by $d-1$ elements. On the other hand, if $a \in B_j$ for some $j$ then the $d$-element $\{a\} \cup (A - A_j)$ represents $\mathcal{K}$. If, however, $a \in A$ then any $d$-element $D \subset A$ containing $a$ represents $\mathcal{K}$, therefore $C$ is really a member of $\mathcal{C}_d(\mathcal{K}(i))$. It is easy to see that there is no other member.

Choose $i = \lfloor k(1 - \frac{1}{d}) \rfloor$. Then the size of $C$, given by the left hand side of (2.1) asymptotically becomes

$$\frac{(d-1)^{d-1}}{d^d(d-1)!} k^d.$$

$\square$

**Upper estimate.** Let $C \in \mathcal{C}_d(\mathcal{K})$ where $\mathcal{K} \subset \binom{\Omega}{\leq k}$. We will prove that $|C| \leq dk^d$. Since we have to consider only the subsets of $C$, so it can be supposed that all members of $\mathcal{K}$ are subsets of $C$.

Proposition 2.1 defines $d$-element subsets $D$ of $C$ each of them is representing $\mathcal{K}$. Moreover, still by Proposition 2.1, their union is $C$. Denote this family by $\mathcal{D}$. We know

$$\cup_{K \in \mathcal{K}} = \cup_{D \in \mathcal{D}} = C, \tag{2.2}$$

$$D \cap K \neq \emptyset \text{ for all } D \in \mathcal{D}, K \in \mathcal{K} \tag{2.3}$$

and $\mathcal{K}$ cannot be represented by a set with less than $d$ element.

Let $I \subset C$. Define the $I$-degree of $\mathcal{D}$ as the number of members of $\mathcal{D}$ containing $I$, that is,

$$\deg_I(\mathcal{D}) = |\{D \in \mathcal{D} : I \subset D\}|.$$

**Lemma 3.1.**

$$\deg_I(\mathcal{D}) \leq k^{d-|I|}.$$

**Proof.** We use induction on $j = d - |I|$. Suppose that $j = d - |I| = 1$, that is, $|I| = d - 1$. If all members of $\mathcal{K}$ meet $I$ then $\mathcal{K}$ can be represented by $d - 1$ elements, a contradiction. Therefore there is a $K \in \mathcal{K}$ which is disjoint to $I$. By (2.3) all the sets $D$ satisfying $I \subset D$ must intersect this $K$, therefore their number is $\leq |K| \leq k$. This case is settled.

Now suppose that the statement is true for $j = d - |I| \geq 1$ and prove it for $j+1 = d-|I|$. Let $|I^*| = d-j-1$. There must exist a $K \in \mathcal{K}, K \cap I^* = \emptyset$ otherwise $\mathcal{K}$ is represented by less than $d$ elements, a contradiction. Let $K = \{x_1, \ldots, x_l\}$ where $l \leq k$. By (2.3) we have

$$\{D \in \mathcal{D} : I^* \subset D\} = \cup_{i=1}^l \{D \in \mathcal{D} : (I^* \cup \{x_i\}) \subset D\}. \tag{2.4}$$

The sizes of the sets on the right hand side are $\deg_{I^* \cup \{x_i\}}(\mathcal{D})$ which are at most $k^{d-j}$ by the induction hypothesis. Using (2.4)

$$\deg_{I^*}(\mathcal{D}) \leq lk^{d-j} \leq k^{d-j+1}$$

is obtained, proving the lemma.                                                   □

Finally, consider any $K = \{y_1, \ldots, y_r\} \in \mathcal{K}$ where $r \leq k$. By (2.3), the families $\{D \in \mathcal{D} : y_i \in D\}$ cover $\mathcal{D}$. Apply the lemma for $I = \{y_i\}$:

$$\{D \in \mathcal{D} : y_i \in D\} \leq k^{d-1}.$$

This implies $|\mathcal{D}| \leq k^d$ and

$$|\cup_{D \in \mathcal{D}} D| \leq |\mathcal{D}|d \leq dk^d.$$

Application of (2.2) completes the proof: $|C| \leq dk^d$.                          □

Let us emphasize the simplest case when the probability of an incorrect data is so small that practically at most one data of an individual can be incorrect. In this case $e = 1, d = 3$, therefore, if the minimal keys have at most $k$ elements, then the 1-error-correcting keys have at most $3k^3$ elements, and this is sharp up to a constant factor. So even in this simple case, the error-correcting keys may be much larger then the keys.

## 4   Further Problems

**1.** Although Theorem 2.1 determines the order of magnitude of $f_1(n, k, d)$, it does give the exact value. We believe that the lower estimate is sharp.

**Conjecture 4.1**

$$f_1(n, k, d) = \max_i \{i + d - 1 + \binom{i + d - 1}{i}(k - i)\}.$$

holds for $n_0(k, d) \le n$.

**2.** Knowing $\mathcal{K}$, can we effectively compute $\mathcal{C}_d$ (for a given $d$)? If $k$ is fixed, then Theorem 1.3 shows that the problem can be decided in polynomial time. If the size of $\mathcal{K}$ is exponential, then this is trivial. We cannot answer the question, e.g. when $\mathcal{K}$ consist polynomially many sets with unbounded sizes.

**3.** It is very easy to characterize the families which can be the family of minimal keys of a database. Can it be done for $\mathcal{C}_d$?

**4.** The investigations of the paper should be extended for the dependency structure of the databases.

**5.** The questions analogous to the results of the present paper can be asked for any other database model, replacing the relational one.

**6.** The following problem sounds similar to the problem treated here, but it is actually very different. Suppose that the data go through a noisy channel, where each data can be distorted with a small probability. Try to add new attributes to make the effective keys for the transmitted database small.

## References

1. Armstrong, W.W., Dependency structures of data base relationship, in: *Information Processing 74*, North-Holland, Amsterdam, pp. 580-583.
2. Demetrovics, J., On the equivalence of candidate keys with Sperner systems, *Acta Cybernet.* 4(1979) 247-252.

# Extension of the Relational Algebra
# to Probabilistic Complex Values

Thomas Eiter[1], Thomas Lukasiewicz[1], and Michael Walter[2, 3]

[1] Institut und Ludwig Wittgenstein Labor für Informationssysteme, TU Wien
Favoritenstraße 9–11, A-1040 Wien, Austria
{eiter,lukasiewicz}@kr.tuwien.ac.at

[2] Institut für Informatik, Universität Gießen
Arndtstraße 2, D-35392 Gießen, Germany

**Abstract.** We present a probabilistic data model for complex values. More precisely, we introduce probabilistic complex value relations, which combine the concept of probabilistic relations with the idea of complex values in a uniform framework. We then define an algebra for querying database instances, which comprises the operations of selection, projection, renaming, join, Cartesian product, union, intersection, and difference. We finally show that most of the query equivalences of classical relational algebra carry over to our algebra on probabilistic complex value relations. Hence, query optimization techniques for classical relational algebra can easily be applied to optimize queries on probabilistic complex value relations.

## 1  Introduction

Databases are a central component of many business and information systems. During the past two decades, relational database systems have replaced earlier systems and have become a standard for data management. Various needs in practice, however, cannot be appropriately managed with current commercial database systems, which are largely based on the plain relational data model.

An important such need is the integration of models of uncertainty into databases. Applications that involve uncertainty abound. Research on this issue can be divided into four categories [5]: (1) handling null values, (2) retrieval of incomplete data, (3) management of vague data (for example, "John is tall") in fuzzy set approaches, and (4) management of ambiguous or imprecise data (for example, "John's salary is between 50K and 70K") in probabilistic approaches. Another important issue is the management of structured objects. The relational model has been early generalized for storing structured objects [16], which was a step towards object-oriented database systems (see [1] for a background on complex values and a historic account).

---

[3] Current address: IBM Germany, Überseering 24, D-22297 Hamburg, Germany.
E-mail: MiWalter@de.ibm.com.

K.-D. Schewe, B. Thalheim (Eds.): FoIKS 2000, LNCS 1762, pp. 94–115, 2000.

In many applications, especially in the business domain, uncertainty stems from ambiguity rather than from vagueness. Several models for incorporating ambiguity into the relational model have thus been proposed so far (e.g., [4,2,5,12,8]; see Section 7 for a discussion of these and further approaches). Informally, they attach a probability to each tuple and/or to each value in a set of possible values of an imprecise attribute of a tuple. The operations of relational algebra are then generalized to combine these probabilities in a suitable way, adopting some underlying assumptions (like independence or disjointness of events).

In this paper, we extend this line of research to databases storing structured objects. In detail, we present a probabilistic data model for complex values. To our knowledge, there is not much work in this direction so far. A probabilistic version of NF2 relations has been presented in [7] (building on earlier work [8] and making some limiting assumptions; see Section 7 for a comparison to our work).

Our model generalizes a similar model of annotated tuples [12] to complex values [1]. Informally, every complex value $v$ is associated with a probability interval $[l, u]$ and an event $e$, forming a quadruple $(v, l, u, e)$. The interval $[l, u]$ represents the likelihood that $v$ belongs to the database, and $e$ records information about how this value was derived. Note that interval probabilities provide a greater flexibility than point probabilities, and seem better suited especially to represent imprecise and subjective probabilistic knowledge. Moreover, we use intervals also for technical reasons (under the assumed probabilistic knowledge, even when using only point probabilities, we generally specify *a set* of probability distributions, rather than *a unique single* distribution). The following is an example of a relation containing probabilistic complex values:

| $v$ | | $l$ | $u$ | $e$ |
|---|---|---|---|---|
| patient      diseases | | 0.7 | 0.9 | $e_1 \vee e_2$ |
| John    {lung cancer, tuberculosis} | | | | |
| patient      diseases | | 0.5 | 0.7 | $e_3$ |
| Jack      {leprosy} | | | | |

Observe that in the above model, probabilities are assigned to a complex value as a whole, and no impreciseness in attributes, given by sets of values with probabilities attached, can be explicitly expressed in the language. It has been shown in [12] that each tuple with imprecise attribute values can be represented by an annotated tuple, and that such a representation can be efficiently computed. Applying similar techniques, complex values with imprecise attributes may be represented by probabilistic complex values as above. To keep our model simple, we do not consider imprecise attributes here.

On top of our model, we define a relational algebra that uses, following [12], generic functions $\otimes$, $\oplus$, $\ominus$ for computing the probability range of the conjunction, disjunction, and difference of two events $e_1$ and $e_2$ from the probability ranges $[l_1, u_1]$ and $[l_2, u_2]$ of $e_1$ and $e_2$, respectively. Instances of these functions are selected according to the relationship between $e_1$ and $e_2$. For example, if $e_1$ and $e_2$ are independent, then the probability range of $e_1 \wedge e_2$ is given by $[l_1 \cdot l_2, u_1 \cdot u_2]$. However, if nothing is known about how $e_1$ and $e_2$ relate, then it is given by

$[\max(0, l_1 + l_2 - 1), \min(u_1, u_2)]$. Such generic functions allow us to remove the explicit or implicit assumptions about joint occurrence of tuples and/or attribute values in relations that are present in other approaches (see [4,2,5,8]).

We further refine [12] by giving a model-theoretic definition of probabilistic combination strategies, which assumes a probabilistic semantics in which probability distributions are defined over a set of possible worlds. Furthermore, we propose probabilistic difference strategies that are not necessarily derived from conjunction strategies and negation. We show that these refinements lead to more precise results in certain cases (see Example 2.8).

The main contributions of this work can be briefly summarized as follows:

- We give a model-theoretic definition of probabilistic conjunction, disjunction, and difference strategies, which is based on a possible worlds semantics.
- We present a data model that is based on probabilistic complex value relations, which generalizes previous data models in the literature [12,1].
- We define an algebra for querying database instances.
- We present equivalence results for query expressions, which can be used for query optimization. Since our model generalizes the one in [12], these results also apply to [12] as a special case. Note that the results on query equivalences in [12] are limited to the relationship between compaction and the standard relational algebra operators.

The rest of this paper is organized as follows. Section 2 gives some preliminaries. Sections 3 and 4 define the data model and the algebra. In Sections 5 and 6, we focus on query equivalences and optimization. Section 7 discusses related work, and Section 8 gives a short summary and an outlook on future research.

Note that for space limitations, proofs of the results are omitted (detailed proofs of the results are essentially given in [18]).

## 2     Probabilistic Background

In this section, we describe the probabilistic background of our approach to probabilistic complex value databases. We assume a semantics in which probabilities are defined over a set of possible worlds (see especially [3,9,17,10]). Note that we adopt some technical notions from [13,14].

The main aim of this section is to give a model-theoretic definition of probabilistic conjunction, disjunction, and difference strategies, which have been introduced by an axiomatic characterization in [12]. Given the probability ranges of two events $e_1$ and $e_2$, these strategies compute the probability range of the events $e_1 \vee e_2$, $e_1 \wedge e_2$, and $e_1 \wedge \neg e_2$, respectively. We allow a variety of different probabilistic conjunction, disjunction, and difference strategies to take into account the different dependencies between the two events $e_1$ and $e_2$.

We assume a set of *basic events* $\mathcal{B} = \{b_1, b_2, \ldots, b_n\}$ with $n \geq 1$. The set of *events* is the closure of $\mathcal{B}$ under the Boolean operations $\neg$ and $\wedge$. As usual, we use $(e_1 \vee e_2)$ to abbreviate $\neg(\neg e_1 \wedge \neg e_2)$. We use $\bot$ and $\top$ to abbreviate the *false event* $(b_1 \wedge \neg b_1)$ and the *true event* $\neg(b_1 \wedge \neg b_1)$, respectively. A *probabilistic pair* $(e, [l, u])$ consists of an event $e$ and an interval $[l, u] \subseteq [0, 1]$, where $l$ and $u$ are rational numbers. We use $\bot$ and $\top$ to abbreviate $(\bot, [0, 0])$ and $(\top, [1, 1])$, respectively.

Informally, each tuple $t$ in our probabilistic complex value database will be associated with a probabilistic pair $(e, [l, u])$. Intuitively, this means that $t$ is identified with $e$ and that the probability of $t$ lies in the interval range $[l, u]$. More precisely, each tuple in a base relation will be assigned a probabilistic pair $(e, [l, u])$ with a basic event $e$. Moreover, each derived tuple $t$ will be assigned a general probabilistic pair $(e, [l, u])$, where $e$ encodes some information on how $t$ is computed from tuples in the base relations.

An *implication* (resp., *negative correlation, positive correlation, independence*) *formula* is an expression $a \rightarrow b$ (resp., $NC(a, b)$, $PC(a, b)$, $Ind(a, b)$) with events $a$ and $b$. A *dependence information* on two events $a$ and $b$ is a subset of $KB^{\star}(a, b) = \{Ind(a, b), NC(a, b), PC(a, b), a \rightarrow b, b \rightarrow a, a \wedge b \rightarrow \bot, \top \rightarrow a \vee b\}$.

Informally, to express that the probability of two events $e_1$ and $e_2$ lies in the intervals $[l_1, u_1]$ and $[l_2, u_2]$, respectively, we will use the two probabilistic pairs $(e_1, [l_1, u_1])$ and $(e_2, [l_2, u_2])$, respectively. The relationship between $e_1$ and $e_2$ will then be encoded by some dependence information $KB \subseteq KB^{\star}(e_1, e_2)$.

A *classical interpretation* $I$ is a truth assignment to the basic events in $\mathcal{B}$, which is extended to all events as usual (that is, $(e_1 \wedge e_2)$ *is true in* $I$ iff $e_1$ and $e_2$ are true in $I$, and $\neg e$ *is true in* $I$ iff $e$ is not true in $I$). We write $I \models e$ iff $e$ is true in $I$. We use $\mathcal{I_B}$ to denote the set of all classical interpretations on $\mathcal{B}$.

A *probabilistic interpretation* $Pr$ is a mapping $Pr : \mathcal{I_B} \rightarrow [0, 1]$ such that all $Pr(I)$ with $I \in \mathcal{I_B}$ sum up to 1. It is extended to all events $e$ as follows:

$$Pr(e) = \sum\nolimits_{I \in \mathcal{I_B}, \, I \models e} Pr(I) \,.$$

It is important to point out that probabilistic interpretations are defined on the set of all classical interpretations and not on the set of all basic events. That is, we do not assume that the basic events are pairwise mutually exclusive. Moreover, we do not assume that the basic events are pairwise independent.

The *truth* of probabilistic pairs, implication formulas, negative correlation formulas, positive correlation formulas, and independence formulas $F$ in a probabilistic interpretation $Pr$, denoted $Pr \models F$, is defined as follows:

$$
\begin{aligned}
Pr &\models (e, [l, u]) && \text{iff} \quad Pr(e) \in [l, u] \,, \\
Pr &\models a \rightarrow b && \text{iff} \quad Pr(a \wedge b) = Pr(a) \,, \\
Pr &\models NC(a, b) && \text{iff} \quad Pr(a \wedge \neg b) = \min(Pr(a), Pr(\neg b)) \,, \\
Pr &\models PC(a, b) && \text{iff} \quad Pr(a \wedge b) = \min(Pr(a), Pr(b)) \,, \\
Pr &\models Ind(a, b) && \text{iff} \quad Pr(a \wedge b) = Pr(a) \cdot Pr(b) \,.
\end{aligned}
$$

A probabilistic interpretation $Pr$ is a *model* of a formula $F$ iff $Pr \models F$. $Pr$ is a *model* of a set of formulas $\mathcal{F}$, denoted $Pr \models \mathcal{F}$, iff $Pr$ is a model of all $F \in \mathcal{F}$. The set $\mathcal{F}$ is *satisfiable* iff a model of $\mathcal{F}$ exists. A formula $F$ is a *logical consequence* of $\mathcal{F}$, denoted $\mathcal{F} \models F$, iff each model of $\mathcal{F}$ is also a model of $F$.

The next result shows that there are combinations of probabilistic pairs $(e_1, [l_1, u_1])$ and $(e_2, [l_2, u_2])\}$ with dependence information $KB \subseteq KB^{\star}(e_1, e_2)$ that are unsatisfiable (note that this fact remains unmentioned in [12]).

**Lemma 2.1.** *Let $p_1 = (e_1, [l_1, u_1])$ and $p_2 = (e_2, [l_2, u_2])$ be two probabilistic pairs and let $KB$ be a dependence information on $e_1$ and $e_2$ such that $KB \cup \{p_1, p_2\}$ is satisfiable. Then, all the following conditions hold:*

1. *If $KB \models e_1 \wedge e_2 \rightarrow \bot$, then $l_1 + l_2 \leq 1$.*
2. *If $KB \models e_1 \rightarrow e_2$, then $l_1 \leq u_2$.*
3. *If $KB \models e_2 \rightarrow e_1$, then $l_2 \leq u_1$.*
4. *If $KB \models \top \rightarrow e_1 \vee e_2$, then $u_1 + u_2 \geq 1$.*

**Example 2.2.** Let $p_1$ and $p_2$ be given by $(e, [.5, 1])$ and $(\neg e, [.6, 1])$, respectively, and let $KB = \emptyset$. Then, $KB \cup \{p_1, p_2\}$ is not satisfiable, since $KB \models e \wedge \neg e \rightarrow \bot$ and $0.5 + 0.6 > 1$ (intuitively, the lower bound 0.6 for the probability of $\neg e$ implies the upper bound $0.4 < 0.5$ for the probability of $e$).

We next define the notion of tight logical consequence for probabilistic pairs. A probabilistic pair $(e, [l, u])$ is a *tight logical consequence* of a satisfiable set of formulas $\mathcal{F}$, denoted $\mathcal{F} \models_{tight} (e, [l, u])$, iff $l$ and $u$ are the infimum and supremum, respectively, of $Pr(e)$ subject to all models $Pr$ of $\mathcal{F}$.

We are now ready to define probabilistic conjunctions, disjunctions, and differences of probabilistic pairs. Let $p_1 = (e_1, [l_1, u_1])$ and $p_2 = (e_2, [l_2, u_2])$ be two probabilistic pairs and let $KB \subseteq KB^*(e_1, e_2)$ such that $KB \cup \{p_1, p_2\}$ is satisfiable. The *probabilistic conjunction, disjunction,* and *difference* of $p_1$ and $p_2$ under $KB$, denoted $p_1 \otimes_{KB} p_2$, $p_1 \oplus_{KB} p_2$, and $p_1 \ominus_{KB} p_2$, respectively, are defined as the probabilistic pairs $(e_1 \wedge e_2, [l, u])$, $(e_1 \vee e_2, [l, u])$, and $(e_1 \wedge \neg e_2, [l, u])$, respectively, where $[l, u]$ such that $(e_1 \wedge e_2, [l, u])$, $(e_1 \vee e_2, [l, u])$, and $(e_1 \wedge \neg e_2, [l, u])$, respectively, are tight logical consequences of $KB \cup \{p_1, p_2\}$ (note that the structure of $KB$ ensures that both $l$ and $u$ are rational).

Informally, to compute the probability range $[l, u]$ of $e_1 \wedge e_2$, $e_1 \vee e_2$, or $e_1 \wedge \neg e_2$ from the probability ranges $[l_1, u_1]$ and $[l_2, u_2]$ of $e_1$ and $e_2$, respectively, we first collect all available dependence information $KB \subseteq KB^*(e_1, e_2)$ on $e_1$ and $e_2$. We then check whether $KB \cup \{(e_1, [l_1, u_1]), (e_2, [l_2, u_2])\}$ is satisfiable. If this is the case, it just remains to compute the unique tight logical consequences $(e_1 \wedge e_2, [l, u])$, $(e_1 \vee e_2, [l, u])$, or $(e_1 \wedge \neg e_2, [l, u])$ of $KB \cup \{(e_1, [l_1, u_1]), (e_2, [l_2, u_2])\}$. Both the satisfiability check and the computation of the tight logical consequence can *effectively* be done by using linear and nonlinear programming techniques.

We next introduce the notions of probabilistic conjunction, disjunction, and difference *strategies*. Let us first give some motivating background.

In query expressions of our algebra, each occurrence of a probabilistic combination operator stands for the probabilistic combination of several pairs of probabilistic pairs. Moreover, each such occurrence will be parameterized with a dependence information $KB_{st} \subseteq KB^*(a, b)$, where $a$ and $b$ are two new distinct basic events. For example, $r_1 \cup^{\oplus_{in}} r_1$ will denote the union of two relations $r_1$ and $r_2$ under the dependence information $KB_{in} = \{Ind(a, b)\}$. This dependence information $KB_{st}$ can now be used in the following ways:

DYNAMIC DEPENDENCE: Given two probabilistic pairs $p_1 = (e_1, [l_1, u_1])$ and $p_2 = (e_2, [l_1, u_2])$, we compute $p_1 \otimes_{KB} p_2$, $p_1 \oplus_{KB} p_2$, and $p_1 \ominus_{KB} p_2$, where $KB$ is given by $KB_{st} \cup \{e_1 \rightarrow a, a \rightarrow e_1, e_2 \rightarrow b, b \rightarrow e_2\}$.

STATIC DEPENDENCE: For any two probabilistic pairs $p_1 = (e_1, [l_1, u_1])$ and $p_2 = (e_2, [l_1, u_2])$, we compute $p_1' \otimes_{KB_{st}} p_2'$, $p_1' \oplus_{KB_{st}} p_2'$, and $p_1' \ominus_{KB_{st}} p_2'$, where

$p'_1 = (a, [l_1, u_1])$ and $p'_2 = (b, [l_1, u_2])$, instead of $p_1 \otimes_{KB} p_2$, $p_1 \oplus_{KB} p_2$, and $p_1 \ominus_{KB} p_2$, respectively (that is, we ignore the concrete events $e_1$ and $e_2$).

DYNAMIC DEPENDENCE has nice properties from the semantic point of view, since it exploits all the (locally) available dependence information. STATIC DE-PENDENCE, in contrast, implies nice computational properties. Firstly, the dependence information $KB_{st}$ is in itself complete (that is, we do not have to compute any other relationships that are implicitly encoded in the structure of some concrete events $e_1$ and $e_2$). Secondly, some specific dependence information $KB_{st}$ often implies nice algebraic properties of $\otimes_{KB_{st}}$, $\oplus_{KB_{st}}$, and $\ominus_{KB_{st}}$, which are known in advance, and can thus be exploited for query optimization.

In the sequel, we implicitly assume STATIC DEPENDENCE (which can be seen as one of the main motivations behind probabilistic combination *strategies*).

Let $KB \subseteq KB^{\star}(a, b)$ be a dependence information on two distinct basic events $a$ and $b$. The *probabilistic conjunction* (resp., *disjunction, difference*) *s-trategy* for $KB$ is the unique function $\otimes$ (resp., $\oplus$, $\ominus$) that associates any t-wo probabilistic pairs $(e_1, [l_1, u_1])$ and $(e_2, [l_2, u_2])$, where $KB \cup \{(a, [l_1, u_1]), (b, [l_2, u_2])\}$ is satisfiable, with the probabilistic pair $(a, [l_1, u_1]) \otimes_{KB} (b, [l_2, u_2])$ (resp., $(a, [l_1, u_1]) \oplus_{KB} (b, [l_2, u_2])$, $(a, [l_1, u_1]) \ominus_{KB} (b, [l_2, u_2])$).

**Example 2.3.** Let $p_1 = (e_1, [l_1, u_1])$ and $p_2 = (e_2, [l_2, u_2])$ be two probabilistic pairs. The probabilistic conjunction, disjunction, and difference strategies for $KB$ among $\emptyset$, $\{Ind(a, b)\}$, $\{PC(a, b)\}$, $\{a \rightarrow b\}$, and $\{a \wedge b \rightarrow \bot\}$ (we refer to these cases by *ignorance, independence, positive correlation, left implication,* and *mutual exclusion,* respectively) are given in Table 1. Note that the probabilistic conjunction and disjunction strategies for ignorance, independence, positive correlation, and mutual exclusion are already known from [12].

We next focus on the properties of probabilistic combination strategies. Let us first introduce some necessary notations.

For probabilistic pairs $p = (e, [l, u])$, we write $\iota(p)$ to denote $[l, u]$. For intervals $[r_1, s_1], [r_2, s_2] \subseteq [0, 1]$, we write $[r_1, s_1] \leq [r_2, s_2]$ to denote $r_1 \leq r_2$ and $s_1 \leq s_2$. For probabilistic pairs $p_1$ and $p_2$, we write $p_1 \sqsubseteq p_2$, $p_1 \equiv p_2$, $p_1 \leq p_2$, and $p_1 \geq p_2$ to denote $\iota(p_1) \subseteq \iota(p_2)$, $\iota(p_1) = \iota(p_2)$, $\iota(p_1) \leq \iota(p_2)$, and $\iota(p_1) \geq \iota(p_2)$, respectively.

Let $KB \subseteq KB^{\star}(a, b)$ with two distinct basic events $a$ and $b$. The probabilistic conjunction (resp., disjunction) strategy $\otimes$ (resp., $\oplus$) for $KB$ is *commutative* iff $p_1 \otimes p_2 \equiv p_2 \otimes p_1$ (resp., $p_1 \oplus p_2 \equiv p_2 \oplus p_1$) for all probabilistic pairs $p_1$ and $p_2$. It is *associative* iff $(p_1 \otimes p_2) \otimes p_3 \equiv p_1 \otimes (p_2 \otimes p_3)$ (resp., $(p_1 \oplus p_2) \oplus p_3 \equiv p_1 \oplus (p_2 \oplus p_3)$) for all probabilistic pairs $p_1$, $p_2$, and $p_3$. We say that $\otimes$ is *distributive* over $\oplus$ iff $p_1 \otimes (p_2 \oplus p_3) = (p_1 \otimes p_2) \oplus (p_1 \otimes p_3)$ for all probabilistic pairs $p_1$, $p_2$, and $p_3$.

For associative probabilistic disjunction strategies $\oplus$ and probabilistic pairs $p_1, p_2, \ldots, p_k$ with $k \geq 1$, we write $\bigoplus_{i \in [1:k]} p_i$ to denote $p_1 \oplus p_2 \oplus \cdots \oplus p_k$.

**Example 2.4.** It can easily be verified that the probabilistic conjunction and disjunction strategies for ignorance, independence, positive correlation, and mutual exclusion are all commutative and associative. Moreover, for positive correlation, the conjunction strategy is distributive over the disjunction strategy.

**Table 1.** Examples of probabilistic combination strategies

| ignorance | $p_1 \otimes_{ig} p_2 = (e_1 \wedge e_2, [\max(0, l_1 + l_2 - 1), \min(u_1, u_2)])$ |
|---|---|
| | $p_1 \oplus_{ig} p_2 = (e_1 \vee e_2, [\max(l_1, l_2), \min(1, u_1 + u_2)])$ |
| | $p_1 \ominus_{ig} p_2 = (e_1 \wedge \neg e_2, [\max(0, l_1 - u_2), \min(u_1, 1 - l_2)])$ |
| independence | $p_1 \otimes_{in} p_2 = (e_1 \wedge e_2, [l_1 \cdot l_2, u_1 \cdot u_2])$ |
| | $p_1 \oplus_{in} p_2 = (e_1 \vee e_2, [l_1 + l_2 - l_1 \cdot l_2, u_1 + u_2 - u_1 \cdot u_2])$ |
| | $p_1 \ominus_{in} p_2 = (e_1 \wedge \neg e_2, [l_1 \cdot (1 - u_2), u_1 \cdot (1 - l_2)])$ |
| positive correlation | $p_1 \otimes_{pc} p_2 = (e_1 \wedge e_2, [\min(l_1, l_2), \min(u_1, u_2)])$ |
| | $p_1 \oplus_{pc} p_2 = (e_1 \vee e_2, [\max(l_1, l_2), \max(u_1, u_2)])$ |
| | $p_1 \ominus_{pc} p_2 = (e_1 \wedge \neg e_2, [\max(0, l_1 - u_2), \max(0, u_1 - l_2)])$ |
| left implication | $p_1 \otimes_{li} p_2 = (e_1 \wedge e_2, [l_2, \min(u_1, u_2)])$ |
| | $p_1 \oplus_{li} p_2 = (e_1 \vee e_2, [\max(l_1, l_2), u_1])$ |
| | $p_1 \ominus_{li} p_2 = (e_1 \wedge \neg e_2, [\max(0, l_1 - u_2), u_1 - l_2])$ |
| mutual exclusion | $p_1 \otimes_{me} p_2 = (e_1 \wedge e_2, [0, 0])$ |
| | $p_1 \oplus_{me} p_2 = (e_1 \vee e_2, [\min(1, l_1 + l_2), \min(1, u_1 + u_2)])$ |
| | $p_1 \ominus_{me} p_2 = (e_1 \wedge \neg e_2, [l_1, \min(u_1, 1 - l_2)])$ |

Rather than defining probabilistic conjunction and disjunction strategies by a rigorous foundation on probability theory, the work in [12] gives a characterization by the postulates BOTTOMLINE, IGNORANCE, IDENTITY, ANNIHILATOR, COMMUTATIVITY, ASSOCIATIVITY, and MONOTONICITY (see [12] for details).

Indeed, all probabilistic conjunction and disjunction strategies satisfy IGNORANCE, (a slight variant of) IDENTITY, and ANNIHILATOR.

**Lemma 2.5.** *Let $KB \subseteq KB^\star(a, b)$ with two distinct basic events $a$ and $b$. Let $\otimes$, $\oplus$, and $\ominus$ be the probabilistic combination strategies for $KB$. Then, the conditions shown in Table 2 hold for all probabilistic pairs $p_1 = (e_1, [l_1, u_1])$ and $p_2 = (e_2, [l_2, u_2])$ such that $KB \cup \{(a, [l_1, u_1]), (b, [l_2, u_2])\}$ is satisfiable.*

*However, there are probabilistic conjunction and disjunction strategies $\otimes$ and $\oplus$ that do not satisfy the postulate BOTTOMLINE, which says that $p_1 \otimes p_2 \leq (e_1 \wedge e_2, [\min(l_1, l_2), \min(u_1, u_2)])$ and $p_1 \oplus p_2 \geq (e_1 \vee e_2, [\max(l_1, l_2), \max(u_1, u_2)])$, respectively, for all probabilistic pairs $p_1 = (e_1, [l_1, u_1])$ and $p_2 = (e_2, [l_2, u_2])$ such that $p_1 \otimes p_2$ and $p_1 \oplus p_2$, respectively, are defined.*

**Example 2.6.** We show that the probabilistic conjunction and disjunction strategies for left implication do not satisfy BOTTOMLINE. Let the two probabilistic pairs $p_1$ and $p_2$ be given by $(e_1, [.2, .7])$ and $(e_2, [.5, .8])$, respectively. It can easily be verified that $\{b \rightarrow a, (a, [.2, .7]), (b, [.5, .8])\}$ is satisfiable. Moreover, we get:

$$p_1 \otimes_{li} p_2 = (e_1 \wedge e_2, [.5, .7]), \text{ but } [\min(l_1, l_2), \min(u_1, u_2)] = [.2, .7],$$
$$p_1 \oplus_{li} p_2 = (e_1 \vee e_2, [.5, .7]), \text{ but } [\max(l_1, l_2), \max(u_1, u_2)] = [.5, .8].$$

**Table 2.** Properties of probabilistic combination strategies

| IGNORANCE | $p_1 \otimes p_2 \subseteq p_1 \otimes_{ig} p_2$ |
|---|---|
| | $p_1 \oplus p_2 \subseteq p_1 \oplus_{ig} p_2$ |
| | $p_1 \ominus p_2 \subseteq p_1 \ominus_{ig} p_2$ |
| IDENTITY | $p_1 \otimes p_2 \equiv p_2$, if $[l_1, u_1] = [1, 1]$, $a \wedge b \to \bot \notin KB$, and $a \to b \notin KB$ |
| | $p_1 \otimes p_2 \equiv p_1$, if $[l_2, u_2] = [1, 1]$, $a \wedge b \to \bot \notin KB$, and $b \to a \notin KB$ |
| | $p_1 \oplus p_2 \equiv p_2$, if $[l_1, u_1] = [0, 0]$, $\top \to a \vee b \notin KB$, and $b \to a \notin KB$ |
| | $p_1 \oplus p_2 \equiv p_1$, if $[l_2, u_2] = [0, 0]$, $\top \to a \vee b \notin KB$, and $a \to b \notin KB$ |
| | $p_1 \ominus p_2 \equiv p_1$, if $[l_2, u_2] = [0, 0]$, $\top \to a \vee b \notin KB$, and $a \to b \notin KB$ |
| ANNIHILATOR | $p_1 \otimes p_2 \equiv \bot$, if $[l_1, u_1] = [0, 0]$ or $[l_2, u_2] = [0, 0]$ |
| | $p_1 \oplus p_2 \equiv \top$, if $[l_1, u_1] = [1, 1]$ or $[l_2, u_2] = [1, 1]$ |
| | $p_1 \ominus p_2 \equiv \bot$, if $[l_1, u_1] = [0, 0]$ or $[l_2, u_2] = [1, 1]$ |

Furthermore, there are probabilistic conjunction and disjunction strategies that do *not* satisfy COMMUTATIVITY (that is, that are *not* commutative).

**Example 2.7.** We show that the probabilistic conjunction and disjunction strategies for left implication do not satisfy COMMUTATIVITY. Let the two probabilistic pairs $p_1$ and $p_2$ be given by $(e_1, [.2, .7])$ and $(e_2, [.5, .6])$, respectively. It can easily be verified that $\{b \to a, (a, [.2, .7]), (b, [.5, .6])\}$ is satisfiable. We get:

$$p_1 \otimes_{li} p_2 = (e_1 \wedge e_2, [.5, .6]) \not\equiv (e_2 \wedge e_1, [.2, .6]) = p_2 \otimes_{li} p_1,$$
$$p_1 \oplus_{li} p_2 = (e_1 \wedge e_2, [.5, .7]) \not\equiv (e_2 \wedge e_1, [.5, .6]) = p_2 \oplus_{li} p_1.$$

Finally, we give an example in which our rigorous model-theoretic approach yields more precise intervals than the axiomatic approach in [12].

**Example 2.8.** Let us consider the case of left implication. Let the two probabilistic pairs $p_1$ and $p_2$ be given by $(e_1, [.2, .7])$ and $(e_2, [.5, .6])$, respectively. It can easily be verified that $\{b \to a, (a, [.2, .7]), (b, [.5, .6])\}$ is satisfiable. We get:

$$p_1 \otimes_{li} p_2 = (e_1 \wedge e_2, [.5, .6]),$$
$$p_1 \oplus_{li} p_2 = (e_1 \vee e_2, [.5, .7]),$$
$$p_1 \ominus_{li} p_2 = (e_1 \wedge \neg e_2, [0, .2]).$$

The approach in [12], in contrast, just produces the probability ranges $[.2, .6]$, $[.5, .7]$, and $[0, .5]$, respectively, which are obtained from $p_1$ and $p_2$ by the computations $p_1 \otimes_{pc} p_2 = (e_1 \wedge e_2, [.2, .6])$, $p_1 \oplus_{pc} p_2 = (e_1 \vee e_2, [.5, .7])$, and $p_1 \ominus p_2 = (e_1, [.2, .7]) \otimes_{ig} (\neg e_2, [.4, .5]) = (e_1 \wedge \neg e_2, [0, .5])$, respectively.

## 3   Data Model

In this section, we define probabilistic complex value relations.

Let $\mathcal{A}$ be a nonempty set of *attribute names* and let $\mathcal{T}$ be a nonempty set of *atomic types*. We define *complex value types* (or simply *types*) by induction as follows. Every atomic type from $\mathcal{T}$ is a type. If $T$ is a type, then the set $\{T\}$ is a type. If $A_1, \ldots, A_k$ with $k \geq 1$ are distinct attribute names from $\mathcal{A}$ and $T_1, \ldots, T_k$ are types, then the mapping $T = \{(A_1, T_1), \ldots, (A_k, T_k)\}$ is a type (called *tuple type*). It is abbreviated by $[A_1 : T_1, \ldots, A_k : T_k]$. We call $A_1, \ldots, A_k$ the *top-level attribute names* of $T$. We use $T.A_i$ to denote $T_i$.

Every atomic type $T \in \mathcal{T}$ is assigned a *domain* $\mathrm{dom}(T)$. We define *complex values* by induction as follows. For all atomic types $T \in \mathcal{T}$, every $v \in \mathrm{dom}(T)$ is a complex value of type $T$. If $v_1, \ldots, v_k$ with $k \geq 0$ are complex values of type $T$, then the set $\{v_1, \ldots, v_k\}$ is a complex value of type $\{T\}$. If $A_1, \ldots, A_k$ with $k \geq 1$ are distinct attribute names from $\mathcal{A}$ and $v_1, \ldots, v_k$ are complex values of types $T_1, \ldots, T_k$, then the mapping $\{(A_1, v_1), \ldots, (A_k, v_k)\}$ is a complex value of type $[A_1 : T_1, \ldots, A_k : T_k]$. It is abbreviated by $[A_1 : v_1, \ldots, A_k : v_k]$.

Given a tuple type $T$, a *complex value tuple* (*cv-tuple*) of type $T$ is simply a complex value of type $T$. For cv-tuples $t = [A_1 : v_1, \ldots, A_k : v_k]$, we use $v.A_i$ to denote $v_i$. A *complex value relation* (*cv-relation*) of type $T$ is a finite set of cv-tuples of type $T$.

A *probabilistic complex value tuple* (*pcv-tuple*) of type $T$ is a mapping $t$ of the kind $\{(\mathsf{data}, v), (\mathsf{lb}, r), (\mathsf{ub}, s), (\mathsf{path}, e)\}$, where $v$ is a cv-tuple of type $T$, $r$ and $s$ are rational numbers with $0 \leq r \leq s \leq 1$, and $e$ is an event. It is abbreviated by $[\mathsf{data} : v, \mathsf{lb} : r, \mathsf{ub} : s, \mathsf{path} : e]$. We use $t.\mathsf{data}$, $t.\mathsf{lb}$, $t.\mathsf{ub}$, $t.\mathsf{path}$, and $t.\mathsf{prob}$ to denote $v$, $r$, $s$, $e$, and $([r, s], e)$, respectively. A *probabilistic complex value relation* (*pcv-relation*) of type $T$ is a finite set of pcv-tuples of type $T$.

A *base pcv-relation* is a pcv-relation $r$ such that $t.\mathsf{path} \in \mathcal{B}$ for all $t \in r$ and that $t_1.\mathsf{path} \neq t_2.\mathsf{path}$ for all $t_1, t_2 \in r$ with $t_1.\mathsf{data} \neq t_2.\mathsf{data}$. A *probabilistic complex value database* is a finite set of base pcv-relations that are defined over pairwise disjoint sets of basic events.

A pcv-relation $r$ is called *compact* iff $t_1.\mathsf{prob} = t_2.\mathsf{prob}$ for all $t_1, t_2 \in r$ with $t_1.\mathsf{data} = t_2.\mathsf{data}$. In the sequel, we identify compact pcv-relations $r$ of type $R$ with pairs $(\delta, \mu)$, where $\delta$ is a cv-relation of type $R$ and $\mu$ is a mapping from $\delta$ to the set of all probabilistic pairs.

Each non-compact pcv-relation can be transformed into a compact pcv-relation by applying a compaction operation: Given a pcv-relation $r$ and a commutative and associative probabilistic disjunction strategy $\oplus$, the *compaction of $r$ under $\oplus$*, denoted $\kappa^{\oplus}(r)$, is defined as the pcv-relation $(\delta, \mu)$, where:

- $\delta = \{v \mid \exists\, w \in r : w.\mathsf{data} = v\}$,
- $\mu(v) = \bigoplus_{w \in r,\, w.\mathsf{data} = v} w.\mathsf{prob}$ for all $v \in \delta$.

In the sequel, we thus assume that all pcv-relations are compact. Moreover, we assume that $t.\mathsf{prob} \not\equiv \bot$ for all tuples $t$ in a pcv-relation $r$ (that is, we make the closed world assumption that $t.\mathsf{prob} \equiv \bot$ for all $t \notin r$).

**Example 3.1.** A compact pcv-relation is shown in Table 3. It contains information about chemical experiments in which several substances are checked for a certain ingredient. Each experiment yields information about the substance analyzed (substance-id), the laboratory (lab), the date (date), the assistants who did the experiment (assistants), and the result ($\alpha$-result).

The probabilistic information in this pcv-relation can be interpreted as subjective belief of an agent. Each pcv-tuple $t$ then means that the probability that $t$.data holds in the real world ranges from $t$.lb to $t$.ub. For example, the first pcv-tuple $t$ could say that the probability that substance S89 was analyzed in laboratory L17 on 02/17/99 by Jack and Jill with positive $\alpha$-result lies between 0.7 and 0.8 (this could mean that we are unsure about the whole information in $t$.data or that we are just unsure about the $\alpha$-result). Another possible interpretation is that the probability that the positive $\alpha$-result describes correctly the properties of substance S89 lies between 0.7 and 0.8.

**Table 3.** A compact pcv-relation

| | | | | | •• | •• | •••• |
|---|---|---|---|---|---|---|---|
| •• ••• •• ••• | $\alpha$••••• •••• ••• | | | $\alpha$•••••• •• | | | |
| S89 | •• • | •• ••• | •• •••••• •• •• | + | 0.7 | 0.8 | $e_1$ |
| | L17 | 02/17/99 | {Jack, Jill} | | | | |
| •• ••• •• ••• | $\alpha$••••• •••• ••• | | | $\alpha$•••••• •• | | | |
| S89 | •• • | •• ••• | •• ••••• •• •• | + | 0.6 | 0.9 | $e_2$ |
| | L10 | 02/13/99 | {Joe, Jim} | | | | |
| •• ••• •• ••• | $\alpha$••••• •••• ••• | | | $\alpha$•••••• •• | | | |
| S64 | •• • | •• ••• | •• ••••• •• •• | − | 0.5 | 0.7 | $e_3$ |
| | L12 | 02/17/99 | {Janet, Jill} | | | | |

## 4    Algebra

In this section, we define an algebra on probabilistic complex value relations.

### 4.1    Selection, Projection, and Renaming

We first define the selection operation on pcv-relations.

Let $x$ be a *tuple variable*. We define *terms* by induction as follows. A term is a complex value $v$, the tuple variable $x$, or an expression $t.A$, where $t$ is a term and $A$ belongs to $\mathcal{A} \cup \{$data, lb, ub$\}$. We define *selection conditions* by induction as follows. If $t_1$ and $t_2$ are terms and $\theta$ belongs to $\{=, \leq, \in, \subseteq\}$, then $t_1\,\theta\,t_2$ is a selection condition (called *atomic selection condition*). If $\phi_1$ and $\phi_2$ are selection conditions, then $\neg\phi_1$ and $(\phi_1 \wedge \phi_2)$ are selection conditions. We use $(\phi_1 \vee \phi_2)$ to abbreviate $\neg(\neg\phi_1 \wedge \neg\phi_2)$.

The *interpretation* of a term $t$ in a pcv-tuple $w$, denoted $[t]_w$, is inductively defined by $[v]_w = v$, $[x]_w = w$, and $[t.A]_w = [t]_w.A$ if $[t]_w.A$ is defined.

A selection condition $\phi$ is *applicable* to a tuple type $T$ iff for all atomic selection conditions $t_1\,\theta\,t_2$ that occur in $\phi$ and all pcv-tuples $w$ of type $T$: $[t_1]_w$, $[t_2]_w$, and $[t_1]_w\,\theta\,[t_2]_w$ are defined. A selection condition $\phi$ is *probability-free* iff it does not contain the expressions lb and ub.

For selection conditions $\phi$ that are applicable to $T$, the *satisfaction* of $\phi$ in a pcv-tuple $w$ of type $T$, denoted $w \models \phi$, is inductively defined as follows:

- $w \models t_1 \, \theta \, t_2$ iff $[t_1]_w \, \theta \, [t_2]_w$,
- $w \models \neg\phi$ iff not $w \models \phi$,
- $w \models (\phi \wedge \psi)$ iff $w \models \phi$ and $w \models \psi$.

Let $r = (\delta, \mu)$ be a pcv-relation of type $R$ and let $\phi$ be a selection condition that is applicable to $R$. The *selection on $r$ with respect to $\phi$*, denoted $\sigma_\phi(r)$, is the pcv-relation $(\delta', \mu')$ of type $R$, where:

- $\delta' = \{v \mid \exists \, w \in r \colon w.\text{data} = v, \, w \models \phi\}$,
- $\mu'(v) = \mu(v)$ for all $v \in \delta'$.

**Example 4.1.** Let us take the pcv-relation given in Table 3. Let the selection condition $\phi$ be defined by

$$\phi = ((\, x.\text{lb} \geq 0.7 \ \vee \ x.\text{data}.\alpha\text{-result} = -) \ \wedge$$
$$\text{Jack} \in x.\text{data}.\alpha\text{-arrangement.assistants}).$$

The result of the selection operation with respect to $\phi$ is shown in Table 4.

**Table 4.** Result of selection

| ● ● ● ● | | | ● ● | ● ● | ● ● ● ● |
|---|---|---|---|---|---|
| $\alpha$ ● ● ● ● ● ● ● ● ● ● ● | | | $\alpha$ ● ● ● ● ● ● | | |
| ● ● ● | ● ● ● ● | ● ● ● ● ● ● ● ● ● | | 0.7 | 0.8 | $e_1$ |
| S89 | L17 | 02/17/99 {Jack, Jill} | $+$ | | | |

We next concentrate on the projection operation on pcv-relations. We define the *subtype* relationship on all types by induction as follows. If $T$ is an atomic type from $\mathcal{T}$, then $T$ be a subtype of $T$. If $T_1$ is a subtype of $T_2$, then $\{T_1\}$ is a subtype of $\{T_2\}$. If $A_1, \ldots, A_k$ with $k \geq 1$ are distinct attribute names from $\mathcal{A}$ and $T_1, \ldots, T_l, S_1, \ldots, S_k$ with $l \leq k$ are types such that $T_1, \ldots, T_l$ are subtypes of $S_1, \ldots, S_l$, then $[A_1 \colon T_1, \ldots, A_l \colon T_l]$ is a subtype of $[A_1 \colon S_1, \ldots, A_k \colon S_k]$.

Let $v$ be a complex value of type $T$ and let $S$ be a subtype of $T$. The *projection of $v$ to $S$*, denoted $\pi_S(v)$, is by induction defined as follows. If $S$ is an atomic type, then $\pi_S(v) = v$. If $v = \{v_1, \ldots, v_k\}$ and $S = \{S'\}$, then $\pi_S(v) = \{\pi_{S'}(v_1), \ldots, \pi_{S'}(v_k)\}$. If $v = [A_1 \colon v_1, \ldots, A_k \colon v_k]$ and $S = [A_1 \colon S_1, \ldots, A_l \colon S_l]$, then $\pi_S(v) = [A_1 \colon \pi_{S_1}(v_1), \ldots, A_l \colon \pi_{S_l}(v_l)]$.

Let $r$ be a cv-relation of type $R$ and let $S$ be a subtype of $R$. The *projection of $r$ to $S$*, denoted $\pi_S(r)$, is the cv-relation $\{\pi_S(t) \mid t \in r\}$ of type $S$.

Let $r = (\delta, \mu)$ be a pcv-relation of type $R$, let $S$ be a subtype of $R$, and let $\oplus$ be a commutative and associative disjunction strategy. The *projection of $r$ to $S$ under $\oplus$*, denoted $\pi_S^\oplus(r)$, is defined as the pcv-relation $(\delta', \mu')$ of type $S$, where:

- $\delta' = \{v \in \pi_S(\delta) \mid \bigoplus_{w \in \delta, \pi_S(w)=v} \mu(w) \neq \bot\}$,
- $\mu'(v) = \bigoplus_{w \in \delta, \pi_S(w)=v} \mu(w)$ for all $v \in \delta'$.

**Example 4.2.** The projection of the pcv-relation from Table 3 to a tuple type over the attribute names substance-id and $\alpha$-result under $\oplus_{pc}$ is given in Table 5.

**Table 5.** Result of projection

| •••• | | | •• | •• | •••• |
|---|---|---|---|---|---|
| •• • •••• •• •••• | $\alpha$•••• •• | | 0.7 | 0.9 | $e_1 \vee e_2$ |
| S89 | $+$ | | | | |
| •• • •••• • ••• | $\alpha$•••• •• | | 0.5 | 0.7 | $e_3$ |
| S64 | $-$ | | | | |

We finally define the renaming operation on pcv-relations. Let $T$ be a type and let $\mathbf{A}$ denote the set of all attribute names that occur in $T$. A *renaming condition* for $T$ is an expression $B_1, \ldots, B_l \leftarrow C_1, \ldots, C_l$, where $B_1, \ldots, B_l$ is a sequence of distinct attribute names from $\mathcal{A}$ and $C_1, \ldots, C_l$ is a sequence of distinct attribute names from $\mathcal{A} - (\mathbf{A} - \{B_1, \ldots, B_l\})$.

Let $T$ be a type and let $N = B_1, \ldots, B_l \leftarrow C_1, \ldots, C_l$ be a renaming condition for $T$. The *renaming of $T$ with respect to $N$*, denoted $\rho_N(T)$, is obtained from $T$ by replacing each attribute name $B_i$ with $i \in [1:l]$ by the new attribute name $C_i$.

Let $v$ be a complex value of type $T$ and let $N = B_1, \ldots, B_l \leftarrow C_1, \ldots, C_l$ be a renaming condition for $T$. The *renaming of $v$ with respect to $N$*, denoted $\rho_N(v)$, is obtained from $v$ by replacing each attribute name $B_i$ with $i \in [1:l]$ by the new attribute name $C_i$.

Let $r$ be a cv-relation of type $R$ and let $N$ be a renaming condition for $R$. The *renaming of $r$ with respect to $N$*, denoted $\rho_N(r)$, is the cv-relation $\{\rho_N(t) \mid t \in r\}$ of type $\rho_N(R)$. Let $r = (\delta, \mu)$ be a pcv-relation of type $R$ and let $N$ be a renaming condition for $R$. The *renaming of $r$ with respect to $N$*, denoted $\rho_N(r)$, is the pcv-relation $(\delta', \mu')$ of type $\rho_N(R)$, where:

- $\delta' = \rho_N(\delta)$,
- $\mu'(v) = \mu(\rho_N^{-1}(v))$ for all $v \in \delta'$.

### 4.2   Join and Cartesian Product

We now define the join operation on pcv-relations.

Two tuple types $T_1$ and $T_2$ over the sets of top-level attribute names $\mathbf{A}_2$ and $\mathbf{A}_2$, respectively, are *join-compatible* iff $T_1.A = T_2.A$ for all $A \in \mathbf{A}_1 \cap \mathbf{A}_2$. The *join* of two such types $T_1$ and $T_2$, denoted $T_1 \bowtie T_2$, is the tuple type $T$ over $\mathbf{A}_1 \cup \mathbf{A}_2$, where $T.A = T_1.A$ if $A \in \mathbf{A}_1$ and $T.A = T_2.A$ if $A \in \mathbf{A}_2$.

Let $v_1$ and $v_2$ be two cv-tuples of join-compatible types $T_1$ and $T_2$ over $\mathbf{A}_1$ and $\mathbf{A}_2$, respectively, with $v_1.A = v_2.A$ for all $A \in \mathbf{A}_1 \cap \mathbf{A}_2$. The *join* of $v_1$ and $v_2$, denoted $v_1 \bowtie v_2$, is defined as the cv-tuple $v$ of type $T_1 \bowtie T_2$, where $v.A = v_1.A$ if $A \in \mathbf{A}_1$ and $v.A = v_2.A$ if $A \in \mathbf{A}_2$.

Let $r_1$ and $r_2$ be two cv-relations of join-compatible types $R_1$ and $R_2$ over $\mathbf{A}_1$ and $\mathbf{A}_2$, respectively. The *join of $r_1$ and $r_2$*, denoted $r_1 \bowtie r_2$, is the cv-relation $r$ of type $R_1 \bowtie R_2$ with $r = \{t_1 \bowtie t_2 \mid t_1 \in r_1, t_2 \in r_2, t_1.A = t_2.A$ for all $A \in \mathbf{A}_1 \cap \mathbf{A}_2\}$.

Let $r_1 = (\delta_1, \mu_1)$ and $r_2 = (\delta_2, \mu_2)$ be two pcv-relations of join-compatible types $R_1$ and $R_2$, respectively, and let $\otimes$ be a probabilistic conjunction strategy. The *join of $r_1$ and $r_2$ under* $\otimes$, denoted $r_1 \bowtie^\otimes r_2$, is defined as the pcv-relation $(\delta, \mu)$ of type $R_1 \bowtie R_2$, where:

- $\delta = \{v \in \delta_1 \bowtie \delta_2 \mid \mu_1(\pi_{R_1}(v)) \otimes \mu_2(\pi_{R_2}(v)) \not\equiv \bot\}$,

- $\mu(v) = \mu_1(\pi_{R_1}(v)) \otimes \mu_2(\pi_{R_2}(v))$ for all $v \in \delta$.

**Example 4.3.** The join of the pcv-relations from Tables 5 and 6 under the probabilistic conjunction strategy $\otimes_{in}$ is given in Table 7.

**Table 6.** Second input pcv-relation of join

| • • •• | | •• | • • | • • •• |
|---|---|---|---|---|
| •• • ••• • ••• ••  $\beta$•••• • ••  S89   — | | 0.8 | 0.8 | $e_4$ |
| •• • ••• • ••• ••  $\beta$•••• • ••  S37   + | | 0.8 | 1.0 | $e_5$ |

**Table 7.** Result of join

| • ••• | | •• | • • | • ••• |
|---|---|---|---|---|
| ••• ••• • •• •••  $\alpha$•••• • ••    $\beta$•••• • ••  S89    +    — | | 0.56 | 0.72 | $(e_1 \vee e_2) \wedge e_4$ |

We next define the Cartesian product as a special case of join. Two tuple types $T_1$ and $T_2$ over the sets of top-level attribute names $\mathbf{A}_1$ and $\mathbf{A}_2$, respectively, are *Cartesian-product-compatible* iff $\mathbf{A}_1$ and $\mathbf{A}_2$ are disjoint. The *Cartesian product* of such types $T_1$ and $T_2$, denoted $T_1 \times T_2$, is the tuple type $T_1 \bowtie T_2$.

Let $r_1$ and $r_2$ be two pcv-relations of Cartesian-product-compatible types $R_1$ and $R_2$, respectively, and let $\otimes$ be a probabilistic conjunction strategy. The *Cartesian product of $r_1$ and $r_2$ under* $\otimes$, denoted $r_1 \times^\otimes r_2$, is the pcv-relation $r_1 \bowtie^\otimes r_2$ of type $R_1 \times R_2$.

## 4.3   Union, Intersection, and Difference

We now define the union, intersection, and difference operation on pcv-relations.

Let $r_1 = (\delta_1, \mu_1)$ and $r_2 = (\delta_2, \mu_2)$ be two pcv-relations of the same type $R$. Let $\otimes / \oplus / \ominus$ be a probabilistic conjunction/disjunction/difference strategy.

The *union of $r_1$ and $r_2$ under* $\oplus$, denoted $r_1 \cup^{\oplus} r_2$, is the pcv-relation $(\delta, \mu)$ of type $R$, where:

- $\delta = \{v \in \delta_1 - \delta_2 \mid \mu_1(v) \oplus \bot \neq \bot\} \cup \{v \in \delta_2 - \delta_1 \mid \bot \oplus \mu_2(v) \neq \bot\} \cup$
  $\{v \in \delta_1 \cap \delta_2 \mid \mu_1(v) \oplus \mu_2(v) \neq \bot\}$,

- $\mu(v) = \begin{cases} \mu_1(v) \oplus \bot & \text{if } v \in \delta_1 - \delta_2 \\ \bot \oplus \mu_2(v) & \text{if } v \in \delta_2 - \delta_1 \\ \mu_1(v) \oplus \mu_2(v) & \text{if } v \in \delta_1 \cap \delta_2. \end{cases}$

**Example 4.4.** The union of the pcv-relations from Tables 5 and 8 under the probabilistic disjunction strategy $\oplus_{pc}$ is given in Table 9.

**Table 8.** Second input pcv-relation of union

| •••• | | •• | •• | •••• |
|---|---|---|---|---|
| •• • ••• • •••• | $\alpha$•• ••• •• | 0.2 | 0.3 | $e_6$ |
| S89 | + | | | |
| •• • ••• • •••• | $\alpha$•• ••• •• | 0.3 | 0.4 | $e_7$ |
| S37 | − | | | |

**Table 9.** Result of union

| •••• | | •• | •• | •••• |
|---|---|---|---|---|
| •• • ••• • •••• | $\alpha$•• ••• •• | 0.7 | 0.9 | $e_1 \vee e_2 \vee e_6$ |
| S89 | + | | | |
| •• • ••• • •••• | $\alpha$•• ••• •• | 0.3 | 0.4 | $e_7$ |
| S37 | − | | | |
| •• • ••• • •••• | $\alpha$•• ••• •• | 0.5 | 0.7 | $e_3$ |
| S64 | − | | | |

The *intersection of $r_1$ and $r_2$ under* $\otimes$, denoted $r_1 \cap^{\otimes} r_2$, is the pcv-relation $(\delta, \mu)$ of type $R$, where:

- $\delta = \{v \in \delta_1 \cap \delta_2 \mid \mu_1(v) \otimes \mu_2(v) \neq \bot\}$,

- $\mu(v) = \mu_1(v) \otimes \mu_2(v)$.

The *difference of $r_1$ and $r_2$ under* $\ominus$, denoted $r_1 -^{\ominus} r_2$, is the pcv-relation $(\delta, \mu)$ of type $R$, where:

- $\delta = \{v \in \delta_1 - \delta_2 \mid \mu_1(v) \ominus \bot \neq \bot\} \cup \{v \in \delta_1 \cap \delta_2 \mid \mu_1(v) \ominus \mu_2(v) \neq \bot\}$,

- $\mu(v) = \begin{cases} \mu_1(v) \ominus \bot & \text{if } v \in \delta_1 - \delta_2 \\ \mu_1(v) \ominus \mu_2(v) & \text{if } v \in \delta_1 \cap \delta_2. \end{cases}$

### 4.4   Relationship to Classical Relational Algebra

It turns out that pcv-relations and the algebra on pcv-relations properly extend classical relations and the classical relational algebra.

Obviously, each tuple $t$ in a classical relation $r$ can be expressed by the pcv-tuple $\varepsilon(t) = [\text{data}: t, \text{lb}: 1, \text{ub}: 1, \text{path}: e_t]$ with $e_t \in \mathcal{B}$ in an appropriate pcv-relation $\varepsilon(r)$. Hence, it now remains to show that the results of our algebraic operations on such pcv-relations corresponds to the results of the classical algebraic operations on the original classical relations.

Note first that each event $t.\text{path}$ in a pcv-tuple $t$ with $[t.\text{lb}, t.\text{ub}] = [1, 1]$ is logically equivalent to $\top$. Moreover, we have the following result.

**Lemma 4.5.** *Let $\otimes$, $\oplus$, and $\ominus$ be the probabilistic combination strategies for any case among ignorance, independence, and positive correlation. Then, the result of applying $\otimes$, $\oplus$, and $\ominus$ to the probabilistic pairs $\bot$ and $\top$ is given in Fig. 1.*

| $\otimes$ | $\bot$ | $\top$ |
|---|---|---|
| $\bot$ | $\bot$ | $\bot$ |
| $\top$ | $\bot$ | $\top$ |

| $\oplus$ | $\bot$ | $\top$ |
|---|---|---|
| $\bot$ | $\bot$ | $\top$ |
| $\top$ | $\top$ | $\top$ |

| $\ominus$ | $\bot$ | $\top$ |
|---|---|---|
| $\bot$ | $\bot$ | $\bot$ |
| $\top$ | $\top$ | $\bot$ |

**Fig. 1.** Probabilistic combinations of $\bot$ and $\top$

This result easily shows that under the probabilistic combination strategies for the cases ignorance, independence, and positive correlation, our selection, projection, renaming, join, Cartesian product, union, intersection, and difference on the pcv-relations $\varepsilon(r)$ correspond to the classical selection, projection, renaming, join, Cartesian product, union, intersection, and difference, respectively, on the original classical relations $r$.

### 4.5   Computational Complexity

We now show that under certain assumptions, the introduced operations on pcv-relations can be done in polynomial time in the size of the input relations. The results of this section are implicit in [18].

Let $KB \subseteq KB^*(a, b)$ be a dependence information on two distinct basic events $a$ and $b$. The satisfiability check for $KB$ is *polynomial-time-computable* iff the satisfiability of $KB \cup \{(a, [l_1, u_1]), (b, [l_2, u_2])\}$ can be decided in polynomial time in the input size of $l_1, u_1, l_2, u_2$. The probabilistic conjunction (resp., disjunction, difference) strategy for $KB$ is *polynomial-time-computable* iff $(a, [l_1, u_1]) \otimes_{KB}$ $(b, [l_2, u_2])$ (resp., $(a, [l_1, u_1]) \oplus_{KB} (b, [l_2, u_2])$, $(a, [l_1, u_1]) \ominus_{KB} (b, [l_2, u_2])$) can be computed in polynomial time in the input size of $l_1, u_1, l_2, u_2$.

**Example 4.6.** The satisfiability checks and the probabilistic combination strategies for the cases ignorance, independence, positive correlation, left implication, and mutual exclusion are all polynomial-time-computable.

In the sequel, we implicitly assume that all involved satisfiability checks and probabilistic combination strategies are polynomial-time-computable. Our first result shows that then all unary operations can be done in polynomial time.

**Theorem 4.7.** *a) Given a not necessarily compact pcv-relation $r$ of type $R$, and a commutative and associative probabilistic disjunction strategy $\oplus$, the compaction $\kappa^{\oplus}(r)$ can be computed in polynomial time in the input size of $r$.*

*b) Given a pcv-relation $r$ of type $R$, a selection condition $\phi$ applicable to $R$, and a renaming condition $N$ for $R$, both the selection $\sigma_{\phi}(r)$ and the renaming $\rho_N(r)$ can be computed in linear time in the input size of $r$.*

*c) Given a pcv-relation $r$ of type $R$, a subtype $S$ of $R$, and a commutative and associative probabilistic disjunction strategy $\oplus$, the projection $\pi_S^{\oplus}(r)$ can be computed in polynomial time in the input size of $r$.*

The next result deals with the binary operations on pcv-relations.

**Theorem 4.8.** *a) Given two pcv-relations $r_1$ and $r_2$ of join-compatible (resp., Cartesian-product-compatible) types $R_1$ and $R_2$, and a probabilistic conjunction strategy $\otimes$, the join $r_1 \bowtie^{\otimes} r_2$ (resp., Cartesian product $r_1 \times^{\otimes} r_2$) can be computed in polynomial time in the input size of $r_1$ and $r_2$.*

*b) Given two pcv-relations $r_1$ and $r_2$ of the same type $R$, and a probabilistic conjunction (resp., disjunction, difference) strategy $\otimes$ (resp., $\oplus$, $\ominus$), the intersection $r_1 \cap^{\otimes} r_2$ (resp., union $r_1 \cup^{\oplus} r_2$, difference $r_1 -^{\ominus} r_2$) can be computed in polynomial time in the input size of $r_1$ and $r_2$.*

Note that the same results also hold for the generalization of our algebraic operations to DYNAMIC DEPENDENCE, if we impose further restrictions on the events in the input relations. For example, if we assume that all events are conjunctions of basic events, or that all events are disjunctions of basic events, or that all events are defined on pairwise disjoint sets of basic events (in these cases, for any $KB \subseteq KB^{\star}(a,b)$, the concrete dependence information $\{F \in KB^{\star}(a,b) \mid KB \cup \{e_1 \rightarrow a, a \rightarrow e_1, e_2 \rightarrow b, b \rightarrow e_2\} \models F\}$ can be computed in polynomial time in the input size of $a$ and $b$).

## 5  Query Equivalences

We now concentrate on query equivalences. We implicitly assume that all involved conjunction and disjunction strategies are commutative and associative.

Our first result shows that the join operation can be reduced to renaming, Cartesian product, selection, and projection like in classical relational algebra.

**Theorem 5.1.** *Let $r_1$ and $r_2$ be pcv-relations of join-compatible types $R_1$ and $R_2$, respectively. Let $\otimes$ and $\oplus$ be a probabilistic conjunction and disjunction strategy. Let $\mathbf{A}_1$ and $\mathbf{A}_2$ denote the sets of top-level attribute names of $R_1$ and $R_2$, respectively. Let $\rho_N$ replace each $A \in \mathbf{A}_1 \cap \mathbf{A}_2$ by the new attribute name $A'$. Let $\phi$ be the conjunction of all $x.A' = x.A$ with $A \in \mathbf{A}_1 \cap \mathbf{A}_2$. Let $R = R_1 \bowtie R_2$.*

$$r_1 \bowtie^{\otimes} r_2 = \pi_R^{\oplus}(\sigma_{\phi}(\rho_N(r_1) \times^{\otimes} r_2)). \tag{1}$$

We next show that most other query equivalences of the classical relational algebra also carry over to our algebra on pcv-relations. The following theorem shows that selections with respect to conjunctive selection conditions can be decomposed, and that sequences of selections can be reordered.

**Theorem 5.2.** *Let $r$ be a pcv-relation of type $R$. Let $\phi_1$ and $\phi_2$ be two selection conditions that are applicable to $R$.*

$$\sigma_{\phi_1 \wedge \phi_2}(r) = \sigma_{\phi_1}(\sigma_{\phi_2}(r)) \tag{2}$$

$$\sigma_{\phi_1}(\sigma_{\phi_2}(r)) = \sigma_{\phi_2}(\sigma_{\phi_1}(r)). \tag{3}$$

The next result shows that sequences of projections can be reordered and that certain selections can be pushed through projections.

**Theorem 5.3.** *Let $r$ be a pcv-relation of type $R$. Let $T$ be a subtype of $R$ and let $S$ be a subtype of $T$. Let $\phi$ be a probability-free selection condition applicable to $T$. Let $\oplus$ be a probabilistic disjunction strategy.*

$$\pi_S^{\oplus}(\pi_T^{\oplus}(r)) = \pi_S^{\oplus}(r) \tag{4}$$

$$\pi_T^{\oplus}(\sigma_{\phi}(r)) = \sigma_{\phi}(\pi_T^{\oplus}(r)). \tag{5}$$

The following theorem shows that selections and projections can be pushed through renaming operations.

**Theorem 5.4.** *Let $r$ be a pcv-relation of type $R$. Let $N$ be a renaming condition for $R$. Let $\phi$ be a selection condition applicable to $\rho_N(R)$ and let $S$ be a subtype of $\rho_N(R)$. Let $\phi'$ and $S'$ be obtained from $\phi$ and $S$, respectively, by performing the renaming $\rho_N^{-1}$. Let $\oplus$ be a probabilistic disjunction strategy.*

$$\sigma_{\phi}(\rho_N(r)) = \rho_N(\sigma_{\phi'}(r)) \tag{6}$$

$$\pi_S^{\oplus}(\rho_N(r)) = \rho_N(\pi_{S'}^{\oplus}(r)). \tag{7}$$

The next theorem shows that joins are commutative and associative, and that certain selections and projections can be pushed through join operations.

**Theorem 5.5.** *Let $r_1$, $r_2$, and $r_3$ be pcv-relations of the pairwise join-compatible types $R_1$, $R_2$, and $R_3$, respectively. Let $\otimes$ and $\oplus$ be conjunction and disjunction strategies such that $\otimes$ is distributive over $\oplus$. Let $\phi_1$ and $\phi_2$ be probability-free selection conditions that are applicable to $R_1$ and $R_2$, respectively. Let $S$ be a subtype of $R_1 \bowtie R_2$. Let $\mathbf{A}_1$, $\mathbf{A}_2$, and $\mathbf{A}$ denote the sets of top-level attribute names of $R_1$, $R_2$, and $S$, respectively. Let the tuple type $S_1$ over $(\mathbf{A} \cup \mathbf{A}_2) \cap \mathbf{A}_1$ be defined by $S_1.A = S.A$ for all $A \in (\mathbf{A} - \mathbf{A}_2) \cap \mathbf{A}_1$ and $S_1.A = R_1.A$ for all $A \in \mathbf{A}_1 \cap \mathbf{A}_2$, and let the tuple type $S_2$ over $(\mathbf{A} \cup \mathbf{A}_1) \cap \mathbf{A}_2$ be defined by $S_2.A = S.A$ for all $A \in (\mathbf{A} - \mathbf{A}_1) \cap \mathbf{A}_2$ and $S_2.A = R_2.A$ for all $A \in \mathbf{A}_1 \cap \mathbf{A}_2$.*

$$r_1 \bowtie^{\otimes} r_2 = r_2 \bowtie^{\otimes} r_1 \tag{8}$$

$$(r_1 \bowtie^{\otimes} r_2) \bowtie^{\otimes} r_3 = r_1 \bowtie^{\otimes} (r_2 \bowtie^{\otimes} r_3) \tag{9}$$

$$\sigma_{\phi_1 \wedge \phi_2}(r_1 \bowtie^{\otimes} r_2) = \sigma_{\phi_1}(r_1) \bowtie^{\otimes} \sigma_{\phi_2}(r_2) \tag{10}$$

$$\pi_S^{\oplus}(r_1 \bowtie^{\otimes} r_2) = \pi_S^{\oplus}(\pi_{S_1}^{\oplus}(r_1) \bowtie^{\otimes} \pi_{S_2}^{\oplus}(r_2)). \tag{11}$$

As Cartesian product is a special case of join, we get the following corollary.

**Corollary 5.6.** *Let $r_1$, $r_2$, and $r_3$ be pcv-relations of the pairwise Cartesian-product-compatible types $R_1$, $R_2$, and $R_3$, respectively. Let $\otimes$ and $\oplus$ be conjunction and disjunction strategies such that $\otimes$ is distributive over $\oplus$. Let $\phi_1$ and $\phi_2$ be probability-free selection conditions that are applicable to $R_1$ and $R_2$, respectively. Let $S$ be a subtype of $R_1 \times R_2$. Let $\mathbf{A}_1$, $\mathbf{A}_2$, and $\mathbf{A}$ denote the sets of top-level attribute names of $R_1$, $R_2$, and $S$, respectively. Let the tuple type $S_1$ over $\mathbf{A} \cap \mathbf{A}_1$ be defined by $S_1.A = S.A$ for all $A \in \mathbf{A} \cap \mathbf{A}_1$, and let the tuple type $S_2$ over $\mathbf{A} \cap \mathbf{A}_2$ be defined by $S_2.A = S.A$ for all $A \in \mathbf{A} \cap \mathbf{A}_2$.*

$$r_1 \times^{\otimes} r_2 = r_2 \times^{\otimes} r_1 \tag{12}$$

$$(r_1 \times^{\otimes} r_2) \times^{\otimes} r_3 = r_1 \times^{\otimes} (r_2 \times^{\otimes} r_3) \tag{13}$$

$$\sigma_{\phi_1 \wedge \phi_2}(r_1 \times^{\otimes} r_2) = \sigma_{\phi_1}(r_1) \times^{\otimes} \sigma_{\phi_2}(r_2) \tag{14}$$

$$\pi_S^{\oplus}(r_1 \times^{\otimes} r_2) = \pi_{S_1}^{\oplus}(r_1) \times^{\otimes} \pi_{S_2}^{\oplus}(r_2). \tag{15}$$

The next result finally shows that union and intersection operations are commutative and associative, and that certain selections can be pushed through union, intersection, and difference. Moreover, we show that projections can be pushed through union, and that intersection is a special case of join.

**Theorem 5.7.** *Let $r_1$, $r_2$, and $r_3$ be pcv-relations of type $R$. Let $\otimes / \oplus / \ominus$ be a probabilistic conjunction/disjunction/difference strategy. Let $\phi$ be a probability-free selection condition that is applicable to $R$ and let $S$ be a subtype of $R$.*

$$r_1 \cup^{\oplus} r_2 = r_2 \cup^{\oplus} r_1 \tag{16}$$

$$(r_1 \cup^{\oplus} r_2) \cup^{\oplus} r_3 = r_1 \cup^{\oplus} (r_2 \cup^{\oplus} r_3) \tag{17}$$

$$r_1 \cap^{\otimes} r_2 = r_2 \cap^{\otimes} r_1 \tag{18}$$

$$(r_1 \cap^{\otimes} r_2) \cap^{\otimes} r_3 = r_1 \cap^{\otimes} (r_2 \cap^{\otimes} r_3) \tag{19}$$

$$\sigma_{\phi}(r_1 \cup^{\oplus} r_2) = \sigma_{\phi}(r_1) \cup^{\oplus} \sigma_{\phi}(r_2) \tag{20}$$

$$\sigma_{\phi}(r_1 \cap^{\otimes} r_2) = \sigma_{\phi}(r_1) \cap^{\otimes} \sigma_{\phi}(r_2) \tag{21}$$

$$\sigma_{\phi}(r_1 -^{\ominus} r_2) = \sigma_{\phi}(r_1) -^{\ominus} \sigma_{\phi}(r_2) \tag{22}$$

$$\pi_S^{\oplus}(r_1 \cup^{\oplus} r_2) = \pi_S^{\oplus}(r_1) \cup^{\oplus} \pi_S^{\oplus}(r_2) \tag{23}$$

$$r_1 \cap^{\otimes} r_2 = r_1 \bowtie^{\otimes} r_2. \tag{24}$$

# 6    Query Optimization

In this section, we briefly concentrate on query optimization.

We have seen that most of the query equivalences of classical relational algebra also hold for the algebra on pcv-relations. Hence, we can use the same query equivalences like in classical relational algebra to move especially selections but also projections as much inside a given query expression as possible:

1. We can use (2) to break up conjunctive selection conditions.
2. We can use (3), (5), (6), (10), (14), (21), (20), and (22) to move selection operations as much inside the query expression as possible.
3. We can use (9), (13), (19), and (17) to structure the query expression in a better way.
4. We can use (4), (5), (7), (11), (15), and (23) to move projection operations as much inside the query expression as possible.

**Example 6.1.** Let $T$ be an atomic type. Let $R_1 = [A\colon T, B_1\colon T, C_1\colon T]$, $R_2 = [A\colon T, B_2\colon T, C_2\colon T]$, $R_3 = [A\colon T, B_3\colon T, C_3\colon T]$, $S_1 = [A\colon T, C_1\colon T]$, $S_2 = [A\colon T, C_2\colon T]$, $S_3 = [A\colon T, C_3\colon T]$, and $S_3 = [A\colon T, C_1\colon T, C_2\colon T, C_3\colon T]$ be tuple types. Let $r_1, r_2$, and $r_3$ be pcv-relations over $R_1$, $R_2$, and $R_3$, respectively. Let $\phi_1$ and $\phi_2$ denote the selection conditions $x.\mathsf{data}.C_1 = v$ and $x.\mathsf{data}.C_2 = x.\mathsf{data}.C_3$, respectively, where $v$ is a complex value of type $T$. Then, the query expression

$$\sigma_{\phi_1 \wedge \phi_2}(\pi_S^{\oplus_{pc}}((r_1 \bowtie^{\otimes_{pc}} r_2) \bowtie^{\otimes_{pc}} r_3))$$

can be transformed into the following equivalent query expression (since the conjunction strategy $\otimes_{pc}$ is distributive over the disjunction strategy $\oplus_{pc}$):

$$\pi_{S_1}^{\oplus_{pc}}(\sigma_{\phi_1}(r_1)) \bowtie^{\otimes_{pc}} \sigma_{\phi_2}(\pi_{S_2}^{\oplus_{pc}}(r_2) \bowtie^{\otimes_{pc}} \pi_{S_3}^{\oplus_{pc}}(r_3)).$$

## 7 Related Work

In this section, we give a brief comparison to related work in the literature.

Our approach generalizes annotated tuples of ProbView [12]. As argued in [12], ProbView generalizes various approaches (like, for example, [2,4]). Cavallo and Pittarelli [4] view relations in a (flat) relational database as probability distribution functions, where tuples in the same relation are viewed as pairwise disjoint events whose probabilities sum up to 1. Drawbacks of this approach have been pointed out in [5]. An extension of the model using probability intervals, which are viewed as constraints on the probabilities, is reviewed in [15]. Barbará et al. [2] have considered a probabilistic extension to the relational model, in which imprecise attributes are modeled as probability distributions over finite sets of values. Their approach assumes that key attributes are deterministic (have probability 1) and that non-key attributes in different relations, are independent. No probabilities can be assigned to outmost tuples.

Fuhr and Rölleke [7] consider a probabilistic version of NF2 relations, extending their approach for flat tuples [8], and define a relational algebra for this model. Probabilities are assigned to tuples and to values of nested tuples (that is, set-valued attributes), which are viewed as events that have an associated event expression. The algebraic operators manipulate tuples by combining value and event expressions appropriately. The probability of a derived tuple is computed from the probabilities of initial tuples by taking into consideration its event expression. The approach in [7] defines an intensional semantics in which probabilities are defined through possible worlds. The evaluation method assumes that in nondeterministic relations (that is, relations with uncertain tuples), joint occurrence of two different values is either always independent or impossible. Our approach has no such severe restriction (we do not make any independence or mutual exclusion assumptions). Furthermore, [7] does not use probability intervals but a single probability value. On the other hand, the algebra in [7] provides nest and unnest operators, which we have not done here.

We see as major drawbacks of the approach in [7] the above non-dependency assumption on relations, which is rarely met in practice, and that the evaluation of event expressions takes exponential time in general, owing to complicated probability sums which need to be computed—this seems the price to pay for a smooth intensional semantics, though.

The probabilistic database model of Dey and Sarkar [5] assigns each tuple in a (flat) relational database a probability value in a special attribute. The classical relational operations are defined adopting different assumptions on the relationship between tuples; in particular, join assumes independence; union and difference assume positive correlation; and compaction assumes disjointness or positive correlation. Our model is more general, since it has complex values, intervals, and allows different strategies (reflecting different relationships between tuples) to be used in the algebraic operations. Based on [5], a probabilistic extension to SQL is developed in [6].

Zimányi [19] presents an approach to querying probabilistic databases based on probabilistic first-order logic. A probabilistic database is axiomatized as a first-order probabilistic theory, which has a possible worlds semantics as in [10]. Tuples $t$ in relations have a trace formula $\phi$ attached, which intuitively selects the worlds in which $t$ is true. The classical relational algebra operations are defined using formulas and manipulate trace formulas. A query is evaluated in two steps: the first step yields a relation of tuples with trace formulas, which are then evaluated using the assertions of the probabilistic theory to obtain a probability for each tuple. Compared to our approach, [19] aims at flat databases and considers no probability intervals (but mentions a possible extension). The approach assumes complete independence of occurrences of distinct tuples in the same or different relations. Furthermore, as with most other approaches, no query equivalences are discussed.

## 8   Summary and Conclusion

In this paper, we generalized the annotated tuple approach in [12] to complex value databases [1]. We presented a probabilistic data model for complex values and defined an algebra on top of it. Moreover, we presented query equivalences and briefly discussed their use for query optimization. It turned out that most of the equivalences of classical relational algebra hold in this generalized model. Hence, many classical query optimization techniques carry over to our model.

Several issues remain for further investigation. One such issue are other operators besides those of classical relation algebra, such as NF2 nest and unnest or the operators in [7,5,2,15]. Moreover, it would be very interesting to more deeply investigate the relationship to purely extensional and purely intensional approaches to probabilistic databases. Finally, an intriguing issue is to extend our approach to object-oriented databases. To our knowledge, few approaches to probabilistic object-oriented databases have been proposed so far (see [11]).

## Acknowledgments

We are very grateful to V. S. Subrahmanian for fruitful discussions. We also want to thank the referees for their useful comments.

This work has been partially supported by an NSF-DAAD grant and the Austrian Science Fund Project N Z29-INF.

## References

1. S. Abiteboul, R. Hull, and V. Vianu. *Foundations of Databases*. Addison-Wesley, Reading, 1995.
2. D. Barbara, H. Garcia-Molina, and D. Porter. The management of probabilistic data. *IEEE Transactions on Knowledge and Data Engineering*, 4(5):387–502, 1992.
3. R. Carnap. *Logical Foundations of Probability*. University of Chicago Press, Chicago, 1950.
4. R. Cavallo and M. Pittarelli. The theory of probabilistic databases. In *Proceedings of the 13th International Conference on Very Large Databases*, pages 71–81. Morgan Kaufmann, 1987.
5. D. Dey and S. Sarkar. A probabilistic relational model and algebra. *ACM Transactions on Database Systems*, 21(3):339–369, 1996.
6. D. Dey and S. Sarkar. PSQL: A query language for probabilistic relational data. *Data & Knowledge Engineering*, 28:107–120, 1998.
7. N. Fuhr and T. Rölleke. A probabilistic NF2 relational algebra for integrated information retrieval and database systems. In *Proceedings of the 2nd World Conference on Integrated Design and Process Technology*, pages 17–30. Society for Design and Process Science, 1996.
8. N. Fuhr and T. Rölleke. A probabilistic relational algebra for the integration of information retrieval and database systems. *ACM Transactions on Information Systems*, 15(1):32–66, 1997.
9. H. Gaifman. Concerning measures in first order calculi. *Israel Journal of Mathematics*, 2:1–18, 1964.
10. J. Y. Halpern. An analysis of first-order logics of probability. *Artificial Intelligence*, 46(3):311–350, 1990.
11. Y. Kornatzky and S. E. Shimony. A probabilistic object-oriented data model. *Data & Knowledge Engineering*, 12:143–166, 1994.
12. L. V. S. Lakshmanan, N. Leone, R. Ross, and V. S. Subrahmanian. ProbView: A flexible probabilistic database system. *ACM Transactions on Database Systems*, 22(3):419–469, 1997.
13. T. Lukasiewicz. Local probabilistic deduction from taxonomic and probabilistic knowledge-bases over conjunctive events. *International Journal of Approximate Reasoning*, 21(1):23–61, 1999.
14. T. Lukasiewicz. Probabilistic deduction with conditional constraints over basic events. *Journal of Artificial Intelligence Research*, 10:199–241, 1999.
15. M. Pittarelli. An algebra for probabilistic databases. *IEEE Transactions on Knowledge and Data Engineering*, 6(2):293–303, 1994.

16. H.-J. Schek and P. Pistor. Data structures for an integrated data base management and information retrieval system. In *Proceedings of the 8th International Conference on Very Large Data Bases*, pages 197–207. Morgan Kaufmann, 1982.

17. D. Scott and P. Krauss. Assigning probabilities to logical formulas. In J. Hintikka and P. Suppes, editors, *Aspects of Inductive Logic*, pages 219–264. North-Holland, Amsterdam, 1966.

18. M. Walter. An extension of relational algebra to probabilistic complex values. Master's thesis, Universität Gießen, 1999.

19. E. Zimányi. Query evaluation in probabilistic relational databases. *Theoretical Computer Science*, 171(1–2):179–219, 1997.

# Persistent Turing Machines
# as a Model of Interactive Computation

Dina Q Goldin

Univ. of Massachusetts - Boston

**Abstract.** *Persistent Turing Machines* (PTMs) are multitape machines
with a persistent worktape preserved between interactions, whose inputs
and outputs are dynamically generated streams of tokens (strings). They
are a minimal extension of Turing Machines (TMs) that express interactive behavior. They provide a natural model for sequential interactive
computation such as single-user databases and intelligent agents.

PTM *behavior* is characterized *observationally*, by *input-output streams*;
the notions of *equivalence* and *expressiveness* for PTMs are defined relative to its behavior. Four different models of PTM behavior are examined:
*language-based*, *automaton-based*, *function-based*, and *environment-based*.
A number of special subclasses of PTMs are identified; several expressiveness results are obtained, both for the general class of all PTMs and for
the special subclasses, proving the conjecture in [We2] that interactive
computing devices are more expressive than TMs.

The methods and tools for formalizing PTM computation developed in
this paper can serve as a basis for a more comprehensive theory of interactive computation.

## 1    Introduction

### 1.1    PTMs vs. Other Models of Computation

*Persistent Turing Machines* (PTMs) are multitape machines with a persistent
worktape preserved between interactions, whose inputs and outputs are dynamically generated streams of tokens (strings) [GW]. They are a minimal extension
of Turing Machines (TMs) that express interactive behavior. They model services over time provided by persistent, object-oriented, or reactive systems that
cannot be expressed by computable functions [MP,We2,WG2,WG3]. They also
provide a natural model for single-user databases, where the current database
instance is modeled as the contents of the persistent worktape.

TMs and PTMs are abstract computing devices useful for representing different forms of computational behavior: TMs model *algorithmic* behavior, where
the output is modeled as a function or a relation of the input, whereas PTM-
s model *sequential interactive behavior* [WG1], where the computing device or
agent *evolves* as it processes the inputs. This evolution is represented by the
change in the contents of the PTM worktape, so PTM output tokens are a
function of both the input tokens and of the evolving worktape contents.

K.-D. Schewe, B. Thalheim (Eds.): FoIKS 2000, LNCS 1762, pp. 116–135, 2000.

## 1.2  PTM Behavior and Expressiveness

PTM behavior is characterized by input-output streams; PTM equivalence and expressiveness are defined relative to its behavior. These are *observation-based* notions, just as for process modeling [Mil]. In fact, a PTM computation can be viewed as a process and modeled with a labeled transition system (LTS) whose individual transitions are Turing-computable and whose states and actions have specific TM-related semantics.

Unlike inputs or outputs, the worktape contents is not directly observable. Though it affects the output, it does not participate directly in the notion of PTM behavior, which is observation-based. Any attempt to model PTM computations with TMs, by making the worktape contents an explicit part of the input, would thus fail to produce models which are equivalent if and only if the corresponding PTMs are.

Models of computation for PTMs, just as models of computation for TMs, can be equivalently expressed by languages, automata, and function-based models. Whereas models of computation for TMs are string-based, models for PTMs are based in input-output streams. An environment-based model of behavior is also defined for PTMs; there has been no analog of this notion for TMs, whose environment is always *algorithmic*. We use these four models of behavior to obtain several expressiveness results, both for the general class of PTMs and for a number of special subclasses.

## 1.3  PTMs as Interaction Machines

PTMs are sequential interaction machines (SIMS) which inherit from TMs the restriction that input tokens must be discrete, and that any model of behavior must ignore time-depended aspects. They are therefore inappropriate for modeling some real-time and embedded devices or physical control processes, whose expressiveness requires the full generality of SIMs. Furthermore, there are multistream interactive behaviors, such as distributed database systems or airline reservation systems, which cannot be modeled by SIMs at all, requiring a model with even more expressiveness – MIMs [WG2,WG3].

We expect that PTM-based models of computation can be generalized to model all sequential computation. We believe that a proper formalization of the notion of a PTM environment will be an important part of this effort. Though there is no "Silver Bullet" in the absolute sense, the problems of correctness testing and verification for interactive software systems may prove tractable – once we are willing to assume reasonable constraints on the system's environment. Notions of equivalence and expressiveness that are *relative* to a PTM's environment, introduced in this work, should prove to be important for formalizing SIMs.

We also expect that single- and multi- agent computation can be modeled within a single formalism. The methods and tools for formalizing PTM computation developed in this paper will serve as a basis for a more comprehensive theory of interactive computation over these models. The resulting models of interactive computation should aid in the formalization of the important aspects of interactive computation, in a hardware- and application- independent fashion.

## 1.4   Summary

Section 2 provides some background concepts and defines PTMs. Section 3 outlines the different models of PTM behavior, identifies several PTM subclasses, and summarizes the expressiveness results about them. Sections 4 through 7 give the details of the four models and obtain the corresponding expressiveness results, followed by a conclusion with a discussion of future work.

In this work, we only consider deterministic TMs and PTMs. Formalization of non-deterministic PTMs involves some interesting and unexpected anomalies which are briefly mentioned in section 8.2; a full treatment of this issue deserves a separate paper.

# 2   Background and Definitions

## 2.1   Turing Machines as Non-interactive Computing Devices

*Turing Machines* are finite computing devices that transform input into output strings by sequences of state transitions [HU]. As is commonly done, we assume that a TM has multiple tapes: a read-only *input* tape, a write-only *output* tape and one or more *internal* work tapes. The contents of the input tape is said to be under the control of the *environment*, whereas the other two tapes are controlled by the PTM. Furthermore, the contents of the input and output tapes is *observable* whereas the work tape is not.

TM computations for a given input are *history-independent* and reproducible, since TMs always start in the same initial state, and since their input is completely determined prior to the start of the computation (they *shut out the world* during the computation). This property of "shutting out the world" during computation characterizes Turing Machines as *noninteractive*:

**Definition 2.1.** Interactive computing devices *admit input/output actions during the process of computation [WG3].*

It is interesting to note that Turing foresaw interactive computation in his seminal paper on TMs [Tu], where he made a distinction between *automatic machines*, now known as TMs, and *choice machines*, which allow choices by an external operator. However, since the motivation for computational devices in [Tu] was to compute functions from naturals to naturals, choice machines were not an appropriate model to use, and they have not been considered since.

## 2.2   Persistent Turing Machines (PTMs)

*Persistence of state* typifies computation as diverse as databases, object-oriented systems, and intelligent agents [AB,ZM,RN]. In this section, we extend TMs by introducing persistence. In the next section, this is coupled with an extension of computational semantics from string- to stream-based, to result in a model for sequential interactive computation [WG1].

**Definition 2.2.** *A* Persistent Turing Machine *(PTM) is a multitape Turing Machine (TM) with a* persistent work tape *whose contents is preserved between successive TM computations. A PTM's persistent work tape is known as its* memory; *the contents of the memory before and after (a single TM) computation is known as the PTM's* state.

*Note*: PTM states are not to be confused with TM states. Unlike for TMs, the set of PTM states is infinite, represented by strings of unbounded length.

Since the worktape (state) at the beginning of a PTM computation step is not always the same, the output of a PTM $M$ at the end of the computation step depends both on the input and on the worktape. As a result, $M$ defines a *partial recursive function* $f_M$ from (*input, worktape*) pairs to (*output, worktape*) pairs of strings, $f_M : I \times W \to O \times W$.

*Example 2.1.* An *answering machine A* is a PTM whose worktape contains a sequence of recorded messages and whose operations are `record message`, `playback`, and `erase`. The Turing- computable function for $A$ is:

$f_A(\texttt{record } Y, X) = (\texttt{ok}, XY); \; f_A(\texttt{playback}, X) = (X, X);$
$f_A(\texttt{erase}, X) = (\texttt{done}, \epsilon).$

Note that both the content of the worktape and the length of input for recorded messages are unbounded. □

An Answering Machine can be viewed as a very simple intelligent agent [RN], whose memory is stored on the worktape. This agent is not *goal-oriented* or *utility-based*; nevertheless, we will show that it exhibits a degree of *autonomy*, which is beyond the capacity of algorithmic agents. A database could also serve as a useful example above, where the current database instance is modeled as the contents of the persistent worktape.

## 2.3   PTM Computation

Individual computational steps of a PTM correspond to TM computations and are string-based. However, the semantics of PTM computations are *stream-based*, where the stream tokens are strings over some alphabet $\Sigma$. The input stream is generated by the *environment* and the output stream is generated by the PTM. The streams have *dynamic* (late, lazy) evaluation semantics, where the next value is not generated until the previous one is consumed. The *coinductive* definition for such streams can be found in [BM].

A *PTM computation* is an (infinite) sequence of Turing-computable steps, consuming input stream tokens and generating output stream tokens:

**Definition 2.3.** *Given a PTM M defining a function $f_M$ and an input stream $(i_1, i_2, \ldots)$, a computation of M consists of a sequence of computational steps and produces an output stream $(o_1, o_2, \ldots)$. The state of the PTM evolves during the computation, starting with the initial state $w_0$; w.l.o.g., we can assume that $w_0$ is an empty string:*

$$f_M(i_1, w_0) = (o_1, w_1); f_M(i_2, w_1) = (o_2, w_2); f_M(i_3, w_2) = (o_3, w_3); \ldots \square$$

*Example 2.2.* For the Answering Machine $A$ (example 2.1), the input stream (record A, erase, record BC, record D, playback, ...) generates the output stream (ok, done, ok, ok, BCD, ...); the state evolves as follows: ($\epsilon$, A, $\epsilon$, BC, BCD, BCD, ...). $\square$

This example represents a single computation of $A$; the fact that input and output actions on streams take place in the middle of computation characterizes PTMs as interactive computing devices. The fact that only a single input stream is involved characterizes PTMs as *sequential interactive devices*, or SIMs [WG1]. Other examples of sequential interactive computation include the lifetime of a single-user database, driving home from work [Wel], holding a dialogue with an intelligent agent [RN], and playing two-person games [Abr].

## 2.4    PTM Interaction Streams

The interaction of PTMs with their *environment* is described by *interaction (I/O) streams*, which interleave inputs and outputs.

**Definition 2.4.** Interaction (I/O) streams *have the form* $(i_1, o_1), (i_2, o_2), \ldots$, *where i's are input tokens generated by the environment (or an observer) and o's are output tokens generated by the PTM (figure 1).*

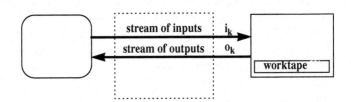

**Fig. 1.** The interaction stream between a PTM and its environment/observer.

Due to the dynamic evaluation semantics of PTM input streams, it is assumed that each input token $i_k$ is generated after the previous output $o_{k-1}$. As a result, later input tokens may depend on earlier outputs and on external (exogenous) events in the environment. Furthermore, outputs may depend not only on the corresponding input but on all earlier ones, resulting in *history dependent* behavior:

*Example 2.3.* The computation in example 2.2 leads to the following interaction stream:

```
(record A,ok),(erase,done),(record BC,ok),(record D,ok),
(playback,BCD),...
```

The fifth output BCD depends on the third and fourth inputs, illustrating *history dependence.* □

The history dependent behavior of PTMs cannot be expressed by TMs whose output is a function of the input. Though history dependence can be simulated in TMs by making the history an explicit part of the input, this would violate the observation-based PTM semantics. In process modeling, observation equivalence is known to be stronger than trace equivalence; similarly, forcing PTM state to be observable cannot be assumed to preserve the expressiveness of the computing device.

## 3    Towards Formalizing PTMs

Being able to determine when two computing devices are equivalent, or when one class of devices is more expressive than another, is an important part of any attempt to formalize a new model of computation. In this section, we formulate these notions in terms of a computing device's *behavior*, and formalize them for PTMs by providing specific models of PTM behavior.

### 3.1    Behaviors, Equivalence, and Expressiveness

The notions of *equivalence* and *expressiveness* of interactive computing devices are intimately related to the notion of their *behavior*, which is exhibited through its interactions with the environment.

*Example 3.1.* *TM behavior* consists of accepting input strings and returning output strings; this can alternately be modeled as a set of input/output pairs, or as a function from inputs to outputs. □

Any model of behavior induces a notion of equivalence for pairs of devices:

**Definition 3.1.** *Two computing devices are* equivalent *if their behavior is the same.*

Furthermore, the notion of equivalence leads to the notion of expressiveness for classes of devices:

**Definition 3.2.** *A class of computing devices $C_1$ is said to be* at least as expressive *as a class $C_2$ if, for every device in $C_2$, there exists an equivalent one in $C_1$. If the converse is not true, $C_1$ is said to be* more expressive *than $C_2$.*

*Example 3.2.* For every Finite State Automaton (FSA), there exists an equivalent Push-Down Automaton, but not vice versa [HU]. Therefore, PDAs are more expressive than FSAs. □

In this paper, we show that PTMs have a richer set of behaviors than TMs, and are therefore more expressive in precisely the same sense that PDAs are more expressive than FSAs in the example above.

## 3.2    Models of PTM Behavior

Just as for TMs, PTM behavior can be modeled in different ways. Whereas models of computation for TMs are based on strings, models for PTMs are based on *interaction streams* (section 2.4). For any PTM $M$, four different models of PTM behavior are examined:

- **Language-based:** $M$ is modeled by its *language*, which is the set of all interaction streams for $M$ (section 4).
- **Automaton-based:** $M$ is modeled by an infinite-state automaton whose edges are labeled by pairs of input/output strings; paths through this automaton are the interaction streams of $M$ (section 5).
- **Function-based:** $M$ is modeled by a recursively defined function from input to output streams; this function has coinductive evaluation semantics [BM], recursing infinitely without reaching a base case (section 6).
- **Environment-based:** $M$ is modeled by a set of finite or infinite interaction sequences that are produced by $M$'s *environment*; this gives us notions of behavior and equivalence that are relative to environments (section 7).

As for TMs, different models of PTM computation are convenient for obtaining different results about their expressiveness. In the next section, we define several specializations of PTMs, as a prelude to proving these results.

Note: Throughout this work, we are assuming that PTMs are deterministic (i.e., based on a deterministic TM). Though these models can be used for non-deterministic PTMs as well, we expect that the correspondence between them will not be as straightforward as in the deterministic case.

## 3.3    Special PTMs and Their Expressiveness

In general, a single computational step of a PTM $M$ is modeled by a computable function $f_M : I \times W \to O \times W$, where $I$, $O$, and $W$ are over $\Sigma^*$ (section 2.2). Several interesting subclasses of PTMs are defined in this section, arising from subcases of this general model.

- **Amnesic PTMs** (section 4.2) ignore the contents of their memory, behaving as if each computational step starts in the same state.
- **Finite-memory PTMs** (section 4.3) have a bound on the amount of available memory.

- **Finite-state PTMs** (section 4.3) have a finite number of states (i.e., $W$ is finite).
- **Simple PTMs** have finite sets of input/output tokens (i.e., $I$ and $O$ are finite). **Binary PTMs** are a subclass of simple PTMs where both $I$ and $O$ have size 2.
- **Consistent PTMs** produce the same output token for a given input token everywhere within a single interaction stream; different interaction streams may have different outputs for a given input [Kos].

Here are some of the results that hold for PTMs and their subclasses:

- Amnesic PTMs have the same expressiveness as sequences of TM computations (section 4).
- Finite-memory PTMs have the same expressiveness as finite-state PTMs (section 4).
- Simple finite-state PTMs have the same expressiveness as finite-state transducers (section 5).
- Simple (binary) finite-state PTMs are less expressive than simple (binary) PTMs (section 5).
- PTMs have the same expressiveness as *effective labeled transition systems* (LTSs), a subclass of LTSs (section 5).
- Amnesic PTMs are less expressive than all PTMs, constituting the lowest level of an *infinite expressiveness hierarchy* for PTMs (section 7).

The remainder of this paper, up to the concluding section, is devoted to a discussion of these results. Note that as a corollary of these results, we prove the conjecture in [We2] that interactive computing devices are more expressive than TMs.

# 4    Language-Based Model of PTM Computation

In this section, we consider the *language-based* model of PTM computation and derive related results summarized in section 3.3.

## 4.1    PTM Languages

The behavior of TMs and other string-based computing devices can be described by a language, which is a set of strings over some finite alphabet. For example, the language of a finite state automaton is the set of strings it accepts [HU]. A set-based notion of languages can likewise be defined for PTMs; *PTM languages* are stream-based rather than string-based.

**Definition 4.1.** *The set of all interaction streams (definition 2.4) for a PTM $M$ constitutes its* language, $\mathcal{L}(M)$.

Despite the change in semantics from strings to streams, the definitions of *equivalence* and *expressiveness* apply to PTMs just as to other computing devices for which a language is defined:

**Definition 4.2. (language-based PTM equivalence and expressiveness)**
*Let $M_1$ and $M_2$ be computing devices whose behavior is modeled by sets of interaction streams; $M_1$ and $M_2$ are equivalent iff $\mathcal{L}(M_1) = \mathcal{L}(M_2)$.*

*Let $C_1$ and $C_2$ be classes of computing devices whose behavior is modeled by sets of interaction streams; $C_2$ is more expressive than $C_1$ if the set of all languages for members of $C_1$ is a proper subset of that for $C_2$.* □

## 4.2    Amnesic PTMs vs. TMs

*Amnesic PTMs* ignore the contents of their memory, behaving as if each computational step starts in the same state. As a result, computations of amnesic PTMs are not history dependent (hence their name).

**Definition 4.3.** *A PTM M is* amnesic *iff $f_M(i, w) = f_M(i, w_0)$ for all inputs $i$ and states $w$, where $w_0$ is M's initial state.* □

In order to compare amnesic PTM languages to those of multitape TMs, we need to consider TM computations over streams of input strings:

**Definition 4.4. (stream-based TM computation)** *Given a TM M defining a function $f_M$ from input to output strings, and an input stream $(i_1, i_2, \ldots)$, a computation of M produces an output stream $(o_1, o_2, \ldots)$, where $f_M(i_k) = o_k$ for each $k$.* □

Amnesic PTMs are no more expressive than stream-based TMs:

**Proposition 4.1.** *The behavior of any amnesic PTM is equivalent to a sequence of TM computations for the corresponding TM.*

**Proof:** Given an input stream $(i_1, i_2, \ldots)$, a computation of an amnesic PTM produces an output stream $(o_1, o_2, \ldots)$, where:

$$f_M(i_1, w_0) = (o_1, w_1); f_M(i_2, w_1) = f_M(i_2, w_0) = (o_2, w_2);$$
$$f_M(i_3, w_2) = f_M(i_3, w_0) = (o_3, w_3); \ldots$$

Since $w_0$ is assumed empty, each computation step of M is the same as a computation of the TM that corresponds to $M$, let us call it $M_0$: for all $k$, $f_{M_0}(i_k) = f_M(i_k, w_0) = o_k$. □

The converse of proposition 4.1 is not true; an arbitrary multitape TM may write something to its work tape and fail to erase it at the end of the computation, so the corresponding PTM is not necessarily amnesic. Nevertheless, it is easy to show that PTMs are at least as expressive as TMs.

**Proposition 4.2.** *For each TM M, there exists a TM $M'$ so that M's stream-based behavior is equivalent to the amnesic PTM based on $M'$.*

**Proof:** For any TM, an equivalent one can be constructed, that always erases its worktape at the end of the computation, guaranteeing that the behavior of the corresponding PTM is amnesic. □

**Theorem 4.1.** *Amnesic PTMs have the same expressiveness as sequences of TM computations.*

**Proof:** Follows from propositions 4.1 and 4.2. □

### 4.3   Finite-State and Finite-Memory PTMs

*Finite-memory PTMs* have a bound on the amount of available memory; this refers to the number of bits that may be stored persistently, without implying a bound on the overall size of all internal worktapes. In contrast, *finite-state PTMs* have a finite number of states; that is to say, the set of all states reachable from the initial state via some sequence of input tokens is finite.

**Theorem 4.2.** *Finite-memory PTMs have the same expressiveness as finite-state PTMs.*

**Proof:** Let $M$ be a finite-memory PTM. If $n$ is the memory bound for $M$, and $c$ is the size of $M$'s alphabet $\Sigma$, then $M$ can have at most $cn$ states. Conversely, let $M$ be a finite-state PTM. If $W$ is the set of $M$'s states and $k$ is the size of $W$, then at most $\log k$ characters are needed to represent any state in $W$. Therefore, one can construct a PTM equivalent to $M$ which has a bound on the amount of memory available to it. □

## 5   Automata-Theoretic Model of PTM Behavior

In this section, we adopt an automata-theoretic view of PTMs, as transducers over an infinite state space. Just as for TMs, this view complements the language-based view (section 4).

### 5.1   Finite-State Transducers and Their Index

All automata are state-based, with labeled transitions between states, and possibly with values associated with states themselves. *Finite-state automata* (FSAs) are the best known and simplest automata, where the set of states is finite, the transition labels are single characters from a finite input alphabet, and the states are associated with one of two values, `accept` and `reject` [HU].

An FSA's *index* is a metric for classifying FSAs; it refers to the number of equivalence classes induced by the FSA's language:

**Definition 5.1. (FSA index)** *Given any FSA A over an alphabet $\Sigma$, where $L(A)$ is the set of all strings accepted by A, let $\mathcal{P}(A)$ be a partition of $\Sigma^*$ into equivalence classes, defined as follows:*

> *for any $x, y \in \Sigma^*$, x and y belong to the same equivalence class in $\mathcal{P}(A)$ iff for all $w \in \Sigma^*$, $xw \in L(A)$ iff $yw \in L(A)$.*

*Then, the size of $\mathcal{P}(A)$ is known as A's index.* □

The index of FSAs is known to be finite; this is the *Myhill-Nerode theorem* [HU].

*Finite-state transducers* (FSTs) extend FSAs, by replacing the binary value at each state with an *output character* from a finite output alphabet $\Delta$. These output characters can be associated with states, as for *Moore machines*, or with transitions, as for *Mealy machines*. For either Moore or Mealy machines, the output is a sequence of output characters of the same length as the input. These two types of FSTs are known to have the same expressiveness [HU]. FST input may also be an infinite stream of characters; the output will be another character stream.

The notion of *index* can be extended to transducers, as follows:

**Definition 5.2. (Index of transducers)** *Given any transducer $A$ over sets of input/output tokens $\Sigma$ and $\Delta$, which maps sequences over $\Sigma$ to sequences over $\Delta$ by a mapping $\mu_A$, let $\mathcal{P}(A)$ be a partition of $\Sigma^*$ into equivalence classes, defined as follows:*

> *for any $x, y \in \Sigma^*$, $x$ and $y$ belong to the same equivalence class in $\mathcal{P}(A)$ iff for all $w \in \Sigma^*$, the last tokens of $\mu_A(x.w)$ and $\mu_A(y.w)$ are the same.*

*Then, the size of $\mathcal{P}(A)$ is known as $A$'s* index. $\square$

The definition above applies whether the set of tokens is finite (i.e., an alphabet) or infinite (i.e., a set of strings), and whether the set of states is finite or infinite. In the case of FSTs, when the sets of tokens and of states are both finite, the index is also known to be finite [TB].

## 5.2 PTMs vs. FSTs

For any *finite-state simple PTM $M$* (section 3.3) with a computable function $f_M$, one can construct an equivalent stream-based *Mealy machine $A$* (section 5.1) and vice versa. The intuition behind such a construction is as follows:

- $M$'s states correspond to $A$'s states, where $w_0$ is $A$'s initial state;
- for any two states $w_1$ and $w_2$, and any input/output pair of tokens $i, o$, $f_M(i, w_1) = (o, w_2)$ iff there is a transition there is a transition between $w_1$ and $w_2$ in $A$ labeled "$i/o$" iff $f_M(i, w_1) = (o, w_2)$.

As a result, these two classes of devices have the same expressiveness:

**Proposition 5.1.** *Finite-state simple PTMs have the same expressiveness as stream-based Mealy machines.*

**Proof:** Follows from the construction above. $\square$

As a corollary to proposition 5.1, finite-state simple PTMs have a finite index (definition 5.2). The same is not true of the class of all simple PTMs:

**Proposition 5.2.** *There exist simple PTMs whose index is infinite.*

**Proof:** The proof is by construction. Let $M$ be a binary PTM which works as follows:

> while $M$'s input stream equals the "template" $\sigma = 0101^2 01^3 01^4 0 \ldots$, $M$'s output bits are all 1's; as soon as there is an "incorrect" input bit, $M$'s output becomes all 0's.

Let $\mu(x)$ be the output string produces by $M$ for any binary input sequence $x$. Let $L$ be the set of all prefixes of $\sigma$ that end in 0; $L$ is countably infinite. It is easy to see that given any pair $x, y$ of distinct elements of $L$, there exists a binary sequence $w$ of the form $1^n$ for some $n \geq 1$ such that the last character of $\mu(x.w)$ is different from the last character of $\mu(y.w)$. $\square$

**Theorem 5.1.** *The class of simple (binary) PTMs is more expressive than the class of (binary) FSTs.*

**Proof:** Follows from propositions 5.1 and 5.2. $\square$

Note that for any given state of any simple PTM, the transition relation is finite (its size is limited by the number of pairs of input and output tokens), just as for an FST. The extra expressiveness of simple PTMs is therefore gained not from the Turing-computability of the individual transitions, but from the unboundedness of the internal state!

## 5.3    PTMs vs. LTSs

There is a well-studied class of transition systems with an infinite set of states, known as *labeled transition systems* (LTSs) [BM]. The transition function of an LTS associates with every state a set of possible *actions*, and specifies a new state reached with each action. The actions are assumed to be observable, whereas the states are not. LTSs are a standard tool for process modeling [Mil]. Depending on the nature of the process being modeled, the actions may represent inputs, or outputs, or a combination of both.

We define a subclass of LTSs that we call *effective*:

**Definition 5.3.** *An LTS is effective if each action is a pair of input, output tokens, and the transition function for the LTS is Turing-computable; that is, there exists a Turing-computable function $\delta$ which, for any pair (state, input token), returns the pair (new state, output token).*

It is easy to see that the class of PTMs is equivalent to the class of effective LTSs under trace equivalence semantics, where the tokens in the I/O streams of the PTM are the same as the labels along the paths of the corresponding effective LTS:

**Proposition 5.3.** *For any PTM $M$, there exists an equivalent effective LTS $T$, and vice versa. Here, $M$ and $T$ are considered equivalent if $L(M)$ is the same as the set of traces for $T$.*

**Proof:** This is similar to the FST construction at the beginning of section 5.2. $\square$

*Example 5.1.* Figure 2 shows the transitions from some state $X$ of an answering machine (example 2.1); the first transition on the figure corresponds to a infinite family of transitions, one for each possible instantiation of the input message.

Though PTMs can be viewed as a special subclass of LTSs, it would be misleading to treat them as nothing more than that. We believe that PTMs cannot be fully appreciated unless all the models of their behavior are treated as incomplete and complementary views of this new device.

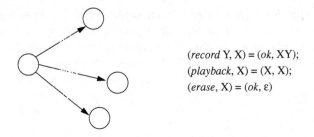

$(record\ Y, X) = (ok, XY);$
$(playback, X) = (X, X);$
$(erase, X) = (ok, \varepsilon)$

**Fig. 2.** Constructing an LTS for the Answering Machine.

# 6   Modeling PTM Behavior by Recursively Defined Functions

We have mentioned in section 3.2 that PTM behaviors can be modeled as a recursively defined mapping from input to output streams. In this section, we define such a mapping $\phi_M$, for any PTM $M$. A similar approach can be found in [Bro].

First, we define two functions over pairs, *1st* and *2nd*, returning the 1st and 2nd component of any pair, respectively. We also define three functions over streams, *head*, *tail*, and *append*; *head($\sigma$)* returns the first token of a stream $\sigma$, *tail($\sigma$)* returns the rest of the stream (which is also a stream), and *append(s, $\sigma$)* appends a token $s$ to the beginning of a stream $\sigma$, returning a new stream.

Streams are assumed to be infinite; successive invocations of *tail* continue returning new streams. Streams are also assumed to be *dynamically bound*: *head* and *tail* have lazy evaluation semantics. Dynamic binding of inputs and outputs is what allows the PTM to be truly interactive: next input is generated only after the previous output is produced, allowing the input and output tokens to be interdependent.

Let $M$ be a PTM where $f_M$ is the corresponding computable function, $f_M$ : $I \times W \to O \times W$. If $\iota$ is the input stream and $w$ is $M$'s current state, the first computational step of $M$ will produce $f_M(head(\iota), w)$. Let $o$ be the first output token and $w'$ be $M$'s new state, they are defined as follows:

$$o = 1st(f_M(head(\iota), w)); \quad w' = 2nd(f_M(head(\iota), w))$$

We can now define a function *frec$_M$* which takes an input stream $\iota$ and a state $w$ and returns an output stream; *frec$_M$* is defined recursively as follows:

$$frec_M(\iota, w) = append(o, frec_M(tail(\iota), w'))$$

Though *frec$_M$* successfully returns the output stream, it takes the state as one of its inputs, which is not what we want. The mapping we want, $\phi_M$, is obtained by currying $M$'s initial state $w_0$ into *frec$_M$*:

$$\text{for any } x, \ \phi_M(x) = frec_M(x, w_0)$$

This definition of $\phi_M$ is based on *coinductive* principles [BM], which are more expressive than the inductive principles underlying Turing computable functions [JR,WG2]. As a result, $\phi_M$ cannot be expressed by any Turing computable function.

**Theorem 6.1.** *For any PTMs $M_1$ and $M_2$, $\mathcal{L}(M_1) = \mathcal{L}(M_2)$ iff $\phi_{M_1} = \phi_{M_2}$.*

**Proof:** The proof is omitted from this abstract; it makes use of coinductive reasoning and coalgebraic methods [BM,JR].

# 7    Environment-Based Approach to PTM Behaviors

So far, PTM behavior has been defined as an *absolute* notion. In this section, we consider a *relative* notion of PTM behavior, defined with respect to the PTM's *environment*. This engenders a different approach to the notion of *expressiveness*, one which looks at *behavioral equivalence classes* within different environments. We believe that this approach will prove more effective for the formalization of interactive systems than the *absolute* one.

Note: The notion of an *environment* presented here is similar to that of an *observer* [WG3]. Whereas the same PTM may be observed by multiple observers, an environment is assumed to remain the same throughout a PTM's "life" (this is not to say that it is *constant*; rather, it obeys the same set of constraints).

## 7.1    Relative Equivalence and Expressiveness

The input stream of any PTM is generated by its *environment*. So far, we have assumed that all the input streams are feasible. However, this is not a reasonable assumption for the context in which interactive systems normally compute. A typical environment will have constraints on the input streams or sequences that it is capable of generating; it can be assumed that a PTM operating within an environment will only receive streams that satisfy the constraints appropriate for that environment. The issue of specifying these constraints, and relating them to the models for various PTM environments is a worthy research topic which is outside the scope of this paper.

We identify the notion of an environment $O$ with that of the inputs that are *feasible* in $O$; within a given environment, PTMs that either *distinguishable* or they *appear equivalent*:

**Definition 7.1. (Environment)** *Given a class $C$ of computing devices with behavior $B$, an environment $O$ for $C$ is a mapping from elements of $C$ to some domain $\beta_O$, $O : C \to \beta_O$, which is consistent, i.e.:*

*for any $M_1, M_2$ in $C$, if $B(M_1) = B(M_2)$, then $O(M_1) = O(M_2)$*

*The elements of $\beta_O$ are known as* feasible behaviors *(within the environment $O$). When $O(M_1) \neq O(M_2)$, we say that $M_1$ and $M_2$ are* distinguishable *in $O$; otherwise, we say that $M_1$ and $M_2$ appear equivalent in $O$.* □

The *consistency* of an environment means that equivalent systems will appear equivalent in all environments; however, systems that appear equivalent in some environments may be distinguishable in others.

*Example 7.1.* So far, we have assumed that all input tokens to the answering machine $\mathring{A}$ (example 2.1) start with one of three commands (`record`, `playback`, `erase`). This is a reasonable assumption in an environment where these commands are selected by pushing one of three possible buttons. If we choose to reject this assumption, the answering machine definition can be extended in various ways:

> when an input token does not start with either of the three commands, a *robust* answering machine will ignore it; a *non-robust* one will erase its tape.

Though these answering machines are not equivalent, they will appear equivalent in any environment where only these three commands are feasible. □

Equivalence and expressiveness of classes of devices can also be defined relative to an environment, in a straightforward fashion:

**Definition 7.2.** *Given some environment $O$, a class $C_2$ of computing devices is appears at least as expressive in $O$ as class $C_1$ if, for every device $M_1 \in C_1$, there exists $M_2 \in C_2$ such that $O(M_1) = O(M_2)$. $C_1$ and $C_2$ appear equivalent in $O$ if $C_1$ also appears at least as expressive as $C_2$ in $O$; otherwise, $C_2$ is appears more expressive in $O$.*

It is possible that two classes may appear equivalent in some environments, but one will be more expressive in a different environment. We will show in this section that this is the case for TMs and PTMs, which appear equivalent in *algorithmic* environments but not in richer ones.

## 7.2 Finite PTM Environments

Unlike the absolute notions of PTM behavior (sections 4 through 6), which were all based on infinite streams, environments do not have to be infinite. Some environments may have a natural limit on their life span (and on the life span of any PTM that "resides" there), and thus a bound on the length of input sequences that they can generate. We expect the study of *finite environments* to prove particularly important in some of the applications of interactive theory of computation, such as for system correctness, where any test of correctness is by definition finite.

**Definition 7.3. (Observations and finite PTM environments)** *Given an arbitrary PTM $M$, any finite prefix of some interaction stream of $M$ (section 2.4) is an* observation *of $M$; its length is the number of pairs in it. A mapping from PTMs to sets of their observations constitutes a* finite PTM environment. *When a finite environment admits observations of length one only, it is known as* algorithmic.

Algorithmic environments are thus finite environments with shortest life span possible, where the instantiation of the computing device is for a single interaction only. This definition of *algorithmic* environments is consistent with [We2]; it reflects the traditional algorithmic view of the nature of computing devices, as presented in a typical undergraduate introduction to the theory of computation [Sip].

If $M_1$ and $M_2$ are *distinguishable* in a finite environment $O$, then $O(M_1) \neq O(M_2)$, i.e., $O(M_1) \oplus O(M_2)$ is not empty. The members of this set are known as *distinguishability certificates* for $(M_1, M_2)$:

**Definition 7.4. (Distinguishability Certificates)** Distinguishability certificates *are observations which are feasible in $O$ for one of the machines but not the other.*

Though equivalence of two PTMs is intractable and cannot be proven (just as for TMs, similar to the halting problem), non-equivalence can be established by finding their distinguishability certificate:

**Proposition 7.1.** *Any two non-equivalent PTMs are distinguishable by some finite-length distinguishability certificate.*

**Proof:** Let $M_1$ and $M_2$ be PTMs which are not language-equivalent; i.e., where $\mathcal{L}(M_1) \neq \mathcal{L}(M_2)$. W.l.o.g., there must be an interaction stream $\sigma \in \mathcal{L}(M_1)$ which is not in $\mathcal{L}(M_2)$. There must exist some $k$ such that the prefix of length $k$ of $\sigma$ is not a prefix of any stream of $\mathcal{L}(M_2)$. Let us choose the smallest such $k$. Then, the prefix of length $k$ of $\sigma$ is the distinguishability certificate for $(M_1, M_2)$. $\square$

It follows from definitions that if two PTMs are distinguishable by some finite observation, there must be some finite environment where they are distinguishable. For amnesic PTMs, algorithmic environments suffice for this purpose:

**Proposition 7.2.** *Any two non-equivalent amnesic PTMs (definition 4.3) are are distinguishable by a certificate of length one.*

**Proof:** Let $M_1$ and $M_2$ be amnesic PTMs which are not language-equivalent; Let $\omega$ be a distinguishability certificate for $(M_1, M_2)$, obtained as in proposition 7.1, and let $(i, o)$ be the last input/out pair in $\omega$. From the definition of amnesic PTMs (definition 4.3), it can be shown that in any environment capable of generating the token $i$, $(i, o)$ will also serve as the distinguishability certificate between $M_1$ and $M_2$. $\square$

Proposition 7.2 asserts that algorithmic environments suffice for distinguishing between all non-equivalent amnesic PTMs. Since the class of TMs has the same expressiveness as the class of amnesic PTMs (proposition 4.1), algorithmic environments suffice for distinguishing between all TMs as well. The same does not hold for the general class of PTMs; we will show in section 7.3 that there exist pairs of PTMs with arbitrarily long distinguishability certificates.

## 7.3   Infinite Expressiveness Hierarchy

Any environment $O$ for a class of devices $C$ with behavior $B$ induces a partitioning of $C$ into equivalence classes, where the members of each class appear equivalent in $O$; we call them *behavioral equivalence classes*. Given a class $C$ of computing devices, an environment $O_1$ is said to be *richer* than $O_2$ if fewer devices in $C$ appear equivalent in it:

**Definition 7.5.** *An environment $O_1$ is* richer *than $O_2$ if the behavioral equivalence classes for $O_1$ are strictly finer than those for $O_2$.*

We define an infinite sequence $\Theta$ of finite PTM environments, $\Theta = (O_1, O_2, \ldots)$, as follows:

**Definition 7.6.** $\Theta = (O_1, O_2, \ldots)$, *where for any $k$ and any PTM $M$, $O_k(M)$ is the set of $M$'s observations of length $\leq k$.*

$O_k$ gives us a relative notion of $M$'s behavior, with respect to environments that can generate at most $k$ input tokens. $O_1$ is an algorithmic environment, with the coarsest notion of behavioral equivalence.

It is easy to see that for any $k$, $O_k$ is consistent (definition 7.1): for any pair of PTMs $M_1$ and $M_2$, if $B(M_1) = B(M_2)$, then $O_k(M_1) = O_k(M_2)$. It is furthermore the case that for the class of PTMs, for any $k$, $O_{k+1}$ is richer than $O_k$:

**Proposition 7.3.** *For any $k$, $O_{k+1}$ is richer than $O_k$.*

**Proof:** It can be shown that $O_{k+1}(M_1) \neq O_{k+1}(M_2)$ whenever $O_k(M_1) \neq O_k(M_2)$. We complete the proof by constructing a sequence of PTMs $(M_1, M_2, \ldots)$ such that for any $k$, $M_k$ and $M_{k+1}$ appear equivalent to $O_k$ but not to $O_{k+1}$. These PTMs are *binary*, with inputs O and 1, and outputs $T$ and $F$. For any $k$, $M_k$ ignores its inputs, outputting $k$ $F$'s followed by all $T$'s. The shortest distinguishability certificate for $(M_k, M_{k+1})$ has length $k + 1$, ending with output $T$ is one case, $F$ in another. $\square$

Proposition 7.3 shows that the environments in $\Theta$ are increasingly richer, producing ever finer equivalence classes for PTM behaviors without reaching a limit.

**Theorem 7.1.** *The environments in $\Theta$ induce an infinite expressiveness hierarchy of PTM behaviors, with TM behaviors at the bottom of the hierarchy.*

**Proof:** Follows from propositions 7.3 and 7.2. $\square$

All the environments in $\Theta$ are *finite*. In contrast, the absolute models of PTM behavior defined in sections 4 through 6 are not finite. The PTM equivalence classes induced by the absolute models can be regarded as the limit point for the infinite expressiveness hierarchy of Theorem 7.1, though this is outside the scope of this paper.

# 8    Conclusions

*Persistent Turing Machines* (PTMs) are multitape machines with a persistent worktape preserved between interactions, whose inputs and outputs are dynamically generated streams of tokens (strings). They are a minimal extension of Turing Machines (TMs) that express interactive behavior. They model services over time provided by persistent, object-oriented, or reactive systems that cannot be expressed by computable functions. They also provide a natural model for single-user databases, where the current database instance is modeled as the contents of the persistent worktape.

## 8.1    Discussion

We have shown how models of computation for PTMs, just as models of computation for TMs, can be equivalently expressed by languages, automata, and function-based models. Whereas models of computation for TMs are string-based, models for PTMs are based on input-output streams. An environment-based model of behavior was also defined for PTMs; there has been no analog of this notion for TMs, whose environment is always *algorithmic*. These four models of behavior were used to obtain several expressiveness results, both for the general class of PTMs and for a number of special subclasses.

PTMs are sequential interaction machines (SIMS) which inherit from TMs the restriction that input tokens must be discrete, and that any model of behavior must ignore time-depended aspects. They are therefore inappropriate for modeling some real-time and embedded devices or physical control processes, whose expressiveness requires the full generality of SIMs. Furthermore, there are multi-stream interactive behaviors, such as distributed database systems or airline reservation systems, which cannot be modeled by SIMs at all, requiring a model with even more expressiveness – MIMs [WG2,WG3]. Despite these restrictions, both TMs and PTMs are robust computational abstractions which serve as a foundation for formal study of algorithmic and sequential interactive computation, respectively.

We expect that PTM-based models of computation can be generalized to model all sequential computation. We believe that a proper formalization of the notion of a PTM environment will be an important part of this effort. Though there is no "Silver Bullet" in the absolute sense, the problems of correctness testing and verification for interactive software systems may prove tractable – once we are willing to assume reasonable constraints on the system's environment. This is analogous to the role of pre- and post- conditions in algorithmic correctness proofs.

We also expect that single- and multi- agent computation can be modeled within a single formalism. The methods and tools for formalizing PTM computation developed in this paper will serve as a basis for a more comprehensive theory of interactive computation over these models. The resulting formalization of interactive computation is expected to be useful in providing a unifying conceptual framework for many areas of Computer Science where the algorithmic model of computation is not sufficient.

## 8.2   Directions for Future Research

It will take much research to achieve the vision outlined above; here, we focus on some immediate extensions of current work.

**Interaction and Non-determinism:**  In this work, it has been assumed that PTMs are deterministic. Abandoning this assumption will mean providing appropriate models for non-deterministic PTM behavior, with corresponding notions of equivalence. We expect that this will yield many surprises; for example, whereas language-based and automata-based notions of equivalence are the same for deterministic systems, this is not the case for non-deterministic systems. Also, for automata-based models, we expect that choosing whether to associate outputs with transitions (Mealy-style) or with states (Mealy-style) has interesting consequences for non-deterministic PTMs that are not present in the deterministic case.

**Minimal PTMs:**  The Myhill-Nerode theorem has been applied to derive the notion of *minimal* FSAs, where all equivalent states are reduced to one. An analogous notion of minimality can be defined for PTMs, so there is exactly one state for each equivalence class over the set of I/O stream prefixes. We believe there is an alternate characterization of such a minimal PTM, in terms of final coalgebras [WG2]; this connection between traditional automata theory and the new field of coalgebras is worth exploring.

**Complexity Issues:**  A theory of interactive computation would not be complete without notions of complexity. Traditionally, complexity is measured in terms of input size; this approach does not suffice for PTMs, where the computations depends on the state as well, and indirectly, on the whole interaction history (section 2.4). In database theory, the notion of data complexity is used instead, where the size of the input is assumed insignificant and only the size of the data (i.e., the PTM state) is considered. The theory of interactive computation will need to integrate both approaches in a coherent and rigorous fashion. It is expected that some techniques will be borrowed from the theory of *interactive proof systems* [Gol].

## 9   Acknowledgements

An earlier version of this work appeared in [GW]. Peter Wegner was unfortunately not able to directly contribute to this paper, due to an accident from which he is still recuperating. However, all my ideas were motivated by his vision of interaction, and would not have been developed without this vision. I would also like to thank the reviewers of this paper, who helped me improve it.

# References

Abr.    Samson Abramsky. Semantics of Interaction, in *Semantics and Logic of Computation*, ed A. Pitts and P. Dibyer, Cambridge, 1997.

AB.     Malcolm Atkinson, Peter Buneman. Types and Persistence in Database Programming Languages, *ACM Computing Surveys* 19:2, 1987

BM.     Jon Barwise, Lawrence Moss. *Vicious Circles*, CSLI Lecture Notes #60, Cambridge University Press, 1996.

Bro.    Manfred Broy. Compositional Refinement of Interactive Systems, *Digital Systems Research Center*, SRC 89, 1992

Gol.    Oded Goldreich. *Modern Cryptography, Probabilistic Proofs and Pseudorandomness*. Springer, 1999.

GW.     Dina Goldin, Peter Wegner. *Behavior and Expressiveness of Persistent Turing Machines*. Technical Report, CS Dept., Brown University, 1999.

HU.     John Hopcroft, Jeffrey Ullman. *Introduction to Automata Theory, Languages, and Computation*. Addison-Wesley, 1979.

JR.     Bart Jacobs, Jan Rutten. *A Tutorial on Coalgebras and Coinduction*. EATCS Bulletin 62, 1997.

Kos.    Sven Kosub. *Persistent Computations*, Theoretische Informatik Tech. Report, U. Wurzburg, 1998.

Mil.    Robin Miler. Operational and Algebraic Semantics of Concurrent Processes, *Handbook of Theoretical Computer Science*, J. van Leeuwen, editor, Elsevier 1990.

MP.     Zohar Manna, Amir Pnueli. *The Temporal Logic of Reactive and Concurrent Systems*, Springer-Verlag, 1992.

RN.     Stuart Russell, Peter Norveig. *Artificial Intelligence: A Modern Approach*, Addison-Wesley, 1994.

Sip.    Michael Sipser. *Introduction to the Theory of Computation*, PWS Publishing Company, 1996.

TB.     B.A. Trakhtenbrot, Y.M. Bardzin, *Finite Automata: Behavior and Synthesis*, American Elsevier, 1973.

Tu.     Alan Turing. On Computable Problems with an Application to the Entscheidungsproblem, *Proc. London Math. Society*, 2:42, 1936.

We1.    Peter Wegner. Why Interaction is More Powerful than Algorithms. *Communications of the ACM*, May 1997.

We2.    Peter Wegner. Interactive Foundations of Computing. *Theoretical Computer Science*, Feb. 1998.

WG1.    Peter Wegner, Dina Goldin. Interaction as a Framework for Modeling. *Conceptual Modeling*, LNCS 1565, Editors P. Chen et al., Springer-Verlag, 1999.

WG2.    Peter Wegner, Dina Goldin. Coinductive Models of Finite Computing Agents, Proc. Coalgebra Workshop (CMCS'99), *ENTCS*, Vol. 19, March 1999.

WG3.    Peter Wegner, Dina Goldin. Interaction, Computability, and Church's Thesis *British Computer Journal*, to be published.

ZM.     Stanley Zdonik and Dave Maier. *Readings in Object-Oriented Database Systems*, Morgan Kaufmann, 1990.

# On Interactions of Cardinality Constraints, Key, and Functional Dependencies

Sven Hartmann

FB Mathematik, Universität Rostock
18051 Rostock, Germany

**Abstract.** Cardinality constraints as well as key dependencies and functional dependencies are among the most popular classes of constraints in database models. While the formal properties of each of the constraint classes are now well understood, little is known about their interaction. The objective of this paper is to discuss how constraints from these classes go together. We propose methods for reasoning about a set of cardinality constraints, key and certain functional dependencies. Moreover, we construct Armstrong databases for these constraints, which are of special interest for example-based deduction in database design.

## 1   Introduction

It is widely accepted now that database systems are best designed first at a conceptual level. The result of this process is a conceptual schema which describes the requirements that the desired database system must achieve, and serves as the basis for the following development phases. In conceptual design great attention is devoted to the modeling of semantics. Integrity constraints specify the way by that the elements of a database are associated to each other. Defining and enforcing integrity constraints helps to guarantee system correctness.

During the last few decades, the area of integrity constraints has attracted considerable research interest. A large amount of different constraint classes has been discussed in the literature and actually used in database design. However, their mathematical rigour often entails complex semantics, and consequently handling them in a proper manner requires a good knowledge about their backgrounds. For an overview on semantics in databases, see e.g. [15,17,18].

The entity-relationship approach to conceptual database design, first introduced by Chen [4], provides a simple way of representing data in the form of entities and relationships among entities. In this approach, cardinality constraints are among the most popular classes of integrity constraints. They impose lower and upper bounds on the number of relationships an entity of a given type may be involved in. For cardinality constraints and generalizations, see [14,20].

Once declared, a conceptual schema can be mapped in an automatic way to a variety of implementation targets such as a relational database. The relational

K.-D. Schewe, B. Thalheim (Eds.): FoIKS 2000, LNCS 1762, pp. 136–155, 2000.

database model, which goes back to Codd [5], has a strong theoretical background which can be reused in most other database models. Extended entity-relationship models support all the major concepts of the relational model. For details and further discussion, we refer to [19].

Codd [5] also introduced functional dependencies, which are to be considered as one of the major concepts of the relational model. In particular, normalization theory up to BCNF is based on the idea of functional dependency. Among functional dependencies, key dependencies are of utmost interest. They are used to identify the tuples in a relation.

Several authors extended functional dependencies to other database models such as object-based databases or temporal databases, see [19,22,23]. It is reasonable to ask how the extensions affect other constructs within these models. As pointed out in [19], results obtained from relational database theory can also be used in the entity-relationship model. This is of interest since the entity-relationship model is not only popular as an intuitive tool for conceptual design, but it becomes more and more prevalent as a mathematical data model upon which real database management systems are built.

While each constraint class mentioned above is now quite well understood, we know little about their interaction. However, in practice the designer of a database will be confronted with the presence of constraints of either class. In order to ensure the correctness of a schema, the designer has (among others) to check the satisfiability of the specified constraint set. Unfortunately, efficient algorithms for consistency and implication checking are still missing for this situation. It should be noted that reasoning about a constraint set containing constraints from different classes happens to be significantly harder than handling the classes separately. It is well-known that constraints from the classes under consideration interact with each other. For example, key dependencies can be used to express certain cardinality constraints, and vice versa. These interactions may cause a database schema to exhibit undesirable properties.

The objective of this paper is to discuss possible interactions between cardinality constraints and key or functional dependencies. In particular, we present methods for reasoning about a set of cardinality constraints, key dependencies and certain functional dependencies, namely non-unary functional dependencies.

This paper is organized as follows. In Section 2, we briefly describe the data model to be used. All our considerations are carried out in the higher-order entity relationship model (HERM, see [19]) which extends the original approach by Chen. In Section 3, we give a formal definition of the constraints mentioned above. Moreover, the consistency and the implication problem for constraint classes are addressed. Section 4 collects some known results about cardinality constraints to be used in further investigations. Section 5 is devoted to the consistency problem, Section 6 to the implication problem. In Section 7 we discuss some problems concerning unary functional dependencies. Due to the lack of space, proofs are omitted or sketched only. The proofs of the major theorems are given in the final section.

## 2    The Data Model

This section briefly describes the basic concepts of the entity-relationship approach. We concentrate ourselves on a characteristic subset of design constructs to be used below.

Let $\underline{E}$ be a non-empty, finite set. In the context of our approach, the elements of $\underline{E}$ are called *entity types*. With each entity type $\underline{e}$ we associate a finite set $\underline{e}^t$ called the domain or population of the type $\underline{e}$ (at moment $t$). The members of $\underline{e}^t$ are entity instances or entities, for short. Intuitively, entities can be seen as real-world objects which are of interest for some application or purpose. By classifying them and specifying their significant properties (attributes), we obtain entity types which are frequently used to model the objects in their domains.

A *relationship type* $\underline{r}$ is a set (or sequence) $\{\underline{e}_1, \dots, \underline{e}_k\}$ of elements from $\underline{E}$. Relationship types are used to model associations between real-world objects, i.e. entities. A relationship or instance of type $\underline{r}$ is a tuple from the cartesian product $\underline{e}_1^t \times \dots \times \underline{e}_k^t$ where $\underline{e}_1^t, \dots, \underline{e}_k^t$ are the domains of $\underline{e}_1, \dots, \underline{e}_k$, respectively, at moment $t$. A finite set $\underline{r}^t$ of such relationships forms the population of $\underline{r}$ at moment $t$.

The relationship types considered so far are often called relationship types of order 1 (cf. [19]). Analogously, relationship types of higher order may be defined hierarchically. Suppose now, we are given entity and/or relationship types of order less then $i > 0$. A set $\{\underline{u}_1, \dots, \underline{u}_k\}$ of them forms a *relationship type* $\underline{r}$ of *order i*. As above, we define relationships of type $\underline{r}$ as tuples from the cartesian product $\underline{u}_1^t \times \dots \times \underline{u}_k^t$ for a moment $t$.

In a relationship type $\underline{r} = \{\underline{u}_1, \dots, \underline{u}_k\}$ each of the entity or relationship types $\underline{u}_1, \dots, \underline{u}_k$ is said to be a *component type* of $\underline{r}$. Additionally, each of the pairs $(\underline{r}, \underline{u}_j)$ is called a *link*.

Let $\underline{S} = \{\underline{r}_1, \dots, \underline{r}_n\}$ be a set of entity and relationship types where with each relationship type $\underline{r}$, all its component types belong to $\underline{S}$, too. Then $\underline{S}$ is called a *database scheme*. Replacing each type $\underline{r}$ in $\underline{S}$ by its population $\underline{r}^t$ at moment $t$, we obtain a database or instance $\underline{S}^t$ of $\underline{S}$.

A database $\underline{S}^t$ is finite if each of the populations $\underline{r}^t$ is finite. In this paper, we are only interested in finite databases. Furthermore, a database $\underline{S}^t$ is *fully-populated* iff none of the populations $\underline{r}^t$ is empty.

From the graph-theoretical point of view, a database scheme $\underline{S}$ can be considered as a finite digraph $\mathfrak{ERD} = (\underline{S}, \mathcal{L})$ with vertex set $\underline{S}$ and a collection $\mathcal{L}$ of arcs. In $\mathfrak{ERD}$ there shall be an arc from $\underline{r}$ to $\underline{u}$ whenever $\underline{u}$ is a component type of the relationship type $\underline{r}$. Hence, the arcs in $\mathfrak{ERD}$ are just the links in the database scheme. The digraph $\mathfrak{ERD}$ is known as the *entity-relationship diagram* of $\underline{S}$. Usually, the entity types are represented graphically by rectangles, the relationship types by diamonds. Using the diagram technique, even complex schemes can be understood and handled.

# 3   Integrity Constraints

In this section, we give formal definitions of the constraints to be studied in the sequel. Assume, we are given a database schema $\underline{S}$ together with an instance $\underline{S}^t$. Let $\underline{r}$ be a relationship type in $\underline{S}$ with population $\underline{r}^t$. If $X \subseteq \underline{r}$ and if $r \in \underline{r}^t$, then we denote the restriction of $r$ to $X$ by $r[X]$.

A *min-cardinality constraint* is a statement $cmin(\underline{r}, \underline{u}) = a$ where $\underline{u}$ is a component type of $\underline{r}$. The population $\underline{r}^t$ satisfies this constraint if every instance $u$ of $\underline{u}$ occurs at least $a$ times in relationships $r \in \underline{r}^t$.

Analogously, a *max-cardinality constraint* is a statement $cmax(\underline{r}, \underline{u}) = b$ where $\underline{u}$ is a component type of $\underline{u}$. The constraint holds in $\underline{r}^t$ iff every instance $u$ of type $\underline{u}$ appears at most $b$ times in relationships of type $\underline{r}$.

Cardinality constraints are usually reflected graphically in the entity-relationship diagram as $(cmin, cmax)$-labels associated to the corresponding links. If no min- or max-cardinality constraint is given for a link $(\underline{r}, \underline{u})$, we may assume $cmin(\underline{r}, \underline{u}) = 0$ and $cmax(\underline{r}, \underline{u}) = \infty$, respectively. It is easy to see that this does not represent a real constraint, but is more or less a technical agreement.

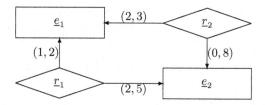

**Fig. 1.** An entity-relationship diagram with labels for the cardinality constraints.

A subset $X \subseteq \underline{r}$ is a *key* for $\underline{r}$ iff the restrictions $r[X]$, $r \in \underline{r}^t$, are pairwise distinct. If $X$ is a key for $\underline{r}$, then the population $\underline{r}^t$ satisfies the *key dependency* $\underline{r} : X \to \underline{r}$.

Finally, a *functional dependency* is a statement $\underline{r} : X \to Y$ where both, $X$ and $Y$ are subsets of $\underline{r}$. The population $\underline{r}^t$ satisfies the functional dependency $\underline{r} : X \to Y$ iff we have $r_1[Y] = r_2[Y]$ whenever $r_1[X] = r_2[X]$ holds for any two relationships $r_1$ and $r_2$ in $\underline{r}^t$. A functional dependency is said to be *unary* if $X$ contains a single component type from $\underline{r}$, and *non-unary* otherwise.

*Example.* Below we give a small example to provide some motivation for the issues we are going to tackle. Consider a part of a university database schema involving the entity types PROFESSOR, ASSISTANT, COURSE, BUILDING, LECTURE HALL and DATE. On this set we define a relationship type LECTURE reflecting assignments of professors and their assistants to courses in combination with the dates and locations they take place at. Figure 2 shows the corresponding diagram.

In this schema, constraints have to be defined to meet the requirements of the university schedule. Let us consider some examples. The cardinality constraints $cmin(\text{LECTURE}, \text{PROFESSOR}) = 3$ and $cmax(\text{LECTURE}, \text{PROFESSOR}) = 6$ state that every professor will give 3 to 6 lectures per term. If every professor has only one assistant per course, then the non-unary functional dependency $\text{LECTURE}:\{\text{PROFESSOR}, \text{COURSE}\} \rightarrow \{\text{ASSISTANT}\}$ holds. Since every lecture hall is situated in only one building, we also have the unary functional dependency $\text{LECTURE}:\{\text{LECTURE HALL}\} \rightarrow \{\text{BUILDING}\}$. Moreover, the key dependency $\text{LECTURE}:\{\text{COURSE}, \text{DATE}\} \rightarrow \text{LECTURE}$ tells us there is only one lecture for every course per day. Other constraints may be defined due to the schedule of the university or deduced from the ones explicitly stated. The questions we deal with are whether such a set of constraints is conflict-free, and which additional constraints may be deduced without being explicitly stated.

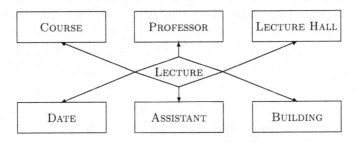

**Fig. 2.** Entity-relationship diagram for our example.

Let $\mathcal{C}, \mathcal{K}$ and $\mathcal{F}$ denote the classes of all possible cardinality constraints, key dependencies or functional dependencies, respectively. In the sequel, if we refer to a constraint, we always mean one from these classes.

A database instance $\underline{S}^t$ satisfies a given constraint $\sigma$ iff $\sigma$ holds for the corresponding population $\underline{r}^t$ in $\underline{S}^t$. Moreover, $\underline{r}^t$ and $\underline{S}^t$ satisfy a set $\Sigma$ of constraints iff $\underline{r}^t$ and $\underline{S}^t$, respectively, satisfy each of the constraints in $\Sigma$.

Let $\Sigma$ be a constraint set defined on the database schema $\underline{S}$. Every database instance $\underline{S}^t$ satisfying all the constraints in $\Sigma$ is said to be *legal* for $\Sigma$. Consequently, $\Sigma$ is said to be *satisfiable* if it admits at least one legal database instance. Again it should be noted that we only pay attention to finite databases.

As pointed out in [13], it is usually not enough to consider satisfiability. Obviously, the empty database is legal for every set of cardinality constraints. However it may happen that there is a type in $\underline{S}$ without instances in any legal database. Examples are given in [13]. For practical reasons, we ask for fully-populated legal databases. A constraint set $\Sigma$ admitting such a database is said to be *consistent*. A fully-populated legal database for $\Sigma$ will also be called a *sample database*. Sample databases, especially the later described Armstrong databases, can be used for database mining and design-by-example.

The *consistency problem* for a constraint class $\mathcal{Z}$ is to decide whether a given set $\Sigma \subseteq \mathcal{Z}$ is consistent or not. For cardinality constraints, the consistency problem has been considered by several authors, e.g. [10,13,20]. It is well-known, that there exist inconsistent sets of cardinality constraints. On the other hand, sets of key or functional dependencies are always consistent. However, the situation may change dramatically if they come together with cardinality constraints.

*Example.* Consider the schema given in Figure 1. The specified set of cardinality constraints is consistent. Now add a key dependency $r_2 : \{e_2\} \to r_2$. It is easy to check, that the resulting constraint set happens to be inconsistent, and the empty database is the only legal one. A further example for this observation is given in Section 7.

If $\Sigma$ is a constraint set and $\sigma$ a single constraint, then $\Sigma$ implies $\sigma$ (denoted by $\Sigma \models \sigma$) if every legal database for $\Sigma$ satisfies $\sigma$, too. Conversely, $\Sigma \not\models \sigma$ holds, if there is a legal database (a *certificate*) for $\Sigma$ violating $\sigma$.

The *implication problem* for a constraint class $\mathcal{Z}$ is to decide whether a given set $\Sigma \subseteq \mathcal{Z}$ implies $\sigma \in \mathcal{Z}$ or not. A constraint set $\Sigma$ is semantically *closed* in $\mathcal{Z}$ if $\sigma \in \Sigma$ whenever $\Sigma \models \sigma$ holds. We denote the closure of a constraint set $\Sigma$ by $C_{\mathcal{Z}}(\Sigma)$. The determination of the closed sets in a constraint class is of special interest. Clearly, $\Sigma \models \sigma$ holds iff $\sigma$ is in the closure of $\Sigma$. Hence the detection of the closed sets in a constraint class $\mathcal{Z}$ completely solves the implication problem for $\mathcal{Z}$. Moreover, it enables us to decide whether constraint sets are equivalent. Database designers usually look for equivalent constraint sets which are better for control and maintenance in real life databases.

It is often argued, that the consistency problem and the implication problem are two sides of the same coin (e.g. [21]). Checking implication can be done by adding the negation of $\sigma$ to $\Sigma$ and testing the resulting set. Conversely, checking inconsistency can be done by testing implication of an unsatisfiable constraint. However, this is only half of the truth. In general, the negation of a constraint from a class $\mathcal{Z}$ is not in $\mathcal{Z}$ again. For example, the negation of a cardinality constraint is an existence constraint, the negation of a functional dependency is an afunctional constraint.

Usually, it is easier to solve the consistency problem than the implication problem, at least for real life constraints. It the remaining sections we shall always start tackling consistency before discussing implication.

Finally, we shall introduce the notions of Armstrong populations and Armstrong databases. Informally, Armstrong databases are sample databases capturing all implications of a constraint set $\Sigma$ in $\mathcal{Z}$. Recall, that if $\Sigma \not\models \sigma$ there is a legal database for $\Sigma$ violating $\sigma$. We call it a *certificate* for $\sigma$. However, there is no a priori guarantee that there exists a single database serving as a certificate for *all* constraints $\sigma \in \mathcal{Z}$ not implied by $\Sigma$.

An *Armstrong population* for $\Sigma$ (with respect to a constraint class $\mathcal{Z}$) is a population $r^t$ of $r$ satisfying all constraints from $\Sigma$, but violating every constraint $\sigma \in \mathcal{Z}$ defined on $r$ with $\Sigma \not\models \sigma$. Analogously, an *Armstrong database* for $\Sigma$ (with respect to $\mathcal{Z}$) is a legal database $\underline{S}^t$ such that $\sigma \in \mathcal{Z}$ holds iff $\Sigma \models \sigma$. Obviously, in an Armstrong database all populations are Armstrong populations.

In order to test whether a constraint follows from an initial set $\Sigma$ we may test whether it holds in the Armstrong database and decide accordingly. Thus, the implication problem reduces to verification in a single example. The concept of Armstrong databases is closely connected to database mining, i.e. the use of given databases for the extraction of constraints. This is an important tool for design-by-example as suggested by Mannila and Räihä [16].

In Section 6, we shall consider Armstrong databases for sets of cardinality constraints, key and functional dependencies. We shall use them in particular, to prove certain constraint sets to be semantically closed.

# 4 Reasoning About Cardinality Constraints

In this section, we shall assemble some terminology and known results concerning cardinality constraints which will be required in the sequel. Throughout, let $\underline{S}$ be a database schema and $\Sigma_C$ a set of cardinality constraints defined on $\underline{S}$. We start with the following trivial observation.

**Lemma 1** *For every link $(\underline{r}, \underline{u})$ in $\underline{S}$ we have*

$$cmin(\underline{r}, \underline{u}) = 0 \text{ and } cmax(\underline{r}, \underline{u}) = \infty, \tag{1}$$

$$cmin(\underline{r}, \underline{u}) = a \text{ implies } cmin(\underline{r}, \underline{u}) = a' \text{ for all } a' \leq a, \tag{2}$$

$$cmax(\underline{r}, \underline{u}) = b \text{ implies } cmax(\underline{r}, \underline{u}) = b' \text{ for all } b' \geq b. \tag{3}$$

The constraints given by (1) are said to be trivial. Put

$$\alpha(\underline{r}, \underline{u}) = \max\{a : (cmin(\underline{r}, \underline{u}) = a) \in \Sigma\}$$
$$\beta(\underline{r}, \underline{u}) = \min\{b : (cmax(\underline{r}, \underline{u}) = b) \in \Sigma\}.$$

Hence, the sharpest constraints explicitly stated in $\Sigma_C$ for a link $(\underline{r}, \underline{u})$ are given by $\alpha(\underline{r}, \underline{u})$ and $\beta(\underline{r}, \underline{u})$. The following claim gives a first result concerning the consistency of $\Sigma_C$.

**Lemma 2** *$\Sigma_C$ is consistent iff there is a function $g : \underline{S} \to \mathbb{N} = \{1, 2, \dots\}$ such that*

$$\alpha(\underline{r}, \underline{u}) \leq \frac{g(\underline{r})}{g(\underline{u})} \leq \beta(\underline{r}, \underline{u}) \tag{4}$$

*holds for every link $(\underline{r}, \underline{u})$.*

Given such a function $g$, it is possible to construct a sample database $\underline{S}^t$ for $\Sigma_C$ where the population $\underline{r}^t$ has size $g(\underline{r})$ for every type $\underline{r}$ in $\underline{S}$. The main problem is to find a suitable function $g$. In [10], we used shortest-path methods in certain digraphs for this purpose.

Let $\mathfrak{D} = (\underline{S}, \mathcal{L} \cup \mathcal{L}^{-1})$ be the symmetric digraph which we obtain from the entity-relationship diagram $\mathfrak{ERD} = (\underline{S}, \mathcal{L})$ by adding to each link $L = (\underline{r}, \underline{u})$ the reverse arc $L^{-1} = (\underline{u}, \underline{r})$. On the arcs of $\mathfrak{D}$ we define a weight function $w : \mathcal{L} \cup \mathcal{L}^{-1} \to \mathbb{Q} \cup \{\infty\}$ by

$$w(L) = \begin{cases} \infty & \text{if } \alpha(\underline{r}, \underline{u}) = 0, \\ 1/\alpha(\underline{r}, \underline{u}) & \text{otherwise,} \end{cases} \quad \text{and} \quad w(L^{-1}) = \beta(\underline{r}, \underline{u}), \quad (5)$$

where $L$ is the original link $(\underline{r}, \underline{u}) \in \mathcal{L}$ and $L^{-1}$ is its reverse.

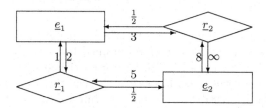

**Fig. 3.** The digraph $\mathfrak{D}$ corresponding to the diagram in Figure 1.

This weight function can be extended to subdigraphs $\mathfrak{D}'$ of $\mathfrak{D}$ by $w(\mathfrak{D}') = \prod_{L \in \mathcal{A}'} w(L)$, where $\mathcal{A}' \subseteq L \cup L^{-1}$ is the collection of arcs in $\mathfrak{D}'$.

Special interest is devoted to directed cycles in $\mathfrak{D}$. A directed cycle $\mathfrak{Z}$ is said to be *critical* if its weight $w(\mathfrak{Z})$ is less than 1, and *subcritical* if its weight equals 1.

The following result was proved by Lenzerini and Nobili [13] and Thalheim [19]. In [10] a polynomial-time algorithm is proposed to construct sample databases or to detect critical cycles using shortest-path methods (namely a variation of the well-known Bellman-Ford algorithm). Hence, the question whether a set $\Sigma_C$ of cardinality constraints is consistent or not can be decided in polynomial time.

**Lemma 3** $\Sigma_C$ *is consistent iff the digraph $\mathfrak{D}$ has no critical cycles.*

The implication problem for cardinality constraints was solved in [11]. The main observation is the following.

**Lemma 4** *Let $\Sigma_C$ be consistent, and $(\underline{r}, \underline{u})$ be a link in $\underline{S}$. Then $\Sigma_C$ implies $cmax(\underline{r}, \underline{u}) = \alpha(\underline{r}, \underline{u})$ iff the link $(\underline{r}, \underline{u})$ lies on a subcritical cycle in $\mathfrak{D}$, and $cmin(\underline{r}, \underline{u}) = \beta(\underline{r}, \underline{u})$ iff the reverse arc $(\underline{u}, \underline{r})$ lies on a subcritical cycle in $\mathfrak{D}$.*

In [11], we called $\Sigma_C$ *strongly consistent* iff it is consistent and $\alpha(\underline{r}, \underline{u}) = \beta(\underline{r}, \underline{u})$ holds whenever link $(\underline{r}, \underline{u})$ or its reverse arc $(\underline{u}, \underline{r})$ lie on a subcritical cycle. Moreover, we proved the following characterization of closed sets of cardinality constraints.

**Lemma 5** *Let $\Sigma_C$ be consistent. Then $\Sigma_C$ is closed in $C$ iff it is strongly consistent and contains all constraints obtained by Lemma 1.*

This solves the implication problem for consistent sets in $C$. Of course, one can also consider inconsistent sets. However, this seems to be of academic use only, and will be omitted here due to space limitations. In [11], we also provided polynomial-time algorithms to detect arcs on subcritical cycles, such that the implication problem for $C$ can be solved efficiently.

In order to prove a set $\Sigma_C$ in $C$ to be closed, we constructed Armstrong databases.

**Lemma 6** *A consistent set $\Sigma_C$ admits an Armstrong database (with respect to $C$) iff it implies a non-trivial max-cardinality constraint for every link in $\underline{S}$.*

Assume, there is a link $(\underline{r}, \underline{u})$ such that $cmax(\underline{r}, \underline{u}) = \infty$ is the only max-cardinality constraint for this link obtained from $\Sigma_C$. Then, for every integer $b$, there must be an instance $u$ of type $\underline{u}$ participating in more than $b$ relationships in an Armstrong population of $\underline{r}$. Hence, the resulting database would be infinite. Since we restricted ourselves to finite databases, there will not be an Armstrong database for this case.

However, if we fix $b$, then there exists a sample database with an instance $u$ involved in more than $b$ relationships of type $\underline{r}$ for every link $(\underline{r}, \underline{u})$ without a nontrivial max-cardinality constraint. Taking such a database for every $b$, we obtain a sequence of sample databases which we shall call an *Armstrong sequence*. Due to [11], every consistent set $\Sigma_C$ admits at least an Armstrong sequence of sample databases (with respect to $C$).

## 5   The Consistency Problem

Sets of key and functional dependencies are always consistent. But as seen in the example of Figure 1, this is not longer true if we are given cardinality constraints, too. The reason for this is the following simple observation (see also [20]).

**Lemma 7** *The key dependency $\underline{r} : \{\underline{u}\} \to \underline{r}$ implies $cmax(\underline{r}, \underline{u}) = 1$, and vice versa.*

Throughout, let $\underline{S}$ be a database schema, and $\Sigma_C, \Sigma_K$ and $\Sigma_F$ denote sets of cardinality constraints, key dependencies and functional dependencies, respectively, defined on $\underline{S}$.

It is noteworthy, that Lemma 7 contains the only nontrivial interaction between cardinality constraints and key dependencies. Let $\Sigma_K^C = \{cmax(\underline{r}, \underline{u}) = 1 : (\underline{r} : \{\underline{u}\} \to \underline{r}) \in \Sigma_K\}$ contain all cardinality constraints obtained from key dependencies in $\Sigma_K$ via Lemma 7.

**Theorem 8** *Let $\Sigma = \Sigma_C \cup \Sigma_K$. Then $\Sigma$ is consistent iff $\Sigma_C \cup \Sigma_K^C$ is consistent.*

The proof of this claim uses structures from combinatorial design theory, namely *resolvable transversal designs*. For details on transversal designs, we refer to [12]. The proof of the theorem is given in Section 9.

*Example.* Theorem 8 shows why the cardinality constraints given in Figure 1 together with the key dependency $\underline{r}_2 : \{\underline{e}_2\} \rightarrow \underline{r}_2$ are not longer consistent. Here $\Sigma_K^C$ contains the additional max-cardinality constraint $cmax(\underline{r}_2, \underline{e}_2) = 1$. This leads to a modification of the weight function $w$ defined by (5) as shown in Figure 4. It is easy to check that the cycle $(\underline{e}_2, \underline{r}_2, \underline{e}_1, \underline{r}_1)$ has weight $1/2$, i.e. is critical.

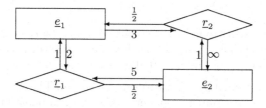

**Fig. 4.** The digraph representing an additional key dependency.

The consistency of $\Sigma_C \cup \Sigma_K^C$ may be checked in polynomial time as proposed in Section 4. In particular, a consistent set of cardinality constraints together with a set of non-unary key dependencies will always be consistent. The same observation holds for functional dependencies. We will state this in a slightly stronger version as follows.

**Theorem 9** *Let $\Sigma = \Sigma_C \cup \Sigma_K \cup \Sigma_F$, and assume that all functional dependencies in $\Sigma_F$ are trivial, non-unary or implied by key dependencies in $\Sigma_K$. Then $\Sigma$ is consistent iff $\Sigma_C \cup \Sigma_K^C$ is consistent.*

Unfortunately, this claim does not hold for arbitrary sets of functional dependencies as shown in Section 7.

# 6 The Implication Problem

We start with some known results on the implication problem for key and functional dependencies, and then use those to obtain generalizations in the presence of cardinality constraints. Delobel and Casey [6] gave a set of inference rules for functional dependencies, which Armstrong [1] proved to be complete. We record these rules for future reference.

**Lemma 10** *Let $\underline{r}$ be a relationship type, and $X, Y, Z$ be subsets of its component types. Then*

$$\underline{r} : X \to Y \text{ holds whenever } Y \subseteq X, \tag{6}$$

$$\underline{r} : X \to Y \text{ and } \underline{r} : Y \to Z \text{ imply } \underline{r} : X \to Z, \tag{7}$$

$$\underline{r} : X \to Y \text{ implies } \underline{r} : X \cup Z \to Y \cup Z. \tag{8}$$

For key dependencies, we may conclude the following rules.

**Lemma 11** *Let $\underline{r}$ be a relationship type, and $X, Y$ be subsets of its component types. Then we have $\underline{r} : \underline{r} \to \underline{r}$ and*

$$\underline{r} : X \to \underline{r} \text{ implies } \underline{r} : Y \to \underline{r} \text{ whenever } X \subseteq Y. \tag{9}$$

According to Armstrong [1], the rules given in Lemma 10 and 11 are correct and complete. Hence, $\Sigma_F$ ($\Sigma_K$) is closed in $\mathcal{F}$ ($\mathcal{K}$) iff it contains all constraints obtained by applying Lemma 10 (11, respectively).

Constraints obtained by (6) are said to be trivial. The Armstrong rules gave rise to a considerable number of papers concerning applications, consequences and alternate rules. For a discussion, see [18]. In [1,2], one finds methods for constructing Armstrong databases for functional dependencies. Attention to combinatorial properties of functional dependencies has been drawn e.g. in [7,8].

As pointed out by Demetrovics and Thi [8], functional dependencies can be represented by closure operations. For a relationship type $\underline{r}$ and any subset $X \subseteq \underline{r}$, we put

$$cl(X) = \{\underline{u} \in \underline{r} : \Sigma_F \models (X \to \{\underline{u}\})\}.$$

This induces a closure operation on the subsets of $\underline{r}$. We call $X$ *functionally closed* (with respect to $\Sigma_F$) if $cl(X) = X$ holds. Conversely, for every closure operation $cl$ on $\underline{r}$, the set

$$\Sigma_F = \{(\underline{r} : X \to Y) : Y \subseteq cl(X)\}$$

is semantically closed in the class $\mathcal{F}$ of functional dependencies.

To continue with, we shall introduce some graph-theoretical notions which turn out to be useful in the future. Assume, we are given a database instance $\underline{S}^t$ of $\underline{S}$. For every link $(\underline{r}, \underline{u})$ we consider a graph $\mathfrak{G}^t(\underline{r}, \underline{u})$ whose vertices are the relationships in $\underline{r}^t$. Two distinct relationships $r_1$ and $r_2$ are connected by an edge in $\mathfrak{G}^t(\underline{r}, \underline{u})$ iff $r_1[\underline{u}] = r_2[\underline{u}]$ holds.

Obviously, $\mathfrak{G}^t(\underline{r}, \underline{u})$ is a collection of vertex-disjoint, complete subgraphs (each of them corresponding to exactly one instance $u$ of type $\underline{u}$). We call $\mathfrak{G}^t(\underline{r}, \underline{u})$ the *representation graph* of the link $(\underline{r}, \underline{u})$ (with respect to the given database instance $\underline{S}^t$). Moreover, let $\mathfrak{G}^t(\underline{r}, X)$ denote the intersection of the representation graphs $\mathfrak{G}^t(\underline{r}, \underline{u})$, $\underline{u} \in X$, for any subset $X$ of $\underline{r}$.

Representation graphs give us useful information on the constraints hold in $\underline{S}^t$.

**Lemma 12** *A database instance $\underline{S}^t$ satisfies*

$$cmin(\underline{r}, \underline{u}) = a \text{ iff all components of } \mathfrak{G}^t(\underline{r}, \underline{u}) \text{ have at least a vertices,}$$
$$cmax(\underline{r}, \underline{u}) = b \text{ iff all components of } \mathfrak{G}^t(\underline{r}, \underline{u}) \text{ have at most b vertices,}$$
$$\underline{r} : X \to \underline{r} \text{ iff } \mathfrak{G}^t(\underline{r}, X) \text{ is edgeless,}$$
$$\underline{r} : X \to Y \text{ iff } \mathfrak{G}^t(\underline{r}, X) \text{ is a subgraph of } \mathfrak{G}^t(\underline{r}, Y).$$

Here *components* mean maximal connected subgraphs, which should not be confused with the component types of relationship types. With the help of representation graphs, we obtain

**Theorem 13** *Let $\Sigma_C$ be consistent. $\Sigma_C \cup \Sigma_K$ is closed in $C \cup K$ iff $\Sigma_C$ is closed in $C$, $\Sigma_K$ is closed in $K$ and we have*

$$\{(\underline{r}, \underline{u}) : (cmax(\underline{r}, \underline{u}) = 1) \in \Sigma_C\} = \{(\underline{r}, \underline{u}) : (\underline{r} : \underline{u} \to \underline{r}) \in \Sigma_K\}. \tag{10}$$

Condition (10) ensures that all implications obtained by Lemma 7 are considered. A key dependency $\underline{r} : X \to \underline{r}$ forces $X$ to be a key for $\underline{r}$. Conversely, $X$ is a *non-key*, if it is not a key. A non-key $X$ is said to be an *antikey*, if every proper superset of $X$ is a key.

To prove Theorem 13 we have, among others, to construct representation graphs $\mathfrak{G}^t(\underline{r}, \underline{u})$, such that the intersection graph $\mathfrak{G}^t(\underline{r}, X)$ contains at least one edge for every non-key $X \subseteq \underline{r}$. This proves $\Sigma \not\models (\underline{r} : X \to \underline{r})$. Actually, it is sufficient to consider antikeys, as every non-key $X$ admits an antikey $Y$ such that $X \subseteq Y$, i.e. $\mathfrak{G}^t(\underline{r}, Y)$ is a subgraph of $\mathfrak{G}^t(\underline{r}, X)$.

As a result, we obtain Armstrong populations for $\Sigma$ with respect to $K$. Mixing them with an appropriate Armstrong database (Armstrong sequence, respectively) for $\Sigma$ with respect to $C$, we obtain the same with respect to $C \cup K$. The main tool of our proof is the following theorem due to Hajnal and Szemeredi [9].

**Theorem 14** *Let $\mathfrak{H}$ be a graph with $m = ts$ vertices and maximum valency less than $t$, then there exists a vertex decomposition of $\mathfrak{H}$ into $t$ sets of $s$ pairwise non-adjacent vertices.*

Details on our proof will be given in Section 9. Theorem 13 gives us an efficient way to decide implication in $C \cup K$.

**Algorithm 15** *Given $\Sigma_C$ and $\Sigma_K$, proceed as follows:*

1. *Determine $\Sigma_K^C$ by applying Lemma 7 to $\Sigma_K$.*
2. *Determine the closure of $\Sigma_C \cup \Sigma_K^C$ in $C$ as proposed in Section 4.*
3. *Determine $\Sigma_C^K$ by applying Lemma 7 to the closure $C_C(\Sigma_C \cup \Sigma_K^C)$.*
4. *Determine the closure of $\Sigma_K \cup \Sigma_C^K$ in $K$ as proposed by Lemma 11.*
5. *$C_C(\Sigma_C \cup \Sigma_K^C) \cup C_K(\Sigma_K \cup \Sigma_C^K)$ gives the closure of $\Sigma_C \cup \Sigma_K$ in $C \cup K$.*

Using similar methods, we are able to obtain results on cardinality constraints and functional dependencies.

**Theorem 16** *Let $\Sigma_C$ be consistent and $\Sigma_F$ contain non-unary functional dependencies only. $\Sigma_C \cup \Sigma_F$ is closed in $C \cup F$ iff $\Sigma_C$ is closed in $C$ and $\Sigma_F$ is closed in $F$.*

This time we have to construct representation graphs $\mathfrak{G}^t(\underline{r}, \underline{u})$ such that for every functionally closed set $X \subseteq \underline{r}$, there is a pair of relationships $r_{1,X}$ and $r_{2,X}$ of type $\underline{r}$ connected by an edge in $\mathfrak{G}^t(\underline{r}, X)$, but not in any of the representation graphs $\mathfrak{G}^t(\underline{r}, \underline{u})$, $\underline{u} \notin X$.

Finally, as a corollary, we obtain the next result.

**Corollary 17** *Let $\Sigma_C$ be consistent and $\Sigma_F$ contain non-unary functional dependencies only. $\Sigma_C \cup \Sigma_K \cup \Sigma_F$ is closed in $C \cup K \cup F$ iff $\Sigma_C \cup \Sigma_K$ is closed in $C \cup K$ and $\Sigma_K \cup \Sigma_F$ is closed in $K \cup F$.*

# 7   Unary Functional Dependencies

Until now, we usually excluded unary functional dependencies. In this section we shall give a brief impression why these dependencies play a special role in the presence of cardinality constraints. However, it is noteworthy that a set $\Sigma_C$ of cardinality constraints will never imply a functional dependency different from those obtained by Lemma 7.

**Lemma 18** *Let $\underline{r}$ be a relationship type, and $\underline{u}, \underline{v}$ be component types of $\underline{r}$. $\Sigma_C$ implies a functional dependency $\underline{r} : \{\underline{u}\} \rightarrow \{\underline{v}\}$ iff it implies $cmax(\underline{r}, \underline{u}) = 1$.*

Conversely, if we are given cardinality constraints *and* functional dependencies, then one may conclude further implications.

*Example.* Consider the schemata in Figure 5. The specified sets of cardinality constraints are both consistent. Assume, we are given the functional dependency $\underline{r} : \{\underline{u}\} \rightarrow \{\underline{v}\}$, too. In every legal database instance, the representation graph $\mathfrak{G}^t(\underline{r}, \underline{u})$ has to be a subgraph of $\mathfrak{G}^t(\underline{r}, \underline{u})$.

For the first schema, the components of $\mathfrak{G}^t(\underline{r}, \underline{u})$ are complete graphs on 4 to 6 vertices, while the components of $\mathfrak{G}^t(\underline{r}, \underline{v})$ are complete graphs on 5 to 7 vertices. The only possible decomposition of components of $\mathfrak{G}^t(\underline{r}, \underline{v})$ into those of $\mathfrak{G}^t(\underline{r}, \underline{u})$ is the trivial one. Hence, both representation graphs are isomorphic. This gives us the new constraints $\underline{r} : \{\underline{v}\} \rightarrow \{\underline{u}\}$ as well as $cmin(\underline{r}, \underline{u}) = 5$ and $cmax(\underline{r}, \underline{v}) = 6$.

For the second schema in Figure 5, the situation is even worse. A similar argumentation shows the specified set of constraints to be inconsistent.

The following result summarizes the observations indicated by the examples. A rigorous exploitation of the argumentation gives further results, which we skip out here due to space limitations.

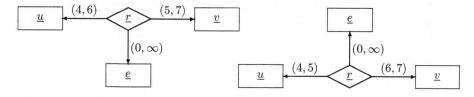

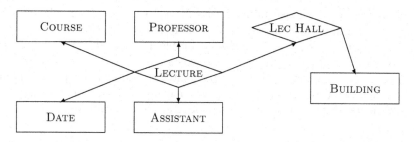

**Fig. 5.** Examples for interactions with a functional dependency $\underline{r} : \{\underline{u}\} \rightarrow \{\underline{v}\}$.

**Lemma 19** *Let $\underline{r}$ be a relationship type, and $\underline{u}, \underline{v}$ be component types of $\underline{r}$. Then*

$$cmax(\underline{r}, \underline{v}) = b \ and \ \underline{r} : \{\underline{u}\} \rightarrow \{\underline{v}\} \ imply \ cmax(\underline{r}, \underline{u}) = b,$$
$$cmin(\underline{r}, \underline{u}) = a \ and \ \underline{r} : \{\underline{u}\} \rightarrow \{\underline{v}\} \ imply \ cmin(\underline{r}, \underline{v}) = a,$$
$$cmax(\underline{r}, \underline{v}) = b, cmin(\underline{r}, \underline{u}) = a \ and \ \underline{r} : \{\underline{u}\} \rightarrow \{\underline{v}\} \ imply \ \underline{r} : \{\underline{v}\} \rightarrow \{\underline{u}\}$$
$$whenever \ b < 2a.$$

An interesting idea to handle unary functional dependencies was given by Biskup et al. [3]. They use these constraints to decompose relationship types by pivoting. In our example from Section 3, the unary functional dependency LECTURE:{LECTURE HALL} → {BUILDING} may be used for this approach. As a result we would obtain the diagram in Figure 6. Here this functional dependency is naturally enforced by the structure of the schema.

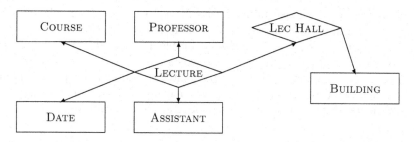

**Fig. 6.** Entity-relationship diagram after decomposition by pivoting.

Decomposition by pivoting is closely related to decomposition into BCNF. A relationship type $\underline{r}$ is in *Boyce-Codd Normal Form* (BCNF) with respect to $\Sigma_F$ if every functional dependency $\underline{r} : X \rightarrow Y$ in $\Sigma_F$ is trivial (i.e. $Y \subseteq X$), or $X$ is a key for $\underline{r}$. Applying Theorem 9 and Corollary 17, we may conclude as follows.

**Theorem 20** *Assume every relationship type $\underline{r}$ is in BCNF. Then $\Sigma = \Sigma_C \cup \Sigma_K \cup \Sigma_F$ is consistent iff $\Sigma_C \cup \Sigma_K^C$ is consistent. In addition, $\Sigma$ is closed in $\mathcal{C} \cup \mathcal{K} \cup \mathcal{F}$ iff $\Sigma_C \cup \Sigma_K$ is closed in $\mathcal{C} \cup \mathcal{K}$ and $\Sigma_K \cup \Sigma_F$ is closed in $\mathcal{K} \cup \mathcal{F}$.*

Recall, that closures in $\mathcal{C} \cup \mathcal{K}$ and in $\mathcal{K} \cup \mathcal{F}$ can be determined applying Algorithm 15 and the Armstrong rules, respectively. This gives us an efficient procedure to check implication under the assumption of BCNF.

## 8    Conclusions

In this paper, we provided an efficient method for reasoning about a constraint set comprising cardinality constraints as well as key and functional dependencies. Reasoning means checking consistency and logical implication. Today, cardinality constraints are embedded in most CASE tools, which are usually based on the entity-relationship model. Although these tools include basic reasoning methods, they do not offer intelligent consistency checking routines for constraint set containing not only functional dependencies, but also cardinality constraints. Applying the ideas presented in this paper, it would be possible to derive interesting properties of schemata, or to detect conflicts among the constraints under discussion.

There are at least two problems which should be investigated in future. In the last section, we gave examples for interactions between cardinality constraints and unary functional dependencies. It would be nice to have a characterization of semantically closed sets in the presence of unary dependencies without additional assumptions such as BCNF.

The second problem concerns Armstrong databases. The Armstrong databases constructed to prove Theorem 13 are extremely large. In order to use Armstrong databases for database mining, they have to be of reasonable size. Thus we are looking for small databases as done in [7] for functional dependencies only. For cardinality constraints, a similar problem is considered in [11]. It would be interesting to decide, whether there exists a sample database where the size of every population is bounded by a given integer. Unfortunately, it is still unknown whether this problem is NP-complete or not. A solution of this question would give us new information on the size of Armstrong databases.

## 9    Proofs of the Main Results

In this section, we shall give proofs for the Theorems 8 and 13.

To begin with, we introduce some notation. A *transversal design* $TD(k, q)$ is a set of $q^2$ tuples from $\{1, \ldots, k\}^q$ such that any two tuples agree in at most one entry. A subset of $q$ pairwise disjoint tuples is said to be a *resolution class*. The transversal design is *resolvable* if it is decomposable into $q$ resolution classes. Resolvable transversal designs are known to exist for fixed $k$ and sufficiently large $q$. In particular, they exist for every prime power $q \geq k$.

*Proof (of Theorem 8).* The necessity is trivial, so we continue with the sufficiency. Since $\Sigma_C \cup \Sigma_K^C$ is consistent, there exists a sample database $\underline{S}^t$. Denote the number of instances of every type $\underline{r}$ by $g(\underline{r})$. We choose a prime power $q$ larger than each of the integers $g(\underline{r})$, and larger than $n$, the number of types in $\underline{S}$. From $\underline{S}^t$ we shall construct a new database $\underline{S}^{t*}$, where every type $\underline{r}$ has $qg(\underline{r})$ instances.

Let $\underline{e}$ be an entity type. For every old instance $e$, we introduce $q$ new instances $(e, 1), \ldots, (e, q)$. Next, let $\underline{r}$ be a relationship type with $k$ component types. Due to our choice of $q$, there is a resolvable transversal design $TD(k, q)$. For every old instance $r$ of $\underline{r}$, fix an own resolution class in the transversal design. Let $r = (u_1, \ldots, u_k)$ be an old instance of $\underline{r}$, and $(i_1, \ldots, i_k)$ a tuple in the associated resolution class. Then we introduce a new instance $((u_1, i_1), \ldots, (u_k, i_k))$. Doing the same for every old relationship and every tuple in the corresponding resolution class, we obtain a new population $\underline{r}^{t*}$ for $\underline{r}$ with exactly $qg(\underline{r})$ instances. We apply the same procedure hierarchically to every relationship type in $\underline{S}$.

Obviously, every new instance $(u, i)$ of a component type from $\underline{r}$ participates in the same number of new relationships as the old instance $u$ did in old relationships. Hence, the new database $\underline{S}^{t*}$ is again a sample database for $\Sigma_C \cup \Sigma_K^C$. It is easy to check, that any two new relationships of a certain type $\underline{r}$ share at most one entry. Therefore $\underline{S}^{t*}$ satisfies every key dependency in $\Sigma_K$, too.    □

The same construction also indicates a proof for Theorem 9.

We now turn to Theorem 13. Its proof requires some preliminary observations. Let $\Sigma_C$ be a consistent and closed set of cardinality constraints. According to Lemma 5, $\Sigma_C$ is strongly consistent. In [11], we gave the following characterization, which is similar to Lemma 2.

**Lemma 21** *Let $\Sigma_C$ be consistent. Then $\Sigma_C$ is strongly consistent iff there exists a function $g : \underline{S} \to \mathbb{N}$ such that*

$$\frac{g(\underline{r})}{g(\underline{u})} = \beta(\underline{r}, \underline{u}), \quad \text{if } \alpha(\underline{r}, \underline{u}) = \beta(\underline{r}, \underline{u}), \tag{11}$$

$$\alpha(\underline{r}, \underline{u}) < \frac{g(\underline{r})}{g(\underline{u})} < \beta(\underline{r}, \underline{u}), \quad \text{otherwise,} \tag{12}$$

*holds for every link $(\underline{r}, \underline{u})$.*

To prove this, we constructed Armstrong databases (Armstrong sequences, respectively) for $\Sigma_C$ where the population $\underline{r}^s$ has size $\lambda g(\underline{r})$ for every type $\underline{r}$ in $\underline{S}$. Here $\lambda$ denotes any sufficiently large integer.

Let $\Sigma_K$ be a closed set of key dependencies, and assume Condition (10) holds. In the sequel, let $\underline{r}$ be a relationship type in $\underline{S}$.

**Lemma 22** *There is an Armstrong population $\underline{r}^t$ of $\underline{r}$ for $\Sigma_K$ (with respect to $\mathcal{K}$), satisfying all constraints in $\Sigma_C$ defined on $\underline{r}$.*

*Proof.* For every component type $\underline{u}$ of $\underline{r}$, put

$$s(\underline{u}) = \begin{cases} \alpha(\underline{r}, \underline{u}) & \text{if } \alpha(\underline{r}, \underline{u}) \geq 2, \\ 1 & \text{if } \beta(\underline{r}, \underline{u}) \leq 1, \\ 2 & \text{otherwise.} \end{cases}$$

Put $m = (\gamma + 2) \prod_{\underline{u} \in \underline{r}} s(\underline{u})$, where $\gamma$ denotes the number of antikeys of $\underline{r}$ (given by $\Sigma_K$). Here, $m$ will be the size of the population $\underline{r}^t$, and every component type $\underline{u}$ of $\underline{r}$ will have exactly $m/s(\underline{u})$ instances. Moreover, each instance of type $\underline{u}$ will participate in exactly $s(\underline{u})$ relationships. Since $\alpha(\underline{r}, \underline{u}) \leq s(\underline{u}) \leq \beta(\underline{r}, \underline{u})$, this ensures that the claimed cardinality constraints in $\Sigma_C$ hold.

Put $\underline{r}^t = \{r_1, \ldots, r_m\}$. On the vertex set $\underline{r}^t$, we shall construct representation graphs $\mathfrak{G}^t(\underline{r}, \underline{u})$. In the beginning, let all vertices in $\underline{r}^t$ be unmarked. For every antikey $X \subseteq \underline{r}$, choose two unmarked vertices $r_{1,X}, r_{2,X}$, and mark them. Next, connect $r_{1,X}$ and $r_{2,X}$ by an edge in every graph $\mathfrak{G}^t(\underline{r}, \underline{u})$ with $\underline{u} \in X$.

Fix a component type $\underline{u}$. For every edge in $\mathfrak{G}^t(\underline{r}, \underline{u})$, choose $s(\underline{u}) - 2$ unmarked vertices from $\underline{r}^t$ and mark them. In addition, let the complete graph on these $s(\underline{u})$ vertices be a component of the graph $\mathfrak{G}^t(\underline{r}, \underline{u})$. In the same way, we proceed for all component types $\underline{u}$.

Let $\mathfrak{H}$ denote the union of the graphs $\mathfrak{G}^t(\underline{r}, \underline{u})$ constructed so far. Again, we fix a component type $\underline{u}$. Note, that at the moment, $\mathfrak{G}^t(\underline{r}, \underline{u})$ consists of a certain number of components of size $s(\underline{u})$ together with a set $I(\underline{u})$ of isolated vertices. Consider the subgraph $\mathfrak{H}'$ of $\mathfrak{H}$ induced by $I(\underline{u})$. Here every vertex has valency at most $\sum_{\underline{v} \neq \underline{u}} (s(\underline{v}) - 1)$. Due to our choice of $m$, we have $\sum_{\underline{v} \neq \underline{u}} (s(\underline{v}) - 1) < m/s(\underline{u})$ and thus maximum valency less than $m/s(\underline{u})$. Applying the Theorem of Hajnal and Szemeredi (Theorem 14) to $\mathfrak{H}'$, its vertex set $I(\underline{u})$ may be decomposed into subsets of size $s(\underline{u})$, such that the vertices within a subset are pairwise non-adjacent. We add the complete graph on each of these subsets as a component to $\mathfrak{G}^t(\underline{r}, \underline{u})$. The resulting graph $\mathfrak{G}^t(\underline{r}, \underline{u})$ will be the representation graph of $\underline{u}$. We apply the same procedure to each of the component types $\underline{u}$ of $\underline{r}$.

It remains to show that the constructed population $\underline{r}^t$ has the desired properties. Let $cmin(\underline{r}, \underline{u}) = a$ and $cmax(\underline{r}, \underline{u}) = b$ be cardinality constraints in $\Sigma_C$. The representation graph $\mathfrak{G}^t(\underline{r}, \underline{u})$ consists of a collection of vertex-disjoint complete graphs on $s(\underline{u})$ vertices each (the components of $\mathfrak{G}^t(\underline{r}, \underline{u})$). Each component corresponds to an instance of type $\underline{u}$ participating in exactly $s(\underline{u})$ relationships. Since $a \leq \alpha(\underline{r}, \underline{u}) \leq s(\underline{u}) \leq \beta(\underline{r}, \underline{u}) \leq b$, the claimed constraints hold. This proves $\underline{r}^t$ to satisfy $\Sigma_C$.

Let $\underline{r} : Y \to \underline{r}$ be a key dependency in $\Sigma_K$. Assume, the intersection graph $\mathfrak{G}^t(\underline{r}, Y)$ contains an edge. Due to our construction, there must be an antikey $X$ with $Y \subseteq X$. This forces $Y$ to be a non-key which gives a contradiction. Hence, $\mathfrak{G}^t(\underline{r}, Y)$ is edgeless and the key dependency holds. This proves $\underline{r}^t$ to satisfy $\Sigma_K$.

Finally, let $\underline{r} : Y \to \underline{r}$ be a key dependency not in $\Sigma_K$. Since $Y$ is a non-key, there exists an antikey $X$ with $Y \subseteq X$. The intersection graph $\mathfrak{G}^t(\underline{r}, X)$ contains an edge connecting $r_{1,X}$ and $r_{2,X}$. Since $\mathfrak{G}^t(\underline{r}, X)$ is a subgraph of $\mathfrak{G}^t(\underline{r}, Y)$, this edge is also in the later one. Thus the key dependency $\underline{r} : Y \to \underline{r}$ is violated. Therefore, $\underline{r}^t$ is an Armstrong population for $\Sigma_K$ with respect to $\mathcal{K}$.    □

For further reference, put $g_r(\underline{r}) = m$ and $g_r(\underline{u}) = m/s(\underline{u})$ for every component type of $\underline{r}$. These values denote the number of instances of $\underline{r}$ and $\underline{u}$ in the population just constructed.

Let $g : \underline{S} \to \mathbb{N}$ be a function satisfying (11,12), let $q$ be a sufficiently large prime power, and let $\lambda$ and $\mu$ be sufficiently large integers such that

$$\mu > g_r(\underline{r}) - \alpha(\underline{r}, \underline{u}) g_r(\underline{u}),$$
$$\mu > \beta(\underline{r}, \underline{u}) g_r(\underline{u}) - g_r(\underline{r}), \quad \text{if } \beta(\underline{r}, \underline{u}) \text{ is finite},$$

hold for every link $(\underline{r}, \underline{u})$ in the schema $\underline{S}$.

Again, let $\underline{r}$ be a fixed relationship type of $\underline{S}$. It must be emphasized, that the population $\underline{r}^t$ constructed above usually satisfies cardinality constraints not in $\Sigma_C$. However, it can be applied to obtain the following stronger result. Suppose that $\Sigma_C$ contains a non-trivial max-cardinality constraint for every link $(\underline{r}, \underline{u})$.

**Lemma 23** *There is an Armstrong population $\underline{r}^z$ of $\underline{r}$ for $\Sigma_K$ (with respect to $\mathcal{K}$), which is also an Armstrong population for $\Sigma_C$ (with respect to $\mathcal{C}$).*

*Proof.* To begin with, put $h_r(\underline{r}) = \mu g(\underline{r}) - g_r(\underline{r})$ and $h_r(\underline{u}) = \mu g(\underline{u}) - g_r(\underline{u})$ for every $\underline{u} \in \underline{r}$. Let us check, that $h_r$ satisfies (11,12). If $\alpha(\underline{r}, \underline{u}) = \beta(\underline{r}, \underline{u})$, we have $g(\underline{r})/g(\underline{u}) = \beta(\underline{r}, \underline{u})$ and $g_r(\underline{r})/g_r(\underline{u}) = s(\underline{u}) = \beta(\underline{r}, \underline{u})$. This implies (11). If $\alpha(\underline{r}, \underline{u}) < \beta(\underline{r}, \underline{u})$, we have

$$1 \leq g(\underline{r}) - \alpha(\underline{r}, \underline{u}) g(\underline{u})$$
$$g_r(\underline{r}) - \alpha(\underline{r}, \underline{u}) g_r(\underline{r}, \underline{u}) < \mu \leq \mu(g(\underline{r}) - \alpha(\underline{r}, \underline{u}) g(\underline{u}))$$
$$\alpha(\underline{r}, \underline{u}) \mu g(\underline{u}) - \alpha(\underline{r}, \underline{u}) g_r(\underline{u}) < \mu g(\underline{r}) - g_r(\underline{r}),$$

which implies the left side of (12). The right side holds analogously.

By Lemma 21, there is an Armstrong population $\underline{r}^s$ for $\Sigma_C$ (with respect to $\mathcal{C}$) such that $\underline{r}^s$ is of size $\lambda h_r(\underline{r})$ and every component type $\underline{u}$ has $\lambda h_r(\underline{u})$ instances. Again, $\lambda$ denotes a sufficiently large integer. Applying the construction presented in the proof of Theorem 8, we obtain an Armstrong population $\underline{r}^{s*}$ for $\Sigma_C$ (with respect to $\mathcal{C}$) such that any two relationships have at most one entry in common. $\underline{r}^{s*}$ is of size $q\lambda h_r(\underline{r})$ and every component type $\underline{u}$ has $q\lambda h_r(\underline{u})$ instances.

Next, we take $q\lambda$ copies of the population $\underline{r}^t$ obtained in Lemma 23, and join them with the population $\underline{r}^{s*}$ just constructed. Let $\underline{r}^z$ denote the resultant population. Due to our construction, $\underline{r}^z$ satisfies every constraint in $\Sigma_K \cup \Sigma_C$. Since $\underline{r}^{s*}$ is a subpopulation, no cardinality constraint not in $\Sigma_C$ holds in $\underline{r}^z$. Moreover, since $\underline{r}^t$ from Lemma 23 is a subpopulation, $\underline{r}^z$ satisfies no key dependency not in $\Sigma_K$. This proves the claim.    □

The population $\underline{r}^z$ obtained above is of size $h(\underline{r}) = q\lambda\mu g(\underline{r}) = q\lambda g_r(\underline{r}) + q\lambda h_r(\underline{r})$. Analogously, every component type $\underline{u}$ of $\underline{r}$ has $h(\underline{u}) = q\lambda\mu g(\underline{u})$ instances.

Now, we are ready to prove Theorem 13.

*Proof (of Theorem 13).* Condition (10) is an easy consequence of Lemma 7. This shows the necessity. We shall proceed with the sufficiency.

Assume, $\Sigma_C$ contains a non-trivial max-cardinality constraint for every relationship type in $\underline{S}$. To prove $\Sigma_C \cup \Sigma_K$ to be closed in $\mathcal{C} \cup \mathcal{K}$, we shall construct a database $\underline{S}^z$ satisfying all constraints in $\Sigma_C \cup \Sigma_K$, but no constraint not in $\Sigma_C \cup \Sigma_K$.

The idea is to comprise the populations constructed above. For every entity type $\underline{e}$ in the database schema $\underline{S}$, we take $h(\underline{e}) = q\lambda\mu g(\underline{e})$ instances. Afterwards, we add the populations $\underline{r}^z$ hierarchically to the database. Finally, we obtain a database $\underline{S}^z$. As shown above, $\underline{S}^z$ satisfies all constraints in $\Sigma_C \cup \Sigma_K$, but no other constraint from $\mathcal{C} \cup \mathcal{K}$. Hence, $\Sigma_C \cup \Sigma_K$ is closed in the class of cardinality constraints and key dependencies. Moreover, $\underline{S}^z$ is an Armstrong database for $\Sigma_C \cup \Sigma_K$ (with respect to $\mathcal{C} \cup \mathcal{K}$).

If $\Sigma_C$ does not contain a non-trivial max-cardinality constraint for every relationship type in $\underline{S}$, we may conclude in a similar way. However, this time, we do not obtain an Armstrong database, but an Armstrong sequence of sample databases.                                                                    $\square$

# References

1. W.W. Armstrong, Dependency structures of database relationship, Information Processing 74 (1974) 580-583.
2. C. Beeri, M. Dowd, R. Fagin and R. Statman, On the structure of Armstrong relations for functional dependencies, J. ACM 31 (1984) 30-46.
3. J. Biskup, R. Menzel, T. Polle and Y. Sagiv, Decomposition of relationships through pivoting, in: B. Thalheim (ed.), Conceptual Modeling (Springer, Berlin, 1996) 28-41.
4. P.P. Chen, The Entity-Relationship Model: Towards a unified view of data, ACM Trans. Database Syst. 1 (1984) 9-36.
5. E.F. Codd, A relation model of data for large shared data banks, Commun. ACM 13 (1970) 377-387.
6. C. Delobel and R.G. Casey, Decompositions of a database and the theory of Boolean switching functions, IBM J. Res. Dev. 17 (1973) 374-386.
7. J. Demetrovics, Z. Füredi and G.O.H. Katona, Minimum matrix representation of closure operations, Discrete Appl. Math. 11 (1985) 115-128.
8. J. Demetrovics and V.D. Thi, Some results about functional dependencies, Acta Cybern. 8 (1988) 273-278.
9. A. Hajnal and E. Szemeredi, Proof of a conjecture of Erdős, in: P. Erdős, A. Renyi and V.T. Sos (eds.), Combinatorial theory and its applications, Colloq. Math. Soc. János Bolyai 4 (North-Holland, Amsterdam, 1970) 601-623.

10. S. Hartmann, Graph-theoretic methods to construct entity-relationship databases, in: M. Nagl (ed.), Graph-theoretic concepts in computer science, LNCS 1017 (Springer, Berlin, 1995) 131-145.

11. S. Hartmann, On the consistency of int-cardinality constraints, in: T.W. Ling, S. Ram and M.L. Lee (eds.), Conceptual Modeling, LNCS 1507 (Springer, Berlin, 1998) 150-163.

12. D. Jungnickel, T. Beth and H. Lenz, Design Theory (BI, Mannheim, 1985).

13. M. Lenzerini and P. Nobili, On the satisfiability of dependency constraints in Entity-Relationship schemata, Inf. Syst. 15 (1990) 453-461.

14. S.W. Liddle, D.W. Embley and S.N. Woodfield, Cardinality constraints in semantic data models, Data Knowl. Eng. 11 (1993) 235-270.

15. D. Maier, The theory of relational databases (Computer Science Press, Rockville, 1983).

16. H. Mannila and K. Räihä, Design by example: an application of Armstrong relations, J. Comput. Syst. Sci. 33 (1986) 126-141.

17. J. Paredaens, P. De Bra, M. Gyssens and D. Van Gucht, The structure of the relational database model (Springer, Berlin, 1989).

18. B. Thalheim, Dependencies in Relational Databases (Teubner, Stuttgart, 1991).

19. B. Thalheim, Foundations of Entity-Relationship Modeling, Ann. Math. Artif. Intell. 6 (1992) 197-256.

20. B. Thalheim, Fundamentals of cardinality constraints, in: G. Pernul and A.M. Tjoa (eds.), Entity-relationship approach, LNCS 645 (Springer, Berlin, 1992) 7-23.

21. D. Theodorates, Deductive object oriented schemas, in: B. Thalheim (ed.), Conceptual modeling, LNCS 1157 (Springer, Berlin, 1996) 58-72.

22. G.E. Weddell, Reasoning about functional dependencies generalized for semantic data models, ACM Trans. Database Syst. 17 (1992) 32-64.

23. J. Wijsen, J. Vandenbulcke and H. Olivie, Functional dependencies generalized for temporal databases, in: R. Elmasri, V. Kouramajian and B. Thalheim (eds.), Entity-Relationship approach, LNCS 823 (Springer, Berlin, 1994) 99-109.

# Capturing LOGSPACE
# over Hereditarily-Finite Sets

Alexander Leontjev and Vladimir Sazonov*

Program Systems Institute of Russian Academy of Sciences
Pereslavl-Zalessky, 152140, Russia
sazonov@logic.botik.ru

**Abstract.** Two versions of a set theoretic $\Delta$-language are considered as theoretical prototypes for "nested" data base query language where data base states and queries are represented, respectively, as hereditarily-finite (HF) sets and set theoretic operations. It is shown that these versions correspond exactly to (N/D)LOGSPACE computability over HF, respectively. Such languages over sets, capturing also PTIME, were introduced in previous works, however, descriptions of LOGSPACE over HF [A.Lisitsa and V.Sazonov, TCS (175) 1 (1997) pp. 183–222] were not completely satisfactory. Here we overcome the drawbacks of the previous approaches due to some new partial result on definability of a linear ordering over finite extensional acyclic graphs and present a unified and simplified approach.

## 1   Introduction

Now it is widely adopted the natural way of characterizing expressive power of (theoretical versions) of data base query languages in terms of a kind of logic over finite structures or in terms of computational complexity. Vice versa, given a complexity class such as PTIME or LOGSPACE, we could ask whether there exists a natural query language corresponding to this class. This way database theory is related with descriptive complexity theory and finite models theory (cf., for example, [1]).

Following this general approach we consider in this paper two versions of a set theoretic $\Delta$-language as theoretical prototypes for "nested" data base query language where *data base states* and *queries* are interpreted, respectively, as *hereditarily-finite (*HF*) sets* and *set theoretic operations*. It is shown that these versions correspond exactly to (N/D)LOGSPACE computability over HF, respectively.

Such languages over sets, capturing also PTIME, were introduced in previous works [30,32,33,34,35,24,25,26], however the case of LOGSPACE already considered in [24] was not completely satisfactory developed there. Two approaches to defining and capturing LOGSPACE computability over HF were

---

* The second author is supported by a grant of the Ministry of Education of Russian Federation. The final version of the paper was also prepared during his visiting in 1999 the University of Siegen, Germany.

K.-D. Schewe, B. Thalheim (Eds.): FoIKS 2000, LNCS 1762, pp. 156–175, 2000.

presented. In one of them there were problems with the closure under compositions of queries, whereas LOGSPACE was described precisely. In another one the problems with composition of queries were resolved by some complication of the notion of LOGSPACE computability over HF (anyway, there is no unique, canonical or most preferable definition for the case of HF) with the syntax of the corresponding query language rather unnatural, however formally effective (computable). The latter involves an infinite family of constants for some technically defined set theoretic operations.

It makes no sense to describe in this paper these two approaches, especially the second one which is somewhat overcomplicated — a price payed for the achieved advantage mentioned above. However, here we overcome their drawbacks by presenting a *unified and simplified approach*. Actually, all of them prove to be *equivalent* due to some new partial result (Proposition 4.1) on definability of a linear ordering over finite extensional acyclic graphs. (Cf. also Note 2.1 and Footnote 8.)

To deal with computability over HF-sets we assume in this paper that (a) HF-sets, (b) membership relation between sets and (c) computable set operations are naturally represented, respectively, by (a') vertices of acyclic graphs, (b') the graph edges and (c') corresponding graph transformers.

Cf. op. cit., specifically [33,24,25,26], for a more extensive general introduction to the subject.

After preliminaries and technical introduction in Sect. 2 we introduce $\Delta$-languages of set theoretic operations in Sect. 3. Main result on capturing NLOGSPACE and DLOGSPACE over HF is presented and proved in Sect. 4.

## 2    Preliminaries and Technical Introduction

### 2.1    Hereditarily-Finite Sets

The universe HF of "pure" *hereditarily-finite sets* is defined inductively as the least class of sets such that

- if $x_1, \ldots, x_n \in \mathrm{HF}$, $n \geq 0$, then $\{x_1, \ldots, x_n\} \in \mathrm{HF}$ (with the order and duplication of $x_i$ considered as irrelevant).

In particular, we have the *empty* set $\emptyset \in \mathrm{HF}$ (the case of $n = 0$) and also $\{\emptyset\}$, $\{\{\emptyset\}\}$, $\{\emptyset, \{\emptyset\}\}$, etc. $\in \mathrm{HF}$. Actually, for real data base applications we have to consider, as in [33,26], a more general universe $\mathrm{HF}(\mathcal{A}, \mathcal{U})$ with *urelements* (or atoms, elementary data) $\mathcal{U}$ and database *attributes* $\mathcal{A}$ (or labels):

- $\mathcal{U} \subseteq \mathrm{HF}(\mathcal{A}, \mathcal{U})$ and
- if $x_1, \ldots, x_n \in \mathrm{HF}(\mathcal{A}, \mathcal{U})$ and $A_1, \ldots, A_n \in \mathcal{A}$, $n \geq 0$, then $\{A_1 : x_1, \ldots, A_n : x_n\} \in \mathrm{HF}(\mathcal{A}, \mathcal{U})$ where $A_i : x_i$ are elements $x_i$ labeled by the attributes $A_i \in \mathcal{A}$.

We may take $\mathcal{A} = \mathcal{U} =$ a set of finite strings in an alphabet, or we may include in $\mathcal{A} = \mathcal{U}$ also integers and other datatypes. Also, we could take $\mathcal{U} = \emptyset$ in favor of $\mathcal{A}$, essentially without any loss of generality. As an example of a data represented as such a set consider

$$\{ \texttt{STUDENT:I.Ivanov, BIRTH\_YEAR:1981, DEPT:CS,}$$
$$\texttt{STUDIES:Logic, STUDIES:Data\_Base\_Theory} \} \, .$$

Here CS (Computer Science Department) may be also a complicated data (set) of analogous form, etc. with any deep nesting if necessary:

$$\texttt{CS} = \{ \texttt{ADMIN:..., LECTURERS:..., STUDENTS:...} \} \, .$$

(In principle, it even may eventually refer again to the first displayed set corresponding to a concrete student I.Ivanov. However, this paper mostly does not account such possibilities for cycling. Cf. also Footnote 2 below.) This way *nested* or *complex* data [3,8,9,10,11,14,19,22] (or, more general, cycling, *semistructured, Web-like* data [2,4,21,22,28], cf. especially [7,26]) may be represented as hereditarily-finite (possibly cycling, called also antifounded or hyper-) sets with attributes and urelements. Note, that any ordinary relational database may be presented as a hereditarily-finite set of the *nesting depth* = 3 (DB = a *set* of relations each of which is a *set* of tuples i.e. of the "plain" *sets* $\{A_1 : x_1, \ldots, A_n : x_n\}$ with different attributes $A_i$ and with $x_i$ urelements).

For simplicity, only the case of pure HF-sets (without attributes and urelements, i.e. essentially the case of $\mathcal{A} = \mathcal{U} = \emptyset$) will be considered below. Note, that some natural linear ordering $<_{HF}$ of HF will play an essential role. Eventually, it is needed to imitate Turing machine tape and to order computation steps. To adapt (as in [33]) the considerations of this paper to the general case of $HF(\mathcal{A}, \mathcal{U})$ some *linear orderings* $<_{\mathcal{A}}$ and $<_{\mathcal{U}}$ should be additionally assumed which may be then extended to a linear order on the whole universe $HF(\mathcal{A}, \mathcal{U})$.

*Here is a natural place to jump temporary to Sect. 3 for getting an idea of a query $\Delta$-language over* HF.

## 2.2   Computability over HF

PTIME and, respectively, (N/D)LOGSPACE denote computability by a Turing machine in the time polynomial in the length of the input and, respectively, by a (nondeterministic/deterministic) Turing machine using the working tape of the length logarithmic in the length of the input. The typical inputs and outputs for a Turing machine are finite strings in a finite alphabet or, slightly more general (by using an appropriate evident encoding), finite graphs, etc. It is well-known that DLOGSPACE $\subseteq$ NLOGSPACE $\subseteq$ PTIME, and it is an *open question* whether $\subseteq$ are, in fact, proper inclusions [13].

There is a problem of some ambiguity of the notion of NLOGSPACE computability of functions in contrast to predicates: different nondeterministically chosen ways of computation may give different results. There is a reasonable direct approach to define what is NLOGSPACE computable function. However, we will actually work in terms of an equivalent notion of $FO^{\otimes}_{<}$-definability described below in Sect. 2.4 where this problem naturally disappears.

The key notion for this paper is the following definition of (say, PTIME or LOGSPACE) *computability* of operations $q : HF^m \to HF$ over HF-sets, instead of finite strings. Here $q(\bar{s}) = a$ means informally, for any $\bar{s}, a \in HF$, that $\bar{s}$ is a *data base state* and $a$ is an *answer* to the *query* $q$ about the state $\bar{s}$. Say, $\bar{s}$ may be a nested relational data base state with $a$ some other nested relation retrieved or (re)constructed from $\bar{s}$ by $q$.

Let $\nu : \text{Codes} \to HF$ be any surjective encoding of HF-sets. We say that $q$ is (PTIME, etc.) computable *with respect to* $\nu$ if the following diagram commutes for some (PTIME-, etc.-) computable transformation $Q$ between codes:

$$
\begin{array}{ccc}
HF^m & \xrightarrow{q} & HF \\
\nu^m \uparrow & & \uparrow \nu \\
\text{Codes}^m & \xrightarrow{Q} & \text{Codes}
\end{array}
\qquad q(\nu(\bar{c})) = \nu(Q(\bar{c})) \qquad (1)
$$

for all $\bar{c} \in \text{Codes}$. Using of Codes is essential here because Turing machine or any real computer does not "uderstand" immediately abstract HF-sets.

> *Computers deal with* Codes. *Peoples deal with abstract "high level" entities, say, with HF-sets.*

For the case of PTIME or (N/D)LOGSPACE we must denote corresponding classes of set-theoretic operations like $\mathcal{PTIME}_\nu$, $\mathcal{NLOGSPACE}_\nu$ or $\mathcal{DLOGSPACE}_\nu$ to emphasize that the corresponding notion of computability over HF *depends* on an encoding $\nu$. Note, that for the case of graph encoding $\gamma$ considered in Sect. 2.3 $\mathcal{NLOGSPACE}_\gamma$ or $\mathcal{DLOGSPACE}_\gamma$, unlike $\mathcal{PTIME}_\gamma$, are very *sensitive* to small variations of this $\gamma$. At least, only for some specific versions of $\gamma$ we can obtain reasonable results for LOGSPACE computability over HF.

In general, let $\mathcal{C}$ denote some *notion of computability* over Codes, for example corresponding to some complexity class. More precisely, $\mathcal{C}$ is a recursive set of *programs* in a reasonable (probably resource restricted) programming language, such as the language of Turing machines. We associate with $\mathcal{C}$ the corresponding class of computable transformers $\text{Codes}^m \to \text{Codes}$, $m = 1, 2, \ldots$. Define $\mathcal{C}_\nu$ as the class of $\mathcal{C}$-computable operations (and predicates) over HF with respect to $\nu$.

Strictly speaking, $\mathcal{C}$ is a class of programs rather than a class of corresponding computable transformers of Codes. In particular, this means that given a program $p \in \mathcal{C}$ and any its input $x$, the result of applying $p$ to $x$ considered as a universal function $U(p, x) = p(x)$ is computable in both arguments $p$ and $x$.

Note, that for any given program $Q : \text{Codes}^m \to \text{Codes}$ (from a fixed class $\mathcal{C}$) it may be problematic to decide whether there exists (actually, unique, if any) $q$ making the above diagram commutative. I.e. $Q$ may be "non-coherent" with $\nu$. We say that the class $\mathcal{C}_\nu$ of computable operations $q$ over HF has an *effective syntax* if (at least) there exists a recursive (not necessary $\mathcal{C}$-computable) family of programs $Q_\pi \in \mathcal{C}$, $\pi = 0, 1, \ldots$, with all corresponding $q_\pi \in \mathcal{C}_\nu$ existing and exhausting the class $\mathcal{C}_\nu$. (Here the programs $Q_\pi$ need not exhaust $\mathcal{C}$.)

Alternatively and more "realistically", we may let $\pi$ to range over formal expressions of a language $L$, instead of natural numbers. (We assume that $L$ itself is a recursive set of expressions.) In this case $q_\pi$ and $Q_\pi$ may be considered, respectively, as *denotational* and *operational semantics* of any expression (program) $\pi$ in this language. In contrast to $\mathcal{C}$, each $L$-program $\pi$ will have a corresponding $q$. In this paper we shall take in the role of $L$ appropriate versions $\Delta'$ of a natural set-theoretic language $\Delta$ (cf. Sect. 3) with a clear denotational semantics and with *tractable* operational semantics, say, in terms of LOGSPACE computability.

> *Thus, our goal is to find a reasonable encodings $\nu_1$ and $\nu_2$ and a set-theoretic languages $\Delta_1$ and $\Delta_2$ with reasonable denotational and operational semantics which correspond exactly to $\mathcal{NLOGSPACE}_{\nu_1}$ and, respectively, $\mathcal{DLOGSPACE}_{\nu_2}$.*

As we argued above, we cannot avoid choosing some encodings $\nu_i$ here. Moreover, in principle there may be different choices for the corresponding pairs $\langle \nu_i, \Delta_i \rangle$.

*Note 2.1.* In previous paper [24] some versions of encodings $\nu$ and of languages $\Delta'$ corresponding to LOGSPACE w.r.t. $\nu$ were found. However, as we noted in the Introduction, in one approach considered in [24] the class of LOGSPACE computable set-theoretic operations was not proved to be closed under compositions, and in another approach the syntax of considered version of $\Delta'$ was, however effective (in the above defined sense), not sufficiently explicitly or naturally presented. In the present paper we will demonstrate even technically simpler approach lacking those drawbacks and actually equivalent to both mentioned approaches (cf. formulas (10) and (12) in [24]) which were considered at the time of writing of [24] as presumably essentially different.

## 2.3    Graph Encoding of HF

An important example of Codes for HF is the class of all finite *acyclic pointed (rooted) graphs*[1] ($\mathcal{AG}$), i.e. graphs $G$ with no cycles and with a distinguished point (vertex) $p$ in each. (We could also consider an $m$-tuple of points distinguished.) Then any computability notion $\mathcal{C}$ will determine a *class of computable graph transformers* $\mathcal{AG} \to \mathcal{AG}$. Let $\gamma : \mathcal{AG} \to \text{HF}$ (or even $\gamma : \mathcal{G} \to \text{HF}$ for *any* class $\mathcal{G}$ of graphs; cf. a generalization below) be Mostowski's *general collapsing*

---

[1] Another interesting and essentially different version of Codes is the class of *finite trees*.

operation (an encoding of HF-sets by graphs) which assigns a set $\gamma(G, p) \in$ HF to each $\mathcal{AG}$ $\langle G, p \rangle$ in such a way that

$$\gamma(G, p) = \{\gamma(G, p') : p \to_G p' \text{ for some child } p' \text{ of } p \text{ in } G\} \ .$$

In particular, if $p$ has no children in $G$ then $\gamma(G, p) = \emptyset$. E.g. for $G$ consisting just of three edges $p_3 \to p_2 \to p_1$ and $p_3 \to p_1$ we have $\gamma(G, p_1) = \emptyset$, $\gamma(G, p_2) = \{\emptyset\}$ and $\gamma(G, p_3) = \{\emptyset, \{\emptyset\}\}$. Note, that for the case of general universe HF($\mathcal{A}$) with attributes we should consider graphs with $\mathcal{A}$-labeled edges.

We shall also write $p \in_G q$ instead of $q \to_G p$ and define formally any graph $G$ as a first-order structure $\langle |G|, \in_G \rangle$ with $|G|$ its set of vertices and with the binary relation $\in_G$ for its edges. Sometimes we will apply $\gamma$ to graphs with several kinds of edges (of various "colors"), i.e. with additional binary relations (such as a linear order $\prec_G$ on $|G|$), where $\in_G$ is just the *main* graph relation. Even *more general*, we may consider that $\gamma(G, p)$ is defined also for *any* graph, not necessary acyclic. Just apply $\gamma$ to the *initial acyclic (or well-founded)* part of $G$, denoted as $\mathbf{WF}(G)$. Here $\mathbf{WF}(G) \rightleftharpoons \langle W, \in_G |_W \rangle$ with $W \subseteq |G|$ the least set of vertices such that if for any fixed vertex $y \in |G|$ all its children $y \to_G x$ are in $W$ then we must have also $y \in W$. [2]

Let $\mathcal{G}$ be any class of finite pointed graphs, quite arbitrary or a special one such as $\mathcal{EG}$, $\mathcal{AG}$, $\mathcal{EAG}^*$, $\mathcal{EAG}^*_{\prec}$ or $\mathcal{EAG}^*_{<}$, etc. defined below. Then the restriction of $\gamma$ to $\mathcal{G}$ defines corresponding encoding of HF-sets with Codes = $\mathcal{G}$ which will be called a *graph encoding* defined by $\mathcal{G}$. So, we may specify explicitly only $\mathcal{G}$, corresponding restricted $\gamma$ being implicitly assumed.

Define *extensional* finite graphs ($\mathcal{EG}$) as those for which the ordinary set-theoretic *extensionality axiom* holds:

$$G \models \forall v \in x(v \in y) \ \& \ \forall v \in y(v \in x) \Rightarrow x = y \ ,$$

or, equivalently, different vertices in $G$ must have different sets of children.

We will use abbreviations like $\mathcal{EAG}^*_{\prec}$, $\mathcal{EG}^*$, etc. with superscript $*$ and/or subscript $\prec$ to designate that the graphs considered involve additional relations for the transitive closure $\in_G^*$ of the main graph relation $\in_G$ and, respectively, for *any* linear order $\prec_G$ on the vertices of a graph $G$. Let also subscript $<$ denote the *canonical linear order* $<_G$ on vertices of any $\mathcal{EAG}$ $G$ which is inherited from the linear order $<_{\mathrm{HF}}$ defined below in (2) via collapsing $\gamma : |G| \to$ HF. Note, that for different vertices $p_1, p_2$ in $\mathcal{EAG}$ $G$ we should evidently have $\gamma(G, p_1) \neq \gamma(G, p_2)$. Actually, any finite $G \in \mathcal{EAG}$ is isomorphic to *initial part* i.e. to a finite *transitive part* of HF.

---

[2] There exists more radical approach based on arbitrary graphs allowing cycles or infinite chains which leads to so called *hypersets* satisfying *anti-foundation axiom*. Cf. [5] for general hyperset theory and [34,35,25,26] for corresponding versions of bounded hyperset theory and its $\Delta$-language. In particular this approach allows considering "cycling" sets like $\Omega = \{\Omega\}$ Such (hereditarily-finite) hypersets may be used to represent so called Web-like Data Bases (WDB) i.e. databases organized analogously to World-Wide Web with arbitrary hyper-links; cf. [26]. It is also interesting to extend the results of the present paper for LOGSPACE from well-founded sets to hypersets.

It can be shown that $=$ and $\in$ over HF are PTIME computable w.r.t. encoding $\gamma : \mathcal{AG} \to$ HF. I.e. '$\gamma(G_1, p_1) = \gamma(G_2, p_2)$' and '$\gamma(G_1, p_1) \in \gamma(G_2, p_2)$' are decidable in PTIME for arbitrary $\langle G_1, p_1 \rangle, \langle G_2, p_2 \rangle \in \mathcal{AG}$. However, it is hardly the case for (N/D)LOGSPACE (due to PTIME completeness of the corresponding problem for $=$; cf. [9]). "Restricting" $\gamma$ to the class $\mathcal{EAG}_<$ (which is, strictly speaking, not a part of $\mathcal{AG}$) and considering its corresponding version $\gamma : \mathcal{EAG}_< \to$ HF makes this problem easier — computable in NLOGSPACE. It becomes even DLOGSPACE computable in the case of $\mathcal{EAG}_<^*$, i.e. when the transitive closure $\in_G^*$ of the main graph relation is also immediately available. (Cf. Proposition 4.1 below.) The additional relations $<_G$ and $\in_G^*$ in $G$ help very much by giving more information on the input, the information which otherwise should be recovered by the cost of some computational resources. Thus, we just change a little the initial notion of Codes $= \mathcal{AG}$, but this change is crucial.

It is evidently inevitable considering something like the above enriched classes of graphs $\mathcal{EAG}_<$ or $\mathcal{EAG}_<^*$ unless (N/D)LOGSPACE $=$ PTIME or $<_G$ and $\in_G$ are formally definable by suitable means (say, in the language $\mathrm{FO}^\odot$ considered in Sect. 2.4; we have only partial, however important, result of Proposition 4.1).

*Actually, this paper is devoted to machine independent description of two classes of computable set theoretic operations: $\mathcal{NLOGSPACE}_{\mathcal{EAG}_<}$ and $\mathcal{DLOGSPACE}_{\mathcal{EAG}_<^*}$ for graph encoding $\gamma$ restricted to corresponding classes of graphs $\mathcal{EAG}_<$ and $\mathcal{EAG}_<^*$.*

*Agreement.* It makes a sense to consider any such graph $G$ in the form of a finite relational structure

$$G = \langle |G|; =_G, \in_G, \in_G^*, <_G, V_G \rangle$$

with $\in_G^*$ and $<_G$ probably omitted depending on the considered class of graphs such as $\mathcal{EG}, \mathcal{AG}, \mathcal{EAG}_<$. Here $=_G$ is *one more* predicate on the finite set $|G|$ which is required to be an *equivalence relation*. Strictly speaking, in this case we should consider as vertices of this graph just corresponding equivalence classes. We postulate that there is an edge $[v] \to [u]$ between any two such classes/vertices $[u]$ and $[v]$ if $u \in_G v$ (i.e. $v \to_G u$) holds for some representatives of these classes, and analogously for $\in_G^*$ and $<_G$. We assume that $V_G$ is an unary predicate on $|G|$ representing just one of these classes and corresponding to a distinguished vertex of the graph. Then the notions of extensionality, acyclicity or the like of graphs represented in this form are defined in terms of the corresponding quotient. In particular, it is required that $\in_G^*$ and $<_G$ behave as intended (i.e. as transitive closure and canonical ordering) on the quotient. Relations of any given structure $G$ of the above form, except $=_G$, may be evidently improved with preserving quotient of $G$ (up to isomorphism) so that $=_G$ becomes *congruence relation* w.r.t. other relations[3]. In this case we should consider an isomorphism between $G_1$ and $G_2$ rather as a relation $\leftrightarrow \subseteq |G_1| \times |G_2|$ which preserves all relations on these graphs, including $=_{G_1}$ and $=_{G_2}$, and the distinguished elements (classes) $V_{G_1}$ and $V_{G_2}$. We may call such an isomorphism as *generalized* one, or isomorphism

---

[3] i.e. such equivalence relation $=_G$ that $G \models x = x' \ \& \ y = y' \ \& \ x \in y \Rightarrow x' \in y'$, etc.

*up to* the congruence relations $=_{G_i}$, in comparison with the ordinary (bijective) isomorphisms. Evidently, for ($\in$-)isomorphic graphs $\langle G_1, p_1 \rangle$ and $\langle G_2, p_2 \rangle$ we have $\gamma(G_1, p_1) = \gamma(G_2, p_2)$.

## 2.4 Definability of Graph Transformers by Logical Means

To define a graph transformer $Q : \bar{G} = \langle G_1, \ldots, G_n \rangle \longmapsto G$ (determined up to a graph isomorphism) we may use, say, some extension FO$'$ of the first-order language

$$\mathrm{FO}(\in_1, \ldots, \in_n; =_1, \ldots, =_n; <_1, \ldots, <_n; \in_1^*, \ldots, \in_n^*; V_1, \ldots, V_n)$$

over a tuple of graphs $\langle G_1, \ldots, G_n \rangle$ considered as many-sorted structure (with $\in_i$, $=_i$, $<_i$, $\in_i^*$ and $V_i$ interpreted, respectively, as $\in_{G_i}$, $=_{G_i}$, $<_{G_i}$, $\in_{G_i}^*$ and $V_{G_i}$). In this case it is reasonable to consider that $|G| \subseteq |\tilde{G}| \rightleftharpoons |G_1|^{k_1} \times \cdots \times |G_n|^{k_n}$, $\in_G \subseteq |\tilde{G}| \times |\tilde{G}|$, $=_G \subseteq |\tilde{G}| \times |\tilde{G}|$, etc., for some $k_1, \ldots, k_n \geq 1$, and define $|G|$, $\in_G$, $=_G$, etc. by FO$'$-formulas $|G|(\tilde{v})$, $\tilde{u} \in_G \tilde{v}$, $\tilde{u} =_G \tilde{v}$ of $k = k_1 + \ldots + k_n$ and $2k$ free variables, respectively. Actually, we may take $=_G$ to be *partial equivalence relation* (i.e. any transitive and symmetric relation) on $\tilde{G}$ and define $|G|(\tilde{v}) \rightleftharpoons \tilde{v} =_G \tilde{v}$. This approach to formal definability of graph transformers relies on the well known concept of first-order interpretations between theories or structures (cf. [17,36]).

Thus, we will use the extension FO$'$ = FO$^\otimes$ of the language FO by new predicate forming construct $[\lambda \bar{x} \bar{y}.\varphi(\bar{x}, \bar{y}, \bar{z})]^\otimes$ for any definable (in FO$^\otimes$) relation $\lambda \bar{x} \bar{y}.\varphi(\bar{x}, \bar{y}, \bar{z})$ of two lists of variables $\bar{x}$ and $\bar{y}$ of the same length. Other free variables $\bar{z}$ of $\varphi$ are considered as parameters. We call this construct the "horizontal" *transitive closure* and define its meaning in any $G$ by

$$[\lambda \bar{x} \bar{y}.\varphi(\bar{x}, \bar{y})]^\otimes (\bar{u}, \bar{v}) \quad (\text{or } \varphi^\otimes(\bar{u}, \bar{v})) \quad \text{iff} \quad \varphi(\bar{u}, \bar{u}_1), \varphi(\bar{u}_1, \bar{u}_2), \ldots, \varphi(\bar{u}_n, \bar{v}) \text{ hold}$$

for some $n \geq 0$ and $\bar{u}_1, \ldots, \bar{u}_n \in |G|$). It may *arbitrarily* participate in any other FO$^\otimes$-formula as a predicate.

Note, that to be $\mathcal{EAG}$ is evidently FO$^\otimes$-definable property of graphs. Cf. also Note 4.1 in Sect. 4 for the case of $\mathcal{EAG}_<^{(*)}$.

We may consider also *deterministic* version $\odot$ of transitive closure $\otimes$ which works as $\otimes$ for any formula $\varphi(\bar{x}, \bar{y})$ when it defines a "deterministic" (partial) *mapping* $\bar{x} \longmapsto \bar{y}$. Otherwise, applying $\odot$ gives, say, the false predicate (or, alternatively, $\odot$ preliminary corrects $\varphi$ to make it "deterministic").

FO$^\otimes$ and FO$^\odot$ are essentially identical to the languages FO + TC and FO + DTC, respectively, considered in [17,18]. (Actually, in [17,18] TC and DTC coincide with the *reflexive* versions of this $\otimes$- and $\odot$-constructs.) However, the denotation TC (and $*$) will be occupied in our paper for the "vertical" transitive closure in the universe of sets HF:

$$u \in \mathrm{TC}(v) \rightleftharpoons u \in^* v \rightleftharpoons [\lambda xy.x \in y]^\otimes (u, v) \ .$$

I.e. we use TC and $*$ just in connection with the relation $\in$. Actually, let $\in_G^*$ coincide with $\in_G^\otimes$.

## 2.5   Recalling Some Results from Descriptive Complexity Theory over Finite Models

It is proved in [17] that the notion of definability in $FO_\prec + $ *positive* $\otimes$ in finite structures *linear ordered* by $\prec$ is equivalent to NLOGSPACE computability. Moreover, $FO_\prec + $ *positive* $\otimes$ has the same expressive power in these structures as the *full* $FO_\prec + \otimes$, i.e. as $FO_\prec^\otimes$ [18]. This result is equivalent to the statement CoNLOGSPACE = NLOGSPACE (cf. also [37]) which have been widely believed previously as false. The same holds for $FO_\prec^\ominus$ and DLOGSPACE, but easier. (In particular, we have $FO \subseteq$ DLOGSPACE.) Therefore, we may freely interchange the notions $FO_\prec^{\otimes/\ominus}$ and (N/D)LOGSPACE where $\prec$ denotes a linear order. More-over, we may consider that the notion of (N/D)LOGSPACE *computable graph transformers* $\mathcal{EAG}_\prec^{(*)} \to \mathcal{EAG}_\prec^{(*)}$ is already defined due to Sect. 2.4.

We will need also the well-known extension FO + LFP of FO by the *least fixed point* construct

$$\textbf{the-least } P.[P(\bar{x}) \leftrightarrow \varphi(\bar{x}, P)]$$

with the predicate variable $P$ occurring in $\varphi$ positively. This construct is based on an iterative computation of the least predicate $P$ satisfying the condition in the brackets. (Start with $P_0 \rightleftharpoons \emptyset$ and continue by $P_{n+1} \rightleftharpoons \lambda \bar{x}.\varphi(\bar{x}, P_n(\bar{x}))$, up to stabilization $P \rightleftharpoons P_n = P_{n+1}$ of this monotonic sequence.) It actually subsumes $\otimes$ and $\ominus$. It was shown in [16,27,38] that definability in $FO_\prec + $ LFP over finite (linear ordered!) models exactly corresponds to PTIME computability. Cf. also analogous results for PTIME and DLOGSPACE in terms of recursive or, respectively, primitively recursive (global) functions, instead of predicates, in finite segments of natural numbers [29,15].

# 3   $\Delta$-Languages of Set Theoretic Operations

Define inductively $\Delta^*$-*formulas* and $\Delta^*$-*terms* by the clauses

$$\langle \Delta^*\text{-terms}\rangle ::= \langle \text{variables}\rangle \mid \emptyset \mid \{a, b\} \mid \bigcup a \mid \{t(x) : x \in^{(*)} a \,\&\, \varphi(x)\}$$

$$\langle \Delta^*\text{-formulas}\rangle ::= a = b \mid a \in^{(*)} b \mid \varphi \,\&\, \psi \mid \varphi \vee \psi \mid \neg\varphi \mid \forall x \in^{(*)} a\varphi(x) \mid \exists x \in^{(*)} a\varphi(x)$$

where $\varphi$ and $\psi$ are any $\Delta^*$-formulas, $a, b$ and $t$ are any $\Delta^*$-terms and $x$ is a variable not free in $a$. The brackets around $*$ mean that there are two versions of the membership relation: $\in$ and its transitive closure $\in^*$. Then $\Delta_0^*$-*formulas* are defined as those $\Delta^*$-formulas involving only atomic terms (i.e. just variables or the constant $\emptyset$). We write $\Delta$ ($\Delta_0$) when $\in^*$ is not used at all. The sub-language $\Delta$ corresponds to the *basic* [12] or *rudimentary* [20] set-theoretic operations. Note, that our using the term $\Delta$ is not completely fixed in our different papers, but the main idea is that $\Delta$-formulas involve only *bounded* quantification $\forall x \in^{(*)} a$ and $\exists x \in^{(*)} a$. That is why, according to traditions of mathematical logic and set theory, we use the name $\Delta$ for our language and for various its versions. All other constructs of $\Delta$ are also in a sense "bounded". But, for example, the unrestricted *power-set operation* $\mathcal{P}(x) \rightleftharpoons \{y : y \subseteq x\}$ is considered as intuitively "unbounded", "impredicative". Note, that $\mathcal{P}(x)$ is also evidently related with exponentiation, and therefore it is computationally intractable. In general, let $\Delta'$ denote some reasonable, still "bounded", extension of the class of basic operations.

We shall use set variables, $\Delta^*$-terms and formulas both as syntactic objects and as denotations of their values in HF. For example, $\Delta$-separation $\{x \in a : \varphi(x)\}$ for $\varphi \in \Delta$ gives 'the set of all $x$ in the set $a$ for which $\varphi(x)$ holds' and is a partial case of the construct $\{t(x) : x \in a \;\&\; \varphi(x)\}$ = 'the set of all values of $t(x)$ such that …'. Also $x \in \{a, b\}$ iff $x = a$ or $x = b$, $x \in \bigcup a$ iff $\exists z \in a(x \in z)$ and $\in^*$ is a transitive closure of the membership relation $\in$ on HF, i.e. $x \in^* y$ iff $x \in x_1 \in x_2 \in \ldots \in x_n \in y$ for some $n \geq 0$ and $x_1, \ldots, x_n$ in HF. The meaning of logical symbols & ('and'), $\vee$ ('or'), $\neg$ ('not'), $\forall$ ('for all'), $\exists$ ('exists') is well known. Bounded quantifiers $\forall x \in^{(*)} a$ and $\exists x \in^{(*)} a$ have the same meaning as the ordinary unbounded ones except the variable $x$ ranges only over the (transitive closure of the) set (denoted by) $a$.

Note that bounded quantifiers may be eliminated from $\Delta^{(*)}$-language:

$$\exists x \in^{(*)} a \psi(x) \Leftrightarrow \{x \in^{(*)} a : \psi(x)\} \neq \emptyset \;,$$
$$\forall x \in^{(*)} a \psi(x) \Leftrightarrow \{x \in^{(*)} a : \neg\psi(x)\} = \emptyset \;.$$

Any $\Delta'$-term $t(\bar{x})$ evidently defines a set-theoretic operation

$$\lambda \bar{x}.t(\bar{x}) : \mathrm{HF}^n \rightarrow \mathrm{HF} \;.$$

For example, we may define in $\Delta^*$ the *transitive closure* of a set $y$ as $\mathrm{TC}(y) \rightleftharpoons \{x : x \in^* y\}$. Ordered singletons, pairs, triples, etc. are defined in $\Delta$ as $\langle u \rangle \rightleftharpoons u$, $\langle u, v \rangle \rightleftharpoons \{\{u\}\{u, v\}\}$ and $\langle u, v, w \rangle \rightleftharpoons \langle\langle u, v \rangle, w\rangle$, etc. It follows that $\langle\langle \bar{y} \rangle, z\rangle = \langle \bar{y}, z \rangle$, $\bigcup\langle u, v \rangle = \{u, v\}$ and for any set of ordered pairs $r$ the set of all the components of these pairs is defined in $\Delta$ as $\mathbf{field}(r) \rightleftharpoons \bigcup\bigcup r$.[4]

As in [33], we may define in the $\Delta$-language many other useful operations on sets, e.g. the *Cartesian product* $A \times B$, *Cartesian power* $A^k$ and *disjoint unions* $A + B$ and $\sum_{i \in I} A_i$ of any two sets $A$ and $B$ and of a $\Delta$-definable family of sets $A_i$, etc.[5]

As usual, any set $g$ of ordered pairs may be considered as a (directed) graph. Moreover, for arbitrary set $g$ we may just ignore its elements which are not ordered pairs. Any pair $\langle g, p \rangle \in \mathrm{HF}$ with $g$ a graph and $p$ its vertex is just a *pointed graph* in the framework of set theory. If $p \notin \mathbf{field}(g)$ then it is considered as an *isolated* vertex.

---

[4] Here the double union $\bigcup\bigcup$ is related with the above specific definition of ordered pairs. Note, that in the case of HF($\mathcal{A}$)-sets with attributes the ordered pair $\langle u, v \rangle$ could be defined more naturally from a practical point of view as $\{\mathrm{Fst} : u, \mathrm{Snd} : v\}$ for some two special labels (attributes) Fst and Snd.

[5] It can be shown [31,32,35] that $\Delta$ defines exactly all *provably-recursive set-theoretic operations* in Kripke-Platek set theory [6] without foundation axiom. In this sense this language is sufficiently complete from the point of view of its expressive power.

We will use extensively the fact that any $\Delta^{(*)}$-formula $\varphi$ is equivalent to a $\Delta_0^{(*)}$-formula [12]. Cf. also [32,35] for corresponding proof-theoretic considerations and formal *reductions*, as in lambda calculus, with $\Delta_0^{(*)}$-formulas being *normal forms* for $\Delta^{(*)}$-formulas. For example, the formula $\langle u, v \rangle = w$ is equivalent (and may serve as an abbreviation) to $\Delta_0$-formula

$$\exists s, p \in w (\forall x \in w(x = s \lor x = p) \,\&\, u \in s \,\&\, u, v \in p \,\&$$
$$\forall x \in s(x = u) \,\&\, \forall x \in p(x = u \lor x = v)) \;.$$

Then $\langle u, v \rangle \in z$ is equivalent to $\exists w \in z(\langle u, v \rangle = w)$ and therefore also reducible to $\Delta_0$. Analogously may be expressed $w = \bigcup u$, etc.[6]

*Note 3.1.* Such abbreviations for $\langle u, v \rangle = w$, $w = \bigcup u$, $u = \emptyset$, $u = \{\emptyset\}$, etc. may be also used in the framework of the language $\mathrm{FO}(\in, =)$ (instead of $\Delta_0$) when working in a graph $G$ (instead of HF).

However, there are notions which are hardly definable in $\Delta^*$ such as the *canonical* or *lexicographical linear ordering* $<_{\mathrm{HF}}$ on HF described by the

**Axiom for $<_{\mathrm{HF}}$:**

$$x < y \Leftrightarrow \exists u \in y \setminus x (\{v \in x : u < v\} = \{v \in y : u < v\}) \;. \tag{2}$$

Note, that (2) defines $<_{\mathrm{HF}}$ uniquely, but only *implicitly*. This ordering evidently coincides with that induced by the Ackerman's bijection $\mathbf{Ack} : N \to \mathrm{HF}$, $N = \{0, 1, 2, \dots\}$, the most popular encoding of the universe HF by natural numbers:

$$\mathbf{Ack}(2^{n_1} + 2^{n_2} + \dots + 2^{n_j}) = \{\mathbf{Ack}(n_1), \mathbf{Ack}(n_2), \dots, \mathbf{Ack}(n_j)\}$$

for any $j \geq 0$ and $n_1 > n_2 > \dots > n_j \geq 0$. In particular, $\mathbf{Ack}(0) = \emptyset$. Note, that very simple singleton operation $x \longmapsto \{x\}$ corresponds to the arithmetical exponential $k \longmapsto 2^k$ with respect to $\mathbf{Ack}$, which is surely intractable. It follows that, however corresponding linear ordering $<_{\mathrm{HF}}$ seems a good candidate to extend $\Delta$-language, we must consider, instead of $\mathbf{Ack}$, other encodings for the universe HF like the graph encoding (collapsing) $\gamma$ described in the Sect. 2.3.

We may extend $\Delta$ also by a set-theoretic *collapsing* operation

$$C : \mathrm{HF} \to \mathrm{HF}$$

which is a *restriction* of the general collapsing $\gamma$ to the case of (pointed) $\mathcal{EAG}$s considered as elements of the universe HF. So, $C(\langle g, p \rangle)$ is the set in HF corresponding to the point $p$ of $g$ under $\gamma$. If $g$ is not an extensional or an acyclic graph then let $C(\langle g, p \rangle) = \emptyset$.

---

[6] Note, that $\Delta_0^*$-formulas are just first-order formulas with bounded quantifiers in the language $\in, \in^*$. By this reason and by the above considerations $\Delta^*$, involving rather complex set-theoretic operations, may be also considered as an *analogue of first-order logic language*. There is also corresponding proof-theoretic conservativeness result [32,35], relative to $\Delta_0$-formulas, for Kripke-Platek set theory without foundation axiom (corresponding to $\Delta$) over set theory consisting only of Extensionality Axiom (which is "almost" first-order logic).

Collapsing operation plays a fundamental role. It reflects in the framework of set theory our informal "understanding" of sets of sets, etc. in terms of graphs. From the database point of view $\langle g, p \rangle$ is a data representing a "plan" of constructing another data, i.e. a set corresponding to the vertex $p$. Collapsing is just a *legal possibility to realize such plans* which a reasonable query language should give.

> This is related with *two levels of representing data* in a database: (i) (comparatively) low level, here via graphs (in general case — with labeled edges), and (ii) high, abstract level — via HF-sets. *Philosophically, this is probably the main point of the set-theoretic approach to (what is called now semistructured or Web-like) databases.*

We will need two other versions of C:

- $C^{\circ}(\langle g, <_g, \in_g^*, p \rangle) \rightleftharpoons C(\langle g, p \rangle)$ if $<_g$ is the canonical linear order on the vertices of $\mathcal{EAG}$ $g$ and $\in_g^*$ is the transitive closure of $\in_g = \{\langle u, v \rangle : \langle u, v \rangle \in g\}$, and $C^{\circ}(\langle g, <_g, \in_g^*, p \rangle) \rightleftharpoons \emptyset$, otherwise. I.e. $C^{\circ}$, unlike C, is properly defined only on $\mathcal{EAG}_<^* \subseteq$ HF, i.e. on the canonically ordered $\mathcal{EAG}^*$s.
- $C^{\otimes}(\langle g, <_g, p \rangle) \rightleftharpoons C(\langle g, p \rangle)$ if $<_g$ is the canonical linear order on the vertices of $\mathcal{EAG}$ $g$, and $\rightleftharpoons \emptyset$, otherwise. I.e. $C^{\otimes}$, unlike C and $C^{\circ}$, is properly defined only on $\mathcal{EAG}_< \subseteq$ HF, i.e. on the canonically ordered $\mathcal{EAG}$s.

The reason of using the superscripts $\otimes$ and $\circ$ in C will be clear later in Theorem 4.1. (Note that $C^{\otimes}$ was called $\hat{C}$ in [24].)

Another particularly important construct is *recursive $\Delta'$-separation* **Rec**:

$$\textbf{the-least } p.[p = \{x \in a : \varphi(x, p)\}] \ .$$

It must be considered as a term which denotes the least solution $p \subseteq a$ of the equation in the square brackets (for $\varphi \in \Delta'$ satisfying a reasonable "positivity" condition for the variable $p$).

We will also consider an extension of $\Delta^*$-language by a new kind of terms $r^{\otimes}$ (instead of formulas, as for the case of FO in Sect. 2.4) to denote the "horizontal" *transitive closure* of any relation (set of pairs) $r$. (Do not mix denotations $r^{\otimes}$ and $r^{\circ}$ with $C^{\otimes}$ and $C^{\circ}$ defined above and having completely different meaning.) It will be called $\Delta^{\otimes}$, with corresponding $\Delta^{\otimes}$-*terms* and $\Delta^{\otimes}$-*formulas*. Evidently, $\otimes$ is definable by **Rec**.[7] *Deterministic* version $\circ$ of $\otimes$ is formally defined as

$$r^{\circ} \rightleftharpoons \text{Det}(r)^{\otimes} \text{ where } \text{Det}(r) \rightleftharpoons \{\langle x, y \rangle \in r : \exists!z(\langle x, z \rangle \in r)\} \ .$$

Analogously, we use denotations $\Delta_<$ or $\Delta_{\leq}^{\otimes}$ if the predicate for $<_{\text{HF}}$ is included in the language.

The following characterization of the language $\Delta^* + \textbf{Rec} + C$ have been obtained in [30,32,33].

---

[7] Strictly speaking, we must write $\Delta^{*\otimes}$ instead of $\Delta^{\otimes}$ because $\otimes$ does not cover the full strength of $*$. However, for simplicity, we will use $\Delta^{\otimes}$ for $\Delta^{*\otimes}$. Thus, TC is not definable even in $\Delta + \textbf{Rec}$ because TC $\notin \mathcal{PTIME}_{\gamma'}$ for some specific version $\gamma'$ of $\gamma$ (cf. [33,35]) such that, moreover, $\mathcal{PTIME}_{\gamma'}$ coincides with the class of operations over HF which are definable in an appropriate extension of $\Delta + \textbf{Rec}$.

**Theorem 3.1.** *The class of operations over* HF *definable in the language* $\Delta^* +$ **Rec** $+\,$**C** *coincides with the class* $\mathcal{PTIME}_\gamma$ *of operations computable in polynomial time under graph representation* $\gamma$ *of* HF-*sets or, equivalently, computable by graph transformers definable in* FO $+$ LFP. $\qquad\square$

It is essentially used in the proof of this theorem that $<_{\mathrm{HF}}$ is definable in $\Delta^* +$ **Rec** [33]. In particular, in the formulation we need not mention any linear ordering in defining graph transformers in FO $+$ LFP. Also, $\mathcal{AG}$s or $\mathcal{EAG}$s may be equally used as Codes here, as well as C may be replaced by $\mathrm{C}^\otimes$ or $\mathrm{C}^\odot$.

## 4  Main Result on Capturing LOGSPACE over HF

The following proposition is essential for proving the main result on capturing LOGSPACE over HF (cf. Cases 2 and 8 in the proof). Let $G_1$ and $G_2 \in \mathcal{EAG}^*_<$ be arbitrary two graphs (each supplemented with canonical linear order $<_i \rightleftharpoons <_{G_i}$ and transitive closure $\in_i^*$ of $\in_i \rightleftharpoons \in_{G_i}$, $i = 1, 2$). For any two vertices $x \in |G_1|$ and $y \in |G_2|$ of these graphs let

$$x \sim_{1,2} y \;\rightleftharpoons\; \gamma(G_1, x) = \gamma(G_2, y) \ ,$$

$$x \sqsubset_{1,2} y \;\rightleftharpoons\; \gamma(G_1, x) \subset \gamma(G_2, y) \ ,$$

$$x <_{1,2} y \;\rightleftharpoons\; \gamma(G_1, x) <_{\mathrm{HF}} \gamma(G_2, y) \ .$$

**Proposition 4.1.** *The relations* $x \sim_{1,2} y$, $x \sqsubset_{1,2} y$ *and* $x <_{1,2} y$ *between vertices of any two graphs* $G_1$ *and* $G_2$ *in* $\mathcal{EAG}^*_<$ *(respectively, in* $\mathcal{EAG}_<$*) are uniformly definable by* $\mathrm{FO}^\odot$-*formulas (respectively, by* $\mathrm{FO}^\otimes$-*formulas).*

*Proof.* Define $\mathrm{FO}^\odot$-formulas (omitting subscripts in $\sim_{1,2}$, $\sqsubset_{1,2}$ and $<_{1,2}$):

$$\mathrm{next}^G_x(u, u') \rightleftharpoons u \in^* x \;\&\; u' \in^* x \;\&\; u < u' \;\&\; \neg \exists w \in^* x(u < w < u') \ ,$$

$$\mathrm{Next}_{x,y}(u, v; u', v') \rightleftharpoons \mathrm{next}^1_x(u, u') \;\&\; \mathrm{next}^2_y(v, v') \ ,$$

$$I_{x,y}(u, v) \rightleftharpoons \mathrm{Next}^\odot_{x,y}(\emptyset, \emptyset; u, v) \ ,$$

$$x \sim y \rightleftharpoons \forall u \in^* x \exists v \in^* y I_{x,y}(u, v) \;\&\; \forall v \in^* y \exists u \in^* x I_{x,y}(u, v) \;\&$$
$$\forall u, u' \in^* x \forall v, v' \in^* y[I_{x,y}(u, v) \;\&\; I_{x,y}(u', v') \Rightarrow$$
$$(u \in_1 u' \Leftrightarrow v \in_2 v') \;\&\; (u \in_1 x \Leftrightarrow v \in_2 y)] \ ,$$

$$x \sqsubset y \rightleftharpoons x \not\sim y \;\&\; \forall u \in_1 x \exists v \in_2 y(u \sim v) \ ,$$

$$E(u, v; x, y) \rightleftharpoons u \in_1 x \;\&\; v \in_2 y \;\&\; u \not\sim v \;\&$$
$$(\forall u' \in_1 x | u' >_1 u)(\exists v' \in_2 y | v' >_2 v)(u' \sim v') \;\&$$
$$(\forall v' \in_2 y | v' >_2 v)(\exists u' \in_1 x | u' >_1 u)(u' \sim v') \ .$$

Note that the formula $I_{x,y}(u, v)$ relates vertices $u \in |G_1|$ and $v \in |G_2|$ lying in the transitive closures of $x \in |G_1|$ and $y \in |G_2|$, respectively, according to their positions in restricted linear orders $<_1$ and $<_2$. It follows from the recursive definition (2) of $<$ over HF that recursively

$$x < y \Leftrightarrow x \sqsubset y \lor (\exists u, v)(E(u, v; x, y) \;\&\; u < v) \ .$$

Therefore we can define explicitly in $FO^\odot$

$$x < y \rightleftharpoons x \sqsubset y \vee \exists u, v(E^\odot(u, v; x, y) \;\&\; u \sqsubset v) \;.$$

$\square$

(It follows that the classes of IC-$FO^\otimes$- ([24]) and $FO^\otimes$-transformers of $\mathcal{EAG}_<$s coincide, what resolves a question 5 from Sect. 13 in [24]. Analogously the classes of IC-$FO^\odot$- and $FO^\odot$-transformers of $\mathcal{EAG}^*_<$s coincide.)

Remember, that *any* class of finite pointed graphs $\mathcal{G}$, in particular $\mathcal{G} = \mathcal{EAG}^{(*)}_<$, defines corresponding graph encoding of HF-sets with Codes $= \mathcal{G}$. Given any $\Delta'$ and class(es) of TRANSFORMERS of graphs from $\mathcal{G}$ to $\mathcal{G}$, we may consider the following abbreviation (introduced in [24])

$$\Delta' \sim_{\mathrm{HF}} \left( \mathcal{G} \xrightarrow[\text{TRANSFORMERS}_2]{\text{TRANSFORMERS}_1} \mathcal{G} \right)$$

of the statement:

'$\Delta'$-*definable operations over* HF *coincide with those computable by* TRANSFORMERS$_i$ *for* $i = 1, 2$'.

One of the classes of transformers may be omitted in this denotation. If both are present then it is asserted that they compute the *same* class of operations over HF, namely those $\Delta'$-definable (even if these classes of TRANSFORMERS are different).

*Note 4.1.* (Cf. [24].) Fortunately, we can check even in FO correctness of the input and output codes, i.e. the membership relations '$G \in \mathcal{EAG}^*_<$' and '$G \in \mathcal{EAG}_<$'. (This will be used in the proof of Theorem 4.1, Case 6). Extensionality and all axioms of a strict linear and canonical ordering $<$ are evidently expressible by FO-formulas. Then acyclicity of any finite graph $G$ follows from an additional axiom $x \in y \Rightarrow x < y$ which, of course, must hold on $\mathcal{EAG}_<$s. This allows to use $\in$-induction in proving that $<$ is uniquely defined by these axioms on any $\mathcal{EAG}_<$. Finally, the relation $\in^*_G$ is completely characterized on all the structures satisfying these axioms by the formula $x \in^* y \Leftrightarrow x \in y \vee \exists z \in y(x \in^* z)$ also by using $\in$-induction (on $y$).

Finally, we are ready to formulate and prove the Main Result of this paper:

**Theorem 4.1 (On Capturing LOGSPACE over HF).**

$$\Delta^\otimes_< + C^\otimes \sim_{\mathrm{HF}} \left( \mathcal{EAG}_< \xrightarrow[\text{NLOGSPACE}]{FO^\otimes} \mathcal{EAG}_< \right) \sim_{\mathrm{HF}} \mathcal{NLOGSPACE}_{\mathcal{EAG}_<} \quad (3)$$

$$\Delta^\odot_< + C^\odot \sim_{\mathrm{HF}} \left( \mathcal{EAG}^*_< \xrightarrow[\text{DLOGSPACE}]{FO^\odot} \mathcal{EAG}^*_< \right) \sim_{\mathrm{HF}} \mathcal{DLOGSPACE}_{\mathcal{EAG}^*_<} \quad (4)$$

*Moreover, in both cases any definable set-theoretic operation may be equivalently represented by a term of the form $C^{\otimes/\circ}(t(\bar{x}))$ with $t(\bar{x})$ involving no collapsing ("external collapsing normal form"), and definable predicates need not use collapsing at all.*[8]

*Proof. of* (3), *direct part.* For each term $t(\bar{x}) = t(x_1, \ldots, x_n)$ in $\Delta_<^{\otimes} + C^{\otimes}$ (representing a query $q$ in the commutative diagram (1)) we will define in $FO^{\otimes}$ by induction on the construction of $t$ a corresponding graph transformer

$$[\![t]\!] : \bar{G} = \langle G_1, \ldots, G_n \rangle \longmapsto G_{t(\bar{x})} : (\mathcal{EAG}_<)^n \to \mathcal{EAG}_<$$

($Q$ — in terms of (1)) with $G_i = \langle |G_i|; =_i, \in_i, <_i, V_i \rangle$. Here $x_i$ is simultaneously a set-theoretic variable of the term $t$ and a first-order variable denoting corresponding distinguished vertex of $G_i$; i.e. $G_i \models x_i \in V_i$ is assumed in the corresponding context. We define $[\![t]\!]$ by a tuple of $FO^{\otimes}$-formulas

$$G_{t(\bar{x})} = \langle \tilde{u} =_{t(\bar{x})} \tilde{v}, \tilde{u} \in_{t(\bar{x})} \tilde{v}, \tilde{u} <_{t(\bar{x})} \tilde{v}, \tilde{v} \in V_{t(\bar{x})} \rangle$$

(depending on variables $\tilde{u}, \tilde{v}, \bar{x}$) over many-sorted structure $\bar{G} = G_1, \ldots, G_n$. Here we assume that $\bar{G} \models$ '$\tilde{u} =_{t(\bar{x})} \tilde{v}$ is a partial equivalence relation on $\tilde{u}, \tilde{v}$' and that $|G_{t(\bar{x})}| = \{\tilde{u} : \tilde{u} =_{t(\bar{x})} \tilde{u}\}$.

Analogously, for each formula $\varphi(\bar{x})$ in $\Delta_<^{\otimes} + C^{\otimes}$ we will define by induction on the construction of $\varphi$ a corresponding $FO^{\otimes}$-formula $[\![\varphi]\!](\bar{x})$ over many-sorted structure $\bar{G} = G_1, \ldots, G_n$.

*Case 1.* If $t(\bar{x})$ is just a variable $x_i$ then let $G_t \rightleftharpoons G_i$: $u =_{t(\bar{x})} v \rightleftharpoons u =_i v$, $u \in_{t(\bar{x})} v \rightleftharpoons u \in_i v$, $u <_{t(\bar{x})} v \rightleftharpoons u <_i v$, and $v \in V_{t(\bar{x})} \rightleftharpoons v \in V_i$.

*Case 2.* $t(\bar{x})$ is $\{t_1(\bar{x}), t_2(\bar{x})\}$. By induction hypothesis, terms $t_1(\bar{x})$ and $t_2(\bar{x})$ have corresponding two $FO^{\otimes}$-definable graph transformers $\bar{G} \longmapsto G_{t_1(\bar{x})}$ and $\bar{G} \longmapsto G_{t_2(\bar{x})}$, $G_{t_i(\bar{x})} = \langle u_i =_{t_i} v_i, u_i \in_{t_i} v_i, u_i <_{t_i} v_i, u_i \in V_{t_i} \rangle$.

Let us abbreviate $\tilde{u} \rightleftharpoons u_1', u_1, u_2$ and analogously for $\tilde{v}, \tilde{w}$ and $\tilde{z}$. Extend denotation $u_i \in |G_{t_i}|$ to tuples of variables $\tilde{u}$:

$$\tilde{u} \in |G_{t_1}| \rightleftharpoons u_1' =_{t_1} \emptyset \,\&\, u_1 \in |G_{t_1}| \,\&\, u_2 =_{t_2} \{\emptyset\} \ ,$$

$$\tilde{u} \in |G_{t_2}| \rightleftharpoons u_1' =_{t_1} \{\emptyset\} \,\&\, u_1 =_{t_1} \{\emptyset\} \,\&\, u_2 \in |G_{t_2}| \ .$$

(Here and below Note 3.1 is used for defining in $FO$ of $u = \emptyset$ and $u = \{\emptyset\}$ and other set theoretic formulas.) The mappings $u_1 \longmapsto \emptyset, u_1, \{\emptyset\}$ and $u_2 \longmapsto \{\emptyset\}, \emptyset, u_2$ give natural bijections between old and new versions of $|G_{t_1}|$ and $|G_{t_2}|$.

---

[8] In [24] the first approach to NLOGSPACE over HF (discussed in the Introduction) was based on such a syntax with *external* collapsing, and only for such restricted language we were able to obtain a result analogous to (3) or (4). Now we see that, by using Proposition 4.1 in the proof below, this artificial restriction may be avoided and, in particular, corresponding class of (N/D)LOGSPACE computable operations and predicates is closed under compositions.

Also note, that new versions of $|G_{t_1}|$, $|G_{t_2}|$ and the set $V_t$ defined below are disjoint and, moreover, $V_t$ is a singleton set.

Define $G_t$ by the following formulas where the FO$^\otimes$-definitions of $=_{t_1,t_2}$ and $<_{t_1,t_2}$ are given in Proposition 4.1:

$$\tilde{u} \in V_t \rightleftharpoons u_1' =_{t_1} \emptyset \ \& \ u_1 =_{t_1} \emptyset \ \& \ u_2 =_{t_2} \emptyset \ ,$$

$$|G_t| \rightleftharpoons |G_{t_1}| \cup |G_{t_2}| \cup V_t \ ,$$

$$\tilde{u} \in_t \tilde{v} \rightleftharpoons (\tilde{u}, \tilde{v} \in |G_{t_1}| \ \& \ u_1 \in_{t_1} v_1) \vee (\tilde{u}, \tilde{v} \in |G_{t_2}| \ \& \ u_2 \in_{t_2} v_2) \vee$$
$$(\tilde{u} \in |G_{t_1}| \ \& \ u_1 \in V_{t_1} \ \& \ \tilde{v} \in V_t) \vee (\tilde{u} \in |G_{t_2}| \ \& \ u_2 \in V_{t_2} \ \& \ \tilde{v} \in V_t) \ ,$$

$$\tilde{u} =_t^0 \tilde{v} \rightleftharpoons (\tilde{u}, \tilde{v} \in |G_{t_1}| \ \& \ u_1 =_{t_1} v_1) \vee (\tilde{u}, \tilde{v} \in |G_{t_2}| \ \& \ u_2 =_{t_2} v_2) \vee$$
$$(\tilde{u} \in |G_{t_1}| \ \& \ \tilde{v} \in |G_{t_2}| \ \& \ u_1 =_{t_1,t_2} v_2) \vee$$
$$(\tilde{u} \in |G_{t_2}| \ \& \ \tilde{v} \in |G_{t_1}| \ \& \ v_1 =_{t_1,t_2} u_2) \ ,$$

$$\tilde{u} =_t \tilde{v} \rightleftharpoons \forall \tilde{z} \in_t \tilde{u} \exists \tilde{w} \in_t \tilde{v}(\tilde{z} =_t^0 \tilde{v}) \ \& \ \forall \tilde{w} \in_t \tilde{v} \exists \tilde{z} \in_t \tilde{u}(\tilde{z} =_t^0 \tilde{v}) \ ,$$

$$\tilde{u} <_t^0 \tilde{v} \rightleftharpoons (\tilde{u}, \tilde{v} \in |G_{t_1}| \ \& \ u_1 <_{t_1} v_1) \vee (\tilde{u}, \tilde{v} \in |G_{t_2}| \ \& \ u_2 <_{t_2} v_2) \vee$$
$$(\tilde{u} \in |G_{t_1}| \ \& \ \tilde{v} \in |G_{t_2}| \ \& \ u_1 <_{t_1,t_2} v_2) \vee$$
$$(\tilde{u} \in |G_{t_2}| \ \& \ \tilde{v} \in |G_{t_1}| \ \& \ v_1 <_{t_1,t_2} u_2) \ ,$$

$$\tilde{u} <_t \tilde{v} \rightleftharpoons (\exists \tilde{z} \in_t \tilde{v} \setminus \tilde{u})(\forall \tilde{w} \in_t \tilde{u} \cup \tilde{v}|\tilde{z} <_t^0 \tilde{w})(\exists \tilde{h} \in_t \tilde{u} \cap \tilde{v})(\tilde{w} =_t^0 \tilde{h}) \ .$$

Here $(\exists \tilde{z} \in_t \tilde{v} \setminus \tilde{u})$ abbreviates $(\exists \tilde{z} \in_t \tilde{v}|\forall \tilde{z}' \in \tilde{u}(\tilde{z} \neq_t^0 \tilde{z}'))$, $(\forall \tilde{w} \in_t \tilde{u} \cup \tilde{v}|\tilde{z} <_t^0 \tilde{w})$ abbreviates $(\forall \tilde{w}|(\tilde{w} \in_t \tilde{u} \vee \tilde{w} \in_t \tilde{v}) \ \& \ \tilde{z} <_t^0 \tilde{w})$, and analogously for $(\exists \tilde{h} \in_t \tilde{u} \cap \tilde{v})$. Note, that $=_t$ coincides with $=_t^0$ on $|G_{t_1}| \cup |G_{t_2}|$, and the same for $<_t$ and $<_t^0$.

*Case 3.* $t(\bar{x})$ is $\bigcup a(\bar{x})$. By induction hypothesis, the term $a$ has corresponding FO$^\otimes$-definable graph transformer $\tilde{G} \longmapsto G_{a(\bar{x})}$,

$$G_{a(\bar{x})} = \langle u =_a v, u \in_a v, u <_a v, u \in V_a \rangle \ .$$

Abbreviate $\tilde{u} \rightleftharpoons u', u$ and extend denotation $u \in |G_a|$ to tuples of variables $\tilde{u}$:

$$\tilde{u} \in |G_a| \rightleftharpoons u' =_a \{\emptyset\} \ \& \ u \in |G_a|$$

Define $G_t$ by the following formulas

$$\tilde{u} \in V_t \rightleftharpoons u' =_a \emptyset \ \& \ u =_a \emptyset \ ,$$

$$|G_t| \rightleftharpoons |G_a| \cup V_t \ ,$$

$$\tilde{u} \in_t \tilde{v} \rightleftharpoons (\tilde{u}, \tilde{v} \in |G_a| \ \& \ u \in_a v) \vee$$
$$(\tilde{u} \in |G_a| \ \& \ \exists \tilde{z} \in |G_a| \exists \tilde{w} \in V_a(u \in_a z \in_a w) \ \& \ \tilde{v} \in V_t) \ ,$$

$$\tilde{u} =_t \tilde{v} \rightleftharpoons \forall \tilde{z} \in_t \tilde{u} \exists \tilde{w} \in_t \tilde{v}(z =_a v) \ \& \ \forall \tilde{w} \in_t \tilde{v} \exists \tilde{z} \in_t \tilde{u}(z =_a v) \ ,$$

$$\tilde{u} <_t \tilde{v} \rightleftharpoons (\exists \tilde{z} \in_t \tilde{v} \setminus \tilde{u})(\forall \tilde{w} \in_t \tilde{u} \cup \tilde{v}|z <_a w)(\exists \tilde{h} \in_t \tilde{u} \cap \tilde{v})(w =_a h) \ .$$

*Case 4.* $t(\bar{x})$ is $\text{TC}(a(\bar{x}))$. This differs from Case 3 only by the definition

$$\tilde{u} \in_t \tilde{v} \rightleftharpoons (\tilde{u}, \tilde{v} \in |G_a| \ \& \ u \in_a v) \vee (\tilde{u} \in |G_a| \ \& \ \exists \tilde{w} \in V_a(u \in_a^\otimes w) \ \& \ \tilde{v} \in V_t) \ .$$

*Case 5.* $t(\bar{x})$ is $\{s(\bar{x}, y) : y \in a(\bar{x}) \ \& \ \varphi(\bar{x}, y)\}$. By induction hypothesis, there are FO$^\circledast$-definable graph transformers $[\![s]\!] : \bar{G}, G' \longmapsto G_{s(\bar{x}, y)}$, $[\![a]\!] : \bar{G} \longmapsto G_{a(\bar{x})}$ and a predicate $[\![\varphi]\!]$ over $\bar{G}, G'$ where

$$G_{s(\bar{x}, y)} = \langle u =_{s(\bar{x}, y)} v, u \in_{s(\bar{x}, y)} v, u <_{s(\bar{x}, y)} v, v \in V_{s(\bar{x}, y)} \rangle$$

in the language of $\bar{G}, G'$ (with $u$ and $v$ being for simplicity single variables) and

$$G_{a(\bar{x})} = \langle \tilde{y} =_{a(\bar{x})} \tilde{z}, \tilde{y} \in_{a(\bar{x})} \tilde{z}, \tilde{y} <_{a(\bar{x})} \tilde{z}, \tilde{y} \in V_{a(\bar{x})} \rangle$$

in the language of $\bar{G}$ (with variables $\bar{x}, y$ ranging, respectively, over $\bar{G}, G'$ to denote distinguished vertices of these graphs).

Let us rewrite $G_{s(\bar{x}, y)}$ in the language of $\bar{G}$ by substituting $G_{a(\bar{x})} = \langle \tilde{y} =_{a(\bar{x})} \tilde{z}, \tilde{y} \in_{a(\bar{x})} \tilde{z}, \tilde{y} <_{a(\bar{x})} \tilde{z}, \tilde{y} \in V_{a(\bar{x})} \rangle$ in place of $G' = \langle |G'|, =', \in', <', V' \rangle$ (i.e. by substituting the formulas $=_a$, $\in_a$, $V_a$, respectively, in place of the predicates $=', \in'$ and $V'$ and with the variables $\tilde{y}$ ranging over $|G_{a(\bar{x})}|$ playing the role of variable $y$ ranging over $|G'|$; variables $\bar{x} = x_1, \ldots, x_n$ are still ranging over $|\bar{G}| = |G_1|, \ldots, |G_n|$). Denote the result as

$$G_{s(\bar{x}, \tilde{y})} = \langle u =_{s(\bar{x}, \tilde{y})} v, u \in_{s(\bar{x}, \tilde{y})} v, u <_{s(\bar{x}, \tilde{y})} v, v \in V_{t(\tilde{y})} \rangle \ .$$

Analogously $[\![\varphi]\!](\bar{x}, \tilde{y})$ is obtained from $[\![\varphi]\!](\bar{x}, y)$.

Abbreviate $\tilde{u} \rightleftharpoons u, \tilde{y}, \tilde{y}', \tilde{v} \rightleftharpoons v, \tilde{z}, \tilde{z}', \tilde{w} \rightleftharpoons w, \tilde{p}, \tilde{p}'$ and define $G_t$ by the following formulas

$$\tilde{u} \in |G^0_{t(\bar{x})}| \rightleftharpoons u \in |G_{s(\bar{x}, \tilde{y})}| \ \& \ \tilde{y} \in |G_{a(\bar{x})}| \ \& $$
$$\exists \tilde{y}_1 \in V_{a(\bar{x})} (\tilde{y} \in_{a(\bar{x})} \tilde{y}_1) \ \& \ [\![\varphi]\!](\bar{x}, \tilde{y}) \ \& \ \tilde{y}' =_{a(\bar{x})} \{\emptyset\} \ ,$$

$$\tilde{u} \in V_{t(\bar{x})} \rightleftharpoons u =_{s(\bar{x}, \tilde{y})} \emptyset \ \& \ \tilde{y} =_{a(\bar{x})} \emptyset \ \& \ \tilde{y}' =_{a(\bar{x})} \emptyset \ ,$$

$$|G_{t(\bar{x})}| \rightleftharpoons |G^0_{t(\bar{x})}| \cup V_{t(\bar{x})} \ ,$$

$$\tilde{u} =^0_{t(\bar{x})} \tilde{v} \rightleftharpoons \tilde{u}, \tilde{v} \in |G^0_{t(\bar{x})}| \ \& \ u =_{s(\bar{x}, \tilde{y}), s(\bar{x}, \tilde{z})} u' \ ,$$

$$\tilde{u} \in^0_{t(\bar{x})} \tilde{v} \rightleftharpoons \tilde{u}, \tilde{v} \in |G^0_{t(\bar{x})}| \ \& \ \exists u' \in_{s(\bar{x}, \tilde{z})} v(u =_{s(\bar{x}, \tilde{y}), s(\bar{x}, \tilde{z})} u') \ ,$$

$$\tilde{u} \in_{t(\bar{x})} \tilde{v} \rightleftharpoons \tilde{u} \in^0_{t(\bar{x})} \tilde{v} \vee (\tilde{u} \in |G^0_{t(\bar{x})}| \ \& \ u \in V_{s(\bar{x}, \tilde{y})} \ \& \ \tilde{v} \in V_{t(\bar{x})}) \ ,$$

$$\tilde{u} =_t \tilde{v} \rightleftharpoons \forall \tilde{z} \in_t \tilde{u} \exists \tilde{w} \in_t \tilde{v} (\tilde{z} =^0_t \tilde{v}) \ \& \ \forall \tilde{w} \in_t \tilde{v} \exists \tilde{z} \in_t \tilde{u} (\tilde{z} =^0_t \tilde{v}) \ ,$$

$$\tilde{u} <^0_{t(\bar{x})} \tilde{v} \rightleftharpoons \tilde{u}, \tilde{v} \in |G^0_{t(\bar{x})}| \ \& \ u <_{s(\bar{x}, \tilde{y}), s(\bar{x}, \tilde{z})} u' \ ,$$

$$\tilde{u} <_t \tilde{v} \rightleftharpoons (\exists \tilde{z} \in_t \tilde{v} \setminus \tilde{u}) (\forall \tilde{w} \in_t \tilde{u} \cup \tilde{v} | \tilde{z} <^0_t \tilde{w}) (\exists \tilde{h} \in_t \tilde{u} \cap \tilde{v}) (\tilde{w} =^0_t \tilde{h}) \ .$$

*Case 6.* $t(\bar{x})$ is $C^\circledast(a(\bar{x}))$. By induction hypothesis, the term $a$ has corresponding FO$^\circledast$-definable graph transformer $\bar{G} \longmapsto G_{a(\bar{x})}$,

$$G_{a(\bar{x})} = \langle u =_a v, u \in_a v, u <_a v, u \in V_a \rangle \ .$$

It follows from the Note 4.1 that there exists also FO$^\circledast$-definable predicate $\mathcal{EAG}_<(z)$ which, given a vertex $z$ of a graph (in our case of the graph $G_{a(\bar{x})}$ in $\mathcal{EAG}_<$), decides whether $z$ considered as an HF-set corresponds to a quadruple $z = \langle g, e, l, p \rangle$ such that (i) $g$ (as an HF-set of pairs) is extensional acyclic graph, (ii) $e$ is a partial equivalence relation, (iii) $l$ (also as an HF-set of pairs) is the canonical linear ordering on this graph, and, finally, (iv) $p$ is a distinguished vertex of the graph $g$ (possibly isolated one).

Define $G_t$ by the following formulas

$$u \in |G_t| \rightleftharpoons (\exists z \in V_a \exists glpv \in |G_a|$$
$$(\mathcal{EAG}_<(z) \ \& \ z = \langle g, e, l, p \rangle \ \& \ (\langle u, v \rangle \in g \vee \langle v, u \rangle \in g \vee u = p))) \vee$$
$$(u \in V_a \ \& \ \neg \mathcal{EAG}_<(u)) \ ,$$
$$u \in V_t \rightleftharpoons (\exists z \in V_a \exists glp \in |G_a|$$
$$(\mathcal{EAG}_<(z) \ \& \ z = \langle g, e, l, p \rangle \ \& \ u = p)) \vee (u \in V_a \ \& \ \neg \mathcal{EAG}_<(u)) \ ,$$
$$u \in_t v \rightleftharpoons \exists z \in V_a \exists glp \in |G_a|(\mathcal{EAG}_<(z) \ \& \ z = \langle g, e, l, p \rangle \ \& \ \langle u, v \rangle \in g) \ ,$$
$$\tilde{u} =_t \tilde{v} \rightleftharpoons \forall \tilde{z} \in_t \tilde{u} \exists \tilde{w} \in_t \tilde{v}(z =_a v) \ \& \ \forall \tilde{w} \in_t \tilde{v} \exists \tilde{z} \in_t \tilde{u}(z =_a v) \ ,$$
$$u <_t v \rightleftharpoons \exists z \in V_a \exists glp \in |G_a|(\mathcal{EAG}_<(z) \ \& \ z = \langle g, e, l, p \rangle \ \& \ \langle u, v \rangle \in l) \ ,$$

*Case 7.* of $t \rightleftharpoons r^\otimes$ relies on the construct $\otimes$ of $FO^\otimes$ analogously to and even simpler than Case 6.

*Case 8.* of $\varphi \rightleftharpoons t_1 = t_2$ or $t_1 < t_2$ is based immediately on Proposition 4.1.

*Case 9.* of $\varphi \rightleftharpoons t_1 \in t_2$ (as well as that of bounded quantification) is reducible to those considered:

$$t_1 \in t_2 \Leftrightarrow \exists x \in t_2(x = t_1) \Leftrightarrow \{x \in t_2 : x = t_1\} \neq \emptyset \ .$$

*Case 10.* of the term $\emptyset$ and of boolean connectives is trivial.

*Proof of (3), converse part, and "external collapsing normal form".* Let $f(\bar{x})$ be any $n$-ary operation over sets $FO^\otimes$-computable by a graph transformer $F$ : $\mathcal{EAG}_< \to \mathcal{EAG}_<$. We may consider that $\mathcal{EAG}_< \subseteq HF$ and $F : HF \to HF$. Then $f$ can be represented as the following $(\Delta^\otimes_< + C^\otimes)$-definable operation, in fact a composition (applied from right to left)

$$f = C^\otimes \circ F \circ G$$

where $G$ is an $n$-ary $\Delta^*_<$-definable operation over sets transforming input sets $x_1, \ldots, x_n$ into their well-founded extensional graph representation (with the distinguished vertex in each graph):

$$G(x_1, \ldots, x_n) = \langle \langle \in |_{TC(\{x_1\})}; < |_{TC(\{x_1\})}, x_1 \rangle, \ldots, \langle \in |_{TC(\{x_n\})}; < |_{TC(\{x_n\})}, x_n \rangle \rangle$$

$F$ is evidently also $\Delta^\otimes$-definable by imitating in $\Delta^\otimes$ its $FO^\otimes$-description. (Input graph for $F$ is considered as set of a specific kind; corresponding output graph is defined by using $\Delta$-definable notion of Cartesian product and by imitating unbounded quantifiers of $FO^\otimes$ and the logical construct $\otimes$ by bounded quantifiers and set-theoretic version of $\otimes$ in $\Delta^\otimes$.) Finally, collapsing operation $C^\otimes$ serves to 'extract' a resulting set from its graph representation.

Evidently, $F$ and $G$ do not use collapsing. If $f : HF^n \to \{$**true**,**false**$\}$ is an NLOGSPACE computable predicate then we will have $f = F \circ G$ and we need not use collapsing at all.

*Proof of* (4) essentially coincides with that of (3). We should only replace (i) $\otimes$ by $\odot$, (ii) $C^{\otimes}$ by $C^{\odot}$, (iii) $\mathcal{EAG}_<$ by $\mathcal{EAG}^*_<$ and add (i) $\in^*_i$ in the denotation of $G_i$, (ii) $\tilde{u} \in^*_{t(\bar{x})} \tilde{v}$ in the denotation of $G_{t(\bar{x})}$ for each term $t$, (iii) $\in^* |_{\mathrm{TC}(\{x_i\})}$ in the definition of $G(\bar{x})$, and respectively extend the proof.

$\square$

# References

1. Abiteboul, S., Hull, R., Vianu, V.: Foundations of Databases. Addison-Wesley, Reading-Massachusetts, 1995
2. Abiteboul, S.: Querying semi-structured data. Database Theory — ICDT'97, 6th International Conference, Delphi, Greece, January 1997, Proceedings. Lecture Notes in Computer Science **1186** Springer (1995) 1–18
3. Abiteboul, S., Beeri, C.: On the power of languages for the manipulation of complex objects. INRIA research report **846** (1988). Abstract in Proc. International Workshop on Theory and Applications of Nested Relations and Complex Objects. Darmstadt (1987)
4. Abiteboul, S., Vianu, V.: Queries and computation on the Web. Database Theory — ICDT'97, 6th International Conference, Delphi, Greece, January 1997, Proceedings. Lecture Notes in Computer Science **1186** Springer (1995) 262–275
5. Aczel, P.: Non-Well-Founded Sets. CSLI Lecture Notes. No **14** (1988)
6. Barwise, J.K.: Admissible Sets and Structures. Springer, Berlin, 1975
7. Buneman, P., Davidson, S., Hillebrand, G., Suciu, D.: A query Language and Optimization Techniques for Unstructured Data. Proc. of SIGMOD, San Diego, 1996
8. Val Breazu-Tannen and Subrahmanyam, R.: Logical and computational aspects of programming with sets/bags/lists, a manuscript, 1991.
9. Dahlhaus, E.: Is SETL a suitable language for parallel programming — a theoretical approach. Börger, E., Kleine Buning, H., Richter, M.M. ed. CSL'87. LNCS **329** (1987) 56–63
10. Dahlhaus, E., Makowsky, J.: The Choice of programming Primitives in SETL-like Languages. ESOP'86. LNCS **213** (1986) 160–172
11. Dahlhaus, E., Makowsky, J.: Query languages for hierarchic databases. Information and Computation **101** (1992) 1–32
12. Gandy, R.O.: Set theoretic functions for elementary syntax. Proc. Symp. in Pure Math. Vol. **13**, Part II (1974) 103–126
13. Garey, M.R. and Johnson, D.S.: Computers and Intractability: A Guide to the Theory of NP-Completeness. W.H.Freeman and Company, New York, 1979.
14. Grumbach, S., Vianu, V.: Tractable query languages for complex object databases. Rapports de Recherche N **1573**. INRIA. 1991
15. Gurevich, Y.: Algebras of feasible functions. FOCS **24** (1983) 210–214
16. Immerman, N.: 'Relational queries computable in polynomial time', in: Proc. 14th. ACM Symp. on Theory of Computing, (1982) 147–152; cf. also Inform. and Control **68** (1986) 86–104.
17. Immerman, N.: Languages which captures complexity classes. SIAM J. Comput., **16** 4 (1987) 760–778
18. Immerman, N.: Descriptive and computational complexity. Proceedings of Symposia in Applied Mathematics, **38** (1989) 75–91
19. Immerman, N., Patnaik, S. and Stemple, D.: The expressiveness of a family of finite set languages. Theoretical Computer Science, **155**, N 1 (1996) 111–140

20. Jensen, R.B.: The fine structure of the constructible hierarchy. Ann. Math. Logic **4** (1972) 229–308

21. Kosky, A. : Observational properties of databases with object identity. Technical Report MS-CIS-95-20. Dept. of Computer and Information Science, University of Pennsylvania (1995)

22. Kuper, G.M., Vardi, M.Y.: A new approach to database logic. Proc. 3rd ACM Symp. on Principles of Database Systems 1984

23. Levy, A.: A hierarchy of formulas in set theory. Mem. Amer. Math. Soc. No. 57 (1965) 76pp. MR 32 N 7399

24. Lisitsa, A. and Sazonov, V.Yu: Delta-languages for sets and LOGSPACE computable graph transformers. Theoretical Computer Science **175**, 1 (1997), 183–222

25. Lisitsa, A. and Sazonov, V.Yu: Linear ordering on graphs, anti-founded sets and polynomial time computability, Theoretical Computer Science **224**, 1-2 (1999) 173-213. (Cf. also earlier versions in Proc. of the 4th International Symp. 'Logical Foundations of Computer Science', Yaroslavl, Russia, 1997, Springer LNCS **1234** (1997), 178–188, and http://dimacs.rutgers.edu/TechnicalReports/1997.html.)

26. Lisitsa, A. and Sazonov, V.Yu: Bounded Hyperset Theory and Web-like Data Bases. In: Georg Gottlob, Alexander Leitsch, Daniele Mundici (Eds.): Computational Logic and Proof Theory, 5th Kurt Gödel Colloquium, KGC'97, Vienna, Austria, August 25–29, 1997, Proceedings. LNCS **1289**, Springer, (1997) 172–185. (Cf. also http://dimacs.rutgers.edu/TechnicalReports/1997.html.)

27. Livchak, A.B.: Languages of polynomial queries. Raschet i optimizacija teplotehnicheskih ob'ektov s pomosh'ju EVM, Sverdlovsk, 1982, p. 41 (in Russian).

28. Mendelzon, A. O., Mihaila, G.A., Milo, T. : Querying the World Wide Web. Draft, available by ftp: milo@math.tau.ac.il (1996)

29. Sazonov, V.Yu.: Polynomial computability and recursivity in finite domains. Elektronische Informationsverarbeitung und Kybernetik. **16**, N7 (1980) 319–323

30. Sazonov, V.Yu.: Bounded set theory and polynomial computability. All Union Conf. Appl. Logic., Proc. Novosibirsk (1985) 188–191 (In Russian)

31. Sazonov, V.Yu.: The Collection Principle and the Existential Quantifier. Logikomatematicheskie problemy MOZ., Vychislitel'nye sistemy **107** (1985) 3O–39 (In Russian). (English translation in: Amer. Math. Soc. Transl. (2) **Vol. 142** (1989) 1–8)

32. Sazonov, V.Yu.: Bounded set theory, polynomial computability and $\Delta$-programming. Application aspects of mathematical logic. Computing systems **122** (1987) 110–132 (In Russian) Cf. also a short English version of this paper in: LNCS **278** Springer (1987) 391–397

33. Sazonov, V.Yu.: Hereditarily-finite sets, data bases and polynomial-time computability. Theoretical Computer Science **119** Elsevier (1993) 187–214

34. Sazonov, V.Yu.: A bounded set theory with anti-foundation axiom and inductive definability. Computer Science Logic, 8th Workshop, CSL'94 Kazimierz, Poland, September 1994, Selected Papers. LNCS **933** Springer (1995) 527–541

35. Sazonov, V.Yu: On Bounded Set Theory. Invited talk on the 10th International Congress on Logic, Methodology and Philosophy of Sciences, Florence, August 1995, in Volume I: Logic and Scientific Method, Kluwer Academic Publishers, 1997, pp. 85–103

36. Shoenfield, J. R.: Mathematical Logic. Addison-Wesley, Reading, MA, 1967

37. Szelepcsényi, R.: 1987, The method of forcing for nondeterministic automata. Bull. European Association Theor. Comp. Sci. (Oct. 1987) 96–100

38. Vardi, M.Y.: The complexity of relational query languages. Proc. of the 14th. ACM Symp. on Theory of Computing, (1982) 137–146

# Non-situation Calculus and Database Systems*

Pedro A. Matos and João P. Martins

Instituto Superior Técnico
Technical University of Lisbon
{pedro,jpm}@gia.ist.utl.pt

**Abstract.** Non-situation calculus is a way to describe dynamic worlds using first order logic, where a theory is written from the viewpoint of a situation (the propositional fluents hold in that situation). We introduced some functions to allow describing propositional fluents that hold in other situations. We define "progression" as a transformation that changes the situation represented by a non-situation calculus. The semantics counterpart of progression, function $\Delta$, transforms an interpretation of a non-situation calculus relative to a situation into an interpretation of a non-situation calculus relative to another situation.

We propose using non-situation calculus to study database dynamics by representing a database as a non-situation calculus theory, by representing transactions as changes and by associating the database that results from executing a transaction to the progression of the theory.

## 1 Introduction

Non-situation calculus (nsc) is way to write theories describing situations in dynamic worlds using first order logic with equality $\approx$. In nsc, we choose a situation to be represented by a theory and the propositional fluents that hold in that situation don't have to refer the situation (hence the name "non-situation calculus"). Non-situation calculus was developed to study some reasoning about action and change systems [3,5,18,11,1,7,4] in which the representation propositional fluents don't refer explicitly the situation. These have been called "meta-level time" approaches [16].

Non-situation calculus is closely related to situation calculus (sc) [10] using reified propositions.[1] Let $s$ be a situation and $p$ a reified proposition. In sc, the fact that "it is true that $p$ in $s$" is written as $\mathtt{holds}(p, s)$, that is, predicate $\mathtt{holds}$ means "it is true that ... in ... ". In nsc, choose a situation to be represented by

---

* We wish to thank the members of the member of GIA for their comments and support. This work was partially supported by PRAXIS XXI projecto 2/2.1/TIT/1568/95 - Raciocínio sobre mudança utilizando Senso Comum and ID-MEC - Grupo de Inteligência Artificial.

[1] Reify means "turn into an object". Reified propositions are propositions that are turned into objects of the domain of discourse, that is, objects about which other propositions can be written. The use of reified propositions in first order logic was introduced in [9].

K.-D. Schewe, B. Thalheim (Eds.): FoIKS 2000, LNCS 1762, pp. 176–191, 2000.
© Springer-Verlag Berlin Heidelberg 2000

a theory, for example $s$, and a unary predicate, say $h$, to identify the propositional fluents that hold in that situation (we call this a *non-situation calculus relative to $s$ using $h$*). The fact that propositional fluent $p$ holds in situation $s$ is written as $h(p)$, that is, predicate $h$ means "it is true that ... in $s$".

When using nsc relative to $s$ using $h$, the propositional fluents always hold in situation $s$. This apparent limitation of the nsc approach can be overcome by introducing an appropriate set of functions, including function "$\delta$", used to represent the change between two situations, function "TSP" (for Temporally Shifted Propositions), used to represent that a proposition holds after a change is executed, and function ";", used to compose changes, as described in Sect. 2.

Using these functions, it is possible to study the relation between sc and nsc. We defined a syntactic transformation from nsc to sc (we called it $R$, from "Reify", because this transformation can be seen as the reification of the situation represented by nsc) and another from sc to nsc (similarly, we called it $D$, from "De-reify", because it can be seen as the de-reification of the situation). We compose these transformations into another transformation which we called "progression"[2] that can be though of as changing both the situation represented by a nsc and the predicate used to identify the propositional fluents by a nsc.

Furthermore, we present function $\Delta$, which is the semantic counterpart of progression. Consider interpretation $\mathcal{I}$ of the parameters of nsc relative to $s1$ using $h_{s1}$, that interprets all the parameters of logic including $h_{s1}$, which establishes all the reified propositions that hold in that situation. Furthermore, consider situation $s2$ and a predicate symbol $h_{s2}$. $\Delta(\mathcal{I}, s1, h_{s1}, s2, h_{s2})$ is the interpretation of parameters of nsc relative to $s2$ using $h_{s2}$ that describes the same facts as $\mathcal{I}$, but now from the viewpoint[3] of $s2$. In Sect. 3, we discuss both the progression and $\Delta$.

As we said before, nsc is a way to write theories that describe situations in dynamic worlds. In Sect. 4, using some inspiration from the work of Reiter [12,14], we propose using nsc to model databases and to study its dynamics. The idea is to associate a database to a nsc theory that describes a situation and to associate a transaction to a change. In this framework, the database that results from executing a transaction is represented by the theory that results from executing the progression corresponding to the change.

Finally, in Sect. 5, we draw conclusions.

## 2   Non-situation Calculus

Non-situation calculus is an approach to write theories describing worlds, where different theories are used to describe the world in different situations. Let $\mathcal{L}_{NSC(s,h)}$ be the language we use to write a nsc theory relative to $s$ using $h$. This language is similar to a language of a form of sc using reified propositions,

---

[2]  The term progression has been used by other authors [15,11,7], with different technical meanings.

[3]  The term viewpoint was used in [6], who proposed a semantics for contextual reasoning which relates theories that describes different points of view.

$\mathcal{L}_{SC}$. The difference is on the predicates of the language: the fact that propositional fluent $p$ holds in situation $s$ is written in $\mathcal{L}_{SC}$ as $\text{holds}(p, s)$ whereas in $\mathcal{L}_{NSC(s,h)}$ it is written as $h(p)$. Furthermore, when we say that $\mathcal{L}_{NSC(s,h)}$ is the language of nsc, we mean that the situation the nsc is relative to is $s$ and the predicate used to describe the propositional fluents is $h$.

## 2.1 Situations and Changes

As in McCarthy and Hayes [10], we take a situation to be "complete state of the universe at an instant of time". Recently, Reiter [13] proposed a different use of sc in which situations are associated to histories of action executions. To distinguish between Reiter's and the original McCarthy and Hayes' sc, the former has been called the "Toronto variant". When we refer to sc, we mean the original sc.

A change represents the difference between two situations and is reified in nsc. We follow McCarthy and Hayes' and use function $\text{result}$,[4] which takes as its first argument a reified change $c$ and as its second argument a situation $s$. The term "$\text{result}(c, s)$" represents the situation that results from change $c$ occurring in situation $s$.

## 2.2 Introducing New Functions

A nsc theory relative to $s$ using $h$ describes the world from the viewpoint of $s$, that is, propositional fluents are always relative to $s$. Restricting the propositional fluents to those which hold in situation $s$ is not a limitation of this approach when compared to sc since this restriction can be easily overcome by introducing functions "$\delta$", "TSP", and "$;$":

- term "$\delta(s_1, s_2)$", when $s_1$ and $s_2$ are two situations, represents the change that transforms $s_1$ in $s_2$. We call this term the *differential change between $s_1$ and $s_2$*;
- term "$\text{TSP}(c, p)$", when $p$ is a reified proposition and $c$ is a change, represents that after executing the change $c$, proposition $p$ holds. We call this term the *temporal shifting of reified proposition $p$ by $c$*; and
- term "$c_1 ; c_2$", when $c_1$ and $c_2$ are changes, represents the change which corresponds to executing $c_1$ and then $c_2$. We call this term the *succession* of $c_1$ and $c_2$.

---

[4]  Even though it is outside the scope of this paper, this use of function $\text{result}$ is actually a generalization of McCarthy and Hayes' use since their function's first argument is an action, which is a special kind of change.

We present some axioms that describe some properties of these functions,

$$\forall s \; 0 \approx \delta(s, s) \tag{1}$$

$$\forall s_1 \forall s_2 \forall c \; \delta(s_1, \mathtt{result}(c, s_2)) \approx \delta(s_1, s_2) \, ; c \tag{2}$$

$$\forall s_1 \forall s_2 \; s_1 \approx \mathtt{result}(\delta(s_2, s_1), s_2) \tag{3}$$

$$\forall p \; p \approx \mathtt{TSP}(0, p) \tag{4}$$

$$\forall c_1 \forall c_2 \forall p \; \mathtt{TSP}(c_1 \, ; c_2, p) \approx \mathtt{TSP}(c_1, \mathtt{TSP}(c_2, p)) \tag{5}$$

according to which: (1) the differential change between $s$ and itself is the null change, represented as $0$; (2) the differential change between $s_1$ and the result of executing $c$ in $s_2$ is the succession of the differential change between $s_1$ and $s_2$, and $c$; (3) the result of executing $\delta(s_2, s_1)$ in $s_2$ is $s_1$; (4) $p$ is the same as temporally shifting $p$ by executing $0$; and (5) temporally shifting $p$ by executing $c_1 \, ; c_2$ is the same as temporally shifting by $c_1$ the reified proposition that is obtained by temporally shifting $p$ by $c_2$.

The intended meaning of $\mathtt{TSP}$ is made clearer in terms of sc. In sc, we may write the axiom (6), according to which term $\mathtt{TSP}(c, p)$ is such that it holds in situation $s$ iff $p$ holds in situation $\mathtt{result}(c, s)$.

$$\forall s \forall c \forall p \; (\mathtt{holds}(p, \mathtt{result}(c, s)) \Leftrightarrow \mathtt{holds}(\mathtt{TSP}(c, p), s)) \tag{6}$$

By the way of example, when considering nsc relative to $\mathtt{S1}$ using $\mathtt{h_{S1}}$, if we use term $\mathtt{on(A, Table)}$ to represent the reified proposition that block $\mathtt{A}$ is on $\mathtt{Table}$, the fact that block $\mathtt{A}$ is on $\mathtt{Table}$ in situation $\mathtt{S2}$ is represented as $\mathtt{h_{S1}(TSP(\delta(S1, S2), on(A, Table)))}$.

We say that theories containing axioms (1)–(5) are *transformable*. Some properties of these theories are discussed in Sect. 3.

## 2.3   A Blocks World Example

In this section, we present a classical example of dynamic systems, a blocks world containing two blocks, $\mathtt{A}$ and $\mathtt{B}$, in which two situations are considered. In situation $\mathtt{S1}$, block $\mathtt{A}$ is on $\mathtt{B}$, and situation $\mathtt{S2}$ is the result of unstacking block $\mathtt{A}$, i.e., $\mathtt{S2}$ is $\mathtt{result(unstack(A, B), S1)}$, as represented in Fig. 1.

This blocks world is represented as the nsc theory $\Gamma_1$ relative to $\mathtt{S1}$ using $\mathtt{h_{S1}}$ that contains the axioms (1)–(5) (the theory is transformable), and axioms (7), describing some atomic wffs that holds in $\mathtt{S1}$.

$$
\begin{aligned}
&\mathtt{h_{S1}(on(A, B))} \\
&\mathtt{h_{S1}(on(B, Table))} \\
&\mathtt{h_{S1}(clear(A))} \\
&\mathtt{h_{S1}(TSP(\delta(S1, S2), on(A, Table)))} \\
&\mathtt{h_{S1}(TSP(\delta(S1, S2), on(B, Table)))} \\
&\mathtt{S2 \approx result(unstack(A, B), S1).}
\end{aligned}
\tag{7}
$$

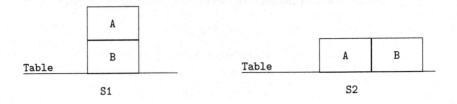

**Fig. 1.** Blocks world in situations S1 and S2.

## 3   Changing the Viewpoint

In this section, we present two transformations: $R$, from nsc theories to sc theories; and $D$, from sc theories to nsc theories. These transformations are used to transform a nsc theory relative to a situation using a predicate into another nsc theory relative to another situation using another predicate, a transformation we call "progression".

### 3.1   Transformations $R$ and $D$

Let $s$ be a constant symbol, let $h$ be a unary predicate, let $\gamma$ and finite transformable $\Gamma$ be in $\mathcal{L}_{NSC(s,h)}$. $R(\gamma, s, h)$ is the result of replacing the occurrences of $h(p)$ for $\mathtt{holds}(p, s)$ (for any $p$) in $\gamma$.

Formally, $R$ is defined as

$$R(\gamma, s, h) = \begin{cases} \mathtt{holds}(p, s), & \text{if } \gamma = h(p), \\ \gamma, & \text{if } \gamma \text{ is atomic and } \gamma \neq h(p), \\ \neg R(\gamma_1, s, h), & \text{if } \gamma = \neg\gamma_1, \\ R(\gamma_1, s, h) \Rightarrow R(\gamma_2, s, h), & \text{if } \gamma = \gamma_1 \Rightarrow \gamma_2, \\ \forall v\ R(\gamma_1, s, h), & \text{if } \gamma = \forall v\ \gamma_1, \end{cases}$$

and $R(\Gamma, s, h) = \{R(\gamma, s, h) \mid \gamma \in \Gamma\}$.

According to Theorem 5.1 (theorems are presented in the appendix), $\Gamma \vdash \gamma$ iff $R(\Gamma, s, h) \cup \{(6)\} \vdash R(\gamma, s, h)$. Notice that $R(\Gamma, s, h)$ only contains propositions that hold in situation $s$. The point of adding $\{(6)\}$ is to extend the set of derivable propositions to include propositions (other than tautologies) referring other situations than $s$.

Let $s$ and $h$ be as before, let $\gamma$ and finite transformable $\Gamma$ be in $\mathcal{L}_{SC}$. $D(\gamma, s, h)$ is the result of replacing $\mathtt{holds}(p, s)$ for $h(p)$ (for any $p$) and $\mathtt{holds}(p, s_1)$ for $h(\mathtt{TSP}(\delta(s, s_1), p))$ (for any $p$ and $s_1 \neq s$).

Formally, $D$ is defined as

$$D(\gamma, s, h) = \begin{cases} h(p), & \text{if } \gamma = \text{holds}(p, s), \\ h(\text{TSP}(\delta(s, s_1), p)), & \text{if } \gamma = \text{holds}(p, s_1) \text{ and } s_1 \neq s, \\ \gamma, & \text{if } \gamma \text{ is atomic and } \gamma \neq \text{holds}(p, s_1), \\ \neg D(\gamma_1, s, h), & \text{if } \gamma = \neg\gamma_1, \\ D(\gamma_1, s, h) \Rightarrow D(\gamma_2, s, h), & \text{if } \gamma = \gamma_1 \Rightarrow \gamma_2, \\ \forall v\ D(\gamma_1, s, h), & \text{if } \gamma = \forall v\ \gamma_1, \end{cases}$$

and $D(\Gamma, s, h) = \{D(\gamma, s, h) \mid \gamma \in \Gamma\}$.

According to Theorem 5.2, $\Gamma \cup \{(6)\} \vdash \gamma$ iff $D(\Gamma, s, h) \vdash D(\gamma, s, h)$.

By the way of example, $R(\text{h}_{\text{S1}}(\text{on}(\text{A}, \text{B})), \text{S1}, \text{h}_{\text{S1}})$ is $\text{holds}(\text{on}(\text{A}, \text{B}), \text{S1})$, and $D(\text{holds}(\text{on}(\text{A}, \text{B}), \text{S1}), \text{S2}, \text{h}_{\text{S2}})$ is $\text{h}_{\text{S2}}(\text{TSP}(\delta(\text{S2}, \text{S1}), \text{on}(\text{A}, \text{B})))$.

## 3.2    Progressing a Theory

Given the two transformations $R$ and $D$, a new transformation of a nsc theory relative to situation $s_1$ using $h_{s_1}$ into a nsc theory relative to situation $s_2$ using $h_{s_2}$ can be built. We define transformation $RD$ by equation (8), and say that $RD(\gamma, s_1, h_{s_1}, s_2, h_{s_2})$ is the *progression of $\gamma$ relative to $s_1$ using predicate $h_{s_1}$ to $s_2$ using predicate $h_{s_2}$*, trivially generalizable to theories.

$$RD(\gamma, s_1, h_{s_1}, s_2, h_{s_2}) = D(R(\gamma, s_1, h_{s_1}), s_2, h_{s_2}) \tag{8}$$

It follows from Theorems 5.1 and 5.2 that if $s_1$ and $s_2$ are constant symbols, if $h_{s_1}$ and $h_{s_2}$ are unary predicates, if $\gamma$ and finite transformable theory $\Gamma$ are in $\mathcal{L}_{NSC(s_1, h_{s_1})}$, then $\Gamma \vdash \gamma$ iff $RD(\Gamma, s_1, h_{s_1}, s_2, h_{s_2}) \vdash RD(\gamma, s_1, h_{s_1}, s_2, h_{s_2})$.

## 3.3    An Example of the Progression of a Theory

We present the progression of a theory describing the blocks worlds relative to S1 using $\text{h}_{\text{S1}}$ to S2 using $\text{h}_{\text{S2}}$, $RD(\Gamma_1, \text{S1}, \text{h}_{\text{S1}}, \text{S2}, \text{h}_{\text{S2}})$.

According to the transformations definitions, the axioms in (1)–(5) are progressed into themselves, since $\text{h}_{\text{S1}}$ doesn't occur in any of these axioms. The axioms in (7) are transformed into axioms in (9).

$$\begin{aligned} &\text{h}_{\text{S2}}(\text{TSP}(\delta(\text{S2}, \text{S1}), \text{on}(\text{A}, \text{B}))) \\ &\text{h}_{\text{S2}}(\text{TSP}(\delta(\text{S2}, \text{S1}), \text{on}(\text{B}, \text{Table}))) \\ &\text{h}_{\text{S2}}(\text{TSP}(\delta(\text{S2}, \text{S1}), \text{clear}(\text{A}))) \\ &\text{h}_{\text{S2}}(\text{TSP}(\delta(\text{S2}, \text{S1}), \text{TSP}(\delta(\text{S1}, \text{S2}), \text{on}(\text{A}, \text{Table})))) \\ &\text{h}_{\text{S2}}(\text{TSP}(\delta(\text{S2}, \text{S1}), \text{TSP}(\delta(\text{S1}, \text{S2}), \text{on}(\text{B}, \text{Table})))) \\ &\text{S2} \approx \text{result}(\text{unstack}(\text{A}, \text{B}), \text{S1}) \end{aligned} \tag{9}$$

Notice that since $RD(\Gamma_1, \text{S1}, \text{h}_{\text{S1}}, \text{S2}, \text{h}_{\text{S2}})$ is transformable, $\text{h}_{\text{S2}}(\text{on}(\text{A}, \text{Table}))$ is derivable from this theory and similarly for $\text{h}_{\text{S2}}(\text{on}(\text{B}, \text{Table}))$.

### 3.4   The Semantics of Non-situation Calculus Progression

Non-situation calculus is a way to write first order logic theories, and therefore a standard tarskian semantics may be used. In order to introduce notation, we present tarskian semantics (our presentation is strongly based in [2]). Furthermore, we define function $\Delta$, the semantic counterpart of progression.

An interpretation of a first order language defines a meaning to the parameters of the language. Formally, an *interpretation* $\mathcal{I}$ assigns:

1. the quantifier $\forall$ to a non-empty set $|\mathcal{I}|$, the universe of $\mathcal{I}$;
2. each $n$-ary predicate symbol $P$ to a $n$-ary relation $P^{\mathcal{I}} \subseteq |\mathcal{I}|^n$;
3. $n$-ary function symbols to $n$-ary functions from $|\mathcal{I}|^n$ to $|\mathcal{I}|$ (e.g. $f$ to $f^{\mathcal{I}}$ : $|\mathcal{I}|^n \to |\mathcal{I}|$);
4. constants to elements of $|\mathcal{I}|$ (e.g. $c$ to $c^{\mathcal{I}}$).

To establish the meaning of a nsc calculus wff, we need to define the meaning of a term, which in general may contain variables. This is achieved by considering a function that assigns each variable in $V$ to an element of $|\mathcal{I}|$ and extending this function to the set of all terms.

Given a function $s$ from the set of variables $V$ to $|\mathcal{I}|$, define the *extension* $\overline{s}$ (relative to $\mathcal{I}$) recursively as follows:

1. if $v$ is a variable, then $\overline{s}(v) = s(v)$;
2. if $c$ is a constant, then $\overline{s}(c) = c^{\mathcal{I}}$;
3. if $t_1, \dots, t_n$ are terms and $f$ is an $n$-ary function symbol, then

$$\overline{s}(f(t_1, \dots, t_n)) = f^{\mathcal{I}}(\overline{s}(t_1), \dots, \overline{s}(t_n)).$$

Furthermore, for $v \in V$ and $d \in |\mathcal{I}|$, $s(v|d)$ is the function from the set of variables $V$ to $|\mathcal{I}|$ that is equal to $s$ for every argument except for $v$. When the argument is $v$, the result is $d$. Formally,

$$s(v|d)(x) = \begin{cases} s(x), \text{ if } x \neq v \\ d, \quad \text{ if } x = v. \end{cases}$$

Let $\mathcal{I}$ be an interpretation, $\gamma$ be a wff, and $s$ be a function from the set of variables $V$ to $|\mathcal{I}|$. The definition of the relation $\mathcal{I}$ *satisfies* $\gamma$ *with* $s$, written $\models_{\mathcal{I}} \gamma[s]$, is recursive:

1. $\models_{\mathcal{I}} (t_1 \approx t_2)[s]$ iff $\overline{s}(t_1) = \overline{s}(t_2)$;
2. for $n$-ary predicate $P$ different from $\approx$, it is the case that $\models_{\mathcal{I}} P(t_1, \dots, t_n)[s]$ iff $\langle \overline{s}(t_1), \dots, \overline{s}(t_n) \rangle \in P^{\mathcal{I}}$ ($P^{\mathcal{I}}$ is the *extent* of $P$ in $\mathcal{I}$);
3. $\models_{\mathcal{I}} (\neg \gamma_1)[s]$ iff $\not\models_{\mathcal{I}} \gamma_1[s]$;
4. $\models_{\mathcal{I}} (\gamma_1 \Rightarrow \gamma_2)[s]$ iff $\not\models_{\mathcal{I}} \gamma_1[s]$ or $\models_{\mathcal{I}} \gamma_2[s]$ or both;
5. $\models_{\mathcal{I}} (\forall v\, \gamma_1)[s]$ iff, for every $d \in |\mathcal{I}|$, $\models_{\mathcal{I}} \gamma_1[s(v|d)]$.

An interpretation $\mathcal{I}$ is a *model* of a wff $\gamma$, written $\models_{\mathcal{I}} \gamma$, when $\models_{\mathcal{I}} \gamma[s]$, for every $s$. This notion is easily extended for a set of wffs $\Gamma$. A theory $\Gamma$ *logically implies* $\gamma$ when for every interpretation $\mathcal{I}$ and every function $s$ such that $\models_{\mathcal{I}} \Gamma[s]$, it is the case that $\models_{\mathcal{I}} \gamma[s]$.

Given this presentation of tarskian semantics, we are in position to discuss the semantics of progression. An interpretation $\mathcal{I}$ in nsc relative to $s1$ using $h_{s1}$ is an interpretation that defines the meaning of the parameters, including the meaning of the predicate $h_{s1}$ that identifies the propositional fluents that holds in situation $s1$. In this sense, we can associate this interpretation with $s1$.

Furthermore, an interpretation also identifies the propositions that holds in any other situation. Consider situation $s2$, which is the situation that results when change $\delta(s1, s2)$ occurs in $s1$. If reified proposition $p$ occurs in $s2$, then the interpretation is such that $\mathrm{TSP}(\delta(s1, s2), p)$ holds in $s1$. This shows that an interpretation of parameters of nsc relative to $s1$ using $h_{s1}$ contains enough information to decide which propositions hold in any situation.

If we change the viewpoint from which propositions are written using progression, the interpretation of parameters should be changed accordingly (the predicate that represents the propositional fluents has changed). Function $\Delta$ is used to represent the changed interpretation of parameters: $\Delta(\mathcal{I}, s1, h_{s1}, s2, h_{s2})$ is an interpretation of parameters in $\mathcal{L}_{NSC(s2, h_{s2})}$ that interprets all the parameters as in $\mathcal{I}$ except for $h_{s2}$. The interpretation of $h_{s2}$ is such that if $p^{\mathcal{I}} \in h_{s1}^{\mathcal{I}}$, then $\mathrm{TSP}(\delta(s2, s1), p)^{\mathcal{I}} \in h_{s2}^{\Delta(\mathcal{I}, s1, h_{s1}, s2, h_{s2})}$. [5]

Formally, $\Delta(\mathcal{I}, s1, h_{s1}, s2, h_{s2})$ is an interpretation of parameters that assigns

1. the quantifier $\forall$ to $|\mathcal{I}|$;
2. each $n$-ary predicate symbol $P$, different from $h_{s1}$, to a $n$-ary relation $P^{\mathcal{I}} \subseteq |\mathcal{I}|^n$;
3. unary predicate $h_{s2}$ to the set $\{\mathrm{TSP}(\delta(s2, s1), p)^{\mathcal{I}} | p^{\mathcal{I}} \in h_{s1}^{\mathcal{I}}\}$;
4. $n$-ary function symbols to $n$-ary functions from $|\mathcal{I}|^n$ to $|\mathcal{I}|$ (e.g. $f$ to $f^{\mathcal{I}}$ : $|\mathcal{I}|^n \to |\mathcal{I}|$);
5. constants to elements of $|\mathcal{I}|$ (e.g. $c$ to $c^{\mathcal{I}}$).

This function is such that when $\mathcal{I}$ is a model of a closed transformable theory $\Gamma_{s1}$, then $\Delta(\mathcal{I}, s1, h_{s1}, s2, h_{s2})$ is a model of $RD(\Gamma_{s1}, s1, h_{s1}, s2, h_{s2})$, as proved in Theorem 5.3.

## 3.5    An Example of Changing the Viewpoint of an Interpretation

As an example of function $\Delta$, consider an interpretation of the language of nsc relative to S1 using $h_{S1}$ satisfying axioms (1)–(5), $\mathcal{I}$, such that

$$\models_{\mathcal{I}} h_{S1}(\mathrm{on}(A, B))$$
$$\models_{\mathcal{I}} h_{S1}(\mathrm{on}(B, \mathrm{Table}))$$
$$\models_{\mathcal{I}} h_{S1}(\mathrm{clear}(A))$$
$$\models_{\mathcal{I}} h_{S1}(\mathrm{TSP}(\delta(S1, S2), \mathrm{on}(A, \mathrm{Table})))$$
$$\models_{\mathcal{I}} h_{S1}(\mathrm{TSP}(\delta(S1, S2), \mathrm{on}(B, \mathrm{Table}))).$$

---

[5]  Note that $h_{s2}^{\Delta(\mathcal{I}, s1, h_{s1}, s2, h_{s2})}$ is the extent of $h_{s2}$ according to $\Delta(\mathcal{I}, s1, h_{s1}, s2, h_{s2})$.

The interpretation that results from changing the viewpoint from S1 to S2 using $h_{S2}$, $\Delta(\mathcal{I}, S1, h_{S1}, S2, h_{S2})$ is such that

$$\models_{\Delta(\mathcal{I}, S1, h_{S1}, S2, h_{S2})} h_{S2}(\mathrm{TSP}(\delta(S2, S1), \mathrm{on}(A, B)))$$
$$\models_{\Delta(\mathcal{I}, S1, h_{S1}, S2, h_{S2})} h_{S2}(\mathrm{TSP}(\delta(S2, S1), \mathrm{on}(B, \mathrm{Table})))$$
$$\models_{\Delta(\mathcal{I}, S1, h_{S1}, S2, h_{S2})} h_{S2}(\mathrm{TSP}(\delta(S2, S1), \mathrm{clear}(A)))$$
$$\models_{\Delta(\mathcal{I}, S1, h_{S1}, S2, h_{S2})} h_{S2}(\mathrm{on}(A, \mathrm{Table}))$$
$$\models_{\Delta(\mathcal{I}, S1, h_{S1}, S2, h_{S2})} h_{S2}(\mathrm{on}(B, \mathrm{Table})).$$

## 3.6   Comparing with Other Work

The other meta-level time approaches [3,5,18,11,1,7,4] that we mentioned are not directly comparable to our approach. For instance, Gelfond and Lifschitz [4] proposed the language $\mathcal{A}$ for describing actions and proposed a semantics based on states and transition functions, where a state is a set containing fluent names (which are symbols used to represent propositional fluents) and a transition function is a mapping from an action name and a state into another state. The transition function depends on the description of the actions in the domain description. The reason why this approach is not comparable with nsc is that adding more action descriptions may result in a nonmonotonic behavior and therefore language $\mathcal{A}$ should be compared with nsc with some sort of nonmonotonic complement, such as circumscription.

Similar coments could be made to the other approaches, except for the work of Lin and Reiter [7]. These authors describe the progression of basic action theories. After summarizing their method, we compare their progression with ours.

Consider a first order language $\mathcal{L}$ with sorts *action*, *situation* and *object*. Define $\mathcal{L}_{st}$ as the restriction of this language that doesn't mention any other situation term but $st$, does not quantify over situation variables and do not mention Poss or $<$ (predicate Poss identifies executable actions and $s1 < s2$ means that situation $s2$ is reachable from situation $s1$ by executing executable actions). Furthermore, consider $\mathcal{L}_{st}^2$, the second order extension of $\mathcal{L}_{st}$ by predicate variables of arity $object^n$.

A basic action theory $\mathcal{D}$ is a theory of the form

$$\mathcal{D} = \Sigma \cup \mathcal{D}_{ss} \cup \mathcal{D}_{ap} \cup \mathcal{D}_{una} \cup \mathcal{D}_{S0},$$

where:

- $\Sigma$ contains

$$S0 \not\approx \mathrm{do}(a, s)$$
$$\mathrm{do}(a1, s1) \approx \mathrm{do}(a2, s2) \Rightarrow (a1 \approx a2 \wedge s1 \approx s2)$$
$$\forall P. P(S0) \wedge \forall a \forall s (P(s) \Rightarrow P(\mathrm{do}(a, s))) \Rightarrow (\forall s) P(s)$$
$$\neg s < S0$$
$$s < \mathrm{do}(a, s') \Leftrightarrow (\mathrm{Poss}(a, s') \wedge s \leq s').$$

- $\mathcal{D}_{ss}$ contains successor state axioms, which are axioms of the form

$$\text{Poss}(a, s) \Rightarrow (F(x, do(a, s)) \Leftrightarrow \Phi_F(x, a, s));$$

- $\mathcal{D}_{ap}$ contains precondition axioms of the form

$$\text{Poss}(A(x), s) \Rightarrow \Psi_A(x, s)),$$

where $A(x)$ is an action and $\Psi_A(x, s)$ is a wff in $\mathcal{L}_s$.
- $\mathcal{D}_{una}$ contains the unique names axioms for actions, that is, for any two different actions $A1(x)$ and $A2(y)$ we have that

$$A1(x) \not\approx A2(y)$$

and

$$A(x1, \dots, xn) \approx A(y1, \dots, yn) \Rightarrow x1 \approx y1 \wedge \dots \wedge xn \approx yn;$$

- $\mathcal{D}_{S_0}$ contains the initial database, a first order theory in $\mathcal{L}_{S0}$.

Given a basic action theory $\mathcal{D}$, the authors characterize the progression $\mathcal{D}_{S_\alpha}$ of $\mathcal{D}_{S0}$ in response to $\alpha$. In order to do so, first introduce relation $\sim_{S_\alpha}$.

**Definition 3.1.** *Consider two interpretations $M$ and $M'$ with the same domain for sorts action and object. We say that $M' \sim_{S_\alpha} M$ iff*

- *$M'$ and $M$ interpret all the predicate and function symbols which do not take any argument of sort situation identically;*
- *$M$ and $M'$ agree on all fluents at $S_\alpha$: for every predicate fluent $F$ and any variable assignment $\sigma$,*

$$M' \models F(x, do(\alpha, S0))[\sigma] \text{ iff } M \models F(x, do(\alpha, S0))[\sigma].$$

Lin and Reiter's definition of progression follows.

**Definition 3.2.** *A set of sentences $\mathcal{D}_{S_\alpha}$ in $\mathcal{L}_{S_\alpha}^2$ is a progression of the initial database $\mathcal{D}_{S0}$ to $S_\alpha$ (with respect to $\mathcal{D}$) iff for any interpretation $M$, $M$ is a model of $\mathcal{D}_{S_\alpha}$ iff there is a model $M'$ of $\mathcal{D}$ such that $M \sim_{S_\alpha} M'$. ([7, Definition 4.2])*

Both Lin and Reiter's notion of progression and ours are used to find the theory that describes a situation given a theory that describes another situation. However, in our method, we characterize the progression syntactically, that is, given a theory that represents a situation, we transform that theory into a theory representing another situation using syntactic transformations $R$ and $D$. As a direct consequence, the bad surprising result that Lin and Reiter obtained, that the progression of a first order theory may result in a second order theory, doesn't occur in nsc since replacing an atomic formula for another atomic formula in a first order formula doesn't produce a second order formula.

# 4    Using Non-situation Calculus to Model Database Systems

One example of application of nsc, inspired on the work of Reiter [12,14], is to model databases and to study the dynamics of databases. As stated earlier, nsc is used to model dynamic worlds. Moreover, a database is a dynamic system in the sense that we can execute procedures to change the database, the transactions. Therefore, it is possible to use nsc to model databases.

In order to use nsc to model a database, we have to decide a priori which is the predicate symbol that is going to be used to describe the propositional fluents. Allowing only one predicate to be changed in different situations is a strong restriction when compared, for example, with Lin and Reiter's approach where many predicates are allowed to be changed from situation to situation. This restriction, however, is the price to pay for a simple characterization of progression.

We represent a database in a given situation as a nsc theory relative to that situation using the chosen predicate symbol to identify the propositional fluents and we represent database transactions as nsc changes. At this point, it is important to stress that transactions are represented declaratively, that is, the theory that represents the database determines which propositions hold after any transaction is executed. This raises a problem concerning the difficulty of finding appropriate axiomatizations, which is related to the infamous frame problem[6] [10]. The solution to this problem is outside the scope of this paper, and we assume that some method is being followed to solve it.

Given this representation of a database, we are interested in characterizing the dynamics of databases. The characterization of a database dynamics can be done syntactically and semantically. Syntactically, given a database represented by a nsc theory $\Gamma_{s1}$ relative to $s1$ using $h$ and a transaction represented by change $c$ such that $\Gamma_{s1} \vdash s2 \approx \texttt{result}(c, s1)$, the database that results from executing this transaction is obtained by progressing $\Gamma_{s1}$ to $s2$, $RD(\Gamma_s, s1, h, s2, h)$. Note that the predicate symbol used to describe the propositional fluents both in $\Gamma_{s1}$ and in $RD(\Gamma_s, s1, h, s2, h)$ is the same even though the predicates are different.

Semantically, the characterization of the change is done using function $\Delta$: given an interpretation of parameters $\mathcal{I}$ of the nsc relative to $s1$ using $h$, as the result of executing change $c$ we should change this interpretation to interpretation $\Delta(\mathcal{I}, s1, h, s2, h)$.

The point we want to make is that the update of a database, which corresponds to the execution of a transaction in the database, doesn't require any kind of inference. Instead, it can be seen as changing the viewpoint of the theory that represents the database, and that operation doesn't need any kind of inference.

It is interesting to notice that the problem raised by Lin & Reiter [7] of "reasoning about databases containing mixed facts - facts about the current and

---

[6] Some solutions have been proposed to this problem and the interested readers are referred to [17].

initial situation", raised when they were discussing perceptual actions, is solved by our approach by realizing that mixed facts hold in different progressions, that is, a proposition in a database representing a situation can be represented in a database representing a different situation by progressing one of the propositions to the situation in which the other proposition holds.

# 5    Conclusions

We present an approach to write first order logic theories to describe dynamic worlds in a meta-level time approach, that is, we use a theory to describe a situation and the propositional fluents holding in that situation don't have to refer the situation. Furthermore, we introduce some functions in order to describe propositional fluents that hold in other situations.

We present the syntactic transformation of this theory into another nsc theory relative to another situation using another predicate to describe the propositional fluents that hold in that situation, an operation we called "progression", and discuss the semantics of nsc progression, that is, function $\Delta$ that is used to transform an interpretation of a nsc relative to a situation using a predicate into an interpretation of a nsc relative to another situation using another predicate.

One of the good results that is obtained by this definition of progression is that progressing a first order theory always results in a first order theory, a result that doesn't hold in Lin and Reiter's characterization of progression.

Non-situation calculus can be used to model databases and to study the dynamics of databases. We characterize the dynamics of databases both syntactically, using the new definition of progression, and semantically, using function $\Delta$.

Given a theory that represents a database in a situation and a transaction which is associated to a change, the theory that represents the database that results from executing the transaction can be obtained by progressing the theory to the situation that results from executing the change. In summary, executing a transaction in a database corresponds to changing the viewpoint from which the theory that represents the database is written.

# Appendix

**Theorem 5.1.** *Let $s$ be a constant, let $\gamma$ and finite transformable $\Gamma$ be in $\mathcal{L}_{NSC(s,h)}$. Then, $\Gamma \vdash \gamma$ iff $R(\Gamma, s, h) \cup \{(6)\} \vdash R(\gamma, s, h)$.*

**Theorem 5.2.** *Let $s$ be a constant, let $\gamma$ and finite transformable $\Gamma$ be in $\mathcal{L}_{SC}$. Then $\Gamma \cup \{(6)\} \vdash \gamma$ iff $D(\Gamma, s) \vdash D(\gamma, s)$.*

Both Theorems 5.1 and 5.2 were proved in [8].

Before proving lemma 5.1 and Theorem 5.3, note that since the constants and functions are interpreted in the same way both in $\mathcal{I}$ and $\Delta(\mathcal{I}, s_0, h_{s_0}, s_1, h_{s_1})$

and the universes $|\mathcal{I}|$ and $|\Delta(\mathcal{I}, s_0, h_{s_0}, s_1, h_{s_1})|$ are the same, the extension of a function from $V$ to $|\mathcal{I}|$ (relative to $\mathcal{I}$) is the same as the extension of a function from $V$ to $|\Delta(\mathcal{I}, s_0, h_{s_0}, s_1, h_{s_1})|$ (relative to $\Delta(\mathcal{I}, s_0, h_{s_0}, s_1, h_{s_1})$).

**Lemma 5.1.** *Let $\mathcal{I}$ be an interpretation of $\mathcal{L}_{NSC(s_0, h_{s_0})}$ and a model of (1)–(5) and let $s$ be a function from $V$ to $|\mathcal{I}|$. When $\gamma \in \mathcal{L}_{NSC(s_0, h_{s_0})}$ is such that if there is an occurrence of a free variable $v$ in $\gamma$ then, for every $d \in |\mathcal{I}|$, $\models_{\mathcal{I}} \gamma[s(v|d)]$ iff , for every $d \in |\mathcal{I}|$, $\models_{\Delta(\mathcal{I}, s_0, h_{s_0}, s_1, h_{s_1})} RD(\gamma, s_0, h_{s_0}, s_1, h_{s_1})[s(v|d)]$, then it is the case that $\models_{\mathcal{I}} \gamma[s]$ iff $\models_{\Delta(\mathcal{I}, s_0, h_{s_0}, s_1, h_{s_1})} RD(\gamma, s_0, h_{s_0}, s_1, h_{s_1})[s]$.*

*Proof.* This lemma is proved by induction on $\gamma$. For readability, $\Delta(\mathcal{I})$ is used for $\Delta(\mathcal{I}, s_0, h_{s_0}, s_1, h_{s_1})$ and $RD(\gamma)$ for $RD(\gamma, s_0, h_{s_0}, s_1, h_{s_1})$.

Suppose that $\gamma$ is atomic. Then, it is either $t_1 \approx t_2$ or $h_{s_0}(t_1)$ or $P(t_1, \dots, t_n)$, for $n$-arity predicate $P$ different from $\approx$ and $h_{s_0}$.

- Consider that $\gamma = t_1 \approx t_2$. It is the case that $\models_{\mathcal{I}} t_1 \approx t_2[s]$ iff $\bar{s}(t_1) = \bar{s}(t_2)$, from which it is the case that $\models_{\Delta(\mathcal{I})} t_1 \approx t_2[s]$. According to $RD$ definition, $RD(t_1 \approx t_2) = t_1 \approx t_2$. Therefore, $\models_{\mathcal{I}} t_1 \approx t_2[s]$ iff $\models_{\Delta(\mathcal{I})} RD(t_1 \approx t_2)[s]$.
- Consider that $\gamma = h_{s_0}(t_1)$. According to the definition of $\Delta$, it follows that $\models_{\mathcal{I}} h_{s_0}(t_1)[s]$ iff $\models_{\Delta(\mathcal{I})} h_{s_1}(\text{TSP}(\delta(s_1, s_0), t_1))[s]$. The result follows by considering that it is the case that either $s_0 = s_1$ or $s_0 \neq s_1$.
  - Consider that $s_0 = s_1$. Given the definition of $\Delta$, since $\mathcal{I}$ is a model of (1)–(5), $\Delta(\mathcal{I})$ is also a model of (1)–(5). Furthermore, these interpretations satisfy $t_1 \approx \text{TSP}(\delta(s_1, s_0), t_1)$ with any $s$, from which it follows that $\models_{\Delta(\mathcal{I})} h_{s_1}(\text{TSP}(\delta(s_1, s_0), t_1))[s]$ iff $\models_{\Delta(\mathcal{I})} h_{s_1}(t_1)[s]$. Observing that $RD(h_{s_0}(t_1)) = h_{s_1}(t_1)$, it is the case that $\models_{\mathcal{I}} h_{s_0}(t_1)[s]$ iff $\models_{\Delta(\mathcal{I})} RD(h_{s_0}(t_1))[s]$.
  - Consider that $s_0 \neq s_1$. Since $RD(h_{s_0}(t_1)) = h_{s_1}(\text{TSP}(\delta(s_1, s_0), t_1))$, it is the case that $\models_{\mathcal{I}} h_{s_0}(t_1)[s]$ iff $\models_{\Delta(\mathcal{I})} RD(h_{s_0}(t_1))[s]$.
- Consider that $P(t_1, \dots, t_n)$, for $n$-arity predicate $P$ different from $h_{s_0}$. According to the definition of $\Delta$, $\models_{\mathcal{I}} P(t_1, \dots, t_n)[s]$ iff $\models_{\Delta(\mathcal{I})} P(t_1, \dots, t_n)[s]$. Since $P$ is different from $h_{s_0}$, $RD(P(t_1, \dots, t_n)) = P(t_1, \dots, t_n)$. Therefore, $\models_{\mathcal{I}} P(t_1, \dots, t_n)[s]$ iff $\models_{\Delta(\mathcal{I})} RD(P(t_1, \dots, t_n))[s]$.

Therefore, for $\gamma$ atomic, $\models_{\mathcal{I}} \gamma[s]$ iff $\models_{\Delta(\mathcal{I})} RD(\gamma)[s]$, from which when $\gamma$ is such that if there is an occurrence of a free variable $v$ in $\gamma$ then, for every $d \in |\mathcal{I}|$, $\models_{\mathcal{I}} \gamma[s(v|d)]$ iff, for every $d \in |\mathcal{I}|$, $\models_{\Delta(\mathcal{I})} RD(\gamma)[s(v|d)]$, then it is the case that $\models_{\mathcal{I}} \gamma[s]$ iff $\models_{\Delta(\mathcal{I})} RD(\gamma)[s]$, for $\gamma$ atomic.

Suppose that $\gamma = \neg\gamma_1$ and that when $\gamma_1$ is such that if there is an occurrence of a free variable $v$ in $\gamma_1$ then, for every $d \in |\mathcal{I}|$, $\models_{\mathcal{I}} \gamma_1[s(v|d)]$ iff, for every $d \in |\mathcal{I}|$, $\models_{\Delta(\mathcal{I})} RD(\gamma_1)[s(v|d)]$, then it is the case that $\models_{\mathcal{I}} \gamma_1[s]$ iff $\models_{\Delta(\mathcal{I})} RD(\gamma_1)[s]$. It must be proved that when $\neg\gamma_1$ is such that if there is an occurrence of a free variable $v$ in $\neg\gamma_1$ then, for every $d \in |\mathcal{I}|$, $\models_{\mathcal{I}} (\neg\gamma_1)[s(v|d)]$ iff, for every $d \in |\mathcal{I}|$, $\models_{\Delta(\mathcal{I})} RD(\neg\gamma_1)[s(v|d)]$, then it is the case that $\models_{\mathcal{I}} (\neg\gamma_1)[s]$ iff $\models_{\Delta(\mathcal{I})} RD(\neg\gamma_1)[s]$.

Assume that $\neg\gamma_1$ is such that if there is an occurrence of a free variable $v$ in $\neg\gamma_1$ then, for every $d \in |\mathcal{I}|$, $\models_{\mathcal{I}} (\neg\gamma_1)[s(v|d)]$ iff, for every $d \in |\mathcal{I}|$, $\models_{\Delta(\mathcal{I})} RD(\neg\gamma_1)[s(v|d)]$. Either there are free variables in $\neg\gamma_1$ or not.

- If there are free variables in $\neg\gamma_1$, then let $v$ be a free variable. Then, $\models_{\mathcal{I}}$ $(\neg\gamma_1)[s(v|s(v))]$ iff $\models_{\Delta(\mathcal{I})} RD(\neg\gamma_1)[s(v|s(v))]$. Since $s(v|s(v)) = s$, the result follows.

- If there are no free variables in $\neg\gamma_1$, then it remains to be proved that $\models_{\mathcal{I}} (\neg\gamma_1)[s]$ iff $\models_{\Delta(\mathcal{I})} RD(\neg\gamma_1)[s]$. According to satisfaction definition, $\models_{\mathcal{I}}$ $(\neg\gamma_1)[s]$ iff $\not\models_{\mathcal{I}} \gamma_1[s]$. According to the inductive hypothesis, it follows that $\not\models_{\mathcal{I}} \gamma_1[s]$ iff $\not\models_{\Delta(\mathcal{I})} RD(\gamma_1)[s]$. From satisfaction definition, it follows that $\not\models_{\Delta(\mathcal{I})} RD(\gamma_1)[s]$ iff $\models_{\Delta(\mathcal{I})} (\neg RD(\gamma_1))[s]$. Since $\neg RD(\gamma_1) = RD(\neg\gamma_1)$, it follows that $\models_{\mathcal{I}} (\neg\gamma_1)[s]$ iff $\models_{\Delta(\mathcal{I})} RD(\neg\gamma_1)[s]$.

Therefore, the result follows for $\gamma = \neg\gamma_1$.

Suppose that $\gamma = \gamma_1 \Rightarrow \gamma_2$, that when $\gamma_1$ is such that if there is an occurrence of a free variable $v$ in $\gamma_1$ then, for every $d \in |\mathcal{I}|$, $\models_{\mathcal{I}} \gamma_1[s(v|d)]$ iff, for every $d \in |\mathcal{I}|$, $\models_{\Delta(\mathcal{I})} RD(\gamma_1)[s(v|d)]$, then it is the case that $\models_{\mathcal{I}} \gamma_1[s]$ iff $\models_{\Delta(\mathcal{I})} RD(\gamma_1)[s]$, and that when $\gamma_2$ is such that if there is an occurrence of a free variable $v$ in $\gamma_2$ then, for every $d \in |\mathcal{I}|$, $\models_{\mathcal{I}} \gamma_2[s(v|d)]$ iff, for every $d \in |\mathcal{I}|$, $\models_{\Delta(\mathcal{I})} RD(\gamma_2)[s(v|d)]$, then it is the case that $\models_{\mathcal{I}} \gamma_2[s]$ iff $\models_{\Delta(\mathcal{I})} RD(\gamma_2)[s]$. It must be proved that when $\gamma_1 \Rightarrow \gamma_2$ is such that if there is an occurrence of a free variable $v$ in $\gamma_1 \Rightarrow \gamma_2$ then, for every $d \in |\mathcal{I}|$, $\models_{\mathcal{I}} (\gamma_1 \Rightarrow \gamma_2)[s(v|d)]$ iff, for every $d \in |\mathcal{I}|$, $\models_{\Delta(\mathcal{I})} RD(\gamma_1 \Rightarrow \gamma_2)[s(v|d)]$, then $\models_{\mathcal{I}} (\gamma_1 \Rightarrow \gamma_2)[s]$ iff $\models_{\Delta(\mathcal{I})} RD(\gamma_1 \Rightarrow \gamma_2)[s]$.

Assume that $\gamma_1 \Rightarrow \gamma_2$ is such that if there is an occurrence of a free variable $v$ in $\gamma_1 \Rightarrow \gamma_2$ then, for every $d \in |\mathcal{I}|$, $\models_{\mathcal{I}} (\gamma_1 \Rightarrow \gamma_2)[s(v|d)]$ iff, for every $d \in |\mathcal{I}|$, $\models_{\Delta(\mathcal{I})} RD(\gamma_1 \Rightarrow \gamma_2)[s(v|d)]$. Either there are free variables in $\gamma_1 \Rightarrow \gamma_2$ or not.

- If there are free variables in $\gamma_1 \Rightarrow \gamma_2$, then let $v$ be a free variable in $\gamma_1 \Rightarrow \gamma_2$. Then, $\models_{\mathcal{I}} (\gamma_1 \Rightarrow \gamma_2)[s(v|s(v))]$ iff $\models_{\Delta(\mathcal{I})} RD(\gamma_1 \Rightarrow \gamma_2)[s(v|s(v))]$. Since $s(v|s(v)) = s$, the result follows.

- If there are no free variables in $\gamma_1 \Rightarrow \gamma_2$, then it remains to be proved that $\models_{\mathcal{I}} (\gamma_1 \Rightarrow \gamma_2)[s]$ iff $\models_{\Delta(\mathcal{I})} RD(\gamma_1 \Rightarrow \gamma_2)[s]$. According to satisfaction definition, $\models_{\mathcal{I}} (\gamma_1 \Rightarrow \gamma_2)[s]$ iff either $\not\models_{\mathcal{I}} \gamma_1[s]$ or $\models_{\mathcal{I}} \gamma_2[s]$ or both. Since, according to the inductive hypothesis, it is the case that $\not\models_{\mathcal{I}} \gamma_1[s]$ iff $\not\models_{\Delta(\mathcal{I})} RD(\gamma_1)[s]$, and $\models_{\mathcal{I}} \gamma_2[s]$ iff $\models_{\Delta(\mathcal{I})} RD(\gamma_2)[s]$, it follows that either $\not\models_{\mathcal{I}} \gamma_1[s]$ or $\models_{\mathcal{I}} \gamma_2[s]$ or both iff either $\not\models_{\Delta(\mathcal{I})} RD(\gamma_1)[s]$ or $\models_{\Delta(\mathcal{I})} RD(\gamma_2)[s]$ or both, from which, according to satisfaction definition, it follows that $\models_{\mathcal{I}} (\gamma_1 \Rightarrow \gamma_2)[s]$ iff $\models_{\Delta(\mathcal{I})} (RD(\gamma_1) \Rightarrow RD(\gamma_2))[s]$. Since $RD(\gamma_1) \Rightarrow RD(\gamma_2) = RD(\gamma_1 \Rightarrow \gamma_2)$, it follows that $\models_{\mathcal{I}} (\gamma_1 \Rightarrow \gamma_2)[s]$ iff $\models_{\Delta(\mathcal{I})} RD(\gamma_1 \Rightarrow \gamma_2)[s]$.

Therefore, the result follows for $\gamma = \gamma_1 \Rightarrow \gamma_2$.

Suppose that $\gamma = \forall x\ \gamma_1$ and that when $\gamma_1$ is such that if there is an occurrence of a free variable $v$ in $\gamma_1$ then, for every $d \in |\mathcal{I}|$, $\models_{\mathcal{I}} \gamma_1[s(v|d)]$ iff, for every $d \in |\mathcal{I}|$, $\models_{\Delta(\mathcal{I})} RD(\gamma_1)[s(v|d)]$, then it is the case that $\models_{\mathcal{I}} \gamma_1[s]$ iff $\models_{\Delta(\mathcal{I})} RD(\gamma_1)[s]$. It must be proved that when $\forall x\ \gamma_1$ is such that if there is an occurrence of a free variable $v$ in $\forall x\ \gamma_1$ then, for every $d \in |\mathcal{I}|$, $\models_{\mathcal{I}} (\forall x\ \gamma_1)[s(v|d)]$ iff, for every $d \in |\mathcal{I}|$, $\models_{\Delta(\mathcal{I})} RD(\forall x\ \gamma_1)[s(v|d)]$, then it is the case that $\models_{\mathcal{I}} (\forall x\ \gamma_1)[s]$ iff $\models_{\Delta(\mathcal{I})} RD(\forall x\ \gamma_1)[s]$.

Assume that $\forall x\ \gamma_1$ is such that if there is an occurrence of a free variable $v$ in $\forall x\ \gamma_1$ then, for every $d \in |\mathcal{I}|$, $\models_{\mathcal{I}} (\forall x\ \gamma_1)[s(v|d)]$ iff, for every $d \in |\mathcal{I}|$, $\models_{\Delta(\mathcal{I})} RD(\forall x\ \gamma_1)[s(v|d)]$. Either there are free variables in $\forall x\ \gamma_1$ or not.

- If there are free variables in $\forall x \ \gamma_1$, then let $v$ be a free variable. Then, $\models_{\mathcal{I}} (\forall x \ \gamma_1)[s(v|s(v))]$ iff $\models_{\Delta(\mathcal{I})} RD(\forall x \ \gamma_1)[s(v|s(v))]$. Since $s(v|s(v)) = s$, the result follows.

- If there are no free variables in $\forall x \ \gamma_1$, then it remains to be proved that $\models_{\mathcal{I}} (\forall x \ \gamma_1)[s]$ iff $\models_{\Delta(\mathcal{I})} RD(\forall x \ \gamma_1)[s]$. According to satisfaction definition, $\models_{\mathcal{I}} (\forall x \ \gamma_1)[s]$ iff, for every $d \in |\mathcal{I}|$, $\models_{\mathcal{I}} \gamma_1[s(x|d)]$. It is either the case that $x$ occurs free in $\gamma_1$ or not.

  - If $x$ occurs free in $\gamma_1$, then, according to the inductive hypothesis, it follows that, for every $d \in |\mathcal{I}|$, $\models_{\mathcal{I}} \gamma_1[s(x|d)]$ iff, for every $d \in |\mathcal{I}|$, $\models_{\Delta(\mathcal{I})} RD(\gamma_1)[s(x|d)]$.

  - If $x$ doesn't occur free in $\gamma_1$, then there are no free variables in $\gamma_1$, and, therefore, according to [2, theorem 22A],[7] for every $d \in |\mathcal{I}|$, $\models_{\mathcal{I}} \gamma_1[s(x|d)]$ iff $\models_{\mathcal{I}} \gamma_1[s]$. According to the inductive hypothesis, it follows that $\models_{\mathcal{I}} \gamma_1[s]$ iff $\models_{\Delta(\mathcal{I})} RD(\gamma_1)[s]$, and, according to [2, theorem 22A], it follows that $\models_{\Delta(\mathcal{I})} RD(\gamma_1)[s]$ iff, for every $d \in |\mathcal{I}|$, $\models_{\Delta(\mathcal{I})} RD(\gamma_1)[s(x|d)]$.

  In both cases, it follows that, for every $d \in |\mathcal{I}|$, $\gamma_1[s(x|d)]$ iff, for every $d \in |\mathcal{I}|$, $\models_{\Delta(\mathcal{I})} RD(\gamma_1)[s(x|d)]$. According to satisfaction definition, it follows that $\models_{\Delta(\mathcal{I})} RD(\forall x \ \gamma_1)[s]$ iff $\models_{\Delta(\mathcal{I})} (\forall x \ RD(\gamma_1))[s]$. Observing that $\forall x \ RD(\gamma_1) = RD(\forall x \ \gamma_1)$, it follows that $\models_{\mathcal{I}} (\forall x \ \gamma_1)[s]$ iff $\models_{\Delta(\mathcal{I})} RD(\forall x \ \gamma_1)[s]$.

Therefore, the result follows for $\gamma = \forall x \ \gamma_1$. $\qquad\square$

**Theorem 5.3.** *Let $\mathcal{I}$ be an interpretation of parameters in $\mathcal{L}_{NSC(s_0, h_{s_0})}$ and a model of closed transformable theory $\Gamma_{s_0}$. Then, $\Delta(\mathcal{I}, s_0, h_{s_0}, s_1, h_{s_1})$ is a model of $RD(\Gamma_{s_0}, s_0, h_{s_0}, s_1, h_{s_1})$.*

*Proof.* If $\mathcal{I}$ is a model of $\Gamma_{s_0}$, then, for each $\gamma \in \Gamma_{s_0}$, $\models_{\mathcal{I}} \gamma$. According to model definition, for each function $s$ from $V$ to $|\mathcal{I}|$, $\models_{\mathcal{I}} \gamma[s]$. According to lemma 5.1, since $\Gamma_{s_0}$ is closed, $\models_{\mathcal{I}} \gamma[s]$ iff $\models_{\Delta(\mathcal{I}, s_0, h_{s_0}, s_1, h_{s_1})} RD(\gamma, s_0, h_{s_0}, s_1, h_{s_1})[s]$. Since this result holds for any $s$, it follows that $\models_{\Delta(\mathcal{I}, s_0, h_{s_0}, s_1, h_{s_1})} RD(\gamma, s_0, h_{s_0}, s_1, h_{s_1})$. Since $\gamma$ is any element of $\Gamma_{s_0}$, it follows that $\Delta(\mathcal{I}, s_0, h_{s_0}, s_1, h_{s_1})$ is a model of $RD(\Gamma_{s_0}, s_0, h_{s_0}, s_1, h_{s_1})$. $\qquad\square$

# References

1. Gerhard Brewka and Joachim Hertzberg. How to Do Things with Worlds: on Formalizing Actions and Plans. *Journal of Logic and Computation*, 3(5):517–532, 1993.
2. Herbert B. Enderton. *A mathematical introduction to logic.* Academic Press Inc., 1972.
3. Richard E. Fikes and Nils J. Nilsson. STRIPS: A New Approach to the Application of Theorem Proving to Problem Solving. *Artificial Intelligence*, 2:189–208, 1971.

---

[7] This theorems states that "Assume that $s_1$, $s_2$ are functions from $V$ to $|\mathcal{U}|$ which agree in all variables (if any) which occur free in the wff $\phi$. Then $\models_{\mathcal{U}} \phi[s_1]$ iff $\models_{\mathcal{U}} \phi[s_2]$."

4. Michael Gelfond and Vladimir Lifschitz. Representing action and change by logic programs. *Journal of Logic Programming*, 17:301–321, 1993.

5. Mathew L. Ginsberg and David E. Smith. Reasoning about Action I: A Possible Worlds Approach. *Artificial Intelligence*, 35:165–195, 1988.

6. Fausto Giunchiglia and Chiara Ghidini. Local model semantics, or contextual reasoning = locality and compatibility". In *Principles of Knowledge Representation and Reasoning: Proceedings of the Sixth International Conference*, pages 282–289, 1998.

7. Fangzhen Lin and Ray Reiter. How to progress a database. *Artificial Intelligence*, 92:131–167, 1997.

8. Pedro A. Matos. Some properties of non-situation calculus. Technical report, Grupo de Inteligência Artificial, Instituto Superior Técnico, U-niversidade Técnica de Lisboa, Lisboa, Portugal, 1999. Available as `http://www.gia.ist.utl.pt/~pedro/techrep/nsc.ps`.

9. John McCarthy. First order theories of individual concepts and propositions. In *Machine Intelligence*, volume 9, pages 129–148. Ellis Horwood, 1979. Available as `http://www-formal.stanford.edu/jmc/concepts.html`.

10. John McCarthy and P. Hayes. Some philosophical problems from the standpoint of artificial intelligence. In *Machine Intelligence*, volume 4, pages 463–502. Edinburg University Press, 1969.

11. Edwin P. D. Pednault. ADL and the State-Transition Model of Action. *Journal of Logic and Computation*, 4(5):465–512, 1994.

12. Raymond Reiter. On formalizing database updates: Preliminary report. In *Proc. 3rd International Conference on Extending Database Technologies*, pages 10–20, 1992.

13. Raymond Reiter. Proving properties of states in the situation calculus. *Artificial Intelligence*, 64:337–351, 1993.

14. Raymond Reiter. The projection problem in the situation calculus: A soundness and completeness result, with an application to database updates. In *Proceedings of the International Conference on Knowledge Representation and Reasoning*, 1996.

15. Stanley J. Rosenschein. Plan synthesis: A logical perspective. In *Proceedings of the Seventh International Joint Conference on Artificial Intelligence*, pages 331–337, 1981.

16. Erik Sandewall and Yoav Shoham. Non-monotonic Temporal Reasoning. In Dov Gabbay, C. J. Hogger, and J. A. Robinson, editors, *Handbok of Artificial Intelligence and Logic Programming*, volume 4, pages 439–498. Oxford University Press, 1994.

17. Murray Shanahan. *Solving the Frame Problem – A Mathematical Investigation of the Common Sense Law of Inertia*. The MIT Press, 1997.

18. Marianne Winslett. Reasoning about action using a possible models approach. In *Proceedings of the Seventh National Conference on Artificial Intelligence*, pages 89–93, 1988.

# Dealing with Modification Requests During View Updating and Integrity Constraint Maintenance

Enric Mayol and Ernest Teniente

Universitat Politècnica de Catalunya, Facultat d'Informàtica
Jordi Girona Salgado 1-3, Edifici C6, E-08034 Barcelona, Catalonia
[mayol|teniente]@lsi.upc.es

**Abstract.** An important problem that arises when updating a deductive database is that of integrity constraint maintenance. That is, given a consistent database and an update request, to obtain all possible updates of base facts such that the request is satisfied and no integrity constraint is violated. This problem becomes more complex when view updates are also taken into account. In this paper we define a method for view updating and integrity constraint maintenance in deductive databases. We propose a new method that is sound and that improves current methods by dealing with three kinds of updates: insertion, deletion and modification updates on base and derived predicates. Moreover, due to the inclusion of an specific modification operator, the own definition of the method deals with key information of base and derived predicates.

**Keywords.** view updating, integrity constraint maintenance

## 1 Introduction

Several problems may arise when updating a deductive database [18]. A well-known problem is that of enforcing database consistency. A deductive database is called consistent if it satisfies a set of integrity constraints. When performing an update, deductive database consistency may be violated. That is, the update, together with the current contents of the database, may falsify some integrity constraint.

The classical approach to deal with this problem is that of integrity constraint checking, which is concerned with detecting whether a given update violates some integrity constraint (see for example [8]). If a violation is detected, the update is rolled back in its entirety. The main drawback of this approach is that the user may not know which additional changes are needed to satisfy all the integrity constraints.

An alternative approach is that of integrity constraint maintenance [14,20,3], [17,13,1], which tries to repair integrity constraint violations by performing additional updates, other than the requested ones, to restore database consistency.

Deductive databases contain also deductive rules that allow to deduce new (view or derived) facts from those (base) facts explicitly stored in the database.

K.-D. Schewe, B. Thalheim (Eds.): FoIKS 2000, LNCS 1762, pp. 192–213, 2000.

Then, a request to update a derived fact must be translated into correct updates of the underlying base facts, since the view extension is completely defined by the application of the deductive rules. This problem is known as view updating [9,10,20,5,17,7,13].

View updating and integrity constraint maintenance are strongly related. On one side, an update obtained as a result of translating a view update request can violate an integrity constraint. On the other, repairing an integrity constraint defined through some derived predicate may require to perform a view update. Moreover, as shown in [17], integrity constraint maintenance and view updating cannot be performed as two independent steps because this would allow to consider repairs that could invalidate the requested view update. We propose a new method that addresses the problems of view updating and integrity constraint maintenance. Given a view update request, the main goal of this method is to obtain all possible translations that satisfy both the request and all integrity constraints.

Our method extends the Events Method [17] by taking into account information about the keys of base and derived predicates. This allows us to consider three basic update operators: insertion, deletion and modification; and to incorporate the treatment of key integrity constraints into the own definition of the method. Moreover, we can obtain translations that are not obtained when a modification is handled as a deletion followed by an insertion. A preliminary version of this method was presented in [15].

This paper is organized as follows. Next section reviews basic concepts of deductive databases. Section 3 reviews event and transition rules, that will be used by our method. Section 4 is devoted to the definition of our method. Section 5 compares our method with previous research. Finally, Section 6 summarizes our conclusions.

## 2   Deductive Databases

We briefly review the basic concepts of deductive databases [11]. We consider a first order language with a universe of constants, a set of variables, a set of predicate names and no function symbols. We will use names beginning with a capital letter for predicate symbols and constants and names beginning with a lower case letter for variables.

A *term* is a variable symbol or a constant symbol. We assume that possible values for the terms range over finite domains. If $P$ is an $m$-ary predicate symbol and $t_1, \ldots, t_m$ are terms, then $P(t_1, \ldots, t_m)$ is an *atom*. The atom is *ground* if every $t_i$ $(i = 1, \ldots, m)$ is a constant. A *literal* is defined as either an atom or a negated atom. A *fact* is a formula of the form: $P(t_1, \ldots, t_m) \leftarrow$, where $P(t_1, \ldots, t_m)$ is a ground atom. We assume that each $m$-ary predicate has a subset of arguments $t_i$ $(i = 1, \ldots, k$ with $m \geq k \geq 1)$ that form the *key* of that predicate.

A *deductive rule* is a formula of the form[1] $P(t_1, \ldots, t_k, t_{k+1}, \ldots, t_m) \leftarrow L_1 \wedge \cdots \wedge L_n$, with $n \geq 1$, where $P(t_1, \ldots, t_k, t_{k+1}, \ldots, t_m)$ is an atom denoting the conclusion, and $L_1, \ldots, L_n$ are literals representing conditions. Any variable in $P(t_1, \ldots, t_k, t_{k+1}, \ldots, t_m), L_1, \ldots, L_n$ is assumed to be universally quantified over the whole formula. A derived predicate $P$ may be defined by means of one or more deductive rules.

An *integrity constraint* is a closed first-order formula that every state of the deductive database is required to satisfy. We deal with constraints in *denial form* $\leftarrow L_1 \wedge \cdots \wedge L_n$ with $n \geq 1$, where each $L_i$ is a literal and variables are assumed universally quantified over the formula. We associate to each integrity constraint an inconsistency predicate $Ic_j$, where $j$ is a positive integer. Then, we would rewrite the former denial as $Ic_1 \leftarrow L_1 \wedge \cdots \wedge L_n$. More general constraints can be transformed in denials by using [12].

We assume that the database contains a distinguished derived predicate $Ic$ defined by the $n$ clauses $Ic \leftarrow Ic_j$, that is one rule for each integrity constraint $Ic_j$ of the database. Note that $Ic$ will only hold in those states of the database that violate some integrity constraint and that it will not hold for those states that satisfy all constraints.

To enforce the concept of key, we assume that associated to each predicate $P(t_1, \ldots, t_k, t_{k+1}, \ldots, t_m)$ there is a key integrity constraint that we define as:

$$Ic_k \leftarrow P(t_1, \ldots, t_k, t_{k+1}, \ldots, t_m) \wedge P(t_1, \ldots, t_k, t'_{k+1}, \ldots, t'_m)$$
$$\wedge [t_{k+1}, \ldots, t_m] \neq [t'_{k+1}, \ldots, t'_m]$$

These constraints are not explicitly defined since they are implicitly handled by our method.

A *deductive database* $\mathcal{D}$ is a triple (EDB, IDB, IC), where EDB is a set of facts, IDB a set of deductive rules and IC a set of integrity constraints. The set EDB of facts is called the *extensional* part of the database and the set of deductive rules and integrity constraints is called the *intensional* part.

Database predicates are partitioned into base and derived predicates. A *base predicate* appears only in the extensional part and (possibly) in the body of deductive rules. A *derived predicate* appears only in the intensional part. Any database can be defined in this form [2]. We deal with *hierarchical* databases [11] and, as usual, we require the database to be *allowed* [11]; that is, any variable that occurs in a deductive rule has an occurrence in a positive literal of the body of the rule.

*Example 2.1.*  The following deductive database will be used during the paper:
    (F1)      Unemp_benef($\underline{Ann}$, 500)
    (F2)      Unemp_benef($\underline{Joan}$, 100)
    (F3)      Sick-leave($\underline{Bob}$)
    (R1)      Worker($p, c$) $\leftarrow$ Works($p, c$) $\wedge$ ¬Sick-leave($p$)
    (R2)      $Ic_1(\underline{p}, a, \underline{c}) \leftarrow$ Unemp_benef($p, a$) $\wedge$ Worker($p, c$)
This database contains three base predicates and a derived one:

---
[1] Underlined arguments correspond to the key arguments of that predicate.

- Unemp_benef($p, a$) states that a person $p$ receives an unemployment benefit of an amount $a$.
- Works($p, c$) states that a person $p$ works in a company $c$.
- Sick-leave($p$) states that a person $p$ leaves from work granted by serious illness.
- Worker($p, c$) states that a person $p$ is a worker if he/she works in a company $c$ and he/she is not sick-leave.

It contains also one integrity constraint $Ic_1$, stating that it is not possible to receive an unemployment benefit and to be a worker at the same time. Key integrity constraints are illustrated by underlining key arguments of each predicate and state that a person may not have two different unemployment benefits and that a person may not work in two different companies. □

## 3   The Augmented Database

Our method is based on a set of rules that define the difference between two consecutive database states. This set of rules, together with the original database, form the Augmented Database $A(\mathcal{D})$ [16,19], which explicitly defines the insertions, deletions and modifications induced by an update.

The definition of the Augmented Database is based on the concept of *event*. For each predicate $P$ in a given deductive database $\mathcal{D}$, an *insertion event predicate* $\iota P$, a *deletion event predicate* $\delta P$ and a *modification event predicate* $\mu P$ are used to define the precise difference of deducible facts of consecutive database states.

More precisely, rules about $\iota P$, $\delta P$ and $\mu P$ in the Augmented Database, called *event rules*, define exactly the facts about $P$ that are inserted, deleted or modified in the extension of $P$ by the application of some transaction $T$. Rules about $\iota P$, $\delta P$ and $\mu P$ depend on the definition of $P$ in $\mathcal{D}$, but they are independent of any transaction $T$ and of the extensional part of $\mathcal{D}$.

A more formal declarative definition of $\iota P$, $\delta P$ and $\mu P$ is given by the following equivalences[2]:

$$\forall \boldsymbol{k}, \boldsymbol{x}(\iota P(\underline{\boldsymbol{k}}, \boldsymbol{x}) \Leftrightarrow P^n(\underline{\boldsymbol{k}}, \boldsymbol{x}) \wedge \neg \exists \boldsymbol{y} P(\underline{\boldsymbol{k}}, \boldsymbol{y}))$$
$$\forall \boldsymbol{k}, \boldsymbol{x}(\delta P(\underline{\boldsymbol{k}}, \boldsymbol{x}) \Leftrightarrow P(\underline{\boldsymbol{k}}, \boldsymbol{x}) \wedge \neg \exists \boldsymbol{y} P^n(\underline{\boldsymbol{k}}, \boldsymbol{y}))$$
$$\forall \boldsymbol{k}, \boldsymbol{x}, \boldsymbol{x}'(\mu P(\underline{\boldsymbol{k}}, \boldsymbol{x}, \boldsymbol{x}') \Leftrightarrow P(\underline{\boldsymbol{k}}, \boldsymbol{x}) \wedge P^n(\underline{\boldsymbol{k}}, \boldsymbol{x}') \wedge \boldsymbol{x} \neq \boldsymbol{x}')$$

For example, given the derived predicate Worker($p, c$), $\iota$Worker($John, C1$) denotes an insertion event corresponding to predicate Worker: Worker($John, C1$) will be true after the application of the transaction and it is false before. On the other hand $\delta$Worker($Mary, C2$) denotes a deletion event: Worker($Mary, C2$) will be false after the application of the transaction and it is true before; while $\mu$Worker($Peter, C1, C2$) denotes a modification event: Worker($Peter, C1$) is true

---

[2] Here $\boldsymbol{k}$, $\boldsymbol{x}$, $\boldsymbol{x}'$ and $\boldsymbol{y}$ are vectors of variables and $P^n$ denotes the evaluation of $P$ in the new state of the database.

before the application of the transaction and Worker($Peter, C2$) will be true in the new state.

If $P$ is a base predicate, $\iota P$, $\delta P$ and $\mu P$ facts represent insertions, deletions and modifications of base facts. Therefore, we assume from now on that a transaction $T$ is a set of base event facts.

If $P$ is a derived predicate, $\iota P$, $\delta P$ and $\mu P$ represent induced insertions, deletions and modifications, respectively. If $P$ is an inconsistency predicate, $\iota P$ represents a violation of the corresponding integrity constraint. For inconsistency predicates, $\delta P$ and $\mu P$ facts are not defined, since we assume that the database is consistent before the update.

An event ($\iota P$, $\delta P$ and $\mu P$) is said to be base (resp., derived) iff $P$ is base (resp., derived).

In addition to the event rules, the Augmented Database may also contain a set of *transition rules* associated to each derived or inconsistency predicate $P$. Transition rules of predicate $P$ define predicate $P$ in the new state of the database (denoted by $P^n$).

*Example 3.1.* Consider a derived predicate $P$ defined by the rule $P(\underline{k}, x) \leftarrow Q(\underline{k}, x) \wedge \neg R(\underline{k}, x)$. Transition and event rules associated to predicate $P$ are the following:

$$P_1^n(\underline{k}, x) \leftarrow Q(\underline{k}, x) \wedge \neg \delta Q(\underline{k}, x) \wedge \neg \mu Q(\underline{k}, x, x') \wedge \neg R(\underline{k}, x)$$
$$\wedge \neg \iota R(\underline{k}, x) \wedge \neg \mu R(\underline{k}, x, x')$$
$$P_2^n(\underline{k}, x) \leftarrow Q(\underline{k}, x) \wedge \neg \delta Q(\underline{k}, x) \wedge \neg \mu Q(\underline{k}, x, x') \wedge \delta R(\underline{k}, x)$$
$$P_3^n(\underline{k}, x) \leftarrow Q(\underline{k}, x) \wedge \neg \delta Q(\underline{k}, x) \wedge \neg \mu Q(\underline{k}, x, x') \wedge \mu R(\underline{k}, x, x')$$
$$P_4^n(\underline{k}, x) \leftarrow \iota Q(\underline{k}, x) \wedge \neg R(\underline{k}, x) \wedge \neg \iota R(\underline{k}, x) \wedge \neg \mu R(\underline{k}, x', x)$$
$$P_5^n(\underline{k}, x) \leftarrow \iota Q(\underline{k}, x) \wedge \delta R(\underline{k}, x)$$
$$P_6^n(\underline{k}, x) \leftarrow \iota Q(\underline{k}, x) \wedge \mu R(\underline{k}, x, x')$$
$$P_7^n(\underline{k}, x) \leftarrow \mu Q(\underline{k}, x', x) \wedge \neg R(\underline{k}, x) \wedge \neg \iota R(\underline{k}, x) \wedge \neg \mu R(\underline{k}, x'', x)$$
$$P_8^n(\underline{k}, x) \leftarrow \mu Q(\underline{k}, x', x) \wedge \delta R(\underline{k}, x)$$
$$P_9^n(\underline{k}, x) \leftarrow \mu Q(\underline{k}, x', x) \wedge \mu R(\underline{k}, x, x'')$$
$$P^n(\underline{k}, x) \leftarrow P_j^n(\underline{k}, x) \qquad\qquad (j = 1, \ldots, 9)$$
$$\iota P(\underline{k}, x) \leftarrow P^n(\underline{k}, x) \wedge \neg \exists y P(\underline{k}, y)$$
$$\delta P(\underline{k}, x) \leftarrow P(\underline{k}, x) \wedge \neg \exists y P^n(\underline{k}, y)$$
$$\mu P(\underline{k}, x, x') \leftarrow P(\underline{k}, x) \wedge P^n(\underline{k}, x, x') \wedge x \neq x'$$

Transition rules define all possible ways of satisfying a derived fact $P(K, X)$ in the new state of the database. For instance, the fourth transition rule states that $P(K, X)$ will be true in the updated database if $Q(K, X)$ has been inserted by the transaction $T$, $R(K, X)$ is false in the current database, $R(K, X)$ will not be inserted by $T$ and no modification from $R(K, X')$ to $R(K, X)$ is given by $T$. Subscripts are only needed to distinguish among several transition rules of a derived predicate. $\qquad\square$

Description and discussion of the procedure for automatically deriving an Augmented Database can be found in [19], where several simplifications are proposed. We would like to note that in several cases transition rules corresponding to a predicate $P$ may be completely removed. In the paper we will use the simplified version of transition and event rules.

**Definition 3.1.** Given a deductive database $\mathcal{D}$, the *Augmented Database* $A(\mathcal{D})$ of $\mathcal{D}$ consists of $\mathcal{D}$, its transition rules and its event rules. □

*Example 3.2.* Relevant event rules of Example 2.1 are the following[3]:

(I2)      $\imath\text{Worker}(\underline{p}, c) \leftarrow \imath\text{Works}(\underline{p}, c) \wedge \neg\text{Sick-leave}(\underline{p}) \wedge \neg\imath\text{Sick-leave}(\underline{p})$

(C0)      $\imath Ic \leftarrow \imath Ic_1(\underline{p}, a, c)$

(C1)      $\imath Ic_1(\underline{p}, a, c) \leftarrow \text{Unemp\_benef}(\underline{p}, a) \wedge \neg\delta\text{Unemp\_benef}(\underline{p}, a) \wedge$
$\neg\text{Aux2}(\underline{p}, a) \wedge \imath\text{Worker}(\underline{p}, c)$

(C5)      $\imath Ic_1(\underline{p}, a, c) \leftarrow \mu\text{Unemp\_benef}(\underline{p}, a', a) \wedge \imath\overline{\text{Worker}}(\underline{p}, c)$

(A2)      $\text{Aux2}(\underline{p}, c) \leftarrow \mu\text{Unemp\_benef}(\underline{p}, a, a')$

□

The event definitions prevent certain event facts to occur simultaneously. That is, some event facts are *mutually exclusive* and they may not be true at the same time. This is formalized by the following rules:

$$\forall \boldsymbol{k}, \boldsymbol{x} \; (\imath P(\underline{\boldsymbol{k}}, \boldsymbol{x}) \Rightarrow \neg\exists \boldsymbol{y} \; (\imath P(\underline{\boldsymbol{k}}, \boldsymbol{y}) \wedge \boldsymbol{x} \neq \boldsymbol{y})$$
$$\forall \boldsymbol{k}, \boldsymbol{x} \; (\imath P(\underline{\boldsymbol{k}}, \boldsymbol{x}) \Rightarrow \neg\exists \boldsymbol{y} \; \delta P(\underline{\boldsymbol{k}}, \boldsymbol{y}))$$
$$\forall \boldsymbol{k}, \boldsymbol{x} \; (\imath P(\underline{\boldsymbol{k}}, \boldsymbol{x}) \Rightarrow \neg\exists \boldsymbol{y}, \boldsymbol{y}' \; \mu P(\underline{\boldsymbol{k}}, \boldsymbol{y}, \boldsymbol{y}'))$$
$$\forall \boldsymbol{k}, \boldsymbol{x} \; (\delta P(\underline{\boldsymbol{k}}, \boldsymbol{x}) \Rightarrow \neg\exists \boldsymbol{y} \; \imath P(\underline{\boldsymbol{k}}, \boldsymbol{y}))$$
$$\forall \boldsymbol{k}, \boldsymbol{x} \; (\delta P(\underline{\boldsymbol{k}}, \boldsymbol{x}) \Rightarrow \neg\exists \boldsymbol{y} \; \mu P(\underline{\boldsymbol{k}}, \boldsymbol{x}, \boldsymbol{y}))$$
$$\forall \boldsymbol{k}, \boldsymbol{x}, \boldsymbol{x}' \; (\mu P(\underline{\boldsymbol{k}}, \boldsymbol{x}, \boldsymbol{x}') \Rightarrow \neg\exists \boldsymbol{y} \; \imath P(\underline{\boldsymbol{k}}, \boldsymbol{y}))$$
$$\forall \boldsymbol{k}, \boldsymbol{x}, \boldsymbol{x}' \; (\mu P(\underline{\boldsymbol{k}}, \boldsymbol{x}, \boldsymbol{x}') \Rightarrow \neg\exists \boldsymbol{y} \; \delta P(\underline{\boldsymbol{k}}, \boldsymbol{y}))$$
$$\forall \boldsymbol{k}, \boldsymbol{x}, \boldsymbol{x}' \; (\mu P(\underline{\boldsymbol{k}}, \boldsymbol{x}, \boldsymbol{x}') \Rightarrow \neg\exists \boldsymbol{y} \; (\mu P(\underline{\boldsymbol{k}}, \boldsymbol{x}, \boldsymbol{y}) \wedge \boldsymbol{x}' \neq \boldsymbol{y}))$$

## 4 Definition of the Method

The purpose of our method is to update a deductive database and to enforce, at the same time, that no integrity constraint is violated. Given an update request that may contain updates of derived facts, our method automatically translates it into all possible transactions that, if applied to the database, would satisfy the requested update and would guarantee that the integrity constraints remain satisfied.

**Definition 4.1.** An *update request* is a conjunction of non-mutually exclusive event facts[4]. □

---

[3] The whole Augmented Database of Example 2.1 is given in Appendix A.

[4] The order of the literals in the conjunction is not relevant, since all of them must be satisfied.

**Definition 4.2.** A transaction is a set of non-mutually exclusive base event facts. □

**Definition 4.3.** Given a deductive database $\mathcal{D}$, its augmented database $A(\mathcal{D})$[5] and an update request $u$, a *translation* of $u$ is a transaction $T_i$ such that:

1. $A(\mathcal{D}) \cup T_i \models u$
2. $A(\mathcal{D}) \cup T_i \not\models \imath Ic$     □

The first condition states that the update request is a logical consequence of the database updated according to $T_i$, while the second condition states that no integrity constraint will be violated in the updated database since no insertion of $Ic$ will be induced by $T_i$. Note that, since we assume that no integrity constraint is violated in $\mathcal{D}$, ensuring that $\imath Ic$ is not induced is sufficient to guarantee that no constraint is violated in the updated database.

**Definition 4.4.** A translation $T_i$ is a *minimal translation* if no proper subset of $T_i$ is also a translation.     □

For instance, the request of inserting the fact that Joan is a worker of BP and deleting the fact that Bob leaves sick would correspond to the update request $u = \{\text{Worker}(\underline{Joan}, BP) \land \text{Sick-leave}(\underline{Bob})\}$. A minimal translation of $u$ is $T_1 = \{\imath\text{Worker}(\underline{Joan}, BP), \delta\text{Sick-leave}(\underline{Bob}), \delta\text{Unemp\_benef}(\underline{Joan}, 100)\}$.

Given a deductive database $\mathcal{D}$ where no integrity constraint is violated, its corresponding augmented database $A(\mathcal{D})$ and an update request $u$, our method aims at obtaining all minimal translations $T_i$ of $u$. Each $T_i$ is obtained by having some failed SLDNF derivation of $A(\mathcal{D}) \cup \{\leftarrow u \land \neg \imath Ic\}$ succeed. This is achieved by including in the translation set $T_i$ each positive base event fact selected during the failed derivation. At the end, we have that there is an SLDNF refutation of $\leftarrow u \land \neg \imath Ic$ by considering $A(\mathcal{D}) \cup T_i$ as input set.

Different ways to make failed derivations succeed correspond to the different translations $T_i$ of $u$. If no translation is obtained, it is not possible to satisfy the update request by changing only the extensional database. When an integrity constraint becomes violated by some update, our method proposes additional updates to repair this violation. In contrast, key information is managed through the own definition of the method by rejecting those translations that violate some key integrity constraint.

## 4.1   Example

The following example illustrates the steps performed by our method to obtain the translations that satisfy a given update request.

---

[5] Note that $A(\mathcal{D})$ already includes $\mathcal{D}$.

*Example 4.1.* Consider again the database of Example 2.1 and its relevant event rules given in Example 3.2. Assume that the update $\imath$Worker($\underline{Ann}, UPC$) is requested.

Translations that satisfy this request are obtained by having some failed derivation of $A(\mathcal{D}) \cup \{\leftarrow \imath$Worker($\underline{Ann}, UPC$)$\wedge \neg\imath Ic\}$ succeed. The relevant part of this derivation is shown in Figure 1, where selected literals are underlined and circled labels are references to the rules of the method defined in Section 4.2.

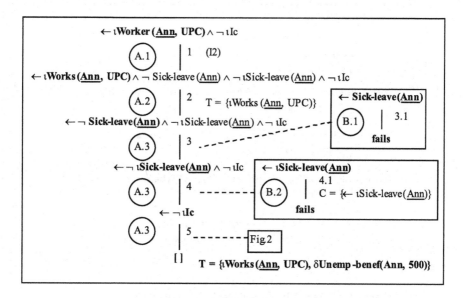

**Fig. 1.** Derivation tree of Example 4.1

Step 1 is an SLDNF resolution step. At step 2 the selected literal is $\imath$Worker($\underline{Ann}, UPC$), which is a positive base event. To get a successful derivation, we must include it in the input set and use it as input clause. Therefore, it is added to the translation set $T$. Step 3 is again an SLDNF resolution step.

At step 4 the selected literal is $\neg\imath$Sick-leave($\underline{Ann}$). To get a success for this branch $\imath$Sick-leave($\underline{Ann}$) must not hold. Then, we have to guarantee that the subsidiary tree rooted at $\leftarrow \imath$Sick-leave($\underline{Ann}$) fails finitely. This corresponds to guarantee that the current transaction $T = \{\imath$Works($\underline{Ann}, UPC$)$\}$ does not contain an insertion of Sick-leave($\underline{Ann}$).

The subsidiary derivation is shown in the box enclosed to step 4. To ensure failure of this derivation we must guarantee that $\imath$Sick-leave($\underline{Ann}$) will not be included into $T$ later on during the derivation process. This is achieved by means of an auxiliary set $C$ that contains conditions to be satisfied during the whole derivation process. These conditions correspond to some of the goals reached in the subsidiary derivations, as shown at step 4.1 of Figure 1 where the condition $\leftarrow \imath$Sick-leave($\underline{Ann}$) is included in $C$. Hence, before adding a base event to $T$ we must guarantee that it does not falsify any of the conditions of $C$.

At step 5 the selected literal is $\neg \imath Ic$ and, as before, we must proceed with the corresponding subsidiary derivation to guarantee that $\leftarrow \imath Ic$ fails finitely. This corresponds, in this case, to enforce that the resulting transaction does not violate any integrity constraint. In Figure 2 we show how our method enforces the failure of this subsidiary tree. We only show one branch of the derivation because the other branches fail finitely without modifying the translation set.

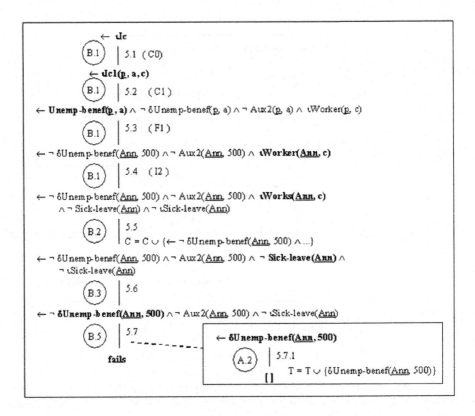

**Fig. 2.** Subsidiary tree for step 5

Steps 5.1, 5.2, 5.3, 5.4 and 5.6 are SLDNF resolution steps where $A(\mathcal{D})$ acts as input set. Step 5.5 is an SLDNF resolution step where $T$ acts as input set, but the current goal is also included into $C$ to ensure that it will remain falsified during the whole derivation process.

At step 5.7, we make the current goal to fail by considering the base event fact $\delta$Unemp_benef($\underline{Ann}$, 500). This is achieved by means of a subsidiary derivation that behaves as the initial one, which ends up with the inclusion of $\delta$Unemp_benef($\underline{Ann}$, 500) to $T$ after verifying that the new translation set does not falsify any of the conditions in $C$ (see step 5.7.1). Note that, in fact that $\delta$Unemp_benef($\underline{Ann}$, 500) is a repair required to satisfy $Ic_1$ which is violated by the current transaction $T = \{\imath$Works($\underline{Ann}, UPC$)$\}$.

After this step, the subsidiary derivation rooted at $\leftarrow \imath Ic$ fails finitely. Then, the initial derivation of Figure 1 succeeds and the translation process is finished obtaining the translation $T = \{\imath \text{Works}(\underline{Ann}, UPC),\ \delta \text{Unemp\_benef}(\underline{Ann}, 500)\}$, which satisfies the original update request and preserves database consistency.

Two additional alternatives exist to force the failure of the derivation of Figure 2, by selecting any of the remaining literals at step 5.7. Although these derivations are not shown in the above figure, neither of them leads to other possible translations. Our method detects these situations because it determines that the base event facts to be included into $T$ contradict some condition in $C$. □

## 4.2   Formalization of the Method

As shown in the previous example, our method is an interleaving of two activities: satisfying the update request by including base event facts into the translation $T$; and ensuring that the updates induced by these events are not contradictory with the requested update nor with the integrity constraints. These two activities are performed, respectively, during the *Constructive* and the *Consistency Derivation*, as defined below.

Let $u$ be an update request. A transaction $T$ is a translation of $u$ if there is a *Constructive Derivation* from $(\leftarrow u \wedge \neg \imath Ic\ \emptyset\ \emptyset)$ to $([]\ T\ C)$. Positive base events selected during this derivation are included in $T$, since they correspond to the updates needed to satisfy $u$, while other positive literals correspond to database queries. Consistency of the negative literals $\neg L_j$ selected during a constructive derivation is provided by considering a subsidiary *Consistency Derivation* from $(\{\leftarrow L_j\}\ T\ C)$ to $(\{\}\ T'\ C')$.

To define these derivations, we need to introduce the following conventions:

- Given a goal $G_i$ of the form $\leftarrow L_1 \wedge \cdots \wedge L_k$, $G_i \backslash L_j$ refers to the goal obtained by removing the literal $L_j$ from $G_i$. Notice that if $G_i = \leftarrow L_j$, then $G_i \backslash L_j = []$.
- In a consistency derivation, $F_i = \{H_i\} \cup F_i'$ refers to the set of goals to be falsified, with $H_i$ corresponding to the goal considered in the current branch.

*Constructive Derivation.*      A *Constructive Derivation* from $(G_1\ T_1\ C_1)$ to $(G_n\ T_n\ C_n)$ via a safe selection rule $R$ is a sequence $(G_1\ T_1\ C_1)$, $(G_2\ T_2\ C_2)$, $\ldots$, $(G_n\ T_n\ C_n)$ such that for for each $i = 1,\ldots,n$ $G_i$ has the form $\leftarrow L_1 \wedge \cdots \wedge L_k$, where $R(G_i) = L_j$ and $(G_{i+1}\ T_{i+1}\ C_{i+1})$ is obtained according to one of the following rules:

**A1)**  If $L_j$ is positive and it is not a base event, then $G_{i+1} = S$, $T_{i+1} = T_i$ and $C_{i+1} = C_i$, where $S$ corresponds to:
- if $L_j$ is a ground evaluable predicate that evaluates to true, then $S = G_i \backslash L_j$;
- if it is not an evaluable predicate, then $S$ is the resolvent of some clause in $A(\mathcal{D})$ with $G_i$ on the selected literal $L_j$.

**A2)** If $L_j$ is a positive base event and there is a substitution $\sigma^6$ such that
  **A21)** if $L_j\sigma \in T_i$, then $G_{i+1} = G_i \backslash L_j\sigma$, $T_{i+1} = T_i$ and $C_{i+1} = C_i$.
  **A22)** if $L_j\sigma \notin T_i$ and
  1. $L_j = \imath P(\boldsymbol{k}, \boldsymbol{x})$ and $\neg\exists \boldsymbol{y}\ \imath P(\boldsymbol{k}\sigma, \boldsymbol{y}) \in T_i$ and $\neg\exists \boldsymbol{z}\ P(\boldsymbol{k}\sigma, \boldsymbol{z})$ holds in $\mathcal{D}$
  2. $L_j = \delta P(\boldsymbol{k}, \boldsymbol{x})$ and $\neg\exists \boldsymbol{x}'\ \mu P(\boldsymbol{k}\sigma, \boldsymbol{x}\sigma, \boldsymbol{x}') \in T_i$ and fact $P(\boldsymbol{k}, \boldsymbol{x})\sigma$ holds in $\mathcal{D}$
  3. $L_j = \mu P(\boldsymbol{k}, \boldsymbol{x}, \boldsymbol{x}')$, $\delta P(\boldsymbol{k}, \boldsymbol{x})\sigma \notin T_i$, $\neg\exists \boldsymbol{y}'\ \mu P(\boldsymbol{k}\sigma, \boldsymbol{x}\sigma, \boldsymbol{y}') \in T_i$, $(\boldsymbol{x} \neq \boldsymbol{x}')\sigma$ and fact $P(\boldsymbol{k}, \boldsymbol{x})\sigma$ holds in $\mathcal{D}$
  If $C_i = \{\leftarrow Q_1, \ldots, \leftarrow Q_k, \ldots, \leftarrow Q_n\}$ and there exist consistency derivations

$$\text{from}\quad (\{\leftarrow Q_1\}\, T_i \cup \{L_j\sigma\}\, C_i)\quad \text{to}\quad (\{\}\, T^1\, C^1),\quad \ldots,$$
$$\text{from}\quad (\{\leftarrow Q_n\}\, T^{n-1}\, C^{n-1})\quad \text{to}\quad (\{\}\, T^n\, C^n)\quad,$$

  then $G_{i+1} = G_i\backslash L_j\sigma$, $T_{i+1} = T^n$ and $C_{i+1} = C^n$.
  Notice that if $C_i = \emptyset$, then $G_{i+1} = G_i\backslash L_j\sigma$, $T_{i+1} = T_i \cup \{L_j\sigma\}$ and $C_{i+1} = C_i$.
**A3)** If $L_j$ is a negative literal and there exist a consistency derivation from $(\{\leftarrow \neg L_j\}\, T_i\, C_i)$ to $(\{\}\, T'\, C')$, then $G_{i+1} = G_i\backslash L_j$, $T_{i+1} = T'$ and $C_{i+1} = C'$.

Step A1 is an SLDNF resolution step where $A(\mathcal{D})$ acts as input set.

Step A2 deals with base event literals. In particular, A21 deals with an event that already belongs to $T_i$ and it corresponds to an SLDNF resolution step with input set $T_i$. In A22 base event facts are included in $T_i$, when this inclusion does not contradict mutually exclusiveness of events, the event definition nor any of the conditions $C_i$ already included in $C$. This may cause, in some cases, new inclusions into $T_i$. If the selected base event is not ground, it must be instantiated by considering possible values. In general, there exist as many alternatives as possible ways to instantiate the selected event.

Step A3 ensures the consistency of the selected literal by considering a corresponding consistency derivation for that literal. Again, new events can be included in $T_i$ as a result of this subsidiary derivation.

*Consistency Derivation.* A *consistency derivation* from $(F_1\, T_1\, C_1)$ to $(F_n\, T_n\, C_n)$ via a safe selection rule $R$ is a sequence $(F_1\, T_1\, C_1)$, $(F_2\, T_2\, C_2)$, $\ldots$, $(F_n\, T_n\, C_n)$ such that for each $i = 1, \ldots, n$, if $H_i =\leftarrow L_1 \wedge \cdots \wedge L_k$ and if $F_i$ has the form $\{H_i\} \cup F_i'$, where $R(H_i) = L_j$ for some $j = 1, \ldots, k$, then $(F_{i+1}\, T_{i+1}\, C_{i+1})$ is obtained according to one of the following rules:

**B1)** If $L_j$ is positive and it is not a base event, then $F_{i+1} = S' \cup F_i'$, $T_{i+1} = T_i$ and $C_{i+1} = C_i$, where $S'$ corresponds to: if $L_j$ is an evaluable predicate that evaluates to true and $k > 1$, then $S' = \{H_i\backslash L_j\}$, but if it evaluates to false, then $S' = \emptyset$; if $L_j$ is not evaluable, then $S'$ corresponds to the set of all resolvents of clauses in $A(\mathcal{D})$ with $H_i$ on the selected literal $L_j$, if $[] \notin S'$.

---

[6] Note that if the literal $L_j$ is ground, the substitution $\sigma$ corresponds to the identity substitution.

**B2)** If $L_j$ is a positive base event, $S'$ corresponds to the set of all resolvents of clauses in $T_i$ with $H_i$ on the selected literal $L_j$. If $[] \notin S'$, then $F_{i+1} = S' \cup F'_i$ and $T_{i+1} = T_i$. If $S' = \emptyset$ or $L_j$ is not ground then $C_{i+1} = C_i \cup \{H_i\}$, otherwise $C_{i+1} = C_i$.

**B3)** If $L_j$ is a negative literal and $\neg L_j$ is not a base event, then if $k > 1$ and there exist a consistency derivation from $(\{\leftarrow \neg L_j\} \ T_i \ C_i)$ to $(\{\} \ T' \ C')$, then $F_{i+1} = \{H_i \backslash L_j\} \cup F'_i$, $T_{i+1} = T'$ and $C_{i+1} = C'$.

**B4)** If $L_j$ is a negative base event and if $\neg L_j \notin T_i$ and $k > 1$, then $F_{i+1} = \{H_i \backslash L_j\} \cup F'_i$, $T_{i+1} = T_i$ and $C_{i+1} = C_i$.

**B5)** If $L_j$ is a negative literal, then if there exist a constructive derivation from $(\leftarrow \neg L_j \ T_i \ C_i)$ to $([] \ T' \ C')$, then $F_{i+1} = F'_i$, $T_{i+1} = T'$ and $C_{i+1} = C'$.

Step B1 is an SLDNF resolution step where $A(\mathcal{D})$ acts as input set.

Step B2 corresponds to an SLDNF resolution step with the input set $T_i$, but it may require the addition of the current goal to $C_i$, if the selected literal is a non-ground base event or if it does not belong to $T_i$. This is required to ensure that this derivation will not be succeeded by new inclusions into $T_i$.

Steps B3 and B4 permit to continue with the current branch by ensuring that the selected literal $L_j$ is consistent with respect to $T_i$ and $C_i$.

Step B5 falsifies the current branch by satisfying the literal $\neg L_j$ through a constructive derivation.

Consistency derivations do not depend on the particular order in which literals are selected because, in general, it is necessary to explore all possible ways to falsify a goal $H_i$ since each of them could lead to a different translation.

## 4.3   Soundness of the Method

Our method is sound in the sense that, given a deductive base $\mathcal{D}$ and the augmented database $A(\mathcal{D})$, if the method obtains a translation $T$ for an update request $u$, then the application of $T$ to $\mathcal{D}$ leaves the database in a state $\mathcal{D}^n$ such that $u$ holds and all the integrity constraints are satisfied. Soundness of our method is based on the following Lemma.

**Lemma 4.1.** *Let $\mathcal{D}$ be a deductive database, $A(\mathcal{D})$ the augmented database, $u$ an update request and $T$ a translation obtained by our method. Then, there exists an SLDNF refutation of $A(\mathcal{D}) \cup T \cup \{\leftarrow u \wedge \neg \imath Ic\}$.*   □

Lemma 4.1 relates the constructive derivation from $(\leftarrow u \wedge \neg \imath Ic \ \emptyset \ \emptyset)$ to $([] \ T \ C)$ of our method to an SLDNF refutation of $A(\mathcal{D}) \cup T \cup \{\leftarrow u \wedge \neg \imath Ic\}$. Given that SLDNF resolution has been proved sound [4], then the following theorem follows.

**Theorem 4.1 (Soundness of the method).**
*Let $\mathcal{D}$ be a deductive database, $A(\mathcal{D})$ the augmented database, $u$ an update request, such that $u$ is not a logical consequence of $comp(A(\mathcal{D}))$. Let $T$ be a translation obtained by our method. Then, $u \wedge \neg \imath Ic$ is a logical consequence of $comp(A(\mathcal{D}) \cup T)$.*   □

Soundness of our method ensures that if there exists a constructive derivation from $(\leftarrow u \wedge \neg \imath Ic \; \emptyset \; \emptyset)$ to $([] \; T \; C)$, then the database updated according to the translation $T$ satisfies the request and does not violate any integrity constraint. The technical proof is presented in Appendix B.

# 5    Comparison with Previous Work

We compare our method with previous ones proposed to deal with view updating and integrity constraint maintenance. We show first the main extensions of our method with regards to our precursor, the Events Method and we provide afterwards a comparison with the rest of the proposals.

## 5.1    Comparison with the Events Method

The method proposed in this paper extends the Events Method [17] along two different directions. First, by introducing the modification as a new basic update operator in addition to the insertion and to the deletion. Second, by considering key integrity constraints implicitly into the own definition of the method. The main differences provided by these features are the following:

*Basic update operators.*  We have incorporated the modification as a new basic update operator. In contrast, the Events Method handles a modification as a deletion followed by an insertion. Incorporating that new basic update operator has caused some changes on the semantics of previous basic update operators. That is, the meaning of insertion and deletion events is not the same in the Events Method than in our method.

*Example 5.1.*  Consider the following deductive database where $R$ and $Q$ are base predicates, $P$ is a derived predicate, and the attribute $x$ is the key of $P$, $R$ and $Q$.

$$R(1,2)$$
$$Q(1,3)$$
$$P(x,y) \leftarrow R(x,y) \wedge \neg Q(x,y)$$

An update request to add the fact $Q(3,4)$ to the EDB would correspond to an event $\imath Q(3,4)$ in both methods. The same occurs with a request for removing the fact $R(1,2)$, that corresponds to the event $\delta R(1,2)$. However, a request for adding the fact $R(1,3)$ would correspond to an insertion event $\imath R(1,3)$ in the Events Method but it would be a modification event $\mu R(1,2,3)$ in our method. This difference is motivated by taking into account the information provided by the keys of base and derived predicates in the definition of the event predicates.    □

*Minimal translations.* Considering a modification as a new basic update causes also some differences with respect to the minimal translations obtained by our method and by the Events Method. In both cases, a translation $T$ is considered to be minimal, if no proper subset of $T$ is itself a translation. Then, and due to the modification event, a minimal translation in our method may not be considered minimal in the Events Method. For this reason, the number of translations obtained may differ in some cases.

For example, assume that we have obtained two translations $T_1 = \{\delta P(\underline{A}, 1)\}$ and $T_2 = \{\mu P(\underline{A}, 1, 3)\}$. As no proper subset of $T_1$ nor $T_2$ is itself a translation, both are considered minimal in our method.

In the Events Method, these two translations correspond to $T_1 = \{\delta P(A, 1)\}$ and $T_2 = \{\delta P(A, 1),\ \iota P(A, 3)\}$. In this case, $T_2$ is not minimal, because there is a subset of it ($T_1$) that is itself a translation. Then the Events Method would only generate the translation $T_1 = \{\delta P(A, 1)\}$.

*Maintenance of key integrity constraints.* The Events Method does not consider the concept of key of a predicate. Therefore, to state that a certain attribute corresponds to the key of a predicate, key integrity constraints must be defined explicitly.

Having to define key integrity constraints explicitly increases significantly the number of constraints in the database. Moreover, this method cannot take advantage of the particular semantics of these constraints since it does not provide an specific treatment for them. In contrast, we do not need to define key integrity constraint and their treatment is specifically performed by the own definition of the method.

## 5.2   Comparison with Other Relevant Work

[17] already provides an exhaustive comparison and a clear illustration of the main drawbacks of methods proposed up to then (namely, [6,9,10]). Therefore, we will compare only with those methods that are not covered by [17]. This section is aimed at illustrating several drawbacks of these methods by means of examples.

We would like to remark first that none of these methods deals with modifications as a basic update operator. That is, they consider only insertions and deletions. Moreover, they do not take into account the information about the keys of the predicates and, then, they do not include maintenance of key constraints in the management of updates during the translation process. The differences provided by these features have already been illustrated in Section 5.1.

*Wüthrich's Method* [20]. This method presents two main limitations:

- *There exist translations that are not obtained by the method*: Wüthrich's method implicitly assumes that there is an ordering to deal with the deductive rules and integrity constraints involved in the update request that would lead to the generation of a translation. However, this ordering does not always exist.

*Example 5.2.* Given the request insert(Edge($A, C$)) on the following database:

Node($A$)                                        Edge($A, B$)

Node($B$)                                        Edge($B, A$)

$Ic_1 \leftarrow$ Node($x$) $\wedge \neg \exists y$Edge($x, y$)     $Ic_2 \leftarrow$ Node($x$) $\wedge \neg \exists z$Edge($z, x$)

$Ic_3 \leftarrow$ Edge($x, y$) $\wedge \neg$Node($x$)        $Ic_4 \leftarrow$ Edge($x, y$) $\wedge$ Node($y$)

Wüthrich's method does not obtain any translation to the request, while we obtain the translation

$$T \quad = \quad \{\imath\text{Edge}(A, C), \ \imath\text{Node}(C), \ \imath\text{Edge}(C, D), \ \imath\text{Node}(D), \ \imath\text{Edge}(D, B)\} .$$

□

– *Non-generation of Minimal Translations*: Wüthrich's method does not necessarily generate minimal translations, because it does not check, whether a base fact is already present in the EDB when suggesting to insert or to delete it.

*Example 5.3.* Given the following database and an update request to insert($P(A)$):

$$S(A, B)$$
$$P(x) \leftarrow Q(x) \wedge R(x)$$
$$R(x) \leftarrow S(x, y)$$

Wüthrich's method could obtain only the non-minimal translation

$$T = \{\text{insert}(Q(A)), \ \text{insert}(S(A, C))\} .$$

In contrast, we would always obtain the minimal translation $T = \{\imath Q(A)\}$.

□

*Console, Sapino and Theseider's Method* [5]. This method presents one important limitation:

– *Restrictions on the Integrity Constraints*: this method can only handle flat integrity constraints, i.e. constraints defined in terms of base predicates only. Moreover, it considers also two additional restrictions: constraints must be in denial form and must have at most two literals in the body or either they must be (non-cyclic) referential integrity constraints. Those are important restrictions to the expressive power of the integrity constraints they can handle.

*Lobo and Trajcevsky's Method* [13]. This method presents two main drawbacks:

- *Restrictions on the Integrity Constraints*: it requires the set of constraints to be resolution complete. That is, it must not be possible to derive new (implicit) integrity constraints from a given set of integrity constraints. For instance, constraints $Ic_1 \leftarrow Q(x) \wedge \neg R(x)$ and $Ic_2 \leftarrow R(x) \wedge S(x)$ are not resolution complete, since a third integrity constraint can be deduced from them: $Ic_3 \leftarrow Q(x) \wedge S(x)$. The problem is that, as far as we know, there is no mechanism to derive sets of integrity constraints that are resolution complete.
- *Invalid Translations*: it may obtain translations that do not satisfy the request:

  *Example 5.4.* Given the following database and an update request to insert($Q(B, 2)$):

  $$S(A, 1)$$
  $$Q(x, y) \leftarrow \neg P \wedge S(x, y)$$
  $$P \leftarrow S(x, y) \wedge \neg T(y)$$

  This method would obtain two translations: $T_1 = $ delete($S(A, 1)$), insert($S(B, 2)$)} and $T_2 = \{$insert($T(1)$), insert($S(B, 2)$))}. However, none of them satisfies the requested update, since insert($S(B, 2)$) induces $P$ and, hence, it falsifies insert($Q(B, 2)$). In contrast, there exist two correct translations that our method obtains: $T_1 = \{\delta S(A, 1), \imath S(B, 2), \imath T(2)\}$ and $T_2 = \{\imath T(1), \imath S(B, 2), \imath T(2)\}$ and that are not obtained by Lobo and Trajcevsky's method.  □

*Decker's Method* [7]. The main limitation of this method is that it cannot manage appropriately update requests that involve rules with existential variables. The reason is that its derivations flounder when a literal corresponding to a non-ground base predicate is selected, thus impeding to reach the empty clause.

For example, this method does not obtain any translation to the update request insert($P$) in a database with only one rule: $P \leftarrow S(x)$. Nevertheless, in our method, there exist as many translations as possible values of $x$ for which $S(x)$ is not true can be inserted.

Moreover, this method does not always take into account base facts during the translation process. Therefore, this method may not obtain correct translations since it flounders because it does not take the EDB into account. For instance, consider the update request to insert($P$) in a database:

$$R(A, B)$$
$$P \leftarrow Q(A)$$
$$Ic_1 \leftarrow Q(x) \wedge R(x, y) \wedge \neg S(y)$$

Decker's method is not able to obtain any translation to insert($P$). However, there exist two translations $T_1 = \{\imath Q(A), \delta R(A, B)\}$ and $T_2 = \{\imath Q(A), \imath S(B)\}$, and both are obtained by our method.

## 6   Conclusions and Further Work

We have proposed a new method for view updating and integrity constraint maintenance. Our method considers three basic update operators: insertions, deletions and modifications on base and derived predicates. Moreover, information about the keys of the database predicates is taken into account by the own definition of the method. We have proven soundness of our method and we have compared it with previous proposals showing by means of examples that we are able to deal with certain situations the others cannot handle appropriately.

We have not considered the computational cost required in the general case to obtain all minimal translations since our aim has been to provide a method that extends the functionalities of the previous ones. However, it is obvious that this approach may not be efficient enough in some applications. Therefore, further work is required to provide efficient methods for view updating and integrity constraint maintenance.

## References

1. Bidoit, N.; Maabout, S. "A Model Theoretic Approach to Update Rule Programs". *Proc. of the International Conference of Database Technology ICDT'97*. Delphi, Greece, January 1997. LNCS Vol. 1186.
2. Bancilhon, F.; Ramakrishnan, R. "An Amateur's Introduction to Recursive Query Processing". *ACM SIGMOD International Conference on Management of Data*. Washington D.C., 1986.
3. Ceri, S.; Fraternali, P.; Paraboschi, S.; Tanca, L. "Automatic Generation of Production Rules for Integrity Maintenance". *ACM Transactions on Database Systems* Vol. 19 no. 3, Sept. 1994, pp.367-422.
4. Clark, K.L. "Negation as Failure". in Gallaire, H.; Minker, J. (Eds.). *Logic and Databases*. Plenum Press, New York 1978, pp. 293-322.
5. Console, L.; Sapino, M.L.; Theseider,D. "The Role of Abduction in Database View Updating". *Journal of Intelligent Information Systems* Vol.4, pp.261-280.
6. Decker, H. "Drawing Updates from Derivations". *Proc. Int. Conf. on Database Theory (ICDT'90)* Paris (France) 1990, pp. 437-451.
7. Decker, H. "One Abductive Logic Programming Procedure for two kind of Updates". *Proc. Workshop DINAMICS'97 at Int. Logic Programming Symposium*. Port Jefferson (New York), 1997.
8. García, C; Celma, M.; Mota, L.; Decker, H. "Comparing and Synthesizing Integrity Checking Methods for Deductive Databases". *10th Int. Conf. on Data Engineering (ICDE)*. Houston, USA, 1994, pp. 214-222.
9. Guessoum, A.; Lloyd, J.W. "Updating Knowledge Bases". *New Generation Computing*. Vol. 8, Num. 1, 1990, pp. 71-89.
10. Kakas, A.C.; Mancarella,P. "Database Updates Through Abduction". *Proc. of the 16th VLDB Conference*. Brisbane, Australia, 1990, pp. 650-661.
11. Lloyd, J.W. *Foundations on Logic Programming*. 2nd edition, Springer, 1987.
12. Lloyd, J.W.; Topor, R.W. "Making Prolog More Expressive". *Journal of Logic Programming*. 1984, No. 3, pp. 225-240.
13. Lobo, J.; Trajcevski, G. "Minimal and consistent evolution in knowledge bases". *Journal of Applied Non-Classical Logics*. Vol. 7. no.1-2, 1997, pp. 117-146.

14. Moerkotte, G.; Lockemann, P.C. "Reactive Consistency Control in Deductive Databases". *ACM Transactions on Database Systems*. Vol.16(4), 1991, pp.670-702.

15. Mayol, E.; Teniente, E. "Incorporating Modification Requests in Updating Consistent Knowledge Bases". *Fourth Int. Workshop on the Deductive Approach to Information Systems and Databases*. Catalonia, 1993, pp. 275-300.

16. Olivé, A. "Integrity Checking in Deductive Databases", *Proc. of the 17th VLDB Conference*. Barcelona, Catalonia, 1991, pp. 513-523.

17. Teniente, E.; Olivé, A. "Updating Knowledge Bases while Maintaining their Consistency". *The VLDB Journal*. Vol. 4, Num. 2, 1995, pp. 193-241.

18. Teniente, E.; Urpí, T. "A Common Framework for Classifying and Specifying Deductive Database Updating Problems". *11th Int. Conf. on Data Engineering (ICDE)*. Taipei (Taiwan), 1995, pp. 173-183.

19. Urpí, T.; Olivé, A. "A Method for Change Computation in Deductive Databases". *Proc. of the 18th VLDB Conference*. Vancouver, 1992, pp. 225-237.

20. Wüthrich, B. "On Updates and Inconsistency Repairing in Knowledge Bases". *Int. Conference on Data Engineering (ICDE'93)*. Vienna 1993, pp.608-615.

# Appendix A    Augmented Database of Example 2.1

This appendix shows the whole content of the Augmented Database $A(\mathcal{D})$ of Example 2.1, after applying the simplifications proposed in [19].

(F1)    Unemp_benef($\underline{Ann}$, 500)

(F2)    Unemp_benef($\underline{Joan}$, 100)

(F3)    Sick-leave($\underline{Bob}$)

(R1)    Worker($\underline{p}, c$) ← Works($\underline{p}, c$) ∧ ¬Sick-leave($\underline{p}$)

(R2)    $Ic_1(\underline{p}, a, c)$ ← Unemp_benef($\underline{p}, a$) ∧ ¬Worker($\underline{p}, c$)

(I1)    $\imath$Worker($\underline{p}, c$) ← Works($\underline{p}, c$) ∧
$$\neg\delta\text{Works}(\underline{p}, c) \land \neg\text{Aux1}(\underline{p}, c) \land \delta\text{Sick-leave}(\underline{p})$$

(I2)    $\imath$Worker($\underline{p}, c$) ← $\imath$Works($\underline{p}, c$) ∧ ¬Sick-leave($\underline{p}$) ∧ ¬$\imath$Sick-leave($\underline{p}$)

(I3)    $\imath$Worker($\underline{p}, c$) ← $\imath$Works($\underline{p}, c$) ∧ $\delta$Sick-leave($\underline{p}$)

(I4)    $\imath$Worker($\underline{p}, c$) ← $\mu$Works($\underline{p}, c', c$) ∧ $\delta$Sick-leave($\underline{p}$)

(D1)    $\delta$Worker($\underline{p}, c$) ← $\delta$Works($\underline{p}, c$) ∧ ¬Sick-leave($\underline{p}$)

(D2)    $\delta$Worker($\underline{p}, c$) ← Works($\underline{p}, c$) ∧ $\imath$Sick-leave($\underline{p}$)

(M1)    $\mu$Worker($\underline{p}, c, c'$) ← $\mu$Works($\underline{p}, c, c'$) ∧ ¬Sick-leave($\underline{p}$) ∧ ¬$\imath$Sick-leave($\underline{p}$)

(C0)    $\imath Ic$ ← $\imath Ic_1(\underline{p}, a, c)$

(C1)    $\imath Ic_1(\underline{p}, a, c)$ ← Unemp_benef($\underline{p}, a$) ∧ ¬$\delta$Unemp_benef($\underline{p}, a$) ∧ ¬Aux2($\underline{p}, a$) ∧
$$\imath\text{Worker}(\underline{p}, c)$$

(C2)    $\imath Ic_1(\underline{p}, a, c)$ ← $\imath$Unemp_benef($\underline{p}, a$) ∧ Worker($\underline{p}, c$) ∧ ¬$\delta$Worker($\underline{p}, c$) ∧
$$\neg\text{Aux3}(\underline{p}, c)$$

(C3)   $\imath Ic_1(\underline{p}, a, c) \leftarrow \imath Unemp\_benef(\underline{p}, a) \wedge \imath Worker(\underline{p}, c)$

(C4)   $\imath Ic_1(\underline{p}, a, c) \leftarrow \imath Unemp\_benef(\underline{p}, a) \wedge \mu Worker(\underline{p}, c', c)$

(C5)   $\imath Ic_1(\underline{p}, a, c) \leftarrow \mu Unemp\_benef(\underline{p}, a', a) \wedge \imath Worker(\underline{p}, c)$

(A1)   $Aux1(\underline{p}, c) \leftarrow \mu Works(\underline{p}, c, c')$

(A2)   $Aux2(\underline{p}, a) \leftarrow \mu Unemp\_benef(\underline{p}, a, a')$

(A3)   $Aux3(\underline{p}, c) \leftarrow \mu Worker(\underline{p}, c, c')$

## Appendix B   Soundness of the Method

In this appendix we prove the soundness of our method. First of all, we have to define the concepts of constructive and consistency derivations of level $k$[7].

**Definition B.1.**  *Let $G$ be a goal, $T$ and $T'$ translation sets and $C$ and $C'$ condition sets. A* consistency derivation *of level 0 from $(\{G\}\ T\ C)$ to $(\{\}\ T'\ C')$ is a consistency derivation that does not call any constructive derivation nor any consistency derivation.* □

**Definition B.2.**  *Let $G$ be a goal, $T$ and $T'$ translation sets and $C$ and $C'$ condition sets. A* constructive derivation *of level 0 from $(G\ T\ C)$ to $([]\ T'\ C')$ is a constructive derivation that does not call any consistency derivation, or it calls only consistency derivations of level 0.* □

**Definition B.3.**  *Let $G$ be a goal, $T$ and $T'$ translation sets and $C$ and $C'$ condition sets. A* consistency derivation *of level $k+1$ from $(\{G\}\ T\ C)$ to $(\{\}\ T'\ C')$ is a consistency derivation that calls some constructive or consistency derivation of level $k$.* □

**Definition B.4.**  *Let $G$ be a goal, $T$ and $T'$ translation sets and $C$ and $C'$ condition sets. A* constructive derivation *of level $k+1$ from $(G\ T\ C)$ to $([]\ T'\ C')$ is a constructive derivation that calls some consistency derivation of level $k$.* □

Let $u$ be an update request. Lemma 4.1 states that there exists an SLDNF refutation of $A(\mathcal{D}) \cup T \cup \{\leftarrow u \wedge \neg \imath Ic\}$ for every translation $T$ obtained by our method.

**Lemma 4.1.**  *Let $\mathcal{D}$ be a deductive database, $A(\mathcal{D})$ the augmented database, $u$ an update request and $T$ a translation obtained by our method. Then, there exists an SLDNF refutation of $A(\mathcal{D}) \cup T \cup \{\leftarrow u \wedge \neg \imath Ic\}$.*

---

[7] Note that the concept of level is different from the concept of rank of SLDNF derivation defined by Lloyd [11].

*Proof.* We have to prove that the steps in the above constructive derivation and the subsidiary consistency derivations correspond to SLDNF resolution steps, where clauses of $A(\mathcal{D}) \cup T$ act as input clauses. This proof is performed by induction on the level $k$ of these derivations.

Let $G$ be a goal, $T$ and $T'$ translation sets and $C$ and $C'$ condition sets. We first prove that a consistency derivation corresponds to a finitely failed SLD-NF tree. This result is used afterwards to prove that a constructive derivation corresponds to an SLDNF refutation. Let $k = 0$.

a) Let $CS$ be a consistency derivation of level 0 from $(\{G\}\ T\ C)$ to $(\{\}\ T'\ C')$. Then, the SLDNF derivation tree of $A(\mathcal{D}) \cup T' \cup \{G\}$ fails finitely[8]. It corresponds to the failure of goal $G$.

  – Step B1 corresponds to a SLDNF resolution step with input set $A(\mathcal{D})$.
  – Steps B2 and B4 correspond to SLDNF resolution steps with input set $T = T'$.
  – Steps B3 and B5 are not applicable for $k = 0$.

b) Let $CT$ be a constructive derivation of level 0 from $(G\ T\ C)$ to $([]\ T'\ C')$. Then, there exists an SLDNF refutation of $A(\mathcal{D}) \cup T' \cup \{G\}$. We distinguish two cases:

  1. *No consistency derivation is called:*
     – Step A1 corresponds to a SLDNF resolution step with input set $A(\mathcal{D})$.
     – Step A21 corresponds to a SLDNF resolution step with input set $T' = T$.
       In Step A22 a ground event $L_j$ could be included to $T$ ($T' = T \cup \{L_j\sigma\}$) and no consistency derivation is called ($C = \emptyset$). Therefore, step A2 corresponds to an SLDNF resolution step with input set $T'$.
     – Step A3 is not applicable in this case.

  2. *Some consistency derivation of level 0 is called:*
     – Step A1 corresponds to a SLDNF resolution step with input set $A(\mathcal{D})$.
     – Step A21 corresponds to a SLDNF resolution step with input set $T' = T$.
       In step A22, a ground event $L_j$ could be included to $T$, and so, a consistency derivation of level 0 is called from $(C\ T \cup \{L_j\sigma\}\ C)$ to $(\{\}\ T'\ C')$. We will get a new goal in the constructive derivation if there exists the above consistency derivation. The consistency derivation corresponds to the negation as failure of $C$ with respect to the new input clause $L_j\sigma$. Previous failure of $C$ with respect to $T$ is not altered. Therefore, step A2 correspond to a SLDNF resolution step with input set $T'$.

---

[8] When $G$ is a set of $n > 1$ goals, the root of the tree is an implicit goal $\leftarrow F$ with $n$ decendant branches, one for each goal $H_i$ in $G$.

  – In step A3 it is checked that a consistency derivation of level 0 exists from $(\{\leftarrow \neg L_j\}\ T\ C)$ to $(\{\}\ T'\ C')$, that is, the failure of $\neg L_j$ is checked. This corresponds to a negation as failure rule and, therefore, step A3 is a SLDNF resolution step.

Since the base case has been proved, we now assume that the result is true for derivations of level $k$. Now, we are going to prove that the Lemma 4.1 also holds for derivations of level $k + 1$.

c) Let $CS$ be a consistency derivation of level $k+1$ from $(\{G\}\ T\ C)$ to $(\{\}\ T'\ C')$. Then, the SLDNF derivation tree of $A(\mathcal{D}) \cup T' \cup \{G\}$ fails finitely[8].
  – Step B1 corresponds to a SLDNF resolution step with input set $A(\mathcal{D})$.
  – Step B2 corresponds to a SLDNF resolution step with input set $T'$. Failure of goal $G$ is ensured:
    • for events that belong to $T$ by the own definition of this step.
    • for those base events that will be included into $T$ after this step $(T' - T)$. These events will be included in a constructive derivation of level $k$ (step A2). The goal $G$ is included to set $C$, and therefore, its failure will be ensured by the consistency derivation of step A2.
  – Step B3 corresponds to a SLDNF resolution step with the input set $A(\mathcal{D}) \cup T'$. By induction, the SLDNF derivation tree of $A(\mathcal{D}) \cup T' \cup \{\leftarrow \neg L_j\}$ fails finitely, since a consistency derivation of level $k$ is called.
  – Step B4 corresponds to a SLDNF resolution step with input set $T$.
  – Step B5 corresponds to a SLDNF resolution step with the input set $A(\mathcal{D}) \cup T'$. By induction, there exists a refutation of $A(\mathcal{D}) \cup T' \cup \{\leftarrow \neg L_j\}$, since a constructive derivation of level $k$ is called.

d) Let $CT$ be a constructive derivation of level $k+1$ from $(G\ T\ C)$ to $([]\ T'\ C')$. Then, there exists an SLDNF refutation of $A(\mathcal{D}) \cup T' \cup \{G\}$.
  – Step A1 corresponds to a SLDNF resolution step with input set $A(\mathcal{D})$.
  – Step A21 corresponds to a SLDNF resolution step with input set $T = T'$. In step A22, a ground event $L_j$ could be included to $T$, and so, a consistency derivation of level $k + 1$ is called from $(C\ T \cup \{L_j\sigma\}\ C)$ to $(\{\}\ T'\ C')$. We will get a new goal in the constructive derivation if there exists this consistency derivation. As we have proved in c), the consistency derivation of level $k + 1$ or below corresponds to the negation as failure of $C$ with respect to the new input clause $L_j\sigma$. Previous failure of $C$ with respect to $T$ is not altered. Therefore, step A2 correspond to a SLDNF resolution step with input set $T'$.
  – In step A3, it is checked that a consistency derivation of level $k+1$ exists from $(\{\leftarrow \neg L_j\}\ T\ C)$ to $(\{\}\ T'\ C')$, that is, the failure of $\neg L_j$ is checked. This corresponds to a negation as failure rule and, therefore, step A3 is a SLDNF resolution step.                                                                    □

**Theorem 4.1 (Soundness of the method).** *Let $\mathcal{D}$ be a deductive database, $A(\mathcal{D})$ the augmented database, $u$ an update request, such that $u$ is not a logical consequence of $comp(A(\mathcal{D}))$. Let $T$ be a translation obtained by our method. Then, $u \wedge \neg \imath Ic$ is a logical consequence of $comp(A(\mathcal{D}) \cup T)$.*

*Proof.* Lemma 4.1 states that there exists an SLDNF refutation of $A(\mathcal{D}) \cup T \cup \{\leftarrow u \wedge \neg \imath I c\}$ if there exists a constructive derivation from $(\leftarrow u \wedge \neg \imath I c \; \emptyset \; \emptyset)$ to $([] \; T \; C)$.

By the soundness of the SLDNF resolution, the existence of the SLDNF refutation of $A(\mathcal{D}) \cup T \cup \{\leftarrow u \wedge \neg \imath I c\}$ ensures that $u \wedge \neg \imath I c$ is a logical consequence of $\mathrm{comp}(A(\mathcal{D}) \cup T)$. $\qquad \square$

# Making Decision Trees More Accurate
# by Losing Information

Takao Miura[1], Isamu Shioya[2], and Mikihiro Mori[2]

[1] Dept. of Elect. and Elect. Engineering, Hosei University,
Kajinocho 3-7-2, Koganei, Tokyo, Japan
`miurat@k.hosei.ac.jp`
[2] SANNO College, Kamikasuya 1563, Isehara, Kanagawa, Japan
`shioya@sanno.ac.jp`

**Abstract.** In this investigation we discuss how to improve the quality of decision trees, one of the classification techniques in compensation for small loss of amount of information. To do that, we assume a semantic hierarchy among classes which is ignored in conventional stories. The basic idea comes from relaxing class membership by using the hierarchy and we explore how to preserve the *precision* of classification in a sense of *entropy*.

*Content Areas* – Machine Learning, AI in Databases, AI in Data Mining

## 1 Motivation

*Knowledge acquisition* from databases is a technique by which we can obtain useful information that we didn't have found before. If the intensional information of databases (i.e., schemes) are utilized, the process is called *classification* because the intents of the inputs are defined in advance. A *decision tree* is one of the classification techniques[16,17]. To classify input, we will specify a collection of classes, class membership criteria, attributes to be examined and training data. The tree is a set of conditions to classify input into classes. The technique has many advantages. First we don't need no domain knowledge thus we have the wider applicability. This also leads to efficient generation of the trees. In fact, no back tracking is needed and it takes polynomial time with respect to the number of attributes and inputs. The result is best optimized in a sense of entropy of class membership. It is worth noting that the issue to obtain the *smallest* decision trees is NP-hard.

On the other hand, no background knowledge such as concept hierarchy is utilized and sometimes it may cause *overfitting trees*[2]. That is, we would generate *wide-spread* trees to reason all the training data but we might make wrong classification to the total data, because such classification process would become slow, incorrect, less useful and hard to maintain tasks.

In this work, we propose a new classification methodology. Compared to conventional processes of decision tree generation, our new decision tree algorithm differs from the ones since we heavily utilize the background knowledge

K.-D. Schewe, B. Thalheim (Eds.): FoIKS 2000, LNCS 1762, pp. 213–225, 2000.

of databases. First, we like *useful* trees in a sense that we could interpret it by means of some concepts of our interests without losing generality. On the other hand, we try to avoid wide-spread trees as we said. In this investigation, we pose some conditions on the structure of decision trees such as the number of nodes or height of the trees. Secondly, the result trees may not be optimal compared to the original theory but still keeps the allowable entropy. Finally the trees may be generated in a back-tracking manner but we try to avoid the duplicate calculation. To obtain our goals, we discuss rather tough ideas. That is, we revisit the input and may change the values or class membership dynamically.

In this work, section 2 contains some definitions and some discussion of decision trees. In section 3, we reexamine notion of entropy for decision trees under the new environment. We discuss our relaxation technique in section 4. Section 5 contains some experimental results. After discussing some related works in the next section, we conclude our work in section 7.

## 2    Definitions

In this investigation, we assume *objects* (or *entities*) and *classes* as primitive concepts where an object means a thing in the world of interests and a class its intension. Every object belongs to some classes. Also we use a notion of *attribute* to stress a role of a class, but its value is an object. Given a class $c$, we denote a collection of objects of a class $c$ by $\Gamma(c)$. In this investigation we discuss *table data* $T$ as our testing vehicles :

$$T = \begin{pmatrix} A_1 \dots A_n : \mathcal{C} \\ a_1^1 \dots a_n^1 : c_1 \\ \dots \dots \dots : \dots \\ a_1^k \dots a_n^k : c_k \end{pmatrix} = \begin{pmatrix} \mathcal{A} : \mathcal{C} \\ t_1 : c_1 \\ \dots \\ t_k : c_k \end{pmatrix}$$

Implicitly each row means an object and $t_j$ describes a collection of the characteristic values over a set $\mathcal{A}$ of attributes $A_i, i = 1, .., n$, $\mathcal{C} = \{c_1, .., c_q\} (q \leq k)$ means which class an object belongs to. For simplicity we assume $\mathcal{A}$ and $\mathcal{C}$ are disjoint.

We say $c_1$ ISA $c_2$ for two classes $c_1, c_2$, if we have a constraint $\Gamma(c_1) \subseteq \Gamma(c_2)$, and a *class hierarchy* is a set of ISA where every class has just one *parent* with one exception ⊚E that means an *object class* as a very top, and we assume every class appears in the hierarchy. The hierarchy is called *single* if $\Gamma(c) \cap \Gamma(c') \neq \phi$ means $c$ ISA $c'$ or $c'$ ISA $c$, i.e., $\Gamma(c) \subseteq \Gamma(c')$ or $\Gamma(c') \subseteq \Gamma(c)$. In the following, we assume a single class hierarchy.

A table $T$ is called *consistent*, if there are duplicate rows of different classes $c$ and $c'$, then $c$ ISA $c'$ or $c'$ ISA $c$ holds. In this work, we assume all the tables are consistent. The readers have to note that such rows have been considered as *noises* in traditional approach of decision trees.

*Example 2.1.* Our running example comes from C4.5 book[17] but slightly modified. There are 3 attributes and 3 classes: *Weather, Temperature, WindForce* are attributes by which we decide whether some horse races are held (*Held*), partially held(*Half*) or not (*No*). The readers might see duplicate rows of different classes[1]. We have 60 possible combination of attribute values but only 13 of them appear in 14 rows:

| Weather | Temperature | WindForce | RaceCondition |
|---------|-------------|-----------|---------------|
| Fine | Medium | Windy | Held |
| Fine | High | VeryWindy | Half |
| Fine | VeryHigh | Windless | No |
| Fine | Low | Breeze | Half |
| Fine | Low | Breeze | Held |
| Cloudy | Low | Windy | Held |
| Cloudy | High | Breeze | Held |
| Cloudy | High | VeryWindy | Half |
| Cloudy | Low | Windless | Held |
| Rainy | Low | Windy | No |
| Rainy | VeryLow | VeryWindy | No |
| Rainy | Medium | Windless | Held |
| Rainy | Low | Windless | Held |
| Rainy | Low | Breeze | Half |

☐

*Classification* has been targeted not only for classifying objects correctly into one of the clases but also for developing *how* to do that, because this could make clear *what the objects mean*. In our story, the classification consists of a set of conditions $\alpha_1, .., \alpha_k$ where $\alpha_i$ determines a class in such a way that all the rows in $T$ satisfying $\alpha_i$ belong to the class, the set of rows is denoted by $T_i = \alpha_i(T)$. Each $\alpha_i$ is described as the conjunction of elementary form of $A_i = "a_i"$ and all the $T$ is covered exclusively by $\alpha_1 \vee ... \vee \alpha_k$.

A special attention has been paid on the tree form of the classification, called *decision trees*. Each node corresponds to a branching process, each branch to a condition $A_i = "a_i"$ where $a_i$ is an attribute value on $A_i$ and every path from the root to the leaf makes $\alpha_j$. Branches are generated on an attribute $A$ according to the set of attribute values over $A$ until all the rows satisfying these conditions belong to an identical class.

Induction of decision trees can be made by the following algorithm $\mathtt{DT}(S, AT, AL)$ where $S$ means a set of rows, $AT$ a set of attributes and $AL$ a set of conditions. A table $T$ is given as an input over a set of attributes $A_1, .., A_n$, but in this case, all the classes $c_1, .., c_q$ in $T$ are assumed disjoint, i.e., there is no $c, c'$ such that $\Gamma(c) \cap \Gamma(c') \neq \phi$. We start the algorithm with $\mathtt{DT}(T, \{A_1, .., A_n\}, \phi)$. If it terminates successfully, we get the tree conditions and the corresponding classes of the paths $\alpha_1(d_1), ..., \alpha_k(d_k)$.

(1) If all the rows in $S$ belong to an identical class $d$, we return $AL(d)$ successfully.
(2) Assume otherwise. Select an attribute $A \in AT$, and
(2.1) Make grouping of $S$ on $A$ into $S_1, .., S_w$. Each $S_j$ is generated by the condition $A = "a_j"$ to $S$.
(2.2) For each $S_j$, do $\mathtt{DT}(S_j, AT - \{A\}, AL \cup \{A = "a_j"\})$ in a recursive manner.

---

[1] But, they are consistent as described later.

(2.3) Collect all the results as $AL_1(d_1) \vee .. \vee AL_w(d_w)$. If some $S_j$ fails, we regard the result as distinct *undefined* class.

(3) If $AT$ is empty, return fail.

Conventional story says that the step (2.1) could be replaced by *most* of the rows belong to a class, in other words, noises are allowed. The step (2.3) also might be considered as *gray* zone and the classification might be inherited from the parent. However which attributes should be selected at the step (2) above ?

To select attributes, the original approach has been proposed based on theory of *entropy*, i.e., probabilistic prediction, though several extensions adopt other probabilistic strategies such as *GINI* found in the theory of *binary* decision trees[17]. This is the point of decision trees by which we can obtain effective and much efficient results without inspecting the input many times.

The scenario of the selection is as below : In the input $S$ of $n$ rows, we assume there exist $n_j$ rows of the class $c_j$, uniformly distributed probability $p_j = n_j/n$ of the class membership of $c_j$, and $n = n_1 + .. + n_q, n_i > 0$. The value $\log_2(1/p_j)$ is called *amount of information* of the class membership, and we define $E(S)$, called *entropy*, as the expected amount of information:

$$E(S) = \Sigma_j p_j \log_2(1/p_j) = -\Sigma_j p_j \log_2 p_j \quad .$$

Let $a_1, .., a_w$ be all the attribute values appeared on $A$ in $S$, and $S_1, .., S_w$ be all the groups of $S$ according to the conditions $A = "a_j"$, $j = 1, .., w$. Then we define $n_i^j$ as the number of the rows in $S_j$ that belong to a class $c_i$. Note $n_i = \Sigma_{j=1}^{w} n_i^j$ and $m_j = \Sigma_{i=1}^{q} n_i^j$ is the number of rows of $S_j$. The entropy $V_j$ of the class membership of $S_j$ is, by the definition :

$$-\Sigma_{i=1}^{q}(n_i^j/m_j) \log_2(n_i^j/m_j)$$

and the entropy $E_A(S)$ of the class membership of $S$ over $A$ is defined as :

$$\Sigma_{j=1}^{w}(m_j/n) \times V_j$$

By the above consideration, the *gain* $G_A(S)$ to do branching on $A$ is defined as $E(S) - E_A(S)$. We will select the attribute $A$ by which we obtain the maximum gain.

*Example 2.2.* In our running example, the original entropy $E(T)$ is 1.49261.

At the first step, we obtained the entropy values 1.31889, 0.886169 and 0.911063 on the attributes *Weather, Temperature* and *WindForce*. Thus we select *Temperature* as the first level. All the rows in each case of $VeryHigh$, $Medium$, $VeryLow$ belong to a single class. In the case of $Low$, we got the values 0.964984 and 0.67927 on the attributes *Weather* and *WindForce*, then we select *WindForce*. The story goes like this and finally we get the decision tree. Below is the result of C4.5.

The tree has the height 3 but it seems hard to see the usefulness of leaf levels although the semantics could be well-defined. This is the reason we like to *summarize* a collection of values. Also the readers can see illegal decisions (of C4.5) since there is no causal row about them[2]. Note also $(Low, Breeze, Half)$ is treated as a kind of error.

| (Temperature) | | | |
|---|---|---|---|
| VeryHigh | | | No |
| Medium | | | Held |
| VeryLow | | | No |
| High | (WindForce) | | |
| | VeryWindy | | Half |
| | Windy | | Half(*) |
| | Breeze | | Held |
| | Windless | | Half(*) |
| Low | (WindForce) | | |
| | VeryWindy | | Held(*) |
| | Breeze | | Half(e) |
| | Windless | | Held |
| | Windy | (Weather) | |
| | | Fine | Held(*) |
| | | Cloudy | Held |
| | | Rainy | No |

□

## 3   Entropy in a Class Hierarchy

In the original theory, as we pointed out, the algorithm sometimes generates less precise yet wide-spread trees since it always tries to reason all the input.

Our new decision tree algorithm differs from the ones proposed before since we heavily utilize the background knowledge of class hierarchy in databases. Since the classes $c_1, .., c_q$ have been assumed to be disjoint in the original theory, the entropy $-\Sigma p_i \log_2 p_i$ describes the expected amount of information with respect to *exclusive* class membership. Remember we assume a (single) class hierarchy, we have to re-examine the definition under the new environment.

In a table $T = \begin{pmatrix} t_1 : c_1 \\ .. \\ t_k : c_k \end{pmatrix}$, it seems reasonable for us to consider a row $t_j : c_j$ as an object carrying the values $t_j$ of the *lowest* class $c_j$ that, in fact, means all the ancestors. This is still true even if there are duplicate values in the consistent table.

Assume $e \in \Gamma(c_1)$ and $c_1$ ISA $c_2$. Then $e$ should be in $\Gamma(c_2)$. Given $p_1 = n_1/n_2$ and $p_2 = n_2/n$ where $n_1, n_2$ are the cardinalities of $\Gamma(c_1), \Gamma(c_2)$ respectively, and $n$ means the number of total objects, the probability of the membership is obtained by $p_1 \times p_2 = n_1/n$, thus we consider the probability of $c_1$ membership of $e$ as the one without looking at the hierarchy. Note $\Sigma_{i=1}^q n_i \geq k$ because objects belong to a class and all its ancestors. As the result, we will change the probabilities in the definition of entropy but the (new) class membership can be obtained easily by looking at ISA hierarchy and the input table $T$.

---

[2] Such rows are marked with *.

## 4   Relaxation of Classification

Let us outline our idea and major issues to be attacked. To improve the understandability of decision trees, we will change class membership into higher ones on class hierarchy. In fact, the hierarchy may help pruning the trees in a much efficient and clever way. By this technique, we obtain *precise* decision tree in a sense that the trees make classification correctly. But sometimes trivial results[3] are obtained by the generalization of the tree along our class hierarchy. Thus our true issue is how we can obtain precise yet *useful* trees. Of course, such fundamental question should come from the nature of knowledge acquisition, but we start with some assumptions to our decision trees as we said. First, we pose some conditions on the structures of decision trees. Second, the result trees may not be optimal compared to the original theory but is kept to have the allowable entropy. And lastly, the trees may be generated in a back-tracking manner but we try to avoid the duplicate calculation.

To obtain our goals, we revisit the input $T$ and change the values or even class membership dynamically.

### 4.1   Complexity of Classification

It is hard to define *complexity* of decision trees. In fact, none of the number of nodes, the height and the width of the trees or the number of branches could capture the complexity of the *concepts*. But also it is true that too large trees make people confused, that's the reason why *pruning* technique is considered important. In our work, we will put an emphasis on the *size* of the tree and pose some conditions on the trees.

Assume there are $u_j$ distinct values appeared on $A_j$ attribute ($j = 1, .., n$) in $T$, and $u = (u_1 + .. + u_n)/n$. In the worst case, the results might become $u$-ary trees of the height up to $\log_u(u_1 \times ... \times u_n)$, but we might expect $\log_u k$ where $k$ is the number of rows in $T$. In this investigation we discuss the heights of the trees since it can be checked anytime independent of other branches. We assume *pruning ratio* $\alpha$ and the height condition becomes $\alpha \times \log_u k$.

*Example 4.1.* In our example, there are 3 values on *Weather* attribute, 5 values on *Temperature* and 4 values on *Windiness*. Then $u = (3 + 4 + 5)/3 = 4$, thus we get $\log_u k = \log_4 14 = 2$. Bigger $\alpha$ causes deeper trees. In this investigation we set $\alpha = 1.1$, i.e., the height 3, just same as the result of C4.5. □

### 4.2   Rewriting Attribute Values

During the generation of decision trees, the structural condition might fail during the generation of new nodes and branches. In this case, we change the values on a certain attribute into higher abstractions and we will guide the rapid convergence.

---

[3] For example, everything is classified into @E.

This can be done just by *clustering techniques* by numerical semantics such as average salary values. By clustering numerical values, a set of range values are abstracted and we can reduce size of trees. In the case of non-numeric semantics such as *HighSalary, LowSalary*, on the other hand, few technique is known. In this work, we adopt the same idea of Han[5].

As the first abstraction, we change an attribute value by its lowest 'class' that the value belongs to[4]. As the following abstraction steps, we *climb up* the class hierarchy, i.e., we change the value by the next higher class. Eventually we get to the very top @E that means every value is identical.

*Example 4.2.* In our running example, we assume several class hierarchies.

1. On *Weather* attribute, we have *Fine, Cloudy* objects and *Rainy* object which belong to *NotWet* and *Wet* classes respectively that are defined as the subclasses of *DontCare* class.

2. On *Temperature* attribute, we have *VeryHigh, High, Medium, Low* and *Very Low* objects. The first two are the member of *Hot* class, *Medium* is in *Warm* class and the last two in *Cold* class. We assume *Warm* ISA *Comfortable*, *Cold* ISA *Comfortable* and *Hot* ISA *NotGood*. We assume each class ISA *DontCareTemp*.

3. On *WindForce*, we have *VeryWindy, Windy, Breeze* and *Windless* objects. The first two are the member of *Wind* class while the last two in *NoWind* class. We assume each class ISA *DontCareWin*.

4. Finally on result classes, we assume *Half* is a special case (sub class) of *Held* case, thus *Half* ISA *Held*.

For instance, we may change both *Fine, Cloudy* into *NotWet*, then into *DontCare*.

Note the entropy in our example is now 1.265982 since $p_{Held} = 11/14$, $p_{Half} = 4/14$ and $p_{No} = 3/14$ where $p_c$ means the probability of the class $c$. □

In the above process, the attribute values are grouped together and the decision trees become useful. In fact, we might lose some amount of information and the entropy must be reduced eventually[5].

Let us consider the details. Assume we change the values $\{a_1, .., a_w\}$ on an attribute $A$ appeared only in the set $S$, $S \subseteq T$, of rows to be considered. Note there should be no change of entropy on other attributes. The set $S$ has been decomposed into $S_1, .., S_w$ but now some of them are combined into $S'_1, .., S'_{w'}, w' \leq w$. This is because, for instance, $S_1, S_2$ have been generated by the conditions $A = "a_1", A = "a_2"$ respectively, but $a_1, a_2$ now become identical, then $S_1$

---

[4] Or we generate a special object of the class and replace by it.

[5] The entropy does not decrease linearly because of the intermediate values.

and $S_2$ must be in the same (new) component. The entropy $V_1$ of $S_1$ is obtained by

$$-(1/m_1)\Sigma_{i=1,..,q}n_i^1 \times \log_2(n_i^1/m_1)$$

where $m_1$ is the cardinality of $S_1$, $n_i^1$ is the number of the rows of $S_1$ that belong to a class $c_i$.

In a similar manner, we have $V_2$ obtained by

$$-(1/m_2)\Sigma_{i=1,..,q}n_i^2 \times \log_2(n_i^2/m_2)$$

When $S_1$ and $S_2$ are combined, the new entropy $V_{12}$ becomes

$$-(1/(m_1+m_2))\Sigma_{i=1,..,q}(n_i^1+n_i^2) \times \log_2((n_i^1+n_i^2)/(m_1+m_2))$$

Thus the total change becomes $V_{12} - (V_1 + V_2)$, but this formula says there can't be continuous reduction of entropy though it might be to 0 (in the case of @E).

Then we must have a question similar to the original story, *which attribute should be selected ?* It seems reasonable to select one from *not-yet-processed* attributes since part of decision trees have been generated. To reduce the selection overhead, we utilize the list of $E_A(S)$ values because they had been calculated to develop the trees. Here our choice depends on the minimum gain of entropy $E(S) - E_A(S)$. This is because $E_A(S)$ of the minimum gain carries the maximum entropy and the change of the attributes values could make effective to reduce branching.

## 4.3    Relaxing Class Membership

By rewriting the attribute values we may expect the reduction of decision trees (and the entropy). Unfortunately we might get some inconsistency in total. In this subsection we discuss this issue and how to resolve it.

After changing the attribute values in $S$ where $S \subseteq T$, there might be duplicate rows $t : c_1, t : c_2$ in $T$ but of distinct classes. By the definition, the result is consistent if $c_1$ is the ancestor of $c_2$ (or vice versa). In this case we change class membership and we replace all the class membership by the least general class among them.

More important is the case that, when $c_1, c_2$ are disjoint, no object can belong to both $c_1$ and $c_2$, and the result becomes inconsistent. We fix this problem by changing the class membership of one of the rows. Using a single class hierarchy, we can have the least common ancestor $c_0$ of $c_1, c_2$. Then we select one of $c_1$ or $c_2$ that has the *smaller* distance to $c_0$, say $c_1$, and we change the two rows by $t : c_0, t : c_2$. The row $t : c_1$ is now assumed not to be in the class $c_1$ but in $c_0$, which means the class membership of $c_1$ is relaxed to $c_0$, since $c_1$ ISA $c_0$. Note that the changes may arise among different branches in the partially developed trees and the duplicate check should be made to the relevant rows.

*Example 4.3.* Since *Half* ISA *Held*, We could change a row (*Fine, Low, Breeze*) of *Half* class into the one of *Held* class. □

The change of class membership causes the reduction of the total entropy. In fact, the probability $n_1/k$ of the lowest class $c_1$ is decreased to $(n_1 - 1)/k$ while the probability $n_0/k$ of the lowest class $c_0$ is increased to $(n_0 + 1)/k$ where $n_0, n_1$ mean the number of rows of $\Gamma(c_0), \Gamma(c_1)$ in $T$ and $k$ means the number of rows in $T$. The amount of information of $c_1$ is changed from $(n_1/k)\log_2(n_1/k)$ into :

$$((n_1 - 1)/k)\log_2((n_1 - 1)/k) = (n_1/k)\log_2(n_1/k) - (1/n)\log_2(n_1/k)$$

Similarly, the one of $c_0$ becomes

$$((n_0 + 1)/k)\log_2((n_0 + 1)/k) = (n_0/k)\log_2(n_0/k) + (1/k)\log_2(n_0/k)$$

In total, $(1/k)(\log_2 n_0 - \log_2 n_1)$ is reduced from the entropy by this change. If there are $v_{ij}$ changes from $c_i$ to $c_j$, then the amount $(1/k)\Sigma_{i,j}v_{ij} \times (\log_2 n_j - \log_2 n_i)$ is reduced.

## 4.4 Preserving the Usefulness

What we have described so far is how to relax $T$ to obtain sufficiently useful decision trees, but as pointed out, we want to obtain *useful* ones. That means we have to avoid the drastic reduction of the entropy. In this subsection, we summarize the change of entropy from several aspects and discuss how to combine them into our new algorithm.

By changing class membership based on relaxing the attribute values on $A$, we lose $(1/k)\Sigma_{i,j}v_{ij} \times (\log_2 n_j - \log_2 n_i)$ from the original (very beginning) entropy $E(T)$. This is the one we have to watch. Here we give a *global threshold ratio* $\beta$ $(0.0 \leq \beta \leq 1.0)$ and we will accept the change if $E(T)$ changes within this ratio, that is to say :

$$|(1/k)\Sigma_{i,j}v_{ij} \times (\log_2 n_j - \log_2 n_i)|/|E(T)| \leq \beta$$

If the change is unacceptable, we will stop the process since the reason comes from the way to cluster values.

Let us discuss the net effect against the selection steps of attributes to a set $S$ of rows. As for $E_A(S)$, we have already discussed the amount of the change of the entropy on $A$. Now let us discuss $E_B(S)$ where $B$ is different from $A$ but will be relaxed in future or the one already processed before. We assume that $E_B(S)$ has been already obtained for the purpose of the attribute selection. Whenever we change the class membership, we will examine $B$-values (or $B = "b_w"$) and count the number $v_{i,j}^w$ of the changes from $c_i$ to $c_j$ to each $b_w$. The total amount of the reduction of the entropy is summarized as below :

$$\Sigma_{i,j}(v_{i,j}^w/m_w) \times (\log_2 n_j^w - \log_2 n_i^w)$$

where $n_j^w$ is the number of the rows of the class $c_j$ in the group component by $B = "b_w"$ and $m_w$ the cardinality of the component.

By this result we can examine whether the change amount falls into the allowable range compared to the best optimized selection in the original decision trees. For this purpose we give a *selection threshold ratio* $\gamma$ $(0.0 \leq \gamma \leq 1.0)$, and we will examine whether the ratio of the change by the original $E_B(S)$ is within $\gamma$. If it is not the case, we will go back to the attribute selection steps in a recursive manner.

For the attributes that are not-yet-selected, this result allows us to avoid the recalculation for the selection of attributes in repeated processes.

## 4.5   New Decision Tree Algorithm

Now let us describe our *new decision tree* algorithm by putting all the considerations together into one. Our new decision trees can be generated by the following algorithm $\mathtt{NDT}(S, AT, AL)$ where $S$ means a set of rows, $AT$ a set of attributes and $AL$ a set of conditions. We have three threshold values $\alpha$ (pruning ratio), $\beta$ (global threshold) and $\gamma$ (selection threshold). A table $T$ is given as an input over a set of attributes $A_1, .., A_n$, and we start the algorithm with $\mathtt{NDT}(T, \{A_1, .., A_n\}, \phi)$. If it terminates successfully, we get the tree conditions and the corresponding classes of the paths $\alpha_1(d_1), ..., \alpha_k(d_k)$ as before.

(1) If all the rows in $S$ belong to an identical class $d$, we return $AL(d)$ successfully. If all the rows are identical but of different (consistent) classes, we change the class membership by the least general class and count the number of changes. If the amount of the change goes beyond the $\beta$ ratio, we quit the process for the failure. If the amount goes beyond the attribute selection ratio, we will return to the attribute selection steps in a back-track manner.

(2) Assume otherwise. First we calculate all the $E_A(S)$ for all the attributes $A$ that are not-yet-processed.

(3) If the partial tree is not within allowance level defined by $\alpha$,

(3.1) Select an attribute $A$ of the minimum gain and relax it.

(3.2) Rewrite attribute values on $A$ and adjust the change of the entropy.

(3.3) If there happen duplicate rows of disjoint classes, we change the class membership and count the number of changes according to the attribute values. If the amount of the change goes beyond the $\beta$ ratio, we quit the process for the failure. If the amount goes beyond the attribute selection ratio, we will return to the attribute selection steps in a back-track manner.

(3.4) Adjust all the $E_A(S)$ values and go back to (1).

(4) The tree is now allowable, and select an attribute $A \in AT$ of the maximum gain.

(4.1) Make grouping of $S$ on $A$ into $S_1, .., S_w$. Each $S_j$ is generated by the condition $A = "a_j"$ to $S$.

(4.2) For each $S_j$, do $\mathtt{NDT}(S_j, AT - \{A\}, AL \cup \{A = "a_j"\})$ in a recursive manner. If it comes back to re-select attributes, goto (2).

(4.3) Collect all the results as $AL_1(d_1) \vee .. \vee AL_w(d_w)$. If some $S_j$ fails, we regard the result as distinct *undefined* class.

(5) If $AT$ is empty, return fail.

The steps (4) to (5) are the same to the original except re-selection of attributes. Note the relaxation changes the contents of the processes while the duplicate calculations are carefully avoided.

*Example 4.4.* Here we assume $\alpha = 1.0, \beta = 0.15, \gamma = 0.15$, and we may have the height 3.

With the initial entropy 1.265982 of the input and the ISA hierarchy, we select *Temperature* as the first attribute to be examined with the minimum entropy 0.637596.

With *Temperature=High*, NDT generates two branches on *WindForce* iwth the entropy 0.0: *windForce=VeryWindy* (*Half* Class) and *WindForce=Breeze* (*Held* Class).

With *Temperature=Low*, NDT generates 3 branches on *WindForce* with the entropy 0.452846: *Breeze* (this causes duplicate rows since *Weather* values are identical, but we get *Held* class because of *Half* and *Held* class membership), *Windless* (*Held* class) and *Windy*. The case *Windy* generates the new branches on *Weather*. The attribute values are *Cloudy* and *Rainy* which are unified as *DontCare* and so is true for the class membership *DontCareRace*. And the process terminates with the allowable thresholds. The readers can check the final result more easily:

| (Temperature) | | |
|---|---|---|
| VeryHigh | | No |
| Medium | | Held |
| VeryLow | | No |
| High | (WindForce) | |
| | VeryWindy | Half |
| | Breeze | Held |
| Low | (WindForce) | |
| | Windy | DontCareRace |
| | Breeze | Held |
| | Windless | Held |

When we assume $\alpha = 1.0, \beta = 0.08, \gamma = 0.15$ and $\alpha = 0.5, \beta = 0.08, \gamma = 0.15$ respectively, we have two distinct results of the height 2:

| (WindForce) | | |
|---|---|---|
| VeryWindy | (Temperature) | |
| | High | Half |
| | VeryLow | No |
| Windy | (Temperature) | |
| | Medium | Held |
| | Low | DontCareRace |
| Breeze | | (undefined) |
| Windless | (Temperature) | |
| | VeryHigh | No |
| | Medium | Held |
| | Low | Held |

| (WindForce) | | |
|---|---|---|
| VeryWindy | (Temperature) | |
| | High | Half |
| | VeryLow | No |
| Windy | (Temperature) | |
| | Medium | Held |
| | Low | DontCareRace |
| Breeze | | (undefined) |
| Windless | (Temperature) | |
| | VeryHigh | No |
| | Medium | Held |
| | Low | Held |

□

## 5    Experimental Results

We examined *Car Evaluation Database* in ML Library by which we rank accept-ability of cars according to price and technical quality. The database contains all the 1728 combinations over 6 attributes without any noise, duplicate nor missing values. The decision depends on *buying* (buying price; vhigh, high, med, low), *maint* (price of the maintenance; vhigh, high, med, low), *doors* (number of doors; 2,3,4, more), *persons* (capacity in terms of persons to carry; 2, 4, more), *lug-boot* (the size of luggage boot; small, med, big) and *safety* (estimated safety of the car ; low, med, high). Decisions consist of *unacc* (unacceptable), *acc* (acceptable), *good* and *vgood* (very good).

We added ISA hierarchy (50 relationships) among types/classes: *buying* (9 re-lationships/4 level), *maint* (9/4), *doors* (9/4), *persons* (4/3), *lug-boot* (5/3),*safety* (5/3) and decisions (9/4). Below is a *decision* hierarchy:

```
unacc ISA BadCar, acc ISA OkCar, good ISA OkCar,
vgood ISA ExcellentCar, BadCar ISA Worthless, OkCar ISA Worthy,
ExcellentCar ISA Worthy, Worthless ISA DontCare, Worthy ISA DontCare
```

By using C4.5, we got 182 branches (from the root to leafs) with the height 5 and 3.7% of error-ratio after pruning.

On th eother hand, in our approach with $\alpha = 1.0, \beta = 0.15, \gamma = 0.15$, we got 102 branches (rules) of the height 6 as below:

unacc (27), acc (26), good (0), vgood (2), BadCar (0), OkCar (9), ExcellentCar (0), Worthless (0), Worthy (6), DontCare (32)

This says we got much simplified decision rules by introducing the hierarchy with the allowable reliability. However we found 32 rules of *DontCare* for this simplification which means we lose some decision because of the abstraction though the decision tree is not incorrect.

## 6    Related Works

*Knowledge discovery in databases* (KDD) is one of the hot research topics and now focused by many database researchers[1,3,4,8,15,18]. It is nothing but knowl-edge acquisition activity but differs from using database as background (domain) knowledge. KDD processes could be captured as general framework for meta-model manipulation[6]. Rules queries on databases are interpreted as rules/con-straints discovery and knowledge acquisition as scheme discovery. Then very ambitious paradigm might be established and applied to wide range of applica-tions. Series of works show how to obtain new database schemes that are suitable for current database instances[11,9,10,12,19,13].

From the viewpoint of machine learning, a theory of logic-based inductive in-ference has the strong relation with KDD[18]. However utilized is only the scheme information but not characteristics of instances nor domain-specific knowledge except a few[7]. It is not easy to discover implicit conditions to give property values, but there exist quantitative and qualitative methods as well known[3,18].

# 7   Conclusion

In this work, we have proposed a new classification methodology for the purpose of precise and useful decision trees. Our new decision tree algorithm utilizes the background knowledge of databases, that is, we relax the attribute values and class membership while keeping the quality of the trees in a sense of entropy. Although the algorithm takes more than polynomial time in the worst cases, the duplicate calculation could be carefully avoided.

# References

1. Agrawal, R., Srikant, R.: Fast Algorithms for Mining Association Rules, *VLDB* (1994), 487-499.
2. Diettrich, T.: Overfitting and Undercomputing in Machine Learning, *ACM Comp.Survey* 27-3 (1995), pp.326-327
3. Fayyad, U.M., Piatetsky-Shapiro, G., Smyth, P. and Uthurusamy, R. (Eds).: Advances in Knowledge Discovery and Data Mining, *MIT Press* (1996)
4. Han, J., Cai, Y. and Cercone, N.: Knowledge Discovery in Databases : An Attribute Oriented Approach, *VLDB* (1992), 547-559
5. Han, J. and Fu, Y.: Discovery of Multiple-Level Association Rules from Large Databases, *VLDB* (1995), 420-431.
6. Imielinski ,T. and Mannila, H.: A Database Perspective on Knowledge Discovery, *CACM* 39-11 (1996), 58-64.
7. Kietz,J.U. and Morik, K.: A Polynomial Approach to the Constructive Induction of Structural Knowledge, *Machine Learning* 14 (1994), pp.193-217.
8. Mannila, H.: Methods and Problems in Data Mining, *Intn'l Conf. on Database Theory* (ICDT), pp.41-55 (1997).
9. Miura, T. and Shioya, I.: Mining Type Schemes in Databases, *Conference and Workshop of DEXA* (1996), 369-384
10. Miura, T. and Shioya, I.: Knowledge Acquisition for Classification Systems, proc. *ICTAI* (1996), pp.110-115.
11. Miura, T. and Shioya, I.: Paradigm for Scheme Discovery, proc.*CODAS* (1996), pp.101-108.
12. Miura, T. and Shioya, I.: On Complex Type Hierarchy, *Conference and Workshop of DEXA* (1997)
13. Miura, T. and Shioya, I.: Learning Concepts from Databases, *Conference and Workshop of DEXA* (1998)
14. Miura, T. and Shioya, I.: Incremental Update of Decision Trees for Temporal Information, Proc.*KRDB* (1999)
15. Ng, R. and Han, J.: Efficient and Effective Clustering Methods for Spatial Data Mining, *VLDB* (1994), pp.144-155.
16. Quinlan, J.R: Induction of Decision Trees, *Machine Learning* 1-1 (1986), pp.81-106.
17. Quinlan, J.R.: C4.5 - Programs for Machine Learning, Morgan Kauffman (1993)
18. Piatetsky-Shapiro, G. and Frawley, W.J. (ed.): Knowledge Discovery in Databases, *MIT Press* (1991)
19. Shioya, I. and Miura,T. : Clustering Concepts from Databases, proc. *ICTAI* (1998), pp.95-102

# High-Level Logic Programming

## Mauricio Osorio[1] and Fernando Zacarias[2]

[1] Universidad de las Americas, CENTIA
Sta. Catarina Martir, Cholula
72820 Puebla, México
`josorio@mail.udlap.mx`
[2] Benemerita Universidad Autonoma de Puebla
Facultad de Ciencias, Computacion
75579 Puebla, México
`fzacarias@diplomado.cs.buap.mx`

**Abstract.** We introduce the paradigm of High-Level Logic Programming. This paradigm is the consolidation of our recent results on disjunctions, sets, partial-order clauses and aggregation. We show how these concepts are integrated in a natural way into the standard logic programming framework. For this purpose, we present several well known examples from the literature that support this claim. Our approach to define the declarative semantics of HLL (High-Level Logic) programs consists on a translation of them to datalog disjunctive programs and then to use D1-WFS-COMP.

## 1 Introduction

The evolution of this research is shown in the papers [15,16,17,18,27,23,28,24,26], [25]. The aim of our research is to define high-level logic programming that includes negation, disjunctions, sets and partial-order clauses [17]. One main goal is to model set-of and aggregate operations, which are of considerable interest in deductive databases. A central concept in most of the works that include sets is one which we call *collect-all*. This concept has independently been adopted by several languages, e.g., SEL [18], SuRE [16], COL [2], Relationlog [21] and LDL1 [3]. The idea is that a program needs only to define explicitly what are the members of the set and, by assuming a *closed world*, the set becomes totally defined. Moreover, all the just mentioned works, have defined a precise semantics for restricted classes of programs and they agree on the common subclasses. Also, a common assumption is to consider only finite sets.

From our research of the following works on sets and aggregation: [18,16,2,21], [31,13,17,30,10,19,29] we have obtained a partial definition of the intended semantics of a POL program (a restricted form of a HLL program). One important goal is to find a pair $< transl, SEM >$, where $transl$ is a computable function from the class of POL programs to the class of normal programs such that the semantics of the translated programs, given by $SEM$, is consistent with the intended semantics of the original program. In [27] the authors gave a first major

K.-D. Schewe, B. Thalheim (Eds.): FoIKS 2000, LNCS 1762, pp. 226–240, 2000.
© Springer-Verlag Berlin Heidelberg 2000

step finding such a suitable pair $< transl, SEM >$ for the restricted class of *cost-monotonic POL* programs. In this case $SEM$ came out to be WFS$^+$ [11]. The class of *cost monotonic* programs is actually a large class that includes most of the examples and classes considered in the literature. Moreover, the semantics SEM of *cost-monotonic* programs can be computed efficiently, without having to translate the given POL program to its respective normal program [17,26]. Our current research suggests that also many *non cost-monotonic POL* programs that have a clear intended meaning, as the difficult examples suggested in [31] can be correctly expressed using the pair just mentioned.

In this paper we discuss that the semantics D1-WFS-COMP defined in [1] can also via used to express the semantics of POL programs via the *alt_trans* translation defined in [24]. Since D1-WFS-COMP allows disjunctions then D1-WFS-COMP can be used to provide a declarative semantics for HLL programs, i.e. extended partial-order programs with disjunctions.

## 2   High-Level Logic Programs

We will now give a brief informal introduction to HLL programs to give an intuition of the style of programming in this language and also to provide some context for discussing the semantic issues it raises. HLL clauses have the structure of normal clauses [20], i.e., they are of the form:

$$A_1; \ldots; A_n \leftarrow L_1, \ldots, L_m$$

where $A_1; \ldots A_n$ represents the disjunction $A_1 \vee \ldots \vee A_n$ which is the head of the clause, $L_1, \ldots, L_m$ its body, and $m \geq 0$. Each $A_i$ $(1 \leq i \leq n)$ is an atom, and for each $L_i$ $(1 \leq i \leq m)$ is a literal (an atom or the negation of an atom). Atoms could be as usual, i.e. of the form $p(\bar{t})$, where $p$ is a user-defined predicate, but also we have two new forms of atoms, $f(\bar{t}) = e$ and $f(\bar{t}) \geq e$, where $f$ represents a user-defined function. Note that $\bar{t}$ represents a tuple of terms; and $e$ represents an expression, which is a composition of user-defined functions. A High-level logic program is a set of program clauses.

The 'logical' view of logic programming is that a program is a theory and computation is logical inference. In the classical approach to logical programming, the inference mechanism is faithful to *logical consequence* in classical first-order logic. This paper adopted the *canonical model* approach, where the inference mechanism is faithful to truth in the "intended" model of the program.

To represent finite sets, we use two constructors, $\{x \backslash t\}$ and $\phi$. The notation $\{x \backslash t\}$ refers to a set in which $x$ is one element and $t$ is the remainder of the set. We permit as syntactic sugar $\{expr\}$ to stand for $\{expr \backslash \phi\}$, and $\{e_1, e_2, \ldots, e_k\}$, where all $e_i$ are distinct, to stand for $\{e_1 \backslash \{e_2 \backslash \ldots \{e_k \backslash \phi\}\}\}$. To illustrate the set constructor, matching $\{X \backslash T\}$ against a ground set $\{a, b, c\}$ yields three different substitutions, $\{X \leftarrow a, T \leftarrow \{b, c\}\}$, $\{X \leftarrow b, T \leftarrow \{a, c\}\}$, and $\{X \leftarrow c, T \leftarrow \{a, b\}\}$. One should contrast $\{X \backslash T\}$ from $\{X\} \cup T$.

We now present several examples to explain the paradigm.

*Example 2.1.* The definition of set-intersection shows how set patterns can finesse iteration over sets (the result is $\phi$ if any of the input sets is $\phi$, as desired):

intersect($\{$X\_$\}$, $\{$X\_$\}$) $\geq$ $\{$X$\}$.

This function works as follows: For a function call intersect($\{1, 2, 3\}$, $\{2, 3, 4\}$), we have the following two clauses: intersect($\{1, 2, 3\}$, $\{2, 3, 4\}$) $\geq$ $\{2\}$, and intersect($\{1, 2, 3\}$, $\{2, 3, 4\}$) $\geq$ $\{3\}$. Since the *lub* of $\{2\}$ and $\{3\}$ is $\{2, 3\}$, we obtain intersect($\{1, 2, 3\}$, $\{2, 3, 4\}$) = $\{2, 3\}$.

*Example 2.2 (Reach, [26]).* The definition of a transitive-closure operation using partial-order clauses illustrates a basic use of the paradigm. The function reach below takes a node (in a directed graph) as input and finds the set of reachable nodes from this node.

reach(X) $\geq$ $\{$X$\}$.
reach(X) $\geq$ reach(Y) $\leftarrow$ edge(X,Y).

As the graph may be cyclic, our intended operational semantics employs memoization in order to detect cyclic function calls that may arise.

*Example 2.3 (Nullables).* For a more substantial example of transitive-closures and one which combines set-terms, predicates and partial-order clauses, we define below the set of its nullable nonterminals of a context-free grammar.

grammar($\{[$p, q$]$, $[$q$]$, $[$r, a$]\}$).
belongKleene($[\,]$, \_).
belongKleene($[$X$]$, $\{$X\_$\}$).
belongKleene($[$X, Y$|$Z$]$, S) $\leftarrow$ belongKleene($[$X$]$, S), belongKleene($[$Y$|$Z$]$, S).
null($\{[$H$|$R$]$\_$\}$)$\geq\{$H$\}$ $\leftarrow$ grammar(G), null(G) = S, belongKleene(R,S).

For convenience, we represent the production rules of the grammar as a set of lists, where each list represents a rule: the first element of the list is the left-hand side of the rule and the rest of the list is right-hand side of the rule. In this example our set of productions is $\{p \rightarrow q, q \rightarrow \epsilon, r \rightarrow a\}$. The predicate belongKleene(X,S) is true if X$\in$S*, where the string X is represented by a list, and S is a set. The function null computes the set of *nullables* of grammar, i.e. the set of nonterminal symbols such each of them derives the empty string.

The following example is taken from [31], where Van Gelder classifies it as not monotonic and he claims that it appears to make intuitive sense.

*Example 2.4 (Party Invitation Problem, [31]).*

accept(X) $\leftarrow$ rel-all(X) = S, sum$_2$(S) $\geq$ 0.
rel-all(X) $\geq$ $\{[$Y,C$]\}$ $\leftarrow$ accept(Y), compatible(X,Y,C).

The above clauses express the criterion that a person will attend a party if he or she has sufficient compatibility with the rest of the people coming to the party. We express this criterion by requiring that the sum of all compatibilities, positive and negative, to be nonnegative. We omit the definition sum$_2$ and we assume that its intended meaning is to add the second argument of every element is S. Consider the database of facts:

```
compatible(a,b,1).    compatible(a,c,1).
compatible(b,a,1).    compatible(b,c,1).
```

The intended semantics of the program (as suggested in [31]) defines all accept(a), accept(b) and accept(c) to be true. That is exactly what we get in our approach.

In the following example we note that our inequalities can be used to define functions over different domains, not just finite sets.

*Example 2.5 (Shortest Distance).* The formulation of the shortest-distance problem is one of the most elegant and succinct illustrations of partial-order clauses:

```
edge(a,b,1).
edge(a,c,2).
edge(b,d,5).
edge(c,d,3).
edge(d,a,1).
short(X,Y) ≤ C  ←  edge(X,Y,C).
short(X,Y) ≤ C+short(Z,Y)  ←  edge(X,Z,C).
```

This definition for short is very similar to that for reach. The relation edge(X,Y,C) means that there is a directed edge from X to Y with distance C. which is non-negative. A possible interpretation to our program is obtained if we let short$(X,Y)$=0, for every pair of vertices $X, Y$. However, this is not the intended model. In the intended model, short(a,b)=1, short(a,d)=5, and so on. The reader should wait to the next section to fully understand the semantics of these programs. Finally, note that the domain of the short function is totally-ordered. This knowledge can be used to tailor a very efficient implementation for this program, resembling Dijkstra's algorithm (see [25]).

*Example 2.6 (Travel, [4]).*

```
visit-europe(john) ; visit-australia(john).
happy(X)  ←  visit-europe(X).
happy(X)  ←  visit-australia(X).
bankrupt(X)  ←  visit-europe(X), visit-australia(X).
prudent(X)  ←  ¬ visit-europe(X).
prudent(X)  ←  ¬ visit-australia(X).
dissappointed(X)  ←  ¬ visit-europe(X), ¬ visit-australia(X).
```

According to [4] we expect that prudent(john) to be true, ¬ dissapointed(john) to be true, and ¬ bankrupt(john) to be true. We get these results with our approach.

The following is a well known example that can not be handled adequately by Circumscription.

*Example 2.7 (Poole's Broken arm, [8]).*

```
left-use(X)  ←  ¬ ab(left,X).
ab(left,X)  ←  left-brok(X).
```

```
right-use(X)  ←  ¬ ab(right,X).
ab(right,X)  ←  right-brok(X).
left-brok(fred) ; right-brok(fred)  ←.
make-cheque(X)  ←  left-use(X).
make-cheque(X)  ←  right-use(X).
disabled(X)  ←  left-brok(X), right-brok(X).
```

The well known semantics D-WFS and DSTABLE derive that Fred is not disabled (see [8]). We get the same answer in our approach. Moreover, DSTABLE (but not D-WFS) derives that Fred can make out a cheque. We get also this result in our approach.

*Example 2.8 (Basic-Disjunctions).*

```
h(a1).                    h(a2).                    h(b).
p(a1); q(a1).             p(a2); q(a2).
c(X)  ←  ¬ p(X), ¬ q(X). s(1) ≥ {X}  ←  ¬ c(X), h(X).
```

Due to the disjunction p(a1) ; q(a1) we expect that c(a1) is false. For a similar reason c(a2) should be also false. Since h(a1) as well as h(a2) are both true then s(1) ≥ {a1,a2} must be true. On the other hand, by negation as failure, c(b) should be true and hence we expect s(1)={a1,a2} to be true. This how behaves our declarative semantics.

*Example 2.9 (Partial-order disjunctions).*

```
s ≥ {1}; s ≥ {2}.            s ≥ {3}.
```

Our declarative semantics defines s ≥ {1,3}; s ≥ {2,3} to be true, s = {1,3}; s = {2,3} to be false and finally s = {1,3}; s = {2,3}; s= {1,2,3} to be true. We claim that this is the intended meaning of the program.

# 3    Declarative Semantics

We first introduce the declrative semantics for disjunctive propositional programs. Then we show how define the declarative semantics of any high level program.

## 3.1    Propositional Programs

We may denote a (general) clause $C$ as: $a_1; \ldots; a_m \leftarrow l_1, \ldots, l_n$, where $m > 0$, $n \geq 0$, each $a_i$ is a propositional atom, and each $l_i$ is a propositional literal. When $n = 0$ the clause is considered as $a_1 \vee \ldots \vee a_m \leftarrow true$, where $true$ is a constant atom with its intended interpretation. Sometimes, is better to denote a clause by $\mathcal{A} \leftarrow \mathcal{B}^+, \neg \mathcal{B}^-$, where $\mathcal{A}$ contains all the head atoms, $\mathcal{B}^+$ contains all the positive body atoms and $\mathcal{B}^-$ contains all the negative body atoms. We also use $body(C)$ to denote $\mathcal{B}^+ \cup \neg \mathcal{B}^-$. When $\mathcal{A}$ is a singleton set, the clause reduces to a normal clause. A definite clause ([22]) is a normal clause lacking of negative literals, that is $\mathcal{B}^- = \emptyset$. A *pure* disjunction is a disjunction consisting solely of positive or solely of negative literals. A (general) program is a finite set of clauses. As in normal programs, $HEAD(P)$ to denote the set of atoms ocurring in heads in $P$. We use $\models$ to denote the consequence relation for classical first-order logic. It will be useful to map a program to a normal program. Given a clause $C := \mathcal{A} \leftarrow \mathcal{B}^+, \neg\mathcal{B}^-$, we write *dis-nor(C)* to denote the set of normal clauses:

$$\{a \leftarrow \mathcal{B}^+, \neg(\mathcal{B}^- \cup (\mathcal{A} \setminus \{a\})) | a \in \mathcal{A}\}.$$

We extend this definition to programs as follows. If $P$ is a program, let *dis-nor(P)* denotes the normal program: $\bigcup_{C \in P} dis{-}nor(C)$. Given a normal program $P$, we write $Definite(P)$ to denote the Definite program that we obtain from $P$ just by removing every negative literal in $P$. Given a Definite program, by $MM(P)$ we mean the unique minimal model of $P$ (that always exists for definite programs, see [22]).

**Definition 3.1 (Definition of *def* and *sup*).**
*Let $P$ be a normal program. Let $a$ be an atom in a given signature $\mathcal{L}$ (such that $\mathcal{L}_P \subseteq \mathcal{L}$), by the definition of $a$ in $P$, we mean the set of clauses: $\{a \leftarrow body \in P\}$, that we denote by $def(a)$. We define*

$$sup(a) := \begin{cases} false & \text{if } def(a) = \emptyset \\ body_1 \vee \ldots \vee body_n & \text{otherwise} \end{cases}$$

*where $def(a) = \{a \leftarrow body_1, \ldots, a \leftarrow body_n\}$*

**Definition 3.2 (comp(P) ([9])).**
*For any normal program $P$, we define comp(P) over a given signature $\mathcal{L}$ (where $\mathcal{L}_P \subseteq \mathcal{L}$) as the classical theory $\{a \leftrightarrow sup(a) : a \in \mathcal{L}\}$[1].*

We use an example to illustrate the above definitions. Let $P$ be the program:
    p; q ← ¬r.
    p ← s, ¬t.
Then $HEAD(P) = \{p, q\}$, and $dis - nor(P)$ consists of the clauses:
    p ← ¬r, ¬q.
    q ← ¬r, ¬p.
    p ← s, ¬t
$Definite(dis - nor(P))$ consists on the clauses:
    p ← true.
    q ← true.
    p ← s.
$MM(Definite(dis\text{-}nor(P)))=\{p, q\}$. Finally, $comp(dis\text{-}nor(P))$ over $\mathcal{L}_P$ consists on the formulas
    p ↔ true ∨ s.
    q ↔ true.

---

[1]    In the standard definition $\mathcal{L}$ is $\mathcal{L}_P$. Our paper requires this more general definition

$r \leftrightarrow false.$

$s \leftrightarrow false.$

What are the minimal requirements we want to impose on a semantics for disjunctive programs? Certainly we want that disjunctive facts, i.e. clauses in the program with empty bodies to be true. Dually, if an atom does not occur in any head, then its negation should be true. These ideas are straightforward generalizations of the case on normal programs.

## Definition 3.3 (Semantics ([5]).

*A semantics over a given signature $\mathcal{L}$, is a binary relation $\vdash_s$ between logic programs and pure disjunctions which satisfies the following conditions:*

1. *If $P \vdash_s \alpha$ and $\alpha \subseteq \alpha'$, then $P \vdash_s \alpha'$.*
2. *If $\mathcal{A} \leftarrow true \in P$ for a disjunction $\mathcal{A}$, then $P \vdash_s \mathcal{A}$.*
3. *If $a \notin HEAD(P)$ for some atom $a$, then $P \vdash_s \neg a$.*

*It is an implicit assumption that every atom that occurs in $P$, $\alpha$, $\alpha'$, $\mathcal{A}$, or $a$ must belong to $\mathcal{L}$.*

*For any program $P$ we define its minimal semantics as:*

$SEM_{min}(P, \mathcal{L}) := \{\mathcal{A}|$ $\mathcal{A}$ *is a pure disjunction that belongs to every semantics over $\mathcal{L}$ of $P\}$*

This means that the minimal semantics of a program is defined only by the rules 1,2 and 3 just defined. For normal programs we defined a semantics as a binary relation between normal programs and literals that satisfies rules 2 and 3 given above, that is, we get rid of rule 1. For rule 2 note that of course $\mathcal{A}$ reduces to an atom.

Again, the key concept of this approach is the idea of a *transformation* rule.

The following transformations are defined in [5,8] and generalize the corresponding definitions for normal programs.

## Definition 3.4 (Basic Transformation Rules).

*A transformation rule is a binary relation on $Prog_{\mathcal{L}}$. The following transformation rules are called* basic. *Let a program $P \in Prog_{\mathcal{L}}$ be given.*

**RED$^+$:** *Replace a rule $\mathcal{A} \leftarrow \mathcal{B}^+, \neg\mathcal{B}^-$ by $\mathcal{A} \leftarrow \mathcal{B}^+, \neg(\mathcal{B}^- \cap HEAD(P))$.*
**RED$^-$:** *Delete a clause $\mathcal{A} \leftarrow \mathcal{B}^+, \neg\mathcal{B}^-$ if there is a clause $\mathcal{A}' \leftarrow true$ such that $\mathcal{A}' \subseteq \mathcal{B}^-$.*
**SUB:** *Delete a clause $\mathcal{A} \leftarrow \mathcal{B}^+, \neg\mathcal{B}^-$ if there is another clause $\mathcal{A}_1 \leftarrow \mathcal{B}_1^+, \neg\mathcal{B}_1^-$ such that $\mathcal{A}_1 \subseteq \mathcal{A}$, $\mathcal{B}_1^+ \subseteq \mathcal{B}^+$, $\mathcal{B}_1^- \subseteq \mathcal{B}^-$.*

*Example 3.1 (Transformation).*
Let $P$ be the program:

$a; b \leftarrow c, \neg c, \neg d.$
$a; c \leftarrow b.$
$c; d \leftarrow \neg e.$
$b \leftarrow \neg c, \neg d, \neg e.$

then $HEAD(P) = \{a, b, c, d\}$, and
$SEM_{min}(P, \mathcal{L}_P) = \emptyset$.
We can apply **RED**$^+$ to get the program $P_1$:

    a; b $\leftarrow$ c, $\neg$c, $\neg$d.

    a; c $\leftarrow$ b.

    c; d $\leftarrow$ true.

    b $\leftarrow$ $\neg$c, $\neg$d, $\neg$e.

If we apply **RED**$^+$ again, we get program $P_2$:

    a; b $\leftarrow$ c, $\neg$c, $\neg$d.

    a; c $\leftarrow$ b.

    c; d $\leftarrow$ *true*.

    b $\leftarrow$ $\neg$c, $\neg$d.

$SEM_{min}(P_2, \mathcal{L}_P) = \{\{c, d\}, \{c, d, a\}, \{c, d, b\}, \{c, d, a, b\}, \{\neg e\}, \ldots,$
$\{\neg a, \neg b, \neg c, \neg d, \neg e\}\}$.

Clearly $\{c, d, a\} \in SEM_{min}(P_2, \mathcal{L}_P)$ means that $c \vee d \vee a$ is a consequence in $SEM_{min}(P_2, \mathcal{L}_P)$. Now, we can apply **SUB** to get program $P_3$:

    a; c $\leftarrow$ b.

    c; d $\leftarrow$ *true*.

    b $\leftarrow$ $\neg$c, $\neg$d.

We will refer to this example again, that we will start calling our *basic example*.

Obviously, the just mentioned transformations are among the minimal requirements a *well-behaved* semantics should have (see [12]). For this reason, every semantics presented in this paper will be invariant under the transformations RED$^+$, RED$^-$ and SUB.

The following transformations are defined in [5,8].

**GPPE:** *(Generalized Principle of Partial Evaluation)* Suppose $P$ contains $\mathcal{A}$ $\leftarrow \mathcal{B}^+$, $\neg \mathcal{B}^-$ and we fix an occurrence of an atom $g \in \mathcal{B}^+$. Then we replace $\mathcal{A} \leftarrow \mathcal{B}^+$, $\neg \mathcal{B}^-$ by the $n$ clauses $(i = 1, \ldots, n)$

$$\mathcal{A} \cup (\mathcal{A}_i \backslash \{g\}) \leftarrow (\mathcal{B}^+ \backslash \{g\}) \cup B_i{}^+, \ \neg \mathcal{B}^- \cup \neg B_i{}^-$$

where $\mathcal{A}_i \leftarrow B_i{}^+$, $\neg B_i{}^- \in P$, (for $i = 1, \ldots, n$) are all clauses with $g \in \mathcal{A}_i$. If no such clauses exist, we simply delete the former clause.

**TAUT:** *(Tautology)* Suppose $P$ contains clause of the form: $\mathcal{A} \leftarrow \mathcal{B}^+$, $\neg \mathcal{B}^-$ and $\mathcal{A} \cap \mathcal{B}^+ \neq \emptyset$, then we delete the given clause.

Let $\mathcal{CS}_1$ be the rewriting system which contains, besides the basic transformation rules, the rules GPPE and TAUT. This system is introduced in [5] and is confluent and terminating as shown in [6].

**Definition 3.5 (D-WFS).** *The disjunctive wellfounded semantics D-WFS is defined as the weakest semantics satisfying SUB, RED$^+$, RED$^-$, GPPE and TAUT.*

Let us note that although the $\mathcal{CS}_1$ system has the nice property of confluence (and termination), its computational properties are not that efficient. In fact, computing the normal form of a program is exponential (even for normal programs, whereas it is known that the WFS ([14]) can be computed in quadratic time).

We introduce our proposed semantics D1-WFS and D1-WFS-COMP and give some important results about them. D1-WFS generalizes a system introduced in [7] from normal to disjunctive programs. Unless stated otherwise we assume that every program is a disjunctive program.

**Definition 3.6 (Dloop).**
*For a program $P$, let $unf(P) := \mathcal{L}_P \backslash MM(Definite(dis-nor(P)))$. The transformation **Dloop** reduces a program $P$ to $P_1 := \{\mathcal{A} \leftarrow \mathcal{B}^+, \neg\mathcal{B}^- \mid \mathcal{B}^+ \cap unf(P) = \emptyset\}$. We assume that the given transformation takes place only if $P \neq P_1$.*

Let **Dsuc** be the natural generalization of **suc** to disjunctive programs, formally:

**Definition 3.7 (Dsuc).**
*Suppose that $P$ is a program that includes a fact $a \leftarrow true$ and a clause $\mathcal{A} \leftarrow Body$ such that $a \in Body$. Then we replace this clause by the clause $\mathcal{A} \leftarrow Body \backslash \{a\}$.*

**Definition 3.8 ($\mathcal{CS}_2$).**
*Let $\mathcal{CS}_2$ be the rewriting system based on the transformations SUB, RED$^+$, RED$^-$, Dloop, Dsuc.*

**Theorem 3.1 (Confl. and termination of $\mathcal{CS}_2$).**
*The system $\mathcal{CS}_2$ is confluent and terminating. It induces a semantics that we call D1-WFS. If we consider only normal programs then its induced semantics corresponds to the well-founded semantics.*

**Proof:**(Sketch) It is easy to verify that each pair of transformations is confluent (also a given transformation with itself). So, the system is confluent. It is also immediate that every transformation reduces the size of the program, so we have termination. Finally, for normal programs, our system defines WFS, as shown in [1], **Q.E.D.**

Consider again $P$ from our *basic example* introduced before. As we noticed before, program $P$ reduces to $P_3$. But $P_3$ still reduces (by RED$^-$) to $P_4$, which is as $P_3$ but the third clause is removed. ¿From $P_4$ we can apply a Dloop reduction to get $P_5$: the single clause $c; d \leftarrow true$. $P_5$ is the normal form of the $\mathcal{CS}_2$ system.

For this example it turns out that D-WFS is equivalent to D1-WFS, but this is false in general. However for normal programs both systems are equivalent since they define WFS, but note that the normal forms for $\mathcal{CS}_1$ and $\mathcal{CS}_2$ are not necessarily the same. An advantage of $\mathcal{CS}_2$ over $\mathcal{CS}_1$ (again for normal programs) is that the normal form of $\mathcal{CS}_2$ is polynomial-time computable (as shown in [7]), while computing the normal form of $\mathcal{CS}_1$ is in general exponential (see [7]).

We now define a very strong semantics that includes the power of *comp*.

**Definition 3.9 (D1-WFS-COMP).**
*For every program P, we define $DCOMP(P):= comp(dis-nor(normal_{cs_2}(P)))$ over $\mathcal{L}_P$. We define D1-WFS-COMP(P) as the set of pure disjunctions that are logical consequences of DCOMP(P).*

It is immediate to see that D1-WFS-COMP is more powerful than D1-WFS. Take for instance the program $P$:

    p; q ← *true*.
    r ← ¬p.
    r ← ¬q.

Then D-WFS$(P)$ = $\{\{p,q\},\{p,q,r\}\}$ =D1-WFS$(P)$, however, D1-WFS-COMP$(P)$ at least derives $r$. In this case D1-WFS-COMP corresponds to STABLE, but this is not always true. Sometimes STABLE is inconsistent, while D1-WFS-COMP is not. Consider $P$ as:

    d; e ← *true*.
    c ← c.
    b ← a.
    a ← b.
    a ← ¬b, ¬c.

Note that STABLE is inconsistent while D1-WFS-COMP is not. This is because DCOMP(P) is:

    d ↔ ¬e.
    e ↔ ¬d.
    a ↔ (b ∨ ¬b).
    c ↔ *false*.

Due to its construction, we see that D1-WFS-COMP is similar to STABLE. However, STABLE is inconsistent more often than D1-WFS-COMP (at least for normal programs).

## 3.2   Datalog Programs

To obtain the semantics of a datalog disyunctive program, we first obtain the ground instanciation of the program and then we proceed as with propositional programs. For instance, the ground instanciation of program  2.6 is:

```
visit-europe(john) ; visit-australia(john) .
happy(john) ← visit-europe(john).
happy(john) ← visit-australia(john).
bankrupt(john) ← visit-europe(john), visit-australia(john).
prudent(john) ← ¬ visit-europe(john).
prudent(john) ← ¬ visit-australia(john).
dissappointed(john) ← ¬ visit-europe(john),
                      ¬ visit-australia(john).
```

## 3.3   Semantics of High-Level Logic Programs

The first step is to obtain the flattened form of every partial-order clause. Consider the following example:

```
f(X) ≥ g(h(X)) ; f(Z) ≥ {m(Z)} ← l(X).
```
then its flattened form is:
```
(f(X) ≥ X1 ← h(X)=X2, g(X2)=X1 ;
f(Z) ≥ Z1 ← m(Z)= Z2, scons(Z2, ∅, Z1)) ← l(X).
```
where *scons* has its well known intended meaning, see [16]. The second step is to transform this formula to a disjunctive clause. With this same example, we get:
```
f(X) ≥ X1; f(Z) ≥ Z1 ← h(X)=X2, g(X2)=X1,
        m(Z)=Z2, scons(Z2, ∅,Z1), l(X).
```
As the third step we translate the clause to its relational form. Again, using this example, we get:
```
f≥(X,X1); f≥(Z,Z1) ← h=(X,X2), g=(X2,X1),
        m=(Z,Z2), scons(Z2, ∅, Z1), l(X).
```
These steps can easily be defined for the general case. We suggest the reader to see [24] to check the details.

The fourth step is to add axioms that relate the predicate symbols $f_=$ with $f_≥$ for each functional symbol f. Let us consider again our example. The axioms for f in this case are as follows:

```
(1)     f=(Z, S)  ←   f≥ (Z, S),  ¬ f >(Z, S).
(2)     f>(Z, S)  ←   f≥(Z,S1),  S1 > S.
(3)     f≥(Z, S)  ←   f>(Z,S1),  S1 > S.
(4)     f≥ (Z, ⊥).
(5)     f≥(Z,C) ← f ≥(Z,C1), f≥(Z,C2),  lub(C1,C2,C).
```

We understand that S1 > S means that S1 ≥ S and S1 ≠ S. And $lub(C_1, C_2, C)$ interprets that $C$ is the least upper bound of $C_1$ and $C_2$. The first two clauses are the same (modulo notation) as in definition 4.2 in [31]. Clause (5) is not useful for total-order domains. It is easy to see that symmetric definitions can be provided for $f_≤$ symbols.

Now we need to instanciate the translated program. In this paper we restrict our attention to finite ground programs. By adding simple type declarations we can ensure to get a finite ground program. In this case, we borrow the declaration style of Relationlog and assume that the original program defines (as in our current example):

```
TYPE a, b, c: el.
PREDICATE l(el).
FUNCTION f(onedigit) --> {el}.
FUNCTION h(onedigit) --> {el}.
FUNCTION m(onedigit) --> {el}.
FUNCTION g({el}) --> {el}.
```

So, with eight new constant symbols we can represent the codomain of s. Therefore, the definition of lub, scons and > can be given by a finite extensional database. Thus, we can now apply our approach as with finite propositional programs.

Let us consider again the *Reach* program again. Assume also that we include its type definition as follows:

```
TYPE 1,2,3: node.
```

```
PREDICATE edge(node,node).
FUNCTION r(node) ← {node}.
r(X) ≥ {X}.
r(X) ≥ r(Z) ← edge(X,Z).
```

The relevant clauses of the translated program are:

```
TYPE 1,2,3: node.
```
PREDICATEedge(node, node), $r_\geq$(node, {node}), $r_=$(node, {node}),
          $r_>$(node, {node}).
PREDICATEscons(node, {node}), lub({node}, {node}), {node} > {node}.

$r_\geq$(X, Y) ← scons(X, ∅, Y).[2]
$r_\geq$(X, Z) ← edge(X, Y), $r_=$(Y, Z).
$r_\geq$(X, s).
$r_\geq$(Z, S) ← $r_\geq$(Z, S1), S1 > S.
$r_\geq$(Z, S) ← $r_\geq$(Z, S1), $r_\geq$(Z, S2), lub(S1,S2,S).
$r_=$(Z, S) ← $r_\geq$(Z, S), ¬ $r_>$(Z,S).
$r_>$(Z, S) ← $r_\geq$(Z, S1), S1 > S.

As alredy mentioned, the type restrictions are used to ensure that predicates
lub, scons and > can be defined by a finite datalog extensional database. For
instance, for lub we can declare:

```
lub(s, s12, s12).
lub(s12, s13, s123).
```

and so on. Where s represents the empty set, s12 represents the $\{1, 2\}$ set. We
only need 8 constants to represent all our required sets.

Now consider the following EDB respect to edge:

$EDB_1 = \{$edge$(1, 2).$ edge$(3, 1).\}.$

It turns out that WFS defines a total model that agrees with the intended model.
In this model $r_=(3,$ s123$)$ is true. STABLE as well as D1-WFS-COMP define
the intended model. Now, consider the following EDB:

$EDB_2 = \{$edge$(1, 2).$ edge$(3, 1).$ edge$(1, 1).\}.$

We expect to keep the same semantics and this indeed true for WFS, STABLE
and D1-WFS-COMP. Now consider the EDB:

$EDB_3 = \{$edge$(1, 2).$ edge$(3, 1).$ edge$(2, 1).\}.$

WFS defines most of the atoms as undefined and the stable semantics is inconsistent. However D1-WFS-COMP defines only one model, which is the intended
model. Assume that we write rc for $r_\geq$, re for $r_=$, and rns for $r_>$. Then, some
rules that DCOMP produce of the above program are:

```
rc(1,a1).
rc(2,a2).
rc(3,a3).
re(1,a1) < - > (-rns(1,a1)).
re(2,a2) < - > (-rns(2,a2)).
re(3,a3) < - > (-rns(3,a3)).
rc(2,a1) < - > ((re(1,a1)) | (re(2,a1)) | (rns(2,a1))).
```

---

[2] To get rid of the set-constructor that has a variable as an argument in $r_\geq$(X, {X}).

```
rc(3,a1) < - > ((re(1,a1)) | (re(3,a1)) | (rns(3,a1))).
rc(1,a2) < - > ((re(1,a2)) | (re(2,a2)) | (rns(1,a2))).
rc(2,a12) < - > ((re(1,a12)) | (re(2,a12)) | (rc(2,a1)) | (rc(2,a1))).
re(2,a1) < - > (-rns(2,a1) & rc(2,a1)).
rc(3,a13) < - > ((re(3,a13)) | (rns(3,a13)) | (rc(3,a1)) | (rc(3,a1))).
re(3,a1) < - > (-rns(3,a1) & rc(3,a1)).
rc(1,a12) < - > ((re(1,a12)) | (re(2,a12)) | (rc(1,a2)) | (rc(1,a2))).
re(1,a2) < - > (-rns(1,a2) & rc(1,a2)).
```

Our program has only one model, which is the intended model.

We computed the semantics all our examples by hand and also by using several programs that our students have written as well as the theorem prover OTTER.

## 4   Conclusion

We presented our notion of high-level logic programming. It includes standard logic programming plus disjunctions, sets and partial-order clauses. We presented several and different challenging problems considered in the literature. Our approach defines the intended meaning of each of them. Our paradigm combines several ideas from our earlier work and it seems promising. Future research is required to fully understand it.

## Acknowledgments

This research was supported in parts by grants from CONACyT (C065-E9605) and Departamento de Computación del CINVESTAV, IPN.

## References

1. J. Arrazola, J. Dix y M. Osorio. Confluent term Rewriting Systems for Non-Monotonic Reasoning. Computacin y Sistemas, II (2-3). pp. 104-123, 1999. México.
2. S. Abiteboul and S. Grumbach, "A Rule-Based Language with Functions and Sets," *ACM Transactions on Database Systems*, 16(1):1-30,1991.
3. C. Beeri, S. Naqvi, et al, "Sets and Negation in a Logic Database Language (LDL1)," *Proc. 6th ACM Principles of Database Systems*, pp. 21-37, 1987.
4. S. Brass, J. Dix, T. Przymusinski, "Super Logic Programs," *Proc. of the Fifth Intern. Conf. on Principles of Knowledge Repr. and Reasoning (KR '96)*, L. C. Aiello, J. Doyle and S. C. Shapiro (eds.), Morgan Kaufmann, San Francisco 1996.
5. Stefan Brass and Jürgen Dix. Characterizations of the Disjunctive Stable Semantics by Partial Evaluation. *Journal of Logic Programming*, 32(3):207–228, 1997. (Extended abstract appeared in: Characterizations of the Stable Semantics by Partial Evaluation *LPNMR, Proceedings of the Third International Conference, Kentucky*, pages 85–98, 1995. LNCS 928, Springer.).

6. Stefan Brass and Jürgen Dix. Characterizations of the Disjunctive Well-founded Semantics: Confluent Calculi and Iterated GCWA. *Journal of Automated Reasoning*, to appear, 1998. (Extended abstract appeared in: Characterizing D-WFS: Confluence and Iterated GCWA. *Logics in Artificial Intelligence, JELIA '96*, pages 268–283, 1996. Springer, LNCS 1126.).

7. Stefan Brass, Ulrich Zukowski, and Burkhardt Freitag. Transformation Based Bottom-Up Computation of the Well-Founded Model. In J. Dix, L. Pereira, and T. Przymusinski, editors, *Nonmonotonic Extensions of Logic Programming*, LNAI 1216, pages 171–201. Springer, Berlin, 1997.

8. Gerhard Brewka and Jürgen Dix. Knowledge representation with logic programs. Technical report, Tutorial Notes of the 12th European Conference on Artificial Intelligence (ECAI '96), 1996. Also appeare d as Technical Report 15/96, Dept. of CS of the University of Koblenz-Landau. Will appear as Chapter 6 in *Handbook of Philosophical Logic*, 2nd edition (1998), Volume 6, Methodologies.

9. Keith L. Clark. Negation as Failure. In H. Gallaire and J. Minker, editors, *Logic and Data-Bases*, pages 293–322. Plenum, New York, 1978.

10. Dovier, A., Omodeo, E. G., Pontelli, E., and Rossi, G. "{log }: A Logic Programming Language with Finite Sets," *Proc. 8th International Conference of Logic Programming*, pp. 111–124, Paris, June 1991.

11. Jürgen Dix. A Framework for Representing and Characterizing Semantics of Logic Programs. In B. Nebel, C. Rich, and W. Swartout, editors, *Principles of Knowledge Representation and Reas oning: Proceedings of the Third International Conference (KR '92)*, pages 591–602. San Mateo, CA, Morgan Kaufmann, 1992.

12. Jürgen Dix. A Classification-Theory of Semantics of Normal Logic Programs: II. Weak Properties. *Fundamenta Informaticae*, XXII(3):257–288, 1995.

13. G. Ganguly, S. Greco, and C. Zaniolo, "Minimum and maximum predicates in logic programs", *Proceedings of the ACM Symposium on Principles of Database Systems*, pp 154-163, 1991.

14. Allen van Gelder, Kenneth A. Ross, and John S. Schlipf. The well-founded semantics for general logic programs. *Journal of the ACM*, 38:620–650, 1991.

15. B. Jayaraman, "Implementation of Subset-Equational Programs," *Journal of Logic Programming*, 11(4):299-324, 1992.

16. D. Jana, "Semantics of Subset-Logic Languages," dissertation submitted to SUNY-Buffalo, 1994.

17. B. Jayaraman, M. Osorio and K. Moon, "Partial Order Programming (revisited)", *Proc. AMAST*, Springer-Verlag, July 1995.

18. Jayaraman, B. and Plaisted, D. A., "Programming with Equations, Subsets, and Relations," *Proc. North American Conference of Logic Programming 89*, pp. 1051-1068, Cleveland, October 1989.

19. Kuper, G. M., "Logic Programming with Sets," *JCSS*, 41(1):44-64, 1990.

20. J. Lloyd, "Foundations of Logic Programming," (2 ed.) Springer-Verlag, 1987.

21. M. Liu., 'Relationlog: A typed extension to Datalog with Sets and Tuples," *Proc. ISLP95* pp. 83-97. MIT Press. June 1995.

22. John W. Lloyd. *Foundations of Logic Programming*. Springer, Berlin, 1987. 2nd edition.

23. Mauricio Osorio y B. Jayaraman Integrating the Completion and the Well Founded Semantics. Titulo del libro: Progress in Artificial Intelligence IB-ERAMIA 98. Ed. Springer-Verlag. ISBN 3-540-64992-1. pp 230-241. Alemania 1998.

24. M. Osorio and B. Jayaraman, "Aggregation and Negation as Failure", *New Genetation Computing*, 17(3), 1999.

25. M. Osorio, B. Jayaraman and J. C. Nieves "Declarative Pruning in a Functional Query Language", accepted ICLP99.

26. Mauricio Osorio, B. Jayaraman and D. Plaisted "Theory of partial-order programming," in *Science of computer programming Journal, (34)3*, 1999.

27. M. Osorio, B. Jayaraman, "Aggregation and WFS$^+$", In J. Dix, L. Pereida, and T. Przymusinski, editors, *Nonmonotonic Extensions of Logic Programming*, LNAI 1216, pp. 71-90. Springer, Berlin 1997

28. Mauricio Osorio, "Semantics of Partial order programming," presented at JELIA98, Germany, Oct. 1998 appears in *Proc. JELIA98*, pp. 47-61, LNAI 1489, Springer-Verlag, 1998.

29. K. Ross, "Modular Stratification and Magic Sets for DATALOG Programs with negation", *Journal of the ACM*, Vol. 41, No. 6, November 1994, pp. 1216-1266.

30. K.A. Ross and Y. Sagiv, "Monotonic Aggregation in Deductive Databases," *Proc. 11th ACM Symposium on Principles of Database Systems*, pp. 114-126, San Diego, 1992.

31. A. Van Gelder, "The Well-Founded Semantics of Aggregation," *Proc. ACM 11th Principles of Database Systems*, pp. 127-138, San Diego, 1992.

# Clausal Deductive Databases and a General Framework for Semantics in Disjunctive Deductive Databases

Dietmar Seipel

University of Würzburg, Dept. of Computer Science
Am Hubland, D – 97074 Würzburg, Germany
@seipel@informatik.uni-wuerzburg.de
Tel. +49 931 888 5026, Fax. +49 931 888 4600

**Abstract.** In this paper we will investigate the novel concept of *clausal deductive databases* (cd–databases), which are special normal deductive databases – i.e. deductive databases which may contain default negation in rule bodies – over a meta–language $\mathcal{L}^{cd}$ with a fixed set of predicate symbols, namely *dis*, *con*, and some *built–in* predicate symbols. The arguments of the literals in $\mathcal{L}^{cd}$ are given by disjunctive and conjunctive clauses of a basic first–order language $\mathcal{L}$ (which are considered as terms in $\mathcal{L}^{cd}$). On the other hand, *disjunctive deductive databases* (dd–databases) extend normal deductive databases by allowing for disjunctions (rather than just single atoms or literals) in rule heads – next to default negation in rule bodies.

We will present an *embedding* of dd–databases into cd–databases: a dd–database $\mathcal{D}$ is transformed into a cd–database $\mathcal{D}^{cd}$, which talks about the clauses of $\mathcal{D}$ – rather than just the literals. Thus, cd–databases provide a *flexible framework* for declaratively specifying the semantics of dd–databases. We can fix a standard *control strategy*, e.g. stable model or well–founded semantics, and vary the *logical description* $\mathcal{D}^{cd}$ for specifying different semantics. The *transformed database* $\mathcal{D}^{cd}$ usually consists of a part $\mathcal{D}^{\otimes}$ which naturally expresses the rules of $\mathcal{D}$, and two generic parts which are independent of $\mathcal{D}$: $\mathcal{D}^{logic}$ specifies *logical inference rules* like resolution and subsumption, and $\mathcal{D}^{cwa}$ specifies non–monotonic inference rules like *closed–world–assumptions*.

In particular we will show that the *hyperresolution* consequence operator $\mathcal{T}_{\mathcal{D}}^s$ for dd–databases without default negation can be expressed as a standard consequence operator $\mathcal{T}_{\mathcal{D}^{cd}}$, for a suitable transformed database $\mathcal{D}^{cd}$, where $\mathcal{D}^{logic} = \mathcal{D}^{cwa} = \emptyset$. For dd–databases with default negation we can show that the semantics of *stable models* can be characterized by adding suitable sets $\mathcal{D}^{logic}$ and $\mathcal{D}^{cwa}$. Moreover, we will define a new semantics for dd–databases which we will call *stable state semantics*; it is based on Herbrand states rather than Herbrand interpretations.

## Keywords

disjunctive deductive databases, clausal logic programming, program transformations, non–monotonic reasoning, stable models, closed–world–assumptions

K.-D. Schewe, B. Thalheim (Eds.): FoIKS 2000, LNCS 1762, pp. 241–259, 2000.

# 1   Introduction

In the last twenty years the concept of relational databases has been extended in various ways, e.g. to deductive databases, object–oriented databases, and active databases [17, 25]. *Deductive databases* [2] provide a very powerful formalism for representing knowledge in the form of facts – which correspond to the tuples in a relational database – and different forms of inference rules. The *semantics* of normal deductive databases with rules that may contain default negation in rule bodies, is well–understood, and it is defined using special concepts of *non–monotonic reasoning*. The most prominent approaches are the *stable model semantics* [8] and the *well–founded semantics* [24]. *Disjunctive deductive databases* [11] allow for disjunctions – rather than just single atoms or literals – in rule heads, next to default negation in rule bodies; thus it becomes possible to specify knowledge with uncertain conclusions. For disjunctive deductive databases, the situation is much more complicated; there exist various generalizations of the stable model semantics [16, 5] and the well–founded semantics [11, 1], including some semantics dealing with three or more truth values[1].

In this paper we will investigate the novel concept of *clausal deductive databases*, which are special normal deductive databases over a meta–language $\mathcal{L}^{cd}$ with a small set of predicate symbols which are talking about the clauses of a basic first–order language $\mathcal{L}$. E.g., the following inference rule is an allowed rule:

$$r = dis(X_d) \leftarrow complement(X_d, X_c) \wedge not\, con(X_c).$$

The arguments of the so–called cd–atoms $dis(X_d)$ and $con(X_c)$ can be arbitrary disjunctive or conjunctive formulas $X_d, X_c \in \mathcal{L}$, respectively. In addition, there are so–called bi–atoms, e.g. $complement(X_d, X_c)$, $subsumes(X_d, X_d')$ or $resolvent(X_1, X_2, X_d)$, with special *built–in* predicate symbols with a fixed, natural interpretation known from predicate logic. The rule $r$ above represents a *closed–world–assumption* for inferring knowledge (the disjunction $X_d$) in the absence of the complementary knowledge (the conjunction $X_c$)[2].

CD–databases provide a flexible *framework for specifying semantics* of dd–databases in a *declarative* way. It is based on the idea of transforming a dd–database $\mathcal{D}$ into a cd–database $\mathcal{D}^{cd}$, the cd–*transformation* of $\mathcal{D}$, and then defining the (disjunctive) semantics of $\mathcal{D}$ based on a well–understood (normal) semantics for $\mathcal{D}^{cd}$. We will show that the (disjunctive) stable model semantics of $\mathcal{D}$ can be characterized by simply using the (normal) stable model semantics of $\mathcal{D}^{cd}$. In a more refined approach we will use a special *fixpoint condition* based on $\mathcal{D}^{cd}$ for defining a new semantics, called *stable state semantics*, which is able to give plausible interpretations for dd–databases for which standard semantics (e.g. stable or partial stable models) are *inconsistent*, i.e. do not provide any interpretations.

For some extensions of deductive databases without default negation we will show that it is possible to use the principle of reasoning known from the definite consequence operator $\mathcal{T}_\mathcal{D}$, as given by Lloyd [10]. We will define a *generic*

---

[1]   *true, false, undefined, overdefined*, etc.
[2]   possible instantiations could be $X_d = \neg p(a) \vee \neg q(b)$ and $X_c = p(a) \wedge q(b)$

*consequence operator* $\mathcal{T}_{\mathcal{D}}^{\odot,\geq} : 2^{\mathcal{X}} \to 2^{\mathcal{X}}$ that is parameterized with a natural transformation, which maps $\mathcal{D}$ to a definite deductive database $\mathcal{D}^{\odot}$, and with a subsumption relation $\geq$. We will prove that $\mathcal{T}_{\mathcal{D}}^{\odot,\geq}$ is *monotonic* and *continuous* on the lattice $\langle 2^{\mathcal{X}}, \subseteq \rangle$. Then the disjunctive hyperresolution consequence operator $\mathcal{T}_{\mathcal{D}}^{s} : 2^{D_{HB_{\mathcal{D}}}} \to 2^{D_{HB_{\mathcal{D}}}}$ of Minker and Rajasekar [13] for dd–databases $\mathcal{D}$ without default negation – whose disjunctive Herbrand base is denoted by $D_{HB_{\mathcal{D}}}$ – is formulated as a definite consequence operator $\mathcal{T}_{\mathcal{D}}^{\odot,\geq}$ for $\mathcal{X} = \{dis(\alpha)|\alpha \in D_{HB_{\mathcal{D}}}\}$. The transformation $\mathcal{D}^{\odot}$ can be extended for the case of dd–databases with default negation by adding a definite representation of the *logical axioms* for binary resolution and subsumption and by adding suitable *closed–world–assumptions*, cf. Reiter [18].

The advantage of transforming a disjunctive deductive database $\mathcal{D}$ into a normal deductive database $\mathcal{D}^{cd}$ is that it becomes possible to use *standard techniques* for defining a semantics and *standard tools* for evaluating a database under this semantics [4, 15, 19, 23, 26]. In a first, prototypical implementation we have used the system Smodels developed by Niemelä [15], which can compute well–founded and stable model semantics for normal deductive databases.

Also other semantics of disjunctive deductive databases have been characterized or computed based on *transformations*. E.g., Brass and Dix [1] have used *partial evaluation* for defining their *disjunctive well–founded semantics*; Seipel et al. [21] have used the tu–*transformation* for characterizing *partial stable models*; Fernández et al. [6] and Seipel [22] have used the *evidential transformation* for characterizing *total stable models*, and *evidential stable models*, respectively.

The rest of the paper is organized as follows: In Section 2 we present the syntax of dd–databases and the stable model semantics. In Section 3 we define the syntax of cd–databases, and we also define clausal Herbrand interpretations for dd–databases. In Section 4 we develop the generic $\mathcal{T}_{\mathcal{D}}$–operator, and we show how the disjunctive consequence operator $\mathcal{T}_{\mathcal{D}}^{s}$ can be formulated. Section 5 deals with a characterization of the stable models semantics using clausal logic programming, and a generalization that is called *stable state semantics*.

## 2    Basic Definitions and Notations

### 2.1    Syntax of Disjunctive Deductive Databases

Given a first order language $\mathcal{L}$, a *disjunctive deductive database (dd–database)* $\mathcal{D}$ consists of logical inference rules of the form

$$r = A_1 \vee \ldots \vee A_k \leftarrow B_1 \wedge \ldots \wedge B_m \wedge not\, C_1 \wedge \ldots \wedge not\, C_n, \qquad (1)$$

where $A_i, i \in \langle 1, k \rangle$, $B_i, i \in \langle 1, m \rangle$, and $C_i, i \in \langle 1, n \rangle$, are atoms in the language $\mathcal{L}$, $k, m, n \in \mathbb{N}_0$, and *not* is the negation–by–default operator.[3] The set of all

---

[3] By $\mathbb{N}_+$ we denote the set $\{1, 2, 3, \ldots\}$ of positive natural numbers, whereas $\mathbb{N}_0$ denotes the set $\{0, 1, 2, \ldots\}$ of all natural numbers. $\langle n, m \rangle$ denotes the interval $\{n, n+1, \ldots, m\}$ of natural numbers.

*ground instances* of the rules in $\mathcal{D}$ is denoted by $gnd\,(\mathcal{D})$. A rule is called a *fact* if $m = n = 0$, and it is called a *denial rule* if $k = 0$. A rule (or database) is called *positive–disjunctive* if it does not contain default negation (i.e. $n = 0$). It is called *normal* if $k = 1$, and *definite* if $k = 1$ and $n = 0$. A rule $r$ of the form (1) above is denoted for short as

$$r = \alpha \leftarrow \beta \wedge not\cdot\gamma,$$

where $\alpha = A_1 \vee \ldots \vee A_k$, $\beta = B_1 \wedge \ldots \wedge B_m$, and $\gamma = C_1 \vee \ldots \vee C_n$.[4] $\alpha$ is called the *head* of $r$, $\beta$ is called the *positive body*, and $not\cdot\gamma$ is called the *negative body* of $r$.

The Herbrand base $HB_{\mathcal{D}}$ of a dd–database $\mathcal{D}$ contains all ground atoms over the language of $\mathcal{D}$, and $HL_{\mathcal{D}} = HB_{\mathcal{D}} \cup \{ \neg A \,|\, A \in HB_{\mathcal{D}} \}$ contains all literals over $HB_{\mathcal{D}}$. The semantics of dd–databases will be based on a set of ground disjunctions, a so–called Herbrand state, or a set of Herbrand interpretations.

1. The *disjunctive*, the *negative*, the *general*, and the *conjunctive Herbrand base* of $\mathcal{D}$ are given by $DHB_{\mathcal{D}}$, $NHB_{\mathcal{D}}$, $GHB_{\mathcal{D}}$, and $CHB_{\mathcal{D}}$, respectively:

$$DHB_{\mathcal{D}} = \{ A_1 \vee \ldots \vee A_k \mid A_i \in HB_{\mathcal{D}}, \text{ for } i \in \langle 1, k \rangle,\ k \in \mathbb{N}_0 \},$$
$$NHB_{\mathcal{D}} = \{ \neg A_1 \vee \ldots \vee \neg A_k \mid A_i \in HB_{\mathcal{D}}, \text{ for } i \in \langle 1, k \rangle,\ k \in \mathbb{N}_0 \},$$
$$GHB_{\mathcal{D}} = \{ L_1 \vee \ldots \vee L_k \mid L_i \in HL_{\mathcal{D}}, \text{ for } i \in \langle 1, k \rangle,\ k \in \mathbb{N}_0 \},$$
$$CHB_{\mathcal{D}} = \{ L_1 \wedge \ldots \wedge L_k \mid L_i \in HL_{\mathcal{D}}, \text{ for } i \in \langle 1, k \rangle,\ k \in \mathbb{N}_0 \}.$$

2. An *Herbrand state* is a set $S$ of formulas. It is called *disjunctive*, *negative*, *general* and *conjunctive*, if $S \subseteq DHB_{\mathcal{D}}$, $S \subseteq NHB_{\mathcal{D}}$, $S \subseteq GHB_{\mathcal{D}}$, and $S \subseteq CHB_{\mathcal{D}}$. respectively.

We will sometimes also write $HB_{\mathcal{L}}$, $HL_{\mathcal{L}}$, $DHB_{\mathcal{L}}$, $NHB_{\mathcal{L}}$, $GHB_{\mathcal{L}}$, and $CHB_{\mathcal{L}}$, if we are interested in the language $\mathcal{L}$ rather than the database $\mathcal{D}$. Disjunctions and conjunctions will be treated like sets of literals. Thus, we will identify a disjunction $L_1 \vee \ldots \vee L_k \in GHB_{\mathcal{D}}$ with its permutations $L_{\pi(1)} \vee \ldots \vee L_{\pi(k)}$. The empty disjunction (conjunction) with $k = 0$ literals will be denoted by $\Box_d$ ($\Box_c$). Note that $\Box_d$ is an element of all of $DHB_{\mathcal{D}}$, $NHB_{\mathcal{D}}$, and $GHB_{\mathcal{D}}$, and that $\Box_c$ is an element of $CHB_{\mathcal{D}}$. Note also that singleton disjunctions or conjunctions with $k = 1$ literals are identified with literals; as a consequence we get $GHB_{\mathcal{D}} \cap CHB_{\mathcal{D}} = HL_{\mathcal{D}}$. The common *subsumption* relation for ground disjunctions $\alpha = L_1 \vee \ldots \vee L_n \in GHB_{\mathcal{D}}$, $\alpha' = L'_1 \vee \ldots \vee L'_m \in GHB_{\mathcal{D}}$, is defined by $\alpha \trianglerighteq \alpha'$ iff $\{ L_1, \ldots, L_n \} \subseteq \{ L'_1, \ldots, L'_m \}$. The *canonical form* of a general Herbrand state $S \subseteq GHB_{\mathcal{D}}$ is defined as the set $can_{\trianglerighteq}(S)$ of minimal elements of $S$ w.r.t. subsumption, and the *expanded form* of $S$ is defined as the set $exp_{\trianglerighteq}(S)$ of all $\alpha \in GHB_{\mathcal{D}}$ that are subsumed by some $\alpha' \in S$:

$$can_{\trianglerighteq}(S) = \{ \alpha \in S \mid \not\exists \alpha' \in S : \alpha' \neq \alpha,\ \alpha' \trianglerighteq \alpha \},$$
$$exp_{\trianglerighteq}(S) = \{ \alpha \in GHB_{\mathcal{D}} \mid \exists \alpha' \in S : \alpha' \trianglerighteq \alpha \}.$$

---

[4] Note that $\gamma$ is a disjunction, and, according to De Morgan's law, $not\cdot\gamma$ is taken to be a conjunction.

Obviously, it holds $can_{\triangleright}(S) \subseteq S \subseteq exp_{\triangleright}(S)$. For a literal $L \in HL_{\mathcal{D}}$ we define the *formal complement* $\neg \cdot L = \neg A$, if $L = A \in HB_{\mathcal{D}}$ is an atom, and $\neg \cdot L = A$, if $L = \neg A \in HL_{\mathcal{D}}$ is a negated atom. For a general disjunction $\alpha = L_1 \vee \ldots \vee L_k \in GHB_{\mathcal{D}}$ we define the conjunction

$$\neg \cdot \alpha = \neg \cdot (L_1 \vee \ldots \vee L_k) = \neg \cdot L_1 \wedge \ldots \wedge \neg \cdot L_k \in CHB_{\mathcal{D}}$$

to be the *formal complement* of $\alpha$ according to the De Morgan pattern, and likewise we define $\neg \cdot \beta = \neg \cdot L_1 \vee \ldots \vee \neg \cdot L_k$ for $\beta = L_1 \wedge \ldots \wedge L_k \in CHB_{\mathcal{D}}$.

## 2.2   Stable Model Semantics

An *Herbrand interpretation* of a dd–database $\mathcal{D}$ is given by a subset $I \subseteq HB_{\mathcal{D}}$. It defines a mapping $I: HB_{\mathcal{D}} \rightarrow \{t, f\}$ assigning a truth value "t" (*true*) or "f" (*false*) to each $A \in HB_{\mathcal{D}}$: $I(A) = t \Leftrightarrow A \in I$. [5] $I$ *satisfies* of a ground rule $r = \alpha \leftarrow \beta \wedge not \cdot \gamma$ if

$$I(\beta) \wedge I(not \cdot \gamma) = t \Rightarrow I(\alpha) = t,$$

where $I(not \cdot \gamma) = \neg I(\gamma)$. $I$ is an *Herbrand model* of $\mathcal{D}$ if $I$ satisfies all ground instances $r \in gnd(\mathcal{D})$ of the rules of $\mathcal{D}$. $I$ is a *minimal model* of $\mathcal{D}$ if $I$ is an Herbrand model of $\mathcal{D}$ and there is no other Herbrand model $J$ of $\mathcal{D}$ such that $J \subsetneq I$. The set of all minimal models of $\mathcal{D}$ is denoted by $\mathcal{MM}_2(\mathcal{D})$. For positive–disjunctive deductive databases $\mathcal{D}$ the semantics is given by $\mathcal{MM}_2(\mathcal{D})$.

The semantics of dd–databases in general is defined based on a more general class of Herbrand models, the *stable models*. These are defined in terms of the minimal models $M$ of the *Gelfond–Lifschitz transformation* (GL–transformation, [8, 16]) of $\mathcal{D}$, which is a special ground positive–disjunctive database $\mathcal{D}^M$ derived from those rules of $gnd(\mathcal{D})$ whose negative body is true in $M$ (i.e. $C_i \notin M$, for all $C_i$ in $not \cdot \gamma = not C_1 \wedge \ldots \wedge not C_n$).

**Definition 2.1 (Stable Models, [8, 16]).**
Let $M$ be a Herbrand interpretation of a disjunctive deductive database $\mathcal{D}$.

1. The GL–transformation $\mathcal{D}^M$ of $\mathcal{D}$ w.r.t. $M$ is

$$\mathcal{D}^M = \{ \alpha \leftarrow \beta \mid \text{there exists } \alpha \leftarrow \beta \wedge not \cdot \gamma \in gnd(\mathcal{D}),$$
$$\text{such that } M(not \cdot \gamma) = t \}.$$

2. $M$ is called *stable model* of $\mathcal{D}$ if $M \in \mathcal{MM}_2(\mathcal{D}^M)$. The set of all stable models of $\mathcal{D}$ is denoted by $STABLE_2(\mathcal{D})$.

---

[5] For $A_i \in HB_{\mathcal{D}}$, $i \in \langle 1, k \rangle$, and a connective $\oplus \in \{\vee, \wedge\}$ we define $I(A_1 \oplus \ldots \oplus A_k) = I(A_1) \oplus \ldots \oplus I(A_k)$. For $k = 0$, the empty disjunction $\square_d$ (i.e. $\oplus = \vee$) evaluates to $I(\square_d) = f$, whereas the empty conjunction $\square_c$ (i.e. $\oplus = \wedge$) evaluates to $I(\square_c) = t$.

*Example 2.1.* For the dd–database

$$\mathcal{D}_{win} = \{ \; win(X) \leftarrow move(X, Y) \wedge not \; win(Y) \; \} \; \cup \; S,$$
$$S = \{ \; move(a, b) \vee move(a, c), \; move(b, d), \; move(c, d) \; \},$$

we get a set with two stable models, which coincide on the subset $I$ of atoms:

$$\mathcal{STABLE}_2(\mathcal{D}_{win}) = \{ \; \{ \; move(a, b) \; \} \cup I, \; \{ \; move(a, c) \; \} \cup I \; \},$$
$$I = \{ \; move(b, d), \; move(c, d), \; win(b), \; win(c) \; \}.$$

For $M = \{ \; move(a, b) \; \} \cup I$ we get that $M(not \; win(y)) = \mathsf{t}$ iff $y \in \{a, d\}$, and thus we get $M \in \mathcal{MM}_2(\mathcal{D}_{win}^M)$ for the GL–transformation $\mathcal{D}_{win}^M$:

$$\mathcal{D}_{win}^M = \{ \; win(x) \leftarrow move(x, y) \mid x \in \{a, b, c, d\}, \; y \in \{a, d\} \; \} \; \cup \; S.$$

All of the atoms in $I$ and the disjunction $move(a, b) \vee move(a, c)$ are consequences of $\mathcal{D}_{win}$ under the stable model semantics.

## 3    Clausal Deductive Databases

In the context of default negation and disjunction one can generalize the notion of a (total) Herbrand interpretation in two ways.

Firstly, one can allow for a third truth value "u" (*undefined*), which leads to partial Herbrand interpretations $I \colon HB_\mathcal{D} \rightarrow \{ \; \mathsf{t}, \mathsf{f}, \mathsf{u} \; \}$. If a semantics is given by a set $\mathcal{I}$ of partial Herbrand interpretations, then a general Herbrand state $S \subseteq GHB_\mathcal{D}$ containing all disjunctive consequences $\alpha \in GHB_\mathcal{D}$ that hold in all $I \in \mathcal{I}$ can be assigned to $\mathcal{D}$. Partial Herbrand interpretations have been used by Przymusinski, cf. [16], who generalized the concept of stable model to *partial stable models*. There exists a characterization of the partial stable models of a disjunctive deductive database $\mathcal{D}$ in terms of the stable models of a naturally transformed database $\mathcal{D}^{tu}$, cf. [21].

Secondly, a semantics can also be given by a set $S$ of so–called *clausal Herbrand interpretations*, which are special general Herbrand states, without referring to total or partial Herbrand interpretations at all. In this paper we will introduce the new concept of a *clausal deductive databases*, which are special normal deductive databases over a restricted set of predicate symbols. In Section 5, we will transform a dd–database $\mathcal{D}$ into a corresponding cd–database $\mathcal{D}^{cd}$ and then derive the clausal Herbrand models of $\mathcal{D}$ by simply applying the standard stable model semantics to $\mathcal{D}^{cd}$.

### 3.1    Partial and Clausal Herbrand Interpretations

A *partial Herbrand interpretation* of a disjunctive deductive database $\mathcal{D}$ is given by a subset $I \subseteq HL_\mathcal{D}$, such that $I$ does not contain both an atom $A \in HB_\mathcal{D}$ and its negation $\neg A$, i.e. $I \cap \neg I = \emptyset$. It defines a mapping $I \colon HB_{\mathcal{D}} \to \{\, \mathsf{t}, \mathsf{f}, \mathsf{u}\,\}$ on ground atoms by

$$I(A) = \begin{cases} \mathsf{t}, & \text{iff } A \in I \\ \mathsf{f}, & \text{iff } \neg A \in I \\ \mathsf{u}, & \text{otherwise.} \end{cases}$$

If for each atom $A \in HB_{\mathcal{D}}$, $I$ contains either $A$ or $\neg A$, then $I$ defines a *total Herbrand interpretation* or Herbrand interpretation for short. In this case, it is sufficient to represent $I$ by its set of true atoms (since there are no undefined atoms), which we did in Section 2. The truth values of disjunctions $\alpha \in GHB_{\mathcal{D}}$ and conjunctions $\beta \in CHB_{\mathcal{D}}$ are defined based on the *Boolean operations* "$\vee$", "$\wedge$" and "$\neg$" in three–valued logic, which are given in Figure 1. The *truth ordering* on the three truth values is given by $\mathsf{f} \leq_t \mathsf{u} \leq_t \mathsf{t}$.

| $\wedge$ | t | f | u |
|---|---|---|---|
| t | t | f | u |
| f | f | f | f |
| u | u | f | u |

| $\vee$ | t | f | u |
|---|---|---|---|
| t | t | t | t |
| f | t | f | u |
| u | t | u | u |

| $\neg$ | |
|---|---|
| t | f |
| f | t |
| u | u |

**Fig. 1.** Boolean operations in three–valued logic

A *clausal Herbrand interpretation* is given by a general Herbrand state $S \subseteq GHB_{\mathcal{D}}$ that is closed under binary resolution and subsumption. Obviously, we can *abbreviate* a clausal Herbrand interpretation $S$ simply by its set $can_{\unrhd}(S)$ of minimal elements w.r.t. subsumption. If $can_{\unrhd}(S) \subseteq HL_{\mathcal{D}}$, then we can consider $S$ as a partial Herbrand interpretation $I = can_{\unrhd}(S)$ of $\mathcal{D}$. Conversely, a partial Herbrand interpretation $I$ can be considered as a special clausal Herbrand interpretation $exp_{\unrhd}(I)$. Every set $\mathcal{S}$ of clausal (or partial) Herbrand interpretations defines a clausal Herbrand interpretation $\mathcal{S}^{\cap} = \cap_{S \in \mathcal{S}} S \subseteq GHB_{\mathcal{D}}$, where $\mathcal{S}^{\cap} = GHB_{\mathcal{D}}$, if $\mathcal{S} = \emptyset$

The *semantics* of a disjunctive deductive database $\mathcal{D}$ will be given by a set $\mathcal{S}$ of clausal Herbrand interpretations, and a formula $\alpha$ is a consequence under $\mathcal{S}$ if $\alpha \in \mathcal{S}^{\cap}$.

### 3.2 Syntax of Clausal Deductive Databases

Consider a first order language $\mathcal{L}$ and the set $Lit_{\mathcal{L}}$ of all literals that can be built in the language $\mathcal{L}$. Additionally, consider a set $\mathcal{V}$ of variable symbols for formulas. Disjunctive (conjunctive) *formulas* are defined inductively: every atom $A \in Lit_{\mathcal{L}}$ and every $X \in \mathcal{V}$ is both a disjunctive and a conjunctive formula, and, if $t_1, \ldots, t_n$ are disjunctive (conjunctive) formulas, then so is $t_1 \vee \ldots \vee t_n$ ($t_1 \wedge \ldots \wedge t_n$).

A *cd–atom* is given by $dis(t_d)$ or $con(t_c)$, where $t_d$ is a disjunctive formula and $t_c$ is a conjunctive formula. If $X_d, X_d', X_d''$ are disjunctive formulas, and

$X_c, X'_c, X''_c$ are conjunctive formulas, and $X \in Lit_{\mathcal{L}} \cup \mathcal{V}$, then the following are *built–in atoms* (bi–atoms):

$$positive(X_d), \; negative(X_d),$$
$$subsumes(X_d, X'_d), \; resolvent(X_d, X'_d, X''_d), \; empty\_dis(X_d),$$
$$conjunction(X_c, X'_c, X''_c), \; empty\_con(X_c),$$
$$literal(X), \; complement(X_d, X_c).$$

A *clausal deductive database* (*cd–database*) $\mathcal{C}$ consists of *cd–rules* of the form

$$r = A \leftarrow B_1 \wedge \ldots \wedge B_m \wedge not\, C_1 \wedge \ldots \wedge not\, C_n, \tag{2}$$

where $A$ is a cd–atom, and the $B_i$, $i \in \langle 1, m \rangle$, and $C_i$, $i \in \langle 1, n \rangle$, are cd–atoms or bi–atoms, and *not* is the negation–by–default operator. A cd–rule is called a cd–fact if $m = n = 0$. For example, the following is a cd–rule:

$$dis(X'_d \vee \neg p(Y, a)) \leftarrow$$
$$\quad dis(X_d \vee q(c)) \wedge subsumes(X_d, X'_d) \wedge$$
$$\quad complement(X_d, X_c \wedge \neg q(d)) \wedge not\, con(X_c \wedge \neg q(d)) \wedge$$
$$\quad not\, literal(X_c).$$

Built–in predicate symbols are not allowed in rule heads, although built–in predicates could of course be defined by logical rules as well. For simplicity reasons, however, we assume that their definition is given by a standard *built–in Herbrand interpretation*

$$I_{\mathcal{L}}^{bi} = \{\, positive(\alpha) \mid \alpha \in DHB_{\mathcal{L}} \,\} \cup \{\, negative(\alpha) \mid \alpha \in NHB_{\mathcal{L}} \,\} \cup$$
$$\quad \{\, literal(\gamma) \mid \gamma \in HB_{\mathcal{L}} \,\} \cup \{\, complement(\alpha, \neg \cdot \alpha) \mid \alpha \in GHB_{\mathcal{L}} \,\} \cup$$
$$\quad \{\, empty\_dis(\Box_d) \,\} \cup \{\, empty\_con(\Box_c) \,\} \cup$$
$$\quad \{\, subsumes(\alpha_1, \alpha_2) \mid \alpha_1, \alpha_2 \in GHB_{\mathcal{L}}, \, \alpha_1 \trianglerighteq \alpha_2 \,\} \cup$$
$$\quad \{\, resolvent(A \vee \alpha_1, \neg A \vee \alpha_2, \alpha_1 \vee \alpha_2) \mid A \in HB_{\mathcal{L}}, \, \alpha_1, \alpha_2 \in GHB_{\mathcal{L}} \,\} \cup$$
$$\quad \{\, conjunction(\beta_1, \beta_2, \beta_1 \wedge \beta_2) \mid \beta_1, \beta_2 \in CHB_{\mathcal{L}} \,\}.$$

The built–in predicate symbols *conjunction* and *resolvent* are not really necessary in cd–databases, since they can be replaced using the junctors "$\wedge$" and "$\vee$", respectively. However, it will be very convenient to have them.

The *ground instance* $gnd(\mathcal{C})$ of a cd–database $\mathcal{C}$ is obtained replacing all variable symbols for formulas by ground formulas from $GHB_{\mathcal{L}} \cup CHB_{\mathcal{L}}$ and by also grounding the literals from $Lit_{\mathcal{L}}$ in $\mathcal{C}$, such that the resulting rules are proper cd–rules.[6] For a general Herbrand state $S \subseteq GHB_{\mathcal{L}}$ we define $dis(S) = \{\, dis(\alpha) \mid \alpha \in S \,\}$ and $con(S) = \{\, con(L_1 \wedge \ldots \wedge L_k) \mid L_i \in S \cap HL_{\mathcal{L}}, \text{ for } i \in \langle 1, k \rangle, \, k \in \mathbb{N}_0 \,\}$. Note that $con(\Box_c) \in con(S)$. Finally, $S^{cd} = dis(S) \cup con(S) \cup I_{\mathcal{L}}^{bi}$ denotes the total Herbrand interpretation of $\mathcal{C}$ that is derived from $S$.

---

[6] This implies that the obvious typing condition for variable symbols for formulas must be obeyed.

# 4 Clausal Deductive Databases Without Default Negation

The idea of clausal logic programming without default negation will be based on the observation that the disjunctive hyperresolution consequence operator, which has been defined by Minker and Rajasekar [13] for positive–disjunctive d-eductive databases $\mathcal{D}$, can be formulated using a generic definite hyperresolution consequence operator $\mathcal{T}_{\mathcal{D}}^{\odot,\geq}$, which is parameterized with a suitable subsumption relation. Thus reasoning with disjunctive hyperresolution can be reduced to reasoning with definite hyperresolution on a suitable domain. For hypothetical and for probabilistic deductive databases, cf. [3, 25], the generic operator $\mathcal{T}_{\mathcal{D}}^{\odot,\geq}$ can be used, too, which will be shown in another paper.

We will consider the following definition[7] of the disjunctive hyperresolution consequence operator $\mathcal{T}_{\mathcal{D}}^{s} : 2^{DHB_{\mathcal{D}}} \rightarrow 2^{DHB_{\mathcal{D}}}$ :

$$\mathcal{T}_{\mathcal{D}}^{s}(S) = \{\, \alpha \vee \alpha_1 \vee \ldots \vee \alpha_m \in DHB_{\mathcal{D}} \mid$$
$$\text{there exists a rule } \alpha \leftarrow B_1 \wedge \ldots \wedge B_m \in gnd\,(\mathcal{D}),$$
$$\text{such that } \{\, B_1 \vee \alpha_1, \ldots, B_m \vee \alpha_m \,\} \subseteq S \,\}.$$

Minker and Rajasekar [13] have shown that $\mathcal{T}_{\mathcal{D}}^{s}$ is *monotonic* and *continuous* on the complete lattice[8] $\langle 2^{DHB_{\mathcal{D}}}, \subseteq \rangle$. In [20], $\mathcal{T}_{\mathcal{D}}^{s}$ has been related to the model-generation operator of Fernández and Minker [7], and it was shown that the latter is monotonic but not continuous.

## 4.1 The Generic $\mathcal{T}_{\mathcal{D}}$–Operator

Consider a deductive database $\mathcal{D}$ without default negation (e.g. a positive–disjunctive, probabilistic or hypothetical deductive database, cf. [20, 25, 3]), and a partial ordering $\mathcal{O}_{\mathcal{D}} = \langle \mathcal{X}, \geq \rangle$ that is assigned to $\mathcal{D}$. The generic $\mathcal{T}_{\mathcal{D}}$–operator

$$\mathcal{T}_{\mathcal{D}}^{\odot,\geq} : 2^{\mathcal{X}} \rightarrow 2^{\mathcal{X}}$$

is based on a transformation "$\odot$" and the subsumption relation "$\geq$" of $\mathcal{O}_{\mathcal{D}}$. Firstly, $\mathcal{D}$ is transformed, such that $gnd\,(\mathcal{D}^{\odot})$ consists of definite ground rules $\alpha \leftarrow \beta_1 \wedge \ldots \wedge \beta_m$, where $\{\, \alpha, \beta_1, \ldots, \beta_m \,\} \subseteq \mathcal{X}$. Secondly, a set $X \subseteq \mathcal{X}$ is expanded to a set $exp_{\geq}(X) = \{\, \alpha \in \mathcal{X} \mid \exists\, \alpha' \in X : \alpha' \geq \alpha \,\} \subseteq \mathcal{X}$, cf. Subsection 2.1. Then the $\mathcal{T}_{\mathcal{D}}$–operator induced by $\langle \odot, \geq \rangle$ is

$$\mathcal{T}_{\mathcal{D}}^{\odot,\geq}(X) = \{\, \alpha \in \mathcal{X} \mid \text{there exists } \alpha \leftarrow \beta_1 \wedge \ldots \wedge \beta_m \in gnd\,(\mathcal{D}^{\odot}),$$
$$\text{such that } \{\, \beta_1, \ldots, \beta_m \,\} \subseteq exp_{\geq}(X) \,\}.$$

---

[7] It is equivalent to the definition of [13]. Since disjunctions are considered as sets of atoms, it is not necessary to work with smallest factors.

[8] For a definition of monotonic and continuous operators $\mathcal{T}$ and complete lattices see Lloyd [10]. Continuity ensures that fixpoint iteration terminates with the least fixpoint of $\mathcal{T}$ within at most $\omega$ steps.

**Theorem 4.1 (Properties of the Generic $\mathcal{T}_D$–Operator).**
The operator $\mathcal{T}_D^{\circledcirc,\geq} : 2^X \to 2^X$ is *monotonic* and *continuous* on the complete lattice $\langle 2^X, \subseteq \rangle$.

The proof is given in the appendix. The properties of fixpoint iteration with subsumption have also been analysed in [9] with special interest in the process of *differential* fixpoint iteration.

## 4.2   Positive–Disjunctive Deductive Databases

For positive–disjunctive deductive databases $\mathcal{D}$ we consider $X = dis(D_{HB_\mathcal{D}})$, and we will present two natural ways for formulating the disjunctive consequence operator $\mathcal{T}_D^s$ as a generic $\mathcal{T}_D$–operator. This gives an alternative proof that $\mathcal{T}_D^s$ is monotonic and continuous. Moreover, in the next section the second transformation will be extended to dd–databases with default negation.

**Transformation 1.** The first approach uses the built–in predicate *subsumes*:

$$\mathcal{D}^\circledcirc = \{\ dis(X) \leftarrow dis(B_1 \vee X) \wedge \ldots \wedge dis(B_m \vee X) \wedge subsumes(\alpha, X)\ |$$
$$\text{there exists } \alpha \leftarrow B_1 \wedge \ldots \wedge B_m \in \mathcal{D}\ \} \cup I_\mathcal{D}^{bi},$$

where $X \in \mathcal{V}$ is a variable symbol for formulas, and the common concept of subsumption for ground disjunctions $\alpha, \alpha' \in D_{HB_\mathcal{D}}$ is used, i.e. $\alpha \geq \alpha'$ iff $\alpha \trianglerighteq \alpha'$. Then the $\mathcal{T}_D^s$–operator on disjunctive Herbrand states $S$ can be characterized using the generic $\mathcal{T}_D$–operator and the expansion for disjunctive Herbrand states:

$$\mathcal{T}_D^{\circledcirc,\trianglerighteq}(dis(S) \cup I_\mathcal{D}^{bi}) = dis(exp_\trianglerighteq(\mathcal{T}_D^s(S))) \cup I_\mathcal{D}^{bi}.$$

*Example 4.1.* For $\mathcal{D} = \{\ a \vee b \leftarrow c,\ c \vee d\ \}$ we get

$$\mathcal{D}^\circledcirc = \{\ dis(X) \leftarrow dis(c \vee X) \wedge subsumes(a \vee b, X),$$
$$dis(X) \leftarrow subsumes(c \vee d, X)\ \} \cup I_\mathcal{D}^{bi}.$$

The rule $dis(X) \leftarrow dis(B_1 \vee X) \wedge subsumes(\alpha, X)$ that is derived from $a \vee b \leftarrow c$ has one disjunction $B_1 \vee X$ in its body, which extends $B_1 = c$ by some disjunction $X$ that must be subsumed by $\alpha = a \vee b$. In a fixpoint iteration with $\mathcal{T}_D^{\circledcirc,\geq}$, first the fact $dis(c \vee d)$ is derived (amoung other facts). In the second iteration, using the ground instance $dis(a \vee b \vee d) \leftarrow dis(c \vee a \vee b \vee d) \wedge subsumes(a \vee b, a \vee b \vee d)$, which is obtained for $X = a \vee b \vee d$, and the fact $dis(c \vee d)$, it is possible to derive the fact $dis(a \vee b \vee d)$, since $c \vee d \trianglerighteq c \vee a \vee b \vee d$ and $subsumes(a \vee b, a \vee b \vee d) \in I_\mathcal{D}^{bi}$.

**Transformation 2.** Another way of transforming a positive–disjunctive deductive database $\mathcal{D}$ is

$$\mathcal{D}^\circledcirc = \{\ dis(\alpha \vee X_1 \vee \ldots \vee X_m) \leftarrow dis(B_1 \vee X_1) \wedge \ldots \wedge dis(B_m \vee X_m)\ |$$
$$\text{there exists }\ \alpha \leftarrow B_1 \wedge \ldots \wedge B_m \in \mathcal{D}\ \},$$

with variable symbols $X_i \in \mathcal{V}$ ($i \in \mathbb{N}_+$) for formulas. If subsumption "$\geq$" for ground disjunctions $\alpha, \alpha' \in D_{HB_D}$ is defined as identity (where disjunctions are treated as sets), i.e. $\alpha \geq \alpha'$ iff $\alpha = \alpha'$, then the disjunctive consequence operator $\mathcal{T}_D^s$ on disjunctive Herbrand states $S$ coincides with the generic $\mathcal{T}_D$–operator:

$$\mathcal{T}_D^{\odot, \unrhd}(S) = dis(\mathcal{T}_D^s(S)).$$

*Example 4.2.* For $\mathcal{D} = \{\, a \vee b \leftarrow c, \; c \vee d \,\}$ we get

$$\mathcal{D}^{\odot} = \{\, dis(a \vee b \vee X_1) \leftarrow dis(c \vee X_1), \; dis(c \vee d) \,\}.$$

In a fixpoint iteration with $\mathcal{T}_D^{\odot, \unrhd}$, first the fact $dis(c \vee d)$ is derived. In the second iteration, using the ground instance $dis(a \vee b \vee d) \leftarrow dis(c \vee d)$ of the first rule (obtained for $X_1 = d$) and the fact $dis(c \vee d)$, it is possible to derive the fact $dis(a \vee b \vee d)$.

## 5    Clausal Deductive Databases with Default Negation

We will transform a disjunctive deductive database $\mathcal{D}$ into a corresponding clausal deductive database $\mathcal{D}^{cd} = \mathcal{D}^{\odot} \cup \mathcal{D}^{logic} \cup \mathcal{D}^{cwa} \cup I_D^{bi}$, which we call the cd–*transformation* of $\mathcal{D}$. It consists of four parts: a set

$$\mathcal{D}^{\odot} = \{\, dis(\alpha \vee X_1 \vee \ldots \vee X_m) \leftarrow$$
$$dis(B_1 \vee X_1) \wedge \ldots dis(B_m \vee X_m) \wedge$$
$$not\, con(C_1) \wedge \ldots \wedge not\, con(C_n) \,|$$
$$\text{there exists} \ \ \alpha \leftarrow B_1 \wedge \ldots \wedge B_m \wedge not\, C_1 \wedge \ldots \wedge not\, C_n \in \mathcal{D} \,\},$$

of rules obtained from $\mathcal{D}$ (by extending *Transformation 2* of Section 4.2), with variable symbols $X_i \in \mathcal{V}$ ($i \in \mathbb{N}_+$) for formulas, a set $\mathcal{D}^{logic}$ of logical rules for relating the predicate symbols $dis$ and $con$, a set $\mathcal{D}^{cwa} = \{\, r_{neg}^{cwa} \,\}$ with a *closed–world–assumption*, and the built–in interpretation $I_D^{bi}$. The cd–facts in $I_D^{bi}$ and the cd–rules in $\mathcal{D}^{logic} \cup \mathcal{D}^{cwa}$ are *generic*; they depend only on the Herbrand base $HB_D$, and not on the structure of the rules of $\mathcal{D}$.

We will prove that the stable models of the cd–transformation $\mathcal{D}^{cd}$ correspond to the stable models of $\mathcal{D}$. Thus, we have shown a very natural way of computing the stable models of a disjunctive deductive database $\mathcal{D}$ based on the stable models of a normal deductive database $\mathcal{D}^{cd}$. Furthermore, we will extend the set $\mathcal{STABLE}_2(\mathcal{D})$ to a set $\mathcal{STABLE}_{cd}(\mathcal{D})$ of so–called *stable states*, which are clausal Herbrand interpretations of $\mathcal{D}$ that are derived using a special *fixpoint condition* for $\mathcal{D}^{cd}$. Stable states form a useful new semantics for dd–databases, which is different from the stable model semantics. In contrast, the well–founded model $I_{wfs}$ of $\mathcal{D}^{cd}$, which is the least partial stable model in the knowledge ordering, is not suitable for defining a state semantics.

## 5.1   The Generic Rules

The following cd–rules represent *closed–world–assumptions*; they allow for deriving certain disjunctions if their complemantary conjunctions cannot be derived:

$$r_{neg}^{cwa} = dis(X_d) \leftarrow$$
$$negative(X_d) \wedge complement(X_d, X_c) \wedge not\, con(X_c),$$
$$r_{pos}^{cwa} = dis(X_d) \leftarrow$$
$$positive(X_d) \wedge complement(X_d, X_c) \wedge not\, con(X_c),$$
$$r_{gen}^{cwa} = dis(X_d) \leftarrow$$
$$complement(X_d, X_c) \wedge not\, con(X_c).$$

In $\mathcal{D}^{cd}$ we will only use the rule $r_{neg}^{cwa}$ for deriving negative disjunctions $\alpha \in N_{HB_\mathcal{D}}$. In a more general framework for extended–disjunctive deductive databases ([14]) one could as well derive positive or general disjunctions by a closed–world–assumption.

The following axiomatic clauses in the set

$$\mathcal{D}^{logic} = \{\, r_{res}^{logic}, r_{sub}^{logic}, r_{con}^{logic}, r_{lit}^{logic}, r_{emp}^{logic} \,\}$$

describe the correlation between the atoms for disjunctions and conjunctions:

$$r_{res}^{logic} = dis(X_d) \leftarrow$$
$$dis(X_d') \wedge dis(X_d'') \wedge resolvent(X_d', X_d'', X_d),$$

$$r_{sub}^{logic} = dis(X_d) \leftarrow$$
$$dis(X_d') \wedge subsumes(X_d', X_d),$$

$$r_{con}^{logic} = con(X_c) \leftarrow$$
$$con(X_c') \wedge con(X_c'') \wedge conjunction(X_c', X_c'', X_c),$$

$$r_{lit}^{logic} = con(X_c) \leftarrow$$
$$literal(X_c) \wedge dis(X_c),$$

$$r_{emp}^{logic} = con(X_c) \leftarrow$$
$$empty\_con(X_c).$$

## 5.2   Two–Valued Analysis of $\mathcal{D}^{cd}$

We want to investigate the total Herbrand models $I$ of the clausal deductive database $\mathcal{D}^{cd}$. Since $I$ is total, it must assign one of the truth values t or f to each of the atoms $dis(\alpha)$ and $con(\beta)$, for $\alpha \in G_{HB_\mathcal{D}}$, $\beta \in C_{HB_\mathcal{D}}$ – in particular for literals $A, \neg A \in H_{L_\mathcal{D}}$. Due to the subsumption rule $r_{sub}^{logic}$ it must hold $I(\alpha_1 \vee \alpha_2) = I(\alpha_1) \vee I(\alpha_2)$, for all $\alpha_1, \alpha_2 \in G_{HB_\mathcal{D}}$. If $I(dis(\square_d)) = $ t, then we define $I^\otimes = J^\top$, where $J^\top(A) = \top$, for all $A \in H_{B_\mathcal{D}}$, with a fourth truth value

$\top$ (*overdefined*) denoting *inconsistency*. $J^\top$ is considered as a special total Herbrand interpretation of $\mathcal{D}$, where all atoms $A$ are both true and false, and where $J^\top(\Box_d) = \mathsf{t}$. If $I(dis(\Box_d)) = \mathsf{f}$, then $I$ can be represented by an (ordinary) total Herbrand interpretation $I^\otimes$ of $\mathcal{D}$, where

$$I^\otimes(A) = I(dis(A)), \quad \text{for all } A \in HB_\mathcal{D}.$$

Conversely, a total Herbrand interpretation $J$ of $\mathcal{D}$ defines an Herbrand interpretation $J^\odot$ of $\mathcal{D}^{\mathrm{cd}}$ by

$$J^\odot(dis(\alpha)) = J(\alpha), \quad \text{for all } \alpha \in GHB_\mathcal{D},$$
$$J^\odot(con(\beta)) = J(\beta), \quad \text{for all } \beta \in CHB_\mathcal{D}.$$

For a total Herbrand model $I$ of $\mathcal{D}^{\mathrm{cd}}$, it holds $(I^\otimes)^\odot = I$, and for a total Herbrand model $J$ of $\mathcal{D}$, it holds $(J^\odot)^\otimes = J$. A set $\mathcal{I}$ of total Herbrand models of $\mathcal{D}^{\mathrm{cd}}$ can be represented by the set $\mathcal{I}^\otimes = \{ I^\otimes \mid I \in \mathcal{I} \}$ of Herbrand interpretations of $\mathcal{D}$.

**Theorem 5.1 (Characterization of Stable Models).**
Given a disjunctive deductive database $\mathcal{D}$, then it holds

$$\mathcal{STABLE}_2(\mathcal{D}^{\mathrm{cd}})^\otimes = \mathcal{STABLE}_2(\mathcal{D}) \cup \mathcal{J}, \quad \text{where} \quad \mathcal{J} = \emptyset \ \text{ or } \ \mathcal{J} = \{ J^\top \}.$$

The proof is given in the appendix. It would be possible to forbid $(J^\top)^\odot$ as a stable model of $\mathcal{D}^{\mathrm{cd}}$ by adding one of the following rules to $\mathcal{D}^{\mathrm{cd}}$:

$$r_{cons}^{logic} = dis(c_\top) \leftarrow$$
$$dis(X_d) \wedge empty\_dis(X_d) \wedge not\, dis(c_\top),$$

$$r_{cons}^{logic'} = \leftarrow dis(X_d) \wedge empty\_dis(X_d).$$

$c_\top$ is a new constant symbol for formulas that does not unify with any $\alpha \in GHB_\mathcal{D}$. $r_{cons}^{logic}$ is a cd–rule, and $r_{cons}^{logic'}$ is an equivalent denial rule, which is easier to understand, but is no cd–rule.

## 5.3    Three–Valued Analysis of $\mathcal{D}^{\mathrm{cd}}$

In the following we will investigate the effects of the propagation rules $r_{res}^{logic}$ and $r_{con}^{logic}$ for disjunctions and conjunctions, respectively, and the closed–world–assumption $r_{neg}^{cwa}$ in three–valued logic. We will see that the well–founded model $I_{wfs}$ of the normal deductive database $\mathcal{D}^{\mathrm{cd}}$ is not appropriate for designing a useful state semantics. Likewise, also the partial stable models of $\mathcal{D}^{\mathrm{cd}}$ are not useful, since the well–founded model $I_{wfs}$ is the least partial stable model of $\mathcal{D}^{\mathrm{cd}}$ in the knowledge–ordering[9].

---

[9] i.e. $I_{wfs}$ exactly is the set of consequences under the semantics of partial stable models

**The Conjunction Rule** $r_{con}^{logic}$. Due to $r_{con}^{logic}$ the partial stable models $I$ exhibit the following behaviour for conjunctions $\beta = L_1 \wedge \ldots \wedge L_k \in CHB_\mathcal{D}$:

$$I(con(\beta)) \geq_t u \iff (\forall i \in \langle 1, k \rangle : I(con(L_i)) \geq_t u).$$

$r_{neg}^{cwa}$ supports $dis(\neg L_1 \vee \ldots \vee \neg L_k)$, if $I(con(\beta)) = f$. In this case $I(con(L_i)) = f$ must hold for some $i \in \langle 1, k \rangle$, i.e. $r_{neg}^{cwa}$ also supports $dis(\neg L_i)$. In a state–based semantics it should be possible that the closed–world–assumption can support a negative disjunction $dis(\neg A_1 \vee \neg A_2)$ without supporting one of $dis(\neg A_1)$ and $dis(\neg A_2)$. For three–valued models $I$, such a behaviour is impossible.[10]

*Example 5.1.* The *stable states semantics* of $\mathcal{D} = \{a \leftarrow not\, b, b \leftarrow not\, a\}$ will be given by the three clausal Herbrand interpretations $S_1 = \{a, \neg b\}$, $S_2 = \{\neg a, b\}$, and $S_3 = \{\neg a \vee \neg b\}$. $S_3$ corresponds to the partial Herbrand interpretation $I = S_3^{cd}$ of $\mathcal{D}^{cd}$, where $dis(\neg a \vee \neg b)$ is derived since $con(a \wedge b)$ cannot be derived.

**The Resolution Rule** $r_{res}^{logic}$. $r_{res}^{logic}$ has the following consequence for disjunctions $\alpha_1, \alpha_2 \in GHB_\mathcal{D}$ and atoms $A \in HB_\mathcal{D}$:

If $\alpha_1 \vee \alpha_2$ is the binary resolvent of two disjunctions $A \vee \alpha_1$, $\neg A \vee \alpha_2$, such that $I(dis(A \vee \alpha_1)) \geq_t u$, $I(dis(\neg A \vee \alpha_2)) \geq_t u$, then $I(dis(\alpha_1 \vee \alpha_2)) \geq_t u$.

This is undesirable and unituitive since it could be the case that $I(dis(A)) = u$, and it does not make sense to resolve on undefined atoms.

*Example 5.2.* The *stable state semantics* of $\mathcal{D} = \{a \leftarrow not\, a, b \leftarrow c\}$ will be given by the clausal Herbrand interpretation $S = \{\neg b, \neg c\}$ corresponding to the partial Herbrand interpretation $I = S_3^{cd}$ of $\mathcal{D}^{cd}$. Here $I(dis(a)) = I(dis(a \vee b)) = I(dis(\neg a \vee c)) = u$, but for the resolvent we get $I(dis(b \vee c)) = f$.

## 5.4   Stable State Semantics

Stable states are clausal Herbrand interpretations $S$ of a dd–database $\mathcal{D}$ that are defined by a special *fixpoint condition* $\Gamma_{\mathcal{C}^t}(\Gamma_{\mathcal{C}^u}(S^{cd})) = S^{cd}$ in terms of the $\Gamma_\mathcal{C}$–operators [18] for the cd–transformation $\mathcal{C}^t = \mathcal{D}^{cd}$ and a variant $\mathcal{C}^u$ of $\mathcal{D}^{cd}$.

**Definition 5.1 (Stable States).**

Given a cd–database $\mathcal{C}$ and a dd–database $\mathcal{D}$.

1. The (unique) minimal model of the GL–transformation $\mathcal{C}^I$ of $\mathcal{C}$ w.r.t. a total Herbrand interpretation $I \subseteq HB_\mathcal{C}$ of $\mathcal{C}$ is denoted by $\Gamma_\mathcal{C}(I)$.

---

[10] $dis(\neg A_1 \vee \neg A_2)$ is supported, if $I(con(A_1 \wedge A_2)) = f$. On the other hand, assuming that $dis(\neg A_1)$ and $dis(\neg A_2)$ are not supported, it must hold $I(con(A_i)) \geq_t u$, for $i = 1, 2$, which implies $I(con(A_1 \wedge A_2)) \geq_t u$, and contradicts $I(con(A_1 \wedge A_2)) = f$.

2. A clausal Herbrand interpretation $S$ of $\mathcal{D}$ is called a *stable state* of $\mathcal{D}$ if for the total Herbrand interpretation $I = S^{cd}$ of the cd–databases

$$\mathcal{C}^t = \mathcal{D}^{cd}, \quad \mathcal{C}^u = I \cup \mathcal{D}^{cd} \setminus \{ r_{res}^{logic}, r_{con}^{logic} \}$$

it holds $\Gamma_{\mathcal{C}^t}(\Gamma_{\mathcal{C}^u}(I)) = I$. The set of all stable states of $\mathcal{D}$ is denoted by $\mathcal{STABLE}_{cd}(\mathcal{D})$.

Stable models $I$ of $\mathcal{C}^t = \mathcal{D}^{cd}$ are characterized by $\Gamma_{\mathcal{C}^t}(I) = I$. In the following we will represent clausal Herbrand interpretations (and thus stable states) $S$ by their canonical form $can_{\unrhd}(S)$. As a consequence of Theorem 5.1, for a disjunctive deductive database $\mathcal{D}$, the representation of a stable model of $\mathcal{D}$ as a partial Herbrand interpretation $J \subseteq HL_{\mathcal{D}}$ is a stable state of $\mathcal{D}$.

**Theorem 5.2 (Stable States).**
Given a disjunctive deductive database $\mathcal{D}$, then it hols

$$\mathcal{STABLE}_2(\mathcal{D}) \subseteq \mathcal{STABLE}_{cd}(\mathcal{D}).$$

This shows that the semantics of stable states is at most as strong as the semantics of stable models, i.e. $\mathcal{STABLE}_{cd}(\mathcal{D})^{\cap} \subseteq \mathcal{STABLE}_2(\mathcal{D})^{\cap}$. The following Example 5.3 will give some dd–databases ($\mathcal{D}_2$, $\mathcal{D}_3$, $\mathcal{D}_4$, $\mathcal{D}_5$) where it is strictly weaker. For many prototypical databases which have been investigated frequently in literature we will compare the stable states to the stable models and – for normal databases – to the well–founded model.

*Example 5.3 (Stable States).*

1. For the positive–disjunctive deductive database $\mathcal{D}_1 = \{ a \vee b \}$ we get

$$\mathcal{STABLE}_2(\mathcal{D}_1) = \mathcal{STABLE}_{cd}(\mathcal{D}_1) = \{ \{ a, \neg b \}, \{ \neg a, b \} \}.$$

The intersection is $\mathcal{STABLE}_{cd}(\mathcal{D}_1)^{\cap} = \mathcal{STABLE}_2(\mathcal{D}_1)^{\cap} = \{ a \vee b, \neg a \vee \neg b \}$.
2. For the normal deductive database $\mathcal{D}_2 = \{ a \leftarrow not\, b, b \leftarrow not\, a \}$, we get

$$\mathcal{STABLE}_2(\mathcal{D}_2) = \{ \{ a, \neg b \}, \{ \neg a, b \} \},$$
$$\mathcal{STABLE}_{cd}(\mathcal{D}_2) = \mathcal{STABLE}_2(\mathcal{D}_2) \cup \{ \{ \neg a \vee \neg b \} \}.$$

$\mathcal{STABLE}_{cd}(\mathcal{D}_2)^{\cap} = \{ \neg a \vee \neg b \}$, is weaker than the state $\mathcal{STABLE}_2(\mathcal{D}_2)^{\cap} = \{ a \vee b, \neg a \vee \neg b \}$ derived from the stable models, but stronger than the well–founded model $\emptyset$.
3. For the normal deductive database $\mathcal{D}_3 = \{ a \leftarrow not\, a \}$, which does not possess any (total) stable model, there is unique stable state $S_3 = \emptyset$, which is identical to the well–founded model. A similar structure may for instance *become active* for "$a = win(x)$" within the database $\mathcal{D}_{win}$ of Subsection 2.2, if the state $S$ contains cyclic moves "$move(x, x)$", namely $win(x) \leftarrow move(x, x) \wedge not\, win(x)$.

4. For the normal deductive database $\mathcal{D}_4 = \{\, a \leftarrow not\, b,\ b \leftarrow not\, c,\ c \leftarrow not\, a\,\}$, we get $\mathcal{STABLE}_2(\mathcal{D}_4) = \emptyset$, but there is a unique stable state

$$S_4 = \{\, \neg a \vee \neg b,\ \neg b \vee \neg c,\ \neg a \vee \neg c\,\},$$

which is weaker than the inconsistent state $\mathcal{STABLE}_2(\mathcal{D}_4)^{\cap} = \mathit{GHB}_{\mathcal{D}_4}$ derived from the stable models, but stronger than the empty well–founded model $\emptyset$.

5. For the dd–database $\mathcal{D}_5 = \mathcal{D}_4 \cup \{\, a \vee b \vee c\,\}$ which does not possess any stable or partial stable models, there is a unique stable state $S_5 = S_4 \cup \{\, a \vee b \vee c\,\}$.

6. For the stratified–disjunctive deductive database $\mathcal{D}_6 = \{\, a \leftarrow not\, b\,\}$, we get a unqiue stable state $S_6 = \{\, a,\ \neg b\,\}$, which is the unique (total) stable model of $\mathcal{D}_6$, namely the perfect model of $\mathcal{D}_6$.

7. For both of the stratified–disjunctive deductive databases $\mathcal{D}_7' = \{\, c \leftarrow a,\ c \leftarrow b,\ a \vee b\,\}$ and $\mathcal{D}_7'' = \{\, c \leftarrow not\, a,\ c \leftarrow not\, b,\ a \vee b\,\}$ we get (for $\mathcal{D}_7 \in \{\, \mathcal{D}_7',\mathcal{D}_7''\,\}$)

$$\mathcal{STABLE}_2(\mathcal{D}_7) = \mathcal{STABLE}_{cd}(\mathcal{D}_7) = \{\, \{\, a,\ \neg b,\ c\,\},\ \{\, \neg a,\ b,\ c\,\}\,\}.$$

The intersection is $\mathcal{STABLE}_{cd}(\mathcal{D}_7)^{\cap} = \mathcal{STABLE}_2(\mathcal{D}_7)^{\cap} = \{\, a \vee b,\ \neg a \vee \neg b,\ c\,\}$.

8. For the dd–database $\mathcal{D}_8 = \{\, a,\ \leftarrow a\,\}$, which has got no Herbrand models, there exists one stable state $S_8 = \{\, \Box_d\,\}$, i.e. $\mathcal{STABLE}_{cd}(\mathcal{D}_8)^{\cap} = \mathit{GHB}_{\mathcal{D}_8}$.

Especially for the dd–databases $\mathcal{D}_2$, $\mathcal{D}_3$, $\mathcal{D}_4$, $\mathcal{D}_5$, which are inconsistent under stable model semantics, stable states provide a plausible, consistent semantics.

For positive–disjunctive deductive databases the intersection $\mathcal{STABLE}_{cd}(\mathcal{D})^{\cap}$ of all stable states corresponds to the union of the *minimal model state* $\mathit{MS}_{\mathcal{D}}$ and the *extended generalized closed–world-assumption* $\mathit{EGCWA}_{\mathcal{D}}$, as defined by [11], together with all general disjunctions that can be derived from $\mathit{MS}_{\mathcal{D}}$ – which is a disjunctive Herbrand state – and $\mathit{EGCWA}_{\mathcal{D}}$ – which is represented as a negative Herbrand state – by repeated applications of binary resolution.

# 6   Conclusions

*Extended–disjunctive deductive databases* allow literals to occur in all places where atoms are possible in disjunctive deductive databases cf. [14]. Marek and Truszczyński have introduced *clausal logic programming*, cf. [12], as a further extension: clausal logic programs allow for general disjunctions – rather than atoms – in rule bodies, next to general disjunctions in rule heads. But clausal logic programs do not allow for variable symbols that stand for general disjunctions in their meta–language $\mathcal{L}^{cd}$, and the ideas of transforming disjunctive logic programs to clausal logic programs or relating the semantics of disjunctive logic programs and corresponding clausal logic programs have not been investigated.

In a forthcoming paper we will give a *characterization of the stable states* of a disjunctive deductive database in terms of the stable models of an *annotated* clausal deductive database $\mathcal{D}^{cd,tu}$ by modifying the concept of the tu–transformation known from [21]. We will investigate the new semantics w.r.t.

further desirable properties, such as *modularity* or *independence under partial evaluation (GPPE)*, and compare it with some more semantics.

In the future we will consider the complexity issue of stable state semantics, and we will work on an *efficient implementation*. So far we have used the system Smodels developed by Niemelä [15] for computing well–founded and stable model semantics for normal deductive databases. Smodels uses a *grounding procedure*, which does not work for databases with function symbols like the cd–transformation $\mathcal{D}^{cd}$. Thus, we have written a new grounding procedure for computing the ground instance $gnd(\mathcal{D}^{cd})$, if the Herbrand base $HB_{\mathcal{D}}$ of $\mathcal{D}$ is finite. For a more efficient implementation, the goal is to *back transform* the declarative approach that is working with cd–databases into a procedure that is directly working with dd–databases. This would allow us to use systems that can handle disjunctions directly, e.g. the dlv–system of Eiter, Leone et al. [4], or our system DISLOG [23] for reasoning in disjunctive deductive databases.

In another paper we will also show how reasoning in *hypothetical* [3] and in *probabilistic deductive databases* [25] can be formulated easily in terms of a suitable generic consequence operator $\mathcal{T}_{\mathcal{D}}^{\odot,\geq}$, which gives immediate results about the continuity of the underlying consequence operators without requiring extra proofs.

# References

1. *S. Brass, J. Dix:* A Disjunctive Semantics Based on Unfolding and Bottom–Up E-valuation, GI–Jahrestagung / IFIP World Computer Congress 1994: Fachgespräch "Disjunktive logische Programmierung und disjunktive Datenbanken", Springer, 1994, pp. 83–91.
2. *S. Ceri, G. Gottlob, L. Tanca:* Logic Programming and Databases, Springer, 1990.
3. *P.M. Dung:* Declarative Semantics of Hypothetical Logic Programming with Negation as Failure, Proc. Workshop on Extensions of Logic Programming 1992 (ELP'92), 1992, pp. 45–58.
4. *T. Eiter, N. Leone, C. Mateis, G. Pfeifer, F. Scarcello:* A Deductive System for Non–Monotonic Reasoning, Proc. Fourth Intl. Conf. on Logic Programming and Non–Monotonic Reasoning 1997 (LPNMR'97), Springer LNAI 1265, 1997, pp. 363–374.
5. *T. Eiter, N. Leone, D. Sacca:* On the Partial Semantics for Disjunctive Deductive Databases, Annals of Mathematics and Artificial Intelligence, vol. 17(1/2), 1997, pp. 59–96.
6. *J.A. Fernández, J. Lobo, J. Minker, V.S. Subrahmanian:* Disjunctive LP + Integrity Constrains = Stable Model Semantics, Annals of Math. and AI, vol. 8 (3–4), 1993, pp. 449–474.
7. *J.A. Fernández and J. Minker:* Bottom–up computation of perfect models for disjunctive theories, Journal of Logic Programming, vol. 25 (1), 1995, pp. 33–51.
8. *M. Gelfond, V. Lifschitz:* The Stable Model Semantics for Logic Programming, Proc. Fifth Intl. Conference and Symposium on Logic Programming 1988 (ICSLP'88), MIT Press, 1988, pp. 1070–1080.
9. *G. Köstler, W. Kießling, H. Thöne, U. Güntzer:* The differential fixpoint operator with subsumption, Proc. Intl. Conference on Deductive and Object–Oriented Databases 1993 (DOOD'93), Springer LNCS 760, 1993, pp. 35–48.

10. *J.W. Lloyd:* Foundations of Logic Programming, second edition, Springer, 1987.
11. *J. Lobo, J. Minker, A. Rajasekar:* Foundations of Disjunctive Logic Programming, MIT Press, 1992.
12. *V.W. Marek, M. Truszczyński:* Nonmonotonic Logic – Context–Dependent Reasoning, Springer, 1993.
13. *J. Minker, A. Rajasekar:* A Fixpoint Semantics for Disjunctive Logic Programs, Journal of Logic Programming, vol. 9(1), 1990, pp. 45–74.
14. *J. Minker, C. Ruiz:* On Extended Disjunctive Logic Programs, Proc. Intl. Symposium on Methodologies for Intelligent Systems 1993 (ISMIS'93), Springer LNAI 689, 1993, pp. 1–18.
15. *I. Niemelä, P. Simons:* Efficient Implementation of the Well–founded and Stable Model Semantics, Technical Report 7/96, Univ. Koblenz – Landau, 1996.
16. *T.C. Przymusinski:* Stable Semantics for Disjunctive Programs, New Generation Computing, vol. 9, 1991, pp. 401–424.
17. *R. Ramakrishnan:* Database Management Systems, McGraw–Hill, 1998.
18. *R. Reiter:* A Logic for Default Reasoning, Artificial Intelligence, vol. 13, 1980, pp. 81–132.
19. *K. Sagonas, T. Swift, D. Warren:* XSB as an Efficient Deductive Database Engine, Proc. ACM SIGMOD Intl. Conf. on the Management of Data 1994 (SIGMOD'94), pp. 442–453.
20. *D. Seipel, J. Minker, C. Ruiz:* Model Generation and State Generation for Disjunctive Logic Programs, Journal of Logic Programming, vol. 32(1), 1997, pp. 48–69.
21. *D. Seipel, J. Minker, C. Ruiz:* A Characterization of Partial Stable Models for Disjunctive Deductive Databases, Proc. Intl. Logic Programming Symposium 1997 (ILPS'97), MIT Press, 1997, pp. 245–259.
22. *D. Seipel:* Partial Evidential Stable Models For Disjunctive Databases, Proc. Workshop on Logic Programming and Knowledge Representation (LPKR'97) at the International Symposium on Logic Programming 1997 (ILPS'97), Springer LNAI 1471, 1998, pp. 66–84.
23. *D. Seipel:* DISLOG – A Disjunctive Deductive Database Prototype, Proc. Twelfth Workshop on Logic Programming (WLP'97), 1997, pp. 136–143. DISLOG is available at "http://www-info1.informatik.uni-wuerzburg.de/databases/DisLog".
24. *A. Van Gelder, K.A. Ross, J.S. Schlipf:*, Unfounded Sets and Well–Founded Semantics for General Logic Programs, Proc. Seventh ACM Symposium on Principles of Database Systems, 1988 (PODS'88), pp. 221–230.
25. *C. Zaniolo, S. Ceri, C. Faloutsos, R.T. Snodgrass, V.S. Subrahmanian, R. Zicari:* Advanced Database Systems, Morgan Kaufmann, 1997.
26. *U. Zukowski, S. Brass, B. Freitag:* Improving the Alternating Fixpoint: The Transformation Approach, Proc. 4th Intl. Conf. on Logic Programming an Non–Monotonic Reasoning 1997 (LPNMR'97), Springer LNAI 1265, 1997, pp. 40–59.

# Appendix

### Theorem 4.1 (Properties of the Generic $T_D$–Operator)
The operator $T_D^{\odot,\geq} : 2^{\mathcal{X}} \to 2^{\mathcal{X}}$ is *monotonic* and *continuous* on the complete lattice $\langle 2^{\mathcal{X}}, \subseteq \rangle$.

*Proof.* (i) Firstly, we prove *monotonicity*:

$$X_1 \subseteq X_2 \;\Rightarrow\; exp_\geq(X_1) \subseteq exp_\geq(X_2) \;\Rightarrow\; T_D^{\odot,\geq}(X_1) \subseteq T_D^{\odot,\geq}(X_2).$$

(ii) Secondly, for proving *continuity*, consider a directed set $\mathcal{Y} \subseteq 2^{\mathcal{X}}$ of subsets of $\mathcal{X}$. Let $X = \cup_{Y \in \mathcal{Y}} Y$. Then $\cup_{Y \in \mathcal{Y}} exp_\geq(Y) = exp_\geq(X)$. Obviously, it holds $\cup_{Y \in \mathcal{Y}} T_D^{\odot,\geq}(Y) \subseteq T_D^{\odot,\geq}(X)$. Conversely, if $\alpha \in T_D^{\odot,\geq}(X)$, then there must exist a rule $\alpha \leftarrow \beta_1 \wedge \ldots \wedge \beta_m \in gnd\,(\mathcal{D}^\odot)$, such that $\{\beta_1, \ldots, \beta_m\} \subseteq exp_\geq(X)$. Thus, there must exist sets $Y_{j_1}, \ldots, Y_{j_m} \in \mathcal{Y}$, such that $\beta_i \in exp_\geq(Y_{j_i})$. I.e. there exist elements $\beta_i' \in Y_{j_i}$, such that $\beta_i' \geq \beta_i$. Since $\mathcal{Y}$ is directed, there must exist a set $Y_{j_0} \in \mathcal{Y}$, such that $\{\beta_1', \ldots, \beta_m'\} \subseteq Y_{j_0}$. Thus, $\{\beta_1, \ldots, \beta_m\} \subseteq exp_\geq(Y_{j_0})$, and $\alpha \in T_D^{\odot,\geq}(Y_{j_0}) \subseteq \cup_{Y \in \mathcal{Y}} T_D^{\odot,\geq}(Y)$. $\square$

### Theorem 5.1 (Characterization of Stable Models)
Given a disjunctive deductive database $\mathcal{D}$, then it holds

$$STABLE_2(\mathcal{D}^{cd})^\otimes = STABLE_2(\mathcal{D}) \cup \mathcal{J}, \quad \text{where } \mathcal{J} = \emptyset \text{ or } \mathcal{J} = \{J^\top\}.$$

*Proof.* (i) Consider a total model $I$ of $\mathcal{D}^{cd}$, such that $I(dis(\Box_d)) = \text{f}$, and consider the corresponding Herbrand interpretation $I^\otimes$ of $\mathcal{D}$. It is not necessary to deal with atoms $dis(\alpha)$ for non–singleton negative disjunctions $\alpha \in NHB_\mathcal{D}$ during the fixpoint evaluation of $\mathcal{D}^{cd}$: amoung the rules $(r_{neg}^{cwa})^I$ the ones in $\{dis(\neg A) \leftarrow negative(\neg A) \wedge complement(\neg A, A) \mid A \in HB_\mathcal{D}, con(A) \notin I\}$ for minimal, i.e. atomary, disjunctions "$\neg A$" are *subsuming* the others. The resolution rule $r_{res}^{logic}$ will consume the atoms $dis(\neg A)$ and produce atoms $dis(\alpha)$ over positive disjunctions $\alpha \in DHB_\mathcal{D}$. The evaluation is equivalent to evaluating the disjunctive deductive database $\mathcal{D}^{I^\otimes}$ together with the set $\mathcal{D}' = \{\leftarrow A \mid A \in HB_\mathcal{D}, con(A) \notin I\}$ of denial rules, using the disjunctive consequence operator $T_{\mathcal{D}''}^s$ for $\mathcal{D}'' = \mathcal{D}^{I^\otimes} \cup \mathcal{D}'$.

(ii) $I \neq (J^\top)^\odot$ is a stable model of $\mathcal{D}^{cd}$ iff it holds $can_\trianglerighteq(T_{\mathcal{D}''}^s \uparrow \omega) = \{A \in HB_\mathcal{D} \mid I^\otimes(A) = \text{t}\}$, i.e. iff $I^\otimes$ is a minimal model $\mathcal{D}^{I^\otimes}$, i.e. iff $I^\otimes \in STABLE_2(\mathcal{D})$.

(iii) As a consequence of (ii) we get $STABLE_2(\mathcal{D}^{cd})^\otimes \subseteq STABLE_2(\mathcal{D}) \cup \{J^\top\}$. Every stable model $J \in STABLE_2(\mathcal{D})$ can be perceived as $J = I^\otimes$ for the total Herbrand interpretation $I = J^\odot$ of $\mathcal{D}^{cd}$. Thus, according to (ii) we get $J \in STABLE_2(\mathcal{D}^{cd})^\otimes$. $\square$

# Partial Evaluations in a Set-Theoretic Query Language for the WWW

Yury P. Serdyuk

Program Systems Institute of Russian Academy of Sciences,
Pereslavl-Zalessky, 152140, Russia
Yury@serdyuk.botik.ru

**Abstract.** We present an approach to handle unavailable data sources during query execution over WWW which is based on partial evaluations. Syntax of the set-theoretic query language $\Delta$ and some examples of queries are given. We define an *ordinary* and a *lazy* semantics for this language. Moreover, we introduce a universe of *non-well-founded hereditarily finite protosets* and an approximation relation on this universe in order to compare the partial answers to a query. A theorem about properties of the above semantics, in particular about correctness of lazy semantics is formulated.

## 1 Introduction

Adequate handling of unavailable data sources is one of the problems and characteristic peculiarities of query systems for the WWW. This unavailability of some HTML-pages during query execution is not an exceptional situation for the WWW and may be caused by various reasons: wrong typing of URL-addresses of the required pages, very slow response time due to overloading of network traffic, refuse of communication channel supplied by space satellite, temporarily down web-server, etc.

Typically, the query execution requires a significant amount of resources and a long time for answering (due to data transmission over the global net). So the simple resubmission of a failed query may be a very inefficient procedure. Some solutions to this problem but only in the relational database context were proposed, for example in [4] and [14].

Our approach consists in dividing the query answer into two parts: a *computed* part, i.e. a set of required URL-addresses, and a *lazy* part as a new, complementary query. The resulting query answer, which possibly is not yet computed and therefore consists of two parts, may be placed again into the WWW as a new HTML-page for further use. Thus, we have more general view on the WWW allowing both completely computed pages and pages with secondary queries that may be executed later. Such "embedded" queries, which are presented immediately in web-documents, are called *virtual data* in [5]. Then, a complete answer to a query can be composed from the already computed part and the answer to the secondary query, if all the necessary data sources for this query will be available.

K.-D. Schewe, B. Thalheim (Eds.): FoIKS 2000, LNCS 1762, pp. 260–274, 2000.

More formally spoken we model the web by a graph with vertices representing web-documents and edges corresponding to hyperlinks between documents. Moreover, all vertices in this graph are partioned into two classes: *active* vertices which represent web-documents that are both available for viewing through some web-browser and completely computed, i.e. with an "empty" secondary query, and *inactive* vertices, otherwise.

In this paper we consider the set-theoretic query language $\Delta$ proposed in [13] and further extended to web-like (in other terms, semi-structured) databases in [7]. We describe a new semantics for $\Delta$ taking into account the activity of web-documents. The essence of our set-theoretic approach to query languages for semi-structured databases which are represented by graphs consists in the following.

Let $G = \langle V, E \rangle$ be a directed graph with a set $V$ of vertices and a set $E$ of edges. If $v \in V$ is a vertex, then the pair $\langle G, v \rangle$ is called a *pointed graph*. Then an arbitrary set $s$ (consisting of sets of sets, etc.) defines such a pointed graph. Just let $TC(s)$ be the transitive closure of $s$. Informally, all "intermediate" sets of $s$ are constructed, starting with $\emptyset$ and including the set $s$ itself. Then the pair

$$\langle \langle TC(s), \ni \rangle, s \rangle \qquad ,$$

where $\ni$ is an inverse membership relation on $TC(s)$, is the pointed graph we need. In this way any set may be encoded by a pointed graph, and the above representation is called the canonical "picture" of the set $s$.

On the other side, if $G$ is a graph then each of its vertices $v$ defines a set $[\![v]\!]^G$ according to the corecursive definition

$$[\![v]\!]^G = \{[\![u]\!]^G | (v \to u) \in E\} .$$

From the above definition one can see that if the graph has cycles, then some sets may contain themselves as elements in some level of nesting. Such kind of sets are known as *hypersets* or *non-well-founded sets*.

Now, let $t(\bar{x})$ be a set-theoretic term of $n$ set variables ($\bar{x} = x_1, \ldots, x_n$). For example, $t(\bar{x})$ can be a term of the $\Delta$- language which will be described below. It denotes a set-theoretic operation of $n$ arguments according to its natural semantics. As sets are represented (encoded) by pointed graphs, there should be corresponding transformer of graphs

$$\langle G, v_1, \ldots, v_n \rangle \longmapsto \langle G', v' \rangle \quad .$$

Here the points $v_1, \ldots, v_n$ and $v'$ correspond to the arguments $x_1, \ldots, x_n$ and to the resulting set $t(\bar{x})$, respectively, and the set-theoretic values of $x_i$ and $t(\bar{x})$ coincide with $[\![v_i]\!]^{G_i}$ and $[\![v']\!]^{G'}$, respectively. We may also consider terms without free variables, but with constants corresponding to input graph vertices $v_1, \ldots, v_n$.

In general, the evaluation of a term $t$ on a pointed graph $< G, v_1, ..., v_n >$ may be considered as a process of appropriately extending this graph ($G'$ extends $G$) by new vertices and related edges, which correspond to sets that are the results of the evaluation of the subterms of the term $t$, including $t$ itself.

Such a representation of abstract objects by concrete objects, namely sets by graphs, which in addition are "understandable" by computers, proves to be efficient from the point of view of computational complexity: all operations, definable in the $\Delta$-language, are computable in polynomial time in terms of graphs and vice versa (see [9]).

In order to model the activity of web-documents we will regard graphs as triples $G =< V, E, A >$, where $A : V \rightarrow \{0,1\}$ is an *activity* function. Here $A(v) = 1$ means that the vertex $v$ is *active*. In this case a pointed graph $< G, v >$ gives a value $[\![v]\!]_A^G$ defined as

$$[\![v]\!]_A^G = \langle A(v), \{[\![u]\!]_A^G | (v \rightarrow u) \in E\} \rangle$$

We will call such kind of pairs *protosets* due to the work [10]. If $p = \langle m, s \rangle$ is a protoset, then $m = 0$ informally says that $p$ is not "complete" as a set and may have more elements than those "explicitly" belonging to $s$. The intuition behind protosets as incompletely defined sets is given in more detail in the same paper. Note, that here protosets may be non-well-founded, unlike those in [10].

If we evaluate a term $t$ over protosets, we are interested not only in the resulting protoset, but also in those elements that complete the given protoset. As the main contribution of the current work it turns out that we may always construct a $\Delta$-term $r$ defining the "uncomputed" part of the term $t$. More formally, the evaluation result of a term $t$ on a pointed graph $\langle G, v_1, ..., v_n \rangle$ with activity function $A$ is a pair

$$\langle [\![v']\!]^{G'}, r \rangle,$$

where $\langle G', v' \rangle$ is an extension of the source graph $\langle G, v_1, ..., v_n \rangle$, i.e., $G' = \langle V', E', A' \rangle$, where $V \subseteq V'$, $E \subseteq E'$, $A = A'|_V$, and $r$ is the secondary term.

We assume that $A'(v') = 1$ holds in the resulting graph, if $r$ defines or simply is equal to the empty set. The specific property of the lazy semantics, which will be defined later on, consists in that independent from the activity of the vertex $v'$, which represents the computed part of the term $t$, this part will include only active values, i.e., only those vertices $u$ for which $A'(u) = 1$. Informally, in the context of the WWW this means that the hyperlinks collected in the computed part of the query may be clicked with a successful transition to the required pages.

The paper is organized as follows. In Section 2 we present a syntactic variant of the set-theoretic language $\Delta$ for querying web-like databases and provide illustrative examples of its use. In Section 3 we define the ordinary, "non-lazy" semantics of the $\Delta$-language. Its specifics consists in the assumption that all vertices of the graph by which we model the web are active. In this case arguments and results of the queries are graphs with all vertices being active, and the secondary query will be absent. As protosets, all of them will have the same first component equal to 1. Therefore, they may be considered (after "stripping" their first components) as the ordinary sets. More formally, we define the ordinary semantics of the $\Delta$-language in terms of elements of $HF_1$, the universe of non-well-founded (hereditarily finite) sets.

In Section 4 we define the lazy semantics in terms of elements of $HFP_1$ which is a new universe of non-well-founded hereditarily finite protosets.

In Section 5 we introduce an approximation relation on $HFP_1$ in order to compare query answers with respect to their precision degrees. Here also the main Theorem is formulated which states that lazy semantics:

(i) coincides with ordinary semantics under the activity of all data sources;
(ii) guarantees, that only active sources hit to the computed part of the answer;
(iii) supplies more and more precise answers under monotone extension of the set of active data sources;
(iv) is correct.

In this paper we do not consider the very intriguing and important questions of using the secondary queries stored as data in database in subsequent queries. This would require linguistic reflection [15,12], i.e., the introduction of a Lisp-like operation **eval** into query language, and the composition of query results, which in general may be incompletely computed. Some algorithms and results concerning related problems may be found in [3,6].

The $\Delta$-language has been implemented both with ordinary and lazy semantics.

## 2   A Query Language $\Delta$ for the WWW

The possibility to use the set-theoretic language $\Delta$ as query language for web-like databases (in other terms, semi-structured databases [1]) was shown in [7]. The main idea is that sets whose elements are again sets, etc. may be naturally represented by vertices of a graph, and membership relations $v \in u$ by edges $u \to v$ of that graph. Generally, an element $v$ of set $u$ may have an attribute label $l$, what is denoted as $l : v \in u$. This may be represented by a labelled edge $u \xrightarrow{l} v$.

On the other hand, the WWW also has a graph structure. Here, the graph vertices represent the web-documents with unique URL-addresses of the form

http://www.botik.ru/PSI/index.html

while the graph edges are the hypertext links between web-documents. There are no restrictions for references. Thus, the presence of cycles in a hypertext structure is a typical situation. But the cycles in the membership relation such as $u \in v_1 \in v_2 \in ... \in v_n \in u$ $(n \geq 0)$ are forbidden in the usual set theory by the Foundation axiom. If this axiom is replaced by the Anti-Foundation Axiom this problem disappears. In particular, the resulting non-standard set theory has the universe $HF_1$ of non-well-founded hereditarily-finite sets among its models.

In practice, a notion of "locality" is very important in the web-context. Two web-documents are **local** with respect to each other, if they are placed on the same web-server (more precisely, have the same hostname-component in their URL's). Formalizing this notion of locality requires to introduce in the set-theoretical language a basic binary predicate *Local*. This predicate is satisfied for pairs of relatively local documents. This predicate is important for the problem of reducing the query search space, which will be demonstrated in some query examples below.

## 2.1 Syntax

The syntax of the $\Delta$-language for WWW-querying is defined as follows:

$\Delta$-terms ::= $\mathbf{c}\,|\,x\,|\,\emptyset\,|\,\{l_1 : t_1, ..., l_n : t_n\}\,|\cup t\,|TC(t)|LTC(t)|$
$\qquad \{l : x\,|\,l : x \in t \,\&\, \phi(l, x)\,\}\,|\{l : t'(x)\,|\,l : x \in t\}\,|$
$\qquad D(s, t)\,|\,\mathbf{fix}\,q.[\,q = q \cup \{l : x\,|\,l : x \in t \,\&\, \phi(q, l, x)\}, p\,]$

$\Delta$-formulas ::= $T\,|\,F\,|\,l = m\,|\,s = t\,|\,l : s \in t\,|\,\neg\phi\,|\,\phi_1 \,\&\, \phi_2\,|\,\phi_1 \vee \phi_2\,|$
$\qquad \forall l : x \in t\,\phi(l, x)\,|\,\exists l : x \in t\,\phi(l, x)$

Here, $\mathbf{c}$ is a constant (URL-address), $x$ is a set variable and $t, t', t_i, s$ are $\Delta$- terms, $l, l_i, m$ are labels, i.e. words from a given language $\mathcal{L}$. The operator $\cup t$ is the set-theoretical union of the family $t$ of sets. $TC(t)$ is the transitive closure of the set $t$. In WWW-terms this is a set of all web-documents reachable from page $t$. $LTC(t)$ is defined in the same way as $TC(t)$, but references among web-documents may be only local. Formally, a reference $u \overset{l}{\rightarrow} v$ is local iff $Local(u, v) = true$.

$\{l : x\,|\,l : x \in t \,\&\, \phi(l, x)\,\}$ and $\{l : t'(x)|l : x \in t\}$ are the constructs of selection (comprehension) and image, respectively. The construct $\mathbf{fix}$ for inflationary fixed points denotes the least solution of the equation

$$q \;=\; q \cup \{l : x\,|\,l : x \in t \,\&\, \phi(q, l, x)\} \quad,$$

that is the result of stabilizing the sequence $q_0, q_1, q_2, \ldots$ of sets, where $q_0 = p$ and $q_{i+1} = q_i \cup \{l : x\,|\,l : x \in t \,\&\, \phi(q_i, l, x)\}$.

The operation $D(s, t)$ is a "pure" set-theoretic equivalent of the decoration operation (in other terms, Mostowski surjection) which is well-known in non-well-founded set theory [11]. The original decoration of a graph $G = \langle V, E \rangle$ is a function $d_G$ on $V$, such that

$$d_G(v) = \{d_G(u)|(v \rightarrow u) \in E\}\,.$$

For example, if $G = \langle \{v_1, v_2, v_3\}, \{v \rightarrow v_1, v \rightarrow v_2, v_2 \rightarrow v_3\}\rangle$, then $d_G(v) = \{\emptyset, \{\emptyset\}\}$.

Let $s$ be a some set the elements of which may be ordered pairs $\langle u, v \rangle$ of sets. Following Mostowski such pairs can be encoded as sets $\{u, \{u, v\}\}$. Then we define a function $G$ on arbitrary sets $s$ by

$$G(s) = \langle\{v|<u, v >\in s \vee <v, u >\in s\}, \{v \rightarrow u|<u, v >\in s\}\rangle.$$

The operation $D(s, t)$ of the $\Delta$-language is theninterpreted as $D(s, t) = d_{G(s)}(t)$, where the argument $t$ of the function $d_{G(s)}$ is treated as a vertex of the graph $G(s)$. In fact, we will apply the above decoration operation in the context of labelled sets or graphs, respectively.

## 2.2   Query Examples

*Example 2.1.*   We would want to know whether Java and Web are among the research interests on Mathematics department of Indiana University. Thus, we want to find on the web-site of this department all pages labelled by words "Java" or "Web":
$$\{\, l : x \,|\, l : x \,\in\, LTC(www.math.indiana.edu)\,\&$$
$$(\, l = "Java" \,\vee\, l = "Web"\,)\,\}. \qquad \Box$$

*Example 2.2.*   To which web-sites references exist from the web-site of the above department? Concretely, we want to collect all references from a given web-site to external sites. With some syntactical abbreviations, which are expressible through basic constructs of the $\Delta$-language, this query looks as:
$$\{\, l : x \,|\, l : x \,\in\, y \,\in\, LTC(www.math.indiana.edu)\,\&$$
$$\neg(\, l : x \,\in\, LTC(www.math.indiana.edu\,)\,)\,\}. \qquad \Box$$

*Example 2.3.*   Find all pages on a given site (say, www.math.indiana.edu),from which the main (home) page of this site is reachable. The corresponding query (in some lightened syntax without labels) which uses the **fix**-construct is shown below:
$$\textbf{fix}\, q\,.\,[\, q \,=\, q \cup \{\, x \,|\, x \,\in\, LTC(www.math.indiana.edu)\,\&$$
$$(\,(www.math.indiana.edu \,\in\, x)\,\vee\,(\exists z \in q.\, z \in x)\,)\,\}\,,\,\emptyset\,]. \qquad \Box$$

*Example 2.4.*   The answers to all queries are always stored on the "local" computer, where the query system is executed. Then, we have the possibility to copy a complete remote web-site (more precisely, its hypertextual, topological structure) to the local computer. First we represent this remote site as a set of edges (hyperlinks), and then we reconstruct its original structure by decoration :
$$D(\{\, l : \langle x, y \rangle \,|\, x, y \,\in\, LTC(\{root : www.math.indiana.edu\})\,\&$$
$$(\, l : x \in y)\}\,,\, www.math.indiana.edu\,).$$
Note, that having a local copy of a remote site, we may now query this site locally. $\qquad \Box$

## 3   *W*-Structures and Ordinary Semantics

We begin with the definition of the ordinary, "non-lazy" semantics of the $\Delta$-language. This semantics models the situation when all data sources in the web are active.

### 3.1   W-Structures and Local Bisimulation

As stated above we take into account in our web-model the notion "locality", both when all sources are active and in more general case with some inactive sources. Namely, we define the ordinary semantics on so called *W-structures* which are graphs with "localities":

$$W = \langle V, E, Local \rangle \,,$$

where $V$ is a (finite) set of vertices denoting web-documents, $E \subseteq \mathcal{L} \times (V \times V)$ is a finite set of edges labelled by words from a given language $\mathcal{L}$ and $Local \subseteq V \times V$ is an equivalence relation. Any equivalence class with respect to $Local$ denotes a set of web-documents placed on the same site.

**Notation.** The triple $\langle l, u, v \rangle \in E$ will be denoted as $u \xrightarrow{l} v$.

According to this model two HTML-pages are assumed to be equal, if they are placed on the same web-server and contain equally labelled hyperlinks pointing to equal or identical pages. In particular, a page and its copy on "mirroring" site will not be equal.

Formally, this understanding of page "equality" is realized by an extended definition of the well-known notion of bisimulation:

**Definition 3.1.** A *local bisimulation* on the W-structure $W = \langle V, E, Local \rangle$ is a relation $R \subseteq V^2$, such that for any $u, v \in V$

$$u \, R \, v \Rightarrow (Local(u,v) \,\&$$
$$\forall (u \xrightarrow{l} u') \in E \; \exists (v \xrightarrow{l} v') \in E$$
$$((Local(u,u') \Rightarrow u'Rv') \,\&$$
$$(\neg Local(u,u') \Rightarrow u' = v')) \,\&$$
$$\forall (v \xrightarrow{l} v') \in E \; \exists (u \xrightarrow{l} u') \in E$$
$$((Local(v,v') \Rightarrow u'Rv') \,\&$$
$$(\neg Local(v,v') \Rightarrow u' = v'))$$

$\square$

Let $\approx_W = \bigcup \{R \mid R \subseteq V^2$ is a local bisimulation on $W\}$.

## 3.2 Transformers of W-Structures

In accordance with the idea exposed in the introduction, we define the ordinary, "non-lazy" semantics of the $\Delta$-language through the (inflationary) **transformer IT of terms and formulas on W-structures** of the form

$$IT :< W, t > \mapsto < W', v' >,$$
$$IT :< W, \phi > \mapsto < W', b >,$$

where $t$ is a closed $\Delta$-term, $\phi$ a closed $\Delta$-formula, and $W'$ is an extension of the source structure $W$ :

$$W' = < V \cup V_l, E', Local' > \,,$$

such that $V \cap V_l = \emptyset$, $E \subseteq E'$, $Local' = Local \cup \{< u, v > \mid u, v \in V_l\}$, $v' \in V \cup V_l$, and $b \in \{T, F\}$. Here $V_l$ models the set of web-documents created by the term (query) $t$ (or formula $\phi$) evaluation on the computer, where the query system is executed.

Informally, this transformer treats the set-theoretic operations of the $\Delta$-language (the explicit enumeration, the union, the transitive closure and others) in terms of modifications (namely, extensions) of the original $W$-structure.

In addition, for the $\Delta$-formulas the transformer indicates besides the extension rules (since formulas contains terms), how the truth values are computed.

As an abbreviation for the sequential transformation of $\Delta$-terms $t_1, \ldots, t_n$, starting with the structure $W$, where

$$IT(< W, t_1 >) = < W_1, v_1 >,$$
$$IT(< W_{i-1}, t_i >) = < W_i, v_i >, \quad 2 \leq i \leq n,$$

and $W_i = < V \cup V_{l_i}, E_i, Local_i >, 1 \leq i \leq n$, we will use the generalized IT-transformer

$$IT :< W, t_1, ..., t_n >\mapsto< W', v_1, ..., v_n >,$$

where $W' = < V \cup V_l, E_n, Local_n >$, and $V_l = \bigcup V_{l_i}$. In particular, $v_1, ..., v_n \in V \cup V_l$.

## Notations.

1. Let $W = < V, E, Local >$ be some W-structure. Then, we suppose that in the $\Delta$-language there exists a constant $\mathbf{c}$ for each vertex $v \in V$, which denotes this vertex.
2. If $\phi(l, x)$ is a formula with free variables $l$ and $x$, then $\phi[m, t]$ is the result of substitution of $m$ and $t$ in each free occurence of $l$ and $x$ in the formula $\phi$, respectively.
3. $\equiv$ denotes syntactical identity.
4. In the sequel, structures $W'$ and $W_1$ have form: $W' = < V \cup V_l, E', Local' >$ and $W_1 = < V \cup V_1, E_1, Local_1 >$.

## 3.3    Transformer IT: Fragments of the Definition

In the following we present the characteristic clauses of the inductive definition of IT. In all cases, unless otherwise specified, it is assumed that

$$IT(< W, s >) = < W_1, v_1 >,$$
$$IT(< W, t >) = < W', v' >,$$

and $V_l = V_1 \cup \{v'\}, v' \notin V \cup V_1$.

Recall, that $< W', v' >$ is the extended resulting structure, where $v'$ represents the computed value of $t$.

**1a.** $t \equiv \mathbf{c}_\mathbf{v}$.
Here $IT(< W, t >) = < W, v >$.

**2a.** $t \equiv \cup s$.
Here $E' = E_1 \cup \{v' \overset{m}{\rightarrow} w | \exists l \in \mathcal{L} \exists u \in V \cup V_1 (v_1 \overset{l}{\rightarrow} u \in E_1 \& u \overset{m}{\rightarrow} w \in E_1)\}$.
This is the ordinary definition of the set-theoretic union in graph terms.

**3a.** $t \equiv \{l_1 : t_1, ..., l_n : t_n\}$.
Let $IT(< W, t_1, ..., t_n >) = < W_1, v_1, ..., v_n >$, where $v_1, ..., v_n \in V \cup V_1$. Then $E' = E_1 \cup \{v' \overset{l}{\rightarrow} v_i | 1 \leq i \leq n\}$.

**4a.** $t \equiv TC(s)$.
Here $E' = E_1 \cup \{v' \overset{l}{\rightarrow} u | exists\ a\ path\ v_1 \overset{l_1}{\rightarrow} u_1 \overset{l_2}{\rightarrow} u_2 \rightarrow ... \overset{l_n}{\rightarrow} u_n, n \geq 1$, in $W_1$ such that $l_n = l$ and $u_n = u\}$.
This is a habitual definition of the set-theoretic transitive closure again in graph terms.

**5a.**$t \equiv LTC(s)$.

Here $E'$ is defined as in 4a with additional condition for the path: $\forall 1 \leq i \leq n, Local(v_1, u_i)\}$.

**6a.**$t \equiv \{l : x | l : x \in s \,\&\, \phi(l, x)\}$. (Here $l, x$ are bounded variables, where the values of $l$ are the labels).

Then $E' = E_1 \cup \{v' \xrightarrow{m} u | (v_1 \xrightarrow{m} u) \in E_1 \,\&\, IT(< W_1, \phi[m, \mathbf{c_u}] >) = < W'', T >$ for some W-structure $W''$ $\}$.

Here $IT(< W_1, \phi[m, \mathbf{c_u}] >)$ gives the truth value of $\phi[m, \mathbf{c_u}]$ on structure $W_1$.

**1b.** $\phi \equiv T(F)$.

Then $IT(< W, \phi >) = < W, T(F) >$.

The transformer IT behaves on logical constants as identity map.

**2b.** $\phi \equiv l = m$.

Then $IT(< W, \phi >) = < W, b >$, where

$$b = \begin{cases} T, & \text{if } l \equiv m, \\ F, & \text{otherwise} \end{cases}$$

**3b.**$\phi \equiv l : s \in t$. Let $IT(< W, s, t >) = < W_1, v_1, v_2 >$. Then $IT(< W, \phi >) \quad = \quad < W_1, b >$, where

$$b = \begin{cases} T, & \text{if } \exists v_1' \in V \cup V_1 (v_2 \xrightarrow{l} v_1') \in E_1 \,\&\, v_1 \approx_{W_1} v_1', \\ F, & \text{in other case.} \end{cases}$$

Here we use a bisimulation relation to treat the equality predicate in the $\Delta$-language.

**4b.**$\phi \equiv \forall l : x \in t \, \psi(l, x)$. Let $IT(< W, t >) = < W_1, v_1 >$. Then $IT(< W, \phi >) = < W_1, b >$, where

$$b = \begin{cases} T, & \text{if } \forall (v_1 \xrightarrow{m} u) \in E_1 \; IT(< W_1, \psi[m, \mathbf{c_u}] >) = < W'', T > \\ & \text{for some structure } W'' \text{ depending on } u, \\ F, & \text{in other case.} \end{cases}$$

Original graph transformers for $\Delta$-language are described in [7,13].

**Definition 3.2 (Semantics of terms).**
If $t$ is closed $\Delta$-term , and $IT(< W, t >) = < W', v' >$, then a **denotation of term $t$ on the structure W** (denoted as $[\![t]\!]^W$ or simply $[\![t]\!]$, if the structure W is known from the context) is a set $[\![v']\!]^{W'}$ defined corecursively as

$$[\![v']\!]^{W'} = \{l : [\![u]\!]^{W'} | (v' \xrightarrow{l} u) \in E'\} ,$$

the existence of which is guaranteed in the universe $HF_1$.                          □

# 4   $W_A$-Structures and Lazy Semantics

The web in which some data sources may be inactive is modelled by extended W-structures that are supplied by an *activity function* $A : V \to \{0, 1\}$. Such extended structures will be called as $W_A$-structures, and they have the general form:

$$W_A = \langle V, E, Local, A \rangle.$$

Correspondingly, the lazy semantics of the $\Delta$-language is defined through **the transformer LC** (lazy computation) **of terms and formulas on $W_A$-structures**:

$$LC :< W_A, t >\mapsto< W'_{A'}, v', r >,$$
$$LC :< W_A, \phi >\mapsto< W'_{A'}, \phi' >,$$

where $t, r$ are $\Delta$-terms, $\phi, \phi'$ are $\Delta$-formulas, $W'_{A'} =< V \cup V_l, E', Local', A' >$, $V \cap V_l = \emptyset$, $E \subseteq E'$, $Local' = Local \cup \{< u, v > | u, v \in V_l\}$, $A = A'|_V$ and $v' \in V \cup V_l$. Note also that terms and formulas may contain free variables in this case.

Informally, in the triple $< W'_{A'}, v', r > v'$ is the semantic part of the answer to the query $t$, namely the computed part of the term $t$, and $r$ is the syntactic part of the answer to the query, i.e. the uncomputed, "lazy" part of the term $t$.

As above, the sequential transformation of $\Delta$-terms $t_1, \ldots, t_n$ starting with structure $W_A$ will be presented by generalized LC-transformer of the form

$$LC :< W_A, t_1, \ldots, t_n >\mapsto< W'_{A'}, < v_1, r_1 >, \ldots, < v_n, r_n >>.$$

**Definition 4.1.**
An *active local bisimulation* on the $W_A$-structure $W_A = \langle V, E, Local, A \rangle$ is a relation $R \subseteq V^2$, such that for any $u, v \in V$

$$u\,R\,v \Rightarrow (Local(u, v) \,\&\, A(u) = A(v) = 1 \,\&$$
$$\forall(u \xrightarrow{l} u') \in E\, \exists(v \xrightarrow{l} v') \in E$$
$$((Local(u, u') \Rightarrow u'R\,v') \,\&$$
$$(\neg Local(u, u') \Rightarrow u' = v'))\,\&$$
$$\forall(v \xrightarrow{l} v') \in E\, \exists(u \xrightarrow{l} u') \in E$$
$$((Local(v, v') \Rightarrow u'R\,v') \,\&$$
$$(\neg Local(v, v') \Rightarrow u' = v'))$$

holds.     □

Let $\approx_{W_A} = \bigcup\{R \,|\, R \subseteq V^2$ is active local bisimulation on $W_A\}$.

**Definition 4.2.** If $A_1, A_2 : V \to \{0, 1\}$ are activity functions, then define $A_1 \sqsubseteq A_2$, iff $\forall v \in V\; A_1(v) \leq A_2(v)$.     □

Especially note that a very strong definition of bisimulation is a necessary condition for the monotonicity of lazy semantics under the corresponding extension of set of the active data sources. In order to achieve in general the semantics to be monotonic, then whenever formula $\phi$ has some truth value on the $W_A$-structure, then the same value must be preserved on any $W_{A'}$-structure, such that $A \sqsubseteq A'$.

## 4.1   Two Variants of Lazy Semantics

In the following we present two variants of the lazy semantics for the $\Delta$-language called *rough* and *precise*, respectively. The difference between them may be easily explained by an example.

*Example 4.1.* Let us consider the term $\cup p$, where

$$p = \langle 0, \{\langle 0, x \rangle, \langle 1, \{\langle 0, y \rangle, \langle 1, z \rangle\}\rangle\}\rangle$$

is a protoset. Then the pair $\langle e, r \rangle$ consisting of the protoset $e = \langle 0, \emptyset \rangle$ and the secondary term $r \equiv \cup p$ will be a denotation of the term $\cup p$ in the rough variant of semantics (see for example cases 4a, 5a, 6a, clause a) in the definition of transformer **LC**). In general, this means that if an inactive protoset, i.e., a protoset of form $\langle 0, s \rangle$ for some set $s$, occurs in the denotation of some subterm of the term under consideration, then the elements of $s$ will not be taken into account in the denotation of a basic term.

In contrast, the pair $\langle e', r' \rangle$ consisting of the inactive protoset $e' = \langle 0, \{\langle 1, z \rangle\}\rangle$ and some secondary term $r'$ will be a denotation of the same term in the precise variant of the semantics. In other words, this variant takes into account the known elements of the incompletely defined protosets in order to give the maximally precise denotation of basic term.    □

Though we are stopping in the middle of one's course in the rough semantics, it nevertheless turns out to be useful enough for practical needs.

We now give below the definition of the rough semantics, leaving the precise variant for forthcoming papers.

## 4.2    Transformer LC: Fragments of the Definition

When the set of terms $l_i : t_i$ in the enumeration construct $\{l_1 : t_1, ..., l_n : t_n\}$ is given by a property $\phi(l, t)$, we will use the metanotation $\{|l : t|\phi(l, t)|\}$ instead.

In all following clauses, unless stated differently, we assume that

$$LC(< W_A, s >) = < W_{A_1}, v_1, r_1 > \text{ and}$$
$$LC(< W_A, t >) = < W'_{A'}, v', r >,$$

with

$$W_{A_1} = < V \cup V_1, E_1, Local_1, A_1 >,$$
$$W'_{A'} = < V \cup V_l, E', Local', A' >,$$
$$V_l = V_1 \cup \{v'\}, v' \notin V \cup V_1,$$

and

$$A' = \begin{cases} A_1 \cup \{< v', 1 >\}, & \text{if } r \overset{*}{\Rightarrow} \emptyset, \\ A_1 \cup \{< v', 0 >\}, & \text{otherwise.} \end{cases}$$

Here $x \overset{*}{\Rightarrow} y$ means "$x$ can be rewritten to $y$". For example, $\cup \{\emptyset, \emptyset\} \overset{*}{\Rightarrow} \emptyset$ ).

**1a.** $t \equiv c_v$.
Then $LC(< W_A, t >) = < W_A, v, \emptyset >$.

**2a.** $t \equiv x$.
Then $r \equiv x$, $E' = E$, $A' = A \cup \{< v', 0 >\}$,
i.e., any free variable always is transformed to the secondary term with adding "empty" vertex to resulting structure.

**3a.** $t \equiv \{l_1 : t_1, ..., l_n : t_n\}$.
Let $LC(< W_A, t_1, .., t_n >) = < W_{A_1},$
$< v_1, r_1 >, .., < v_n, r_n >>$, where $v_i \in V \cup V_1, 1 \le i \le n$. Then

$r \equiv \{|l_i : t_i| \ 1 \leq i \leq n \ \& \ A_1(v_i) = 0|\}$,

$E' = E_1 \cup \{v' \xrightarrow{l_i} v_i | 1 \leq i \leq n \& A_1(v_i) = 1\}$.

Here, the secondary term $r$ enumerates all uncomputed terms-arguments.

**4a.** $t \equiv \cup s$.

**a):** If $A_1(v_1) = 0$, then $r \equiv \cup s$ and $E' = E_1$.

**b):** If $A_1(v_1) = 1$, then

$r \equiv \cup \{ FstLevel : r_1, SndLevel : r_2 \}$, where

$FstLevel, SndLevel$ are any two new labels, and

$r_1 \equiv \cup \{| l : \mathbf{c_u} \ \ |\exists l \in \mathcal{L} \exists u \in V \cup V_1 \, ( v_1 \xrightarrow{l} u \in E_1 \ \& \ A_1(u) = 0 \,) |\}$,

$r_2 \equiv \{| m : \mathbf{c_w} \ \ |\exists l \in \mathcal{L} \ \exists u \in V \cup V_1 \, ( v_1 \xrightarrow{l} u \in E_1 \ \& $

$A_1(u) = 1 \ \& \ u \xrightarrow{m} w \in E_1 \ \& \ A_1(w) = 0 \,) |\}$, and

$E' = E_1 \cup \{v' \xrightarrow{m} w | \exists l \in \mathcal{L} \exists u \in V \cup V_1 \, ( v_1 \xrightarrow{l} u \in E_1 \ \& \ A_1(u) = 1 \ \& \ u \xrightarrow{m} w \in$

$E_1 \ \& \ A_1(w) = 1 \,) \}$.

In this case, term $r$ describes all vertices unreachable from $v_1$ on pathes with length 2 (due to inactivity some vertices on these pathes).

In the following, let

$$R(l, u) \ \rightleftharpoons \ "exists\, a\, path\ v_1 \xrightarrow{l_1} u_1 \xrightarrow{l_2} u_2 \rightarrow ... \xrightarrow{l_n} u_n \ in \ W_{A_1},$$
$$such\, that\, l_n = l \ \& \ u_n = u"$$

**5a.** $t \equiv TC(s)$.

**a):** If $A_1(v_1) = 0$, then $r \equiv TC(s)$ and $E' = E_1$.

**b):** If $A_1(v_1) = 1$, then

$r \equiv TC(\{|l : \mathbf{c_u}| R(l, u) \ \& \ \forall 1 \leq i \leq n{-}1 A(u_i) = 1 \& A(u_n) = 0|\}$, $E' = E_1 \cup \{v' \xrightarrow{l}$

$u| R(l, u) \ \& \ \forall 1 \leq i \leq n A(u_i) = 1\}$.

Here, the term $t$ is constructed as in 4a with the exception that the pathes of arbitrary length are considered.

**6a.** $t \equiv LTC(s)$.

**a):** If $A_1(v_1) = 0$, then $r \equiv LTC(s)$ and $E' = E_1$.

**b):** If $A_1(v_1) = 1$, then

$r \equiv \cup \{ Vertices : r_1, TheirLTC's : r_2 \}$,

where again $Vertices, TheirLTC's$ are any two new labels, and

$r_1 \equiv \{l : \mathbf{c_u}| R(l, u) \ \& \ \forall 1 \leq i \leq n - 1 \ A_1(u_i) = 1 \& A_1(u_n) = 0|\}$, $r_2 \equiv \{l :$

$LTC(\mathbf{c_u}) | R(l, u) \ \& \ \forall 1 \leq i \leq n - 1 \ A_1(u_i) = 1 \& A_1(u_n) = 0|\}$, $E' = E_1 \cup \{v' \xrightarrow{l}$

$u| R(l, u) \ \& \ \forall 1 \leq i \leq n \ A_1(u_i) = 1\}$.

In the definition of secondary term $r$ we take into account the subtle property of operation $LTC(t)$, that if the term $t$ is complex, i.e., $t \not\equiv \mathbf{c}$, then the local transitive closure is computed "without looking inside" to the sets, denoted by constants in $t$ (to be distinguished from ordinary $TC$ – see definition of $Local'$ for transformers IT or LC ).

**7a.** $t \equiv \mathbf{fix}\, q.[\,q = q \cup \{1 : x | 1 : x \in t \ \& \ \phi(q, l, x)\}, \ p\,]$

Here, we will explain the "lazy" semantics of given construction only informally ( the precise formulation is too cumbersome).

The ordinary computation of the **fix** operation is performed by construction of the sequence of sets:

$$q_0 = p,$$

$$q_{i+1} = q_i \cup \{l : x \mid l : x \in t \,\&\, \phi(q_i, l, x)\}$$

until to the stabilization of this sequence.

The lazy computation of **fix** is finished, if either

(a) the sequence has been stabilized on, say, $q_n$ , and all elements of this sequence have been completely computed; in this case, $< q_n, \emptyset >$ is the result of the lazy computation of $t$,

or

(b) if the next in turn $q_i$ has not been computed completely; in this case the result is

$$< \emptyset, t >, \qquad \text{if } i = 0,$$

or

$$< q_{i-1}, r >, \quad \text{if } i > 0,$$

where $r \equiv \mathbf{fix}\, \mathrm{q}.[\mathrm{q} = \mathrm{q} \cup \{1 : \mathrm{x} \mid 1 : \mathrm{x} \in \mathrm{t} \,\&\, \phi(\mathrm{q}, 1, \mathrm{x})\}, \mathrm{q_{i-1}}]$.

Add, that above $q_i$ is considered as completely computed, if all $q' \in q_i$ are completely computed also (this needed in order to the clause (ii) in Main Theorem would be true).

**1b.** $\phi \equiv l : s \in t$.

Let $LC(< W_A, s, t >) = < W_{A_1}, < v_1, r_1 >, < v_2, r_2 >>$. Then
$LC(< W_A, \phi >) = < W_{A_1}, \phi' >$, where

$$\phi' = \begin{cases} T, & \text{if } A_1(v_1) = 1 \,\& \\ & [\exists v_1' \in V \cup V_1 (v_2 \xrightarrow{l} v_1') \in E_1 \,\& \, v_1 \approx_{W_{A_1}} v_1'] \\ F, & \text{if } A_1(v_1) = A_1(v_2) = 1 \,\& \\ & \neg[\exists v_1' \in V \cup V_1 (v_2 \xrightarrow{l} v_1') \in E_1 \,\& \, v_1 \approx_{W_{A_1}} v_1'] \\ \phi, & \text{in other cases .} \end{cases}$$

**Definition 4.3 (Lazy semantics of terms).**
For a $\Delta$-term $t$ we have $LC(< W_A, t >) = < W'_{A'}, v', r >$, where $W_A = < V, E, Local, A >$. Then, a *(lazy) denotation of term* $t$ *on the structure* $W_A$, denoted as $[\![t]\!]^{W_A}$, or simply $[\![t]\!]^A$, is a value $[\![v']\!]^{W'_{A'}}$, defined by corecursive identity

$$[\![v']\!]^{W'_{A'}} = \langle A'(v'), \{l : [\![u]\!]^{W'_{A'}} \mid (v' \xrightarrow{l} u) \in E'\} \rangle . \qquad \square$$

The above pairs generalize the notion of "protoset" [10] to the non-well-founded case.

**Definition 4.4.** An *active denotation of a term* $t$ *on the structure* $W_A$ (denoted as $[\![t]\!]_a^{W_A}$ or simply $[\![t]\!]_a^A$) is a set $[\![v']\!]_a^{W'_{A'}}$ defined as

$$[\![v']\!]_a^{W'_{A'}} = \{l : [\![u]\!]_a^{W'_{A'}} \mid (v' \xrightarrow{l} u) \in E' \,\& A'(u) = 1\}. \qquad \square$$

## 5    Main Theorem

In order to state our main theorem, we have to define what it means that a (non-well-founded) protoset approximates another protoset, otherwise said, that it is clarified by it. First of all, there is precise definition of the universe $HFP_1$ of non-well-founded hereditarily-finite protosets as the largest set $x$, such that

$$x = \{0,1\} \times \mathcal{P}_{<\omega}(x) \,,$$

where, $\mathcal{P}_{<\omega}(x)$ is the set of all finite subsets of $x$. $HFP_1$ is the generalization of the well known universe $HF_1$ of non-well-founded hereditarily-finite sets. The existence of this universe can be proved by using the Anti-Foundation Axiom [2].

**Notation.** If $x \in HFP_1$, then we write $x^0$ for the first component of $x$, and $x^1$ for the second component.

Moreover, we adopt the slight modification to work in the universe $HFP_1^{\mathcal{L}}$ – the universe of protosets with elements labelled by words from the set $\mathcal{L}$.

**Definition 5.1.** An *approximation relation* on $HFP_1^{\mathcal{L}}$ is any binary relation $R_{\sqsubseteq}$ such that for any $x, y \in HFP_1^{\mathcal{L}}$

$$x\, R_{\sqsubseteq}\, y \Rightarrow [x^0 = y^0 = 1 \;\&\; \forall l : x' \in x^1 \,\exists l : y' \in y^1\, x'\, R_{\sqsubseteq}\, y'\, \&$$
$$\forall l : y' \in y^1 \,\exists l : x' \in x^1\, x'\, R_{\sqsubseteq}\, y'\,] \vee$$
$$[x^0 = 0 \;\&\; \forall l : x' \in x^1 \,\exists l : y' \in y^1\, x'\, R_{\sqsubseteq}\, y'\,]\ \text{holds.}$$

*We say that $x$ approximates $y$ (or $y$ clarifies $x$) and denote this as $x \sqsubseteq y$, iff there exists an approximation relation $R_{\sqsubseteq}$, such that $x\, R_{\sqsubseteq}\, y$.* □

Again, our relation $\sqsubseteq$ is an extension of approximation preorder from [10] to non-well-founded case.

**Theorem 5.1.**

(i) *Let $t$ be a closed $\Delta$-term, $W =< V, E, Local >$, and $W_1 =< V, E, Local, \mathbb{1} >$, where $\mathbb{1} : V \to \{1\}$ is the constant function. Then*
$$[\![t]\!] = [\![t]\!]_a^*,$$
*i.e., the ordinary and the lazy semantics coincide in case of absence of in-active sources.*

(ii) *Let $W_A =< V, E, Local, A >$ and for any $\Delta$-term $t$ (where $t \not\equiv \mathbf{c}$) let*
$$LC(< W_A, t >) =< W'_{A'}, v', r >,$$
*where $W'_{A'} =< V \cup V_l, E', Local', A' >$. Then*
$$v' \in V_l \Rightarrow \forall (v' \xrightarrow{l} u) \in E'\, A'(u) = 1,$$
*i.e., in the computed part of the term (query) only active sources are present.*

(iii) *Let $A_1$ and $A_2$ be activity functions with $A_1 \sqsubseteq A_2$. Then, for any $\Delta$-term $t$ we get*
$$[\![t]\!]^{A_1} \sqsubseteq [\![t]\!]^{A_2},$$
*i.e., under extending the set of active sources we obtain more and more precise answers.*

(iv) *Let $W_A =< V, E, Local, A >$ and $LC(< W_A, t >) =< W'_{A'}, v', r >$ be as in (ii). Then we get*
$$(a)\ [\![t]\!]^A \sqsubseteq [\![t]\!]^*,$$
$$(b) \text{for any } A_1,\ (\,0\,,\,(\,[\![r]\!]^{A_1}\,)^1\,) \sqsubseteq [\![t]\!]^{A_1}$$
$$(\text{ in particular, }\ [\![r]\!]_a^* \subseteq [\![t]\!]_a^*),$$
*i.e., the lazy semantics is correct.*                                 □

**Acknowledgements.** I very grateful to Vladimir Sazonov and Alexei Lisitsa for fruitful conversations of this work.

# References

1. Abiteboul S. Querying semistructured data, in: ICDT'97, LNCS, vol. 1186, Springer, 1997, pp. 1- 18.
2. Aczel P. Non-Well-Founded Sets. CSLI Lecture Notes, no. 14, 1988.
3. Aliffi D., Dovier A., Rossi G. From set to hyperset unification, The Journal of Functional and Logic Programming, Volume 1999, no. 11, pp. 1-48.
4. Bonnet P., Tomasic A. Partial answers for unavailable data sources, in: Proceedings of the Conference on Flexible Query Answering Systems, Roskilde, Denmark, 1998, pp. 43-54.
5. A.Deutsch, M.Fernandez, D.Florescu, A.Levy, D.Maier, D.Suciu. Querying XML Data, IEEE Data Engineering Bulletin, September 1999, vol. 22, no. 3, pp.10 - 18.
6. Dovier A., Piazza C., Policriti A. Fast (hyper)set equivalence, in: B.Jayaraman, G.Rossi, eds., DPS'99 Workshop on Declarative Programming with Sets, Paris, September 28, 1999.
7. Lisitsa A.P., Sazonov V.Yu. Bounded hyperset theory and Web-like data bases, in: 5th Kurt Gödel Colloquium, KGC'97, LNCS, vol. 1289, Springer,1997, pp.172-185.
8. Lisitsa A.P., Sazonov V.Yu. $\Delta$-languages for sets and LOGSPACE-computable graph transformers, Theoretical Computer Science, vol. 175, no. 1, 1997, pp. 183 - 222.
9. Lisitsa A.P., Sazonov V.Yu. Linear ordering on graphs, anti-founded sets and polynomial time computability, Theoretical Computer Science, vol. 224, no. 1-2, 1999, pp. 173-213.
10. Mislove M.W., Moss L.S., Oles F.J. Non-well-founded sets modeled as ideal fixed points, Information and Computation, vol. 93, no. 1, 1991, pp.16-54.
11. Moschovakis Y.N. Notes in set theory, Springer-Verlag, New York, 1994.
12. Neven J., Van den Bussche J., Van Gucht D., Vossen G. Typed query languages for databases containing queries, Information Systems, 1999, to appear.
13. Sazonov V.Yu. Hereditarily finite sets, data bases and polynomial-time computability, Theoretical Computer Science, vol. 119, no. 2, 1993, pp. 187 - 214.
14. Vrbsky S.V., Liu J.W.S. APPROXIMATE : A query processor that produces monotonically improving approximate answers, Transactions on Knowledge and Data Engineering, vol. 5, no. 6, December 1993, pp. 1056-1068.
15. Van den Bussche J., Van Guch D., Vossen G. Reflective programming in the relational algebra, Journal of Computer and System Sciences, vol. 52, no. 3, pp. 537-549, 1996.

# Minimum Matrix Representation
# of Some Key System

Krisztián Tichler[1,2]

[1] Department of Computer Science, Eötvös Loránd University (ELTE)
1088 Budapest, Hungary
[2] Alfréd Rényi Institute of Mathematics
1053 Budapest, Hungary
krisz@math-inst.hu

**Abstract.** Consider a matrix satisfying the following two properties. There are no two rows of the matrix having the same entries in two cyclically neighbouring columns. On the other hand for each subset of the columns not containing a cyclically neighbouring pair there are two rows having the same entries in these columns.

In this paper the magnitude of the minimal number of the rows of such a matrix will be determined for given number of columns. Using the same method, the analogue question can be answered for some other Sperner-systems, too. The heart of the proof is a combinatorial lemma, which might be interesting in itself.

**Keywords.** relational database, keys, antikeys, labelled directed tree, extremal problems

## 1 Introduction

A relational database system of the scheme $r(a_1, a_2, \ldots, a_n)$ can be considered as a matrix, where the columns correspond to the *attributes* $a_i$'s (for example name, date of birth, place of birth, etc.), while the rows are the *n-tuples* of the relation $r$. That is, a row contains the data of a given *individual*.

Let us denote the set of columns of a given $m \times n$ matrix $\mathbf{M}$ by $\Omega$. $K \subseteq \Omega$ is a *key*, if two rows, that agree in the columns of $K$, agree in any column. Keys play an important role in the theory of databases. A database can be considered as a matrix and if we know the connection between the columns of a key and the other columns, it is clearly sufficient to store the columns of the key. For a summary of combinatorial problems and results of database theory see for example [8].

A key is called a *minimal key*, if it does not include other keys. The system of minimal keys is clearly a non-empty *Sperner-system* (i.e. no member can include another member). On the other hand for any non-empty Sperner-system $\mathcal{K}$ there is a matrix $\mathbf{M}$ in which the family of minimal keys is exactly $\mathcal{K}$ [1,3,4]. In this case we say, that $\mathbf{M}$ *represents* $\mathcal{K}$.

However it is not clear, what the minimum of $m$ is, for which a matrix exists, which has $m$ rows and represents $\mathcal{K}$. Denote this minimum by $s(\mathcal{K})$. The

K.-D. Schewe, B. Thalheim (Eds.): FoIKS 2000, LNCS 1762, pp. 275–287, 2000.

problem was widely studied, if $|\Omega| = n$ and $\mathcal{K} = \mathcal{K}_k^n$ consists of all subsets of $\Omega$ of $k$ elements [6,5,7,2]. In many cases the exact value was determined.

$A \subseteq \Omega$ is an *antikey* if it is not a key. An antikey is called a *maximal antikey*, if other antikeys do not include it. If $\mathcal{K}$ is the system of minimal keys, denote the system of maximal antikeys by $\mathcal{K}^{-1}$. There is a strong connection between $s(\mathcal{K})$ and $|\mathcal{K}^{-1}|$, the magnitude of $s(\mathcal{K})$ is between $|\mathcal{K}^{-1}|$ and its square root. More precisely ([5])

$$|\mathcal{K}^{-1}| \leq \binom{s(\mathcal{K})}{2} \quad \text{and} \quad s(\mathcal{K}) \leq 1 + |\mathcal{K}^{-1}| \tag{1.1}$$

hold. Most of the results proved the sharpness of the lower bound until now.

It is quite natural to ask $s(\mathcal{K})$ for other Sperner-systems. While nearly nothing is known about it, the best thing we can do is to start with a simple structure. Methods for simple Sperner-systems may give ideas for solving this problem for more difficult structures. Suppose, that the Sperner-system contains only sets of two elements, for example if the Sperner-system is the circle. This problem was rised by G.O.H. Katona. Let $|\Omega| = n$, and $\mathcal{C}_n$ the circle on the columns, i.e. $\mathcal{C}_n = \{\{1,2\}, \{2,3\}, \ldots, \{n-2,n-1\}, \{n-1,n\}, \{n,1\}\}$. ($n$ is associated with $n$th column of the matrix.) The aim of this paper is to determine the magnitude of $s(\mathcal{C}_n)$. The result is somewhat surprising, because it is closer to the upper bound of (1.1). Examining the method of the proof, a more general theorem can be obtained for other Sperner-systems.

Finishing the introduction, let us say a few more words about the motivation. Suppose, that little *a priori* information is known about the structure of a given database. If some theorem ensures the validity of certain inequalities among some parameters of databases and we have information on the actual values of a part of these parameters then some statement can be conluded for the other parameters of the given matrix. In our case, we have a theorem between the number of columns, system of minimal keys and the minimal number of rows. So if we know the number of the columns and the number of the rows is less than this minimum, then the system of minimal keys can not be this one.

Finally, consider the following database scheme showing that neighbouring attribute-pairs can be the system of keys of minimal cardinality. Suppose that we have objects rotating uniformly (for example planets or stars in an astronomial database). For every object a fixed position of it is given. The attributes are the angle between the actual position and the fixed one at the integer points of time (with some unit). It is easy to see, that two neighbouring attributes determine all the data of an object (so the angular velocity modulo $2\pi$), while two other columns do not. Unfortunately, there are other types of minimal keys of greater cardinality. Instead of this system of minimal keys, we study the above simpler Sperner-system.

## 2    Summary of the Results

Before stating the theorems, two constants must be defined. Let $\kappa$ be the unique real root of the polynomial $P(x) = 23x^3 - 23x^2 + 9x - 1$, i.e. numerically

$$\kappa = \frac{1}{3} - \frac{2}{3\sqrt[3]{46}} \left( \sqrt[3]{\sqrt{\frac{27}{23}} + 1} - \sqrt[3]{\sqrt{\frac{27}{23}} - 1} \right)$$

and let us introduce the notation

$$\lambda = \kappa \log_2 \frac{1 - \kappa}{2\kappa} + \frac{1 - 3\kappa}{2} \log_2 \frac{1 - \kappa}{1 - 3\kappa}.$$

Note, that $\kappa \approx 0.177008823\ldots$ , and $\lambda \approx 0.405685231\ldots$ .

### Theorem 2.1

**A.** *For every $0 < \varepsilon < \frac{1}{2}$ there exists an $n^*$, such that for $n > n^*$*

$$|\mathcal{C}_n^{-1}|^{1-\varepsilon} \le s(\mathcal{C}_n) \le |\mathcal{C}_n^{-1}| + 1. \tag{2.1}$$

**B.**

$$\frac{\log_2 s(\mathcal{C}_n)}{n} \longrightarrow \lambda. \tag{2.2}$$

Exploiting our method, we were able to prove a more general theorem.

Let $\mathcal{G}_n$ be a Sperner-system on the underlying set $V$, $|V| = n$. Furthermore, a partition $V = \bigcup_{i=0}^{k} V_i$, $|V_i| = n_i$, $n_0 + n_1 + \ldots + n_k = n$, $V_i = \{w_1^{(i)}, \ldots, w_{n_i}^{(i)}\}$, $0 \le i \le k$ of $V$ is given satisfying the following properties. For every $1 \le i \le k$, $1 \le j \le n_i - 1$ $\{w_j^{(i)}, w_{j+1}^{(i)}\} \in \mathcal{G}_n$ holds. On the other hand for every $K \in \mathcal{G}_n$ different from the above sets $w_j^{(i)} \in K \cap (V \setminus V_0) \Rightarrow j = 1$ or $j = n_i$ holds for $1 \le i \le k$, $1 \le j \le n_i$. Assume , that $n_i \to +\infty$, $1 \le i \le k$ and $n_0 = o(n)$ then the following holds.

### Theorem 2.2

**A.** *For every $0 < \varepsilon < \frac{1}{2}$ there exists an $n^*$, such that for $n > n^*$*

$$|\mathcal{G}_n^{-1}|^{1-\varepsilon} \le s(\mathcal{G}_n) \le |\mathcal{G}_n^{-1}| + 1. \tag{2.3}$$

**B.**

$$\frac{\log_2 s(\mathcal{G}_n)}{n} \to \lambda. \tag{2.4}$$

For the sake of better understanding $\mathcal{G}_n$ let us consider a few examples.

**Example 2.3** *Some (maybe only one) disjoint circles and paths, covering every vertex. All lengths tend to infinity. (Vertices are associated with the columns of a matrix.)*

**Example 2.4** *Assume, that a finite grid is given. Devide all edges between neighbouring grid points into n parts with n−1 points (n→∞).*

**Example 2.5** *Let $S_n$ be an arbitrary Sperner-system on $\{1, 2, \ldots, \lceil \frac{n}{\log n} \rceil\}$ not containing $\emptyset, \{1\}, \{2\}$. Add the path $\{1, \lceil \frac{n}{\log n} \rceil + 1\}, \{\lceil \frac{n}{\log n} \rceil + 1, \lceil \frac{n}{\log n} \rceil + 2\}, \ldots, \{n-2, n-1\}, \{n-1, n\}, \{n, 2\}.$*

Although the first theorem is a special case of the second one, we will prove both of them. This is motivated by the several technical difficulties in the proof of the more general theorem, which could cover up the essence of the proof.

## 3   Main Lemma

A tree $F$ is called a *directed tree*, if there is a direction of the edges, so that a vertex $r$ *(root)* has only out-neighbours, and an arbitrary vertex $v \neq r$ has a uniquely determined in-neighbour $n(v)$. $N(v)$ denotes the out-neighbourhood of $v$. The set of the leaves of the tree is denoted by $l(F)$. Let $U$ be a (finite) set. A tree $F = F(U)$ is called *labelled*, if a subset $A(v)$ of $U$ is associated with each vertex $v$ of $F$.

Let $U = \{1, 2, ..., m\}$ $(m \geq 2)$. Consider the family of directed labelled trees $\mathcal{F} = \mathcal{F}^{(m)}$, for which the vertices of each tree $F \in \mathcal{F}$ are labelled as follows. The label of the root $r$ of $F$ is $A(r) = U$. For an arbitrary vertex $v$ of $F$ there is a disjoint partition $N(v) = N_0(v) \cup N_1(v)$ of its out-neighbourhood and the following hold:

$$A(v) \subseteq A(n(v)) \quad (v \neq r), \tag{3.1}$$

$$|A(v)| \geq 2, \tag{3.2}$$

$$w_1, w_2 \in N_i(v) \Rightarrow A(w_1) \cap A(w_2) = \emptyset \ (i=0,1), \tag{3.3}$$

$$w_1 \in N_i(v), w_2 \in N_{1-i}(v) \Rightarrow |A(w_1) \cap A(w_2)| \leq 1 \ (i=0,1). \tag{3.4}$$

Introduce the notation $T(m) = \max\limits_{F \in \mathcal{F}^{(m)}} |l(F)|$. As an example, consider the following labelled directed tree $F$ of $\mathcal{F}^{(9)}$.

**Example 3.1** $A(r) = \{1, 2, 3, 4, 5, 6, 7, 8, 9\}$, $N(r) = \{v_1, v_2, v_3\}$, $A(v_1) = \{1, 2, 3, 4, 5\}$, $A(v_2) = \{6, 7\}$, $A(v_3) = \{3, 6, 8\}$, $N(v_1) = \{v_4, v_5, v_6, v_7\}$, $A(v_4) = \{1, 2, 3\}$, $A(v_5) = \{4, 5\}$, $A(v_6) = \{1, 5\}$, $A(v_7) = \{3, 4\}$, $N(v_4) = \{v_8, v_9\}$, $A(v_8) = \{1, 3\}$, $A(v_9) = \{2, 3\}$, $l(F) = \{v_2, v_3, v_5, v_6, v_7, v_8, v_9\}$. *It is an easy exercise, that $F$ satisfies the properties (3.1)-(3.4).*

**Lemma 3.2** *For every $0 < \varepsilon < \frac{1}{2}$ there exists an $M$ depending only on $\varepsilon$, so that for every integer $m \geq 2$:*

$$T(m) \leq M^2 m^{1+\varepsilon}. \tag{3.5}$$

# 4    Proof of the Main Lemma

Before estimating $T(m)$, an easy technical lemma is needed.

**Lemma 4.1** *For arbitrary integers $m_1, m_2, \ldots, m_k \geq 2$ the following hold:*

$$T(m_1) + T(m_2) + \ldots + T(m_k) \leq T(m_1 + m_2 + \ldots + m_k), \tag{4.1}$$
$$\text{if } m_1 < m_2 \text{ then } T(m_1) < T(m_2). \tag{4.2}$$

*Proof.* In order to prove (4.1) it is sufficient to see that $T(m_1) + T(m_2) \leq T(m_1 + m_2)$. Let two directed labelled trees, $F_1$ and $F_2$ be given with the disjoint labels $U_1$ and $U_2$ at their roots respectively, $|U_i| = m_i$, $|l(F_i)| = T(m_i)$ $(i=1,2)$. Suppose, that these trees have properties (3.1)-(3.4). Now consider the following directed labelled tree $F$. Its root has degree 2, and connected with the roots of $F_1$ and $F_2$, which are subtrees of $F$. The label of the root of $F$ is $U_1 \cup U_2$, the other labels are unchanged. It is clear, that $F$ has properties (3.1)-(3.4) and $|l(F)| = T(m_1) + T(m_2)$.

In order to prove (4.2) take a directed tree $F$ satisfying properties (3.1)-(3.4) and suppose, that the label $U$ is at its root, $|U| = m_1$, $|l(F)| = T(m_1)$. Then consider the following directed labelled tree $F'$. Let $U_1$ be an arbitrary set, satisfying $|U_1| = m_2 - m_1 + 1 (\geq 2)$, $|U_1 \cap U| = 1$. The root of the tree $F'$ has label $U \cup U_1$ and degree 2, and connected with the root of $F$ and a new point of label $U_1$. It is obvious, that $F'$ has properties (3.1)-(3.4) and $|l(F')| = T(m_1) + 1$. ∎

*Proof (of Lemma 3.2).* Let $0 < \varepsilon < \frac{1}{2}$ be a fixed positive number. We use induction on $m$. Let the integer $c = c(\varepsilon)$ be so large, that $\left(1 - \left(\frac{1}{4}\right)^{1/\varepsilon}\right)^\varepsilon < 1 - \frac{1}{c}$, $2 < c^\varepsilon$. Note, that these two conditions imply $\frac{1}{c} < \left(1 - \frac{1}{c}\right)^{1/\varepsilon}$. Moreover choose the integer $M = M(\varepsilon)$ so large, that $M^{2+\varepsilon} > 2c^2 T(c^2)$.

The inequality $T(m) \leq \binom{m}{2}$ obviously holds, which implies, that (3.5) is true for $m \leq M$.

Let $m > M$ be an arbitrary integer. Suppose, that (3.5) is true, for every integer less than $m$. Consider a tree $F \in \mathcal{F}^{(m)}$, for which $|l(F)|$ is maximal. If $r$ denotes the root, then let $N(r) = \{v_1, v_2, \ldots, v_s, v_{s+1}, \ldots, v_t\}$ where $N_0(r) = \{v_1, v_2, \ldots, v_s\}$ and $N_1(r) = \{v_{s+1}, v_{s+2}, \ldots, v_t\}$ is the decomposition in the definition of $F$. Choose $m_i = |A(v_i)|$ and let $F_i$ be the subtree, defined by $v_i$ as a root $(1 \leq i \leq t)$. Observe, that $|l(F)|$ can be maximal only if $T(m_i) = |l(F_i)|$ for every $1 \leq i \leq t$. So it is sufficient to prove, using the short notation $T'(m) =$

$\frac{T(m)}{M^2}$, the inequality

$$\sum_{i=1}^{t} T'(m_i) \leq m^{1+\varepsilon}. \tag{4.3}$$

Now let us decompose the set of indices $1 \leq i \leq t$ into 4 parts:

$$P = \{i|\ m_i \leq c^2\},$$
$$Q = \{i|\ c^2 < m_i \leq \tfrac{m}{c}\},$$
$$R = \{i|\ \tfrac{m}{c} < m_i \leq m(1 - \tfrac{1}{c})^{1/\varepsilon}\},$$
$$S = \{i|\ m(1 - \tfrac{1}{c})^{1/\varepsilon} < m_i\}.$$

By the definition of $c$ and $M$ these sets are disjoint. Note, that the first condition on $c$ implies

$$S \subseteq \{i|\ \left(\tfrac{m-m_i}{m}\right)^{\varepsilon} < \tfrac{1}{4}\}. \tag{4.4}$$

*Case 1:* $S \neq \emptyset$. Let $j \in S$. By the symmetry of the definition of $F$ we may assume, that $1 \leq j \leq s$. (3.3) obviously implies $\sum_{\substack{i=1 \\ i \neq j}}^{s} m_i \leq m - m_j$ and (3.2)-(3.4)

imply $\sum_{i=s+1}^{t} m_i \leq m - m_j + (t-s) \leq 2(m-m_j)$. These inequalities and (4.1) lead to

$$\sum_{i=1}^{t} T'(m_i) = T'(m_j) + \sum_{\substack{i=1 \\ i \neq j}}^{t} T'(m_i) \leq T'(m_j) + T'(m-m_j) + T'(2m-2m_j).$$

$$\tag{4.5}$$

Using the induction hypothesis we obtain

$$T'(m_j) \leq m_j^{1+\varepsilon} \leq m^{1+\varepsilon} - (m-m_j)m^{\varepsilon}, \tag{4.6}$$
$$T'(m-m_j) \leq (m-m_j)^{1+\varepsilon}, \tag{4.7}$$
$$T'(2m-2m_j) \leq (2m-2m_j)^{1+\varepsilon}. \tag{4.8}$$

Observe, that

$$(2m-2m_j)^{1+\varepsilon} = 2^{1+\varepsilon} \cdot (m-m_j)^{1+\varepsilon} \leq 3 \cdot (m-m_j)^{1+\varepsilon}. \tag{4.9}$$

By (4.9) we have

$$(m-m_j)^{1+\varepsilon} + (2m-2m_j)^{1+\varepsilon} \leq 4 \cdot (m-m_j)^{1+\varepsilon} = (m-m_j)m^{\varepsilon}\left(4 \cdot \left(\tfrac{m-m_j}{m}\right)^{\varepsilon}\right).$$

$$\tag{4.10}$$

By (4.4) the last factor of the right hand side in the big parantheses can be upperestimated by 1. Now comparing this, (4.5)-(4.8) and (4.10) we get inequality (4.3).

Case 2: $S = R = \emptyset$. Then the summation from 1 to $t$ acts on $P \cup Q$. By the induction hypothesis we have

$$\sum_{i=1}^{t} T'(m_i) \leq \sum_{i \in P \cup Q} m_i^{1+\varepsilon} = \sum_{i \in P \cup Q} m_i \left(\tfrac{m_i}{m}\right)^{\varepsilon} m^{\varepsilon}. \tag{4.11}$$

By the definition of $Q$ and the second condition on $c$ we get $\left(\tfrac{m_i}{m}\right)^{\varepsilon} \leq \tfrac{1}{2}$ for $1 \leq i \leq t$, on the other hand (3.3) obviously implies

$$\sum_{i=1}^{t} m_i = \sum_{i=1}^{s} m_i + \sum_{i=s+1}^{t} m_i \leq m + m = 2m.$$ These two inequalities and (4.11) prove (4.3).

Case 3: $S = \emptyset, R \neq \emptyset$. Then $\sum_{i=1}^{t} T'(m_i) = \sum_{i \in P} T'(m_i) + \sum_{i \in Q} T'(m_i) + \sum_{i \in R} T'(m_i)$ holds. By the induction hypothesis and the definition of $R$ we have

$$\sum_{i \in R} T'(m_i) \leq \sum_{i \in R} m_i^{1+\varepsilon} = m_i \left(\tfrac{m_i}{m}\right)^{\varepsilon} m^{\varepsilon} \leq \frac{1}{2} \sum_{i \in R} 2m_i (1 - \tfrac{1}{c}) m^{\varepsilon} =$$

$$= \frac{1}{2} \left(\sum_{i \in R} (m_i + m_i - \tfrac{m_i}{c})\right) m^{\varepsilon} - \frac{1}{2} \left(\sum_{i \in R} \tfrac{m_i}{c}\right) m^{\varepsilon}. \tag{4.12}$$

By the definition of $R$ and the condition $R \neq \emptyset$

$$\frac{1}{2} \left(\sum_{i \in R} \tfrac{m_i}{c}\right) m^{\varepsilon} \geq \frac{1}{2c^2} m^{1+\varepsilon} \tag{4.13}$$

can be obtained. The choice of $M$, (4.2), and $|P| \leq m$ ensures

$$2c^2 \sum_{i \in P} T'(m_i) \leq \frac{2c^2 m T(c^2)}{M^2} < m \cdot M^{\varepsilon} < m^{1+\varepsilon}. \tag{4.14}$$

So, by (4.13)-(4.14) the last term of (4.12) can be lowerestimated in absolute value by $\sum_{i \in P} T'(m_i)$. The summation on $Q$ can be made as in Case 2:

$$\sum_{i \in Q} T'(m_i) \leq \sum_{i \in Q} m_i \left(\tfrac{m_i}{m}\right)^{\varepsilon} m^{\varepsilon} \leq \frac{1}{2} \sum_{i \in Q} m_i m^{\varepsilon}. \tag{4.15}$$

Prove the inequality

$$\sum_{i \in Q} m_i + \sum_{i \in R} (m_i + (m_i - \tfrac{m_i}{c})) \leq 2m. \tag{4.16}$$

Consider an $i \in R$. It may be assumed without loss of generality, that $1 \leq i \leq s$. By (3.3), the set $A(v_i)$ can have a non-empty intersection only with $A(v_j)$s satisfying $s+1 \leq j \leq t$. These sets are disjoint. Here $m_j > c^2$ holds for $j \in Q \cup R$, hence the number of sets $A(v_j), j \in Q \cup R$, having a non-empty intersection with $A(v_i)$ is at most $\frac{m}{c^2}$. The choice $i \in R$ implies $|A(v_i)| > \frac{m}{c}$. So by (3.4) at most one cth of the elements of $A(v_i)$ can be an element of some $A(v_j)$, $j \in Q \cup R$. In other words at least $m_i - \frac{m_i}{c}$ element is not covered by some $A(v_j)$ belonging to $s+1 \leq j \leq t$, $j \in Q \cup R$. Hence we have

$$\sum_{\substack{i=s+1 \\ i \in Q \cup R}}^{t} m_i + \sum_{\substack{i=1 \\ i \in R}}^{s} \left(m_i - \tfrac{m_i}{c}\right) \leq m \text{ and } \sum_{\substack{i=1 \\ i \in Q \cup R}}^{s} m_i + \sum_{\substack{i=s+1 \\ i \in R}}^{t} \left(m_i - \tfrac{m_i}{c}\right) \leq m,$$

proving (4.16).

By (4.12)-(4.16) inequality (4.3) is valid in this case, too. ∎

## 5   Proof of the Theorems

**Lemma 5.1 A.** $\mathcal{C}_n^{-1} = \{\{a_1, a_2, \ldots, a_l\} \mid 2 \leq a_j - a_{j-1} \leq 3, 2 \leq a_1 - a_l + n \leq 3\}$.
**B.** If $\mathcal{C}_n^* = \{A \in \mathcal{C}_n^{-1} \mid 1 \in A\}$, then

$$|\mathcal{C}_n^*| = \sum_{\substack{t=0 \\ t \equiv n(2)}}^{\lfloor \frac{n}{3} \rfloor} \binom{\frac{n-t}{2}}{t}, \tag{5.1}$$

**C.** $s(\mathcal{C}_n) \to +\infty$.

*Proof (Part A).*
Consider an arbitrary subset $K$ of $\Omega$ the above form, it is clearly a maximal antikey. Conversely, if $K$ is an antikey, then it can not contain a key, i.e. a neighbouring pair. On the other hand, a set, that skips at least 3 neighbouring element of $\Omega$ can not be a maximal antikey, because we can add an element to this set, the neighbours of which are not in the set.

*Proof (Part B).*
An arbitrary element $\{1, a_1, \ldots, a_l\}$ of $\mathcal{C}_n^*$ uniquely determines a partition of the set $\Omega$ into intervals of size two and three: $\{1, \ldots, a_1 - 1\}$, $\{a_1, \ldots, a_2 - 1\}, \ldots, \{a_l, \ldots, n\}$. Conversely, if such a partition into intervals of size two and three is given, then the set of the left endpoints of the intervals determine an element of $\mathcal{C}_n^*$. The right hand side of (5.1) is the number of such partitions (if the number of intervals of size three is $t$, then the number of the intervals is $\frac{n-t}{2}$).

*Proof (Part C).*
It follows easily from (1.1), part A and part B since $n \to +\infty$. ∎

**Lemma 5.2** *Suppose, that the matrix* **M** *is a minimum representation of the Sperner-system* $\mathcal{K}$*, then the following hold:*

**(i)** *for every* $A \in \mathcal{K}^{-1}$ *there exist two rows, that are equal in* $A$.
**(ii)** *there are no two rows, that are equal in a (minimal) key* $K \in \mathcal{K}$.

*Proof.* Obvious. ∎

Note, that this statement can be reversed in a certain sense, see [5].

*Proof (of Theorem 2.1 Part A).* Our task is to determine the "density" of the pairs of rows, which are associated with the elements of $\mathcal{C}_n^{-1}$ by (i). Of course, these pairs are different, otherwise there would be two rows, that are equal in the union of two maximal antikeys, which is a key, hence contains neighbouring elements, contradicting (ii). Let $\mathbf{M} = [a_{ij}]_{s(\mathcal{C}_n) \times n}$ be a matrix, that represents $\mathcal{C}_n$.

Notice, that at least one from every three antikeys passes through 1, i.e.

$$\frac{1}{3}|\mathcal{C}_n^{-1}| \le |\mathcal{C}_n^*| \le |\mathcal{C}_n^{-1}|. \tag{5.2}$$

Let $U = \{1, \dots, s(\mathcal{C}_n)\}$ be the set of indices of the rows. The equalities of the entries in a given column $j$ determine a partition of $U$ or more generally of its arbitrary subset $W$. Let us denote the elements of cardinality at least 2 of this partition by $\mathcal{P}_W^j$. Formally let $W \subseteq U$ and $j$ be a positive integer. Let us introduce the notation

$$\mathcal{P}_W^j = \begin{cases} \{A \subseteq W \mid |A| \ge 2;\ i_1, i_2 \in A \Rightarrow a_{i_1 j} = a_{i_2 j}; \\ \qquad i_1 \in A, i_2 \in W \backslash A \Rightarrow a_{i_1 j} \neq a_{i_2 j}\} & \text{if } 1 \le j \le n-1, \\ \emptyset & \text{if } j \ge n. \end{cases}$$

We will build (i.e. define recursively) a labelled directed tree $F$. Let the label of the root $r$ of $F$ be $A(r) = U$. If $\mathcal{P}_U^1 = \{U_1, U_2, \dots U_t\}$ for some $t$, then let $N(r) = \{v_1, v_2, \dots v_t\}$ and its labels $A(v_i) = U_i$, $1 \le i \le t$. Suppose, that we have already defined a vertex $v$ of the tree, and its label $A(v)$. Furthermore assume, that $A(v) \in \mathcal{P}_W^j$ for some $W \subseteq U$ and $1 \le j \le n-1$. If $\mathcal{P}_{A(v)}^{j+2} = \{A_1, A_2, \dots, A_s\}$ and $\mathcal{P}_{A(v)}^{j+3} = \{A_{s+1}, A_{s+2}, \dots, A_t\}$, then let $N(v) = \{v_1, v_2, \dots, v_t\}$ and $A(v_k) = A_k$ $(1 \le k \le t)$.

The leaves of the tree $F$ will be those vertices, for which $t = 0$. Observe, that $|A_k \cap A_l| \le 1$ $(1 \le k \le s,\ 1 \le l \le t)$, otherwise there would be two rows, which are equal in the columns of the key $\{j+2, j+3\}$ contradicting (ii). We can see, that $F \in \mathcal{F}^{(s(\mathcal{C}_n))}$.

Consider a set of at least two elements containing the indices of the rows, that agree in an arbitrary element of $\mathcal{C}_n^*$. Such a set exists by (i) and it is a subset (equal in fact in this simpler case) of some $A(v)$, $v \in l(F)$ by Lemma 5.1.A and the definition of the tree $F$. On the other hand two different elements of $\mathcal{C}_n^*$ can not be associated with the same element of $l(F)$, otherwise by the definition of $F$

there would be at least two rows, that agree in a neighbouring pair of columns, contradicting (ii). So we obtained the inequality

$$|l(F)| \geq |\mathcal{C}_n^*|. \tag{5.3}$$

By Lemma 3.2 we obtain

$$|l(F)| \leq T(s(\mathcal{C}_n)) \leq M^2 s(\mathcal{C}_n)^{1+\varepsilon}. \tag{5.4}$$

The first part of the theorem follows from (5.2)-(5.4) and Lemma 5.1.C.

*Proof (of Part B).*

It is sufficient to calculate the magnitude of the largest term on the right hand side of (5.1). This will give a lower estimate, and $\frac{(n+6)}{6}$ times this gives an upper estimate.

Let us consider the quotient of two consecutive terms of the sum and examine when will it be 1. After simplifications it becomes

$$\frac{(\frac{n-t}{2} - t + 3)(\frac{n-t}{2} - t + 2)(\frac{n-t}{2} - t + 1)}{(\frac{n-t}{2} + 1)t(t - 1)} = 1.$$

Introducing the notation $x = \frac{t}{n}$ and rearranging it we obtain

$$23x^3 - (23 + \tfrac{96}{n})x^2 + (9 + \tfrac{68}{n} + \tfrac{112}{n^2})x - (1 + \tfrac{12}{n} + \tfrac{44}{n^2} + \tfrac{48}{n^3}) = 0. \tag{5.5}$$

Consider the polynomial $P_n(x)$ on the left hand side of (5.5) as the $n$th member of a sequence of functions. The polynomials $P_n(x)$ have no root for $|x| > 100$. On the other hand this sequence uniformly tends to $P(x)$ in the finite interval $[-100, 100]$. From this it follows after a short consideration, that (5.5) has a unique real solution $\kappa_n$ if $n$ is sufficiently large and $\kappa_n \to \kappa$, i.e. $\kappa_n = \kappa + o(1)$.

From this argument it also follows, that if $n$ is large enough the terms in (5.1) are increasing until $\frac{t}{n}$ reaches $\kappa_n$ and decreasing after that. If the index of the maximum term is $t^*$, then $|\kappa_n n - t^*| \leq 2$ holds, so $t^* = (\kappa + o(1))n$. Use this in (5.1)

$$\binom{(\frac{1-\kappa}{2} + o(1))n}{(\kappa + o(1))n} \leq |\mathcal{C}_n^*| \leq \frac{n+6}{6}\binom{(\frac{1-\kappa}{2} + o(1))n}{(\kappa + o(1))n}. \tag{5.6}$$

Using the Stirling formula

$$n! = 2^{n(\log_2 \frac{n}{e} + o(1))}$$

we obtain

$$\binom{cn}{dn} = 2^{n(d\log_2 \frac{c}{d} + (c - d)\log_2 \frac{c}{c-d} + o(1))} \qquad (1 \geq c > d > 0).$$

Using this in (5.6) it is easy to see, that

$$2^{n(\kappa \log_2 \frac{1-\kappa}{2\kappa} + \frac{1-3\kappa}{2} \log_2 \frac{1-\kappa}{1-3\kappa} + o(1))} \leq |\mathcal{C}_n^*| \leq$$

$$\leq 2^{n(\kappa \log_2 \frac{1-\kappa}{2\kappa} + \frac{1-3\kappa}{2} \log_2 \frac{1-\kappa}{1-3\kappa} + o(1))},$$

Part B of the theorem follows from this inequality, (5.2), and part A. ∎

*Proof (of Theorem 2.2 Part A).*

We will follow the proof of Theorem 2.1 and see what is different in this general case.

First of all, we need to select a big part $\mathcal{G}_n^*$ of $\mathcal{G}_n^{-1}$, which will play the role of $\mathcal{C}_n^*$. Note, that every maximal antikey necessarily contains at least one of the first three elements of $V_i$, $1 \leq i \leq k$. The same can be said about the last three elements. So let $W_n = V_0 \cup \bigcup_{i=1}^{k} \{w_1^{(i)}, w_2^{(i)}, w_3^{(i)}, w_{n_i-2}^{(i)}, w_{n_i-1}^{(i)}, w_{n_i}^{(i)}\}$ if $n$ is so large, that $n_i \geq 9$ holds for every $1 \leq i \leq k$. There are at least $\frac{1}{2^{|W_n|}}|\mathcal{G}_n^{-1}|$ maximal antikeys having the same intersection with $W_n$. Let $\mathcal{G}_n^*$ denote these antikeys. We obtained

$$\frac{1}{2^{|W_n|}}|\mathcal{G}_n^{-1}| \leq |\mathcal{G}_n^*| \leq |\mathcal{G}_n^{-1}|. \tag{5.7}$$

By the same argument as in the proof of Lemma 5.1.A, it can be seen that if $A \cap V_i = \{w_{j_1}^{(i)}, w_{j_2}^{(i)}, \ldots, w_{j_l}^{(i)}\}$ then $2 \leq j_{r+1}-j_r \leq 3$, $1 \leq r \leq l-1$ for every $1 \leq i \leq k$. This statement can be reversed. For every $1 \leq i \leq k$ there are 2 indices, $l_{1i} \in \{2,3,4\}$ and $l_{2i} \in \{n_i-3, n_i-2, n_i-1\}$, so that the following holds. Consider an arbitrary subset $A$ of $\Omega$ satisfying $w_{l_{1i}}^{(i)}, w_{l_{2i}}^{(i)} \in A \cap V_i$ and having the above fixed intersection with $W_n$. Furthermore, suppose, that if $A \cap V_i = \{w_{j_1}^{(i)}, w_{j_2}^{(i)}, \ldots, w_{j_l}^{(i)}\}$ then $2 \leq j_{r+1}-j_r \leq 3$, $1 \leq r \leq l-1$ for every $1 \leq i \leq k$ holds. Then $A \in \mathcal{G}_n^*$. (If $w_2^{(i)} \in A$ or $w_3^{(i)} \in A$, then let $l_{1i} = 2$ or 3 respectively. If $w_1^{(i)} \in A$ and $w_3^{(i)} \notin A$, then $w_4^{(i)} \in A$ must hold, so let $l_{1i} = 4$.)

In the next step, we define a labelled directed tree $F$. This tree will be built similarly as in the simpler case. There are two differences. We will not use all of the vertices and we have to tell how to connect the different $V_i$s. Unfortunately, we must use somewhat more difficult notations.

For the sake of convenience let us introduce the notation $t_i = l_{2i} - l_{1i} + 1$, $1 \leq i \leq k$. We can assume (by changing the order of the columns), that $w_h^{(i)}$, $l_{1i} \leq h \leq l_{2i}$ is associated with the $((\sum_{r=1}^{i-1} t_r) + h - l_{1i} + 1)$-th column of $\mathbf{M}$.

Let $U = \{1, \ldots, s(\mathcal{G}_n)\}$ be the set of indices of the rows. For fixed $i$ and $h$ denote the number $j_{i,h} = h + \sum_{l=1}^{i-1} t_l$ shortly by $j$. If $T \subseteq U$ and $1 \leq i \leq k$ then let us introduce the following notation for every positive integer $h$:

$$\mathcal{P}_W^{i,h} = \begin{cases} \{A \subseteq W \mid |A| \geq 2; \ i_1, i_2 \in A \Rightarrow a_{i_1j}=a_{i_2j}; \\ \qquad i_1 \in A, i_2 \in T \backslash A \Rightarrow a_{i_1j} \neq a_{i_2j}\} & \text{if } 1 \leq h \leq t_i, \ h \neq t_i-1, \\ \emptyset & \text{otherwise.} \end{cases}$$

Let the label of the root $r$ of $F$ be $A(r) = U$. If $\mathcal{P}_U^{1,1} = \{U_1, U_2, \ldots U_t\}$ for some $t$, then let $N(r) = \{v_1, v_2, \ldots v_t\}$ and its labels $A(v_i) = U_i$, $1 \leq i \leq t$. Suppose, that we have already defined a vertex $v$ of the tree, and its label $A(v)$. Furthermore assume, that $A(v) \in \mathcal{P}_W^{i,h}$ for some $W \subseteq U$ and $1 \leq h \leq t_i$, $h \neq t_i-1$. There are two cases. In the first case suppose, that $h \neq t_i$ or $i = k$. If $\mathcal{P}_{A(v)}^{i,h+2} = \{A_1, A_2, \ldots, A_s\}$ and $\mathcal{P}_{A(v)}^{i,h+3} = \{A_{s+1}, A_{s+2}, \ldots, A_t\}$, then let $N(v) = \{v_1, v_2, \ldots, v_t\}$ and $A(v_r) = A_r$ $(1 \leq r \leq t)$. Observe, that $|A_r \cap A_l| \leq 1$ $(1 \leq r \leq s, \ 1 \leq l \leq t)$, otherwise there would be two rows, that are equal in the columns of the key $\{j+2, j+3\}$ contradicting (ii). Suppose, that $h = t_i$ and $1 \leq i \leq k-1$. If $\mathcal{P}_{A(v)}^{i+1,1} = \{A_1, A_2, \ldots, A_t\}$, then let $N(v) = \{v_1, v_2, \ldots, v_t\}$ and $A(v_r) = A_r$ $(1 \leq r \leq t)$. The leaves of the tree $F$ will be those vertices, for which $t = 0$. We can see, that $F \in \mathcal{F}^{(s(\mathcal{G}_n))}$.

The same argument as in the proof of Theorem 2.1 shows, that

$$|l(F)| \geq |\mathcal{G}_n^*|. \tag{5.8}$$

By Lemma 3.2 we obtain

$$|l(F)| \leq T(s(\mathcal{G}_n)) \leq M^2 s(\mathcal{G}_n)^{1+\varepsilon}. \tag{5.9}$$

We need a last little observation. $s(\mathcal{G}_n)$ is not just tends to infinity, but it grows exponentially (for example, it follows from (5.1) and (5.10)). So $2^{|W_n|} = 2^{o(n)} \leq s(\mathcal{G}_n)^\varepsilon$ if $n$ is large enough. The theorem follows from (5.7)-(5.9).

*Proof (of Part B).* By the statement on $\mathcal{G}_n^*$ in Part A we obtain

$$|\mathcal{G}_n^*| = \prod_{i=1}^k |\mathcal{C}_{t_i-1}^*|. \tag{5.10}$$

By the definitions of $W_n$ and $t_i$ it is obvious, that $n - |W_n| - k \leq \sum_{i=1}^k (t_i-1) \leq n - |W_n| + 3k$. So by the concluding exponential expression of $|\mathcal{C}_n^*|$ in the proof of Theorem 2.1.B and (5.10) we obtain

$$2^{(n-|W_n|-k)(\lambda+o(1))} \leq |\mathcal{G}_n^*| \leq 2^{(n-|W_n|+3k)(\lambda+o(1))}. \tag{5.11}$$

$\frac{n-|W_n|-k}{n} \to 1$, $\frac{n-|W_n|+3k}{n} \to 1$, (5.7), (5.11), and part A of the theorem proves part B. ∎

## Acknowledgements

I would like to thank for the invaluable help of my supervisor, G.O.H. Katona in writing this paper.

## References

1. W.W. Armstrong, *Dependency structures of database relationship,* Information Processing **74** (North Holland, Amsterdam, 1974) 580-583.
2. F.E. Benett, Lisheng Wu, *On minimum matrix representation of closure operations,* Discrete Appl. Math. **26** (1990) 25-40.
3. J. Demetrovics, *Candidate keys and antichains,* SIAM J. Algebraic Methods **1** (1980) 92.
4. J. Demetrovics, *On the equivalence of candidate keys with Sperner systems,* Acta Cybernet. **4** (1979) 247-252.
5. J. Demetrovics, Z. Füredi, G.O.H. Katona, *Minimum matrix representation of closure operations,* Discrete Appl. Math. **11** (1985) 115-128.
6. J. Demetrovics, G.O.H. Katona, *Extremal combinatorial problems in relational database,* in Fundamentals of Computation Theory 81, Proc. of the 1981 International FCT-Conference, Szeged, Hungary, 1981, Lecture Notes in Computer Science **117** (Springer, Berlin 1981) 110-119.
7. Z. Füredi, *Perfect error-correcting databases,* Discrete Appl. Math. **28** (1990) 171-176.
8. G.O.H. Katona, *Combinatorial and algebraic results for database relations,* in J. Biskup, R. Hull, ed., Database Theory - ICDT '92, Berlin, 1992, Lecture Notes in Comput. Science, **646** (Springer Verlag, Berlin, 1992) 1-20.

# Reflective Relational Machines Working on Homogeneous Databases

Jose Maria Turull Torres

Universidad Tecnológica Nacional, F.R.B.A.
Universidad Nacional de San Luis
Peron 2315, piso 4, depto. P
1040 Capital Federal, ARGENTINA

turull@iamba.edu.ar    turull@unsl.edu.ar

**Abstract.** [1] [2] We define four different properties of relational databases which are related to the notion of homogeneity in classical Model Theory. The main question for their definition is, for any given database, which is the minimum integer $k$, such that whenever two $k$-tuples satisfy the same properties which are expressible in First Order Logic with up to $k$ variables ($FO^k$), then there is an automorphism which maps each of these $k$-tuples onto each other? We study these four properties as a means to increase the computational power of sub-classes of Reflective Relational Machines ($RRM$) of bounded variable complexity. For this sake we give first a semantic characterization of the sub-classes of total $RRM$ with variable complexity $k$, for every natural $k$, with the classes of queries which we denote as $QCQ^k$. We prove that these classes form a *strict* hierarchy in a strict sub-class of $total(CQ)$. And it follows that it is orthogonal with the usual classification of computable queries in Time and Space complexity classes. We prove that the computability power of $RRM^k$ machines is much bigger when working with classes of databases which are homogeneous, for three of the properties which we define. As to the fourth one, we prove that the computability power of $RRM$ with sub-linear variable complexity also increases when working on databases which satisfy that property. The strongest notion, pairwise $k$-homogeneity, allows $RRM^k$ machines to achieve *completeness*.

## 1 Introduction

The $RRM$ (*Reflective Relational Machine* of [1]), is a suitable model for computing queries in the class $CQ$ of *computable queries* ([6]), on classes of finite and relational structures, or relational databases (*db* from now on). It is an extension of the $RM$ (*Relational Machine* of [2]). Recall that a $RM$ is a Turing Machine with the addition of a *relational store* (*rs* from now on), where a countable set of

---

[1] The work presented here was partially done during a visit to the Department of Mathematics of the University of Helsinki.

[2] This work has been partially supported by Grant 1011049 of the Academy of Finland and by Grants of Universidad CAECE and Universidad de Luján, Argentina.

K.-D. Schewe, B. Thalheim (Eds.): FoIKS 2000, LNCS 1762, pp. 288–303, 2000.

relations of bounded arity can be stored. The interaction with the rs is done *only* through $FO$ (First Order Logic) formulae in the finite control of the machine, and the input db as well as the output relation are in rs. Each of these $FO$ formulae, is evaluated in rs according to the transition function of the machine and the resulting relation can be assigned to some relation symbol or index of the appropiate arity in the rs. Note that this kind of interaction with the db and auxiliary relations is what enforces the preservation of isomorphisms in this model of computation, as opposite to Turing Machines. The *arity* of a given relational machine is the maximum number of variables of any formula in its finite control. We will regard the *schema* of a db as a relational signature, that is, a finite set of relation symbols with associated arities. And we will consider a db instance, or db, as a finite structure of a relational signature. In the $RRM$ model the $FO$ queries are generated during the computation of the machine, and they are called *dynamic queries*. Each of these queries is written in a *query tape* and it is evaluated by the machine in one step when a distinguished *query state* is reached. Another important difference w.r.t. $RM$ is that in $RRM$ the relations in the rs can be of arbitrary arity. In [2] it was proved that the $RM$ model is *incomplete*, that is, it cannot compute the whole class $CQ$ on a given signature or db schema. As to the $RRM$ model, in [1] it was proved that it is also incomplete if we restrict the number of different variables which can be used in any $FO$ query generated during a computation, to be less than the size of (the domain of) the input db (that is, if we restrict what is known as the *variable complexity* of the model in that way).

A natural question arises from the incompleteness of these models of computation of queries: which properties, if any, of the input db can increase the class of queries which these classes of incomplete machines can compute, when working with db's which satisfy any of those properties?

In the study of the expressibility, or query computability, of different logics below second order, the presence of a total order relation in the structures (or db's) was shown to be quite relevant ([11], [10]). In [2] it was proved that the class $RM$ is complete when the input db is ordered. This means that for every computable query $q$ there is a machine in the class which computes a query $q'$ such that for every ordered db $I$ of the corresponding schema, it is $q'(I) = q(I)$, and this is not necessary the case if the input db is not ordered. In [9] and [14] *bounded rigidity* in classes of finite and relational structures, or db's, was studied as a property which allows (incomplete) $RM$ to achieve completeness. In the second work, *unbounded* rigidity was also studied with the same purpose, considering (incomplete) reflective relational machines whose variable complexity is bounded by a sub-linear function (to be explained later in this Section). Finally, in [15] bounded and unbounded *partial* rigidity were studied also as a means to increase the computability power of (incomplete) $RM$ and $RRM$ whose variable complexity is bounded by a sub-linear function, respectively. Recall that a database is *rigid* if it has only one automorphism, which is the identity. Let's denote as $FO^k$ the sub-logic of $FO$ where formulae are restricted to use up to $k$ different variables. A class of rigid databases is said to be of *bounded rigidity*, if there is an integer $k$ such that every element in every database in the class is definable in $FO^k$ (up to automorphism), and the class is said to be of *unbounded rigidity*, otherwise. Finally, a database is *partially rigid* if it has a non empty subset of definable elements.

That is, there is a main point leading to a research program, which is finding properties of db's which are "good properties", in the sense that a query language, or any kind of suitable formalism for this matter, which is incomplete, can benefit from these properties and increase its computation power when working on db's which satisfy them.

Up to now, order, rigidity, either bounded or unbounded, and partial rigidity, also either bounded or unbounded, are properties of databases which have been shown to be quite relevant as to computability power. The results presented here show that different notions related to homogeneity are also quite relevant in the same way.

In this paper, following the same research program, we study different notions which are related to the notion of *homogeneity* of classical Model Theory (see [8] among others). We define four different notions, which will be informally explained later in this Section, and we study them as properties of classes of structures, or db's, which allow incomplete $RRM$ to increase their computability power when working on this kind of classes. We only consider *total* machines here, that is, machines which compute total queries. Three of our notions are similar to some properties independently defined in [13], where they are studied in relation to the expressibility of fixed point logics.

The main question for the definition of our properties is, for a given db which is the minimum integer $k$, such that whenever two $k$-tuples have the same $FO^k$ *type* (see below) then there is an automorphism which maps each of these $k$-tuples onto each other?

In order to study the increment in computation power of the $RRM$ when working on db's which satisfy any of our properties, we give first (in Section 2) a semantic characterization for the sub-class of total queries which are computed by $RRM^k$ (i.e., $RRM$ with variable complexity $k$), for every natural $k$. Similarly, $RRM^{O(1)}$ will denote the class of $RRM$ with variable complexity $O(1)$. The restriction to total machines will be denoted as $total(RRM^k)$ and $total(RRM^{O(1)})$, respectively. Consequently, we will denote the sub-class of total computable queries as $total(\mathcal{CQ})$. We do this characterization by defining, for every $k \geq 1$, the class $\mathcal{QCQ}^k \subset total(\mathcal{CQ})$, as the total queries which *preserve* $FO^k$ types realization. Roughly, for every $1 \leq l \leq k$, an $FO^k$ *type* for $l$-tuples is a property of $l$-tuples which is expressible in $FO^k$ by a set of formulae with $l$ free variables. And we say that a db $I$ *realizes* an $FO^k$ type for $l$-tuples if there is an $l$-tuple in $I$ which satisfies the property expressed by that type. Then, by preservation of $FO^k$ types realization, we mean that for every pair of db's of the corresponding schema, and for every property of $k$-tuples which is expressible in $FO^k$, if either both db's have no $k$-tuple which satisfy that property, or both db's have a non empty subset of $k$-tuples which satisfy it (*without minding the cardinalities* of the corresponding subsets), then the relations defined in each db by the query also agree in the same sense, considering the schema of the db's. So that, for every natural $k$, the class $\mathcal{QCQ}^k$ is the sub-class of the computable queries which *cannot distinguish* differences between two non isomorphic db's, which need more than $k$ variables to be expressed in $FO$. It is well known that two db's realize the same $FO^k$ types iff they have the same $FO^k$ theory (i.e., both databases satisfy the same set of $FO^k$ sentences). So that the class $\mathcal{QCQ}^k$ may also be regarded as the sub-class of computable queries which, when evaluated on db's that satisfy the same properties expressible in $FO^k$, the corresponding resulting relations in the two db's also satisfy the same properties expressible in $FO^k$ (considering the schema of the databases as signature for the sentences). The way in which we define the classes $\mathcal{QCQ}^k$ is to some extent implicit in [2] and [5].

We show that, for every $k > 0$, $\mathcal{QCQ}^k = total(RRM^k)$, and we show also that these classes form a *strict* hierarchy inside $total(\mathcal{CQ})$. We denote the whole hierarchy as $\mathcal{QCQ}^\omega$, and this class gives us the semantic characterization for $total(RRM^{O(1)})$.

The properties of preservation of the realization of types in $FO$ with different bounds in the number of variables, for queries, are quite natural, since in the definition of *computable query* ([6]) the very property of preservation of isomorphisms is crucial. And, as it is well known, on finite structures isomorphism is equivalent to the realization of the same $FO$ types. That is, two finite structures (or db's) of the same relational signature (or schema) are isomorphic iff for every $FO$ formula with one free variable either there is no element in the two structures which satisfy that formula, or they both have the *same number* of elements which satisfy it. Note that in defining isomorphism of structures we have considered not only the automorphism type of a given tuple, but also the number of tuples which realize that type in the structure. Actually, if we use $FO$ types, the number of tuples which satisfy a given property can also be expressed in the formula which expresses that property, so that two structures are isomorphic iff they both realize the same $FO$ types (as an example, think of a formula with one free variable which says "$x$ is an isolated node and there are 7 such nodes", in the schema of graphs). As to $FO^k$ types, we cannot express cardinalities of sets of tuples in $FO^k$ beyond a constant. So that even for db's where $FO^k$ types are automorphism types, equivalence in the $FO^k$ types which are realized in two given db's is far from being equivalent to isomorphism.

Then, when we define different restrictions in the types, as to the number of variables which may be used for their definition, what we are actually doing is defining *different levels as to the amount of information on the db which every query really needs* for it to be evaluated on that db. Or *how carefully needs a db be analyzed* for the query to be evaluated on that db.

An interesting characteristic of the hierarchy of the classes $\mathcal{QCQ}^k$, for $k \geq 1$, is the fact that it is orthogonal with the usual classification of the computable queries in complexity classes. That is, in every level in the hierarchy there are queries of *any* complexity class in the usual classification defined by Turing Machine complexity.

We believe that the definition of the classes $\mathcal{QCQ}^k$ and $\mathcal{QCQ}^\omega$ (see also the definition of the class $\mathcal{QCQ}$ later in this Section) is interesting in its own right and independently of the use we make of them here, since no semantic characterization of $RRM^{O(1)}$ is known at present, as to the author's knowledge. They can help in a better understanding of the computability power of the $RRM$ and, particularly, of the signification of different bounds in their variable complexity. To this regard we are building on the seminal work of S. Abiteboul, C. Papadimitriou, M. Vardi and V. Vianu ([2], [4], [5], [3] and [1]). Besides, as the $\mathcal{QCQ}^k$ hierarchy is orthogonal with the usual Time and Space complexity hierarchy, it can be used to define (and study) finer and more precise classes of queries, for instance by intersecting layers in both hierarchies. As to the $RM$, as it is known that the whole class of these machines is equivalent, as to computational power, to the sub-class $RRM^{O(1)}$ (see [3]), then it turns out that $\mathcal{QCQ}^\omega = total(RM)$. So that we get also a semantic characterization for this model. On the other hand, it is not known, for every natural $k$, which sub-class of $RM$ is equivalent to the sub-class $RRM^k$. Though it is clear that $RRM^k$ includes the sub-class of $RM$ of arity $k$, and hence $\mathcal{QCQ}^k$ includes the sub-class of $RM$ of arity $k$, it is not known whether the inclusion is strict, though it is strongly believed to be the case.

As there are many classes of db's for which no bound in the number of variables is enough to define the automorphism types for tuples for every db in the class, we also define a sub-class of the total queries which we denote as $\mathcal{QCQ}$. Queries in this class are defined in such a way that they preserve realization of types built with the number of variables which is actually needed for each db to define the automorphism types for its tuples. This class strictly includes the hierarchy $\mathcal{QCQ}^\omega$. On the other hand, there are computable queries which are not in $\mathcal{QCQ}$, because queries in this class cannot *count* the number of different tuples of the same automorphism type, beyond a fixed bound. So that we have the following picture inside $total(\mathcal{CQ})$, where $\subset$ denotes proper inclusion:

$$\mathcal{QCQ}^1 \subset \ldots \subset \mathcal{QCQ}^k \subset \ldots \subset \mathcal{QCQ}^\omega \subset \mathcal{QCQ} \subset total(\mathcal{CQ}).$$

In Section 3, we define our four notions related to homogeneity. The first three notions which we define are *k-homogeneity*, *strong k-homogeneity* and *pairwise k-homogeneity*. Roughly, a db is *k-homogeneous* if $k$ variables suffice to define the automorphism types for their $k$-tuples. We prove that, for every natural $k$, machines in $total(RRM^k)$ working on such classes of db's augment their computability power to such an extent that, in a sense which will be clarified later (Corollary 3.1), they go through the whole hierarchy $\mathcal{QCQ}^\omega$ and they fall somewhere between $\mathcal{QCQ}^\omega$ and $\mathcal{QCQ}$. A db is *strongly k-homogeneous* if it is $r$-homogeneous for every $r \geq k$. Here we show that, roughly, for every $r > k \geq 1$, the class of queries computable by $total(RRM^r)$ working on such classes of db's strictly includes the class of queries computable by the same machines on classes of db's which are $k$-homogeneous but which are not strongly $k$-homogeneous. And as to the third notion, we say that a class of db's is *pairwise k-homogeneous* if for every pair of db's in the class, and for every pair of $k$-tuples $\bar{a}$ and $\bar{b}$ taken respectively from the two db's, if both $k$-tuples have the same $FO^k$ type, then the two db's are isomorphic and there is an isomorphism mapping one tuple onto the other. We show that, for every $k$, machines in $RRM^k$ working on such classes achieve completeness, provided the classes are recursive and closed under isomorphisms.

We then consider $RRM$ whose variable complexity is bounded by a *sub-linear* function. For our purpose, it is enough to define a sub-linear function as a function over the naturals such that for every $n \in \omega$ it is $f(n) < n$. We will denote as $RRM^{f(n)}$ an $RRM$ whose variable complexity is $f(n)$, that is, the number of variables which may be used in the dynamic queries is bounded by $f(n)$, where $n$ is the size of the domain of the input db. For this case we define our fourth notion of homogeneity, in which the number of variables which we may use for the types for $k$-tuples is given by a function on the size of the db. We denote this notion as $(f(n), k)$-*homogeneity*. And we prove that, roughly, for every sub-linear function $f$ defined over the naturals, the class of queries which can be computed by $RRM^{f(n)}$ machines (which are known to be incomplete, [1]) on classes of db's which are $(f(n), k)$-homogeneous strictly includes the class of queries which can be computed by $RRM^{f(n)}$ machines on classes of arbitrary db's.

So, we conclude to this regard that our different notions related to homogeneity in classes of db's are all relevant regarding computability power.

Finally, we make some considerations regarding a connection of our research with an aspect of db practice, namely, a real world query language $(SQL2)$. Roughly speaking, for every natural $k$, the sub-class of $RM$ of arity $k$ can be considered as being equivalent, as to computation power, to the sub-class of $SQL2$ expressions which are restricted to reference at most $k$ different attribute names. In [3] the equivalence in computation power between the class of $RM$ and the class $RRM^{O(1)}$ was proved, but the arity of each $RM$ is not preserved by that extension. That is, it is not automatically translated into a constant bound for the variable complexity of the corresponding $RRM$. So that, for any given $RRM^k$ machine there exists a $RM$ of arity $k'$, for some $k' \geq k$, which computes the same query. Then, our results in Section 2 mean, regarding $SQL2$, that the class of total queries which can be computed by the sub-class of $SQL2$ expressions restricted to $k'$ different attribute names is roughly characterized by the class $QCQ^k$, for some $k \leq k'$. And they also mean that the class of all $SQL2$ expressions form a strict hierarchy regarding the number of different attribute names which are allowed to be referenced in each expression. We think that this rough characterization of sub-classes of $SQL2$ expressions, yet being quite approximate, is of interest because it helps in understanding the kind of queries which can be computed by this language, and the meaning of the bound in the number of different attribute names which are allowed in the expressions. As to the results in Section 3, they tell us, to this regard, that fixing a given layer in that hierarchy in $SQL2$, the sub-class of $SQL2$ expressions corresponding to that layer can increase its computation power when the input db happens to satisfy any of the four properties which we defined in this paper, to an extent which depends on the particular property which is satisfied by the db, according Theorem 3.1 and Lemmas 3.1, 3.2 and 3.3.

Some of the results presented here appeared in a short paper in [16].

# 2   A Characterization of Sub-classes of RRM

In the present article we will deal only with relational db's, or finite structures whose signature is finite and relational. Let $\sigma$ be a signature (or db schema), and let $I$ be a $\sigma$-structure (or a db of schema $\sigma$). We will denote the domain of $I$ as $dom(I)$. For any $k > 0$, we will denote a $k$-tuple of $I$ as $\bar{a}_k$. This is not to be confused with the $k$-th component of $\bar{a}_k$, which we will usually denote as $a_k$. If $\sigma$ is a finite relational signature, we will denote the set of all finite $\sigma$-structures, or db's of schema $\sigma$, as $\mathcal{S}_{\sigma,fin}$.

Recall that, given a $\sigma$-structure $I$, an $FO^k$ type for an $l$-tuple $\bar{a}_l$ of $I$, with $l \leq k$, is the set of $\sigma$-formulae in $FO^k$ with $l$ free variables, such that every formula in the set is TRUE when interpreted by $I$ for any valuation which assigns the $i$-th component of $\bar{a}_l$ to the $i$-th free variable in the formula, for every $1 \leq i \leq l$. We will say that a structure $I$ *realizes* a type $\phi$ for $k$-tuples, if there exists a $k$-tuple in $dom(I)$ whose type is $\phi$. Let $I_1$ and $I_2$ be two db's of schema $\sigma$ for some schema $\sigma$, and let $k \geq 1$. We will say that $I_1$ and $I_2$ are $FO^k$ *equivalent* if they satisfy the same set of $FO^k$ sentences. We will denote this (equivalence) relation as $\equiv_{FO^k}$.

**Definition 2.1.** *Let $I_1$ and $I_2$ be two db's of schema $\sigma$ for some schema $\sigma$, and let $k \geq l \geq 1$. We will say that $I_1$ and $I_2$ agree on $FO^k$ types for $l$-tuples, if they both realize the same set of $FO^k$ types for $l$-tuples. We will denote this (equivalence) relation as $\equiv_{\tau_{k,l}}$. In case that it is $l = k$, we will denote the relation as $\equiv_{\tau_k}$.*

Note that, for every $k \geq 1$, and for every pair $I_1$, $I_2$ of db's of the same schema, the following holds:

$$I_1 \equiv_{FO^k} I_2 \quad \Longleftrightarrow \quad I_1 \equiv_{\tau_k} I_2 \quad \Longleftrightarrow \quad I_1 \equiv_{\tau_{k,l}} I_2 \text{ for every } k \geq l \geq 1.$$

Further, from the study in [9] it follows that for every $k \geq l \geq 1$, and for every pair $I_1$, $I_2$ of db's of the same schema, if $I_1 \equiv_{\tau_{k,l}} I_2$, then $I_1 \equiv_{\tau_l} I_2$.

In [9] it is shown that, for every $k \geq 1$, every $FO^k$ type for $k$-tuples can be *isolated* through an $FO^k$ formula with $k$ free variables. That is, a single formula defines the same $FO^k$ type for $k$-tuples on *every* database of the same schema. We will call such a formula the *isolating formula* for the corresponding $FO^k$ type for $k$-tuples. Dawar builds these formulae through an inductive definition, and at every stage of the induction a formula which characterizes a sub-type with a bounded quantifier rank is obtained. Then he shows that for a database of size $n$, $n^k$ steps in the induction suffice to build the isolating formula for the corresponding type.

Let's denote by $\equiv_k$ the (equivalence) relation induced in the set of $k$-tuples of a given db $I$, by the equality in the $FO^k$ types of the $k$-tuples. That is, for every $\bar{a}_k$ and $\bar{b}_k$ in $(dom(I))^k$, $\bar{a}_k \equiv_k \bar{b}_k$ iff $\bar{a}_k$ and $\bar{b}_k$ have the same $FO^k$ type for $k$-tuples.

*Remark 2.1.* The following two observations, which will be later used, follow from [2] and [9]: for every schema $\sigma$, for every db $I$ of schema $\sigma$, for every $k \geq 1$, for every $1 \leq r \leq k$ and for every $FO^k$ formula $\varphi$ of signature $\sigma$, with $r$ free variables, the relation which $\varphi$ defines on $I$ is a union of equivalence classes in the relation $\equiv_k$ on $I$, reduced to $r$-tuples; and for every $k \geq 1$, for every $1 \leq r \leq k$, and for every db $I$ of the corresponding schema, equivalence classes in $\equiv_r$ on $I$ are unions of equivalence classes in $\equiv_k$ on $I$, reduced to $r$-tuples.

**Definition 2.2.** *For every $k \geq 1$, we define the class $QCQ^k$ as the class of $l$-ary queries $f \in total(CQ)$, of some schema $\sigma$ and for some $l \leq k$, such that for every pair of db's $I_1$, $I_2$ in $S_{\sigma,fin}$, if $I_1 \equiv_{\tau_k} I_2$ then $f(I_1) \equiv_{\tau_{k,l}} f(I_2)$, with respect to the schema $\sigma$. We also define $QCQ^\omega = \bigcup_{k \in \omega} QCQ^k$.*

That is, queries in $QCQ^k$ preserve realization of $FO^k$ types. In the consideration of the observation after Definition 2.1, queries in $QCQ^k$ may also be regarded as those which preserve "agreement" of $FO^k$ theories. That is, whenever two db's satisfy the same sentences of $FO^k$ (or properties expressible in $FO^k$), the resulting relations of the evaluation of the query on both db's will also satisfy the same sentences of $FO^k$ (considering the schema of the db's as their signature).

Note that queries in the class $CQ$ (computable queries) preserve realization of $FO$ types. This is because, as db's in this context are finite structures, then their $FO$ types are also *isomorphism types*. This is due to the well known fact that finite structures can be described in $FO$ up to isomorphism (their $FO$ theories are *categorical*, see [8]. Preservation of isomorphisms is a crucial property of queries in $CQ$ and, clearly, a query preserves isomorphisms iff it preserves realization of isomorphism (i.e., $FO$) types. So that queries in $CQ$ range, to this regard, from those which need to be aware of every property of the db up to isomorphism (i.e., $FO$ property), to those for which it is enough just with caring about $FO^k$ properties of the db, for some fixed $k$. And the different sub-classes $QCQ^k$, correspond to different degrees of "precision", say, with which the queries in the given sub-class *need* to consider the db for them to be evaluated.

*Remark 2.2.* Let $f \in total(CQ)$, of schema $\sigma$. Note that, for every $k \geq 1$ and for every $i \in \omega$, if $f$ preserves realization of $FO^k$ types for $k$-tuples on every pair of db's in $S_{\sigma,fin}$ then $f$ also preserves realization of $FO^{k+i}$ types for $(k+i)$-tuples on every pair of db's in $S_{\sigma,fin}$. This follows from the very definition of preservation of realization of types by a function, and it can be also derived as a Corollary to Lemma 2.1.

Next, we will give a semantic characterization of the class of total $RRM^k$ machines.

**Theorem 2.1.** *For every $k \geq 1$, the class of total queries which are computable by $RRM^k$ machines is exactly the class $QCQ^k$.*

*Proof.* **a)** ($\subseteq$): Using the Remark after Definition 2.1. **b)** ($\supseteq$): For every query $f \in \mathcal{QCQ}^k$ of schema $\sigma$ we can build a $RRM^k$ machine $\mathcal{M}_f$, which computes $f$. With the input db $I$ in its rs, $\mathcal{M}_f$ builds in its $TM$ tape an encoding of a db $I'$ which will agree with $I$ on the $FO^k$ types for $k$-tuples. For this purpose, $\mathcal{M}_f$ builds every possible db $I'$ of schema $\sigma$ for every possible size $n$, with domain $\{1, \dots, n\}$. For every $k$-tuple in $I'$, $\mathcal{M}_f$ builds the *isolating formula* for its $FO^k$ type as in [9], following its inductive construction up to the step $n^k$. By using these formulae as dynamic queries, $\mathcal{M}_f$ checks whether $I \equiv_{\tau_k} I'$. At that point $\mathcal{M}_f$ computes $f(I')$, and finally it builds $f(I)$ in the rs considering the $FO^k$ types realized in $I'$ which are realized also in $f(I')$.

**Corollary 2.1.** $\mathcal{QCQ}^\omega = total(RRM^{O(1)}) = total(RM)$ and $\mathcal{QCQ}^\omega \subset total(\mathcal{CQ})$.

*Remark 2.3.* Regarding the class $RM$, two different *syntactic* characterizations are known. In [2], it was noted that the class of queries computable by this machines is exactly the same class known as WHILE$^+$. This is the RQL programming language of [7] with the addition of the set of natural numbers as a secondary domain with arithmetic restricted to it. In [5], regarding only *boolean queries*, it was proved that, for every integer $k$ greater than the maximum arity in the corresponding schema, the queries which are computable by $RM$ of arity $k$ are exactly those which can be expressed by a r.e. fragment of the infinitary logic $\mathcal{L}^k_{\infty,\omega}$. Further, if $RM$ are restricted to compute total boolean queries, then the class of queries which are computable by $RM$ of arity $k$ is the class of queries expressible in a *recursive* fragment of $\mathcal{L}^k_{\infty,\omega}$. This logic extends $FO$ by allowing conjunctions and disjunctions over infinite sets of formulae, while restricting the number of variables in every formula to be at most $k$. The union of the logics $\mathcal{L}^k_{\infty,\omega}$ for every $k > 0$ is the logic $\mathcal{L}^\omega_{\infty,\omega}$, where every formula is restricted to use a finite number of variables. And the corresponding r.e and recursive fragments give us a characterization for the whole classes of $RM$ and $total(RM)$, respectively, and considering only boolean queries. As to the author's knowledge it is not known at present a *semantic* characterization for the sub-class of $RM$ of each particular arity.

Now we will show that the classes $\mathcal{QCQ}^k$ form a strict hierarchy inside $total(\mathcal{CQ})$. In [1] it is shown that $RRM$ with sub-linear variable complexity form a strict hierarchy, according to the function which bounds the number of variables in dynamic queries depending on the size of the input database. Their result is related, to some extent, to our next result, by Theorem 2.1.

**Lemma 2.1.** *For every* $k > 0$, $\mathcal{QCQ}^{k+1} \supset \mathcal{QCQ}^k$.

*Proof.* **a)** ($\supseteq$): Trivial, using Theorem 2.1. **b)** ($\neq$): Define the query $f$ in the schema of the graphs as *"nodes in $(k+1)$-subcliques"*. Then, $f \in \mathcal{QCQ}^{k+1}$, but $f \notin \mathcal{QCQ}^k$.

The hierarchy defined by the classes $\mathcal{QCQ}^k$ is not only *strict*, but it is *orthogonal* with respect to the usual complexity classes. Note that, for every $k > 1$, *any* recursive predicate evaluated on the number of equivalence classes in $\equiv_k$

is in $\mathcal{QCQ}^k$. Intuitively, what this hierarchy classifies is how carefully needs the structure or db be analyzed for the query to be evaluated. The lower is the parameter $k$, the *less information* on the db is needed for the query to be evaluated on it.

*Remark 2.4.* In [2] it is stated that $total(RM) \subset \mathcal{L}^{\omega}_{\infty,\omega}$ (see remark after Corollary 2.1). It is also noted there that, as this logic has the so called 0–1 Law, then it follows that $total(RM)$ has also the 0–1 Law. This means that the asymptotic probability of every property which can be expressed in the formalism (or which belongs to the given class) always exist, and is 0 or 1 (see [12]). Then, from Theorem 2.1 and Corollary 2.1, it follows that the boolean queries in the classes $\mathcal{QCQ}^{\omega}$ and $\mathcal{QCQ}^k$, for every $k \geq 1$, also have the 0–1 Law.

## 3    Homogeneous Databases

From the Remark after Definition 2.1, it follows that as we allow for more variables to be used in writing the isolating formulae for types of tuples (as in the Proof of Theorem 2.1), we get a more precise view of the properties which i-dentify a given set of tuples among the whole set in the domain of the db. The limit is $FO$, in which logic we can express the automorphism types for tuples of every length in every db. So, we ask the natural question arising from this observation: how many variables are needed for a given db and for a given integer $k$, to express the properties of $k$-tuples in that db up to automorphism?[3] That is, we look for the minimum integer $k$ such that $FO^k$ types for $k$-tuples are *automorphism types* for $k$-tuples in *that* particular database.

Note that a type, or a property which in one db is enough to define an element up to automorphism (i.e., an automorphism type), may not be enough to define an element in *another* db of the same schema. Let's consider the property "the out degree of $x$ is 2" in the schema of graphs. In some graphs it may certainly identify a set of nodes which cannot be distinguished from each other (for every pair of nodes in the set there are automorphisms in the graph which map one onto the other), so that the property is an automorphism type for those graphs. For instance, think of graphs which are collections of binary trees of depth 1 and out degree 2. But this is not the case for *every* graph. In arbitrary binary trees there may be certainly many nodes with out degree 2, but which may also have some other properties which distinguish one from each other, like the depth of the node in the tree, or the length of the longest chain which begins in it, etc. So, in these other graphs our property is not an automorphism type (strictly speaking, our property about the out degree is not even a *type* in these graphs, since there are other properties which the nodes with out degree 2 also satisfy in the graphs, and types are consistent and maximal sets of properties, see definition at the beginning of Section 2).

On the other hand, it may be the case that for a *given class* of db's the automorphism types are also *isomorphism types*. See Definition 3.3, and the

---

[3] This was suggested to me by Lauri Hella.

example which follows it. In this Section we define different notions regarding what we define as *homogeneity* for its close relation with the classical concept in Model Theory (see [8] among others). For every $k \geq 1$, and for any two $k$-tuples $\bar{a}_k$ and $\bar{b}_k$ of a given db $I$, we will denote as $\equiv_\sim$ the (equivalence) relation defined by the existence of an automorphism mapping one tuple onto the other. That is, $\bar{a}_k \equiv_\sim \bar{b}_k$ iff there exists an automorphism $f$ on $I$ such that, for every $1 \leq i \leq k$ is $f(a_i) = b_i$. Note that, according to what we said above about $FO$ types, we can also define this relation using types. That is, $\bar{a}_k \equiv_\sim \bar{b}_k$ iff, for every formula $\varphi \in FO$ with $k$ free variables $\bar{a}_k$ is in the relation defined by $\varphi$ in $I$ iff $\bar{b}_k$ is also in that relation.

**Definition 3.1.** *Let* $k \geq 1$. *A db* $I$ *is* $k$-homogeneous *if for every pair of $k$-tuples* $\bar{a}_k$ *and* $\bar{b}_k$ *in* $(dom(I))^k$, *if* $\bar{a}_k \equiv_k \bar{b}_k$, *then* $\bar{a}_k \equiv_\sim \bar{b}_k$. *Let* $k \geq 1$, *and let* $\sigma$ *be a schema. A class* $\mathcal{C}$ *of db's of schema* $\sigma$ *is* $k$-homogeneous *if every db* $I \in \mathcal{C}$ *is* $k$-*homogeneous.*

From the definition of the relation $\equiv_\sim$ and from Definition 3.1, it follows that, for every $k \geq 1$, if a db $I$ is $k$-homogeneous, then for every $1 \leq l \leq k$ and for every pair of $l$-tuples $\bar{a}_l$ and $\bar{b}_l$ in $(dom(I))^l$, if $\bar{a}_l \equiv_k \bar{b}_l$, then $\bar{a}_l \equiv_\sim \bar{b}_l$. Note that if a db $I$ is $k$-homogeneous, for some $k$, it is not necessarily $r$-homogeneous for every $r \geq k$. So, we next define a stronger notion regarding homogeneity.

**Definition 3.2.** *Let* $k \geq 1$. *A db* $I$ *is* strongly $k$-homogeneous *if for every* $r \geq k$ *it is* $r$-homogeneous. *Let* $\sigma$ *be a schema. A class* $\mathcal{C}$ *of db's of schema* $\sigma$ *is* strongly $k$-homogeneous *if every db* $I \in \mathcal{C}$ *is strongly* $k$-*homogeneous.*

*Remark 3.1.* Note that every db is strongly $k$-homogeneous for some $k \geq 1$. However, it is clear that this is not the case with *classes* of db's. And it is quite easy to build classes which are not even $k$-homogeneous for any $k$. Let's consider a class of graphs where each one is the disjoint union of two trees as follows. Every tree is built over a linear sub-graph, by adding $> 1$ sons to the maximal node of the linear sub-graph. And in every graph in the class the length of the linear sub-graphs in both trees is the same, and the out degree is different in both of them. The lengths and the out degrees can grow arbitrarily in the class. Now let's take one graph with, say, out degrees $k$ and $(k + 1)$, respectively, in the trees which form it. This graph certainly cannot be $k$-homogeneous, because we can easily choose two $k$-tuples, one from each tree, which have the same $FO^k$ type and for which there is no automorphism mapping one to each other. This is because in $FO^k$ we cannot distinguish between out degrees $k$ and $(k+1)$. Then, as the out degrees are not bounded in the class, it is clear that the class cannot be $k$-homogeneous for no $k$.

It seems that it is not easy to find examples of classes of db's which are $k$-homogeneous, for some $k$, but which are not strongly $k$-homogeneous. However, we believe that such classes do exist. That is, we believe that strong $k$-homogeneity is actually a *stronger* notion than $k$-homogeneity.

In [2] it was noted that the discerning power of a $RM$ of arity $k$ is restricted to $FO^k$ types for $k$-tuples (and the same is also true regarding $RRM^k$ machines, see [1]). So, the following result seems quite natural, and is somehow implicit in Abiteboul and Vianu's work.

If $f$ is a query of schema $\sigma$, and $\mathcal{C}$ is a class of db's of schema $\sigma$, we will denote as $f|_{\mathcal{C}}$ the restriction of $f$ to the class $\mathcal{C}$.

**Theorem 3.1.** *For every $k \geq 1$, there is a set of queries $F$ of some schema $\sigma$ such that if $\mathcal{C}$ and $\mathcal{C}'$ are any two classes of db's of schema $\sigma$, such that $\mathcal{C}$ is $k$-homogeneous and $\mathcal{C}'$ is not $k$-homogeneous, then, for every $f \in F$, $f|_{\mathcal{C}}$ is computable by a $RRM^k$ machine, but it is not the case that for every $f \in F$, $f|_{\mathcal{C}'}$ is computable by a $RRM^k$ machine.*

*Proof.* For every given $k$, and for every db $I$, let's define the $k$-ary query $q_i$, for $i \geq 1$, as the $i$-th equivalence class in the relation $\equiv_{\sim}$ for $k$-tuples in $I$, considering any pre-defined and computable order. These queries are certainly computable by $RRM^k$ machines on $k$-homogeneous classes of db's. But, by the Remark after Definition 2.1, not all of them will be computable by $RRM^k$ machines on classes of db's which are not $k$-homogeneous.

*Remark 3.2.* Note that the subclass of queries which can be computed by $RRM^k$ machines on $k$-homogeneous classes of db's, but which *cannot* be computed by such machines on arbitrary classes of db's, is quite big. Let's consider by case that a $RRM^k$ machine can count the number of equivalence classes in $\equiv_{\sim}$ for $k$-tuples on a $k$-homogeneous db as an intermediate result in its $TM$ tape. This can be done by following the same process as we did in the Proof of Theorem 2.1, and then by counting the isolating formulae for $FO^k$ types on whose realization both databases ($I$ and $I'$) agree. And it should be clear by now that, for any schema $\sigma$, this number cannot be computed by any $RRM^k$ machine on the whole class $\mathcal{S}_{\sigma, fin}$. Then we can use this parameter, which we will call *type index for $k$-tuples* following [2], as the argument for *any* partial recursive predicate in a $RRM^k$ machine. So that the whole class of partial recursive predicates, evaluated on the type index for $k$-tuples of the input database is included in the subclass of queries which can be computed with $RRM^k$ machines, due to $k$-homogeneity. However, $k$-homogeneity is *not enough* to achieve completeness with $RRM^k$ machines, as queries like parity of the size of the input db, parity on the sizes of the equivalence classes in $\equiv_{\sim}$, and isomorphism, are not computable with these machines, even on $k$-homogeneous classes of db's. Let's consider as an example a class $\mathcal{C}$ of graphs which are the disjoint union of some set of cliques of size $k$. This class is clearly $k$-homogeneous. Now, let's consider the equivalence class in $\equiv_k$ of the $k$-tuples of nodes which belong to the same clique. It is clearly also a class in $\equiv_{\sim}$, and for different graphs it can have certainly a different size. But a $RRM^k$ machine cannot count the tuples in this equivalence class.

Next, we will show that the property of *strong $k$-homogeneity* will allow the $RRM^{O(1)}$ machines to get still more power as to computability of queries. But this time we will use machines with variable complexity $r$, for every $r > k$, considering that according to Definition 3.2 the strong $k$-homogeneity of a class implies its $r$-homogeneity, for every $r \geq k$. And this is not the case for

$k$-homogeneous classes which are not strongly $k$-homogeneous. Let's denote by $\{F_r\}_{r \geq k}$ a countably infinite class of sets of queries $F_r$, for every $r \geq k$.

**Lemma 3.1.** *For every $k \geq 1$, there is a class of sets of queries $\mathcal{F} = \{F_r\}_{r \geq k}$ of some schema $\sigma$, such that, if $\mathcal{C}$ and $\mathcal{C}'$ are any two classes of db's of schema $\sigma$, such that $\mathcal{C}$ is strongly $k$-homogeneous and $\mathcal{C}'$ is not strongly $k$-homogeneous, then for every $F_r \in \mathcal{F}$ and for every $f \in F_r$, $f|_{\mathcal{C}}$ is computable by an $RRM^r$ machine, but it is not the case that for every $F_r \in \mathcal{F}$ and for every $f \in F_r$, $f|_{\mathcal{C}'}$ is computable by an $RRM^r$ machine.*

Now we will define a stronger concept regarding homogeneity, but this time involving classes of db's, instead of a single one. We will show that with this stronger notion we can achieve *completeness* with $RRM^k$ machines. Note that in this case we are considering the *whole* class $RRM^k$, including machines which compute partial queries.

**Definition 3.3.** *Let $\sigma$ be a schema, and let $\mathcal{C}$ be a class of db's of schema $\sigma$. Let $k \geq 1$. We say that $\mathcal{C}$ is pairwise $k$-homogeneous, if for every pair of db's $I_1$, $I_2$ in $\mathcal{C}$, and for every pair of $k$-tuples $\bar{a}_k \in (dom(I_1))^k$ and $\bar{b}_k \in (dom(I_2))^k$, if $\bar{a}_k \equiv_k \bar{b}_k$ then there exists an isomorphism $f : dom(I_1) \longrightarrow dom(I_2)$, such that $f(a_i) = b_i$, for every $1 \leq i \leq k$.*

That is, in pairwise $k$-homogeneous classes $FO^k$ types for $k$-tuples are *isomorphism types* for $k$-tuples.

As an example of such classes, let's define the class $\mathcal{T}_r$, for every $r \geq 1$, as a class of trees of arbitrary depth, of out degree bounded by $r$, and where all the nodes at the same depth have the same out degree. So, we can write a formula with one free variable which defines a type for 1-tuples, expressing the distance from the node to the root, the distance from the node to a leaf, and the out degree of every ancestor, as well as the out degree of every descendant, in any of the paths from the node to a leaf (it doesn't matter which path we choose, because in all of them all the nodes at the same depth will have the same degree). This formula can be written with $(r + 1)$ variables (though it should be noted that for trees which are not in the class $\mathcal{T}_r$ we need $(r + 2)$ variables). And it is clear that we can write the $FO^{r+1}$ types for $(r + 1)$-tuples by using a formula of this kind for every component of the tuple, and then by defining, with 2 variables, the directed or undirected path between every pair of components. Finally, the conjunction of all those formulae isolates the desired $FO^{r+1}$ type for $(r+1)$-tuples. Then it is clear that if two $(r+1)$-tuples of two different trees in the class have the same $FO^{r+1}$ type, the trees must be isomorphic, and one tuple can certainly be mapped onto the other. So that the class $\mathcal{T}_r$, for every $r \geq 1$, is pairwise $(r + 1)$-homogeneous.

**Lemma 3.2.** *For every $k \geq 1$, and for every query $f$ of any schema $\sigma$ in $\mathcal{CQ}$, if $\mathcal{C}$ is a class of db's of schema $\sigma$ which is recursive and closed under isomorphisms and which is also pairwise $k$-homogeneous, then there is a $RRM^k$ machine which computes $f|_{\mathcal{C}}$.*

Finally, let's consider $RRM$ with variable complexity $f(n)$. As we observed before in this article, there are many classes of db's for which there is no $k \in \omega$ such that the class is $k$-homogeneous. However it is quite easy to build classes of db's where the number of variables which are needed for automorphism types for tuples is bounded by a *sub-linear* function. This is because as it is well known in $FO^n$ we can characterize a database of size $n$ up to isomorphism, and we cannot count the number of elements with less than $n$ variables. As an example of such classes of databases, think of graphs which are formed by a certain number of isolated nodes and the disjoint union of two trees of depth 1, where the out degree of the trees differs by 1. We can make the number of isolated nodes arbitrary big in relation with the degrees. And it is clear that if we can use a number of variables big enough to separate the trees we can define the automorphism types, and then we can adjust the number of isolated nodes so that the number of variables is bounded by any given recursive and sub-linear function.

We will denote as $\equiv_{f(n),k}$ the equivalence of $FO^{f(n)}$ types for $k$-tuples (that is, types in $FO$, where the number of variables is given by a function on the size of the db).

**Definition 3.4.** *Let $f : \omega \longrightarrow \omega$ be a sub-linear and recursive function, and let $k \geq 1$. A db $I$ is $(f(n), k)$-homogeneous if $k \leq f(|dom(I)|)$ and if, for every pair of $k$-tuples $\bar{a}_k$ and $\bar{b}_k$ in $(dom(I))^k$, if $\bar{a}_k \equiv_{f(n),k} \bar{b}_k$, then $\bar{a}_k \equiv_{\sim} \bar{b}_k$. A class $\mathcal{C}$ of db's of schema $\sigma$ is $(f(n), k)$-homogeneous if every db $I \in \mathcal{C}$ is $(f(n), k)$-homogeneous.*

**Lemma 3.3.** *Let $k \geq 1$. Then, for every sub-linear and recursive function $f$, there is a set of queries $Q$ of some schema $\sigma$, such that if $\mathcal{C}$ and $\mathcal{C}'$ are any two classes of db's of schema $\sigma$, such that $\mathcal{C}$ is $(f(n), k)$-homogeneous and $\mathcal{C}'$ is not $(f(n), k)$-homogeneous, then for every $q \in Q$, $q|_{\mathcal{C}}$ is computable by a $RRM^{f(n)}$ machine, but it is not the case that for every $q \in Q$, $q|_{\mathcal{C}'}$ is computable by a $RRM^{f(n)}$ machine.*

With the classes $\mathcal{QCQ}^k$ we characterized the total queries which preserve realization of $FO^k$ types for $k$-tuples. But, as we noted in the Remark after Definition 3.2, it is not the case that every countably infinite class of databases is $k$-homogeneous for some $k$. So, the queries which preserve realization of $FO$ types for tuples, but which don't preserve realization of $FO^k$ types for $k$-tuples, for any $k$, will not belong to any $\mathcal{QCQ}^k$ class, for no $k$. This is because if we fix some $k \geq 1$, the number of variables which are needed for the automorphism types for $k$-tuples in different databases can be different. And the number of different bounds for the number of variables is actually infinite.

So that for this purpose we need to define a new class of queries in a different way than the one we used before. The intuitive idea behind this new class, is that queries which belong to it preserve, for *any two* db's of the corresponding schema, the realization of types in $FO$ bounded to a number of variables which is *enough* for *both* db's to define tuples up to automorphism. Note that for different pairs of db's these queries will preserve types defined with possibly different number of variables.

**Definition 3.5.** *For any schema $\sigma$, let's denote as $arity(\sigma)$ the maximum arity of a relation symbol in the schema. We define the class $\mathcal{QCQ}$ as the class of queries $f \in total(\mathcal{CQ})$, of some schema $\sigma$ and of any arity, for which there exists an integer $n \geq max\{arity(f), arity(\sigma)\}$, such that for every pair of db's $I_1, I_2$ in $S_{\sigma,fin}$, if $I_1 \equiv_{T_h} I_2$, then $f(I_1) \equiv_{T_h} f(I_2)$, where $h = max\{n, min\{k : I_1 \text{ and } I_2 \text{ are strongly } k\text{-homogeneous}\}\}$.*

**Lemma 3.4.** $total(\mathcal{CQ}) \supset \mathcal{QCQ} \supset \mathcal{QCQ}^\omega$.

*Proof.* The first $\supset$ and the second $\supseteq$ are straightforward. As to the second $\neq$, let's define the query $f$ in the schema of the graphs, as *the nodes belonging to the smaller clique* in the sub-class $\mathcal{G}$ of graphs which are the disjoint union of two cliques whose sizes differ at most by 1. And we define $f$ to be empty if the two cliques are of the same size or if the graph is not in that sub-class. It is not hard to see that $f \in \mathcal{QCQ}$, but $f \notin \mathcal{QCQ}^\omega$.

We should point out a very important difference between queries in $\mathcal{QCQ}$ and queries in $\mathcal{QCQ}^\omega$. A query in the first class has to be aware of every property which a tuple may have in the db, up to automorphism. And this fact can imply that it will not preserve realization of *coarser* types, that is, types defined in $FO$ with fewer variables. In part **b** of the Proof of Lemma 2.1 we showed an example of a query which preserves realization of $FO^{k+1}$ types, but which does not preserve realization of $FO^k$ types. On the other hand, a query $f \in \mathcal{QCQ}^k$, for some $k$, must preserve realization of $FO^k$ types for $k$-tuples in *every pair* of db's in the corresponding schema. And, by the Remark after Definition 2.2, if this is the case, the query $f$ will also preserve the realization of types defined with any bigger number of variables, say $(k + i)$ for some $i \in \omega$, also for every pair of db's in the schema. Now, note that $f$ is sufficiently precise as to consider $FO^{k+i}$ types, but, at the same time, it must also be sufficiently simple so it doesn't separate equivalence classes in $\equiv_k$ in equivalence classes in $\equiv_{k+i}$ which form them (by the Remark after Definition 2.1), arbitrarily, because $f$ must preserve realization of $FO^{k+i}$ types.

Note that the queries based on the type index for $k$-tuples which we mentioned in the Remark after Theorem 3.1 are in $(\mathcal{QCQ} - \mathcal{QCQ}^\omega)$. So that the increment in the computability power of the $RRM^{O(1)}$ machines when working on classes of db's which are homogeneous, is big enough to allow for a $RRM^k$ machine to go through the whole hierarchy $\mathcal{QCQ}^\omega$, and, further, to get out of it into $\mathcal{QCQ}$. So, the next results follow immediately.

**Corollary 3.1.** *There are queries $f$ of some schema $\sigma$ in $(\mathcal{QCQ} - \mathcal{QCQ}^\omega)$ whose restriction to any class of db's of schema $\sigma$ which is $k$-homogeneous, for some $k \geq 1$, is computable by a $RRM^k$ machine. On the other hand, if $g$ is a query of some schema $\rho$ whose restriction to any class of db's of schema $\rho$ which is $k$-homogeneous, for some $k \geq 1$, is computable by a $RRM^k$ machine, then, $g \in \mathcal{QCQ}$.*

## Acknowledgements

I am deeply grateful to Lauri Hella and to Jouko Väänänen for letting me visit the Department of Mathematics of the University of Helsinki, as well as for their partial funding.

# References

1. Abiteboul, S., Papadimitriou, C. and Vianu, V.: The Power of the Reflective Relational Machine. Proc. of 9th IEEE Symposium on Logic in Computer Science (1994)
2. Abiteboul, S. and Vianu, V.: Generic Computation and its Complexity. Proc. of 23th ACM Symposium on Theory of Computing (1991) 209–219
3. Abiteboul, S., Vianu, V.: Computing with first-order logic. Journal of Computer and System Sciences (1994)
4. Abiteboul, S., Vardi, M. and Vianu, V.: Fixpoint Logics, Relational Machines, and Computational Complexity. Proc. of 7th IEEE Conference on Structure in Complexity Theory (1992) 156–168
5. Abiteboul, S., Vardi, M. and Vianu, V.: Computing with Infinitary Logic. Proc. of International Conference on Database Theory (1992)
6. Chandra, A. and Harel, D.: Computable Queries for Relational Data Bases. Journal of Computer and System Sciences **21** (1980) 156–178
7. Chandra, A. and Harel, D.: Structure and Complexity of Relational Queries. Journal of Computer and System Sciences **25** (1982) 99–128
8. Chang, C. and Keisler, H.: Model Theory. 3rd edn. Elsevier North Holland (1992)
9. Dawar, A.: Feasible Computation Through Model Theory. PhD Thesis. University of Pennsylvania, Philadelphia (1993)
10. Gurevich, Y.: Logic and the Challenge of Computer Science. Trends in Theoretical Computer Science. Computer Science Press (1988)
11. Immerman, N.: Upper and Lower Bounds for First Order Expressibility. Journal of Computer and System Sciences **25** (1982) 76–98
12. Kolaitis, P. and Vardi, M.: 0–1 Laws for Infinitary Logic. Proc. of 5th IEEE Symposium on Logic in Computer Science (1990)
13. Seth, A.: When do Fixed Point Logics Capture Complexity Classes?. Proc. of 10th IEEE Symposium on Logic in Computer Science (1995)
14. Turull Torres, J.M.: Query Completeness, Distinguishability and Relational Machines. Models, Algebras and Proofs: Selected Papers from the X Latin American Symposium on Mathematical Logic, Bogotá 1995. Marcel-Dekker (1998) 135–163
15. Turull Torres, J.M.: Partial Distinguishability and Query Computability on Finite Structures. Communicated in the XI Brazilean Symposium on Logic, Salvador, Brazil, 1996. Abstract published in Bulletin of the IGPL **3** (1996)
16. Turull Torres, J.M.: Reflective Relational Machines of Bounded Variable Complexity. Proc. of Short Papers, Third East-European Conference on Advances in Databases and Information Systems, edited by University of Maribor, Slovenia (1999) 193–199

# Author Index